GOD:

AN ANATOMY

Francesca Stavrakopoulou

GOD:

AN ANATOMY

ALFRED A. KNOPF NEW YORK 2022

Contents

Author's Note

This book deals with places, peoples and deities that can be known by many different names – some of which are culturally and politically loaded. Where possible, I have tried to use neutral or general terms without sacrificing historical or geographical precision. In particular, I have deliberately avoided employing the more usual label 'ancient near East'. To be blunt, it is Western-centric and freighted with colonial baggage (much like its older metonym, 'the Orient'). Instead, I refer to 'ancient south-west Asia'. This book also draws on primary sources written in a number of ancient languages. For the benefit of the reader, I have kept transliterations simple, primarily with an eye to helping pronunciation (for example, 'Ashur' rather than 'Assur', 'Asshur', or 'Aššur'). Occasionally, I have jettisoned strict consistency in favour of transliterated words and phrases as they are more commonly seen. Biblical quotations follow the New Revised Standard Version and its versification, although I have modified its (confessional) translation where necessary, especially when dealing with the Bible's pre-Christian texts.

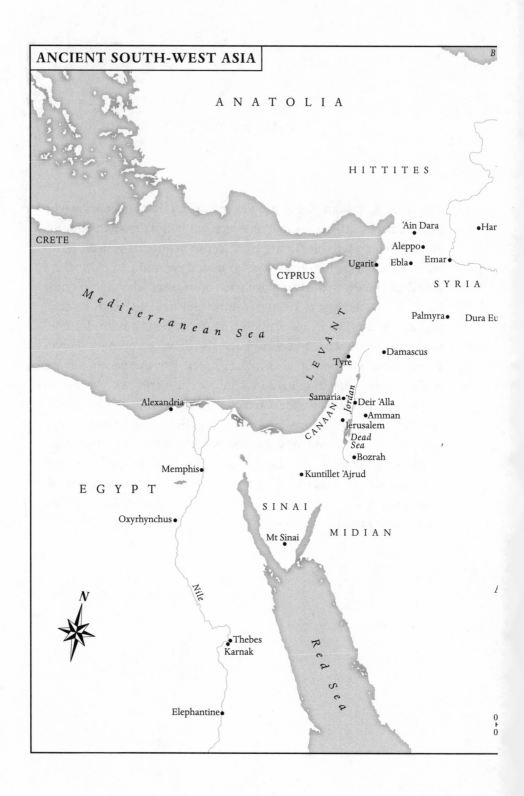

ANCIENT SOUTH-WEST ASIA

B

ANATOLIA

HITTITES

'Ain Dara●

●Har

Aleppo●

CRETE

Ugarit● Ebla● Emar●

CYPRUS

SYRIA

Mediterranean Sea

L
E
V
A
N
T

Palmyra● Dura Eu

●Damascus

Tyre●

Samaria● Deir 'Alla●

Alexandria●

C
A
N
A
A
N

Jordan

●Amman

Jerusalem●

*Dead
Sea*

●Bozrah

Memphis●

●Kuntillet 'Ajrud

EGYPT

SINAI

Oxyrhynchus●

MIDIAN

Mt Sinai●

N

Nile

Red Sea

Thebes●
Karnak●

Elephantine●

0
0

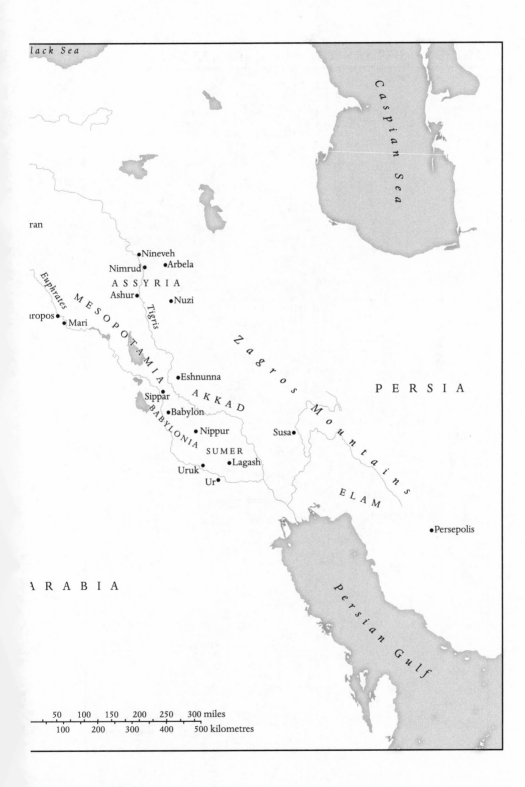

Black Sea

Caspian Sea

Iran

Euphrates

•Nineveh
Nimrud•   •Arbela
A S S Y R I A
Ashur•   •Nuzi

M E S O P O T A M I A

Tigris

uropos• •Mari

Zagros Mountains

P E R S I A

•Eshnunna

A K K A D

Sippar•
•Babylon

B A B Y L O N I A

•Nippur

Susa•

S U M E R

Uruk•   •Lagash
Ur•

E L A M

•Persepolis

A R A B I A

Persian Gulf

| 50 | 100 | 150 | 200 | 250 | 300 miles |

| 100 | 200 | 300 | 400 | 500 kilometres |

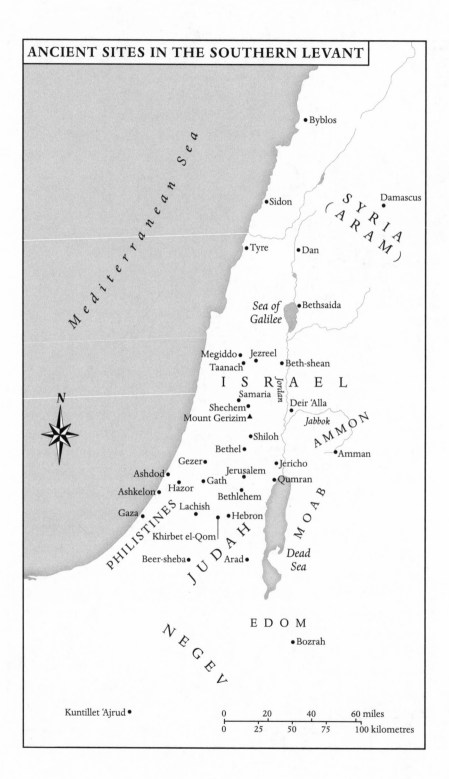

ANCIENT SITES IN THE SOUTHERN LEVANT

Mediterranean Sea

• Byblos

• Sidon

SYRIA
(ARAM)

• Damascus

• Tyre   • Dan

Sea of
Galilee   • Bethsaida

Megiddo •   Jezreel
Taanach •   • Beth-shean

I S R A E L

Samaria   Jordan
•
Shechem •   • Deir ʿAlla
Mount Gerizim ▲

Jabbok   AMMON

• Shiloh

Bethel •   • Amman

Gezer •
Ashdod •   Jerusalem   • Jericho
•   • Gath   • Qumran
Ashkelon •   Hazor
Gaza •   Bethlehem
PHILISTINES   Lachish
•   • Hebron
Khirbet el-Qom

MOAB

Beer-sheba •   Arad •
J U D A H   Dead
Sea

N E G E V

E D O M
• Bozrah

Kuntillet ʿAjrud •

0   20   40   60 miles
0   25   50   75   100 kilometres

PROLOGUE

Think back. Where were you when you first encountered a Bible? I was five, maybe six years old, sitting cross-legged on a scratchy beige carpet, a big picture book open in my lap. The book was a children's illustrated Bible, and its pages smelled delicious – tangy, like poster paints, if faintly musty, like the public library. I can vividly recall what I saw. Abraham had tied up his son Isaac on what looked to me like an unlit bonfire. He had a knife. He was about to stab him and burn him. But he was suddenly stopped by an angel in the sky with yellow hair and a billowing robe, pointing at a fat, fluffy sheep. There were more pictures in the book: an old man on a mountain, carrying two big slabs of stone; another old man in a chariot pulled by horses made of fire. I kept turning the pages. There was a man covered in seaweed, sitting in the belly of a big blue whale. The baby Jesus in a bed of hay, with sheep, cows and a donkey crowding round to look at him. A woman twirling scarves as she danced in front of a head on a plate. I briefly stopped and stared at the picture of the man nailed onto a big wooden cross; he was covered in scratches, blood trickling down the side of his face.

I've never believed in God, but religion has always intrigued me. As I grew up, it was everywhere, pushing its way into view and punctuating the passing of time – from daily school assemblies and Sunday-night TV, to the giddy excitement of Christmas nativity plays and chocolate Easter eggs. But it was during family trips to museums that religion became tangible. Giant stone statues of gods, rounded, fleshy and powerful. Gods draped in tunics and wearing sandals. Gods with toenails, elbows, eyebrows. In other rooms, there were brightly painted coffins with bodies wrapped in strips of dirty fabric, sur-rounded by gods with the faces of animals. A cat. A dog. A bird. A crocodile. Turn a corner and there were more gods, this time carved on tiny polished stones, sitting on thrones in long skirts, with horns on their crowns and monsters at their feet. In museums, I learned that the deities of Egypt, Mesopotamia, Greece and Rome were the gods of the wider world in which the Bible was made. But where were the statues of the God of the Bible himself – the only deity among them to survive into the modern day?

While I was studying theology and religion at university, there was a broad assumption among lecturers and students alike that the God of the Bible is without a body. This was a formless, imageless, invisible deity, who in the Hebrew Bible (the Old Testament) revealed himself in words mysteriously uttered through his prophets, and then in the New Testament became flesh ('incarnate') in Jesus Christ, in order to die for the sins of humanity before resurrecting and ascending back to the heavens. But as I looked closely at the books comprising the Bible, I couldn't find this bodiless God. Instead, these ancient texts conjured a startlingly corporeal image of God as a human-shaped deity, who walked and talked and wept and laughed. A god who ate and slept and felt and breathed. And a god who was distinctly male.

As my undergraduate studies progressed, no one seemed to talk about the body of the biblical God – until one memorable lecture, when the gender politics of modern Christian theology were being discussed. I was excited to discover that feminist theologians had long taken issue with the maleness of God in their scriptures. And yet it soon transpired that the way in which both feminist and traditionalist theologians proposed getting around this sticky issue was to insist that God couldn't possibly have a sex or a gender, because God didn't have a body. I vividly recall protesting in the question-and-answer session at the end of the lecture, 'But lots of biblical texts suggest that God is masculine, with a male body.' 'The problem isn't God,' replied the professor – a highly respected Christian theologian, and a man of the cloth. 'The problem only arises when we take the Bible's descriptions too literally.' He went on to explain that those troublesome biblical portrayals of a corporeal, masculine God were simply metaphorical, or poetic. 'We shouldn't get too distracted by references to his body,' he said. To do so, he claimed, was to engage too simplistically with the biblical texts. Apparently, we had to look not just *at* the texts but *through* the texts, to engage their theological truths.

Everyone else in the room seemed remarkably content with this approach to the God of the Bible, but I found it deeply frustrating. Why *should* I look past the clear image of God as a gigantic man with a heavy tread, weapons in his hands and breath as hot as sulphur? A god who took on a monstrous sea dragon in a physical fight – and won? A god who walked about in his heavenly garden and in the cemeteries of his people? A god who stripped a woman naked and offered her up to be gang-raped and mutilated? A god who sat on a throne in a temple, enjoying the aroma of scorched animal fat as he waited for his dinner? A god who not only had children, but who willingly and wilfully offered up his beloved son to be killed as a sacrifice? How could I not be distracted? Here was a deity just like those I'd visited in museums as a child – a god of ancient myths, fantastic stories and long-lost rituals; a god from the distant past, from a society utterly unlike our own. Those were the terms on which I wanted to encounter him; not as a distant and abstract being, but as the product of a particular culture, at a particular time, made in the image of the people who lived then; a god shaped by their own physical circumstances, their own view of the world – and their own imaginations.

Sitting in that lecture hall, it seemed to me that this potent figure had somehow been theorized away and replaced by the abstract being with whom we are more familiar today: a god celebrated in our cultural rituals, invoked by politicians and celebrities, and praised every Sunday on the TV. A god to whom many of my peers and lecturers expected me to be answerable – whether in this life or the next. A god whose supposed decrees have shaped our own social and cultural conventions about gender, sex and morality, about power and class, about life and death. And then it suddenly dawned on me. Everyone else in the room, my theology professor included, was censoring the

Bible, sanitizing its deity of any mythological, earthy or unsettling characteristics. I was disappointed by them. And disappointed for them.

This is the book I'd have liked to read when I was at university. It tells the story of the real God of the Bible, in all his corporeal, uncensored, scandalous forms. Stripping away the theological veneer of centuries of Jewish and Christian piety, this book disentangles the biblical God from his scriptural and doctrinal fetters to reveal a deity wholly unlike the God worshipped by Jews and Christians today. The God revealed in this book is the deity as his ancient worshippers saw him: a supersized, muscle-bound, good-looking god, with suprahuman powers, earthly passions, and a penchant for the fantastic and the monstrous.

INTRODUCTION

1

DISSECTING THE DIVINE

In June 2018, news platforms across much of the world published a photograph of God. 'Does THIS photograph show the true face of God?' shouted one click-bait headline. 'Science reveals the face of God and it looks like Elon Musk', teased another. Others, including NBC's website, were rather less sensationalist in their headlines: 'The face of God is in the eye of the beholder'. The photograph in question showed a fuzzy black-and-white image of a middle-aged, beardless Caucasian male, with a soft, rounded face and just a hint of a smile (fig. 1). The image was produced by researchers at the University of North Carolina at Chapel Hill, who showed a demographically representative sample of US Christians a series of computer-generated faces embodying certain cultural stereotypes of emotional, ethical, social and spiritual values, and asked them to select those faces perceived to best reflect their mental image of God. Some of the faces were androgynous in appearance, while some were more feminine, and some more masculine. All the faces were grey, like a black-and-white photocopy, but some were lighter skinned and some were darker skinned. Some faces were expressive, some were seemingly blank. But each face was a canvas onto which the experiment's participants were free to project their own assumptions. The results were averaged out and used to create God's e-fit. Unsurprisingly, the study revealed that in the US, God is made in the image of a white American man.[1]

Psychologists and social anthropologists have long understood that

Fig. 1. The face of God, as imagined by a representative sample of US
Christians in a recent study. The fuzzy quality of this computer-generated
image reflects the composite process of the experiment. The study
concluded that those surveyed envisaged God as similar to themselves
in terms of physical appearance, age and race.

a very heavy dose of cognitive bias underlies the construction of the
divine in human societies. But while modern studies like those conducted at Chapel Hill can tell us something of the psychological and
social processes underlying this tendency, this is hardly news. Over two
and a half thousand years ago, in the late sixth or early fifth century
BCE, the Greek intellectual and adventurer Xenophanes of Colophon
had already arrived at a similar conclusion: 'If cattle and horses or lions
had hands, or were able to draw with their hands and do the works
that men can do, horses would draw the forms of the gods like horses,
and cattle like cattle, and they would make their bodies such as they
each had themselves'. For Xenophanes, the human tendency to make
gods in our own image was as much about local cultural preferences
as overarching, lofty ideals, as the diversity of deities in his world
attested: 'The Ethiopians say that their gods are broad-nosed and dark-
skinned, the Thracians that theirs have blue eyes and red hair'. As far
as Xenophanes was concerned, the widespread assumption that the
gods had bodies like those of their worshippers was inextricably linked

to the notion that deities behaved very much like humans – and this was deeply problematic, for it inevitably cheapened the moral nature of the divine. Proof could be found in the Greek myths themselves: 'Homer and Hesiod have attributed to the gods everything that leads to blame and abuse among men – stealing, committing adultery, and deceiving each other', Xenophanes complained. It was an objection rooted in his philosophically driven insistence that a god was inherently and necessarily a being 'in no way like mortals either in body or thought'.[2]

Similar ideas were soon championed by other Greek thinkers, most notably Plato (c. 429–347 BCE), his student Aristotle (c. 384–322 BCE) and subsequent generations of their elitist, learned adherents in the Graeco-Roman world, who theorized that the divine power ultimately undergirding the universe and everything in it was necessarily without a body – an incorporeal, invisible, abstract principle, force or intellect, wholly beyond and distinct from the material world. Not that these rarefied views made much of an impact on the religious lives of ordinary folk. Whether they were schooled in philosophy or not, and no matter the deities they worshipped, most people living in the Graeco-Roman world continued to envisage their gods as corporeal beings with bodies shaped like their own – much as they always had.

But towards the close of the first millennium BCE, and into the early centuries of the Common Era, these erudite philosophical ideas would gradually come to shape the thinking of certain Jewish and Christian intellectuals, so that they began to re-imagine their deity in increasingly incorporeal, immaterial terms, drawing ever-sharper distinctions between the heavenly and the earthly, the divine and the human, and the spiritual and the bodily. It is the broadly Platonic notion of the otherness and unlikeness of the divine to anything in or beyond the universe that has shaped the more formal theological constructions of God in the Western religious imagination. And yet these constructions are built on a conceptual framework very much at odds with the Bible itself, for in these ancient texts, God is presented in startlingly anthropomorphic ways. This is a deity with a body.

In the Beginning

The high god had already spent several days speaking new marvels into being – separating the primeval waters of chaos into heavenly and underworld reservoirs; bringing forth dry land, planting it with fruit trees and crops; appointing the sun and moon to light day and night; and commanding the new-formed land, seas and skies to bring forth animals, fish and birds. Now, he was about to speak again. 'Let us make humankind in our image, according to our likeness', he says to the other deities in his retinue. It is more a declaration than a suggestion, but a good idea, nonetheless, for the humans will be tasked with keeping order in the newly created earthly realm. And so the high god makes the very first human: 'God created the human in his image, in the image of God he created him'. The new creature – *adam*, meaning 'man' or 'human' – bears a bodily resemblance to his divine creator, and is swiftly paired with a female version: 'male and female he created them'. Equipped with god-shaped bodies, humans are rendered superior to the other newly made creatures of the world, over whom they are appointed to rule. Blessing humans with fertility, the high god gives them two tasks: to procreate and dominate. They are to fill this new world with their offspring, and keep the other creatures under control. Satisfied with his creative accomplishments, the high god decides his work is done. The next day, he rests.

In academic circles, there is nothing particularly contentious about this paraphrase of the opening chapter of the book of Genesis. Most biblical scholars would agree that when God says, 'Let *us* make humankind in *our* image, in *our* likeness', he is addressing the other members of the 'divine assembly' – the biblical label given to God's council of lower-ranking deities and divine beings. And most would agree (even if some might squirm a little) that in being made in the image and likeness of the gods, freshly minted humans bear a visual resemblance to their own deities, just as Adam's son Seth is later said to be the 'image' and 'likeness' of his father, and in other biblical texts, divine statues are the 'image' and 'likeness' of the gods they represent.[3] Written in about the fifth century BCE, but drawing on older mythologies, the creation story that now begins the Bible reflects a time when Yahweh – the deity of Jerusalem, now better known as God – had yet to be imagined as the only divine being in the universe. Like the Babylonian deity Marduk, or the Greek god Zeus, this ancient deity had long been cast as the king of the cosmos, but like them, he was far from alone in the heavens. Above all, he was still several centuries away from becoming the immaterial, incorporeal abstraction of later Jewish and Christian theologies. Instead, he was just like any other deity in the ancient world. He had a head, hair and a face; eyes, ears, a nose and a mouth. He had arms, hands, legs and feet, and a chest and a back. He was equipped with a heart, a tongue, teeth and genitals. He was a god who breathed, in and out. This was a deity who not only looked like a human – albeit on a far more impressive, glamourous scale – but who very often behaved like a human. He enjoyed evening strolls and hearty meals; he listened to music, wrote books and made lists. He was a god who not only spoke, but whistled, laughed, shouted, wept and talked to himself. He was a god who fell in love and into fights; a god who squabbled with his worshippers and grappled with his enemies; a god who made friends, raised children, took wives and had sex.

This portrait of God has not been lifted from obscure myths inscribed on long-abandoned clay tablets. It is drawn from the Bible itself – a book as complex as the deity it promotes, not least because the Bible is not a book at all, but a collection of books, falling into two parts. The first is the Hebrew Bible, known in Judaism as Tanakh, and in Christianity as the Old Testament, and it is an anthology of ancient texts, originally crafted as scrolls. Most of these texts are themselves complex compilations of diverse literary traditions, and the majority were composed between the eighth and second centuries BCE in Judah, a small southern polity in the ancient Levant – the region we know today as Palestine, Israel, Jordan, Lebanon and western Syria. In the eighth century BCE, Judah was a kingdom captured by Assyria; at the beginning of the sixth century BCE, it was conquered again, this time by the Babylonians. By the fifth century BCE, Judah had become a Persian province, and in about 333 BCE, it was incorporated into Alexander the Great's vast empire. Some Hebrew Bible texts tell of Judah's changing political fortunes, while others are stories about legendary heroes and myths about the very distant past. Some are collections of oracles attributed to various prophets, and others are compilations of poetry, ritual songs, prayers and teachings. But none of these texts have reached us in their 'original' form. Instead, all were subject to creative and repeated revision, addition, emendation and editing across a number of generations, reflecting the shifting ideological interests of their curators, who regarded them as sacred writings.

It is this long process of creative curation that has given narrative shape to the biblical story of God's relationship with 'Israel', the people in whom he takes a special interest. The first five books of the Hebrew Bible tell of the founding of this relationship. Following the creation of the world and the great flood, God forges a covenant (or contract) relationship with the Israelites' ancestors – Abraham, his son Isaac and grandson Jacob – promising them a multitude of descendants in return for their obedience, which is to be demonstrated primarily by their worship of him alone. When the Israelites find themselves enslaved in Egypt, God liberates them, tasking Moses both to lead them to the 'promised land' of Canaan and to instruct them in God's teaching (*torah*) – the regulations which will shape their ongoing relationship with the deity, including instructions for the glorious temple they are to build in their divinely granted homeland. Collectively, these five books – Genesis, Exodus, Leviticus, Numbers, Deuteronomy – are known as the Torah, and together they rework what were probably competing traditions about ancestors and origins into a broadly coherent narrative about 'Israelite' identity.

The crafting of the past is continued in the books of Joshua, Judges, Samuel and Kings. Together, this second block of material tells of the conquest and settlement of Canaan and the reigns of the first Israelite monarchs: Saul, then David, who makes Jerusalem his capital, followed by Solomon, who builds God a temple there. These books continue with stories about the fracturing of the kingdom into two, after Solomon's death: Israel, in the north, and Judah, in the south. The fates of the kingdoms are traced, skipping briskly past the Assyrian defeat of the kingdom of Israel in the late eighth century BCE, and ending in the early sixth century BCE with the Babylonian conquest of Judah, the destruction of Jerusalem and the exile of its elites to

Mesopotamia – events depicted as a punishment from God for generations of religious malpractice. The biblical portrayal of the past resumes in the books of Ezra and Nehemiah, which focus on the return of the exiles in the late sixth and fifth centuries BCE. In spite of their former transgressions, this group is now the divinely elected, 'purified' remnant of the ancient people of God – a notion similarly expressed in some of the prophetic works dating to this period. Restored to divine favour and back in the homeland, they rebuild Jerusalem and its temple, and recommit themselves to the divine teaching Moses had mediated.

Historically, only the later episodes of this biblical story broadly dovetail with known realities, at best consigning Abraham, Isaac, Jacob, Moses, and even David and Solomon, to the realms of fable – and at worst, to sheer fantasy. But from the ninth century BCE onwards, archaeological evidence points to the existence of the separate Iron Age kingdoms of Israel and Judah, and corroborates the names of some of their kings. Mesopotamian records confirm the Assyrian destruction of Israel in the late eighth century BCE, and the Babylonian defeat of Judah in the early sixth century BCE; Mesopotamian annals also attest to the forced migration of some higher-status groups from both kingdoms – a common imperial strategy designed to curtail local uprisings in conquered territories – and there is sufficient evidence to suggest that some deportees did indeed return from Babylonia to Judah in the late sixth or early fifth century BCE.[4]

But non-biblical material can also flag the limitations of the Bible's portrayal of the past, warning us that it cannot be taken as a comprehensive or reliable 'record' of history. In the books of Kings, for example, a ninth-century BCE ruler of the northern kingdom of Israel, named Omri, is presented as a figure of marginal significance, whose only noteworthy accomplishment is the founding of a new capital city, Samaria. But an inscribed stela set up by Mesha, king of neighbouring Moab, celebrates the regaining of sizable Moabite territories from 'Omri king of Israel' and his successor, both of whom had 'oppressed Moab for a long time'. The longevity of Omri's territorial and dynastic legacy is also reflected in Assyrian texts of the ninth and eighth centuries BCE, in which the kingdom of Israel is frequently designated 'Omri-land' and its various kings as 'sons of Omri'. The possibility that the Judahite writer of the books of Kings has not only minimized but suppressed Omri's significance is signalled by an oblique, fleeting reference to 'the rest of the acts of Omri, and the power that he showed'.[5]

The partisan perspectives of the biblical writers and editors are also evident in an overarching insistence that the Jerusalem temple served as the only 'legitimate' site of Yahweh worship. Other ritual sites are downplayed as mere shrines, or disparagingly dismissed as idolatrous, and are said to have been closed down by especially virtuous kings of Judah. And yet archaeological evidence corroborates the existence of several Yahweh temples throughout the first millennium BCE, including one in a state-sponsored fortress in Arad, on Judah's southern border, dated to the eighth century BCE; another built by Judahite immigrants on the Egyptian island of Elephantine in the fifth century BCE; and yet another, operating from the fifth to the second centuries BCE, on Mount Gerizim in the West Bank. Scholars are agreed that the religious realities of Yahweh worship were far more diverse, and far less centralized, than the biblical story asserts.

To put it bluntly, the Hebrew Bible offers a highly ideological and frequently unreliable portrayal of the past. It is a story told from the perspective of pro-Jerusalem writers and editors, for it was the trauma of Judah's conquest in the sixth century BCE, and Jerusalem's gradual regeneration in the Persian era, that triggered the literary activities giving rise to the texts of the Hebrew Bible as we find them today. With the restoration of the city's temple, which served as both a religious and administrative centre, Jerusalem's priestly and scribal cultures flourished. During this 'Second Temple' period, old texts were reshaped and new literary works were crafted – and much of this literature was filtered through the lens of exile, return and restoration. But although these texts tend to present the exile and return as the experience of all Judahites, this was not the case. Only the elites and some among the professional classes had been deported to Babylonia, and the majority remained there.[6] Meanwhile, other Judahite groups had already migrated to Egypt during the years of political upheaval, and many more would relocate to towns and cities along the prospering trade routes criss-crossing the eastern Mediterranean, Mesopotamia and the Levant. As the cultural contours of the imperial landscape shifted to Persia and then to Greece, Aramaic and Greek became the dominant literary languages of Jewish communities (as those of Judahite descent had come to be known). Consequently, by the beginning of the Common Era, many Jewish groups outside Roman Palestine – and some within – were reading and hearing their sacred texts in Aramaic and Greek translation.

Among them were members of the Jesus movement – a minor Jewish cult, whose adherents believed their executed teacher had resurrected, heralding the imminent arrival of the Kingdom of God and the universal justice and peace it would bring. The movement had emerged in Roman Palestine, but was recruiting devotees from both Gentile and Jewish communities across the empire. Although we know it better as Christianity, this movement would ostensibly remain a Jewish sect for several generations, and its members quite naturally regarded the texts we now find in the Hebrew Bible as their own sacred scriptures.

Like other Jewish groups, the earliest Christians also produced their own writings, including those that would eventually comprise the New Testament. Written in Greek between the mid first and early second centuries CE, these texts quickly circulated around the empire. The earliest are letters written by Paul to Christian groups in cities across the eastern Mediterranean in the mid-50s, two to three decades after Jesus was executed, urging his readers to ready themselves for impending and miraculous change. The Gospels of Matthew, Mark and Luke (as they would soon be called) offer varied portrayals of Jesus' life, supernatural powers and teachings, and were written in the closing decades of the first century, while John probably dates to about 100 CE. By the early second century CE, the other texts we now find in the New Testament had been produced, including some falsely attributed to Paul, others purportedly written by some of Jesus' disciples, and the apocalyptic account of the expected cosmic transformation, known as the book of Revelation. These texts were far from being the only authoritative gospels, epistles and 'revelations' circulating among early Christian communities, but they would become the most important.[7] By the third century CE, they were increasingly being described as the new 'testament' (or 'covenant') – a label indexing their elevated status as sacred writings both completing and eclipsing the old 'testament' of Christianity's Jewish roots. Collectively known as 'the books' (in Greek, *ta biblia*), the Bible would arguably become the most significant book in global history – and its deity the God of Western cultures.

God's body is nowhere denied in the Bible. It is simply assumed – whether or not mortals were privileged enough to catch a glimpse of it. And according to biblical texts, many were. Following their exodus from Egypt, a committee of Israelite elders had ascended Mount Sinai and seen first God's feet, then the deity himself. Among them, of course, was Moses, who is said to have enjoyed regular meetings with God, talking to him 'face to face, as one would speak to a friend'.[8] Moses is not the only one claimed to have experienced God's physical presence. In Genesis, Abraham walks alongside him, and Jacob has a wrestling match with him. In the books bearing their names, the prophets Isaiah and Ezekiel each see God sitting on his throne, while Amos sees him standing in one of his temples. In the Gospels, Jesus not only boasts he has seen God, but is also said to have seated himself alongside God in the heavens, at his right hand. It is a companionable pairing reputedly witnessed by members of the Jesus movement, including a talkative young man called Stephen in the book of Acts, and the enraptured, if terrified, writer of Revelation, known as John of Patmos, both of whom see God sitting enthroned in the heavens, with Christ seated or standing next to him.[9] In all these biblical stories, and many more besides, it was simply a given that God had a body. The sensational aspect in their telling was that God had allowed people to see it – such a rare privilege that, during the Second Temple period (*c.* 515 BCE–70 CE), God was increasingly understood to have long hidden his body from the world, rendering it unseeable – and hence invisible – to most mortals.[10]

But an unseen body is not the same as a non-existent body. Underpinning the hiddenness of God was a religious regulation which had crept its way into earlier versions of the Ten Commandments in the Second Temple period: 'You shall not make for yourself a carved image, whether in the likeness of what is in the heavens above, or what is on the earth below, or what is in the waters beneath the earth'.[11] It is a striking insertion, for it suggests that material images of God were once a normative feature of Israelite and Judahite religion – otherwise there would be no need for the ban.[12] And in this, Israel and Judah were no different from their neighbours, for – alongside other sacred objects – statues and figurines of deities had long played a part in south-west Asian religions. It was well understood that the gods were usually unobservable in their 'natural' heavenly habitat. But they might deign to reveal themselves in the earthly realm as material images in a cult place (a site of worship). More than a symbol or representation, a cult image was a material manifestation of divine presence: the statue was not only identified with the deity, but *was* the deity.

It is all too easy to dismiss this as a characteristic of unsophisticated or 'primitive' religious cultures, but this is to misunderstand the people of the past – and their gods. This was a world in which perceptions of reality were neither limited nor defined by the physical, but stretched along a continuum from the natural to the supra-natural. The cosmic membrane separating the earthly from the otherworldly was highly porous and malleable, so that divinity in all its myriad forms could break through into the world of humans, whether it was perceived as a strange scent on the wind, a fleeting shape glimpsed from the corner of the eye, or felt at a powerful place in the landscape. But divinity was at its most tangible when materialized in images of the gods. It was by means of cooperation between deities and worshippers, facilitated by ritual experts, that the earthly substance of the statue was transformed into a different category of being. As ritual specialists in Mesopotamia had put it, the divine statue was 'born in heaven and made on earth'.[13] As extraordinary beings, deities were thus unconstrained: they could remain unseen and at a distance in the heavens while simultaneously revealing themselves as stars in the sky, statues in temples, figurines in the home, or unseen but perceptible forces permeating the earthly realm.[14]

The biblical ban on divine images is often held to signal the incorporeal nature of God, marking him out as a deity distinct from any other in the ancient world – a deity impossible to craft in clay or metal, wood or stone, by virtue of being bodiless. But the Bible's promotion of imageless worship indicates no such thing. The cults of various Egyptian, Assyrian, Babylonian and Phoenician deities all experienced periods of aniconic worship, despite the fact that these deities were understood to have bodies.[15] The prohibition of divine images in the Ten Commandments points instead to a growing emphasis on the hiddenness of God's body, as a closely related tradition in Deuteronomy indicates. Here, Moses reminds the Israelites of their encounter with God on the way to the Promised Land, when they had gathered at the foot of the holy mountain in the wilderness to listen as the deity spelled out the terms of the covenant. Having descended onto the mountaintop, God himself was veiled from view, for all the Israelites could see was the heavenly fire and dark cosmic cloud shrouding the mountain's peak. 'Since you saw no form when Yahweh spoke to you from the middle of the fire', Moses says, 'watch yourselves very closely, lest you act corruptly by making a carved image for yourselves'.[16] In this text, the imageless worship of God was to be preferred to creating a statue of a deity the Israelites hadn't actually seen, but had only heard speaking.

This emerging theological emphasis on the hiddenness of God would eventually give rise to the abstract, incorporeal deity of Judaism and Christianity – a deity no longer shrouded by fire and clouds, but only wondrous, inscrutable mystery. But Judaism and Christianity are post-biblical religions, and their disembodied deity is a later re-imagining of a god who was far from enigmatic. For the God of the Bible was a deity who not only had a body, but a personal name, a backstory, a family and a host of companions in the heavens.

Curriculum Vitae

God's real name is Yaho. Or Yahu. Or perhaps just Yah. It is impossible to know for sure, because the original, Hebrew-speaking devotees of this god used a writing system comprising only consonants, much like modern Hebrew and Arabic today. And so in ancient inscriptions, the deity's name appears only as 'Yhw', 'Yh' and 'Yhwh', leaving us uncertain as to how it was vocalized. It is the longer form, 'Yhwh', that is more commonly found in the ancient Hebrew literature of the Bible, but although many of these texts would be read aloud in worship, it remains difficult to know how the name was pronounced, for by the third century BCE, when this deity had already been venerated for centuries, it had become unutterable: a name too dangerous and powerful for human mouths to articulate. But later scholars in the Graeco-Roman world would have no such scruples. They appear to have vocalized it as 'ya-we' or 'ya-ve', and so 'Yahweh' is the name by which this deity has come to be known.[17] Given the thorough-going theological revision of the literature which now forms the Hebrew Bible, Yahweh is often assumed to have been a distinctively solitary deity, devoid of divine colleagues and a family. But the religious realities of his early history were very different.

As one of many deities in the Late Bronze and Early Iron Age Levant, Yahweh was originally a god rooted within a polytheistic world – and remained comfortably so for much of his early career. This was a world in which the gods were imagined as a sprawling heavenly household, broadly reflecting the family bonds and social structures of their human worshippers. In most Levantine societies, this pantheon was headed by the aged progenitor of the cosmos, the god El or (in some dialects) Il – a name functioning both as a proper noun and the generic Semitic term for 'deity'. Beneath him were ranked a younger generation of gods, each charged with a particular portfolio in the management of the universe – from storms, seas, sunlight and starlight, to fertility, birth, warfare and death. As frontline deities, these were the most prominent gods of ancient Levantine societies, and those most closely tied to the political and territorial identities of their worshippers.

Thanks particularly to a wealth of literature dated to the fourteenth and thirteenth centuries BCE, recovered from the remains of an ancient city-state called Ugarit, on the Syrian coast, El's multi-tiered household has come into sharper focus. He was understood to be the gentle father of the gods, enjoying a comfortable semi-retirement from the day-to-day running of the cosmos, accompanied by his consort, the mother goddess Athirat. Between them, they had 'seventy sons' – a collective term for the frontline deities. These included Ugarit's special patron, the powerful storm-god Baal, and his sister Anat, a fearsome warrior, as well as the boisterous sea-god Yam and the underworld king of death, Mot, each of whom dwelt in his own domain located at the very edge of the divine realm. Ranked beneath them were the relatively minor deities of practical skills and cultural arts, including architecture and design, healing, music and magic, while below them was a collection of divine attendants and messengers, who variously served the gods and commuted between the heavens and the earthly realm. Despite their differences in rank, the gods met together as a divine council or assembly, chaired by El in his role as the highest god, to decide on matters both divine and mortal.

Ugarit's pantheon was typical of Levantine religions in the late second and early first millennium BCE, when early forms of Yahweh worship emerged. The pantheon's shape and composition was determined by the very human idea that to be a god isolated from any other was to be bereft of the benefits of collaboration, status and kinship. In short, it was to be socially impotent – and frankly useless, therefore, to mortals. Against this cultural backdrop, certain theological claims asserting that Yahweh had only ever been a solitary deity look more than a little implausible. And the Bible itself reveals that this god was far from alone.

A fragment of ancient poetry in the book of Deuteronomy not only locates Yahweh within a pantheon, but also reveals exactly who his father was. It describes the separation of humans into distinct groups ('peoples' or 'nations'), and explains why each group was allocated a particular deity to act as its special patron. But the deity supervising this division of divine labour is not Yahweh, but Elyon – a title of El reflecting his role as the 'Most High' god of the pantheon:

> When Elyon ['Most High'] apportioned the nations,
> when he divided humankind,
> he fixed the boundaries of the peoples
> according to the number of the divine sons;
> for Yahweh's portion was his people,
> Jacob [Israel] his allotted share.[18]

Here, Yahweh appears as just one among El's many divine children.[19] Other ancient pieces of poetry in the Hebrew Bible tell us something of Yahweh's early career. They too employ mythic motifs that run against the theological preferences of later biblical writers and editors, suggesting that they reflect older traditions about the earliest history of the biblical God. Far from portraying Yahweh as the supreme king and creator of the cosmos, they present him instead as a minor but ferocious storm deity, at the margins of the inhabited world, in an ancient place variously known as Seir, Paran and Teman – cast in the Bible as a dangerous, mountainous wilderness, seemingly located south of the Negev desert, beyond the Dead Sea, in what used to be called Edom and is now southern Jordan.[20]

As a god of such a place, Yahweh might have been akin to a group of disruptive deities known in the southern Levant as the Shadday gods – a name identifying them as deities of the 'steppe' or 'wilderness'. And naturally, they too were subordinate to El. A remarkable discovery at Deir 'Alla, the site of an ancient city in the eastern Jordan valley, offers a glimpse of these desert-dwelling deities. Inside a building destroyed by an earthquake in about 800 BCE, archaeologists found several fragments of a lengthy inscription, which had once adorned a plastered wall. Pieced together, it describes a series of visions received by a seer called Balaam ben Beor, who would later make a cameo appearance in the biblical book of Numbers as a prophet of El.[21] The inscription reveals that a delegation of deities had warned Balaam that the Shadday gods had banded together against their high god, El, and were threatening to sew up the heavens in thick cloud, casting the world into darkness. 'So will be done, with naught surviving; no one has seen [the likes of] what you have heard!' the gods declare to the panicked seer.[22]

While the heavenly rebellion and its associated cosmic calamity is typical of ancient south-west Asian myths, it is the portrayal of El as the heavenly overlord of the Shadday gods that is particularly remarkable, for it parallels one of the most prominent titles given to El in the Hebrew Bible. In Genesis, the god of the Israelite patriarchs Abraham, Isaac and Jacob is not usually named Yahweh, but El Shadday, as the deity himself insists: 'I am El Shadday', the God of the Bible announces to Abraham, 'I will make my covenant between me and you, and will make you exceedingly numerous'.[23] The deity makes a similar promise to Jacob: 'I am El Shadday! Be fruitful and multiply; a nation and a company of nations shall come from you, and kings shall spring from you'.[24] Traditionally (if mistakenly) translated as 'God Almighty', 'El Shadday' means something like 'El of the wilderness', and appears to have been the name of a well-known local manifestation of the great high god El in and around the territories identified today as Palestine, Israel and Jordan. It is El to whom Abraham, Isaac and Jacob build altars and make offerings in the land of Canaan, marking it out as the territory their divinely promised descendants will inherit. And it is El whom even these biblical writers recognize as being the god of their assumed ancestors.

Scholars have long suspected that El, not Yahweh, was the original god of the people known in the Bible as 'Israel'; his name not only occurs in the traditions of the patriarchs, but is embedded in the name of Israel itself (*yisra-el*), and is explicitly revealed in the divine name of a temple Jacob is said to have built at the ancient city of Shechem, in what is now the West Bank: 'He erected an altar there and called it "El, god of Israel" '.[25] Yahweh would gradually come to usurp his father El by supplanting him as the head of the pantheon. But quite how this happened remains frustratingly unclear. It is possible that the transition was tied to the socio-political conditions that gave rise to the emergence of the kingdoms of Israel and Judah early in the first millennium BCE. With kingship and statecraft came ideologies of militarized power – and the need for kings to exhibit themselves as warriors endorsed by fearsome divine fighters. As a storm god, Yahweh was naturally a god of warfare, equipped with weapons of thunder, lightning and rainclouds, and it was Yahweh's personal patronage the kings of Israel and Judah claimed. And as the patron deity of these kings, so Yahweh became the tutelary god of their small kingdoms, and the deity increasingly promoted at the ancient temples and sanctuaries within their bounds, whose economic and ritual heft further enabled and enhanced the performance of royal power.[26]

While this might account for the political prioritization of Yahweh, and even the deity's acquisition of some of El's traditional roles, titles and sanctuaries, it is still unknown exactly how or when Yahweh came to be understood as the head of the pantheon – and it is impossible to say whether or not this view of the pantheon was shared by ordinary Israelites and Judahites, for whom the religious ideologies of statehood remained relatively unimportant. What is more certain is that cultural memories of El's traditional role persisted, suggesting they remained too potent, or too deeply ingrained, to be ignored or excised from the religious traditions on which biblical authors and editors subsequently drew. Instead, a different theological strategy was employed: in a spectacularly transparent attempt at spin-doctoring, some writers sought to downplay Yahweh's apparent supplanting of his mythic father by insisting that Yahweh was El all along: 'I am Yahweh', the deity says to Moses, in Exodus. 'I appeared to Abraham, Isaac and Jacob as El Shadday, but by my name Yahweh I did not make myself known to them'.[27]

Yahweh's origins might well be murky, but by the ninth century BCE, he was firmly established as the head of the local pantheons of two kingdoms located in the territories belonging today to modern Israel and Palestine: Judah, with Jerusalem serving as its capital, and, to its north, Israel, governed primarily from the city of Samaria, the impressive remains of which are located in today's West Bank. Of the two, the kingdom of Israel was by far the stronger: with ten times the people power of Judah, its flourishing economy was rooted in the fertile soils of its hilly spine and lush lowlands, which together produced the olive oil, wine and wheat on which its economy and trade depended. Israel was a relatively prominent player on the southern Levantine stage, while Judah was often little more than its smaller, weaker, poorer neighbour.[28] These kingdoms were just two of a number of regional polities, among them the Philistines, who lived along the coast of present-day southern Israel and the Gaza Strip; the kingdoms of Ammon, Moab and Edom, in what is now modern Jordan; the Phoenicians, whose principal cities now lie within modern Lebanon and coastal southern Syria; and the Aramaeans, who dominated much of the rest of Syria. By the eighth century BCE, these peoples were subsumed within the vast expanse of the Assyrian Empire, which now stretched from its Mesopotamian homeland in today's Iraq to encompass the lands we now know as Iran, Turkey, Syria, Lebanon, Israel, the Palestinian territories and Jordan.

But the imperial subjugation of the kingdoms of Israel and Judah did not dislodge the cultural characteristics indigenous to these small southern Levantine societies. Within both kingdoms – which shared not only an oft-contested border, but a language (Hebrew), treaties and trade agreements, similar social and religious practices, and myths about common ancestors and gods – Yahweh was acclaimed as the 'national' or state deity, and the divine patron of each kingdom's royal household. A number of other deities, who likely played their part in the polytheistic governance of the cosmos, were worshipped alongside him, with the most prominent among them being Yahweh's wife, the goddess Asherah. The biblical writers cannot help but reveal that she was worshipped alongside Yahweh in his temples in Jerusalem and Samaria, while inscriptions dating to the eighth century BCE attest to worshippers seeking blessings from 'Yahweh and his Asherah'. This goddess was a local iteration of one of the oldest deities in the Levant, beloved for millennia by numerous societies across the region. Indeed, her name betrays something of her former life: 'Asherah' is the Hebrew version of 'Athirat', the name of the mother of the gods at Ugarit – and El's consort. It would appear that, in supplanting his mythological father, Yahweh also took his wife. While the domestic arrangements of this biblical Oedipus might have been perfectly straightforward for an ancient deity and his worshippers, they would prove intolerable for later biblical writers, who engaged in so determined a campaign of defamation against the goddess that she would come to be locked out of the heavens forever.

Historically, the goddess's fall broadly reflects the decline of traditional, state-sponsored polytheism – a decline triggered by the Assyrian annihilation of the kingdom of Israel in about 722 BCE, and the Babylonian destruction of Judah in 587 BCE. As patron deity and divine warrior of his peoples, Yahweh had seemingly failed to protect them. It would prompt a profound theological and cultural shift among certain priestly and scribal groups, some of them in exile, whose work would begin to shape the central traditions reflected in the Hebrew Bible, and eventually craft a new image of their god – the deity who would become the God of the Bible. Despite the destruction of his kingdoms, Yahweh himself had not been defeated, they insisted.

Rather, he had engineered the collapse of the states of Israel and Judah in punishment of his worshippers' religious deviancy: the worship of other gods. Yahweh would come to be presented as a god intolerant of other deities, and Yahweh worship would become increasingly monolatrous.

Readers of the Bible might be surprised by this brief historical overview of Yahweh's early career. After all, the ancient editorial voices dominating the biblical portrayal of the past insist on a competing, alternative story, in which it is claimed that, from the beginning, God was only ever a solitary, unchanging deity, devoid of divine colleagues; a universal being in exclusive command of the cosmos, its course and its creatures. But this story is a product of a later theological worldview – and its narrative of religious history is unreliable. The texts that form the Bible were never intended to be a coherent account of the past, and they do not agree on either the central features or the smaller details of the religious landscape they present. Just as an atlas can only offer a constructed version of the world, compiled from a selection of political, cultural and social preferences (the changing names and borders of nations; disused quarries and railway lines) and frozen moments in time (the shifting shapes of coastlines, ice caps, forests and deserts), so too the Bible comprises a diverse collection of material, crafted and reworked over time with the force and flux of competing ideologies.

By mapping God's body, rather than the Bible itself, we can better navigate the transformation of this ancient southern Levantine deity into the God with whom we are now culturally more familiar. Despite the theological changes wrought by the emergence of ancient Judaism and early Christianity, the one aspect of this deity that remained unchanged was his corporeality. By virtue of having a body, he endured as a powerful social agent in the lives of his worshippers across the centuries of the Bible's formation. In exploring the body of this ancient deity as his worshippers imagined him, we can access their world. We can meet the real God of the Bible.

Part I

FEET AND LEGS

2

GROUNDED

A little over forty miles north-west of Aleppo, in northern Syria, set high above a valley, there lie the remains of a gateway to heaven: an ancient temple, the meeting place of the heavenly and earthly planes. A colossal carved lion, its teeth and claws bared, guards the approach. Surrounded by walls of black basalt, its floor paved with pale flagstones, the temple is the dwelling place of a long-lost deity, worshipped by the Syro-Hittites – close cultural cousins of the ancient Israelites and Judahites. Partially destroyed in the eighth century BCE, and devastated again in a Turkish airstrike in 2018, this temple at 'Ain Dara is the closest we can come to the temple that stood in Jerusalem at the same time. Its structure and iconography map so precisely onto the biblical description of Solomon's temple, it is as though they shared the same divine blueprint.

When I visited the temple in 2010, shortly before the war in Syria began, wild summer flowers dotted the grass at the temple's edges, dappling the feet of guardian beings and lions lining the base of its now broken walls. I took off my shoes and walked barefoot up the warm, shallow steps to the entrance of the temple's outer courtyard. And then I saw them: two giant footprints, each about a metre in length, carved into the limestone threshold; neatly paired, they were pointing into the temple. The toes and balls of each footprint were softly, deeply rounded, as though they had been pressed firmly into wet sand. I stepped into these enormous, yet delicate feet. They dwarfed my own. I was standing in the bare footsteps of a god. As I looked ahead of me, I could see the vastness of the deity's stride into the temple: the left foot had been imprinted again a few metres inside the temple, this time on the entrance to the vestibule; ten metres or so beyond that was the right footprint, inside the holy of holies – the innermost sanctum, where the deity dwelt (Plate 1).[1] The god had arrived home, and I was there to witness it.

This was the grand residence of a deity whose precise identity has long since been forgotten. But although this god would fade from view, their bodily presence was clearly marked by those giant footprints, travelling in just one direction: inside. There were no exiting footprints; no indication that the deity had left the temple. Rather, the footprints signalled the permanent presence of the god within. It is this sense of material presence that lies at the heart of ancient ideas about deities. The perceived reality of the gods was bound up with the notion that for anything or anyone to exist – and persist – is to be present and placed in some tangible form. It is to be engaged with and within the physical world. The footprints at 'Ain Dara communicated precisely this sense of placement. They marked the exact place of the deity within the world of humans. At this spot, where the heavenly and earthly realms met, the god was manifest and accessible to worshippers. The deity took on a social life.

The power of the footprint to communicate complex ideas about social presence says as much about what it is to be human as it does about what it is to be a god. When we see footprints, we recognize them as material traces of being; a frozen moment of movement or stillness; a memorial – however fleeting – to a reality by which we configure ourselves in the world and with those around us. Footprints capture something of the extraordinary and the familiar about human life – the orchestrated and haphazard, the durable and flimsy. A toddler's excited footsteps imprinted in sand or snow. Celebrity shoe-prints set in concrete on Hollywood Boulevard. Muddy shoes accidentally tracked across a kitchen floor. The footprints of a group of *Australopithecus afarensis*, some of our earliest bipedal hominid ancestors, solidified in volcanic ash, three and a half million years ago, in Laetoli, northern Tanzania.[2] The famous dusty boot-print of Apollo 11 astronaut Buzz

Aldrin on the surface of the moon. A footprint isn't simply a trace or a representation of the foot. It is a material memory of its owner treading upon the surface on which the print appears, conjuring the presence of the whole body – the whole person.[3] Our feet are not simply the pedestals on which we stand, or the motors by which we move, but the foundations of our presence in the world.

The impressions made by our feet have imprinted themselves into the religious cultures we have created. The footprints of gods and other extraordinary beings are celebrated and venerated all over the globe: divine or mystical beings are said to have left their footprints in rock art across Scandinavian and British sites of the Late Bronze and Iron Ages. On an island sacred to the ancient Inca in Lake Titicaca, separating Bolivia from Peru, the footsteps of the sun god Inti are displayed. In southern Botswana, the giant hunter Matsieng left his footprints in wet earth around a waterhole.[4] The extent to which the footprint appears in the ritual settings of human communities across time and space is remarkable.

Some of the earliest examples of divine footprints derive from the ancient sanctuaries of deities who once travelled the lands bordering the Mediterranean. According to Herodotus, the enormous footprint of Heracles could be seen in a rock by a river in Scythia – a print Lucian mockingly claimed to be bigger than the footprint of the god Dionysus, next to it.[5] The Egyptian goddess Isis left impressions of her feet across the Graeco-Roman world: at Maroneia, in Greece, for example, her supersized prints appear alongside those of one of her consorts, Serapis. This divine couple is also invoked in a first-century BCE inscription upon a marble slab in Thessaloniki, beneath which the goddess has approvingly left her footprints.[6]

Such is the power of divine footprints that they often became sites of competing religious claims. Most famous, perhaps, is the depression in rock akin to an enormous footprint on Sri Pada, a high peak in south-central Sri Lanka. For Tamil Hindus, it is the print of Shiva, left as he danced creation into existence; for Buddhists, the footprint belongs to Gautama Buddha, who pressed his foot into a sapphire beneath the rock; for Muslims, it is the print left by Adam as he trod on the mountain following his expulsion from Eden; for Christians, it is the footprint of Saint Thomas, who is claimed to have brought Christianity to the region.[7] Jerusalem, too, has its share of contested holy footprints. As he ascended to heaven, Muhammad is said to have left a single footprint upon the exposed spur of bedrock enshrined beneath the Dome of the Rock, in Jerusalem. But for Christian pilgrims and Crusaders of the medieval period, the footprint on this sacred rock belonged to Jesus, whose foot is also said to be imprinted on the Mount of Olives, where it has been venerated since at least the fifth century CE.[8] Whether the work of geological erosion, local folklore or ritual art, each of these footprints communicates something of both the earthiness and otherworldliness of a divine or holy being.

As my own feet rested in the footprints of an ancient deity in Syria, I better understood why the biblical God is so frequently concerned with the placement of his feet – and why we find his footprints all over the Bible and the landscapes its texts describe. In Genesis, Adam and Eve hear Yahweh's footsteps approaching as he walks in the Garden of Eden; later in the same book, Abraham sees Yahweh standing with two other divine beings beneath a group of sacred trees, and subsequently goes for a walk with him. Soon after, Abraham's grandson, Jacob, encounters Yahweh standing next to him in a sacred space at Bethel.[9] In the book of Exodus, Moses meets God several times. When he first sees Yahweh in his corporeal form, the deity is standing on a magical rock in the wilderness. Later, when Moses ascends Mount Sinai with a group of tribal elders, God is seen again – along with a stunning close-up of the heavenly floor on which his feet rest:

> Moses and Aaron, Nadab and Abihu, and seventy of the elders
> of Israel went up, and they saw the God of Israel. And under
> his feet there was something like a brick pavement of lapis
> lazuli, like the very heavens for clarity.[10]

When the biblical story moves to Jerusalem, God's feet are there, too. This time, they are surrounded by the fragrant trees of an Eden-like temple garden, which, Yahweh says, 'glorify where my feet rest'.[11] 'This is the place for the soles of my feet, where I will reside among the people of Israel forever', he declares of his temple in the city.[12] It is the place to which generations of his worshippers would flock to encounter the presence of the divine.

In the Bible, God's feet are crucial to his social existence – fundamental to his very being – and so they are the bodily features by which he often renders himself evident in the world. The force of his feet splits mountains. They shake the earth as he strides out from the desert. They crush the bodies of his enemies. They transform dust and dirt into holy ground. Like indelible tracks worn into the earth along ancient pathways, the precise locations at which Yahweh plants his feet impact the landscape: his sure-footed presence in the earthly realm transforms a piece of ground into a place, and a place into sacred space.

Almost four million years ago, three changes in the bodies of our primeval ancestors enabled us to climb down from the trees to live upon the ground: our brains grew larger and more powerful; our thumbs and fingers became more dexterous; and our spines, hips and legs changed shape and alignment, so that we could habitually walk upright on two feet. In the popular drama of human evolution, our brains and hands tend to play the starring roles, with the feet cast as supporting members of the anatomical ensemble. According to the usual script, habitual human bipedalism freed up the hands so that they could spend less time propelling our bodies about and more time working with the brain in carrying out increasingly complex tasks. It was with our hands and our heads that human animals conquered the world; our feet simply got us about.

And yet, as the social anthropologist Tim Ingold argues, the relegation of our feet to mere motors was not simply a product of evolution. It was also a 'head-over-heels' conceptual shift in European intellectual perception, millions of years later, brought about by the dominance of the stiff leather boot.[13] With the invention of the boot came the enclosing of the foot, dulling its sensory capacities, limiting its use as a tool to grasp and manipulate objects, and distancing our feet from the ground. The pervasive presence of the booted foot altered Europeans' bodily experience of the natural world – so much so, that, by the time human evolutionary theory had become firmly established in the modern West, the boot was already a colonial and cultural marker of 'civilization', along with chairs, pavements, military parade grounds and motorized vehicles, all of which elevated us away from the earthy messiness of the 'primitive', uncontrollable world. But as our feet lost touch with the ground, so we lost touch with our feet.

By contrast, our religious ancestors were far more grounded – and so too were their gods. The deities of the ancient Levant kept their feet firmly planted on the earth, imparting something of the divine to the places at which they stood. Indeed, sacred space had long been marked by the material presence of supra-natural powers. Across the Levant, for thousands of years before Yahweh worship emerged, the presence of these supra-natural powers was often manifested by standing stones. Heavyweight, hardy and enduring, and taller than they were wide, these roughly hewn stone slabs ranged in size from just a foot or so high to towering monoliths. They were erected into a standing position, singly or in small groups, at places of power in the landscape – locations deemed to mark magical points of access to other realms. Their upright stance transformed the 'natural' stone into a social presence: the stone stood up like a person.

By the Early Bronze Age (c. 3100–2000 BCE), standing stones could be found in a range of settings: at isolated, open-air locations at a distance from human communities; at outdoor locations on the out-skirts of walled settlements; and inside buildings or compounds within settlements.[14] Archaeologists are still uncertain about the precise ways in which these stones were understood to function during this period. What is more certain, however, is that, by the Middle Bronze Age (c. 2000–1500 BCE), standing stones were identified with extraordinary beings: they marked the presence of deities, deified ancestors and other supernatural powers, who 'stood' at places at which the membrane between the human realm and otherworldly planes was at its most permeable (fig. 2).

The identification of standing stones with a divine presence con-tinued throughout the Late Bronze Age (c. 1550–1200 BCE) and the Iron Age (1200–539 BCE). During this long period, these stones were common – though not uniform – features of temples and other ritual spaces across the southern Levant. Whether these sacred spaces were sited inside

Fig. 2. A row of standing stones, ranging in height from one to three metres, at the ancient site of Gezer, Israel. Set up in the Middle Bronze Age (*c.* 2000–1500 BCE), the stones stood as a social group, materializing the presence of otherworldly beings or powers. The squat block in the foreground is a large limestone basin, likely used in rituals.

towns and cities, on their fringes, or at more remote locations in the wider landscape, their standing stones simultaneously monumental- ized, memorialized and manifested the robust, grounded presence of the divine. Over thousands of years, the sturdy base of a standing stone implanted into the earth had gradually come to mark the presence of a deity or otherworldly being dwelling in the material world. And these very ancient ideas about divine presence played a crucial role in shaping the God of the Bible and the places at which he stood.

Standing stones populated the urban temples and outdoor sanctu- aries associated with Yahweh worship, as archaeological excavations confirm. Some of these were very ancient, as at early Iron Age Shechem, near modern Nablus in the West Bank. Here, three stones had already stood for several centuries in a large fortified cult place; although it is now broken, the largest of these is estimated to have been almost three metres high. Others were more recent installations. Within a Judahite fortress at Arad, in the Negev desert, an eighth- century BCE temple dedicated to Yahweh contained a standing stone

Fig. 3. Jerusalem's Israel Museum is now home to the inner
sanctum of an eighth-century BCE temple dedicated to Yahweh,
uncovered during excavations at Judah's fortress town of Arad.
The standing stone bears faint traces of red pigment. In
the foreground are two incense altars.

almost a metre tall, originally decorated with red pigment (fig. 3). At
the same time, a sanctuary just inside the city of Dan, in the very north
of the neighbouring kingdom of Israel, contained several groups of
standing stones, some accompanied by incense burners and the bones
of sacrificial animals. These sites represent just a handful of those
exhibiting standing stones in their cult places, demonstrating that
they were a familiar presence across the religious landscape.[15] Today,
these stones might look unexpectedly modest – even a little undignified –
for time has stripped them of all but the barest traces of their social
lives. But something of their sacred presence and numinous power
can be seen on two coins from the Phoenician cities of Tyre and Byblos,
in what is now Lebanon. Although these coins were minted in the
Roman period, both exhibit far older Levantine religious motifs: one
shows a standing stone enshrined within a high-status temple courtyard; the other depicts a pair of standing stones beneath a sacred
tree, an offering of incense burning on an ornate brazier before them
(fig. 4).

Fig. 4. Drawings of two third-century CE coins from Byblos (left) and Tyre (right). Both present standing stones in cultic settings. On the Byblos coin, the stone stands in a pillared temple precinct. The Tyrian coin shows a pair of stones on a platform, flanked by a sacred tree and an incense burner. Beneath them is inscribed the legend 'Ambrosial Rocks'.

Given their ubiquity across the Levant, it is no surprise to find that the biblical writers were well acquainted with standing stones. More significantly, the terminology they use to refer to these objects and their cult places reflects the age-old association of the standing presence of the divine and sacred space: in the Hebrew Bible, a standing stone is called a *massebah*, derived from the word meaning 'standing', while a sacred location at which these stones were placed is a *maqom*, a term commonly translated 'place', but which more precisely means 'a standing place'.

This specialized religious terminology is artfully employed in a highly idealized account in Genesis about the supposed origins of a temple at Bethel – a sacred site located atop a small mountain within the wider environs of what is now Ramallah, in the West Bank. Dating to at least the Middle Bronze Age, the site's biblical name betrays its very ancient and prestigious origins: 'Bethel' tends to be translated as 'House of God', but it more literally means 'House of El', suggesting it was a temple originally sacred to Yahweh's predecessor. As with many other religious sites and stories, however, it was later claimed by Yahweh worshippers as their own, giving rise to the legend in Genesis, in which the temple is founded by one of the great ancestors of Israel, Jacob.

As he travels through the promised land of Canaan on a quest for a wife, Jacob beds down for the night in the open, using a slab of stone as a large pillow. He dreams, and sees a staircase (not a ladder) on which messenger gods are travelling up and down between the earth and the heavens – a clear indication that this is a place at which humans can access the divine. Suddenly, Yahweh is standing next to him. He introduces himself as the ancestral deity of Jacob's forebears, Abraham and Isaac, and promises blessings of perpetual fertility and immovable territory in return for allegiance from Jacob and his descendants. When he awakes, Jacob realizes he has been sleeping in the dwelling place of the deity. 'Yahweh is in this standing-place!' he exclaims, giddy with the tremulous zeal of the newly converted. 'How awesome is this standing-place!'* He sets up the rock on which he slept as a standing stone (*massebah*), anoints it with sacred oil and pledges to make offerings to Yahweh there.[16] At Bethel, Yahweh not only stands in the place marked by a standing stone, but identifies with the stone itself: 'I am the god of Bethel, whom you anointed there in the *massebah*', he later reminds Jacob.[17]

Today, the ancient temple at Bethel is lost to pilgrims, tourists and archaeologists, for much of the ancient city lies hidden beneath the long-established West Bank town of Beitin – one among many towns and villages caught up in bitter territorial disputes between primarily Orthodox Jewish settlers and local Palestinian communities.[18] But ancient Bethel was long known to have been one of the most authoritative and prosperous religious sites in the region throughout the Iron Age and well into the Roman period. Consequently, its temple was also a fierce competitor to its near neighbour in Jerusalem.[19] Only a little over ten miles apart, the temples in Bethel and Jerusalem were powerful political and economic hubs located in related but rival territories during the first half of the first millennium BCE: Bethel, in the punchy

---

* As tempting as it is to hear a Californian accent in reading Jacob's exclamation, the term 'awesome' in its biblical usage carries the sense of an overwhelming but reverent fear of the divine.

kingdom of Israel and – later – the Assyrian province of Samerina, was a sanctuary of prestigious ancestral pedigree under the administrative patronage of the state, while Jerusalem, of course, was the capital of the smaller, weaker kingdom of Judah, and its temple served as the ritual powerhouse of the ruling Davidic dynasty.

As high-status political and economic centres, as well as important cult places, Bethel and Jerusalem each relied on Yahweh's footfall to maintain their position as the powerful – and profitable – place at which the deity was present. Bethel might have boasted of being the standing place of God, but Jerusalem countered with the claim it was the place at which God had chosen to permanently rest his feet. It is a claim reflected in Yahweh's biblical assertions that the Jerusalem temple was 'my sanctuary, the place of my feet' and 'the place for the soles of my feet, where I will reside forever'.[20] But these were not expressions of quiet, restful domesticity. They were proprietorial: whether divine or human, feet communicated ownership and identity throughout ancient south-west Asia. And the God of the Bible used his to stamp his authoritative presence onto the world of his worshippers.

Underfoot

In a world in which writing tended to be the preserve of scribal guilds, religious specialists and the elites for whom they worked, cylinder seals, stamp seals, tokens and amulets were frequently used as markers of identity, functioning in ways not dissimilar to our own personal signatures, PINs and fingerprints today. For wealthier members of society, small stone or bone seals comprising images or a few words were pressed or rolled into wet clay to validate legal documents and movable property, such as storage jars of wine, olives and grain. Whether prosperous or poor, however, people's clothing, sandals, or body parts also served a similar function.

Clay tablets from the Late Bronze Mesopotamian town of Nuzi, in the northern reaches of modern-day Iraq, illustrate the ways in which children's footprints were used as items of identity and exchange. Dated to between 1500 and 1350 BCE, some of them are imprinted with

the feet of 'ownerless' children (foundlings and orphans) alongside a
record of their newly assigned parents, marking the adoptive family's
responsibility for the child and the child's new social identity. At about
the same time, in Emar, a city on the upper Euphrates in what is now
Syria, the young children of impoverished families might also have
been pawned or sold into servitude, or given over to local businesses
by means of a similar process. Records from Emar reveal this is precisely what a woman called Ku'e and her husband, Zadamma, had to
do. Unable to feed their family, they sold their two-year-old daughter,
year-old twin boys and a baby girl to a religious specialist called Baal-
malik, who paid a mere sixty shekels for the children and later appears
to have trained the two boys to be diviners. Clay tablets recording the
sale are accompanied by further tablets, each impressed with a child's
footprint and a record of their name, serving as contracts of receipt
for Baal-malik.[21] These children's feet quite literally marked their new
social identities.

Property sales, too, might also be accomplished by means of the
foot. In several Mesopotamian cities, tracts of land were transferred in
a series of legal rituals which included references to the seller raising
a foot from the parcel of land to be released, and the buyer setting a
foot on the land to claim its new ownership.[22] Similar practices are
reflected in the Bible, in which land is taken by walking upon it, or
transferred to another by the seller removing a sandal and symbolically
giving it to the buyer. In some traditions, a dead man's land – and the
womb of his widow – might be contracted or released by his kinsman
by means of similar sandal rituals conveying his social and legal right
to claim ownership and occupancy of his dead kinsman's property.[23]

These body rituals underlie the dominant territorial ideologies
of the Bible, in which God vows to give the land of Canaan to the
Israelites: in Deuteronomy, Yahweh promises the Israelites that 'every
place where the soles of your feet tread will be yours'; in Genesis, he
commands Abraham to 'walk through the length and breadth of the
land' of Canaan, 'for I will give it to you'.[24] The proprietorial function
of Abraham's striding feet is a function shared with a divine figure
properly known as 'the Satan' ('the Accuser'), God's minister of justice
in the book of Job, whose task it is to 'go to and fro on the earth' and

'walk up and down on it', policing its inhabitants and punishing those unfaithful to God.[25] In each of these verses, the biblical writers are deliberately engaging in the rhetoric and performance of political power – all prosecuted via the feet.

For thousands of years, from the early third millennium BCE and continuing into the Roman era, the acquisition of lands by means of conquest was regularly publicized in royal inscriptions across south-west Asia and the eastern Mediterranean, describing a king 'setting his foot' or 'bringing down' his sandals on vanquished territories and their peoples. It is an idea beautifully illustrated on the inner soles of King Tutankhamun's ceremonial sandals, which are decorated with gold-lined images of the trussed-up bodies of foreign enemies upon which he trod (Plate 3). Like the pharaoh, the biblical God also used his sandals to mark the subjugation of an enemy: 'On Edom I hurl my shoe!' he boasts in the Psalms, refocusing what might appear to Western eyes as a divine temper tantrum into a violent act of territorial expansion into a neighbouring nation.[26]

Yahweh's shoes were not as ornate as Tutankhamun's, but they were no less authoritative. Cult images of southern Levantine gods suggest they usually wore delicate leather sandals not dissimilar to flip-flops. They might have been relatively simple in style, but the gods' shoes were sandals of status. Unlike the fibrous or leather sandals worn by mere mortals, the purpose of divine shoes was not to protect the feet, but to highlight a deity's sure-footed power. The ideological, rather than practical purpose of divine footwear is evident in a small statue of one of Yahweh's immediate cultural predecessors – a high god from fourteenth-century BCE Hazor, in what is today modern Israel. Seated in ceremonial glory on a now-missing throne, the deity wears sandals accessorized with snazzy wedged heels, giving him an additional authoritative lift (Plate 4).[27] Wedged sandals like these would also become the power shoes of choice for both the fearsome kings of the late Assyrian Empire and the divine beings who protected their thrones. In the British Museum, traces of pigments on the ninth-century BCE wall panels of a royal palace at Kalhu – better known as Nimrud – vividly attest to their force. Accessorized with blood-red soles, they were shoes of deadly dominion.

Across ancient south-west Asia, the divinely derived power of royal feet had long been exhibited on iconographic monuments displayed in temples, palaces, and even on mountainsides, showing the successful king trampling the landscapes and bodies of the subjugated. One of the most dynamic examples is the victory stela of the formidable Mesopotamian king Naram-Sin (*c.* 2254–2218 BCE), grandson of the world's first emperor, Sargon of Akkad (Agade). Now in the Louvre, it was originally set up in the city of Sippar, in what is today Iraq, and is dated to about 2250 BCE. It monumentalizes Naram-Sin's defeat of a powerful people called the Lullubi, who dwelt in the eastern foothills of the Zagros mountains. Naram-Sin is depicted as a triumphant, muscular monarch, striding up a steep, rocky landscape towards the gods' sacred mountain, above which the starburst emblems of the high gods glitter. As he ascends, his eyes fixed on the peak of the divine mount in the heavens, he pins the broken bodies of his barefooted enemies under his sandalled feet, his obedient troops marching in file below him. Naram-Sin is thought to have been one of the first Mesopotamian kings to declare himself divine, and the iconography of this stela vividly promotes his deification: godlike in stature, he dwarfs both his soldiers and enemies as he ascends from the earthly realm into the heavenly plane. Wearing the horned crown of the gods as he tramples the world into submission, he has become just like one of the deities who brought order to the universe by subduing the forces of chaos and disruption under their feet (Plate 2).

The subjugation of chaos was one of the most widespread mythological themes of ancient south-west Asian religions. The creation of the world was frequently understood to have been the result of a divine battle against chaos – often personified as a gigantic and primordial seven-headed sea monster. Although the myth varied in its details across south-west Asian civilizations, its basic shape was the same: a fearless young warrior deity takes on the monster in hand-to-hand combat, each using an arsenal of cosmic forces and magical weapons to attempt to defeat the other. After a lengthy and brutal struggle, the monster is vanquished, the victorious deity trampling its body in an assertion of supremacy. In some traditions, the god then dismembers and rearranges the corpse, creating a carefully contained watery roof for the skies, which separates the heavenly realm from the earthly realm, and an aqueous cosmic floor to separate the earth from the underworld. Having imposed order upon chaos, the warrior deity is rewarded with kingship over the other gods, and his own temple.

The best-known example of this mythic trope is found in the Babylonian epic Enuma Elish, a masterpiece of the late second millennium BCE, in which the mighty god Marduk defeats the fearsome Tiamat, the ancient mother of the gods and embodiment of the primeval salt-sea. Its vivid celebration of Marduk's victory displays the cosmic power of the god's trampling feet:

> He flung down her carcass, he took his stand upon it . . .
> The Lord trampled upon the frame of Tiamat,
> with his merciless mace he crushed her skull.
> He cut open the arteries of her blood . . .
> He split her in two, like a fish for drying,
> half of her he set up and made as a cover, heaven.
> He stretched out the hide and assigned watchmen,
> and ordered them not to let her waters escape.[28]

In the Bible, the battle is fought between Yahweh and the aqueous chaos monster, whose various names attest to its dangerously disordered, unbounded nature: Leviathan ('Twisty One'), Rahab ('Overflow'), Yam ('Sea'), Nahar ('River-Flood'), Tannin ('Dragon' or 'Sea Monster') and Tehom ('Deep') – many of which are the same names given to Baal's watery arch-enemy in the older Ugaritic myths of the battle with disorder. In several biblical texts, Yahweh is praised for 'driving back' Yam, 'breaking the heads of the sea monsters', 'piercing Rahab', 'smashing the heads of Leviathan', dismembering and 'cutting openings' in the corpse of chaos 'for springs and torrents'.[29] According to the book of Job, this enormous watery monster has scaly skin akin to rows of tightly packed shields. Flames shoot from its mouth, scorching smoke pours forth from its nostrils, and when it sneezes, it flashes lightning. As it thrashes about and roars in might, the dragon makes its primal waters boil, whipping up a foam so thick it looks white-haired. It terrifies even the other deities in Yahweh's retinue. 'Are not even the gods overwhelmed at the sight of it?' Yahweh asks. 'No one is so fierce as to dare stir it up – who can stand before it? Who can confront it and be safe – under the whole heaven, who?'[30] The answer to these questions, of course, is Yahweh, who subjugates the chaos monster by hooking it like a fish, filleting its body and trampling it under his feet.

Elsewhere in the Hebrew Bible, God follows up his victory over the monster by pinning its watery body beneath his throne in his temple in Jerusalem. 'Yahweh sits enthroned over the flood! Yahweh sits enthroned as king forever!' went the ancient ritual refrain.[31] Here, temple mythology dovetailed with a distinctly royal ideology: Yahweh was explicitly cast as a divine king, seated in glory in a throne room in his temple, the fearsome chaos monster now his subservient prisoner, its waters compelled to roar a hymn of praise to Yahweh's superior might:

> Yahweh is king, he is robed in majesty;
> Yahweh is robed, he is girded with strength;
> he has established the world – it shall never be moved.
> Your throne is established from of old,
> you are from everlasting.
> The river-floods have lifted up, O Yahweh,
> the river-floods have lifted up their voice;
> the river-floods lift up their roaring.
> More majestic than the thunders of mighty waters,
> more majestic than the waves of the sea,
> majestic on high is Yahweh![32]

Echoes of the divine defeat of chaos reverberate throughout the Bible, as the mythic trampling, dissection and abuse of its watery form is recycled in other texts: in Exodus, Yahweh bisects the sea to enable Moses and the Israelites to escape Egypt; in the Gospels, Jesus walks like a god on raging waters; and in the book of Revelation, the archangel Michael battles a seven-headed dragon in the final apocalypse.[33] Adopting and adapting the mythic motif of God's battle with monstrous chaos, these traditions demonstrate just how pervasive the ancient myth continued to be. Picking up motifs drawn from the Greek myth of Bellerophon's slaying of the Chimera, it would later find its way into the popular legend of Saint George and the dragon, and become a stock image of hellish turmoil in the wall paintings, tapestries and illuminated manuscripts of medieval Europe.[34]

But in the Hebrew Bible, the only proper place for chaos was beneath the feet of the deity enthroned in his temple in Jerusalem. The building itself was located on the deity's 'holy mountain', Zion, where the vast elevated plaza known in Jewish tradition as Har Habayit ('Temple Mount') and in Islamic tradition as Haram al-Sharif ('Noble Sanctuary') stands today. Even in the Iron Age, Zion was less a mountain and rather more a hill. But within the bounds of sacred topography, the temple's lofty location was mythic, rather than strictly geological. To step into any temple was to ascend into the heavenly sphere – the world of the gods, located in the skies atop a gigantic mythological mountain at the centre of the world. Rooted in the underworld, stretching up through the earthly realm and reaching into the heavens, this cosmic mountain was the vertical axis of the universe. It was commonly known in mythological and ritual texts across the Levant as the 'holy mountain', the 'mountain of the gods', or the 'mount of assembly', and was the site at which the gods gathered to feast, hold council meetings to debate the day-to-day running of the cosmos, and to enjoy the attentions of their worshippers. Whether sited on a mountain, a hill, a rocky outcrop, or even a raised, artificial platform, in the imagined realities of ancient Levantine religions, a temple was necessarily and schematically located at the apex of the cosmic mountain.[35]

It is for this reason that the God of the Bible, like his contemporaries across the sea on Mount Olympus, is often encountered on mountaintops. Be it Sinai or Horeb in the wilderness, Carmel, Tabor, Ebal or Gerizim in the highlands, or Zion or the Mount of Olives in Jerusalem, divine presence is particularly associated with high points in the landscape and the mythological motif of the cosmic mountain. It is an idea beautifully expressed in a small poetic fragment embedded in the book of Amos, in which Yahweh's footsteps on the mountaintops demonstrate his dominion and his role as guarantor of cosmic order:

> For, look!
> The one who forms the mountains, creates the wind,
> reveals his plan to mortals,
> makes the morning darkness,
> and treads on the heights of the earth –
> Yahweh, God of Hosts, is his name![36]

As a king enthroned on the cosmic mountain, Yahweh enjoyed the affectations of ancient, princely rule typical of many other deities across south-west Asia – including a permanent dwelling place of impressive quality. A high-status urban construction, sponsored by the local king and reflecting the religious worldviews of social elites, the Jerusalem temple had much in common with other Levantine temples of the second and first millennia BCE. Constructed of large stone blocks and sweet-smelling cedar (a favourite fragrance of many deities), temples were power structures for both humans and gods. Most were set on a large raised terrace, accessed by steps, and separated from the 'ordinary' world by a walled precinct, into which gateways were cut. These gates opened onto an open-air courtyard, where animal sacrifices and other communal (and potentially messy) rituals were performed. In larger temples, courtyards might also contain sacred trees and plants, pens to hold sacrificial animals, and small workshops, where specialized temple crafts, such as pottery, weaving and herb processing, were carried out.

Most Levantine temples were rectangular in shape, and accessed at the short, eastern side by more ascending steps, a twin-pillared porch and a large set of doors, which might be plated with bronze or other shiny materials to manifest the gleaming brightness of the heavenly realm. These gave entry to a large enclosed space, roofed with wooden beams and scented with incense and perfumed oils, within which more exclusive – and now mostly unknown – rituals were performed. In this space, usually at the very back of the building, behind a wall or screen, was an elevated chamber – the inner sanctum (known in the Bible as the 'holy of holies'), where the deity's statue, standing stone or symbol was housed. Throughout the temple complex, including within the building itself, the walls and portals were covered with magical, protective symbols of cosmic fecundity. In the Jerusalem temple, these seem to have included sacred palm trees, pomegranates, rosettes and blossoming flowers, as well as images of lions, bulls and other powerful guardian beings. It was a place of intense multi-sensory stimulation for those privileged enough to enter.

The monumentality and iconography of temple architecture served not only to glorify their human commissioners and the deities they honoured, but vividly demonstrated the imposition of the divinely inspired, human-built environment upon unwieldy, uncultivated, 'uncivilized' chaos. But the most important function of a royal temple was as a ritual space at which the presence of deities was not only marked, but maintained. And deities were very high maintenance. Their residences were not simply dwelling places, but divine palaces. The incumbent deity and their assembly of junior gods was attended by a household of 'servants' comprising the temple priesthood, who prepared and served the deities' meals (sacrifices and libations); diviners, prophets and cultic scribes, who smoothed the transmission of divine communication (speaking, interpreting and 'recording' oracles and omens); and other priests and ritual functionaries, who washed, dressed and paraded the gods in the form of cult statues.[37]

Ideologically, if not literally, these temples might include enormous furniture for their supersized deities. In an ancient world in which big was beautiful, the gigantism of the gods and their temple furnishings was both an aesthetic delight and a theological virtue. It is for this reason that in the biblical portrayal of the Jerusalem temple – which in its details speaks more to the rhetoric of political prestige than historical reality – King Solomon is said to have provided Yahweh with enormous household furniture, attesting to the gigantic proportions of his body. These included a huge bronze altar for his sacrificial meals, measuring over thirty-two feet (twenty cubits) in length and breadth and more than sixteen feet (ten cubits) high, a vast water basin over sixteen feet in diameter (ten cubits), and ritual bowls for the god's oils and perfumes, set on stands more than eleven feet high (seven cubits).[38] But the

most important of pieces of furniture could be found in the temple's
holy of holies. Here, two golden cherubim formed the giant throne on
which Yahweh was said to sit. Far from being the winged chubby babies
of Renaissance art, cherubim were frightening divine beings with the
wings of an eagle, the body of a lion, a bull or a person, and a human-
like face. Equipped with speed, strength and steadfast stubbornness,
they served the gods as guardians, and could usually be found supporting the thrones of high gods and their nominated kings, and standing
at the thresholds of temples (fig. 5). The Jerusalem cherubim are said
to have stood a staggering sixteen feet high, matching their equally
enormous wing-span of sixteen feet (ten cubits by ten cubits).[39]
Enthroned upon them, Yahweh's feet rested on the ark of the
covenant – a box-shaped miniature shrine, cast as a golden pedestal, said
to measure four feet long (two and a half cubits) and described in the
books of Chronicles as 'the footstool of our God'.[40] The symbolic significance of this configuration of divine furniture is attested by its
longevity and ubiquity in the religious art of the ancient Levant: royal

Fig. 5. Detail of an ivory plaque from the city of Megiddo, dated to about
1350–1150 BCE. It shows a king seated on a high-backed cherubim throne,
his feet resting on a footstool. Egyptian in style, the cherub has the body
of a lion, the wings of a bird of prey and a human-like face.

gods and goddesses are commonly depicted sitting upon tall, ornate thrones in their temples, their feet resting neatly upon raised, solid-legged, square footstools. When the God of the Bible had declared the Jerusalem temple to be the place for the soles of his feet, he meant it literally. And his worshippers knew it, too:

> Yahweh is king; let the peoples tremble!
> He sits enthroned upon the cherubim; let the earth quake!
> Yahweh is huge in Zion;
> he is exalted over all the peoples . . .
> Extol Yahweh our god;
> worship at his footstool.
> Holy is he![41]

Like the deity at 'Ain Dara in Syria, whose footprints were set in stone as they strode into their temple, the permanence of Yahweh's presence in the Jerusalem temple was made manifest by his feet. Enthroned in exalted glory, this was a deity exuding the confident, stable control of a cosmic king who had little need to rise from his seat; a powerful ruler who could sit and relax, his feet up on his stool, the forces of rebellion quashed under the soles of his shoes. That, at least, was the theological ideal. The religious reality was rather different. The political power play of gods and mortals would gradually come to loosen Yahweh's feet from their place in Zion – and worshippers would find themselves reminded that their deity was neither immovable nor immobile.

3

FOOTLOOSE

In the drizzle of a gloomy day, the triumphal Arch of Titus on Rome's Via Sacra can look strangely sombre: the yellowed marble of its enormous frame darkens to a lacklustre grey, rendering its high-vaulted ceremonial archway a bleak and brooding empty space. But beneath the arch itself, the celebratory monument suddenly springs into life. Gods, people, animals and architecture burst out of the bas-relief friezes decorating the passageway. On one side, Titus stands in a chariot pulled by four magnificent horses, as Virtus and Honos, the divine personifications of military virtue and imperial glory, lead the chariot along the processional way. Behind Titus stands winged Victory, crowning him with the oak and acorn circlet of triumph as he gazes towards the political heart of ancient Rome. Originally painted in bright bursts of colour, the monument was erected to celebrate Titus' emphatic defeat of a rebellious Judaea (Judah) in 70 CE, when he was still but a general, fighting under the command of his father, the emperor Vespasian. The spoils of his victory are depicted on the opposite frieze. Here, a throng of Romans jostle their way along the Via Sacra, struggling under the weight of the sacred swag looted from the Jerusalem temple: a golden table for ritual offerings, its cups still perched upon it; the silver trumpets of the temple's priests; and a huge golden menorah (fig. 6).[1]

Of course, the Romans were not the first to monumentalize the capture of sacred treasures from the temples of the defeated, nor indeed the first to glory in the violation of a deity's dwelling place. But

Fig. 6. The Arch of Titus, on Rome's Via Sacra, celebrates the imperial victory over a rebellious Judaea in 70 CE. One of its friezes shows the parade of sacred objects looted from the Jerusalem temple, which was razed to the ground. The huge menorah (left) and the offering table (right) were once painted in golden hues. The temple's elegant trumpets, criss-crossed in front of the offering table, appear to have been coloured silver.

it is the indignity inherent in the dynamic display on the Arch of Titus that distinguishes it from the visual propaganda of earlier imperial cultures; tottering on their makeshift pallets amid a crush of bodies, the Jerusalem temple's prized possessions are not so much glorious trophies, but objects of derision. The contrast with the celebratory art of the conquering kings of older cultures is striking. The mighty emperors of south-west Asia were no less triumphalist in their exhibition of looted temple treasures, and no less destructive in their despoliation of the divine, but they tended to afford a certain dignity to their sacred booty – publicly, at least. Ancient precursors to the iconography of the Arch of Titus can be seen on the monumental wall panels decorating the ceremonial rooms of late Assyrian palaces. Here, soldiers marching with regimented precision carry aloft their holy cargo with reverent care, as their comrades continue to bludgeon, butcher and burn their way through vanquished cities. They process towards their victorious king, who is often shown standing in his

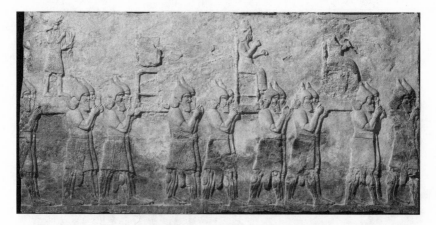

Fig. 7. Part of an Assyrian palace relief from Kalhu (Nimrud), dated to about 730 BCE, showing Levantine gods being conveyed out of their conquered city by victorious Assyrian troops. The cult statues offer a snapshot of the local pantheon: two enthroned deities are followed by a god hidden in a mobile shrine, and a warrior deity, who brandishes a bundle of lightning and a mace.

chariot or sitting on an ornate throne in front of his campaign tent, watching as the wealth of the fallen is paraded before him, his account-ants keeping tally as temple treasures, civic booty, prisoners, refugees and animals file past.

A particularly vivid, though damaged, example of this scene is now in the British Museum. Dated to about 730 BCE, it commemorates the defeat of an unidentified Levantine city by King Tiglath-pileser III. The top register of the panel shows archers attacking the heavily fortified city, while troops hack at the brickwork. Striding past a pile of corpses, soldiers carry off sacks of loot and a couch from an affluent home, while another herds a terrified, skittish ox out of the city. The tumult of the Assyrian raid gives way to a solemn procession in the lower register. Marching two by two, troops convey the gods of the city into exile: carefully positioned on sturdy pallets carried on the soldiers' shoulders, the cult statues progress in stately fashion towards their new home in Assyria. Four deities in the middle of the procession are shown: a fearsome warrior god, wearing a horned crown and bran-dishing his weapons, follows a deity housed in a box-like shrine; ahead of them are two enthroned deities, probably goddesses, clothed in the ankle-length tunics of royal authority. Although their feet are partially obscured by their captors' tall helmets, the towering height of the gods' thrones indicates their feet remain appropriately elevated, their divine authority intact (fig. 7). In a world in which even the gods of other lands were considered dangerously powerful, these statues and their temple furniture are handled with a ritualized reverence. The gods might as well be going on tour to pay willing tribute to another deity in another temple – which is precisely the way in which the capture and exile of divine statues was so often couched in ancient south-west Asian texts and inscriptions.

At the heart of this iconography is the widespread and deeply rooted sense that the imposition and maintenance of order in the earthly realm was a divinely ordained responsibility of kings, who imitated their patron deities by stamping out rebellious forces and upholding the hierarchical power-structures built into the world at its creation. Mortal kings might have had their footstools kicked out from under them as they were pulled from their thrones and forced to prostrate themselves at the feet of a conqueror, but even in defeat, deities continued to be accorded the honour their exalted, enthroned status demanded.

Across ancient south-west Asia, this social dynamic was borne out in the divine realm itself, where the footstool of an enthroned deity functioned as a prop in the bodily performance of power. Seated in glory on a high-legged throne, the footstool not only undergirded the deity's sure-footed presence in their temple, but emphatically elevated their feet above those of other gods and heavenly attendants who stood alongside them. This carefully staged configuration of divine bodies is well attested in the Bible, for it is what Yahweh's prophets are said to have seen. In a text drawing on traditions of the ninth century BCE, Micaiah ben Imlah declares, 'I saw Yahweh sitting on his throne, with all the host of heaven standing to the right and to the left of him'.[2] Centuries later, God was still holding court in the same way: in the second-century BCE book of Daniel, the eponymous seer endures a terrifying but flamboyant vision of the deity sitting enthroned while 'a thousand thousands served him; and ten thousand times ten thousand stood attending him'.[3]

Standing on ceremony in the presence of an enthroned deity was a crucial piece of courtly etiquette in the world of the gods. It was a mark of collegial, collaborative respect, and formally displayed a keenness to leap into action should the high god demand it. Accordingly, upon entry into the divine throne room, gods were expected first to kneel or prostrate themselves at the feet of the divine ruler, and then to stand in polite, ready attendance. Poor manners or a deliberate snub might trigger the most serious of punishments. A telling example of gods behaving badly is found in the Mesopotamian myth of Nergal and Ereshkigal – the earliest known version of which is dated to the fifteenth or fourteenth centuries BCE. When the goddess Ereshkigal, queen of the underworld, sends her official representative up to the heavenly realm to attend a banquet on her behalf, she is enraged to learn that one of the gods, the ambitious, cocky Nergal, refused to rise to his feet in the presence of her vizier. 'Bring him to me . . . that I may kill him!' Ereshkigal commands. In a series of unsettling twists, Nergal descends to the underworld with an army, intending to behead the goddess and seize her throne. But as they grapple in the throne room, Nergal fiercely clutching fistfuls of the queen's hair, she suddenly offers to become his wife and to share with him her underworld kingdom. He relaxes his grip, and she weeps. He cries, and they kiss. He wipes away her tears, accepts her offer and is enthroned alongside her.[4] As challenging as this myth is to the gender-alert sensibilities of modern-day readers, it underscores the ancient conviction that a deity's enthroned status was to be preserved at all costs.

The Bible too betrays ancient anxieties about God's need to defend his throne from challengers. In a poem drawing on much older mythic tropes, a semi-divine tyrant named only as 'Day Star, son of Dawn' ascends Saphon, a traditional name of the Levantine cosmic mountain, in an effort to unseat Yahweh in his role as the enthroned Elyon ('Most High'), the title inherited from El. As he strides up the holy mountain, the trespassing tyrant mutters to himself, revealing his plot:

I will ascend to the heavens;
I will raise my throne above the stars of God;
I will sit on the mount of [the divine] assembly
on the heights of Saphon;
I will ascend to the tops of the clouds,
I will make myself like Elyon![5]

His punishment is swift. He is cast out of the heavens and down into the underworld, the place of the dead. His expulsion is a feature of the ancient myth Christianity later recycled in its story of Lucifer, the star-bright but rebellious 'fallen angel' who is cast out of heaven to take up a new career as the Devil. But unlike Lucifer, who goes on to enjoy a heady existence in the underworld, the tyrant of this biblical poem is subjected to further punishment: his corpse is exhumed and abandoned 'like loathsome carrion' to be trampled underfoot.[6]

Indeed, whether divine or human, no other body was fit, quite literally, for the throne and footstool of the king of the gods. At Ugarit, on the coast of Syria, the throne of Baal on Saphon was said to be so big that appointing his potential successor proves a challenge to the council of gods. The successful candidate must be a warrior of gigantic size and enormous strength, who can run as far and fast as Baal, and wield a lance with sufficient supernatural skill to defeat the most fearsome of cosmic enemies. But when the warrior god impressively named Athtar the Awesome is chosen to sit in Baal's place, he must suffer an embarrassing climbdown: as the other deities disappointedly exclaim, 'his feet do not reach its footstool, his head does not reach its top! '[7]

Dangling feet, unfixed to their royal footstool, were dangerous in the power play of divine politics – after all, some gods were known to have been dragged from heaven by their feet. This was the fate of one of the oldest deities in the cosmos, Anu, the god of primeval heaven in Mesopotamian and Hittite cultures. According to a Hittite myth, Anu's son, Kumarbi, had spent nine years of obedient prostration at his father's feet when he decided to challenge Anu in his throne room. As Anu attempted to fly to the very tops of the heavens to escape, Kumarbi caught him by his heels, pulled him down by his feet and bit off his genitals.[8] To lose a foothold in the divine realm was to be emasculated in the most visceral of ways. Echoes of the story found their way into Greek mythology, too. When Zeus takes the throne from his father, Kronos, who had supplanted and castrated his own father, Ouranos, he is challenged by the monster Typhon, who cuts the tendons from Zeus' feet and hides them in a cave in an effort to unseat him. In some traditions, it is only when his tendons are retrieved and restored to his body that Zeus can finally secure his throne.[9]

Underlying these myths was the widespread notion that the back of the foot was a point of particular vulnerability and weakness in the body – as Achilles is said to have discovered during the fabled battle of Troy. Accordingly, the back of the foot was the place at which hierarchies of power might be disrupted. This idea finds expression in the Hebrew Bible, in which the common myth of divine usurpation is reworked in the story of Jacob, whose name means 'heel taker' or 'supplanter'. Born immediately after Esau, his twin brother, Jacob emerges from the womb gripping the heel of his older sibling, in an action prefiguring his later usurpation of Esau when he tricks him out of his birthright as firstborn. The book of Hosea pointedly draws a parallel with Jacob's attempt to take on God himself in a wrestling match at the River Jabbok: 'In the womb he took his brother by the heel; and in his manhood he strove with God'.[10] Whether a human, a hero, or a god, to keep one's feet fixed firmly in place – both spatially and socially – was to guard against a loss of status.

One of the most vivid biblical accounts of divine usurpation is told in the books of Samuel. The story begins at Shiloh, in the West Bank, where one of Yahweh's oldest temples is thought to have been located. When the Israelites go to war against the Philistines, a formidable people living along Canaan's southern coast, they suffer such a catastrophic defeat that they send word to the Shiloh temple, and ask for Yahweh himself to join their ranks. 'Let us bring Yahweh's ark of the covenant from Shiloh, so that he may come among us and save us from the power of our enemies! '[11] As the footstool of God, the ark was not the wrath-filled box of Hollywood's Indiana Jones movie, but the pedestal on which the deity's feet remained fixed, even as his enthroned statue was processed about his temple – or indeed taken into battle. It is the cult statue of Yahweh that is envisaged by the biblical writers when they affirm that 'the ark of the covenant of Yahweh of Hosts, who is enthroned on the cherubim' duly entered the war camp. The arrival of the deity and his divine entourage ('hosts') prompts such a rapturous response from the Israelite soldiers that the Philistines quickly realize what has happened. 'Gods have come into the camp!' they cry. 'Woe to us! Who can deliver us from the power of these mighty gods?'[12]

The answer, it soon transpires, is Dagan (in Hebrew, 'Dagon'), one of the best-known deities across ancient south-west Asia. The Philistines not only succeed in defeating the Israelites, but capture the ark – and the deity enthroned above it – and carry it back to the city of Ashdod, where they ceremonially install it in Dagan's temple, next to his statue. As was common, the Philistines treated their sacred booty with a holy reverence. Yahweh might have been a prisoner of war, but his capture was cast as an opportunity to pay polite homage to Dagan. It was an opportunity Yahweh turned to his advantage. When the victorious Philistines return to the temple the next morning, they find Dagan flat on his face, prostrate before Yahweh's footstool. Lifting the divine statue from the temple floor, they restore it to its upright position. The following day, however, they were in for another shock – Dagan had not only fallen again, but was dismembered: 'the head of Dagan and both his hands were lying cut off upon the threshold; only the torso of Dagan was left to him'.[13] On the battlefield, Yahweh's sure-footed presence might not have won the day, but in the temple of Ashdod, in the dangerous darkness of the night, his footstool had become a weapon of war. Dagan had not only been floored by Yahweh, but – like a cosmic chaos monster – he had been trampled and dismembered, his body parts kicked to the very edges of the sacred realm.

As both his footstool and a mobile shrine, Yahweh's ark was a part of his person seemingly external to his body, but barely distinguishable from him. The two were one and the same. When Yahweh moved, so did the ark. And when the deity came to rest, the ark did too, as one biblical writer explains, citing what appears to be an ancient incantation: 'Whenever the ark set out, Moses would say, "Arise, O Yahweh,

let your enemies be scattered, and your foes flee before you!"
And whenever it came to rest, he would say, "Return, O Yahweh, to
Israel's teeming myriads!" '[14] Uncomfortable with the deification of the
ark as the weaponized pedestal of Yahweh, other biblical writers
endeavoured to disempower its agency by demythologizing its role.
The ark was carried about in ritual processions, they agreed, and it had
once led Yahweh's worshippers into battle, they confirmed, but it was
merely a box shrine for the Ten Commandments: 'There was nothing
in the ark except the two tablets of stone that Moses had placed there'.[15]
Written into the story of the founding of Yahweh's temple in Jerusalem, this little verse reads like special pleading. And it is at odds with
the ritual refrain sung by worshippers as they watched what was likely
a statue of their deity process about the city and into the temple: 'Rise
up, O Yahweh, and go to your resting place, you and the ark of your
might!'[16]

The insistence that the divine footstool was actually a specialized –
if sacred – container for holy writings marks a relatively early
theological assault on the body of God, whose material presence, once
manifest in the Iron Age temples of ancient Israel and Judah as a divine
statue or cultic object, would gradually come to be replaced in ritual
by the Torah. In synagogues, which emerged only during the latter
half of the Second Temple period (c. 515 BCE–70 CE), this displacement
would come to be underscored by the small 'ark' or shrine in which
the Torah scrolls were housed, which took its name from the ark of
the covenant.[17] But cultural memories of the ark's original role as a
divine footstool or pedestal appear to have persisted, as a remarkable
artefact suggests.

In 2009, excavations at Migdal – ancient Magdala – on the north-
western shore of the Sea of Galilee revealed a large synagogue dated
to the mid first century CE. In its main room was a squat, four-footed
limestone block, beautifully decorated with relief carvings of iconographic and architectural motifs seemingly drawn from the Jerusalem
temple. Along its longer sides are four arched gateways, flanked by
columned pillars, within which stylized palm trees stand. On one of
its shorter sides, two similar gateways each house a large rosette – a
symbol taking pride of place between two more palms on the stone's

Fig. 8. The mysterious carved stone block from an affluent mid-first-century CE synagogue in the ancient city of Magdala, on the shores of the Sea of Galilee. It is decorated with religious symbols associated with the Jerusalem temple, including a large menorah, standing on a pedestal.

top. Its other short side is decorated with two more columns, a pair of amphorae, and a large menorah, standing on or behind a square object which looks not unlike like the stone itself (fig. 8). Scholars remain uncertain as to the function of this extraordinary object, but some suspect it served either as a ritual pedestal for the Torah, or as a shrine modelled on the Jerusalem temple.[18] However it is understood, its shape is remarkably evocative of the biblical footstool of God.

For many, the permanent destruction of the Jerusalem temple in 70 CE meant that synagogues inevitably became the places at which God now set his feet. It was a view that would be endorsed in an anthology of early rabbinic interpretations of the book of Exodus, probably in circulation by the end of the fourth century CE, known as *Mekhilta de-Rabbi Ishmael*, in which it is claimed that 'wherever ten people congregate in the synagogue, the Divine Presence is with them, for it is written [in Psalm 82], "God stands in the congregation of God" '.[19] In Babylonia, then home to the largest population of Yahweh worshippers outside of Palestine, the synagogue of Shaf ve-Yativ in the city of Nehardea was said to have been built with the very dust and stones of the Jerusalem temple itself, where God had set his feet.[20] The synagogue community could point to a scriptural precedent: in the books of Kings, an Aramaean general called Naaman had been so impressed by his encounter with Yahweh's prophet Elisha, he decided to take two sackfuls of Israelite earth back to Aram (the city-state of Damascus) so that he could worship the god of Israel on appropriately holy ground.[21]

There was nothing new about the idea that temple materials or sacred soil could be requisitioned and relocated for cultic service. In 689 BCE, the Assyrian king Sennacherib had destroyed the city of Babylon, but was keen to transfer the ancient prestige of Marduk's Babylonian *akitu* (New Year) temple to the *akitu* temple he was constructing in Ashur. Accordingly, he says, 'I removed dirt from Babylon and piled it in heaps and mounds in that *akitu* house'.[22] Harnessing the material power of sacred ground was one way to maintain the continuity of religious practice as the political ground shifted beneath the feet of gods and mortals. But another was to assert that the gods themselves could voluntarily abandon a temple without fear of undermining their presence in the world of their worshippers. This theological strategy would effect one of the biggest transformations in the social life of the God of the Bible.

Lift Off

Resting on their footstools, the feet of the gods had long embodied order, control and hierarchy in the universe. It was a power pose of cosmic supremacy. But divine footstools also played more nuanced, emotional roles in the body language of the gods. When the Late Bronze Age goddess Athirat pays a visit to her husband El, he is so delighted to see her that 'he unfurrowed his brow and laughed; he set his feet on the footstool, and wiggled his toes'.[23] His footstool is pressed into performative service again when he learns that Baal is dead, having been swallowed into the underworld by Mot, the god of death. El is distraught. He descends from his throne and sits on his footstool, and then lowers himself from his footstool to sit upon the ground to mourn. 'Baal is dead! What has become of the Powerful One?' he cries. 'After Baal I shall go down into the underworld! '[24] Coming down from his throne onto his footstool marks his ritual descent from the heavenly realm into the earthly world – the place of his feet – while his lowering from his footstool onto the ground enacts his descent from the earthly realm into the underworld. With the heavenly gods El and Baal out of place, the universe is catastrophically turned upside down, as Anat exclaims to Shapsh, the sun goddess: 'Dried up are the furrows of the fields, O Shapsh! Dried up are the furrows of El's fields, Baal is neglecting the furrows of the ploughland! Where is mighty Baal? Where is the Prince, master of the earth?'[25] Cosmic order is only restored when El foresees the return of Baal and his rains, and re-seats himself on the throne, pointedly setting his feet on his footstool once again. 'At last I can sit and rest', El declares, 'for alive is mighty Baal!'[26]

In the Jerusalem temple, Yahweh's footstool also functioned as a ritual manifestation of the earthly realm upon which the deity set his feet. In some biblical texts, the divine footstool is an object so large that it subsumes both the temple and the city, rendering Jerusalem itself the giant footrest of the supersized god: 'Yahweh is huge in Zion!' exclaims one psalmist urging pilgrims to Jerusalem: 'Worship at his footstool!'[27] It is a gigantism intensely magnified in the closing chapter of the book of Isaiah, in which God's temple furniture is presented as the very fabric of the cosmos itself: 'Heaven is my throne and the earth is my footstool! What is the house that you would build for me and what is my resting place?' Yahweh bellows.[28]

Yahweh's assertion of corporeal gigantism and its follow-up question about the temple was as much a snipe at his critics as it was a boast of immense cosmic sovereignty. In 597 BCE, over a century before this particular oracle was proclaimed, the kingdom of Judah had been emphatically annexed by Nebuchadnezzar II, king of Babylonia, as he consolidated power across his newly won empire. And with vassalage came desecration. 'He carried off all the treasures of the house of Yahweh . . . he cut in pieces all the objects of gold in the temple of Yahweh, which King Solomon of Israel had made'.[29] God's golden throne and footstool were gone. Within a decade, Babylonian troops had returned, and this time, they sacked the city and destroyed the

very fabric of the temple. In a painfully vivid lament, a ritual singer
cries out to Yahweh:

> Lift up your feet because of the perpetual ruins,
> all that the enemy laid waste in the sanctuary.
> Your foes have roared within your holy place;
> they set up their emblems there.
> At the upper entrance they hacked
> the wooden trellis with axes.
> And then, with hatchets and hammers,
> they smashed all its carved work.
> They set your sanctuary on fire;
> they desecrated the dwelling place of your name,
> bringing it to the ground.[30]

Both the desecration and destruction of the Jerusalem temple threatened to shatter the mythological foundations underlying the claim that
Yahweh's feet were set securely in Zion. The Hebrew Bible reflects the
confusion arising from this disaster: some, like the lamenting poet,
believed Yahweh had 'lifted up his feet' to leave his sanctuary, now it
had been defiled by the destructive presence of his enemies. Others
assumed that the Babylonians had carried him off as a prisoner of war.
Still others held he had permanently rejected Jerusalem because his
priests had failed to attend sufficiently to his needs. However it was
perceived, God's feet had wandered away. 'He has not remembered
his footstool', wept the people of Jerusalem.[31]

Theological counterclaims quickly ensued. Among the urban elites
exiled from Jerusalem to Babylonia in 597 BCE was a priest of Yahweh's
temple, who saw visions of God as he longed for Jerusalem. The deity
had been neither defeated nor repelled, Ezekiel claimed in the book
bearing his name. Instead, he insisted, Yahweh had temporarily vacated
his temple ahead of the foreign invasion he himself had planned, by
wheeling himself out from his dwelling place on what was now his
mobile throne. Ezekiel had seen it all, he said: the two cherubim
flanking God's throne and footstool had become four, matching the
compass of the world, and each of them now perched atop a wheel.

As the cherubim lifted their wings and elevated the throne, the wheels turned, and Yahweh rolled out of his temple – without lifting his feet or leaving his seat.[32]

This highly specialized, esoteric image of the enthroned deity would become a stock feature of later Jewish mysticism, entrancing ancient scholars and visionaries alike. But the wheeled throne was not a notion Ezekiel had desperately plucked from the sky – despite having seen it, he said, when the clouds of heavens had rolled open to reveal their secrets to him.[33] The augmentations customizing Yahweh's cherubim throne were drawn from much older mythologies. Deities across ancient south-west Asia had long employed the services of their attribute animals and attendant monsters to get them about. Some stood on the back of a lion, like the great goddesses Ishtar and Athirat, while others stationed themselves on the back of a bull, like Adad and Baal. Some ceremonially stood on a monstrous snake-headed or lion-bodied dragon, like Marduk of Babylon and Ashur of Assyria (fig. 9), while others stood or sat enthroned upon a cherub – just like Yahweh. Upon their fantastic pedestals, the gods could travel about the heavens, parade about their cities, or settle themselves in exalted glory in their temples. As a powerful storm god, Yahweh had long been known to travel on a cherub, splitting open the skies on clouds heavy with rain, and crashing into the earthly realm with a thunderous shout:

> He bent the heavens and came down,
> and a thick cloud was beneath his feet.
> He rode on a cherub, and flew,
> and came swiftly upon the wings of the wind.
> He made darkness his covering around him,
> his canopy thick clouds dark with water.
> Out of the brightness before him,
> there broke through his clouds hailstones and coals of fire.
> Yahweh thundered in the heavens,
> the Most High uttered his voice.[34]

The storm clouds enveloping Yahweh's cherubic mount were an especially celebrated feature of his divine vigour, and were already imagined

Fig. 9. A large gypsum wall plaque from a residential building in the
Assyrian city of Ashur, dated to the seventh century BCE. It shows
a majestic, bearded deity, likely Ashur himself, standing on the
back of a winged, horned lion. The deity holds his right
hand aloft in a gesture of blessing.

as a sky chariot. 'Sing to God, sing praises to his name!' worshippers
sang in the Jerusalem temple. 'Lift up the charioteer of the clouds! Yah
is his name, therefore exalt before him!'[35] Yahweh appears to have
inherited his role and title as the 'charioteer of the clouds' from the
storm god Baal, whose skill at charging about the heavens was particularly lauded at Ugarit. Combining the throne-and-footstool iconography
of the Jerusalem temple with the ancient motif of the cherub-riding
cloud-charioteer, Ezekiel's god was a deity of cosmic dynamism.
Yahweh had left the temple, but he had not been toppled from his
throne, and nor had he abandoned it. The high god of Jerusalem
remained seated in glory, his feet firmly fixed on his footstool, as he
wheeled out of his city to join his exiles in Babylonia: 'Though I
removed them far away among the nations, and though I scattered
them among the countries, yet I have been a sanctuary to them', he
declared.[36] This was a deity unconstrained by traditional territorial
boundaries and undefeated by the devastation of desecration. On his

mobile throne, he brought the sacred space of Jerusalem to his dispossessed worshippers.

A century or so later, the writer of what is now the final chapter of Isaiah thus adopted a similar strategy to downplay the destruction of the Jerusalem temple. Like Ezekiel, this prophet adapted much older mythological themes to insist that Yahweh remained enthroned, his feet reassuringly planted in the world of his worshippers – no matter where they were. But there was no need for sky chariots and cherubim to illustrate Yahweh's international reach, and no need for a man-made temple to prove his presence. Instead, the gigantism of God proved the deity remained seated in glory. 'Heaven is my throne and the earth is my footstool!' Yahweh emphatically declared.[37] Although his temple in Jerusalem lay in ruins, Yahweh's cosmic supremacy was undiminished, and his feet were still firmly fixed in the earthly realm.

The Jerusalem temple would be rebuilt in the early fifth century BCE, and permanently destroyed by Titus in 70 CE. But the idea that God sat enthroned in the heavens, with his feet resting on the earth, remained irresistibly potent to many early Jewish and Christian writers. Some pressed God's boast in Isaiah into polemical service against the material trappings of temple cults. Others, however, understood the text more literally, and cast the earth itself as the divine footstool of God, later prompting some rabbis and (according to Matthew's Gospel) Jesus of Nazareth to forbid their followers from 'blasphemously' invoking the earth in swearing ritual oaths.[38]

But several Jewish and Christian communities clearly embraced the divine corporeality presented in Isaiah, and quite reasonably assumed that God's body was so gigantic it reached from earth to heaven. It was a scripturally endorsed belief that would become increasingly problematic – particularly for early Christian thinkers, who preferred the divine body to take the form of Christ, rather than that of a supersized deity more akin to the 'pagan' deities of Rome. In the Graeco-Roman world, a certain philosophical distaste for the earthiness of the material world, combined with an increasing spiritual preference for the abstract and the transcendent, had been percolating among the intelligentsia for some time, encouraging a re-evaluation

of the nature of the divine. It was against this backdrop that the archi-
tects of early Christian doctrine sought to understand their own
scriptures, in which God was often presented in disturbingly corporeal
terms. In their intellectual world, Christ was the only incarnation of
God. Those troublesome verses in the scriptures attesting to God's
body would be smoothed, smothered, or superseded by new interpretative frameworks and some fancy philosophical footwork.

A favourite tactic employed by early Christian theologians was
simply to reduce all biblical references to God's body to the symbolic.
When the scriptures instructed people to worship at God's footstool,
it was towards the cross to which Christ's feet were nailed that
worshippers were directed. Another strategy, of course, was simply to
insist that biblical references to God's body parts were metaphorical
and allegorical, and were not to be taken literally. 'Reverence rather
requires . . . an allegorical meaning', wrote Clement of Alexandria
(c. 150–215 CE). 'You must not entertain the notion at all of figure and
motion, or standing or seating, or place, or right or left, as appertaining
to the Father of the universe, although these terms are in Scripture'.
Instead, Clement argued, the biblical ascription of body parts to God
was a divinely directed accommodation to the limitations of human
understanding.[39] Some early Christian theologians navigated the dis-
orientating portrayals of God's feet by bending and stretching the
temporal dimensions in which God was understood to walk in the
world: when Adam and Eve had heard God walking in the garden, it
was actually the sound of Christ as the pre-existent, spoken Word of
God moving towards them.[40]

The extent to which these theological manoeuvres were practised
by ordinary Christians is a matter of considerable debate among scholars. What is more certain, however, is that, by the third century CE, the
Christian exegete and theologian Origen was so appalled by those who
still conceived of God as a cosmic giant that he launched a scathing
attack upon them in one of his famous homilies: 'Those carnal men
who have no understanding of the meaning of divinity suppose . . . that
God has so large a body that they think he sits in heaven and stretches
his feet to the earth.' Rather, he argued, God could not possibly be
corporeal. Influenced by his conviction that scripture often revealed its

truths on ascending levels of spiritual insight (primarily the literal, the moral and the allegorical), Origen contended that the portrayal of God's body in Isaiah was figurative in form and allegorical in nature. It served, he claimed, to illustrate the spiritual gulf between those 'at the most remote part' of God's providence, who were too caught up in the literal, worldly affairs of the created realm, and those at the head end of the Creator God, who sought to acquire a heavenly 'perfection of life and loftiness of understanding' as true Christians.[41]

It was a convoluted, theological abstraction that would influence Christian interpretation of this biblical text and others like it for centuries to come, reflecting an increasingly powerful conceptual shift away from an old-fashioned mythological imagination to a world in which the symbolic and the abstract were granted the highest cultural and theological status. But in rendering the realm of creation in which humans dwelt so estranged from God, Origen and those Church Fathers to follow in his footsteps would contribute to the ongoing theological distancing of the divine from the earthly world of human experience. In doing so, they widened the emerging fissure between the corporeal and the spiritual – and in effect, dislodged God's enormous feet from the Christian world.

4

SENSATIONAL FEET

Despite the blisters and bunions so often wrought by modern footwear, it remains all too easy to overlook the significance of our feet as sophisticated sensory organs – parts of our bodies we can use to feel, grasp and keep 'in touch' with the world. But our ancestors used their feet far more frequently to 'think' with – to understand and manipulate the world in which they walked and worked. Whether threshing and milling grains and seeds, treading fruit, herding animals, rolling manure for firebricks and fertilizer, turning the potter's wheel, weaving textiles and baskets, or measuring distance and time, the world was experienced through people's feet in ways increasingly unfamiliar in the modern age. Our ancestors were far more focused on their feet – literally more grounded – than most of us are today, and this naturally shaped their body practices and religious imaginations.

In the cultures of ancient south-west Asia, the feet were particularly precious sensory organs and had to be looked after. Happy feet were those that were washed and (for the wealthy) oiled several times a day to help prevent swelling, blistering and skin cracking (fig. 10). A good pair of sandals that rarely needed patching was a prized commodity. Travellers petitioned the gods for wide, stable surfaces to walk upon, instead of the slip and scrape of unstable ground; they requested divine protection from thorns, stones, snake bites and shoes that pinch. Curse texts and malevolent incantations often targeted the feet of their victims – shoelessness, skin diseases, hobbling, lameness and toe

68

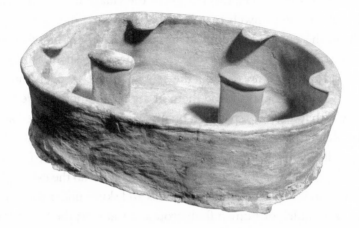

Fig. 10. A late eighth-century BCE basin from a gatehouse in the Judahite city of Lachish, assumed to be a foot bath. The ledges inside these objects are thought to have supported the foot while it was being washed, oiled and dried.

amputation were particularly popular. In some biblical texts, as in other ancient legislative literature, retaliatory punishment or compensation for criminal offences demanded not only 'a life for a life' and 'an eye for an eye', but 'a foot for a foot'.[1]

Within this world, the feet of the gods were as tactile and as sensory as those of their worshippers. Just as human bodies experienced the visceral carnage of warfare, the dry rustle of the threshing floor, or the squelch of the wine press, so too did the bodies of the gods. Mythic texts abound with detailed descriptions of their intense sensory experiences, some of which border on the monstrous. When she goes on the rampage against humans, the fearsome warrior goddess Anat is 'up to her knees [as] she wades in the blood of soldiers, up to her neck in the gore of fighters'. It is a sensation she enjoys so much that when she returns home, she transforms the chairs and tables in her dining hall into an army of living victims, fresh for trampling.[2]

Not one to be outdone by his older Ugaritic cousin, the God of the Bible also showcases his martial expertise by excessive body-trampling. In a particularly graphic scene in Isaiah, the deity recasts

of Islamic law as a guide to divine will. But on occasion, the biblical writers seem to have understood walking with God as a more corporeal activity: Abraham is portrayed as literally walking and talking with Yahweh and two of his divine colleagues on the road from Mamre towards Sodom.[10] And Yahweh enjoys Enoch's company so much that even after 300 years of walking the earth together, the deity decides to lift him into the heavenly realm, where in a rich collection of early Jewish and Christian literature, Enoch continues to travel about heaven's various dimensions, meeting its angelic inhabitants.[11] For Yahweh, walking in step with his worshippers was a form of male bonding – and shaped the very essence of his special relationship with the Israelites, who are consistently gendered as the 'sons' of Jacob [Israel]: 'I will walk among you, and will be God to you, and you, you will be my people'.[12]

It may be that companionship was Yahweh's goal when he went for his evening stroll in the Garden of Eden, for as he walks, he is on the lookout for Adam. But Adam is nowhere to be seen. 'Where are you?' he calls out, like the frustrated loser in a game of hide-and-seek (and laying to rest any idea that the God of the Bible is omniscient and omnipotent). A near-naked Adam emerges from the foliage and shyly confesses to Yahweh that he could 'hear the sound' of him walking, and so had time to conceal his newly realized nudity among the trees.[13] God's feet may have been sensuously receptive to the pleasures of the garden, but they were also very noisy.

Noisy feet were not usually a problem for the gods. Rather, the sonorous impact of divine footfall was a certain indication to humans in the earthly realm of the ongoing activity of their deities. The loud, heavy marching of the gods caused the earth to tremble and the mountains to quake, just as they did when Yahweh processed in imperial victory from his wilderness home to take possession of the land of Canaan. 'O Yahweh, when you went out from Seir, when you marched from the steppe of Edom, the earth trembled!' his worshippers gleefully sang; 'the mountains quaked before Yahweh, he of Sinai, before Yahweh, the god of Israel!'[14] The noise of the gods' footsteps might also function as a siren in the earthly realm, triggering holy war between nations and their deities. In the books of Samuel, an oracle instructs King David to listen out for the sound of the wind in a grove of trees before launching an attack on the Philistines: 'when you hear the sound of marching in the tops of the balsam trees, then be on the alert; for then Yahweh has gone out before you to strike down the army'.[15]

Along with marching, foot-pounding was also particularly popular with warrior deities, and typical of the gods at Ugarit, who frequently punctuated their arguments and declarations of war with ferocious stamping. It was a clear signal of divine rage, as the good-looking hero Aqhat discovered when he refused to give his magical bow and arrows to the goddess Anat: 'I'll make you fall under my feet, pretty-boy, he-man', she threatens, stamping her feet so hard that 'the earth shook'.[16] This ancient idea survived well into later periods, so that even in rabbinic literature, earth tremors were sometimes thought to be caused by God pounding his feet in fury or vengeance.[17] The gods are not often described as having quiet feet – as divine beings, they rarely felt the need to move by stealth. But if they did, they might remove their shoes, so as to muffle the sound of their footsteps, particularly when they risked journeying into the underworld. Pitched as a place of dimmed light and hushed noise, the requirement that visitors to the underworld remove their sturdy travelling shoes not only warned that they might not be able to return home, but lessened the disruptive imposition of their presence.[18]

The removal of footwear mattered far more to the gods in other ways: their worshippers were often expected to take off their shoes before praying or stepping inside a place of worship – an ancient custom inherited by Islam, and required of anyone entering a mosque today. Although this practice is shared with other religious groups (including Hindus, Sikhs and Buddhists), in Islam it arguably derives in part from much older religious preferences, attested in some societies across ancient south-west Asia and the eastern Mediterranean, in which barefootedness played an important sensory role for both humans and gods.

The art and inscriptions of ancient Egypt suggest that barefootedness was a common ritual prerequisite to entering a temple. This was sacred space – the place of the feet of the gods – and so the feet of priests and worshippers were to be unshod and washed before they could tread where the gods stepped. As a further precaution, a ritual known as the 'Bringing of the Foot' was undertaken by priests and other cult functionaries, who used a magical broom to sweep the floor as they backed away from the altar, removing human footprints from the sanctuary.[19] Ritual foot-washing and floor-and-wall cleansing was practised across Mesopotamia, too, where the appropriate management of disruptive 'dirt' inside sacred space demanded not cleaners, but exorcists, skilled in the safe manipulation and eradication of otherworldly dust.[20]

It is against this wider cultural backdrop that certain ritual forms of shoe-removal and foot-washing in the biblical world are best understood. Barefootedness appears to have been the norm for priests in Yahweh's temples, for references to footwear are conspicuously absent in biblical and early Jewish descriptions of priestly vestments, while certain ritual prescriptions attest to the daubing of blood or water on the bare feet and toes of the priests once they moved inside Yahweh's sanctuaries.[21] By the Roman period, most Jewish communities across Palestine were engaging in regular ritual foot-washing. The jugs, troughs and small clay foot basins of older centuries were gradually supplemented or replaced at sacred sites and synagogues with a specially constructed bathing pool called a *mikveh*. This stepped stone structure allowed groups of worshippers to cleanse not only their feet, but their whole bodies, accommodating the communal water-immersion practices popular with groups as diverse as Jerusalem-based Torah scholars, the Dead Sea Scrolls community, and the followers of holy men like John the Baptist and Jesus of Nazareth (fig. 11).[22]

By this time, the priestly prerogative to go barefoot when worshipping Yahweh already appears to have been extended to all those who might step onto Jerusalem's Temple Mount. It was far from sufficient simply to remove sandals – all feet had to be ritually cleansed before they could come into contact with holy ground. To ascend the Temple Mount to God's dwelling place was to enter into the heavens, and as the Jewish philosopher Philo of Alexandria put it, 'the washing of feet . . . means that we should no longer walk on the earth, but sweep through the heights of the ether'.[23] Writing in the first century CE,

Fig. II. A purpose-built *mikveh* at ancient Gamlah, a town in the Upper Galilee. Likely constructed early in the first century CE, it was destroyed in 67 CE, when Gamlah was attacked during the Roman campaign to crush Jewish uprisings against imperial rule.

shortly before the destruction of the temple, Philo claimed that even the hooves of sacrificial animals were washed before they stepped into the temple precinct – after all, 'according to the saying, one should not enter with unwashed feet on the pavement of the temple of God'.[24] It was an ancient religious requirement that had been famously flouted in 167 BCE by the Seleucid king Antiochus IV Epiphanes when he looted the Jerusalem temple to fund his military campaigns. This shocking event triggered painful cultural memories of the Babylonian desecration of the temple in the sixth century BCE, moving a Jewish poet to pen a bitter lament, berating the foreigners who 'arrogantly trampled' the sanctuary of God 'with their sandals'.[25]

It was one thing for 'outsiders' to trample the temple, but quite another for Yahweh's own worshippers to defile the place of his feet in Jerusalem. In the highly volatile context of the Graeco-Roman era, in which religious control of the city was repeatedly sought and contested by both establishment and sectarian Jewish groups, accusations of temple defilement were common. Writing in the first century CE, the Jewish historian Josephus deploys this rhetorical weapon against the Zealots, whom he claims entered the sanctuary 'with polluted feet'.[26] More sensationally, this is precisely what Jesus is also said to have done. A fragmentary papyrus manuscript found amid a cache of documents in an ancient rubbish tip at the Egyptian site of Oxyrhynchus preserves an otherwise unattested story about Jesus and his disciples. Dating from the first half of the second century CE, the text describes Jesus and his disciples wandering about the Jerusalem temple, and the shocked response of a high priest who discovers them there: 'Who gave you permission to walk in this place of purification and look upon these holy vessels when you have not bathed and your disciples have not washed their feet?' the priest demands. Jesus answers back with a vicious denunciation of Jewish purification rites, insultingly belittling their function and the high priest himself: 'You have washed in this running water, in which dogs and pigs have wallowed night and day, and you have washed and scrubbed your outer skin, which harlots and flute-girls also anoint and wash and scrub, beautifying themselves for the lusts of men while inwardly they are filled with scorpions and unrighteousness of every kind.'[27]

While this story is not out of keeping with the Gospels' portrayal of a frequently confrontational and hostile Jesus, its sharp anti-Jewish polemic suggests it is probably a later invention, reflecting disputes among Jewish–Christian communities of the second century CE about the relative value of traditional purity rituals vis-à-vis Christian baptism.[28] Nevertheless, it is a good illustration of the continued perception that 'unclean' feet were not to tread on the temple's holy ground.

After the religiously cataclysmic destruction of the Jerusalem temple by the Roman general Titus in 70 CE, the removal of shoes was a ritual transferred from temple priests to rabbis officiating in synagogues across ancient Palestine. While the Babylonian Talmud suggests it was not a practice necessarily expected in the synagogues of ancient diaspora communities, it was popular among some groups. And it is a tradition in the worship of the Jewish God that has survived in part today: while barefootedness in synagogues is not required, in Orthodox services males of priestly descent (kohanim) will remove their shoes when proclaiming the priestly benediction.

In the ancient world, all these activities reflected the notion that shoes were symbols of power. To wear them inside a temple was to assert a social dominance entirely inappropriate in the presence of the gods – a view that would encourage a social preference among ancient pilgrims across the eastern Mediterranean to travel in barefooted humility. But bare feet were also quiet feet. High-ranking gods – especially those among the oldest generations – enjoyed periods of peace and quiet as much as the rest of us, and might easily be provoked to anger should the smack and slap of noisy sandals in their temples become too loud. Indeed, humans had long been known as inherently noisy creatures. In the Mesopotamian epic Atrahasis, dated to about 1700 BCE, the high god Enlil famously decides to kill off humans with a great flood because, he says, 'the noise of mankind has become too much; I'm losing sleep over their racket'.[29]

It is an episode which speaks to a divine distaste for excessive human noise, well attested for millennia across ancient south-west Asia and the eastern Mediterranean. The truly pious were often character-ized as those who conducted themselves quietly in temples: in an Egyptian text of the Eighteenth Dynasty (c. 1550–1305 BCE), the god Amun was quite understandably said to love 'the silent one more than the one with a loud voice'.[30] In Greece, several centuries later, even Socrates, denounced by his opponents for not 'believing' in the gods of the Athenian state, was teasingly demanding silence from his debat-ing partner, 'for there seems to be a divine presence in this spot'.[31] The God of the Bible similarly preferred limited words and muffled feet. In the book of Ecclesiastes (known in Jewish tradition as Qoheleth), worshippers are advised to 'guard your steps when you go to the house of God . . . let your words be few'.[32] Shoeless feet were quiet feet, and quiet feet were the feet of the devout.

It was not only a divine aversion to human noisiness that encour-aged shoelessness among worshippers. As many of these foot-focused traditions and rituals reveal, barefootedness also expressed concerns across the ancient world about ritual purity: the dust, dirt and decay of the 'ordinary' world outside a temple could not be allowed to pol-lute the purity or 'cleanness' of the ground inside the temple. Ritual washing before (and sometimes after) entering sacred space enabled priests and worshippers to maintain an embodied distinction between

the sacred and profane, and so guard against the dangerous wrath of
the gods, who might punish transgressors with death, or – worse –
reject the whole community by abandoning their dwelling places.

In Roman-era Judah, the bodily dynamics of traditional worship
would render human feet overtly political. Although he is more usually
remembered as a baby-killer, King Herod's legacy is more reliably
represented by his impressive building projects, many of which were
designed to enrich (quite literally) holy sites across his realm. Most
significant was his large-scale renovation of the Jerusalem temple,
which expanded its outer courtyards to accommodate ever larger
numbers of pilgrims and 'foreign' visitors during festivals. But by the
time his ambitious plans had come to fruition, in about 64 CE (nearly
seventy years after his death), non-Jewish people were strictly prohibited from setting foot inside the temple's precincts. Bodily purity was
a ritual state of such importance that allowing anybody other than
Yahweh's own worshippers to approach the deity's dwelling place
risked unclean feet trampling dangerous ritual pollutants across holy
ground. According to Josephus, the stone balustrade surrounding the
temple's precincts carried inscriptions 'giving warning, some in Greek,
others in Latin characters, of the law of purification, to wit that no
foreigner was allowed to enter the holy place'. Some of these inscriptions have been found, the most complete of which is now in the
Istanbul Archaeological Museum. Written in Greek, it reads, 'No foreigner is to enter within the balustrade and forecourt around the sacred
precinct. Whoever is caught will himself be responsible for [his] consequent death' (fig. 12).[33]

Over time, anxieties about ritual impurities carried by the feet
would morph into a fuzzier cultural understanding within many societies that the shoes and feet of humans were potentially antisocial
because of their intense, frequent contact with the ground beyond the
bounds of sacred space. Accordingly, feet and shoes are today carefully
managed outside as well as inside places of worship in a number of
communities. As is well known, it is now customary to remove shoes
upon entering a Muslim home. In Orthodox Jewish communities,
shoes are not to be worn indoors during periods of mourning, nor on
Yom Kippur, when even among liberal Jewish groups, the 'decaying'

Fig. 12. 'No foreigner is to enter within the balustrade and forecourt around the sacred precinct', begins this first-century CE Greek inscription on a marble slab. It was originally set into the barrier separating the large outer court on Jerusalem's Temple Mount from the inner precinct surrounding the temple building.

materials of leather shoes are often to be swapped in favour of bare feet or synthetic fabrics. In some eastern Mediterranean and Middle Eastern societies, it is often inappropriate to show the soles of the feet, and the bottoms of shoes must not come into contact with other parts of the body – a cultural concern powerfully harnessed on screens around the world in 2008, when Iraqi journalist Muntadhar al-Zaidi protested against the Iraq War by throwing his 'polluting' shoes at US President George W. Bush during a press conference.

But just as purity regulations in the ancient world safeguarded divine presence in temples and sanctuaries, so too they protected human communities in their own spaces. Shoe removal at a temple prevented the holiness of sacred ground being tracked unchecked out of the temple and into the streets of the ordinary world. The 'extraordinary' ground of temples contained something of the material properties of divine presence, transmitted from the feet of the gods, which demanded careful handling. Just as a spell-caster might use soil taken from a footprint or dust wiped from the feet of a man to cause him harm, so too the dust from the temple floor on which the gods walked might be used in magical incantations.[34] And the biblical writers were well aware of this. In one of the more unsettling religious laws in the book of Numbers, compiled in about the fifth century BCE, any woman accused of adultery is to be brought into Yahweh's sanctuary, to stand before the priest and the deity. The priest mixes some dust from the floor of the sanctuary into a vessel containing holy water, into which has been dissolved the ink from a written curse. 'May this water that brings the curse enter your bowels and make your womb discharge, your uterus drop!' incants the priest. The woman drinks the potion. If she suffers a miscarriage, she is guilty of adultery, and will be estranged from the community. If she suffers no ill effects, she is innocent, and any child she subsequently bears will be recognized as that of her husband.[35]

It is the numinous power of sacred space, materialized in its very earth and stone, that ultimately underlies ancient religious preferences for shoe removal. Barefootedness enabled the worshipper to come safely but intimately into direct physical contact with the divine. And it is this feet-first approach to the gods which underlies one of the most famous stories of barefooted holy men in Western culture: that of Moses and the burning bush in the book of Exodus.[36] The story is set in the wilderness on Mount Horeb (an alternative name for Sinai), and describes Moses' first encounter with Yahweh. Moses is tending his father-in-law's flock of goats when he comes upon a thornbush that is mysteriously engulfed but undamaged by flames. As he pauses, intending to take a closer look, God calls out to him from within the bush: 'Come no closer! Remove the sandals from your feet, for the place [*maqom*] on which you are standing is holy ground!' Obeying the deity's instructions, Moses approaches the god in the bush. The two have a lengthy conversation, but Moses is compelled to cover his face 'because he was afraid to look at God'. Temporarily blinded, Moses' encounter with the deity is sustained not by sight, but by bare feet – feet that feel the sacred ground in which the bush itself is rooted.[37]

In the southern Sinai, a towering bramble enshrined within a sunny courtyard in the Monastery of the God-Trodden Mount is traditionally identified as the very place where Moses first met Yahweh. Nestled in a rocky gorge at the foot of the holy mountain, the monastery itself is better known as St Catherine's, and was formally founded by the Eastern Roman emperor Justinian in the sixth century CE. It is home to some of the oldest religious art of the Byzantine world, including the stunning golden mosaics that shimmer on the apse and triumphal arch in the Justinian basilica. Here, there are two dazzling images of a po-faced Moses on the holy mountain: one shows him as a rugged young man, taking off his sandals before a bright green bush alive with dancing red flames (Plate 5); the other shows him as an aging, exhausted elder, standing barefoot on Sinai's peak as God's hand plunges out of the sky to give him the Ten Commandments. In both mosaics, Moses continues to model good practice for his monastic audience, for abutting the external wall of the apse is the older fourth-century Chapel of the Burning Bush, next to which the revered bush grows. Today, the monks of St Catherine's are still required to remove their shoes before stepping inside to pray before its holy of holies, said to be located directly above the roots of the sacred bush.

Shoe removal at the Chapel of the Burning Bush is just one of a number of barefooted rituals to survive into the monotheisms of the modern era. Whether Jewish, Christian, or Muslim, and whether habitual or episodic, shoe removal and barefootedness remains a powerful sensory experience in the religious lives of millions of worshippers today, echoing very ancient encounters with sacred ground.

Foot Fetish

Shortly after his election to papal office in 2013, Pope Francis appalled conservative Roman Catholics across the world by bathing, drying and kissing the feet of two women during the foot-washing ceremony of Easter week. Closely aligned to the Last Supper narrative in the Gospel of John, in which Jesus is portrayed as washing his disciples' feet, the Roman Catholic ritual traditionally restricted recipients of the practice to selected male members of the congregation (a convention only enshrined in Holy Week liturgy in 1956). Many critics voiced their discomfort at the Pope's breaching of Church law, protesting that the maleness of the disciples should be faithfully represented by male participants in the rite – the same objection long levelled against those in favour of the ordination of women to the priesthood. But the Pope persisted, and has washed and kissed the feet of women (and those of non-Christians) every Easter since, supporting his actions with a papal decree in 2016 and advising that, where possible, women should be included in the ceremony.

Protestors continued to object. Some insisted it is the authoritative status of Church law, and not institutionalized gender inequality, that necessitates the exclusion of women from the ritual. 'Foot washing is too important to be dragged into a feminist debate', asserted the headline in one Roman Catholic newspaper.[38] Others, however, appeared to be more unsettled by the Pope and his priests performing such an intimate body-ritual with women. From the underbelly of liturgical conservatism re-emerged a deeply rooted misogynistic anxiety about the 'dangerous' sexuality of women – and their feet. In Kazakhstan, for example, Bishop Athanasius Schneider of Astana (now Nur-Sultan) responded to the papal decree by publicly declaring the washing and kissing of women's feet 'improper and even indecent', while in the UK, the Latin Mass Society of England and Wales published a statement expressing concerns about 'the etiquette of men washing the feet of women', as an activity that 'would have been considered inappropriate only a few decades ago in the West'.[39]

To bathe and kiss the feet of another is an act of intense intimacy – embarrassingly so for some Christians, as modern religious commentators have often noted. Consequently, Church theologians are often keen to emphasize the ancient heritage of the ritual in mitigating any discomfort around its intimacy. In the hierarchical societies of first-century CE Roman Palestine, they point out, foot-washing was one of the duties of a servant or slave, whose own body was merely a tool for the servicing of that of his or her overlord. As such, when Jesus washes his disciples' feet at the Last Supper in the Gospel of John, it is to be read as an act of servile humility, enacting the deliberate self-abasement of the 'master' (Jesus) to his 'servants' (the disciples). But in the highly loaded imagery of the Gospel, Jesus' actions also carry a far weightier religious freight – and they are not quite as humble as they might appear. This is a Gospel in which Jesus' actions move beyond the symbolic to serve instead as carefully coded, revelatory performances which point insistently to his divinity. 'You do not know what I am doing, but later you will understand', Jesus says as he crouches at Peter's feet, who is utterly confused by the proceedings, and protesting loudly: 'You will never wash my feet!' he declares.[40] Realizing he has to make things clearer, Jesus tells the disciples he is making their feet ritually 'clean' – in other words, physically ready to enter into the presence of the divine, in keeping with the conventions of Jewish temple practice. 'Unless I wash you, you have no share with me', he says, warning his followers that they will lose their place alongside him if their feet are not ritually pure – and thereby claiming that he himself is the grounded locus of divine presence among his disciples.[41]

This is a divine presence repeatedly manifested by Jesus' feet in early Christian literature. Although first-century CE rabbis were accustomed to their students and followers sitting at their feet, the biblical portrayal of Jesus' feet often elevates his status beyond that of a religious teacher and casts him instead as a divine figure. Like the ancient gods before him, Jesus tramples the chaotic waters of the raging sea into quiet submission. When the sick and infirm are placed at his feet, they are healed by his life-giving powers. In the Gospels, followers frequently fall at Jesus' feet, where some are explicitly said to worship him. It is an action often accompanied by his devotees clutching or kissing his feet, much as gods and their cult statues were grasped and kissed on the feet in myths and rituals throughout ancient south-west Asia and the eastern Mediterranean.[42] In Hebrew Bible texts, on which the earliest Christians drew to support their claims about Jesus' divinity, it is an act of ritual veneration performed in honour of gods and divinely anointed kings. Indeed, in Psalm 2, one of the most important scriptural passages used by early Christians to support their claims that Jesus was the son of God and royal Messiah (in Greek, *Christos*), worshippers are pointedly instructed to kiss the divine feet.[43]

The veneration of Jesus' feet is most explicitly expressed in the story in Luke's Gospel about a woman who seeks out Jesus while he is dining at the house of a Pharisee – a member of a conservative group of Torah specialists. Described as a 'sinner' and given no name (although often assumed to be Mary Magdalene), she positions herself at Jesus' feet as he reclines at the table, weeping so much that she floods tears upon them. She bathes his feet with her tears and rubs them dry with her unbound hair – a style more usually seen publicly on women venerating the gods in a sanctuary or performing mourning rituals. Her flood of tears becomes a rain of kisses ('she has not stopped kissing my feet', Jesus approvingly observes) while she anoints and massages his feet with a rich ointment.[44] The ritualized nature of her actions is impossible to miss: she washes and anoints Jesus' feet as priests in a temple would wash and anoint the cult statue of a god, simultaneously acknowledging and marking its sacred status.

But the intense sensuality of the scene also communicates an eroticism many have found discomforting – including the Pharisee in the story, who is shocked that Jesus should let a sinful woman touch him in such a way. It is a scene emphasizing the overwhelming sensuous excesses of her body. By using her flowing hair, wet skin, and the repeated actions of her mouth and hands to caress Jesus' feet, her actions take on the characteristics of sexual stimulation and erotic play, as seen in visual and literary works across the contemporaneous Graeco-Roman world – including Petronius' *Satyricon*, where long-haired slave-boys anoint the feet of diners at a lascivious banquet, winding garlands around their ankles.[45] It is an experience Luke's Jesus endorses at the close of the story – and is one of the most erotically charged scenes in the Gospels.

Against this backdrop, the story in the later Gospel of John, describing Jesus washing his disciples' feet, looks rather more suggestive. Stripping off his clothes and wrapping a towel around his waist, Jesus positions himself at the feet of his closest companions to perform a bathing ritual of sensory service, wiping his disciples' feet dry with the towel about his groin and encouraging them to do the same to each other. It becomes a sensuous encounter, binding Jesus and his disciples together into a shared and intense bodily relationship.

The erotic undertones of these biblical episodes are often missed by modern readers unfamiliar with the cultural contours of the ancient world and unaccustomed to the notion of a sexualized Christ. But for the earliest followers of Jesus, steeped in Jewish traditions, the feet were already eroticized and closely associated with sexual activity, and in the Hebrew Bible, they often serve euphemistically as a stand-in for genitalia. In the book of Ruth, for example, the eponymous heroine is instructed by her dead husband's mother to seduce the landowner Boaz by oiling herself with perfume, uncovering his 'feet' while he's asleep and positioning herself there. ('And then he will tell you what to do', her mother-in-law adds, with the voice of experience.) Ruth remains at Boaz's 'feet' all night, and succeeds in conceiving a child.[46] Elsewhere in the Hebrew Bible, husbands wet their 'feet' with (or 'in') their wives at home; women's skirts are forcefully lifted to expose their 'feet' in public acts of sexual abuse and humiliation; wanton women whose genitalia deserve to be shamefully exposed are those who 'jingle with their feet' as they walk in sandals and anklets decorated with tiny bells; and adulterous women are those whose feet 'do not stay at home' but walk about the city by night and stand on street corners.[47]

These biblical traditions reflect a sexualizing of the feet attested in Mesopotamian literature of a similar period. In a seventh-century BCE Assyrian text, for example, the scribe god Nabu praises the goddess Tashmetu with enraptured delight as the divine woman 'whose thighs are a gazelle in the plain; whose ankle bones are an apple of Simian; whose heels are obsidian; whose whole being is a tablet of lapis lazuli!'[48] It is a lyrical expression of sexual desire akin to the biblical Song of Songs, in which the male lover revels in the erotic beauty of his beloved's legs and feet: 'How graceful are your feet in sandals, O queenly maiden! Your rounded thighs are like jewels, the work of a master hand!'[49]

Against this rich cultural backdrop, the fetishizing of Jesus' feet as the site of both religious and erotic veneration is unsurprising – and persistent. Extending across centuries of Christianity, sexualized encounters with Christ's feet litter the religious works of theologians, bishops, monks and mystics. In the closing decades of the fourth century, Jerome was battling his sexual urges while on ascetic retreat in the Syrian desert, likening himself to the sensuous sinner of Luke's Gospel: 'Helpless, I cast myself at the feet of Jesus, I watered them with my tears, I wiped them with my hair, and then I subdued my rebellious body with weeks of abstinence'. At around the same time, Bishop Paulinus of Nola was fantasizing about touching the heel of Christ with the tip of his tongue so that he could 'lick the divine feet'.[50] In the twelfth century, the Cistercian monk Bernard of Clairvaux was writing with fevered passion about his desire to move his mouth up the body of Christ, his 'tender lover', kissing first his feet, and then his hand, and then his mouth. In the fifteenth century, the English mystic Margery Kempe was caressing Christ's feet and toes in a series of erotic visions in which he commanded her to treat him as her lover and her husband.[51]

The fixation with divine feet was not confined to Christians during this lengthy period. Within ancient and medieval Judaism, too, some rabbis rhetorically stripped and gazed upon the body of God, fixing their eyes particularly on his feet as the anatomical parts traditionally associated in the Hebrew Bible with the revelation of the divine body. From as early as the second century CE and continuing into the eighth, rabbinic debate about the presence of God frequently circled back to biblical references to God's feet and footstool. In contrast to a theological preference in mainstream Judaism today to read these references metaphorically or symbolically, certain rabbinic traditions celebrated the wonder of God's feet in ways that married the mysterious, transcendent nature of God with ever more tangible ways of experiencing his presence. Accordingly, in some Talmudic and midrashic texts, it is assumed that God leaves humanlike footprints on the rocks and mountains on which he stands; in others, the feet of God are so intimate a part of his body that he conceals them from human eyes, but reveals their impact in the world in the clouds of dust he kicks up as he walks. Even the personified Shekhinah – the 'indwelling' or 'presence' of God in the world – was assumed by some rabbis to have feet, which might be revealed or concealed by clouds, or be soiled or pushed away from the earth by the transgressions of worshippers.[52]

In early Jewish mysticism, intense scholarly speculation about the corporeal nature of God's feet climaxed with the *Shi'ur Qomah* ('measurement of the body') – a literary collection of much older traditions, in circulation by the twelfth century CE. In this work, the measurements of God's body were calculated and the secret names of its anatomical parts discerned. In particular, the claim in the book of Isaiah that the earth was the footstool of God was taken as a handy guide to the enormous size of God's feet, measured in spatial units known as parasangs – each one roughly equivalent to three miles:

> The soles of his feet fill the entire universe, as it is said: '"The heavens are my throne and the earth is my footstool"'. The length of his soles is 30,000,000 parasangs . . . From his foot till his ankle [the distance is] 10,000,500 parasangs in its height [on the right side] and thus also on the left side.[53]

In measuring the feet of God, Jewish mystics were not trying to impoverish the glory of God by rendering him more like a man, as an appalled Maimonides (Rambam) contested in the twelfth century CE. Rather, they were using a specialized religious logic to demonstrate the incomprehensible, uncontainable nature of the divine. To a certain extent, the medieval mystical tradition was keeping alive God's ancient mythological past in ways classical rabbinic Judaism and Western Christianity could not – or would not.

But it is within a collection of medieval mystical traditions known as the *Zohar* that the fetishization of God's feet is most explicitly sexualized. Emerging in thirteenth-century Spain, but claimed to derive from the visions and homilies of a wandering band of Roman-era Palestinian sages and rabbis, the *Zohar* decodes and then recodes biblical texts and Jewish teachings, and is the foundational literature of later Kabbalah and Hasidism. At its heart is the notion that something of the inscrutable, infinite God (*Ein Sof*) can be grasped via the world of the *sefirot* – the ten interactive 'dimensions' or 'emanations' of God in the created world (such as goodness, justice, separation and wisdom) by which humans can experience divine responsiveness. Within this highly esoteric, multilayered theological scheme, God is not only embodied, but the divine body comprises male and female principles, which can engage tenderly and sexually with one another. Encouraged by the biblical tendency to associate the feet with genitalia, the sexualized masculinity of God (a form of the ninth dimension, known as *Yesod*) is frequently correlated with his feet, with which the feminine aspect of the presence of God, the *Shekhinah* (cast as the tenth dimension) engages and unites, erotically and sexually. In the *Zohar*, God's feet become powerfully coded symbols of the spiritualized divine penis.[54]

It is often assumed that this highly specialized, mystical sexualizing of God's feet was a scandalous but anomalous innovation of its time. But this is mistaken. The fetishizing of the divine feet was already a well-established feature of centuries of Jewish and Christian traditions. The medieval mystics contributing to the *Zohar* were simply drawing anew on a rich biblical heritage of cosmic mythology in order to better understand the intimate relationship between God and humans. Deeply embedded within this mythology was the ancient idea that God had always been a sexual deity. And in the Bible, he had the genitals to prove it.

Part II

GENITALS

5

COVER UP

Hidden behind the walls of a monastery in the small Italian town of Bassano Romano is one of the most sensational sculptures in the history of Western art. In the monastery's church of San Vincenzo Martire, tucked away inside a tiny sacristy, is the *Risen Christ* – a masterpiece of Renaissance spirituality, hewn from creamy marble by Michelangelo. Christ stands almost seven feet tall, holding upright the large, heavy cross on which he was killed. He leans casually into the cross, his strong arms comfortably bearing its bulk. Bundled in one hand are the accessories of his execution: a rope, thickly coiled, and the sponge used to wet his drying, dying lips. From his other hand dangles his abandoned death shroud. His face is turned away from the cross as he gazes down at the new world his resurrection has created. His burly body is athletically taut, recalling the classical statuary of Greek culture so beloved by the artist and his contemporaries. Like his Greek forebears, the *Risen Christ* of Bassano Romano is confidently, magnificently nude: beneath a tidy crescent of pubic hair, his petite, relaxed penis rests on a fleshy, rounded scrotum. Jesus' genitals are unashamedly displayed (Plate 6).

The statue was largely ignored until the art world rediscovered it in 1997, which swiftly led to its identification as Michelangelo's first attempt at this particular composition. Commissioned in 1514 for the church of Santa Maria sopra Minerva in Rome, the statue had disappeared from public view when the artist abandoned his nearly completed creation upon discovering a long dark vein in the marble, disfiguring the face of Christ. He began again with a fresh block of stone, and it is this second version that still stands in its intended home in Rome.[1] It too is a nude Christ – or at least it was, until a gaudy bronze loincloth was fixed to the statue in 1546, veiling the penis and testicles from view. Tarnished with age, the modesty device remains to this day. So too do the fluttering draperies and flimsy britches painted in 1565 over the genitals and buttocks of the writhing nude figures populating Michelangelo's monumental *Last Judgement* (1534– 42), in the Sistine Chapel. 'All those figures showing their nakedness so shamelessly', the papal master of ceremonies, Biagio de Cesena, is reported to have exclaimed upon seeing the enormous fresco as it neared completion. The poet Pietro Aretino was equally appalled: 'Your art would be at home in some voluptuous *bagnio* [brothel], certainly not in the highest chapel of the world', he wrote to Michelangelo in 1545. 'Less criminal were it if you were an infidel, than, being a believer, thus to sap the faith of others'.[2]

The censoring of Michelangelo's work was just one of a number of Counter-Reformation strategies adopted by bishops, priests and theologians in the wake of the Council of Trent (1545–63) to tackle what had come to be seen as the scandalous profanity of frontal nudity in Christian art.[3] No matter that Michelangelo, like many of his predecessors and peers, used the nude theologically to celebrate the humanity and masculinity of the divine Christ. For too many, the genitals were both spiritually and morally dangerous, and were thus to be hidden from view.

This was far from a new idea. The genitals have long functioned as a site of religious and cultural anxiety in human societies. Simultaneously associated with sex, reproduction and urination, the places and spaces between our legs trigger deep-rooted social and cultural concerns – particularly about their public display – and are coded with values and meanings in ways many other body parts are not. These values and meanings are closely linked to the generative and changeable physiology of our genitals. After all, they are places of potent physical transformation. Pubic hair grows, greys and fades as we age. Vaginas open, expand and contract during sex and in labour, and are the entry and exit points at which new life is brought into the world. Penises alternate from small and soft to large and hard as erections come and go. Scrotums, labia and clitorises similarly enlarge and engorge, and shrink and retreat, at the stimulus of touch and temperature. Genital skin is recurrently moistened and scented by the body's natural lubricants and the wetness of sexual arousal, or by menstruation, ejaculation and the expulsion of urine. Our genitals are subject to changes in appearance, touch, smell, function and form more than any other part of our bodies. They are powerfully transformative. And like other manifestations of power and transformation, they are potentially dangerous – unless carefully harnessed or managed by the social and cultural preferences of the communities in which we live.

It is for this reason that human societies past and present at once celebrate and denigrate the genitals. Some cultures might decorate, cut, pierce, cover, or expose the genitals of certain groups. In some societies, people might find themselves temporarily or permanently maligned or marginalized given the relative status of their genitalia – menstruating women, the impotent, the infertile, the sick, those who are intersex, or those who are transgender. But it is the covering of the sexual organs that is the most common form of genital regulation in human societies.

In the modern West, as in many other cultures, an adult's genitals are to be covered most of the time. Their uncovering in social settings tends to occur only in certain circumstances: during sex with someone else; in a medical context; or when the social norms surrounding the exposure of the genitals are deliberately flouted, whether subversively, pornographically, or abusively. Our genitals have become our 'private' parts. And yet they remain socially powerful. What we do with our genitalia – and how we do it, where we do it, and with whom – is inextricably linked to the identity politics and associated power play of wider society. From shifting ideas about gender, sexuality, appearance and dress, to nebulous concepts as varied as virginity, adulthood, status and decency, our genitals are in many ways public property, at once privileged and protected, feared and shamed. By covering our genitals, we render them culturally visible.[4]

In the West, our complicated relationship with our genitals has been heavily shaped by the fallout from the most famous of cover-ups: the donning of fig leaves in the Garden of Eden. The story is told in the book of Genesis, in which Eve takes fruit from a forbidden tree and gives it to Adam. They eat, and the eyes of the first man and woman are pointedly said to be 'opened'. They suddenly perceive their bodies differently: they are not simply bare, but 'undressed'. Adam and Eve sew fig leaves together to make coverings to fix around their waists, and further conceal their bodies in the foliage of the garden when they hear God approaching. Having cursed them for their disobedience with a promise of hard agricultural and maternal labour, God expels them from Eden.[5]

In the hands of early Christian theologians, this story about human misbehaviour became a morality tale about the dangers of the flesh. 'They turned their eyes on their own genitals, and lusted after them with that stirring movement they had not previously known', conjectured the fifth-century CE bishop Augustine of Hippo – a Christian convert and reformed womanizer, who knew the hazardous allures of the body all too well.[6] His formulation of humanity's 'original sin' would quickly become a central doctrine of the Western Church. Eve became a temptress who led her husband into religious deviancy. Transgression led to sexualization, rendering innocent nudity shameful nakedness. The first humans fell away from God, exchanging the easy intimacy of the garden for the sweat, pain and unruly sexual desire of the carnal world. Salvation from original sin, congenitally inherited by all humans, was only to be found in Christ – the celibate, sinless counterpart to Adam – who was birthed into the world by Mary – the virginal, uncorrupted foil to Eve. Woeful shame and dangerous lust have infected our genitals ever since.

And yet there is nothing in the biblical story of Eden to suggest that the covering of the genitals reflects the sin of sexuality. Rather, it is a tale about the disobedience of Adam and Eve, and the threat they now pose to God, who shares with his divine colleagues in the heavenly council his worry that, in acquiring wisdom, the humans have become 'like one of us'.[7] They are akin to gods. Their rudimentary clothing marks this transformed, elevated status – a new status further acknowledged by God himself, who replaces their flimsy fig leaves with more durable outfits of leather, made by his own hand. Beyond the bounds of the garden, humans immediately harness their newfound wisdom to do as the gods have always done: they bear children, cultivate crops and rear animals; they kill, travel, play music, build cities, forge tools, craft weapons and perform rituals. In covering their genitals, Adam and Eve reveal not their sexualized self-corruption, but their godlike capacity for the creation of culture.[8]

The distortion of this story by early theologians is just one episode in the long history of a ferocious Christian hostility towards sex and the genitals. It was a hostility shaped in part by the acute ascetic tendencies of certain ancient and classical Greek philosophies, including aspects of Stoicism and Platonism, in which the base and the bodily were sharply distinguished from the sublime and the immaterial. But it was also a view firmly embedded within the earliest authoritative writings of Christianity. In his letter to Christian communities in Roman Galatia, in what is now Turkey, the self-declared apostle Paul draws a pointed distinction between the carnal and the divine: 'Live by the spirit, I say, and do not gratify the desires of the flesh. For what the flesh desires is opposed to the spirit, and what the spirit desires is opposed to the flesh'.[9] For those unwilling or unable to renounce sex, as he told Christians in Corinth, it was better to marry as a means of 'containing' passion, lest the body became so 'aflame' that all self-control would be lost.[10] For Paul, an out-and-proud celibate himself, the holy and the horny could not and should not mix.

It was an austere asceticism seemingly endorsed by Christ himself in texts circulating among early Christian communities across southwest Asia, the Mediterranean and North Africa – including the Gospels (which date from the latter half of the first century CE). Here, Jesus often appears as an extremist who opposes traditional forms of household kinship and its sexual dynamics. He frequently undermines the social worth of marriage and childbirth in favour of an androcentric model of family in which male believers are bound together by faith, not blood: 'Whoever comes to me and does not hate father and mother, wife and children, brothers and sisters, yes, and even life itself, cannot be my disciple'.[11] Although he strongly condemns adultery, divorce and remarriage, the Jesus of the New Testament Gospels presents marriage and childbirth (and by strong implication, sex itself) as a relic of a former age of spiritual ignorance that his death and resurrection would destroy.[12]

By the second century CE, this hostility had intensified. In an important text known as the Acts of Thomas, the risen Jesus suddenly appears in the bedchamber of a couple on their wedding night, urging them not to have sex: 'Know that if you refrain from this filthy intercourse, you become temples holy and pure . . . and you will not be involved in the cares of life and of children, whose end is destruction'. Suffer little children, indeed. Meanwhile, in the Gospel of Thomas (another influential work), Jesus goes further, casting childlessness as a divine blessing: 'The days will come when you will say, "Blessed is the womb which has not conceived and the breasts that have not given suck" '.[13] The conception and raising of children was not only considered a distracting impediment to believers, but a salvific irrelevance. According to Luke's Gospel, Jesus had warned of the futility of sexual reproduction because disaster was coming: 'Woe to those who are pregnant and to those who are nursing infants in those days! For there will be great distress on the earth and wrath against this people'.[14] Indeed, many early Christians – including Paul and the Gospel writers – believed that the world as they knew it was about to end, for it was to be swept away by the Kingdom of God, in which there would be no place for sex nor need for procreation. Instead, believers would enjoy eternal life in celibate, heavenly bodies akin to those of angels.

The world did not come to an end. Yet neither did Christianity die with its first followers. Unsurprisingly, early Christian sex advice appears not to have been wildly popular, for believers continued having children. Although virginity and celibacy would long be idealized as the pious behaviour of the most devout, Christian teaching on marriage and procreation quickly became more accommodating to sexual reproduction, drawing closer to the traditional values of mainstream Jewish groups, for whom marital sex had long been lauded as a pleasurable activity essential to the religious well-being of both husband and wife, and the flourishing of the family. Indeed, sex in marriage was commanded in the Torah by God himself, who had insisted that a newly married man must remain at home for a year in order 'to give pleasure to his wife'.[15] By the second century CE, some Jewish laws were stipulating that a man must have sex with his wife at least once a week, and seek her permission before taking a job that would require prolonged absences from the marital bed.[16]

Against this cultural backdrop, however, sexual activities beyond the bounds of marriage – including adultery, prostitution and same-sex relationships – were deemed antisocial and religiously deviant by both early Jewish and Christian leaders. These activities undermined or upturned the building blocks of marriage, household, kinship and inheritance on which society was constructed. Sexual deviancy was consequently considered offensive to God, for it was contrary to his intentions for humanity. As authoritatively depicted in the first chapter of Genesis, sex was cast as a human activity commanded by God, and yet distanced from him. Set within a cosmic framework of divine creation, its primary purpose was to fulfil God's life-giving instruction that humans 'be fruitful and multiply' – a blessing issued at the point of humanity's creation.[17] The birthing of children was closely tied to the mortality of every generation; humanity could only continue to exist by reproducing – setting them apart from their creator, for whom existence was perpetual. God thus neither needed nor desired sex.

Despite the divine blessing of sex within marriage, an inherent opposition of the sexualized body and the divine was deeply embedded within ancient Jewish and Christian cultures. To a certain extent, it was already modelled in the very language of the scriptures themselves, in which references to the sexualized body were euphemistically controlled or poetically presented. In keeping with long-established cultural norms across ancient south-west Asia, the vocabulary used in literature to describe or refer to the genitals tended towards colloquialism, euphemism, allusion and wordplay. Common linguistic strategies to describe the sex organs included concrete terms for tools and weapons for male genitals (bow, arrow, staff, rod, plough), and domestic or horticultural language for female genitals (water-well, churn, field, garden, fruit). Other body parts frequently served as stand-ins for the genitals, particularly 'hand', 'thigh', 'limb', or 'flesh' for the penis, 'lips' and 'mouth' for the vulva, and 'feet' for the genitals of any type of body.

Abstractions, too, were especially common for male sex organs: 'naked-ness', 'strength' and 'virility' are frequently attested. These linguistic tics are arguably a reflex of common cultural anxieties surrounding the sexual organs – a reflex similarly pervading modern societies. Both British and North American English, for example, enjoy a rich spread of genital vocabulary, from the formal (penis, testicles, vulva, vagina) and the politely veiled (privates, bits, John Thomas, lady garden), to the childish (willy, winky, foo-foo, vajayjay) and the vulgar (cock, prick, pussy, cunt, gash). But in ancient south-west Asian cultures, the literary veiling of the genitals did not render the sexualized body invisible; on the contrary, the elasticity of euphemism made room for deeply erotic reflections on the sexualized body. Take, for example, this sensuous description of bodies readying themselves for sex, in which the wetness of male and female arousal is played out in a flirtatious fantasy:

> I was sleeping but my heart was awake.
> Listen! My lover is knocking!
> 'Open to me, my sister, my love,
> my dove, my perfect one,
> for my head is drenched with dew,
> my locks with the drops of the night!'
> I have taken off my robe;
> am I to put it on again?
> I have bathed my feet;
> am I to get them dirty?
> My lover reached his hand into the opening,
> at which my body thrilled.
> I rose to open to my lover,
> and my hands dripped with myrrh,
> my fingers, flowing myrrh,
> on the handles of the bolt.

This beautiful love lyric appears in the Bible. It is an extract from the Song of Songs (5.2–5), a Hellenistic-era compilation of older medita-tions on the pain and pleasure of sexual desire – a compilation that was so beloved of the scribal cultures of ancient Jerusalem that it found its way into the canonical collections of both Judaism and Christianity.[18] But as the authority of certain religious texts grew – including the Song of Songs – colloquial and euphemistic words for the genitals acquired an additional veneer of reverential modesty: both early Jewish and Christian interpretations of biblical literature increasingly privileged the metaphorical and abstract over the poetic and corporeal, effectively distancing the sacred from the all-too-human realities of sex. What had come to be understood as the written word of God could not be tainted by the gauche, seductive, or scandalous intrusion of genital language.

It was a theological tendency encouraged by the careful separation of the sexualized human body from the divine, which had long been expressed in the Torah and other early Jewish texts in the form of strict ritual regulations surrounding mortals' encounters with sacred space. Scholars are unsure of the extent to which these restrictive regulations were imposed and obeyed, but they indicate nonetheless deep anxiety about the management of human genitals in religious contexts. And carefully managed they were. Just as priests were instructed to remove their shoes and wash their feet before entering the house of God, so too were they ordered to ensure not only that their genitals were covered, but that beneath their long tunics, penises and testicles were tightly secured with close-fitting, high-quality linen underpants, which effectively 'neutralized' – and symbolically neutered – the sexualized bodies of priests.[19] Uncontrolled, loose genitals were clearly not appropriate in the presence of God.

Worse still were 'leaky' genitals, which were considered ritually toxic. According to the book of Leviticus, men who had recently ejaculated, or women who had recently had sex, were considered 'unclean' or 'impure' – in other words, they were unfit for ritual activity, posing a danger both to the sanctity of sacred space and to its personnel. Consequently, these men and women were not to approach such space until they had performed a day-long purification ceremony at home. Menstruating women, or those bleeding after childbirth, were even more dangerous, demanding not only extended periods of ritual purification (of at least a week), but also the day-long purification of anyone who might come into contact with them or the items their bodies had touched. Similar strategies were also employed to deal with anyone suffering a genital discharge prompted by infection or illness. Even after the final destruction of the temple in Jerusalem in 70 CE, these regulations – and the rabbinic debates they sparked – remained potent within Jewish worship, impacting synagogue and study-house attendance for both men and women.[20]

Jewish concerns about the genitals were inevitably carried into early Christian worship and its liturgical precepts. Encouraged by the pro-celibacy theology of salvation promoted by Paul and other prominent community leaders, early Christians of both Jewish and Gentile cultural identity shared (and squabbled over) anxieties about the potential religious hazards of their genitals. As the small house cults of earliest Christian meetings gave way to more formalized, public and increasingly 'sacred' venues of worship, restrictions triggered by the sexualized body intensified. Long before infant baptism became a Christian norm, baptism as an initiation into the faith was originally more akin to a spiritual coming-of-age ritual for adults – and in some communities it was undertaken either wholly undressed or nearly so, in order to ensure the 'holy' water thoroughly coated the body. But this set the sexually mature body and the anxieties it provoked at the very heart of believers' most sacred rites. The transformative power of baptism likely addressed some of these anxieties, as a stunning sixth-century mosaic set into the ceiling of the Arian Baptistery in Ravenna, Italy, would later attest. Flanked by John the Baptist and the god of the Jordan River, an adolescent Jesus is immersed up to his waist in the river waters. He is completely naked – and his genitals are clearly visible. Beardless and youthful, this striking image of Jesus points to the notion of a sin-free nudity akin to that originally enjoyed by Adam and Eve in Eden (Plate 7).

But while childlike nakedness or partial nudity in baptism had been variously encouraged or idealized in the earliest centuries of Christianity, discomfort with the exposed or 'undressed' body steadily grew. These anxieties centred as much on issues of identity and difference as they did theological worries concerning the raw exposure of the flesh, so that Christians increasingly sought to distinguish their immersion rituals from those of traditional Jewish practice, as well as

the bathing cultures of Graeco-Roman civic life, in which nudity or
partial nudity was more usual. Just as significantly, 'naked' baptism
would also trigger wider concerns about the ritual roles of women.
Some early Christian women likely self-administered baptism in small,
private groups to maintain bodily privacy and spare male blushes. But
many feared women had been granted too much ritual power in the
performance of what remains one of Christianity's most important
sacraments. As churches spread and their membership diversified,
apostolic authority birthed powerful priesthoods, rendering baptisms
more public, ceremonial and heavily regulated. Male priests now baptized both men and women – and so genitals and buttocks were hastily
hidden.[21]

For most early Christian communities, however, it was the actively
'polluting' nature of the female sex organs and the ritual risks inherent
in the aftermath of male ejaculation that proved most problematic.
Some groups forbade menstruating and post-partum women both
from baptism and Eucharist, while in many communities the temporary exclusion of women who had recently given birth from all forms
of worship would eventually be extended in the more common rite of
'churching'. In many churches, leaders advised any man or woman
who had recently been exposed to semen to delay their participation
in worship – whether private prayer or communal celebration. Even
the impact of a wet dream upon a man's ability to draw closer to Christ
in worship was a point of contention in the first centuries of the faith.
Understood as an involuntary ejaculation prompted by latent lust or
demonic stimulation, a wet dream muddied the growing conventions
surrounding the careful religious management of the sexualized body.
Some considered it an unwilling if unseemly emission that should not
impinge upon spiritual development and acceptance by Christ. For
others, however, it was a devilish sign of the weak and corrupted flesh
and demanded immediate rectification by means of penitence or
temporary exclusion from worship.[22] Even in sleep, the genitals were
dangerous.

Despite the differences within and between early Jewish and Christian communities, all appeared to agree that the regulation of the
genitals hinged around perceptions of sacred time and sacred place.

deity's 'lower extremities', *shul*, is more commonly used by biblical prophets not to refer to the edges of garments, but to pointedly allude to the fleshy realities of the sexual organs.[27] In this vision in Isaiah, God's genitals are enormous. No wonder the seraphim coyly position their wings over their own. Like temple priests donning underpants, their covering gesture in the divine throne room acknowledges their humble stature in the presence of the well-endowed deity they praise.

The scale of Yahweh's genitalia is to be expected – not only because it belongs to a supersized body, but because Yahweh's cultural father, the aged deity El, was similarly well equipped. In the mythological stories enshrined on the clay tablets of cosmopolitan Ugarit (*c.*1350–1200 BCE), El's penis makes several appearances. In one myth, the god sets out along the serpentine seashore at the edge of the world, where he encounters two young goddesses. They urge him to get an erection and take them in body and marriage. The response is unambiguous: 'El's penis grew as long as the sea, El's penis [grew as long] as the ocean'. Having installed them as brides in his home, he grasps his penis in his right hand and 'shoots' it skyward, like an arrow, to entice his new wives into consummating the marriage. They are suitably impressed with his masturbatory performance. El stoops to kiss them, relishing the pomegranate-sweet taste of their 'lips' – a delicately sensuous double entendre. Penetrative sex quickly follows, and El impregnates the goddesses, who bear him the 'gracious gods' Shahar (Dawn) and Shalem (Dusk).[28]

El's penis may have enthused his young brides, but his primary wife, the great mother goddess Athirat, is not as easily impressed by his penchant for occasional genital exhibition. When she visits her husband in the Baal Cycle of myths, Athirat is on a mission to secure El's approval for the construction of a palace for Baal. Delighted to see her, El assumes her needs are bodily and scrambles to sate her appetites. He offers her rich food and fine wine – and then his penis: 'Does the penis of El the King excite you? Does the love-organ of the Bull arouse you?'[29] Ignoring both his penis and his questions, Athirat simply presses on with her petition. With the world-weary strategy goddesses were often forced to deploy, she tactfully flatters him not with sexual compliments, but appeals to his great wisdom to win her case.

In this story, El's self-titling as 'Bull' is just as revealing as the flaunting of his penis. The bull was an enduring ancient symbol of an aggressively potent, unrestrained hyper-masculinity. It manifested military might, sexual prowess and divine generative power. These were the qualities of the masculine gods of creation, who harnessed the wildness of chaos to impose order upon the cosmos and bring fecundity into the world. It is an ancient and sophisticated constellation of religious ideas, offering an image of a raw, animalized sexual virility that is celebrated in a Sumerian myth dated to about 2000 BCE. In this remarkably vivid tale, the high god Enki* – himself 'engendered by a [divine] bull, begotten by a wild bull' – fertilizes the world by digging irrigation ditches with his penis and creating the great rivers of Mesopotamia with his semen: 'After Father Enki had lifted his eyes across the Euphrates, he stood up full of lust like a rampant bull, lifted his penis, ejaculated, and filled the Euphrates with flowing water . . . By lifting his penis, he brought a bridal gift. The Tigris rejoiced in its heart, like a great wild bull, when it was born'.[30] In the same myth, Enki's penetrative, bodily presence in the heavens, in the meadows and in the rivers stimulates an abundance of rains, a high carp-flood and an accumulation of grains and fruits. As the god of fresh waters, Enki's semen quite literally enlivens the cosmos. It is in these phallic acts of creation that he proves himself a high god and divine progenitor par excellence (fig. 13).

This fertile potency was a characteristic shared across millennia with other masculine deities closely associated with the bull, or to whom the epithet 'Bull' was approvingly applied. These included the Egyptian god of male sexuality, Min, who was consistently depicted in art with an impressively permanent erection; the deity Amun-Re, who frequently adopted Min's phallic iconography (fig. 14); and their venerable colleague Atum, a god of creation, who famously declared that, from the very beginning, he 'came into being ithyphallic'. Alongside El at Ugarit, the god Baal used what is described as his 'tumescent' penis to mate with a heifer, fathering the wild bull who impregnated

---

*   In later Mesopotamian cultures, Enki was better known by his Akkadian name, Ea.

Fig. 13. Enki's innate fertility is vividly portrayed in this detail from a cylinder seal, dated to about 2250 BCE. Known in this particular context by his Akkadian name Ea, his role as the god of fresh water is evident as two fish leap in the abundant streams issuing from his shoulders. His superior status is signalled by his seated position, as another deity politely stands before him.

Fig. 14. A permanent erection was the iconographic hallmark of both the Egyptian god Min and a form of the creator god Amun-Re, who adopted Min's features and pose in his role as Amun-Kamutef ('Amun-the-Bull-of-His-Mother'). This image from the temple complex at Karnak shows Amun-Re as the self-generating ithyphallic god.

the city's cattle. The Assyrian storm-god Adad was often depicted standing atop a great bull, while various unidentified goddesses across the region are depicted upon a divine bull, commanding its virility – an image seemingly recast and abased in the famous Greek myth of Zeus' sexual abduction of Europa, whom he carries off across the sea on his back while disguised as a bull. Among these high-status deities, it is no surprise to find that Yahweh, too, was often understood as the divine bull. Bovine language (the Hebrew term *abbir*) underlies his biblical designation as the 'Mighty One [*abir*] of Jacob' who grants genital fertility to the Israelite tribe of Joseph, and in some biblical texts, Yahweh's cult statue is said to take the form of a bull or a bull calf.[31]

Like the Sumerian god Enki, Yahweh's status as a fertile creator god of the highest order is also confirmed in the Bible with a fleeting portrayal of his sexual encounter with the earthly realm. Although the biblical writers (and their later translators) have done their best to sanitize the story by diluting Yahweh's corporeal sexuality, its erotic features nonetheless suggest that an older myth lurks in the background: the God of the Bible sexually takes the land of Israel as his wife (as signalled by the euphemistic use of the verb 'to know') and excites the cosmos into an aroused, mutually reproductive fecundity as he impregnates his bride at a place called Jezreel ('He Seeds') – a region famed for its rich agricultural soils:

> I will take you for my wife in faithfulness,
> and you will 'know' Yahweh.
> On that day, I will fructify – says Yahweh,
> I will fructify the heavens,
> and they will fructify the earth;
> and the earth will fructify the grain, the wine, and the oil,
> and they will fructify Jezreel;
> and I will seed her for myself in the land.[32]

In this poem in the book of Hosea, dated to about the eighth century BCE, Yahweh's penis may well be veiled from direct view, hidden behind a modesty screen of euphemism and wordplay, but the bodily, sexual connotations are impossible to miss. Like the prophets Isaiah and said to have defeated the great sea monster, piercing its body to expose its innards.[7] And he too appears to hang his bow in the skies: in the biblical story of the Flood, which incorporates motifs drawn from the battle with aqueous chaos, Yahweh memorializes his subjugation of the deadly waters by suspending his war bow in the heavens. 'My bow I have placed in the cloud', he declares. 'When I bring a cloud over the earth, and the bow appears in the cloud, I will remember my covenant which is between me and you and every living being, so that waters shall not again become a flood to annihilate all flesh.'[8] The transformation of his war bow into a rainbow was made easy in biblical Hebrew, in which the word *qeshet* ('bow') is used for both. But the phallic associations of this commemorative sky-sign were clearly recognizable to his worshippers: when the prophet Ezekiel beheld God's genitalia, he likened what he saw to the deity's phallic weapon of war, describing the glorious sight to be as dazzling as 'the bow in a cloud on a rainy day'.[9] The rainbow at which so many of us have looked in delighted wonder is a polychrome vision of God's weaponized penis.

The divine penis inserted itself into the human world in other ways, too – not least on the battlefield. Across ancient south-west Asia, war was not simply a tool of economic and territorial conflict, nor solely a means of ordering the world and its inhabitants into the civilized and the barbaric, the victorious and the defeated. Warfare was idealized as a means of distinguishing the most masculine from the non-masculine. Like their gods, the south-west Asian kings of the second and first millennia BCE understood that the weapons of war represented their virility and masculinity – politically, socially and personally. Written into imperial treaties and international trade policies were divine curses to be triggered should one party renege on the agreed relationship: vassal kings would have their bows broken by the gods; their dynastic lines would be rendered sterile; their bodies would become impotent or effeminate. But just as it took more than a weapon to make a successful warrior, and more than a successful warrior to win a war, so it took more than a penis to make a man, and more than manliness to manifest masculinity. For gods and humans alike, this was a world governed and shaped by a network of multiple of these relationships bordered on the taboo. In some social groups, gender constructs both shifted and intersected with status and power, so that sex between men was slightly less offensive if the penetrated partner was of a lower social category than his lover.[14] But penetrative sex between men of the same social status was unacceptable, for it improperly feminized the receptive partner by diminishing his masculinity. In a text among a collection known as the Middle Assyrian Laws, dated to about 1225 BCE, the punishment threatened for this crime is retributive and severe: the perpetrator is to be raped and then castrated – 'feminizing' him sexually, socially and physically.[15] But the social impact of homoerotic sexual relationships was not restricted to the earthly realm – at least, not as far as some biblical writers were concerned. In the eyes of Yahweh, who had a special concern for the phallic productivity of his worshippers, sex between men could be particularly troublesome. The fertility of semen was best not wasted – whether on menstruating wives, other men's women, or male sexual partners. Consequently, the intrusion of the life-giving, semen-shooting penis into the barren, anal locus of 'dead' faeces was considered a highly toxic impurity, remedied only by the community expulsion or execution of both partners.[16]

From the most masculine to the non-masculine, the penis was the pivot around which ideologies of cultural power turned, and the tool by which social order was calibrated. But it was not confined to war and sex alone. Phallocentric masculinity bound together many other aspects of ancient societies – and the undergirding patriarchal systems by which they were held to flourish. Most crucially, all life within the cosmos was usually understood to be drawn from and depend upon the phallic potency of the divine male.

Cultural Insemination

In 1760, an eminent Swiss physician called Samuel Auguste David Tissot published the revised and expanded results of his research into the dangers of male masturbation, entitled *L'Onanisme, ou dissertation physique sur les maladies produites par la masturbation*. A runaway success, it was to be penetrated or at risk of penetration. Instead, it is the Assyrian who penetrates – with arrows, with spears, with knives, and with a divinely endorsed authority granted by the bow-bearing high god himself.[11] To be a penetrated male was to be downgraded, degraded and devoid of masculinity. To be penetrated was not only to be emasculated – it was to be like a woman.

Across ancient south-west Asia, high-status ideologies of warfare and politics usually ran parallel to cultural norms of sex, gender and sexuality. This was a patriarchal world in which social relationships tended to be structured on unequal terms, distinguishing between the penised and the non-penised, the penetrators and the penetrated, the dominant and the submissive, and the active and the passive. While the deliberate confusion of these distinctions was a prerogative of the gods, the human blurring of gendered and bodily hierarchies could generate considerable social anxiety. Even in the marital bedroom, the distinction between masculine dominance and feminine passivity was often carefully guarded. According to some Mesopotamian sources, a husband was not to allow his wife to be on top during sex, for fear it would rob him of his physical strength for a month. Centuries later, similar exhortations in the Babylonian Talmud would warn husbands that the same sexual position would curse them with diarrhoea.[12] It was a fear of female sexual dominance further reflected in early medieval Jewish debates about the malevolent winged demon, Lilith. By then, some rabbis had recast this ancient Mesopotamian baby-killer as Adam's first errant wife, who had insisted on assuming the dominant position in sex because, she said, she and Adam were of equal status. When her husband refused, she sensibly abandoned the marriage, flying away over Eden's garden wall.[13]

If heterosexual relationships were potentially hazardous, same-sex relationships were especially problematic. While the masculinist focus of ancient south-west Asian literature tended not to notice sex between women, the phallic penetration of male bodies was a concern for some. The erotic dimensions of homosocial relationships were occasionally celebrated in myth and song – both Gilgamesh in Mesopotamia and King David in Judah were said to treasure the love of a man more than that of any woman. But more often than not, the sexual consummation

quickly translated into German, Italian and English, the expanded title
of which rendered even more explicit the potential perils of a man's
sexual self-satisfaction: *Onanism: or, a Treatise upon the Disorders Produced
by Masturbation: or, The Dangerous Effects of Secret and Excessive Venery.*[17]
As an advisor to the Vatican, Tissot's work fortuitously offered scientific
(for its time) condemnation of what Western Christianity regarded as a
heinous activity, offensive to God: in the Bible, the deity had killed the
unfortunate Onan for repeatedly spilling his seed (although in the story,
the poor man's crime is not actually masturbation, but coitus inter-
ruptus).[18] Tissot's manifesto against masturbation might have com-
plemented Church teaching, but it undermined a belief long held in the
West that semen might harbour dangerous – even devilish – powers. It
was a view authoritatively endorsed by Augustine of Hippo, who centuries before had claimed that the sin of Adam and Eve was transmitted
to every subsequent generation via 'corrupted semen'.[19] Instead, Tissot
reasoned, semen was an unadulterated 'essential oil', more vital to the
well-being of the male body than its blood: the loss of one ounce of
semen, he asserted, was as hazardous as a blood loss of forty ounces.
Excessive ejaculation was thus deadly. Worse still, it might strip a man
of his humanity, reducing him to a monstrous non-human being, as
Tissot's description of a compulsive masturbator suggests:

> I found a being that less resembled a living creature, than a
> corpse, lying upon straw, meagre, pale, and filthy, casting forth
> an infectious stench; almost incapable of motion, a watry
> palish blood issued from his nose; slaver constantly flowed from
> his mouth: having diarrhaea [*sic*], he voided his excrement
> into the bed without knowing it . . . he was a spectacle, the
> horrible sight of which cannot be conceived, and it was difficult
> to discover that he had formerly made part of the human
> species.[20]

Although it was widely regarded at the time as a seminal work of
scientific research, Tissot's study was in many ways a product of much
older ideas about the male body. His emphasis on the vitality of semen
echoed the highly influential Greek view, shared by thinkers as

divergent in their opinions as Hippocrates (*c.* 460–370 BCE) and Galen (*c.* 129–215 CE), that semen was the substance or transmitter of the 'vital force' from which each human life derived and on which it survived, from the womb to the tomb. While Greek and later Western ideas about the reproductive capacities of a woman's 'seed' or menstrual blood varied, semen was consistently understood as the agent of life: it sparked existence into being in utero, gifting the child its lifelong store of vitality, which had to be carefully managed lest it lingered too long, like rotting fruit, or spent out entirely, like a leaky trough.

This masculinist conviction about the power of semen not only persisted well into the nineteenth century, but stretched back thousands of years, far beyond the golden age of Greek philosophical science, to the ancient cultures of south-west Asia. From the early third millennium BCE and well into the early centuries of the first millennium CE, there was at the very heart of these cultures a pervasive sense not only that semen was the source of new life, but that it was a substance so potent it was potentially dangerous. Whether divine, semi-divine, or human, semen could impact the materiality of the cosmos and its inhabitants in both enlivening and destructive ways.

In social terms, the high cultural value of semen in ancient south-west Asia inevitably impacted the bodies and status of mortal women. Female bodies were held to shape, birth and nourish children, and their vulvas were considered organs of intense, intoxicating sexual allure. Yet generative power resided in the bodily fluids of men – especially their semen. 'Taken' or 'received' by the womb, semen acted as a clotting agent, curdling the blood residing passively inside the uterus into a fleshy child – an idea vividly illustrated in the Hebrew Bible when Job credits God with his conception: 'Did you not pour me out like milk and curdle me like cheese? You clothed me with skin and flesh, and knit me together with bones and sinews'.[21] The powerful agency of semen is perhaps a notion embedded in the very earliest cuneiform texts (*c.* 3200 BCE), in which the ideogram (or symbol) for 'man' appears to be an actively ejaculating penis, while 'woman' is represented more passively by a pubic triangle.[22] But it is also reflected in the distinctly gendered language of human sexual reproduction in subsequent ancient south-west Asian literatures – including the

Hebrew Bible – in which men are usually said to 'beget' children, while women simply 'bear' them.[23]

Making babies was essentially a male activity – so much so, the penis was closely identified with the other most creative part of the male body: the hand. Both body parts were especially valued as agents of skilled, productive and transformative action. It is no surprise, then, to find that in many south-west Asian texts, the word 'hand' was a common synonym of the penis. The work of one corresponded to the work of the other. And so it is in the Hebrew Bible, in which it is a man's divinely ordained task to bring life into the world by the work of his *yad* ('hand' or 'penis'), whether it be impregnating a woman, keeping livestock, or tilling the land: 'Yahweh your god will make you abundantly prosperous in all the work of your hand/penis, in the fruit of your [woman's] womb, in the fruit of your cattle, and in the fruit of your soil.'[24]

To a certain extent, the cultural privileging of the penis in these ancient societies is a stark reflection of the androcentric, elite perspectives of the scribes creating and compiling the texts on which we rely for information about the worlds in which they lived. This literature tended overwhelmingly to be produced by men, for men – and it was usually about men. But when complications in sex and reproduction arose, women were inevitably rendered more visible in the magical-medical rituals preserved in some scribal compositions, which indicate that women were expected to play a key role in helping to remedy penis problems – particularly in treating childlessness.

Infertility was not widely considered an affliction suffered by men. Childlessness instead signalled 'barren' wives. Men might experience impotence – a condition often caused by the malevolent powers of sorcery, demons, or the restless ghosts of jealous young virgins – yet their fertility was rarely in doubt. The penis might well remain disappointingly flaccid, but the semen held within the body was not believed to be seedless. Magical cures harnessed the fecund forces pervading the cosmos to empower the penis of any man proverbially described in Mesopotamian texts as one whose 'youthful masculinity has left [his] loins, like a runaway donkey'.[25] Some cures were probably quite effective in triggering an erection. In one Assyrian ritual, dated to about

1500 BCE, a woman is to take pulverized iron ore – the very stuff of hard weapons – mix it into oil and instruct her husband to rub it onto his penis, as she massages oil into her vulva. The ritual also recommends other restorative methods, such as talking dirty to him and encouraging him to envisage what (to all intents and purposes) looks to be bestial pornography: his wife tethers a stag to the head of the bed, and a ram at its foot – rutting animals with whom her husband is magically identified. Then, somewhat intimidatingly for her partner, she shouts a powerful incantation:

> The one at the head of my bed, get an erection, make love
>   to me!
> The one at the foot of my bed, get an erection, make love
>   to me!
> My vagina is the vagina of a bitch! His penis is the penis of
>   a dog!
> As the vagina of a bitch holds fast the penis of a dog, [so may
>   my vagina hold fast his penis!][26]

As on earth, so in heaven. In myths across ancient south-west Asia, fertility was almost exclusively a masculine trait, exhibited by male deities. Sterility or barrenness in the world was not a manifestation of divine infertility – but nor was it a reflection of erectile dysfunction among the gods. Rather, it was a result of the deliberate withdrawal or absence of the masculine gods of fertility, who might retreat in response to insult or social disorder, or temporarily relocate to the wilderness or the underworld. The death and sterility their absences triggered starkly underscored their superior control of fecundity. It is a role evident in several traditions: when the Anatolian god Telipinu is suddenly angered, he puts his shoes on the wrong feet, storms out of the divine assembly and takes himself off into the wilderness. The impact is catastrophic: 'Barley and wheat no longer grow; cows, sheep, and humans no longer conceive, and those who are [already] pregnant do not give birth'.[27] Similarly, when the Ugaritic deity Baal is temporarily slain by the death god Mot, 'dried up are the furrows of the fields'; it is only upon his resurrection from the underworld and return to the heavenly realm that 'the heavens rain down oil, the wadis run with honey'.[28] The calamitous impact of a disappearing deity is well known in the Bible, too. When God vows to punish his people with 'a miscarrying womb and dry breasts', he threatens to do so by abandoning them:

> [Israel's] Glory will fly away like a bird –
> no birth, no pregnancy, no conception!
> Even if they bring up children,
> I will bereave them until no one is left.
> Woe to them indeed when I depart![29]

These myths overturn the common – and woefully reductive – misconception that across the ancient pantheons of south-west Asia, goddesses were primarily responsible for fertility. Instead, goddesses more usually looked after the womb, birth and lactation in matters of reproduction. But in the phallic cultures of this ancient world, they inevitably shared with their male peers a divine concern for the well-being and arousal of the human penis, and were frequently called upon to gift or empower the seductive, sexual allure of humans of all genders. Although female deities might well bring into being other deities, semi-divine heroes and humans, they often required both the assent and the semen, blood, tears, spit, sweat, or wet breath of divine masculinity to do so.[30] By contrast, male deities could entirely forgo female cooperation, and create new life alone. In an ancient Egyptian myth, the high god Atum does precisely this when he masturbates the universe into existence. Ejaculating into his mouth, he spits and sneezes out his semen to create the male deity of airy space, Shu, and the female deity of sweet moisture, Tefnut:

> I am the one who acted as husband with my fist:
> I copulated with my hand,
> I let fall into my own mouth,
> I sneezed Shu and spat Tefnut.[31]

As Atum's hand acts as a wife's vagina, so his mouth and nostrils function as birth canals. His divine twins have sex and bring into being

Fig. 16. The essential role of mother goddesses and birth goddesses is captured in this plaque from ancient Eshnunna, dated to about 1800 BCE. The deity cradles a newborn at her breast, while her divine attributes are represented by the infants emanating from her shoulders. The figures at her feet are variously interpreted as foetuses under her protection, or babies lost to miscarriage or stillbirth – threats warded off by the plaque itself.

God emphatically acts alone: 'Yahweh-God formed a human [*adam*] from the dust of the ground [*adamah*], and breathed into his nostrils the breath of life; and the human became a living being'.[35] Less well known, however, is God's use of his breath to create Lady Wisdom, the name biblical scholars give to the goddess figure known as Hokmah in Hebrew texts and Sophia in Greek-language Jewish texts. Popular from at least the fourth century BCE onwards, Lady Wisdom was said to have accompanied God at the creation of the world. In the second-century BCE book of Sirach (also known in Jewish tradition as Ben Sirah, and to Christians as Ecclesiasticus), she boasts of her privileged status and describes her birth from God's body:

> In the assembly of the Most High she opens her mouth,
> in the presence of his hosts she tells of her glory:
> 'I came forth from the mouth of the Most High,

absurd that Adam, the very first man himself, whom God had made and blessed as the pinnacle of his creation, should have been denied the mark of circumcision. And yet, in the Hebrew Bible, neither Noah nor Adam is said to have forsaken his foreskin.

As with many other theological conundrums, the problem was solved by careful rabbinic exposition of biblical texts. Noah, the rabbis declared in the second century CE, was clearly born circumcised, for he is described in Genesis as *tamim*, just like Abraham. But what of Adam? Crucially, the rabbinic answer to this question unveiled God's genitals in the starkest of ways: 'Adam, too, was born [from the earth] circumcised, for it is said, "And God created man in his own image" '.[4] If Adam was made in the image of God, as it is twice claimed in Genesis, he must have been circumcised, the rabbis reasoned, for God was circumcised, too.

This idea is unlikely to have been an innovative theological shift. It reflects instead much older and deeply held assumptions. The elevated religious status of male circumcision in God's own sacred texts rendered it unthinkable that he could have had a foreskin. Culturally, too, there may have been an ancient mythic precedent for divine circumcision. God's direct forerunner, the Late Bronze Age deity El, appears to have undergone circumcision in a ritual preparing him for marriage and sex with the two goddesses he encountered at the seashore. In this Ugaritic myth, El sits enthroned, equipped with phallic symbols of old age and infertility: 'in his hand the staff of sterility; in his hand the staff of widowhood'. El's reversal of the lifelessness held in his hands is revealed in a ritual asserting his sexual fecundity. His foreskin appears to be removed and the wound wrapped by ritual specialists associated with the careful cultivation of sacred vineyards: 'Those who prune the vine pruned him; those who bind the vine bound him; they let his tendril fall like a vine'. Like a budding vine clipped into fruitfulness, so El's circumcised penis brings forth children in his new marriages – infant deities whose own genitalia ('grapes' and 'tendrils') are inspected by a birth goddess to ensure they are in order.[5]

The extent to which this myth was known throughout the Levant is uncertain. But in the Gospel of John (composed around 100 CE), the viticultural imagery of circumcision is used to describe Jesus as the 'true vine', who is 'pruned' by his divine father to bring forth Christ's 'fruitful' disciples.[6] And as late as the fourth century CE, the Christian apologist Eusebius of Caesarea was citing an ancient writer called Philo of Byblos (c. 70–160 CE), who recounts an even older (if convoluted) Phoenician myth in which El circumcises himself before sacrificing his 'only begotten' son, Iedoud ('Beloved') – a story striking in its parallels to that of Abraham, who in Genesis similarly circumcises himself and then attempts to sacrifice his 'only begotten' and 'beloved' son Isaac.[7]

As a form of body modification, male circumcision was well known throughout the ancient world, although not all societies practised it. One of its earliest depictions appears in an ancient Egyptian tomb relief from Saqqara, the great necropolis of Memphis, and is dated to the period of the Sixth Dynasty (c. 2345–2181 BCE). Two naked young men each stand in front of a circumciser seated on the floor at his feet. With one hand, the circumciser gently pulls at the youth's flaccid penis; with the other, he carefully takes a tool to the tip of the penis. Annotations running across the relief present dialogues between the characters. 'Hold him fast; do not let him faint!' says one circumciser to an attendant restraining one of the young men. 'I will do as you command', he responds. The other young man reaches out to place his hand on the head of his circumciser – perhaps to steady his nerves, as well as his gait. 'Sever, indeed, thoroughly', says the man. 'I will proceed carefully', replies his practitioner (fig. 17). While the precise purpose of circumcision in this relief goes unstated, accompanying hieroglyphs indicate the circumcisers are mortuary priests, initiating new members into their guild.[8] As such, circumcision here appears to function as a body ritual manifesting a new social identity or religious status, enabling the circumcised to perform particular roles otherwise unavailable to them.

Indeed, male circumcision in ancient or traditional societies tends to function in this way. Like other forms of religious body modification – including piercing, tattooing, scarification and cutting – male circumcision is a means of 'making' the body. In contrast to the notion of the 'natural' body as a body unchanged and unadorned, the peoples of ancient south-west Asia and Egypt perceived the body as an unfinished, ongoing social project, subject to essential alteration, adjustment

Fig. 17. This painted relief from the tomb of a royal official called Ankhmahor, in Saqqara, is widely held to depict circumcision. Dated to the Sixth Dynasty (*c.* 2345–2181 BCE), its accompanying inscriptions reveal that the circumcisers are mortuary priests. This form of body modification might have played a role in the initiation of new colleagues into their guild.

and reformation. Temporary forms of body modification, including make-up, hair styling, clothing and ritual washing, as well as permanent alterations, helped 'make' and 'remake' the body in ways that materialized particular social identities and abilities.[9]

This understanding of male circumcision stands in contrast to the common misperception that the reduction or removal of the foreskin reflected ancient efforts to maximize genital hygiene – a concern replicated in a number of Western societies today, particularly in the United States and Canada, where circumcision is routinely performed on infant males not as a religious ritual, but a medical convention. But there is little (if any) evidence to suggest that the ancient origins of circumcision lie with a concern about potential health risks festering beneath the foreskin. Blame for this tenacious misperception largely falls on the Greek author Herodotus. Writing in the mid fifth century BCE, he asserts that circumcision was originally a custom of the Egyptians, who 'practise circumcision for the sake of cleanliness, for they set cleanness above seemliness'.[10] But although Herodotus was famously declared the 'father of history', his travelogues turned instead on cultural caricature and parody. Consequently, his description of the Egyptian practice satirizes the 'clean' nature of circumcision: to be 'clean' was not to be hygienic, but to be a body ritually ready for presence or action in sacred space. This seems to be the context of circumcision in the Egyptian relief at Saqqara, and it is the way in which circumcision is presented in Genesis: when God instructs Abraham to circumcise himself and walk with him, the ritual is pitched as the modification necessary to render Abraham unblemished (*tamim*). And the reason why the God of the Bible would perceive the foreskin to be a blemish likely lies with the power of his own penis.

In ancient and traditional societies, circumcision is more usually performed on pubescent or near-pubescent males as a rite of passage, marking on their bodies the maturing of their reproductive sexuality and the transition from boyhood to manhood. But the reduction or removal of the foreskin is more than a symbol of shifting social status. In societies in which a meaningful distinction is drawn between the mysterious hiddenness of the inside of the body, and the more visible, malleable aspects of its outside, rituals often serve to control or negotiate the interplay between the two. This is why social and religious regulations in traditional societies often accrue around the body's orifices. But the deliberate blurring of the distinction between the inside and the outside of the body is also powerfully transformative. Bringing the inside of the body 'out' intensifies its social and religious force. In the religious imagination, traditional male circumcision falls into this category: it 'opens' the penis, bringing the glans 'outside' the body permanently (perhaps mimicking the exposure of the glans in an erection) and thereby enhancing the fertile potency of the penis.

It is no wonder male circumcision was so central to ancient Judaism and its religious precursors. Just as God's penis manifested his life-giving powers, so too he rendered the penises of his male worshippers more fruitful in commanding circumcision. This is made explicit in his covenant with Abraham in Genesis: Yahweh promises to make Abraham 'the ancestor of a multitude' by rendering him 'exceedingly fruitful'[11] – a prospect Abraham initially finds incredible, given that he is nearing one hundred years old, and his elderly wife, Sarah, has always been barren. But male circumcision is the means by which this covenantal blessing is to be brought about, miraculously gifting Abraham and Sarah not only with a son of their own, Isaac, but with generations of Abrahamic descendants, tracked in Jewish tradition via the newborn Isaac, rather than Ishmael, the patriarch's thirteen-year-old son born by the slave-girl Hagar, who in the Bible is quickly rejected by his father after Isaac's birth.

It is for this reason that the heightened fruitfulness of the circumcised penis is closely associated in the Hebrew Bible with the careful cultivation of agricultural fecundity. Maturing fruit trees are held to render a better quality and more bountiful crop if 'circumcised' in their fourth year – much as El's circumcised penis was made fruitful by those who 'prune the vine' at Ugarit.[12] But the close paralleling of circumcised penises and fruiting trees also carries a more unsettling legacy, as the Phoenician myth of El's circumcision appears to have done. Just as the God of the Bible demanded his cut of the agricultural and animal harvest in the form of tithed offerings in his temples, so too he claimed his ancient right to a cut of the human crop: 'The firstborn of your sons you shall give to me. You shall do the same with your oxen and your sheep. Seven days he shall remain with his mother; on the eighth day you shall give him to me.'[13] But while a firstborn animal was to be sacrificed, male infants were to be 'rescued' from death by means of circumcision – the modification of their penises physically marking God's claim to their bodies. Male circumcision not only brought life, but protected newborn males from sacrificial death, transforming a fertility ritual more usually performed on pubescent boys into a birth ritual.[14]

Such was the religious power of the circumcised penis that, by the fifth century BCE, the priests of the Jerusalem temple had developed a complex set of regulations designed to tame its seminal discharge: its potent fertility should only be used to bring 'legitimate' life into the world. Sex outside marriage was discouraged. Sex with a kinsman's woman (whether wife, sister, mother, or daughter) was abhorrent because it risked confusing patrimonial bloodlines. Sex with a 'foreign' woman, who might well worship other gods, risked destabilizing the kinship cohesion of Yahweh's worshippers, and undermined his exclusive claim to their children. And as we have seen, sexually penetrating another man, or an animal, or ejaculating onto the earth, was especially deviant – not for any clear moral objections, but probably because it meant that semen would be wasted, transgressing God's command that his people were to 'be fruitful and multiply'.[15] Enshrined in the Torah, these religious regulations were originally intended only for priests, but they would increasingly be assumed to apply to all male Yahweh worshippers in and beyond the Jerusalem temple.

In an ancient society in which idealized masculinity was closely tied to the social and physiological performance of the penis, Jerusalem's religious elites considered the uncircumcised penis deficient – just as other body parts that did not function optimally (deaf ears, mumbling mouths, disloyal hearts) were also said to be 'uncircumcised'.[16] And if the uncircumcised penis was deficient, so too was its owner. He was perceived as physically, socially and religiously defective, which is why some biblical writers are emphatic in their insistence that only the circumcised can participate in rituals devoted to Yahweh and count themselves among the people of God. This ideology would later go some way to constructing a distinctively masculinized 'ethnic' identity of Yahweh worshippers within early Jewish societies. But its phallocentrism rendered those without functioning genitals or a penis to circumcise excluded from certain forms of worship, and either temporarily or permanently marginalized in their communities: women and alternatively gendered members of society, including those conventionally described as 'eunuchs' and the genitally impaired, were increasingly seen as inherently flawed – and potentially destabilizing in the religious world.[17] Consequently, these lesser bodies demanded careful management, primarily – but not exclusively – by means of rituals understood to contain or counteract the social and religious dangers they manifested.

Eunuchs had long enjoyed or endured a unique status across ancient south-west Asia. Their specialized bodies rendered them powerfully equipped not only to cross boundaries between masculine and feminine spaces, but to traverse the ritualized thresholds of the cosmos, so that they might step safely between divine and human spheres. And yet their mysterious liminality made them potentially dangerous, and they were feared and celebrated in equal measure. Among the masses, their fates were precarious. But within elite contexts, some eunuchs might be elevated to prestigious political and religious positions. Some were identified as eunuchs from birth, but many were castrated males – some voluntarily, some through coercion or force. If they survived castration, the resulting health complications made their lives expensive to sustain, rendering them luxury commodities and status symbols for their wealthy patrons or owners. Eunuchs literally embodied designer chic for royal courts and temples.[18]

It is in these elite settings that eunuchs most frequently appear in the Hebrew Bible: they are members of royal households, performing important political, military and religious roles. But in Judah, their lives changed in the fifth century BCE, when the Persian Empire held sway across the region. Judah's defunct monarchy was replaced by a series of imperially appointed governors, who oversaw the rebuilding of Jerusalem's temple. Its priesthood was reconstituted, and the city's burgeoning theocracy now ministered to a much-reduced community. Against this backdrop, eunuchs' bodies became more problematic. Although most were equipped with a penis (and some were able to have penetrative sex), their sterility rendered them 'a dry tree' in a religious culture in which the fruitful phallus was ever more crucial. They were to be kept away from God's presence, although one of Yahweh's prophets promised they would be granted compensatory access to sacred space in the form of a memorial stela, which would be pointedly erected in the temple and would be 'better than sons and daughters'.[19]

For those members of society without a penis, matters of temple-community membership were more complex, for their bodies deviated even further from the religious ideal of the circumcised male. Female circumcision appears not to have been a practice with which ancient south-west Asian and eastern Mediterranean societies were particularly familiar. Early evidence for the rite anywhere in this region is sporadic and sketchy at best, and tends to be filtered through the pejorative cultural bias of Greek and Roman writers primarily discussing 'exotic' Egyptian communities.[20] Instead, Jerusalem's priests formalized the older tendency to restrict or exclude women from the male-dominated spaces and rituals of the temple, and countered the dangerous impact of their 'leaky' bodies by prohibiting men from having sex with a menstruating woman.[21] They also guarded male infants from the contaminating impact of their own 'female' birth blood. Mothers and babies were to be considered 'unclean' and kept away from both sacred space and those men who might enter it, until their uncleanness had subsided and they had performed the requisite purification rituals. If a woman bore a son, the blood of his circumcision on the eighth day countered the dangerous blood of his mother's body; the baby boy was made 'clean', while she remained in a state of impurity for thirty-three days. If she birthed a daughter, however, a mother's uncleanness was intensified: her body was highly toxic for fourteen days, and she remained impure for a further sixty-six days.[22]

Essentially, the Hebrew Bible was born in a specialized scribal culture in which the circumcised penis was both the ultimate human manifestation of a divinely endorsed, phallocentric masculinity and a bodily performance of 'normative' faithful devotion to God. This speaks to a hierarchy of human bodies, built on relative and varying constructions of gender (including diverse shades of masculinities), deeply embedded within the religious traditions giving rise to early Judaism and Christianity. At the apex of this hierarchy was the circumcised male body, a body itself drawn on a divine paradigm: the body of God. As the cosmic creator, who constructed human males in his own image, it was for many beyond theological doubt that God himself was circumcised, and that this form of body modification among his male worshippers perfected their own penises, making their bodies whole, unblemished and divinely fertile, as it had Abraham.

Manhood

The paradigmatic divine penis inevitably extended into Christianity and onto the body of Jesus of Nazareth. Oddly, though, his is a body about which we know very little. For all its talk about Jesus, one of the most peculiar features of the New Testament is its apparent disinterest

in what he looked like.[23] Certainly, the writers of these texts offer
various observations about the wounds inflicted on Jesus during his
torture and execution, and the nature of his resurrected body. But
nowhere in the biblical canon is there a description of his physical
features. Only one passing detail about the visual appearance of his
body is given: Jesus' penis was circumcised.[24]

This in itself should come as no surprise. After all, Christianity
began as a minor Jewish sect. Jesus of Nazareth was Jewish, as were
most of his first followers. It was only natural that Jesus was assumed
to have been circumcised. But the presumed religious realities of Jesus'
personal life were all too often lost in the highly abstract theologies of
Paul and other early Christian leaders, for whom the resurrected,
heavenly Christ was in many ways more important than Jesus the man.
To a certain extent, the authors of the New Testament Gospels (composed after Paul's letters) tempered this abstraction by focusing on the
earthly, human nature of Christ, offering tales of Jesus' life set in his
own Jewish culture in Roman Palestine. But these tales also served to
bolster first-century Christian theologies; as a subset of Judaism, earliest Christianity necessarily relied upon the Jewish scriptures to
endorse its claims about Jesus' messianic and divine status. Consequently, selected Jewish cultural and religious preferences are used in
the Gospel accounts of the mysterious man from Nazareth to attest
to his bona fide credentials as the alleged embodiment and 'fulfilment'
of both traditional Jewish teaching and practice. And for some early
Christians, there was no denying that this divine man's penis was
appropriately circumcised.

Authoritative confirmation was offered in the Gospel of Luke, in
which Jesus is said to have been circumcised on his eighth day of life,
in accordance with God's regulations in the Torah. Afterwards, when
both he and his mother have emerged from the impurity of the birth,
Jesus is taken to the Jerusalem temple to be presented to God,
because – as the author of Luke states – 'it is written in the law [Torah]
of the Lord, "Every firstborn male shall be designated as holy to the
Lord" '.[25] In this early Christian tradition, at least, Jesus' circumcision
functions in expected ways: it brings Jesus' body into anatomical line
with the masculine, circumcised body of the god of the Jerusalem

temple. But the sexualized fecundity promised by male circumcision would not bear fruit in the New Testament; both the earthly Jesus of Nazareth and the risen, heavenly Christ remain emphatically childless and celibate. Instead, the fruits of his circumcised penis are spiritualized. In the Gospel of John, as we have seen, they are disciples 'pruned' from his 'vine' by his divine father. Meanwhile, in the letter to the Colossians, Christ's circumcision figuratively de-fleshes the base bodies of his followers, transforming them into spiritually charged believers destined for eternal life: 'In him also you were circumcised with a spiritual circumcision, by putting off the body of the flesh in the circumcision of Christ . . . And when you were dead in trespasses and the uncircumcision of your flesh, God made you alive together with him'.[26]

The spiritualizing of circumcision was not only theologically fruitful, but socially strategic. In its early years, the Jesus movement was exhibiting the symptoms of an older cultural malaise suffered by its Jewish parent: circumcision had become a problem. Evidence from as early as the second century BCE indicates that some Jewish men within and beyond Judaea (Judah) were attempting to conceal or reverse their circumcisions. Traces of this practice are evident in I Maccabees (late second century BCE), in which a group of Jewish elites is roundly condemned for building a Greek gymnasium in Jerusalem and 'removing the marks of circumcision' before exercising in the nude. It was an event similarly condemned by the historian Josephus – a Jewish Roman – who claims that the men of Jerusalem's gymnasium 'concealed the circumcision of their private parts in order to be Greeks even when unclothed'.[27] But Greek-style sporting etiquette was not the only motivation for the practice. It might also be triggered by religious 'conversion'. Just as Gentile men across the Mediterranean were often circumcised when they joined diasporic Jewish communities, so those abandoning their traditional Jewish practices for Graeco-Roman gods or Christian worship might seek 'uncircumcision'. This is powerfully presented in the New Testament writings of Paul, in which he advises Jewish followers of Christ against 'epispasm' – the physical reversal of circumcision: 'Was anyone at the time of his call circumcised? Let him not seek to remove the marks of circumcision. Was anyone at the time of his call foreskinned? Let him not seek circumcision.'[28]

As a circumcised Jewish convert to Christ, Paul himself may well have found the prospect of secondary genital modification unappealing. Although he gives no indication of precisely how Jewish men were reversing their circumcisions, other ancient sources suggest it could be achieved in two ways. The easiest method was a temporary (and faintly implausible) fix: circumcision might be camouflaged by donning a sheath. But for those requiring a longer-lasting solution, the process was more complex – and uncomfortable. Weights were attached to the skin at the neck of the penis shaft, piercing any residual remnants of the foreskin, so that it was stretched over the glans to cover as much of the head of the penis as possible. It is described in early rabbinic traditions as *meshikhat orlah* ('drawing down the foreskin'), and appears to have been sufficiently notorious that it rarely required further explanation. But it concerned Jewish leaders enough to institute a lasting change in traditional circumcision. By the mid second century CE, rabbis were instructing circumcisers in their communities not only to cut back the bulk of the foreskin, but to split and peel away the underlying mucous membrane, which fully exposed the corona and prevented the stretching of vestigial skin over the glans. Known as *periah* ('revealing'), it remains the standard method of traditional Jewish circumcision.[29]

The physical removal or reversal of male circumcision had more to do with wider Graeco-Roman constructs of idealized masculinity than intra-Jewish religious resistance; for the Greek intelligentsia and their Roman beneficiaries, the perfect male body was the muscular nude form of the athlete – a corporeal manifestation of disciplined masculine beauty teasingly caricatured in Aristophanes' *Clouds* as 'a rippling chest, radiant skin, broad shoulders, a wee tongue, a grand rump and a petite dick'. Crucially, the penis was to be generously foreskinned, and the testicles present and intact.[30] While circumcised men and various types of eunuchs were well known in the Greek and Roman worlds, their modified genitals often signalled an 'exotic' or discomforting cultural otherness – no matter how 'Greek' or 'Roman' they were in any other way. Within this context, both male circumcision and castration tended to be perceived as a barbaric 'mutilation', potentially generating trans-gressive or uncontrolled sexual appetites. The two forms of genital modification were only marginally distinguished in the second century CE, when forced castration was increasingly outlawed, and the lucrative trade in congenital and voluntary eunuchs was subjected to tighter regulation in the Roman Empire.[31]

Against this backdrop, male circumcision was an inflammatory issue in some Christian communities, as New Testament texts sug-gest. This literature was written and shared by Greek-speaking Christians thoroughly immersed in their own Graeco-Roman cultures – many of whom were growing increasingly hostile to the Jewish origins of their faith. Eventually, most forms of Christianity would abandon circumcision altogether – a position encouraged by Paul's letter to the Galatians, in which he claims that Christians are rendered the offspring of Abraham not by means of the body, but by their faith in Christ: 'There is neither Jew nor Greek, there is neither slave nor free, there is neither male nor female; for all of you are one in Christ Jesus. And if you belong to Christ, then you are Abraham's seed, heirs according to the [covenant] promise.'[32]

Some Christians today often interpret his words as a more 'democ-ratized' (and even superior) understanding of the traditional Jewish idea of covenant – a theological liberation from what they perceive to be the restrictive gender politics and ethnocentrism of Judaism. But this is mistaken. Paul was not rejecting circumcision, nor the validity of the Torah in which it was so keenly promoted; nor was he calling for the emancipation of slaves, nor indeed for the elevation of women to a status equal to men (foreskinned or not). Rather, Paul was assert-ing that even the starkest of social distinctions were eclipsed by believers' shared identity 'in Christ Jesus'. For this reason, he repeatedly argued, there was no need for people to seek a change in their social or cultural positioning – hence his insistence that within a Christian community in which cultural descent of members varied, Gentile genitals should not be cut, while Jewish genitals could continue to be. 'Let each of you lead the life that the Lord has assigned, to which God called you', he wrote. 'This is my rule in all the churches'.[33] Ultimately, neither circumcision nor non-circumcision mattered to Paul, for penises were about to become redundant. With the imminent coming of the Kingdom of God, there would be no need for mortal bodies and no need for sex. Instead, Christians would be returned to the celibate, celestial state in which – they had come to believe – humans were originally created.[34]

But Christian theology has never been wholly successful at reconciling its heavenly aspirations with the material, bodily realities of human existence. Paul's lofty theology not only failed to quell early Christian disputes about the religious significance of circumcised penises, but it also did little to diminish a growing appetite for any fleshy fragments Christ might have left behind before his ascension to heaven. By the fourth century CE, believers had grown increasingly interested in Jesus' own circumcision – and the fate of his foreskin. In a world in which the mortal remains of holy men and heroes were already venerated in Jewish and Graeco-Roman cultures, the purported material fragments of Jesus' earthly life – from the splinters of his cross to his bloodied death shroud – were naturally believed to hold magical powers. A trade in holy relics spread across Christendom, encouraged by legends assuring believers that bits of Christ's body remained in the world.

Proof of the continued existence of Jesus' foreskin was firmly attested in the so-called Arabic Infancy Gospel (c. fifth century CE), an influential text drawing on colourful traditions circulating about Christ's early life. It includes the story of a midwife present at the birth and circumcision of Jesus, who sagaciously stores his severed foreskin in an alabaster container of precious oil and gives it to her pharmacist son – a purveyor of powerful potions and lotions. Although she instructs him not to sell it, it is procured by the 'sinful' woman who anoints Jesus' feet when he is an adult: a canny detail reassuring concerned Christians that the oil touching Jesus' body had already been sanctified by the presence of his holy foreskin within it.[35] The text neglects to tell its readers what subsequently became of Christ's foreskin – but no matter, for it began to pop up with astonishing frequency across the Christian world. East and West, increasing numbers of churches, bishops, mystics and pilgrims all claimed to be in possession of what would come to be known as the Holy Prepuce.

By the thirteenth century, the most famous of Christ's foreskins was believed to be lodged in Rome. It was claimed that a heavenly hand had presented it to Charlemagne (*c*. 742–814 CE) as he prayed in Jerusalem's Holy Sepulchre while on pilgrimage. He had taken it to Western Europe, enshrining it first in his imperial chapel at Aix-la-Chapelle (now Aachen, in Germany), and then at Charroux, in France, before gifting it to Pope Leo III in return for his coronation as the first Holy Roman Emperor, on Christmas Day 800 CE. Leo is said to have kept it in a sacred chest of cypress wood along with other earthly remains of Christ's body – including his umbilical cord and death blood.[36] When Rome was sacked in 1527, during the wars of Pope Clement VII and the Holy Roman Emperor Charles V, the Holy Prepuce disappeared – although this did not prevent its continued appearance in countless churches throughout Christendom. It was last seen in 1983, in the small Italian town of Calcata, where it had apparently been venerated for centuries. And yet, shortly before its ritual exhibition at its annual festival, it again disappeared. The local priest claimed sacrilegious thieves had ransacked his home, stealing the shoebox at the back of his wardrobe in which the holy relic resided for safekeeping. But many believed it was snatched by dark forces within the Vatican.[37]

For centuries, paying pilgrims had flocked to see the Holy Prepuce at sacred sites across medieval Europe, seemingly unconcerned by its mysterious ability to be installed in several places at the same time. After all, said some, it was further proof of the miraculous ability of Jesus' body to regenerate and multiply without diminishing in power – a phenomenon attested by the repeated consumption of Christ's flesh and blood in the Eucharist. Others, however, had long suspected it was evidence of a racket in relics. To counter forgers and sceptics – and no doubt boost church coffers – the authenticity of a Holy Prepuce might be certified by reputable Christian mystics, whose visionary encounters with the divine enabled them to furnish cathedrals and churches with curatorial notes on their relics. But validation might also be sought by means of the taste test: a physician would be appointed by local clergy to nibble a piece of the latest relic to confirm whether it was vegetal matter, animal leather, or human foreskin.[38] Its sanctity might also be confirmed by its flavour. Sacred relics were believed to give off a sweet scent; they surely tasted sweet, too. This was indeed the experience of the thirteenth-century Beguine mystic Agnes Blannbekin, who claimed Christ's foreskin tasted gloriously sweet. Agnes was regularly swallowing the Holy Prepuce, which miraculously manifested itself on her tongue when she received Communion on the annual Feast of the Circumcision. She reported its consistency was 'alike the skin in an egg', and that, when she felt compelled to put her finger in her mouth to touch it, 'that little skin went down her throat on its own', filling her limbs with a sweetness so great it appears to have triggered an orgasmic out-of-body experience.[39]

Intimate encounters with the Holy Prepuce often took on an erotic, fetishistic allure. In the fourteenth century, Christ's foreskin wrapped itself around the finger of Catherine of Siena – an unenclosed nun and mystic, who believed she had been wedded to Christ in a vision. This in itself was not altogether unusual. Catherine shared with many other celibate devotees an understanding that her intensely intimate relationship with Christ was a sacred marriage. But for Catherine, that marriage was marked by the Holy Prepuce she saw encircling her finger like a wedding band. 'You espouse our souls to you with the ring of your flesh', she declared in a passionate prayer to her divine husband.[40] Catherine was a great letter-writer, and repeatedly reminded other brides of Christ in her correspondence that 'we do not marry Christ with rings of gold or silver but with the ring of Christ's foreskin, given in the circumcision and accompanied by pain and the shedding of blood'.[41] For both Agnes Blannbekin and Catherine of Siena, as for other Christian thinkers, the bloodied foreskin was not only a treasured earthly remnant of the divine body, but a material manifestation of the transformative, salvific death of Christ: cast as the first painful wound inflicted on his innocent body, Jesus' circumcision anticipated the piercing of his hands and feet, and the lancing of his side, as he died in agony upon the cross. But the mystical, erotic experiences of these pious women also reflect a deep and devout desire to encounter the corporeal realities of Christ upon and within their own bodies. Like those priests and pilgrims who venerated the Holy Prepuce, Agnes and Catherine sought to enflesh the religious realities of their convictions in ways the more doctrinal, immaterial abstractions of Christian theology and its transcendent, otherworldly God could not.

It was not only relics that helped to perpetuate the vernacular engagement with Christ's fleshy genitals in the West. The circumcision of the infant Jesus became a stock feature of art across medieval and Renaissance Europe. But the visual portrayal of the cleansing cut of his Jewish past was heavily influenced by its common reinterpretation as a precursor to his Passion. Blended with the virulent antisemitism of the West, artistic representations of Christ's circumcision often portrayed a chubby white baby Jesus as the self-sacrificing victim of the bloodthirsty, hooked-nosed Jewish circumcisers surrounding him. Frequently garbed in the imagined vestments of the ancient Jewish priesthood, or topped with the distinctive peaked hat that had become a conventional, malevolent marker of 'Jewishness' in European art, these men are regularly depicted crowding around the child, leering at the large blade menacingly positioned at his tiny genitals.[42] In some works, the ugly caricaturing of Jewish ritual was further embellished by the deliberate mis-gendering of the circumciser as a hideous, villainous woman. In the masculinist world of medieval and Renaissance Christianity, circumcision was still closely associated with castration. The Jewish 'mutilation' of the genitals was therefore cast as a feminizing, sexually abusive wound, fating little boys to an unmanned adulthood.[43] One example among many powerfully illustrates this: a depiction of Jesus' circumcision in Guillaume de Digulleville's widely read trilogy, *The Pilgrimage of Human Life, the Pilgrimage of the Soul and the Pilgrimage of Jesus Christ* (c. 1400), shows a startled infant Jesus raising his arm in an attempt to fend off the snarling woman looming over his genitals. Two other Jewish women huddle behind her, craning their necks to see the cut. By contrast, Jesus' parents stand at a distance behind him, Mary's hands raised in fretful, pleading protest (fig. 18).

Mary's maternal concern for Jesus' penis was even more familiar in the wildly popular representations of the Madonna and child, in which the naked infant was depicted sitting in her lap, her hand or fingers modestly covering his genitals. But in several Renaissance examples of this scene, Mary's hand does not veil his penis. Instead, she gestures towards it, holds it between her fingers, or gently fondles

Fig. 18. Antisemitic motifs abound in this portrayal of Christ's circumcision, featured in an illustrated version of Guillaume de Digulleville's *Pilgrimage* trilogy (*c*. 1400 CE). In particular, the ritual is presented as a cruel and barbaric custom as the circumciser – deliberately misrepresented as a woman – takes a huge pair of shears to the infant's tiny genitals.

it in ways indicative of its very deliberate public exhibition. In some instances, the child's penis appears to serve as an object of veneration to other figures in the composition, who gaze upon it in pious, wondrous adoration.[44] The Madonna's emphatic exhibition of Jesus' genitals not only serves to underscore his fleshy humanity, but foregrounds the mediatory role of the divine penis in Christ's relationship with the world.

Mary's assertive exposure of her son's penis is often met with his responsive approval in paintings employing what art historian Leo Steinberg affectionately calls the 'chin-chuck': as the Madonna presents Jesus' genitals, the Christ child reaches out his little arm and touches his mother's chin. It is a much older artistic motif of erotic endorsement, adapted in medieval Christian art to communicate the complex theological intimacy of Christ and the Virgin: she is not only his mother, but his chosen heavenly consort. The celibacy of their union tempers the genital sexualization of Christ in these images.[45] But this is disrupted in certain Renaissance portrayals of the pietà – another stock scene in Western Christian iconography, mirroring with forceful intent the intimacy of the Madonna and child. In these images, Christ is again held in the Virgin's lap, but this time he is the sexually mature man who has been killed and brought down from the cross. In anguish, his mother cradles his naked, broken body, his groin strategically covered by his dead hand or draped with fabric. But in some versions of the pietà, Christ's penis is startlingly erect beneath his loincloth. A vivid example is an early-sixteenth-century painting attributed to the Flemish artist Willem Key. A bearded, muscular Christ lies dead across his mother's lap, his hand pierced with the gaping wound of a nail. A heavily veiled Mary lifts his head to her own as she bends to kiss his lips. Christ's pelvic and thigh muscles are sharply defined, drawing the gaze to his loincloth, which barely covers his groin. Beneath it, his penis swells into an erection, lifting the folds of the fabric. Christ might be dead, but his penis promises his restoration to life (Plate 8).

It is an intense image of a powerfully sexualized masculine virility, similarly conveyed in contemporaneous portrayals of the Man of Sorrows – the name given to a common devotional image focusing on the bloodied physicality of Christ's suffering, torture and death. One of the most astonishing is a Ludwig Krug engraving (c. 1510–32), in which Christ sits between his mother and the disciple John, looking straight at the viewer. On his head is a thick crown of thorns; the spear slash in his side is clearly visible. He shows the viewer the nail wounds in his hands, which are bound together with rope. A wide loincloth is wrapped around his waist, but it rises up from his groin to wind tightly around Christ's extraordinarily large, thick erection. In this engraving, the physical realities of Christ's death are vividly countered by his active, living corpse: he sits up and raises his hands; his open eyes reveal an all-seeing gaze; and his penis is powerfully erected into life. It is a profoundly theological image (Plate 9).

Single and celibate. Asexual and childfree. In the text-centric modern West, we have become so accustomed to the neutered Christ of the New Testament that it is difficult to comprehend or even perceive the veneration of the sexualized virility of this divine man within those societies preceding our own. But across the visual cultures of late antique, medieval and Renaissance Europe, close attention to Christ's genitals in legends, relics, icons and artwork served not only to highlight his maleness and his humanity, but his death-defying divine virility. Whether newly circumcised, prepubescent, or maturely erect, the divine penis of the post-biblical Christ inherited the sexualized, life-giving agency of the phallic body of the God of the Bible – with one important exception. In the religious imagination, Christ tended to remain tantalizingly chaste and sexually innocent. The God of the Bible did not.

8

DIVINE SEX

In a modern, airy building in Jerusalem, there is an astonishing woman. She has long, thick hair, sweeping down over her shoulders to fall between her breasts. There, twin babies are carefully positioned, their tiny faces turned towards her nipples. She meets the eyes of anyone who looks at her, her face tenderly expressive, her eyebrows slightly raised. Her arms are long and slender, the colour of warm sand. She extends them down the length of her torso, her wrists dressed with bangles, her hands coming together to meet between her legs. Large, leafy tattoos cover her thighs, stencilling her skin with ibexes nibbling budding trees. She holds open her labia, revealing the dark, long opening of her vagina. Her gaze remains steady. She is the wife of God.

This beautiful clay figurine was found in the excavated remains of a Late Bronze Age site in the Shephelah region of what is now modern Israel (Plate 10). Dated to the thirteenth century BCE, she is a manifestation of the high goddess venerated across the southern Levant, an image inexpensively crafted for her worshippers to use in their rituals at home. She was a divine revealer of the secrets of new life, whose open labia manifested a powerful liminality: the inside-and-outside, entrance-and-exit place at which sexual potency, fecundity and birth were located. But in Jerusalem's Israel Museum, her open labia signal that she is little more than a commodified sex object: 'This figurine may represent Asherah, the sacred prostitute', reads the notice positioned next to her in the display case. It is a shocking and misleading caricature, grounded in a centuries-old, biblically derived hostility towards the goddess once venerated as the traditional consort of Yahweh, the God of the Bible.

This hostility seeps through the pages of the Hebrew Bible. In its story of the religious past, the worship of the goddess called Asherah is well known: her statues and symbols are frequently said to stand in temples and sanctuaries across the Iron Age kingdoms of Israel and Judah. But her cult is presented as an abhorrent manifestation of the 'foreign' polytheism polluting the land given by Yahweh to Abraham and his descendants. It is a religious deviancy repeatedly likened to sexual malpractice, so that those 'idolatrous' Israelites and Judahites who stray after other deities are accused of 'whoring' after them, 'sprawling' beneath them, 'getting hot' and acting as an 'adulteress' in betraying their exclusive commitment to God.[1] Metaphorically but authoritatively coupled in the Bible with female prostitution and promiscuity, the veneration of Asherah was consequently imagined by older generations of scandalized historians to have been little more than a titillating sex-cult, in which the goddess functioned as a divine patron of open-air orgies and sacred prostitution – for which there is no compelling evidence.[2] But the sexualized language of the biblical slur against Asherah was adopted unquestioningly as historical fact – giving rise to the distorted assumptions regurgitated alongside the goddess figurine in the Israel Museum today.

More recently, however, Asherah has been rehabilitated, and scholars are now widely agreed that she functioned traditionally as Yahweh's consort. As a number of biblical writers inadvertently confess, his temple in Jerusalem housed Asherah's cult statue; her cult object – a stylized sacred tree – was planted or positioned next to his altars; and kings and queens of Israel and Judah sponsored her worship in their royal sanctuaries.[3] These admissions on the part of the biblical writers are striking. They demonstrate that even their own account of the religious past – as distorted with bias as it is – could not completely ignore so important a goddess.

Asherah's pre-biblical career is best known from Late Bronze Age Ugarit (1550–1200 BCE), where she was known as Athirat. Here, she was the powerful wife of El and the mother of a major group of deities

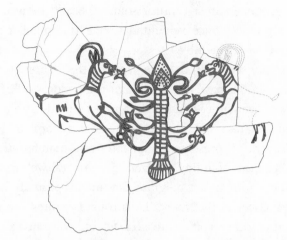

Fig. 19. The sacred tree was a common visual motif across the Levant, and closely associated with goddesses – including Asherah. Dated to the eighth century BCE, this example appears with other religious symbols and inscriptions inked onto large storage jars discovered at Kuntillet 'Ajrud in northern Sinai. Caprids flank the tree, nibbling at its lotus flowers.

Fig. 20. An ivory relief of a high-status goddess, excavated from a thirteenth-century BCE grave in Minet el-Beida, the harbour serving the city of Ugarit. Although her identity is uncertain, she is usually assumed to be Athirat. Enthroned on a mountaintop, the goddess is flanked by caprids, who eat from the fronds in her hands.

known as the 'Seventy Sons', indicating that her partnership with El was extremely fecund. But her role was more than maternal. As El's partner, she was a powerful intercessor, mediating debates and disputes between the gods and petitioning her husband on their behalf. And yet she was more than the First Lady of domestic politics. She was also known as the 'Lady of the Sea' and the 'Lady who tramples the Sea Serpent' – titles suggesting she once played a role in the ordering of the cosmos by commanding or subduing the watery monster with whom so many other deities would later contend. Her influential role in the human politics of Ugarit was also celebrated in her function as a divine wet nurse to Ugarit's kings, who relied on her to nurture and endorse their dynasties. As an ancient goddess of the highest calibre, her presence in the mythological story worlds of her worshippers underscored the authoritative status of the male deity with whom she was partnered. As Athirat of Late Bronze Age Ugarit, this was El. And as Asherah in the Iron Age kingdoms of Israel and Judah, this was Yahweh.

While Asherah's relationship with Yahweh is usually presented as an abomination in the Bible, a collection of ancient Hebrew inscriptions, sensationally unearthed in the 1960s and 1970s, confirms her role as his consort. Dated to the eighth century BCE, these inscriptions present Yahweh and Asherah as a divine power-couple petitioned for protective blessings by their worshippers. One inscription was found above the entrance to a high-status, rock-cut tomb at Khirbet el-Qom in the West Bank. It confers a blessing from 'Yahweh and his Asherah' upon the dead occupant of the tomb, a wealthy man named Uriyahu, who requires divine protection against those who might ransack his grave and disturb his peaceful existence in the underworld. At the same time, other Hebrew-speakers were scribbling appeals to Yahweh and Asherah on votive pottery at a desert waystation at Kuntillet 'Ajrud, a stopover site on a network of ancient trade routes crossing the Sinai. These inscriptions are among a number of petitions scrawled by travellers to secure the blessings of various regional deities for their family and friends at home. Their messages are addressed to gods residing in particular temple locations, including 'Yahweh of Samaria and his Asherah' and 'Yahweh of Teman and his Asherah'. These appeals to distinctive, localized manifestations of the divine couple indicate that the pairing of Yahweh and the goddess was common in sanctuaries across the area. Taken together with the Khirbet el-Qom tomb inscription, these appeals suggest that most Yahweh worshippers did not share the biblical writers' derogatory view of Asherah. Rather, they considered her to be the traditional partner of their high god Yahweh, and they worshipped her as a protective, life-giving goddess, able to mediate divine blessings to Yahweh's people.[4]

But the protective force of Yahweh and Asherah was unable to withstand the onslaught of imperial invasions in their homelands. And it was Asherah who paid the price. Her state cults waned in the aftermath of the Assyrian assault on the kingdom of Israel's capital, Samaria, in 722 BCE, and the later Babylonian destruction of Judah's Jerusalem temple in 587 BCE. Although there is some evidence to suggest that Asherah worship continued in some forms at these and other sites, the imperial destruction of these tiny kingdoms, and the devastating desecration of their temples, irrevocably damaged traditional religion and the local networks – political, economic and social – on which it relied. Asherah would never recover her prestigious position as a state deity and the consort of God. In the late sixth or early fifth century BCE, when Persia was the dominant imperial force throughout the Levant, an elite group descended from Judah's exiles living in Mesopotamia was granted permission to return to Jerusalem and rebuild Yahweh's temple. But in remaking their temple, they also remade their religion. The traditional polytheism of the past was remodelled in the image of what is sometimes described as an 'emergent monotheism', but is more accurately understood as a radical form of pantheon reduction: Yahweh lost his wife, while other members of his divine council were downgraded from deities to minor divine beings, heavenly messengers, or cosmic abstractions. Cultural memories of the wife of God were twisted into the theological distortions now evident in the biblical texts in which she appears. Asherah was recast as a toxic idol and – alongside other members of the former pantheon – blamed for the disasters of earlier generations: she was held responsible for seducing Yahweh's followers away from him, prompting him to punish them with military destruction and territorial displacement.

But a glimpse of the true nature of the divine couple's relationship can be found in an ancient poem in Genesis. It recycles an even older incantation into a ritual song conveying Yahweh's blessings upon the legendary ancestor Joseph. The incantation invokes a series of deities to bestow sexual masculinity and fruitfulness upon Joseph's penis, euphemistically described as his 'taut bow' and 'strong hand'. Included in the divine roll-call is a goddess bearing the title 'Breasts-and-Womb' – a likely epithet of Asherah, given it is used of Athirat, her older incarnation at Ugarit. She is paired in the poem with a deity called 'Father' and 'Most High' – ritual titles of the God of the Bible, inherited from Athirat's husband, El:

> From the God of your ancestor, who supports you,
> from Shadday who blesses you:
> the blessings of Heaven above,
> the blessings of Deep crouching below;
> the blessings of Breasts-and-Womb,
> the blessings of your Father, warrior Most High;
> the blessings of the Everlasting Mountains,
> [the blessings] of the outlying Eternal Hills.[5]

The coupling of 'Father, warrior Most High' and 'Breasts-and-Womb' points to the sexualized collaboration of these deities, paralleling the pairing of 'Heaven' and 'Deep' – the divinized, primeval parts of the universe, whose union birthed and built the very cosmos.[6] The poem hints at an ancient pantheon, in which the coupling of the high god and high goddess is set within the frame of an ordered, fertile creation.

Crucially, the sexualized structuring of the cosmos was as social as it was architectural. In the religious worldviews of ancient southwest Asian cultures, sex was not only procreative and pleasurable, but socially civilizing, binding both the universe and its inhabitants – whether divine or human – into the intense relationships by which life flourished. While a handful of these relationships in the divine realm were celibate or virginal, most were cast as the sexualized pairing of a husband and wife, father and mother, or brother and sister. Sometimes, however, a deity might take a human as a sexual partner.

The God of the Bible was well acquainted with divine–human sex – but at first blush, it appears to be an activity of which he firmly disapproves, as a fleeting myth in Genesis suggests. In this book's story of beginnings, the creation of humanity is swiftly followed by a series of human transgressions: eating banned fruit; the first murder; and then – worst of all – sex with gods. As humans obediently begin to fill the earth with their offspring, a group of junior deities known as the Sons of God (the members of Yahweh's divine council) find the daughters of mortal men so alluring that they 'take' these girls for themselves and have sex with them. The girls give birth to the Nephilim – a mythical warrior race of divine–human hybrids, cast elsewhere in the Bible as fearsome giants.[7] In this fifth-century BCE text, the fault appears to lie not only with the predatory Sons of God, but with mortal men's daughters, too, whose sexual appeal is demonstrably dangerous. God is so appalled at what he describes as human 'wickedness' that he regrets having created a now dangerously warped humanity. He decides to punish them by curbing mortal lifespans to a mere 120 years, but then quickly intensifies the penalty by resolving to kill off humans altogether. He sends the Flood.

This is likely a stripped-back version of a much fuller myth describing the corruption of the earliest humans. It is found in its longer form in a composition called the Book of Watchers, an early version of which is included in a text known as 1 Enoch (c. fourth century BCE). Here, the Sons of God are the Watchers – a group of 200 divine beings who function as God's emissaries (or 'angels'). Unable to resist the charms of mortal women, the Watchers descend from the heavens to have sex with them, but defile their holiness in the process by engaging in what is essentially depicted as cross-species sex. For the women, however, sex with these divine beings is not defiling, but enlightening: the Watchers teach them the divine secrets of magic, medicine and metallurgy, so that they can not only better harness the powers of the cosmos, but render themselves even more beautiful by making and wearing magical jewellery. Meanwhile, the giant Nephilim born to the women go on the rampage; having gobbled up the earth's supply of food, they begin to devour humans. It is only when God's senior emissaries (the archangels Michael, Sariel, Raphael and Gabriel) hear the cries of despair from mortal men that they ask God to intervene and rid the world of all its dangerously corrupted life forms – hence the Flood.

It is a story that would remain popular – and alarming – within ancient Jewish and early Christian circles. Indeed, by the middle of the first century CE, Paul was alluding to it when he insisted that women should keep their heads veiled or covered during prayer and prophecy 'on account of the angels', to prevent them from attracting the attention of the divine beings watching over worship.[8] And by the beginning of the second century, the story had become a repeated motif in Christian teaching, warning human sinners of God's punishing ways, much as the New Testament letters of 2 Peter and Jude suggest.[9] But God's destructive response to sex between deities and humans in Genesis and 1 Enoch is striking in view of other tales in which he engages in sex with human or human-like women himself. Clearly, the primary concern for the God of the Bible is not so much an anxiety about divine sex, nor the sexual transgression of the boundary between the human and divine worlds, but the defence of God's own and exclusive prerogative to have sex.

God's first sexual encounter occurs long before the birth of the Nephilim. In the Garden of Eden, food from the sacred tree might have been off the menu, but sating sexual appetites was divinely ordained. God's pairing of Adam and Eve seemingly comes to fruition when Eve bears Cain – the first human child. But her emphatic declaration at the birth of her son credits God, not Adam, with paternity: 'I have procreated a man with Yahweh!'[10] This more literal translation of the Hebrew is rarely seen. Most renderings of this verse default to a theologically fudged interpretation, so that Eve is merely presented as claiming that Yahweh has 'helped' her to 'acquire a man', as any good fertility god might. But the very language of this Hebrew text signals a bodily dynamic well beyond this, for the woman's words are pointedly precise: she is claiming that Yahweh has fathered her first child.

There is nothing virginal about this birth. Eve's boast is indicative of a female sexual agency wholly unlike the sanitized passivity of her later biblical antitype, the 'Virgin' Mary. Her words reveal she is God's collaborative partner in the creation of new human life. But this pro-active role also points to a long-lost mythic backstory to Eve's character. Although in her biblical form she is a human woman, her choice of vocabulary is the language of goddesses: in asserting that she has 'procreated' a man, she uses a specialized, technical term for divine reproduction also used of goddesses in the myths from Ugarit.[11] Indeed, like the Ugaritic goddess Athirat, Eve is called 'Mother of all Living', and even her name (*hawwah* in Hebrew) likely means 'life giver' or 'living one', evoking an epithet of Athirat in her glorious title 'the Lady, the Living One, the Goddess'.[12] These features of Eve's characterization in Genesis suggest that, before her biblical career, she was more akin to a life-bearing goddess appropriately located in the heavenly Garden of Eden – and hence a most suitable sexual partner for a male deity.

In the Bible, however, God's most significant and sexualized relationship is not with a goddess or a goddess-like figure, but with his other wife, Israel. The personification of a city, territory, nation or social group as a woman is well attested in (often masculinist, patriarchal) cultures across the globe, but in the biblical texts, the female personification of Israel plays a sustained and crucial role in articulating the intense and exclusive relationship between God and his worshippers. It is a relationship so intimate that his love for them is frequently expressed in the language of sexual desire. And yet, in some books of the Hebrew Bible, the erotic tone of this imagery not only moves from the emotional to the physical, but takes on a much darker hue, casting God as a powerful sexual predator, and Israel as a coquettish young girl. The book of Hosea offers a vivid example. Here, Israel is a capricious teenager whose sexual allure so intoxicates God, he falls to scheming obsessively and possessively to make her his wife. 'I will now seduce her', he says of Israel; 'I will take her walking into the wilderness and speak to her heart . . . and there she will cry out'.[13] These words betray more than the romantic fantasy of a love-struck deity. God's language here marks a shift from passion to threat: in claiming he will 'seduce' her, he uses a Hebrew expression more usually employed in the Bible to describe the rape of captive women. And in describing Israel's vocal response, he uses a term that can convey both the noise of sexual gratification and religious joy. God's dangerous sense of sexual entitlement skews his planned attack on the girl into the distorted conviction that she will enjoy her rape – and scream in orgasmic ecstasy.[14]

This image of sexual violation is unsettling enough. But nowhere in the Bible is the portrayal of God's sex life more disturbing than in two stories in the book of Ezekiel. Like other biblical narrators, Ezekiel reasons that the military defeat and imperial subjugation that befell Yahweh's people in the sixth century BCE was a divine punishment for worshipping other gods. Here, too, Israel is cast as God's wife, but her whoring after foreign deities provokes her husband's fury and punishment. According to Ezekiel, her wanton behaviour in marriage is the culmination of a long history of social and sexual deviancy.

Their relationship begins in the wilderness, where God finds an abandoned baby girl, her umbilical cord still attached, deliberately cast away from the rest of humanity: 'You were abhorred on the day of your birth', scorns God, as he reminds her that she had been neither washed of birth blood, nor rubbed with a protective salt scrub and swaddled.[15] And yet God acknowledges her, commanding her to live and grow. Only when she has obediently matured to puberty does he notice her again. Reminiscing lasciviously about this subsequent encounter, God comments: '. . . your breasts were formed, your [pubic] hair had grown; you were naked and bare! I passed by you and looked at you: you were at the age for lovemaking. I spread the corner of my cloak over you, and covered your nakedness; I pledged myself to you and entered into a covenant with you . . . You became mine.'[16]

The voyeuristic tone to his words is not lost in this English translation, which barely manages to soften the graphic sexual nature of his actions: God's gaze is upon the girl's exposed sexual organs, moving him to cover her genitals ('nakedness') with his own – his spreading cloak politely functioning here as an image of his mounting her, much as in the book of Ruth, in which the eponymous heroine urges a sleepy Boaz to have sex with her by spreading the corner of his cloak over her.[17] The sexual euphemisms continue, for it is by penetrating the girl's body that God 'enters into' a binding covenant with her – an unequal power relationship in which the forging of the deity's exclusive and proprietary claim to Israel is presented as the sexual consummation of a man's possession of a bride: 'you became mine'.[18]

Jewish and Christian interpreters have tended to soften and sanitize this encounter – either by reductive means, so that the episode is 'merely' a metaphor or allegory depicting intense religious intimacy, or by fantasizing that romantic notions of a committed, heteronormative love find their archetype in God, so that he is the paradigmatic devoted husband. But this is wishful thinking – and it will not do. Ezekiel's story is reflective of a patriarchal, masculinist culture, in which girls and women tended to be valued and defined in terms of their bodily configurations with men: as daughters, sisters, wives, mothers, or sex-workers. The biblical God cannot and should not be let off the hook. Here, he is a predatory alpha male, whose sexual entitlement entirely shapes the identity and fate of this displaced and vulnerable young girl.

Indeed, it is only after sex that God formally rehabilitates his young bride by means of actions reminiscent of the rituals denied her at birth: he bathes her, washing away the dried blood of birth and the wet blood of puberty, and then rubs her not with salt, but with sacred oil. Her objectification continues as he dresses her in rich fabrics and puts soft leather sandals on her feet; he decorates her with earrings, a nose ring, bangles, a necklace and crown, so that she looks like a statue of a goddess in a temple. He gives her the ritual foods commonly offered to deities – choice flour, honey and fragrant oil – and transfers her from the wilderness to civilization, where she is rapturously celebrated for the beauty God has bestowed upon her. And here she is fixed: an unspeaking, passive ornament of her husband's hegemonic, sexualized masculinity.

For God, this is a fruitful relationship: the girl gives birth to his sons and daughters – God's own worshippers.[19] But it also results in extreme sexual violence. In a battery of fierce denunciations, the deity accuses his wife of adultery and prostitution with his rivals, the gods and kings of other nations: 'Adulterous wife, who takes strangers instead of her husband!' he spits. According to God, her sexual deviancy is so depraved that she pays her lovers for sex with the treasures received from her husband: 'Gifts are given to all whores, but you gave your gifts to all your lovers, bribing them to come to you from all around for your whorings!' He shames her further, accusing her of being in such a permanent state of impure arousal that her vagina constantly drips with wetness.[20] Her punishment is brutal: God gathers her lovers and strips her naked in front of them; her legs are wrenched apart, her genitalia exposed. It is an invitation to gang-rape her. A mob is summoned – to stone her, cut her, stab her and set her home alight. This scene of graphic, frenzied sexual violence is the theological money-shot, for the brutality wrought against his wife triggers in God a climactic gratification, by which his psychosexual anger suddenly appears spent: 'Thus I will satisfy my fury on you, and my jealousy shall turn away from you; I will be calm, and will be angry no longer'.[21] Once she has learned her lesson, he will take her back.

In a parallel narrative, a few chapters later, God again looks back on his alleged cuckolding with venomous fury. This time, Israel is personified as two sisters, Oholah and Oholibah, who represent the cities Samaria and Jerusalem. Their sexual crimes, God claims, begin even before he makes them his brides: in their youth, they seek out the Egyptians, cast as animalized foreigners with penises 'like those of donkeys' and gushing semen 'like that of stallions', who squeeze and fondle the young girls' breasts and ejaculate over them.[22] Even so, God marries them. But the sisters' sexual depravity only worsens – so much so, they seek out lovers who disgust them, and even sacrifice to those lovers the children they have borne their divine husband.[23]

God's violent response is again profoundly disturbing: he gathers his wives' lovers, who strip the sisters naked and abuse them. Oholah's children are seized, and she is put to death by the sword.[24] Her younger sister, Oholibah, endures a more prolonged suffering. God again summons her lovers, instructing them to disfigure his unfaithful wife by cutting off her nose and ears, to expose her genitalia and to burn her children.[25] God then gives his wife her dead sister's cup of 'desolation and horror', commanding her to drink until she is intoxicated with such sorrowful shame that the cup will shatter in her hands. In a startling image of self-harm wrought by abuse, God decrees she will use its jagged pieces to mutilate herself, gnawing on its sherds and hacking off her breasts.[26] Most damaging of all, perhaps, is the moral of the tale: the fate of God's wife is explicitly exhibited in this narrative as a warning to all women, lest they too dishonour their husbands.

These horrifying tales in the book of Ezekiel have proved deeply troubling for many readers – past and present, secular and religious. As endorsements, albeit ancient ones, of male sexual predation, exploitation and misogynistic violence, the value systems evoked in these narratives ostensibly conflict sharply with those of the modern West. They not only degrade and vilify female sexuality, but enshrine the sexual and domestic abuse of girls and women with ongoing biblical authority. Theologically, the sexual grooming and graphic violence God inflicts on his young wife is immensely difficult for some modern-day believers to reconcile with their idealized constructs of God. But for many Jewish and Christian readers, it is more specifically the graphic portrayal of a sexually active deity that has proved unbearable: it has been mistranslated, dismissed as 'mere' allegory, or simply ignored. Indeed, by the second century CE, the story of God having sex with his pubescent bride in Ezekiel was banned by the rabbis from public reading in the synagogue – a ruling attributed to Rabbi Eliezer (c. 100 CE), who was said to have interrupted a man reading aloud the opening words of the story ('Mortal, proclaim to Jerusalem her abominations') with the sarcastic rebuke, 'Why don't you go out and proclaim the abominations of your mother?'[27] For the ancient rabbis, there was no pretence that the lurid, explicit portrayal of divine–human sex was 'simply' symbolic. Ezekiel's story was simultaneously a metaphor and a mythological truth, revealing the torrid nature of the physical relationship between the mother of the people and their God. Better to censor it entirely than to repeat aloud its shocking truths. By contrast, almost all the early Church Fathers refused to recognize the sexualized, gendered bodies of God and Israel in these biblical narratives – even while relying on their corporeal imagery to teach Christians about the concrete, bodily realities of sin and salvation. Origen was staggered by the implication that Ezekiel presents a vision of the corporeality of God and his wife. 'It is said to me: "Don't allegorize, don't explain figuratively!"' he complained. 'Let them give an opinion on this, I ask: Jerusalem has breasts, and at one time they are not bound, and at another they are made firm, and she has an umbilical cord and is reproached because "it was not cut". How is it possible to understand these things without allegorical interpretation?'[28] Origen's approach to these difficult texts would dominate subsequent Christian readings for centuries. In spite of a confessional commitment to the incarnate reality of the divine body of Christ, Church theologians remained incredulous that God's body was ever in full sexualized view in the book of Ezekiel.

These older forms of resistance reading in Jewish and Christian circles continue today. In standard modern translations of the Tanakh and the Christian Bible, the graphic sexual imagery of these troubling texts is softened or obscured with sanitized vocabulary and clunky euphemisms, theologically veiling their portrayal of a sexually active God.[29] But for the ancient writers of biblical books, God was so familiarly corporeal, masculine and sexual, that these characteristics were easily harnessed to tell the story of his intense and turbulent relationship with his people, Israel – a people he expected to desire, love and obey him as a good wife should. In the eyes of the biblical writers, God's traditional wife, Asherah, might have been cast aside, but he himself retained his position as a divine husband, and wedded himself instead to his worshippers.

This is why early Christians could so easily conjure the image of Christ as their Heavenly Bridegroom. It was deeply embedded in their religious DNA. As early as the mid first century CE, Paul was telling Christians in Corinth that they were 'promised in marriage to one husband . . . as a chaste virgin to Christ'.[30] Similarly, in his letter to the Christian community in Rome, Paul cast the intimate relationship between Christ and his Church as the fertile, bodily union of a husband and wife, an image later extended in the book of Revelation and the epistle to the Ephesians to describe the Church as Christ's bride.[31] Both these texts draw on Ezekiel's portrayal of God dressing up his young wife like a goddess statue to describe the sexual allure of Christ's bride, but in Ephesians, the parallels are disturbingly pronounced. Here, Christ not only cleanses and beautifies his bride to render her more desirable and 'holy', but the stark power imbalance of divine–human marriage is used as a paradigm for mortal marriages: 'For the husband is the head of the wife just as Christ is the head of the Church . . . Just as the Church is submissive to Christ, so also wives are to be, in everything, to their husbands'.[32]

These and other early Christian texts would authoritatively endorse the self-portrayal of the Church as the bride of Christ for at least the next thousand years. This was a marriage supposedly ordained by Jesus himself, who in the New Testament Gospels refers to himself as the 'bridegroom' of his followers.[33] But in other ancient Christian texts, Mary Magdalene appears to play the bridal role of the Church itself. In both the Gospel of Mary (second century CE) and the Gospel of Philip (early third century CE), she is cast as the disciple Jesus loves the most; she is his 'beloved' and his 'consort', with whom he not only shares his most authoritative, esoteric teachings, but his physical affection in the form of kisses – much to the irritation of the other disciples.[34] While attempts to argue that Mary Magdalene was originally the wife of Jesus have repeatedly proved unpersuasive, scholars are broadly agreed that she was celebrated in nascent Christianity as a crucial player in the early Jesus movement. Not only was she perceived to have been a prominent member of Jesus' inner circle, but she was held by some to have been commissioned by the newly risen Christ to teach the other disciples about his divinity and his heavenly kingdom. Her elevated status in the Gospels of Mary and Philip reflects the continued potency of these early traditions in some eastern-empire communities, in which she was revered as a great leader of the Church.[35] But as the scholar April DeConick shows, growing anxieties about the religious authority of women, coupled with increasing conflicts between churches in the Roman East and West, led to her marginalization.[36] Eventually, in what would come to be more prominent theological traditions, she would be cast as a prostitute. Like Asherah and Eve before her, Mary Magdalene was overwhelmingly disempowered by her deliberate denigration as the embodiment of sexual deviancy.

The life-giving virility of Christ and his bodily commitment to his Church was vividly drawn on much older biblical models of divine marriage and the masculinized, corporeal sexuality of God.

Throughout the Bible, God engages in sexualized or eroticized relationships with a variety of female or feminized consorts. Some are
deliberately marginalized and vilified; others are cast in the subordinate
role of unruly or obedient bride. All were subjected to a series of
theological distortions later wrought by a misogynistic monotheism,
making space for the continued degrading of the sexualized female
body (whether human or divine) in the religious systems the Bible
would come to shape. But at the heart of God's relationships with
these consorts – even if at times deeply suppressed – was a complex
of ancient ideas in which cosmic creation mapped onto genital generation, divine corporeality mapped onto human physicality, religious
awe mapped onto erotic allure, and spiritual intensity mapped onto
sexual intimacy. On the body of the biblical God, the divine penis was
more than an accessory of patriarchal masculinity. It was the corporeal
manifestation of the divine thrust of all life – heavenly and earthly,
cultural and social – in the cosmos.

Part III

TORSO

9

BACK AND BEYOND

The climb from St Catherine's Monastery to the summit of Jebel Musa, the most sacred mountain in southern Sinai, takes about two and a half hours. At least, it does for those sensible enough to take the winding Camel Path to the top, rather than all 3,750 steps of the painfully steep, boulder-block stairway. Along the way, the tributes and trash of sacred tourism are a constant reminder that this is an ancient pilgrimage trail: ramshackle shrines; rocks daubed with Christian crosses, Arabic blessings and people's names; empty Coke cans and sweet wrappers. When the path joins the narrow stony stairway for the final sharp ascent, the chatter of pilgrims and tourists gives way to a quieter, if breathless, contemplation and a sense of awe that has rendered Jebel Musa a holy place. Known in Judaism and Christianity as Mount Sinai, it is here that Moses is said to have seen God's feet resting on his sky pavement. These are the rocks, tradition has it, from which were hewn the tablets of the Ten Commandments. Here is the very spot where Moses asked to see God's body in its most fulsome glory.

There is no sign of a divine body today. Instead, there are Bedouins of the local Jebeliya tribe, offering blankets to pilgrims and escorting them down to the wooden tea huts just below the summit. There is also a tiny mosque and a little chapel, each constructed of large red blocks of mountain rock. The mosque has stood since the twelfth century CE, but the chapel is surprisingly new. It was built in 1934, following the collapse of its sixteenth-century predecessor – a collapse allegedly caused by local treasure hunters digging for Moses' lost tablets of stone. But the walls of both the mosque and the chapel contain the recycled remnants of a much older building. There was already a bigger church here on the summit in the fourth century CE. And it is thanks to an extraordinary woman named Egeria that we know of its existence. In 381 CE, she left her home in north-west Iberia for a three-year pilgrimage around the holy sites of Egypt and the Levant. While she was away, she wrote regularly to her friends, detailing the places and people she had encountered. In doing so, Egeria created one of the earliest surviving Christian travelogues – a compilation which would be used by later generations of pious men to compile their own guidebooks to God. By December 383 CE, Egeria had begun a month-long expedition around the countless monasteries and churches that once peppered Sinai. Having lodged with one of the small monastic communities living in the southern mountain range, she made the journey up 'Sina' – the Holy Mountain of God. Her account of the experience feels as fresh as the day it was written:

> . . . the toil was great, for I had to go up on foot, the ascent being impossible in the saddle, and yet I did not feel the toil, on the side of the ascent, I say, the toil, because I realised that the desire which I had was being fulfilled at God's bidding. In that place there is now a church, not great in size, for the place itself, that is the summit of the mountain, is not very great; nevertheless, the church itself is great in grace . . . No one, however, dwells on the very summit of the central mountain; there is nothing there excepting only the church and the cave where holy Moses was.[1]

Today, the little red chapel atop Jebel Musa likely stands on the same spot as the church Egeria saw. But it is the cave 'where holy Moses was' that is the most ancient religious feature of the mountain peak: jutting up against the western wall of the chapel is an enormous boulder, split open by a long, low cleft, just big enough to crouch inside.[2] According to ancient tradition, this is the very place in which Moses waited to see God's body. But he didn't quite get what he bargained for.

The oldest version of the story is found in Exodus. It is a book combining ancient myths, old poems, later theologies and several literary sources – some perhaps as early as the eighth century BCE, others as late as the third century BCE. But its basic features have stabilized into an intimate, intense tale of a remarkable series of encounters with God. Having ascended Mount Sinai for one of his regular meetings with the deity, Moses attempts to negotiate an agreement with his god before continuing the arduous journey with the Israelites from Egypt to the Promised Land: 'How shall it be known that I have found favour in your sight, I and your people?' he asks. 'Please, show me your Glory.' It is a bold request to see the divine body that has been hidden by thick clouds during the Israelites' trek through the wilderness. Yahweh agrees – on condition that he will not reveal everything. 'I shall make all my splendour pass before your face . . . but you may not see my face, for no mortal may see me and live'. In its narrative context, it is a capricious assertion, for Yahweh and Moses have already enjoyed a number of conversations 'face to face' – and Moses has survived. But the deity is insistent and directs Moses towards a rock – long since identified as the giant cracked boulder atop Jebel Musa – from where he can view God's teasing appearance. 'While my Glory passes by', Yahweh explains, 'I will put you in a cleft of the rock, and I will cover you with my hand as I pass by; then I will take away my hand, and you shall see my back. But my face shall not be seen.'[3]

It is one of the more carefully choreographed exhibitions of God's anatomy in the Bible. Like a celebrity stretching out a hand to block the paparazzi, God only permits Moses to see him from behind as he moves away. In the story, this is supposed to be a sign of divine favour. And yet, culturally, the back of a god was more usually a devastating sight: it not only signalled divine displeasure, but also presaged definitive disaster in one swift, ritual gesture of power. 'I will show them my back, not my face, in the day of their calamity,' the biblical God frequently threatens – usually in response to his worshippers turning their own backs on him. 'They have turned their backs to me, and not their faces', he despairs, as he rails against his 'stiff-necked' and 'stiff-backed' people.[4] It is a body language common to many societies – including those of the modern West, in which a turn of the back can speak volumes. With our backs turned, we might render ourselves potentially vulnerable to the unseen and unknown, or forcefully dominant in the face of those at whom we choose not to look.

The cultural freight carried by the body language of the back was carefully managed in the religious traditions of ancient south-west Asia and Egypt. The gods were almost always portrayed as straight-backed and solidly upright, whether seated in splendour or standing in authority. Even the Egyptian sky goddess Nut, who bends her long, slender body on all fours over the earth, maintains an impressively straight back in ancient iconography. The solid back of a deity was not only a posture of steadfast and immovable power, but a manifestation of the bony sturdiness at the very core of the god, for running through the divine body was a backbone. Like a mortal body, the uprightness of the divine body was innately structured and maintained by its spine. But this rendered a god's back a crucial – if challenging – target in times of divine conflict or cosmic disaster. Ugarit's myths offer some vivid anatomical images: Baal's eventual triumph over the sea-god Yam is marked by the softening of Yam's skeleton and his collapse upon the ground: 'Yam goes groggy, falls to the ground; his joints go slack, his body slumps'.[5] And the goddesses Athirat and Anat each experience a bone-shaking transformation when faced with dangerous visitors or devastating news: 'her back muscles snap . . . her vertebrae rattle, her spine goes weak'.[6]

The body language of the back shaped worshippers' visual interactions with their deities in temples and other cult places. The gods were rarely – if ever – depicted in two-dimensional religious art with their backs turned towards the viewer. In a world in which sacred images were not simply symbolic representations but magical manifestations, the fixed image of a god's back was a dangerous curse no temple artisan or patron would dare execute, for fear of conjuring divine rejection or (perhaps worse) rendering the deity problematically unseeing. Even three-dimensional portrayals of the gods guarded against the cultural anxieties provoked by the potential sight of a deity's back: ceremonies manoeuvred the statue in ways made safe by the rituals of the priests, while the statues themselves were either clothed in ritually woven 'heavenly' textiles to buffer mortals from the divine back, or inscribed with ritual declarations to magically counter any sense of passive vulnerability on the part of both the worshipper and the deity.

But on the summit of the Holy Mountain, the threat to Moses is contained by careful stage management: strictly speaking, God promises that Moses will see his 'backparts' or 'hindquarters' – the same term used in the Hebrew Bible to describe the buttocks of an animal that are to be cleaned of dung before its sacrifice. The story evokes an image of a divine colossus striding past a diminutive Moses, swinging his giant hand to cover the rocky fissure in which Moses shelters as God passes by. Peering out from his small place of safety, like a child peeping through a crack in a door, Moses can only see Yahweh's 'hindquarters' once the towering deity removes his hand from the rock as he walks away. He sees not the deadly back of God thrust menacingly into the face of an enemy, but the disappearing backside of a celestial celebrity.

The precautions taken by God to protect Moses in this scene are a direct response to Moses' request to behold the divine *kabod* ('glory'). This is not the language of grandiose transcendence or sycophantic flattery. It is an explicit request to encounter the very essence of divine corporeality: Moses wants to see God's luminescent, dazzling body.* The *kabod* of God is the same glowing, fiery emanation the prophet Ezekiel sees surrounding Yahweh's body when he glimpses the divine genitals; the same white-hot, radiant body that (almost four hundred years later) the eponymous hero of the book of Daniel is said to have seen enthroned: it is a white-clad body from which 'a stream of fire issues and flows out'.[7] This is the same blinding brilliance that settles on the top of the Holy Mountain in Sinai 'like a devouring fire', enveloped by thick clouds to protect mortals from its dangerous glare.[8] And it is the same visible, blazing brightness that worshippers across ancient south-west Asia understood their gods to possess.

---

* In the Septuagint (the Greek translation of the Hebrew scriptures, produced in the third to second centuries BCE), Moses' request to see God's body is even more explicit, for Moses says to God not 'show me your Glory', but 'show yourself to me'.

A Sign of the Divine

Wandering around a museum or the ruins of an ancient city, it is easy to forget that the religious past was a place of vivid colour. Worn and weathered images of ancient gods are the muted browns and greys of clay and stone, or the drab, mottled tones of tarnished silver and dulled bronze. The shiny metals, precious stones, vivid paints and deep dyes colouring images of ancient south-west Asian gods may have faded or gone, but enough traces remain, and stories survive, to suggest that the gods were spectacularly colourful. Their skin might be the blood-red of warriors, the hot gold of the sun, the orange of bright amber, the warm black of dark olives, the rich brown of cedars, the translucent white of alabaster, or the sharp silver of the moon. Their very divinity mapped them onto the coloured contours of the cosmos in myriad hues. And emanating from their bodies, shining out from their skin, was the dazzling radiance of a heavenly aura.

One of the clearest iconographic portrayals of this divine radiance is found on a glazed brick used in a decorative frieze in a royal palace at Ashur – the ancient capital of the Assyrian kingdom, located on the Tigris River in what today is Iraq. Now in the British Museum, the painted brick is dated to the brief reign of Tukulti-Ninurta II (c. 890–884 BCE), and depicts the high god Ashur as a winged deity, stretching back his war bow as he moves through the skies, smartly dressed in a skirt pleated with fire and a conical helmet. Radiating from his body are thick wavy lines, bounded towards their outer edges by concentric circles that wrap themselves into the peak of his helmet, the tips of his bow and the hem of his skirt. Protruding from these circles are blazing tongues of fire (fig. 21). This is Ashur's *melammu* – a term used by the Assyrians and their neighbours to refer to the luminous, fiery radiance of divinity. Its range of uses suggests the divine radiance of Assyria's gods was very much like the *kabod* of the God of the Bible.

The visual portrayal of the brilliant nimbus surrounding the bodies of the gods often combined two elements of religious iconography crucial to communicating divine power. One was the twin quiver of arrows worn on the backs of warring deities. A lovely

Fig. 21. The Assyrian high god Ashur, drawing back his war bow in
the heavens. The deity's blazing radiance emanates from his body.
Once brightly coloured, the original image appears on an
enamelled brick from a temple in the city of Ashur and is dated
to the reign of King Tukulti-Ninurta II (*c*. 890–884 BCE).

example is now held in Yale University's Babylonian Collection. Dated
to about 1800 BCE, the moulded clay plaque shows the goddess Ishtar
standing triumphantly on two roaring, recumbent lions, her left leg
extended in victory from the long folds of her skirt as she presses her
foot down on a thickly maned neck. She holds a lowered scimitar in
her right hand, and lifts a bow in her left. On her head is a crown of
divinity, and bound around her chest are the tight straps of her arrow
quivers, criss-crossed on her back. But the warrior and her weaponry
appear almost as one: the tops of the quivers stand tall behind her
shoulders, while their bases shoot out from behind her waist, so that
her military might springs out of her body, just like the fearsome aura
ancient south-west Asian gods came to acquire (fig. 22).

The other motif of divine power often incorporated into the
iconography of divine radiance was the bright light emanating from
the torsos of deities associated with the sun, moon and stars. Although
this feature of divine power was often schematized in emblematic form
as a fiery winged sun disc – a symbol common to ancient south-west

Fig. 22. The goddess Ishtar
(Inanna), armed with her bow,
arrows and a scimitar, standing in
triumph on the backs of roaring
lions. The quivers on her back not
only serve as the equipment of
warfare, but manifest the military
might springing from her body.
This Mesopotamian clay plaque is
dated to about 1800 BCE.

Fig. 23. King Hammurabi of
Babylon standing before Shamash,
the solar god of justice, on the
stela monumentalizing the king's
laws. Shamash's radiance emanates
from his shoulders. Dated to about
1760 BCE, the stela was looted from
its Babylonian home and
transported to Susa in 1158 BCE.

Asian high gods – it was also seen on the gods in their human-like
forms. The famous Hammurabi Stela, now in the Louvre, is better
known for its cuneiform law code drawn up by King Hammurabi of
Babylon (c. 1792–1750 BCE). But it also offers a striking illustration of
divine radiance. In an image carved in relief at the top of the stela,
Hammurabi enshrines his self-proclaimed role as the 'king of justice'
in a scene depicting his meeting with Shamash, the Babylonian sun-god
and divine dispenser of justice. The king stands before the deity, who
is seated in splendour on his imposing throne, his feet resting on a
footstool of mountains. From Shamash's broad shoulders rise his sig-
nature motif of illuminating radiance – thick rays of light, akin to
those that would encircle the Assyrian god Ashur's body almost a
millennium later. The polished stone of the stela may be cool, black

basalt, but the shimmering heat of Shamash's powerful body is almost palpable (fig. 23).

From the third millennium BCE and well into the second, the luminescent radiance of the gods tended to be understood as a material, visible quality, gifted to them by more ancient or senior deities, whether in the form of a weapon, a crown, a cloak, or a bodily aura. But by the end of the second millennium BCE, the dazzling, blazing radiance of the gods' bodies had come to be a defining characteristic of divinity – much as skin tone has become one of the dominant markers of identity in the modern world. When the mighty Babylonian god Marduk was born, for example, he already 'wore on his body the auras of ten gods' and 'five fearsome rays clustered above him', explaining why he was known to his worshippers as the 'Bright One', 'the shining god who illuminates our ways'.[9] In temples, the radiant splendour of the gods was manifest in the polished gold, silver and bronze 'skin' of their cult statues. The manufactured nature of these precious metals did not render them any less godly. They were long believed to have their origins in the heavenly plane. Imbued with a divine radiance imparted by the gods themselves, they had been worked into the fabric of the earthly realm as it was divinely crafted, waiting to be revealed to mortals as and when the gods saw fit.[10] This is precisely the way in which the gods' royal servants and priestly attendants perceived the materials used to construct the cult images in their temples. Well into the first millennium BCE, kings were still boasting of the divine nature of the metals and stones used to create images of the gods. When King Esarhaddon of Assyria (c. 681–669 BCE) speaks of the 'destiny of radiance' gifted by the ancient high god Ea to cult statues, he emphasizes the primeval nature of their raw materials, hewn deep from the innards of creation – the 'quality gold, which no one had worked for any artistic task', and the 'select stones, not overgrown by vegetation' mined from distant mountains.[11]

The dazzling nimbus of the divine body was not only an awesome, corporeal glamour, but the material manifestation of the deity's frightening, forceful charisma. This was often weaponized as the hot, dangerous light with which deities equipped themselves – thus both the underworld warrior deity Nergal and the warring goddess Ishtar are described as wearing a fiery *melammu* like an armoured cloak or tunic. In Ishtar's case, its power is such that it can boil the ocean: 'My *melammu* cooks the fish in the sea', she brags.[12] On land, the divine radiance emanating from a god's body overwhelmed everything within its reach. According to King Ashurbanipal of Assyria (*c.* 668–627 BCE), 'the *melammu* of Ashur and Ishtar overwhelmed [the people of] the land of Elam, and they submitted to my yoke'.[13] The terrifying quality of divine radiance might also be embodied by the gods' own monstrous sidekicks. In the Epic of Gilgamesh, the eponymous hero has to take on the so-called Scorpion-men – fabulously body-queer attendants of the Mesopotamian gods, who not only have the legs of a bird, a snake-headed penis and a scorpion's tail, but 'whose aura is frightful', and whose 'terrifying mantles of radiance drape the mountains' they are tasked to protect.[14]

It is this awesome combination of luminescence, scorching splendour, metallic glare, dangerous fire and a weighty, weaponized force that characterizes the divine radiance of the God of the Bible. He too is 'wrapped in light as with a garment' and 'clothed with glory and splendour' – exalted language that, in English translations, is all too easily mistaken for the magisterial hyperbole of theological metaphor, but in its biblical (Hebrew) context, is the technical terminology used of the palpable, gleaming radiance emanating from God's body.[15] In the book of Habakkuk, the dangerous glare of God's material form is powerfully illustrated in a poem celebrating his role as a warrior. Here, the deity emanates a dazzling splendour from the relative safety of a far-off sacred mountain called Paran, in a southern wilderness known as Teman. But as he marches into the human world, his weapons of light and gleaming brightness come into view, eclipsing even the sun and moon:

> His splendour covers the heavens,
> and the earth is full of his radiance . . .
> He has rays [coming out] from his hand . . .
> The mountains see you and quake,
> waters gush torrents;
> the Deep roars aloud, raising its hand aloft;

Sun and Moon stand still,

at the light of your arrows speeding by,

by the gleaming splendour of your flashing spear;

you stride the earth in fury,

crushing nations in rage.[16]

God's radiance is clearly a double-edged sword for the inhabitants of the earthly realm, which is perhaps why his worshippers are repeatedly warned about the dangers of their god's radiant body. In the book of Isaiah, those who treasure the silver splendour and golden glory of 'foreign' cult statues are cautioned either to walk 'in Yahweh's light' or to take cover from the terrifying, vengeful menace of God's radiance: 'Enter into the rock, and hide in the dust, from the terror of Yahweh, and from the splendour of his majesty!'[17] No wonder God instructs Moses to take the same precaution when he asks to see the divine body atop the Holy Mountain in the wilderness.

For over two thousand years, Jewish and Christian commentators have twisted Moses' rear-view sighting of God into an elaborate allegory, claiming that it speaks to the ultimate unknowability and inscrutability of the divine. Not even the blessed Moses can take in the fullness of God. A notable exception was Joseph ben Isaac (more commonly titled Bekhor Shor), a twelfth-century CE French rabbi and scholar, who was far more comfortable than some of his learned colleagues with embracing the mysterious corporeality deeply embedded within the Torah's vision of God. What Moses experienced on Mount Sinai, he argued, was akin to what a more ordinary mortal can bear of the sun: its overwhelming splendour prevents us from looking directly at it, but we can gasp in wonder at its afterglow.[18] In Exodus, however, God's luminescent backside clearly gives off something more powerful than a wondrous afterglow. When Moses finally descends from the Holy Mountain, clutching the Ten Commandments, his own face is startlingly transformed. But quite how is a matter of some debate, for the ancient Semitic root of the Hebrew term used to describe this transformation probably means 'horn', but is also associated with light. The earliest translations of this peculiar story indicate that, from at least the third century BCE, Moses was understood to have developed horn-like rays of light, so that his face beamed with a divine radiance. Other ancient scholars would assume Moses' face literally grew horns – a symbol of the divine elsewhere in the Bible – giving rise to startling medieval images of Moses as a double-horned being. Either way, Moses undergoes a bodily transformation so profound that the Israelites cannot look him in the face and are afraid to go near him.[19] Moses' visual encounter with God has left its mark on him, rendering him more divine than human.

As the first millennium BCE neared its close, the dazzling brightness of the biblical God had become a standard marker of divinity in earliest Judaism: Ezekiel's glowing god of sixth-century BCE Jerusalem had been recast in the second-century BCE book of Daniel as an ancient deity seated on a flaming throne, with clothing 'as white as snow'; his divine emissary was said to have a face as bright as lightning, and a body gleaming like burnished bronze. It was a vision of God celebrated in 1 Enoch – another influential text of the period – in which 'streams of flaming fire' shoot from beneath the divine throne. 'It was difficult to look at', Enoch confesses. But he cannot look away. He sees God, 'the Great Glory', seated upon the throne. 'His gown shone more brightly than the sun and was whiter than any snow'; the deity is surrounded by flaming fire of such 'magnificence and glory' that not even the multitude of angels standing in attendance dare look upon him.[20] Many of the famous scrolls discovered near Qumran, by the Dead Sea, attest to a first-century BCE Jewish sect who counted themselves as 'the children of righteousness' walking 'in the light' of an archangel called the 'Prince of Light'; their enemies were the 'children of injustice' who were ruled by the 'Angel of Darkness'. In their visions of the heavenly realm, God is surrounded by a celestial entourage of angels, whose bodies are enveloped in light.[21] By the first century CE, Jewish texts commonly portray the divine messengers of God as luminous beings. Dressed in the bright white hues of the stars, shining angels crowd the godly realm. They bring brilliant light into the mundane world of mortals, flash into the prophetic dreams of the living and give illuminating tours of the heavens to the favoured few.

The early followers of Jesus naturally shared these deep-rooted ideas about the iridescent nature of divine bodies. In the New

Testament, the angel who announces Christ's birth to startled shepherds does so in a blaze of shining glory. It is an angel whose 'appearance
was like lightning and his clothing white as snow' who rolls back the
stone of Jesus' tomb, terrifying the Roman sentries who are supposed
to be guarding his corpse.[22] In Luke, two supernatural beings 'in dazzling clothes' are found standing inside the empty tomb, while, in the
Gospel of John, angels dressed 'in white' are discovered sitting in the
darkness of the newly abandoned grave.[23] In the book of Revelation,
the heavenly Christ has a head 'white as white wool, white as snow'.
His eyes blaze with fire, his feet gleam like burnished bronze and his
face is 'like the sun shining with full force'.[24] So well known was the
brightness of divine bodies that Paul felt the need to warn his Corin-
thian correspondents that even Satan himself might appear disguised
'as an angel of light'.[25]

But even the pre-resurrection, earthly Jesus of Nazareth can give
off the unmistakable aura of divine radiance. Unabashedly echoing the
story of Moses' encounter with the divine body on Sinai, an early
tradition used in the Gospels of Matthew, Mark and Luke describes
the divine transfiguration – or metamorphosis – of Jesus at the summit
of a high mountain. 'His face shone like the sun, and his clothes
became dazzling white', notes the author of Matthew; 'his clothes
became dazzling white such that no one on earth could bleach them',
the writer of Mark helpfully explains. In Luke's Gospel, this divine
transformation is pointedly described as Jesus' radiant 'glory', using
the Greek term *doxa* that ancient Jewish scribes had used to translate
the Hebrew term for Yahweh's own bright 'glory', *kabod*.[26] By the end
of the second century CE, this tradition would be further elaborated
in a text known as the Acts of John, in which the transfiguration is an
opportunity for the earthly Jesus to reveal his gigantic, divine body:
'his feet were whiter than snow, so that the ground there was lit up by
his feet, and his head reached to heaven'.[27] By contrast, the writer of
John's Gospel had felt no need for a glorious transfiguration. In this
text, Jesus is already fully divine – a god made flesh, whose radiant
'glory' (*doxa*) is an innate and pre-existent characteristic of his fully
fledged divinity. 'I am the light of the world', Jesus declares.[28] This was
no theological abstraction. It was to claim a divine nature, casting

Christ as the bodily manifestation of the divine light of creation, constructed in opposition to the darkness of primordial disorder, as was carefully spelled out in the prologue to the Gospel:

> All things came into being through him,
> and without him not one thing came into being.
> What has come into being in him was life,
> and the life was the light of all people.
> The light shines in the darkness,
> and the darkness did not overcome it . . .
> The true light, which enlightens everyone,
> was coming into the world.[29]

Christ's brightness was more than symbolic. Early believers imagined his extraordinary heavenly body to be a magnification of the form their own bodies would imminently take in the Kingdom of God. In his writings, Paul had frequently described this transformation using the language of getting dressed (in Greek, *enduo*), as he does in a letter to Christians in Corinth: 'For this perishable body puts on imperishability, and this mortal body puts on immortality'.[30] Throughout the book of Revelation, this wardrobe change is vividly portrayed: in the heavens, those believers who had been martyred on earth or conducted themselves virtuously are given gleaming white robes to wear, so that they too are clothed in the star-bright garments of immortality worn by heaven's divine inhabitants – including the white-robed, radiant Christ himself.[31]

Heavenly radiance was so fundamental to ancient Christian constructs of divinity that it would come to play a defining role in the formulation of doctrine. In 325 CE, the Roman emperor Constantine convened a council of bishops at Nicaea, on the eastern shores of Lake Ascanius in modern-day Turkey. As a new worshipper of Christ (rather than a 'convert' who had wholly abandoned his former gods), Constantine was keen to calm the increasingly vicious disputes among Christian theologians across his empire. At Nicaea, the objective was to settle, once and for all, arguments about the 'true' nature of Christ's relationship, as divine Son, to God the Father. In particular, the council's attention was firmly focused on the long-running feud between Alexander, Bishop of Alexandria, and Arius, his most learned presbyter. Both agreed that God the Father and God the Son were one. But they disagreed on the essential nature or 'substance' (in Greek, *ousia*) of that oneness. The bishop held that God the Son was divine in exactly the same way as God the Father, and that the Son was eternally coexistent with the Father. Arius, on the other hand, argued that the Son could not be co-eternal with the Father, because scripture insisted he was 'begotten' and 'made' by the Father. The Father alone was self-existent and unbegotten. By contrast, the Son was neither self-existent nor unbegotten, for he had a beginning: 'There was before he was not', ran the Arian slogan. The Father's divinity was therefore greater than the Son's. The council sided with Bishop Alexander, and Arius was declared a heretic – a label derived from the language of 'choice' or 'opinion' (in Greek, *hairesis*), but increasingly employed to mean 'sect', and now used as a pejorative term to marginalize those Christians whose views risked undermining either the humanity or divinity of Jesus. But Arian views were shared by numerous Christian communities, particularly across the eastern empire. And so, in the fashion of most councils, an official policy was drawn up, circulated for comments, redrafted and finally agreed.

As signatories to the document, those bishops who had been present at the meeting were expected to hold their congregations accountable to this new policy. Known as the 'Symbol of Nicaea', it was not only a declaration of faith, but a new definition of faith, and would form the basis of what is known as the Nicene Creed. 'We believe in one God, the Father Almighty, maker of all things visible and invisible', the creed began. Then came the doctrinal dismissal of Arian teachings:

> And [we believe] in one Lord Jesus Christ, the Son of God,
> begotten from the Father, only begotten, that is, from the
> substance of the Father, God from God, Light from Light, True
> God from True God, begotten, not made, from one substance
> with the Father . . . as for those who say There was when He
> was not, and Before being born He was not . . . these things
> the Catholic [whole] Church anathemizes.[32]

It is telling that the palpable divinity of the Father and Son was couched in the language of divine radiance: the Son is from the Father, as 'God from God, Light from Light'. It was a claim increasingly mirrored in early Christian art across the empire. The bodily luminescence that once framed the ancient gods of pre-Christian south-west Asia began to appear around Christ as a full-body halo. One of the oldest examples occurs in a mosaic in the Catacomb of Saint Domitilla in Rome. Dated to the time of Pope Damasus (366–84 CE), it presents Christ seated on a throne between Peter and Paul, with a basket of scrolls at his feet, displaying the classic posture of a philosopher or teacher. A huge aura of brilliant lapis light encircles his whole body, its outer edge curling around the top of Peter's head as a divine seal of approval. An accompanying Latin inscription reads, 'You are said to be the Son and are found to be the Father', echoing the Nicene claim that the Son and the Father are of the same divine substance. A few decades later, in the Church of Hosios David, overlooking the Greek city of Thessaloniki, the divine radiance of the Father was emphatically claimed as Christ's own in another mosaic. Here, the prophet Ezekiel's vision of God's blazing glory is theologically recast, reflecting its recycling in the book of Revelation: robed in deep purples and rich reds, with golden sandals on his feet, a youthful Christ sits delicately on the rainbow that was once God's phallic war bow. He is surrounded by a vast gleaming aureole of bright light. From its outer edges emerge the animalized cherubim of the divine chariot throne. Christ holds an unrolled scroll, the first words of which read, 'Behold our God' (Plate 12). The Son of God is clearly to be seen as the perfect likeness of his Father.[33]

The Christian iconography of light is more usually tracked back to the solar symbolism of Greek and Roman sun deities, whose shining halos were quickly grafted onto images of Christ, the Virgin and the apostles.[34] But it is also the much older ancient south-west Asian notion of the divine radiance emanating from the torsos of the gods to encompass their bodies that shapes Christ's dazzling aureole in early Christian art. It was inevitable that the overwhelming *melammu* of Mesopotamian gods and the glorious *kabod* of Yahweh would eventually find their way onto the body of the new Christian god. The metallic gleam of cult statues was mirrored in the use of gold and silver to clad statues and icons of Christ and his heavenly family – a feature later intensified in the highly ornate art of the Byzantine Church, and still common to Eastern and Oriental Orthodox iconographies today. Whether shimmering in the glow of lamps in churches, or flashing bright in the light of outdoor processions, the radiance of these cult images, surrounded by the smoky swirls of incense and oil lamps, rendered them animated, so that they appeared to be brilliantly, phenomenally living.[35]

From Brightness to Whiteness

If the glorious radiance of divine bodies enthralled worshippers, it also left a more sinister and deeply damaging legacy. The early Christian theology of light spoke to an increasingly dualistic religious world-view, in which the bright powers of God were contrasted with the dangerous, devilish forces of darkness, which themselves embodied a much older, seemingly primeval fear of what might lurk in the cover of night. 'God is light and in him there is no darkness at all', claims the writer of the Gospel of John. As Jesus is the embodiment of divine light in this Gospel, so his opponents are cast as evil-doers who 'love darkness rather than light'. It is a theme running through John's story of Jesus, and impossible to miss: as soon as Satan enters Judas, he goes out into the darkness of the night to betray Jesus, who is arrested in the black of night by a detachment of Roman soldiers and temple guards.[36] In the book of Acts, Paul's shift from a traditional form of Judaism to faith in Jesus Christ is said to have been triggered by his literal illumination by a light brighter than the sun shining down on him from heaven; Christ then commissions him to convert Jews and Gentiles 'so that they may turn from darkness to light and from the power of Satan to God, so that they may receive forgiveness of sins and a place among those who are sanctified by faith in me'.[37] To be debt-free of sin and sanctified by faith in Christ is to be in light. To be non-Christian and sullied by Satan is to be in darkness.

The theological coding of evil and sin as 'darkness' in early Christian writings drew heavily on the imagery of light and dark already embedded in some contemporaneous Jewish cosmologies, which themselves shared something in common with Persian Zoroastrianism, in which a divine cast of spirits of light and darkness competed for control of the universe. But in the hands of some Christian writers, the deviancy of 'darkness' would come to acquire a polemical association with those with black skin. It marked a departure from the cultural norms of both ancient Jewish and Graeco-Roman religions, in which black skin might be variously identified with beauty, majesty and wealth, as well as foreignness, erotic exoticism, or xenophobic danger. While these identifications were at times set within a context of perceived ethnic or geographical difference, they were not *primarily* constructed in what might now be considered racialized opposition to lighter skin: across ancient south-west Asia and the eastern Mediterranean, different social groups often classified themselves and others in terms of affiliations of city, homeland, religious practice, or culture (among other markers of identity), but the notion and category of 'race' – as we use the term today – was yet to be conjured.[38] But as early Christian groups negotiated their own self-identity in a context of ongoing difference and dispute (both among themselves and with those around them), the symbolism of blackness was increasingly used to caricature the physical appearance of those cast as deviant, heretical, or sinful.[39]

A popular strategy among the early Church Fathers was to lift particular geographic labels from their scriptures and redeploy them as a means of colouring sinners in need of Christian salvation. This is exactly what the fourth-century Balkan-born theologian Jerome does when he disturbingly caricatures 'Ethiopians' (biblical Kushites) as 'black and cloaked in the filth of sin' to illustrate the tangible, transformative power of Christian baptism and repentance: 'At one time we were Ethiopians in our vices and sins. How so? Because our sins had blackened us. But afterwards we heard the words: "Wash yourselves clean!" And we said: "Wash me and I shall be whiter than snow". We are Ethiopians, therefore, who have been transformed from blackness into whiteness.'[40]

For some Christians, Satan himself had already come to acquire not only the darkness of night, but the blackness of vice. In the Epistle of Barnabas, a highly influential text of the late first or early second century CE, the Devil is called the Black One and held responsible for all the sins that destroy the soul. It is quite a list: idolatry, impertinence, glorification of power, hypocrisy, duplicity, adultery, murder, robbery, arrogance, transgression, deceit, malice, insolence, sorcery, magic, greed and 'the lack of the fear of God'. Satan is also cast as the black opponent of Christ in the late second-century Acts of Peter, in which he is said to attack the souls of Christians with poisoned arrows and is declaimed the source of 'wickedness and the abyss of darkness'.[41] But Satan's blackness could take on even more dangerous forms. According to the fourth-century theologian Athanasius, the young Egyptian monk later known as Saint Antony the Great repeatedly contended with Satan's most devilish devices while he was trying to get on with the business of being a desert-dwelling ascetic. In one of his toughest battles, Antony dealt not with the more usual blows of a demonic beating, but with the Devil himself, manifested as a woman so desirable that Antony had to fill his mind with visions of a worm-filled fiery hell in order to resist her. Satan changed tack, opting for a more direct approach – about which it is now thoroughly repugnant to read. In Athanasius' *Life of Antony*, we are told: '[Satan] appeared, as was fitting, in a form that revealed his true nature: an ugly black boy prostrated himself at Antony's feet, weeping loudly.' The boy confesses his real identity and – in a tone of stunned incredulity – protests that he is usually far more successful at tempting young people into fornication. Antony realizes he is not quite so afraid. '[He] gave thanks to God and strengthened by greater confidence in the face of the enemy, he said, "You are utterly despicable and contemptible, for both your blackness and your age are signs of weakness. You do not worry me any longer"'.[42] As Antony starts to sing a psalm, the boy vanishes.*

---

*   I cite here the more famous Latin version of the *Life of Antony* (circulating only fifteen years or so after the Greek original), for it would quickly become both the better known and more authoritative account in Western Christendom. In this Latin text, the hostility of the original Greek is further intensified by glossing the boy's appearance as 'ugly'.

The Devil might well have left with the painful sound of singing in his ears, but modern-day readers of the *Life of Antony* are more likely to hear alarm bells. The demonization of black people, dressed in tropes of eroticized danger and sinful deviancy, clearly continues to stalk the world in highly damaging and deadly forms today. Something of this can be attributed to the colour-coded dualism inherent within early Christian theology, which lent itself as easily to the whitening of divinity as it did to the blackening of evil. In the iconography of Western Christendom in particular, divine brightness and lightness would morph into corporeal whiteness. Encouraged by the repeated references to the white robes of the heavenly Christ and his angels in New Testament texts, which visually marked divine bodies as bleach-bright, the golden hues of Christ's divinity were increasingly concentrated in his halo, while his skin grew ever lighter and whiter. Across early medieval Europe, on the walls of churches, in illustrated Bibles and prayer books, and in the pictures conjured in sermons, Jesus was made in the image of his light-skinned, wealthier worshippers – and increasingly contrasted with black demons. Pitch-black and pitchforked, they scuttled across religious landscapes, loomed from shadows behind unsuspecting God-fearers, and screamed with rage as Christ yanked them from the gasping mouths of the possessed. The racialized image of Christ as a light-skinned European would not only become a convention of the Western artistic canon, but a tool of political power, social oppression and state-sanctioned killing.

As Europeans invaded other people's homelands in Africa, Asia and the Americas, and began the violent colonial process of brutalizing, exploiting and profiteering from two-thirds of the world, the white-skinned European Christ lent his support to the conquest, oppression, enslavement and trafficking of those cast as black-, brown-, dark- or red-skinned – regardless of whether these people were already deemed appropriately God-fearing or not. By the late fifteenth century, the biblical story of Noah's son Ham had been twisted into an anti-black myth of African origins. The story is told in Genesis 9.18–27, in which Ham sees his father's nakedness, prompting Noah to inflict a curse of perpetual slavery upon Ham's descendants, the Canaanites. Nowhere in this peculiar tale are black colour terms used, and neither here nor anywhere else in the Hebrew Bible are Ham or the Canaanites point-edly associated with dark skin. Instead, in the next chapter in Genesis, Ham is simply said to be the ancestor of many other peoples in the repopulated, post-Flood world, including the Egyptians and the Kush-ites.[43] But from the fourth century CE onwards, scholars would read a false etymology into the name of Ham, incorrectly linking it to words meaning 'dark', 'brown' and 'black', so that in several Christian, Jewish and Islamic traditions, Ham was increasingly assumed to be the ances-tor of all dark-skinned people. By the late fifteenth century, the biblical 'curse of Ham' had become a scriptural proof-text in Western Chris-tendom endorsing the perception of black-skinned people as a divinely ordained caste of slaves innately inferior to lighter-skinned Euro-peans.[44] This distorted story has been a stock chapter in the white supremacist's playbook ever since.

As European empires continued to build on the backs of those they first invaded and then oppressed and exploited, light skin tones were increasingly seen as the inherited physical hallmark of a cosmic supremacy. But it was a position which came with an earthly duty: white colonialism was frequently promoted as a godly and 'civilizing' mission, commanded by Christ to extend salvation to non-white, non-Christians. The Saviour, cast in the New Testament as the paradigmatic form of humanity, made in the image of God, had been whitewashed. Christian salvation would remain a theological justification for the ongoing expansion or retention of both Roman Catholic and Protes-tant European empires well into the twentieth century. An oft-cited sub-Saharan African dictum illustrates this well: 'When the white man came to our country, he had the Bible and we had the land. The white man said to us, "Let us pray." After the prayer, the white man had the land and we had the Bible.'*

For generations, people of colour led the way in countering the colonial hijacking of the Bible, demonstrating how it can offer an

---

* This dictum is so well known that its origins and details can vary in its retelling. This is the version cited in Takatso Mofokeng's 1988 article in the *Journal of Black Theology.*

alternative, liberationist response to imperial oppression and white supremacy, pointing particularly to its emphasis on God's rescue of the Israelites enslaved in Egypt, and the victory of Christ over his death on an imperial cross.[45] But by the time European colonizers had seized vast swathes of Australasia from its indigenous inhabitants, the cultural myth of divine whiteness had already birthed another Western falsehood: the pseudoscientific, physiological classification of people into 'races', complete with cranial and facial diagrams. These diagrams typically racialized and arranged people into an invented, stratified schema. The civilized 'Caucasian' man, equipped with the heavenly curls of a marble-carved Greek god, the straight-cut nose of a Roman emperor and the lily-white skin of the colonial Christ, was placed at the apex of this imagined evolutionary hierarchy. Beneath him were positioned gross caricatures of East Asian people, South-East Asian people, indigenous peoples of the Americas and Australasia, and Jewish people, who had been physiologically othered in the West since at least 1000 CE. A black-skinned African man, depicted as an animalized 'primitive', was at its base.[46]

Some might say the rest is history. Except it's not, as the global Black Lives Matter movement is so clearly and repeatedly prompted to demonstrate in the face of ongoing racial killings and systemic injustices. It is impossible to overstate the continuing social and political ramifications of the theologically endorsed cultural othering of people of colour. A direct line can be drawn from the early Christian demonization of black people to the well-known repugnant episodes and echoes of European colonialism, some of which have *formally* come to an end, while some persist in different forms: the transatlantic slave trade, human zoos, death camps, state-sponsored eugenics, law-enforced segregation, the forced enclosure of indigenous peoples across the Americas and Australasia, South African apartheid, the false 'science' of racialized evolution, to name but a frightful few. But whiteness remains the dominant, collective category of privilege, entitlement and power in much of the world, and continues to uphold the economic disparity, structural inequality and social injustices harming people of colour. And deep within its cultural heart is a racialized theology of light – a theology that has helped to create and sustain a reality in which people of colour continue to be marginalized, vilified and killed.

10

INSIDE OUT

Since its inception in 1995, an exhibition of flayed, dismembered and dissected human corpses has toured the globe, thanks to its now famous creator, the German anatomist Gunther von Hagens. Skinned, sliced and drained of their fluids, these donor cadavers are 'plastinated' with blood-bright silicones and flesh-hued polyesters, and carefully staged in a tableau of social activities. There are copulating bodies, wrestling bodies, singing bodies, gambling bodies, horse-riding bodies, chess-playing bodies, football-kicking bodies. Other corpses are more actively engaged in matters of life and death: there is a heavily pregnant body, the unborn child as viscerally exposed as its mother; a kneeling body, performing CPR on a body collapsed on the floor; a gasping body, wearing a firefighter's helmet and carrying in its arms a dried-up, lifeless skeleton. Each corpse is strategically stripped of its fat and flesh at key sites to reveal the muscles and organs nestled within its bony frame. Alongside the cadavers, internal organs are suspended in glass curiosity cabinets. Pale, lumpy lengths of intestine, stretched out like a rope for hanging. A pair of inflated lungs, hovering overhead like a ghoulish bird. A bulbous heart, frilled and frayed at its seams, dangling like a Halloween bauble. Turned inside out, the body becomes almost monstrous. And yet, like the best horror films, 'Body Worlds' has proved irresistibly popular. With total attendance figures now estimated at over forty-four million, the exhibition is classed by its creator as a form of 'edutainment', rendering the paying public privy to the secrets of the body hidden beneath the skin.[1]

Whether considered edifying, unethical, or grotesque, the ongoing success of 'Body Worlds' is just the latest incarnation of an enduring human fascination for the inside of the body. The spectacle of the innards brings the strangeness of the body's internal organs to the surface in ways the flattened illustrations of medical textbooks cannot, graphically revealing the realities of our insides, more usually experienced only as the sensations wrought by their activities: the rumble of an empty stomach; the gurgling of the intestines; the heaviness of a full bladder; the muffled thump of the heart. Exposing them renders the familiar strange, and the strange familiar.

It was the very strangeness of the innards that gave birth to one of the world's oldest monsters. Known as both Huwawa and Humbaba, he was one of the most fearsome divine beings of ancient Mesopotamian mythology. Clothed with seven layers of divine radiance, with a belt around his waist, he had the body of a giant man, with thick bowed legs, a large flaccid penis, the paws and claws of a lion, and long straggly hair and whiskers. Most horrifying of all, he wore his guts on his face. In literary circles, Huwawa was well known as the guardian of the precious Forest of Cedars – a dwelling place of the gods located in what today is Lebanon. Appointed to this role by the high gods, Huwawa's terrifying appearance combined the mysterious powers of the internal organs with the animalized horrors of the wilderness. Indeed, he had the famously heroic Gilgamesh rooted to the spot when he and his devoted best friend Enkidu entered the Forest of Cedars on a quest for adventure and everlasting fame: 'Fear and terror spread through his sinews and feet. He could not move his feet on the ground; the big toenails of his feet stuck . . . to the path'.[2] Huwawa's repulsiveness was designed to ward off even the boldest of intruders.

Although Gilgamesh and Enkidu managed to defeat Huwawa by tricking him out of his protective auras, punching him in the face and then cutting off his head, Huwawa enjoyed a long afterlife across Mesopotamia. Hundreds of terracotta plaques depicting his monstrous severed head were produced from the late third millennium BCE and into the first. One of the most characterful examples, now displayed in the British Museum, was found in the ancient city of Sippar in southern Iraq. Huwawa's face is alive with tightly packed, lumpy coils of entrails. Like a flesh labyrinth, they twist and turn back on themselves, forming his cheeks and chin, his forehead and ears, and two rows of terrifying teeth set into a wide grimace – an iconographic constellation that would morph into the head of the Gorgon in Greek art. Some plaques were fixed as amulets to the walls of temples, or suspended from doorways in homes, perpetuating Huwawa's mythic role as a powerful guardian. But others were used as magical tools to decipher omens. Inscribed on the reverse with guidelines for interpretation, these clay images of Huwawa's face were employed in a specialist branch of divination known now as extispicy, by which the entrails of a sacrificial animal (usually a sheep) were examined for hidden messages from the gods. Comparing the shape and texture of the animal's intestines to Huwawa's thick fleshy coils enabled the diviner to discern what had been decided in the heavens (Plate 14).[3]

As both an agent of divination and the guardian of the divine Forest of Cedars, Huwawa could guard or give access to the secrets of the gods; his gut-filled face manifested this gatekeeping role in the most visceral way. But the monstrosity of Huwawa's face also embodied the very stuff of fear – a primal emotion, which in ancient south-west Asia was understood to be located not in the brain, but in the gut. Huwawa was a product of a world in which the internal features of the torso embodied the more subjective aspects of existence. Fear and dread were overwhelmingly sensed in the intestines – and most acutely felt in the discomfort and discharge of the bowels, reflecting in part an understanding that emotional upset and physical suffering were barely distinguishable.[4] It is an understanding all too often minimized in the medicalized treatment of the body in the modern world, and yet instinctively reflected in the idioms of our everyday language: we are gutted by disappointment, shit ourselves with fear, and feel sick to our stomachs with worry.

But fear was not the only emotion located and felt within the ancient south-west Asian torso. For both gods and mortals, excitement, lust and distress were also sited within the innards, or, more specifically, the liver and kidneys. In the lower belly, and especially the bowel and womb, the gut feelings of social bonding were sensed: the ache of sympathy, the warmth of compassion and the burn of parental love. Emotions more closely tied to cognitive reflection and intellectual deliberation moved in and around the heart: regret, malice, satisfaction, grief, delight, frustration, ambition. Aspects of this ancient sensorium of the emotions are vividly glimpsed in descriptions of ancient south-west Asian deities: as Anat of Ugarit revelled in the trampling of her enemies, 'her liver shook with laughter, her heart was filled with joy, the liver of Anat with triumph'. When Marduk of Babylon became infuriated by social delinquency and religious neglect in his city, his whole body not only 'shook with anger', but 'his heart fumed; his liver raged.'[5] Like his divine elders, the God of the Bible experienced much of his emotional life as a sensory, physical transformation within his torso.

An oracle in the book of Jeremiah is particularly visceral in its description of the intense emotions experienced by Yahweh. Dated to the early sixth century BCE, its setting is the Babylonian attack on Jerusalem and the destruction of the city's temple complex – described in traditional language as the 'tents' and 'curtains' of the deity. The disaster is engineered by Yahweh himself as a sorry punishment for the religious malpractice of his worshippers. But it will hurt him, as well as them:

> My innards, my innards! I writhe [in pain]!
> Oh, the walls of my heart!
> My heart beats wildly,
> I cannot keep silent.
> I hear the sound of the trumpet,
> the alarm of war!
> Disaster overtakes disaster,
> the whole land is laid waste.
> Suddenly my tents are destroyed,
> my curtains in a moment.[6]

The sensory anguish expressed in these verses is akin to the divine distress articulated by other ancient south-west Asian deities, who physically lament the destruction of their cities and the desecration of their temples: they weep, they groan, they bend double; their hearts race with grief-stricken rage, or are weighed down with the heaviness of regret. And yet most biblical translators and commentators have long preferred to hear in these words the voice of the prophet Jeremiah, rather than the deity himself. After all, it is one thing for God to weep in anguish and cry out in pain – as he so often does in the Bible – but quite another to find him suffering belly cramps and heart palpitations brought on by emotional distress. But in the Bible, Yahweh's internal organs regularly manifest his shifting emotions. When freighted with grief, his heart sickens; when he mournfully sanctions the destruction of Moab, his innards groan and tremble; when he is moved to compassion for his beloved worshippers, his guts sonorously rumble.[7] So familiar were some worshippers with the sensory workings of God's inner organs, his sudden somatic silence is cited as proof that he has physically abandoned them: 'Where is your zeal and your strength, the sounding of your innards, your compassion? They are restrained', his despairing people cry. 'Return, for the sake of your servants!'[8]

Tearful appeals like this, often staged within sacred space as ritual lamentation, were accompanied by the beating of chests and the mournful tones of drums and lyres. It was a practice long known to soothe the inflamed, enraged internal organs of the gods, and just as important to them as the daily ministrations of their priests. To be without specialists skilled in both praise and lamentation was to suffer dire neglect, as the bereft Sumerian goddess Gula complains: 'My lamentation expert no longer cools down my heart! My gudu-priest [cultic expert] no longer sings jubilations!'[9] Regular lamentation was so fundamental to the workings of a temple that, in Mesopotamia, the lamenting musician – gala – was given his own mythological origins. Equipped with a drum in his hand, the gala was created by the clever god Enki precisely to appease the wrathful heart of the fearsome goddess Inanna: 'he fashioned for her the gala, the one whose lament soothes the heart . . . he arranged his tearful laments of supplication'.[10] The sound of these sacred drums not only echoed the lamenters' ritualized beating of their breasts (a widespread mourning action still employed today in grieving for the Jerusalem temple on Yom Kippur), but conceptually and audibly amplified the beating of the deity's heart, gradually bringing the thumping chests of worshippers and the deity into calmer, syncopated harmony.[11]

It was a multi-sensory transformation with which the God of the Bible would also find himself familiar. Biblical texts suggest that ritual drummers and professional lamenters were regular players in the cults of Yahweh and his divine assembly, with women 'skilled in lamentation' performing a particularly prominent role in the ritual expression of religious grief. 'Call for the lamenting women to come! Send for the skilled women to come!' God commands. 'Let them quickly raise a dirge over us, so that our eyes may run down with tears, and our eyelids flow with water'.[12] Painted terracotta figurines of high-status female drummers have been found in cultic contexts at sites across the southern Levant, including those of ancient Israel and Judah.[13] Dating from the eighth to the sixth centuries BCE, Israelite and Judahite examples have tended to be interpreted as symbols of joyful celebration, but with their hand-drums held closely to their chests, they are just as likely to represent some of the sacred lamenters called upon to soothe the hearts of Yahweh and the other gods.

The ever-present threat of divine displeasure demanded the regular performance of ritual laments by religious professionals. But cultic lamentation was at its most urgent when the gods' raging hearts wrought punishment in the form of divine abandonment and earthly warfare. Both professional lamenters and royal mourners were hastily pressed into service to petition the gods for clemency and restoration. One such high-status petitionary was Adad-guppi, the 104-year-old mother or grandmother of King Nabonidus of Babylon (r. 555–539 BCE). Her expertise in ritual mourning is memorialized in two inscribed stelae, both of which were found recycled as paving slabs in the steps leading to the Great Mosque of modern-day Harran (Turkey). The inscriptions reflect on the destruction of Harran's ancient predecessor in 609 BCE, and naturally assume that the city had been given up to military attack by its angry deity, the moon god Sin, and his divine companions. As a lifelong devotee of Sin, Adad-guppi sought to appease the god's anger and secure the rebuilding of his city: 'I was constantly beseeching Sin', she declares in the inscriptions. On her

Fig. 24. Terracotta figurines of female drummers, who likely played
a ritual role in soothing the hearts of the gods. Dated to the eighth
and seventh centuries BCE, these examples are from Achzib, on
the Phoenician coast. But similar figurines – some more
elaborate, and almost all badly worn – have been found
at contemporaneous Israelite and Judahite sites.

knees, she says, she gazed at him 'prayerfully and in humility', repeating the petitionary refrain, 'May your return to your city take place'.
Her whole body was her ritual instrument: 'In order to appease the
heart of my god . . . I did not put on a garment of excellent wool,
silver, gold, a fresh garment; I did not allow perfumes [or] fine oil to
touch my body. I was clothed in a torn garment. My fabric was sackcloth'. Adad-guppi's concentrated endeavours paid off. Sin's 'wrathful
heart quietened down', and he returned to the city.[14]

As the language of the gods and their petitioners indicates, the
soothing, cooling and quietening of divine hearts was more than
poetically figurative. Just as the ritual appeals of worshippers demanded
the sensory engagement of their own bodies, so too the bodies of the
gods were understood to respond with a visceral physicality. And the
God of the Bible was no exception. When Assyrian forces threatened
to overwhelm Yahweh's city of Samaria towards the end of the eighth
century BCE, the cries of his worshippers moved him – and his internal

organs – to mercy: 'How can I give you up . . . how can I hand you over, O Israel?' he asks, as he wonders whether to avert his impending punishment of his people. 'My heart recoils within me', he continues, while a convulsion of compassion in his belly 'rises up warm'.[15] The sensation God experiences here is akin to that felt by the mother of the baby King Solomon famously threatens to carve in half: the gut-wrenching, lurching turn of a parent's innards, triggered by a deep-seated fear for their child.[16] As God feels this same parental pain, the sensation spreads: the strong emotional impulses within his lower abdomen reach up into the cavity of his chest, causing his heart to turn about its decision. Physically, rather than simply metaphorically, the God of the Bible feels a change of heart.

For both humans and deities, this upward anatomical movement was the corporeal process by which feeling also became thinking. 'It did not ascend to my heart', God says, when he claims in the Bible (with some frequency) that a certain idea had not occurred to him.[17] His heart was the body part in which his passions and plans were fused and fleshed, and in this he was no different from any other deity – nor indeed any mortal. Across the cultures of ancient south-west Asia, the heart was a cognitive organ: it was the site of reason and deliberation, decision making and action taking. But it might easily be changed by an uprising of belly-based emotion. And within the divine realm, the consequences of such a change of heart could be devastating: 'Yahweh regretted that he had made man on the earth, and there was pain in his heart. So Yahweh said, "I will wash from the earth the man I cre-ated, both man and beast, creeping things and birds of the air, for I regret that I made them".'[18]

The palpable, corporeal nature of the Bible's ancient language of the heart is often missed by modern-day Western readers, for whom the emotional, thinking heart is rather more emblematic than solidly somatic. Although we might read the changing rhythms of the heart as a gauge of shifting emotion, it serves only symbolically as a sensing, thinking organ. Meanwhile, our thoughts are to be found in our heads, caught somewhere between the neurological activities within the lobes of our brains and the more nebulous, psychological dynamics of our minds – whatever it is that the mind might be. By contrast, in ancient south-west Asia, it was the heart that sensed and made sense of the world beyond the body. Just as the eyes see, and the ears hear, as Moses is said to tell the Israelites, so the heart understands.[19] Conscious thought was quite literally organic – it was a fleshy, feeling part of the inner anatomy.

In the Bible's story world, the perpetual motion and sound of the living heart signalled its fleshy malleability, which in turn textured the quality and worth of its thoughts. A 'hardened' heart was impenetrable and impervious to change; a 'fat' heart was sated of space and dulled in sense, leaving no room for increased understanding; a 'melting' heart was unstable in form, incapable of holding reason and intention within its walls. Like an otherworldly Goldilocks, Yahweh preferred the human heart to be neither too firm, too full, nor too soft. Instead, it was to be just right: a heart 'after my own', he says, in form and function – a 'heart of flesh', to be saturated with religious knowledge and understanding. Those special individuals equipped with such hearts were usually the monarchs divinely ordained to lead Yahweh's people as a 'shepherd' – an exalted ritual title commonly used of kings throughout ancient south-west Asia (and literalized in the biblical story of the rise of David from sheep-herder to king).[20] But Yahweh was not alone in correlating the hearts of his royal shepherds with his own.

In 539 BCE, the Persian king Cyrus II conquered the ancient city of Babylon, incorporating its sizeable territories into his own to create a vast empire. At its eastern edges, it reached as far as the Himalayas; westwards, the new empire encircled the Mediterranean from Thrace in Greece down to Memphis in Egypt. Such a seismic reordering of the world could only have been achieved by a king in possession of a divinely aligned heart. And this is exactly what Cyrus himself claimed. To commemorate his victory over Babylon, he commissioned the inscription adorning the famous Cyrus Cylinder, copies of which were circulated to his new vassals. In this inscription, Cyrus casts himself not as the foreign aggressor, but the rightful liberator of Babylon, specially selected by the mighty Babylonian god Marduk to free his city from the destructive rule of its indigenous rulers, and to restore the angry god to the capital he had abandoned. Cyrus claims that

Marduk scrutinized the innards of mortals to find the man whose heart matched the 'urgings' of his own:

> All [through] the lands together he searched out, tested, and looked for an upright ruler who matched the urgings of his heart. He called out his name: Cyrus, king of Anshan; he pronounced his name to be king over all [the world] . . . And he [Cyrus] shepherded with justice and righteousness all the black-headed people over whom he [Marduk] had given him victory.[21]

Yahweh, too, appears to have felt the same urgings of the heart as Marduk. In a collection of oracles delivered shortly after Cyrus' capture of Babylon, and now found in the book of Isaiah, Yahweh claims it was he himself who had called out Cyrus' name, appointing him as the shepherd – the king who would fulfil all the delights and intentions of God's heart. Yahweh designates Cyrus his messiah ('anointed one'), who will subdue the nations, rebuild Jerusalem, return his displaced people to the city and restore his temple.[22] This prophetic interpretation of wider political events became so central to subsequent reflections on the rebuilding of the Jerusalem temple that Cyrus is even given the last word in the Tanakh. At the very end of 2 Chronicles, which closes the Jewish Bible,* Cyrus declares: 'Yahweh, the God of Heaven, has given me all the kingdoms of the earth, and has charged me with building him a house in Jerusalem, which is in Judah. Whoever is among you of all his people, may Yahweh his god be with him. Let him go up [to worship in Jerusalem]!'[23] Marduk and Yahweh might have been long-term rivals in the territorial politics of the earthly realm, but in the mythological world, their hearts were cannily aligned when it came to the great King Cyrus.

---

*   Fixed several centuries after the texts were composed, the canonical sequence and number of Hebrew Bible books differ in Jewish and Christian traditions. The Jewish Bible (Tanakh) closes with the books of Chronicles and excludes a number of texts canonized in the Christian Old Testament (which itself varies in both the number and sequence of books across denominations).

For both deities, the scrutinizing of human hearts was a process akin to divination. With piercing super-sight, the gods could not only peer into the hearts of worthy rulers, but examine the hearts of the disobedient. When Yahweh decides to flood the world to rid it of mortals, it is because he sees that 'the inclination of the thoughts of their hearts' is evil. Like a diviner skilled in extispicy, he was well known to scrutinize the innards of his worshippers to discover their desires and principles, and judge them accordingly. He is called 'the tester of hearts and entrails' and the god who 'seeks an oracle in every heart and understands every plan and intention'.[24] It is probably for this reason that in Exodus 28, Yahweh's high priest is commanded to wear a chest-covering over his heart, known as the *hoshen mishpat* ('breast-piece of decision'). Crafted with expensive blue, purple and crimson fabrics, and embellished with gold, the breastpiece is filled or studded with twelve precious stones, each inscribed with the name of one of the tribes of Israel. This chest-covering appears to have been a part of the high priest's divinatory tool kit, along with divine lots known as Urim and Thummim, which were kept inside its pocket. The Urim and Thummim were used to divine the will of the deity – a key function of a priest, who was appointed by Yahweh 'to do according to what is in my heart'.[25] In ritual exchange, the stones on the breastpiece likely facilitated Yahweh's divinatory reading of the high priest's heart in his role as the cultic intermediary and representative of the deity's wor-shippers.[26] By wearing these sacred stones 'in the breastpiece of decision on his heart when he goes into the holy place', the high priest 'shall carry the [instrument of] decision for the Israelites over his heart in the presence of Yahweh at all times'.[27]

For some early Christian writers, the mediatory and divinatory skills of the high priest were pointedly usurped by Jesus. In John's Gospel, the divine Son of God is the only one who can communicate God's intentions, because he is 'close to the Father's heart'.[28] Mean-while, God's own divination of human hearts had inevitably become a skill attributed to Christ. In the Gospels of Matthew, Mark and Luke, Jesus reveals that he can 'perceive the thoughts' of his opponents when he asks them, 'Why do you think evil in your hearts?' In the book of Revelation, the divine nature of this skill is rendered even more explicit when the Son of God claims, 'I am the one who searches kidneys and hearts'.[29] It was the age-old ability of the gods to read the hearts of mortals that also underlay early Christian confessions of faith. As Paul wrote in his letter to Jesus-devotees in Rome, it was not enough simply to proclaim faith in Jesus Christ; believers also had to know it – to think it – in their hearts in order to attain eternal salvation: 'If you confess with your mouth that Jesus is Lord and believe in your heart that God raised him from the dead, you will be saved'.[30] For Paul, believing 'in your heart' that Jesus resurrected was not a leap of unthinking faith, but a reasoned decision.

If thinking was an act of the heart, wisdom was hefted within its chambers. The old biblical proverb that 'wisdom is at home in the heart of one who has understanding' was a physiological truism of its time.[31] The legendary King Solomon, famed in the Bible for his wisdom, was said to have asked God for a 'listening heart', and was granted 'very great wisdom, discernment, and breadth of heart as vast as the sand on the seashore . . . he was wiser than anyone else'.[32] But the hearts of gods, of course, were wider and wiser. Stored within them was not only the worldly wisdom humans might hope to acquire, but the distinctive form of wisdom with which the cosmos itself was brought into order. Exclusive, elusive and all-encompassing, it was divine wisdom.

A lengthy Sumerian hymn of praise illustrates well the dizzying breadths and depths of the wise hearts of the gods. It is attributed to the earliest author we are lucky enough to know by name: Enheduanna, a woman whose remarkable literary legacy is all too often eclipsed by that better-known female poet of antiquity, Sappho. Writing over a millennium and a half before Sappho, Enheduanna was the daughter of the powerful King Sargon of Akkad (c. 2334–2279 BCE), who appointed her high priestess of the moon god Nanna (also known as Sin) at the city of Ur (fig. 25). She wrote and compiled a number of religious texts praising various deities and their temples, but her collection of hymns to the goddess Inanna are particularly remarkable for their literary artistry and deeply personal religious passion. In the first of these, Enheduanna pointedly addresses the wise goddess as 'Lady of the Largest Heart', and crafts a richly textured portrait of Inanna as 'the magnificent lady who gathers up the divine powers of heaven and

Fig. 25. Sporting braided hair, elaborate flounced robes and a cap, the
prominent figure in this ritual scene is widely assumed to be
Enheduanna, high priestess of the moon god Nanna. The image
appears on a votive lunar disc, inscribed on its reverse with a
dedication from Enheduanna to Nanna. Now restored, the
object was found in pieces during the excavation of a temple
in Ur, and has been dated to around 2300 BCE.

earth'. For Enheduanna, Inanna is a deity so powerful that her divinity
surpasses even that of the highest gods, An and Enlil, who have willingly ceded their wisdom to her. 'In your vast wisdom, amongst all the
gods . . . you alone are majestic', Enheduanna exclaims. In this poem,
Inanna not only governs the forms of wisdom graciously bestowed
upon mortals, such as expertise in warfare, ritual, economics, sex and
medicine, but curates and controls the divine wisdom underpinning
the very foundations of the cosmos: 'To destroy, to create, to cut apart,
to establish, Inanna, are yours; to turn a man into a woman and a
woman into a man, Inanna, are yours . . . a large and expansive heart,
Inanna, are yours'.[33]

Almost two thousand years later, another poet was crediting just
one deity with the wisdom to create and destroy – and, for him, it was
Yahweh. For the writer of the biblical book of Job, creation and
destruction were precisely the aspects of divine wisdom 'hidden in the

heart' of Yahweh and shared with no other divine being. Not even the primordial gods of the cosmos, who continued to play such a crucial role in the structuring and maintenance of the universe, had access to his wisdom: 'It's not in me', says ancient Tehom (Deep); 'It's not with me', states Yam (Sea); 'We have heard [only] a rumour of it with our ears', claim Abaddon (Destroyer) and Mot (Death).[34] The creative results of divine wisdom were evident in the shape and workings of the cosmos, but the power to hold that wisdom in the heart was Yahweh's alone.

It was a view shared by other biblical writers. In the book of Jeremiah, Yahweh is described as the god who built all three tiers of the cosmos: 'It is he who made the underworld by his power, who established the [earthly] world by his wisdom, and by his understanding stretched out the heavens'. As if to emphasize the exclusivity of Yahweh's cosmological wisdom, a later hand – writing in Aramaic, rather than Hebrew – has inserted a helpful preface to this verse: 'The gods who did not make the heavens and the earth shall perish from the earth and from under the heavens'.[35] The wise and secret heart of Yahweh would continue to be used as proof of his cosmic supremacy. Among the Dead Sea Scrolls, an unusual version of the book of Psalms was found to contain a hymn celebrating the creation of the cosmos by a notably corporeal Yahweh, equipped with a knowing heart: 'Kindness and truth are around his face, truth, uprightness and justice are at the base of his throne. He separated light from darkness, the dawn he established with the knowledge of his heart. Then all his angels saw and sang, for he showed them what they had not known'.[36]

It was the emphatically exclusive character of divine wisdom that had always distinguished it from the wisdom of mortals. While the wisest men of the legendary past – like Solomon – might have amassed the specialist knowledge of earthly wisdom beyond bounds, their wise hearts were by no means akin to those of the gods. And to assume otherwise was deadly. In the sixth century BCE, this is exactly what Yahweh tells an anonymous king in the book of Ezekiel. In a sharp-tongued attack, he condemns to death the king who is so wise of heart he presumes himself a god, and claims Yahweh's throne as his own:

You have said 'I am a god;
I sit in the seat of the gods . . .'
. . . Because you compare your heart
with the heart of a god,
I will therefore bring strangers against you,
the most terrible of the nations . . .
They shall thrust you down to the Pit,
and you shall die a violent death.
Will you still say, 'I am a god',
in the presence of those who kill you?[37]

Spitting with sarcasm, this stinging oracle draws on a much older, possibly pre-biblical myth about the privileged ritual ascent of a king into the heavenly sphere, from where he can be expelled by divine decree should he offend the gods. Further features of the myth are found in a second, closely related oracle in Ezekiel, in which the source of the king's wisdom is indeed revealed to be none other than the heavenly realm: 'You were in Eden, the garden of the gods', Yahweh says to him, 'full of wisdom and perfect in beauty'.[38] These qualities are represented by the divinatory breastplate – elsewhere associated with the high priest – covering the king's chest. But the breastplate serves its purpose, revealing that the king's wise heart has become fatally tarnished: 'Your heart was proud because of your beauty, you corrupted your wisdom because of your splendour'.[39] He is cast out of Eden and into the earthly realm, where he is killed and consigned to the underworld. The lesson in these oracles is as transparent as the fallen king's heart: wisdom and immortality are defining characteristics of divinity, and no mortal should seek or claim to possess both.

A century or so later, in the fifth century BCE, the myth was again reworked, this time into its better-known form, now found in the story of Eden in Genesis 2–3. In this version, the privileged king of old has been replaced by the primal man, Adam.[40] But wisdom is deliberately kept from him and his wife while they dwell in God's garden; it is held at arm's reach, locked within the fruit of the tree 'desired to make one wise' – the tree of the knowledge of good and evil. A mysterious, second tree in the garden holds in its fruits the potential to live forever.

Both trees are strictly off-limits. But it is a divine prohibition the man and woman famously ignore. Eating from the first tree, they consume wisdom and become 'like gods'. Fearing they will now eat from the other tree and taste the fruit of immortality, God expels them from the heavenly garden to a life of earthly mortality.[41] It is a story so well known that it often goes unnoticed that stealing wisdom is not the only crime committed in Eden. Adam and Eve are also guilty of illegally consuming sacred food – carefully cultivated produce that is not to be eaten by humans, but is to be set apart for the gods. This was as serious a misdemeanour as disobedience, and the resulting punishment fits the crime. With visceral precision, God targets the bellies of Eden's criminals: the man will have to work unyielding, cursed earth to fill his stomach, rather than tending the divinely fertile garden; the woman will feel pain in her abdomen in birthing children, but a perpetual appetite for her husband in her loins; deprived of his wings (not his legs),* the serpent will be forced to crawl on the ground on his belly, swallowing dust as he goes.[42] It was common knowledge across ancient south-west Asia that when it came to their food, the gods could be ferociously possessive, exceptionally picky and woefully unforgiving of any culinary calamities. The God of the Bible was no different.

---

* Eden's serpent is best understood as one of the seraphim – the winged, guardian serpents who fly about the divine throne in Isaiah 6.1–8.

11

FROM BELLY TO BOWEL

As dusk descends on Mount Gerizim, one of two peaks overlooking the West Bank city of Nablus, a noisy procession makes its way from a village to an open-air enclosure on the summit. Priests and elders clad in brightly coloured robes are accompanied along the dusty track by men and boys singing and chanting, dressed head to toe in white, some wearing matching baseball caps and welly boots. Shaggy-haired, startled-looking lambs are carried on their shoulders, or half-led, half-dragged to the mountaintop amid the excited swarm of human bodies. Women are singing, too, clutching children and iPhones while they follow the procession. Everyone crowds into the enclosure. Behind camera crews, security guards and a high wire fence, tourists stand on an embankment, watching and waiting. Expectation is in the air, along with the smell of burning wood, carried by smoke billowing from cylindrical fire pits dug deep into the earth. As night falls, the high priest mounts a podium and takes the microphone. Addressing the crowd with age-old prayers, he switches smoothly between ancient forms of Hebrew, Aramaic and modern Arabic. As he finishes, he raises his staff. Large knives flash into view. The lambs' throats are cut. With clapping and jumping, cheers and chants rise up, and the singing begins again. The hot blood of the lambs is smeared on the foreheads of firstborn males there and then, and on doorposts in the village later. The dead lambs are suspended from large metal frames, where they are quickly fleeced, inspected for blemishes and disembowelled. Blood glistens on the hands and arms of the slaughterers, and stains their white tunics a deep crimson. The lambs' innards are carefully burned away on a large grill over a trough of fire, while their carcasses are salted, skewered on long wooden spits and carried to the fire pits. Head first, they are plunged into the smoky depths, and sealed in with a metal grate covered with branches, damp earth and canvas. Later, the roasted meat will be distributed to the worshippers, accompanied by unleavened bread and bitter herbs. This is Passover, Samaritan style.

The Samaritans, as they are known to the outside world, are one of the oldest and longest-lived religious communities in the Middle East. They are also the smallest, numbering only about 750 members, all of whom are related by blood or marriage. Having relocated from Nablus (ancient Shechem) during the First Intifada (1987–93), half the community now lives in the village of Luza on Mount Gerizim, while the other half is to be found in a long-established community in Holon, now a suburb of Tel Aviv. Like their Jewish neighbours, the Samaritans worship Yahweh as the ancient 'God of Israel', and name the biblical Jacob as their ancestor. They too keep Shabbat, circumcise their sons, gather in synagogues, celebrate Pesach (Passover), Shavuot, Yom Kippur and Sukkot, and venerate the Torah as divine teaching. But they also claim to be the true Israelites – the name by which they refer to themselves – who have endured in a land beset by repeated conflict, conquest, displacement and occupation, to worship on the sacred mountain first chosen by the Israelites' God upon their entry into the Promised Land, long before his 'illegitimate' temple in Jerusalem was ever built. The Samaritans believe themselves to be the direct descendants of the tribes of Levi, Ephraim and Manasseh, countering the Jewish tradition that Ephraim and Manasseh were among the 'lost' tribes of Israel, who were deported to Mesopotamia in the late eighth century BCE when Assyria defeated the northern kingdom of Israel and destroyed its capital, Samaria.[1]

Although tiny in number, the Samaritans can do what modern Jews cannot: they can sacrifice animals, as God commanded. It is a practice Jewish worshippers have been unable to undertake since the Roman destruction of the Jerusalem temple in 70 CE. As the only place in which mainstream Judaism has traditionally permitted the ritual offering of animals, the loss of the temple quickly rendered Jewish Pesach a sacrifice-free, domestic festival – notwithstanding recent scandalous attempts by religious activists to slaughter lambs on Temple Mount. In both the Samaritan and Jewish Torah, the Pesach sacrifice is an offering to Yahweh combined with a rushed ritual meal, commemorating the haste of the Israelite exodus from Egypt. The blood of the lambs daubed on the doorposts of homes served to protect the Israelite firstborns from the deadly presence of Yahweh and his supernatural envoy ('the Destroyer'), who 'passed over' Egypt to kill the firstborn sons of the enemy, terrifying a grief-stricken Pharaoh into allowing the Israelites to leave.[2] Historically, however, the origins of this sacrifice are very different.

As attested in most human cultures, food and drink are powerful carriers of religious experience – experiences directly related to the social function of food and drink as makers and conveyors of meaning. This meaning derives not only from the essential role of eating and drinking for our physical well-being and survival, but from the very transience of the food we eat and the liquids we drink. Of all human activities of production, the cultivation, processing and consumption of food is perhaps the most remarkable: no other material product is created as intensively for the precise purpose of being destroyed. This renders food and drink inherently suited to playing a role in rituals expressing both a community's cultural values and its social relationships – including its ties to any ancestors, gods, or spirits who might shape its world. When a community eats together, group identities are fed and nourished by food and drink.[3] Against this backdrop, the sacrificial offering of domestic animals is an especially powerful ritual act. In Samaritanism, Judaism and Christianity, the Passover meal is the central act of an ancient scriptural story articulating a distinctive community identity. But at its heart is a much older agricultural celebration of firstborn animals, in which a community's deities were given their portion of the flocks and herds they had rendered fertile. In a pastoral-agrarian economy, in which ordinary families depended on domesticated animals primarily for their wool, hides, milk, dung and traction power, the slaughter of a young animal for meat was infrequent enough as to be rendered sacred. Accordingly, meat was a delicacy for most people, and was naturally to be shared with the gods who sustained the flocks and herds.[4] Eating together, worshippers and gods were bound together socially, creating and maintaining ties forged on reciprocal hospitality.

The close interrelation of agricultural productivity and divine consumption was written into the earliest south-west Asian stories about the origins of mortals. Humans were created in order to feed the gods – not only with meat, but with the other foodstuffs they and their worshippers also enjoyed eating, including bread, fruit, grain, oil, honey, beer and wine. Provisioning the gods with their daily meals was not to suggest divine weakness or dependency. After all, deities were perfectly capable of feeding themselves. Myths often describe them preparing and sharing meals of bread and wine, sacrificing and eating animals, holding ceremonial feasts and throwing drinking parties – all of which bound them together as an extended heavenly household. But the mortal duty to feed the gods was considered essential to the flourishing of cosmic order.

One of the oldest narratives describing this ordered cosmos is crafted not in words, but in images and symbols. The metre-high Uruk Vase was made for the Sumerian goddess Inanna in about 3100 BCE. It was smashed during the looting of the National Museum in Baghdad at the beginning of the Iraq War in 2003, but has since been returned and restored. This stunning alabaster vessel presents a coherent portrait of the inextricable bonds between agricultural fertility, human endeavour and the worship of the gods. Circling its lowest register are fertile waters, from which ordered rows of barley spring; above them, male and female sheep and goats file dutifully around the vase. In the middle register, the fruits of agricultural plenty are borne aloft in baskets and jugs by nude male priests in a ritual procession. Their destination is depicted on the top register, where an elite female – either the goddess or her human representative – stands in Inanna's temple, surrounded by goats, jugs and baskets overflowing with food (fig. 26).

In Sumerian mythology, the job of feeding the gods was a role initially performed by lower-tier deities, who were tasked with baking bread for the high gods, filling their tables with food, and digging out canals to irrigate fields and transport their crops. When the high god

Fig. 26. Dated to about 3100 BCE, this magnificent alabaster vessel was unearthed in Inanna's sanctuary in Uruk. On the top register, the goddess (or her human representative) accepts one of many offerings from a procession of priests, who carry baskets piled high with the bounty of the earth, manifested by the animals and crops circling the lower registers. Unseen in this photograph are the overflowing baskets and jugs already amassed in Inanna's temple.

Enki is told that they are 'complaining about their life', smashing up
their tools and blaming him for their miserable fate, he devises a way
to call a halt to the unrest. He engages the mother goddess Nammu
and her assistant birth goddesses to shape new life from wet clay.
Mortals are made, and the burden of feeding the gods is imposed on
them.[5] A similar innovation to alleviate the divine workload is attributed to the god Marduk in the Babylonian epic Enuma Elish. 'I shall
compact blood, I shall cause bones to be, I shall make stand a human
being, let "Man" be its name', he declares. 'I shall create humankind,
they shall bear the gods' burden that those may rest'.[6] But to be a
creature of the gods, and to take on their labour, was to be regarded
as a cosmic privilege. The primal human was a prototype of the king,
divinely appointed to shepherd the rest of humanity and ensure the
gods were brought food offerings. In the temple cults of Mesopotamia,
the king was accordingly known as the 'gardener of the gods'; he
oversaw the purity of temples, the fullness of their animal pens, grain
silos, oil presses and wine stores, and ritually tended to the sacred trees
within their precincts.[7]

Echoes of this mortal – and royal – privilege can be detected in
the myths of human and agricultural origins in the Bible. Like his older
divine colleagues across Mesopotamia, Yahweh was well able to cultivate land and grow food himself. And according to Genesis 2, this is
exactly what he did: when 'there was no man to till the soil', Yahweh
planted a garden in Eden, created waterways to irrigate it, and 'made
to grow every tree that is pleasant to the sight and good for food' –
including the two trees set apart for him, which stood at its centre. But
the upkeep of the garden was not work with which God needed to
occupy himself every day. (After all, this was a deity who would elsewhere declare that he liked a day's rest at the end of a busy week.) And
so the first man is created from clay for a very specific purpose:
'Yahweh-God took the man and put him in the Garden of Eden to till
it and to care for it'. Like a king, the primal man is appointed the
gardener of God.

Although Yahweh is not said to receive sacrifices in Eden, the divine
expectation for food is quickly met by Eve's first sons, Cain and Abel,
in Genesis 4. Abel is described as 'a keeper of sheep', and Cain as 'a

tiller of the ground', and they each offer Yahweh a portion of their produce. Abel's lambs are favourably received. But Cain's crops are rejected. His culinary faux pas triggers his second – more infamous – crime: the murder of his brother, whose blood screams out to God as it seeps into the ground and down to the underworld. Like Adam, Cain is sent away from Yahweh's presence, and away from the soil he tills, to scratch an existence from the uncultivated, unyielding dust at the ends of the earth.[8] Readers often suppose a theological preference for blood sacrifice underlies God's distaste for Cain's meat-free option. But this is to misunderstand the cultural climate in which these myths were cultivated – and betrays a common misunderstanding of sacrifice only as ritual killing. Across ancient south-west Asia, most foodstuffs consumed by humans were potential sacrificial offerings, whether animal, cereal, vegetable, fruit, or liquid. But the apportioning of the sacrifice was crucial. God looks with displeasure upon Cain's offering not because crops were inherently inferior to livestock as sacrifices, but because Cain neglects to offer the distinctively sacred portion conventionally set apart for divine consumption – the 'first fruits' of the harvest. He sacrifices what is described only as 'the fruit of the ground'. By contrast, Abel sacrifices the cream of his crop: 'the firstlings of his flock, their fatty parts'.[9] As the first to open the womb, these animals were of the highest cultural and religious value, and so naturally belonged to Yahweh. The pieces he particularly liked were their 'fatty parts' – the succulent slipperiness coating the intestines, kidneys and liver, plus the spongy thickness of the lamb's tail.

Yahweh's preference for particular portions was not only a matter of divine taste, but a mark of godly distinction. Like other rituals, sacrifice was far from a symbolic gesture. It was a loaded, magical performance in which imagined realities about the world were brought into being, enacted, and endorsed by all its participants, the gods included. Setting apart – rendering sacred – certain portions for the deity drew an important distinction between a god and a mortal. Both ate, and in the cult place they ate together, but the exclusive allocation of the firstborn, first fruits and fatty parts to the deity drew on the essential primacy of food to materialize and mark the fundamental difference between gods and mortals – the difference between who

1. Divine footprints, almost a metre long, at an Iron Age temple in 'Ain Dara, north-western Syria. The imprint of another footstep was carved into the floor of the inner sanctum, located at the top of the steps. The remains of this remarkable temple were destroyed in an airstrike in 2018.

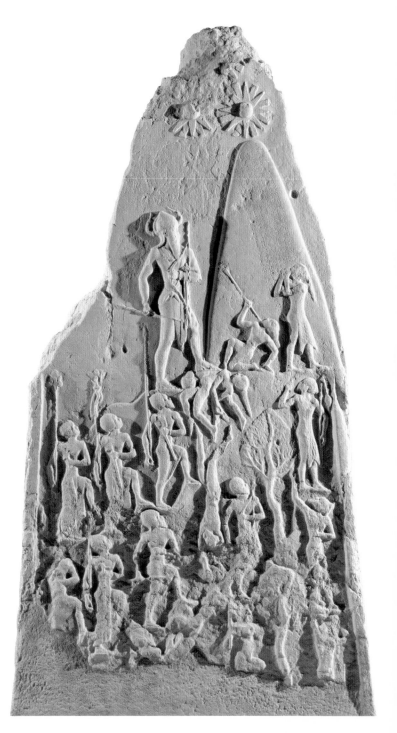

2. Godlike in both stature and dress, Naram-Sin tramples his enemies as he strides towards a tall mountain, its peak reaching into the heavens. Worn inscriptions on the monument indicate it was set up in Sippar in about 2250 BCE, but captured by an Elamite king and taken to Susa in 1158 BCE.

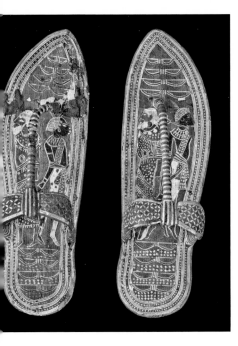

3. A pair of Tutankhamun's ceremonial sandals, manifesting the king's power to trample his opponents. Using conventional visual motifs, the insoles depict the trussed-up bodies of Egypt's traditionally 'foreign' enemies, framed top and bottom by their disabled war bows.

A god from the city of Hazor, wearing edged sandals. Dated to the fourteenth century BCE, this deity is thought to be or Baal. The tabs in the figurine's base suggest it was once fixed to a throne.

5. Moses removes his sandals at the burning bush. In front of him is the commanding hand of God. This glittering sixth-century CE mosaic is one of two depictions of Moses framing the triumphal arch in the basilica in St Catherine's Monastery, Sinai.

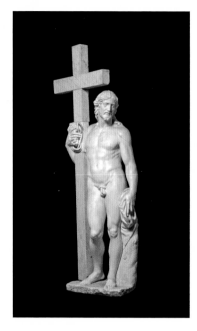

7. A sixth-century CE mosaic in the Arian Baptistery, Ravenna, depicting the baptism of Christ. Flanked by John Baptist and the god of the Jordan Rive Jesus' nudity embodies the childlike innocence of those transformed by th baptismal bestowal of the Spirit, represented by the descending dove.

6. Michelangelo's first attempt at the *Risen Christ*, rediscovered by the art world in 1997 in a monastery sacristy in Bassano Romano, Italy. The second version stands in the Church of Santa Maria sopra Minerva, Rome, where a bronze loincloth was fixed to the statue in 1546.

8. Mary cradles the corpse of a muscular Christ, whose penis swells beneath his loincloth, promising his restoration to life. Dated to the early sixteenth century, the painting is usually attributed to Willem Key.

9. A Ludwig Krug engraving of Christ as the Man of Sorrows, *c.* 1510–1532. Seated between Mary and the apostle John, Christ's open seeing eyes and prominent erectior prefigure his resurrection.

0. Terracotta plaque figurine of goddess, *c.* 1250 BCE. Discovered excavations near Kibbutz Revadim, Israel, she is usually identified as the Levantine high goddess known Yahweh worshippers as Asherah. Holding open her labia, she has babies at her breasts and sacred-tree motifs on her thighs.

11. Goddess and temple imagery abound on this tenth-century BCE ritual object from Taanach, Israel. On the bottom tier, the goddess appears in anthropomorphic form, flanked by lions. Above her, the entrance to a temple is guarded by cherubim. Above that stands the goddess's sacred tree, framed by caprids and lions. The top tier enshrines a sun disc, pedestalled on a horse or bull calf.

12. Christ enthroned on a rainbow within a bright aureole. Dated to the early fifth centu
this mosaic in the Church of Hosios David, Thessaloniki, draws on biblical portrayal
God's bodily radiance to present the Son of God as the likeness of his Father.

13. The early Chris
colour-coding of evil
as 'darkness' and 'blac
would play an increa
prominent theologic
in the Western other
people with black s
Illustrating the biblica
of Jesus' exorcism o
Gadarenes, this mini
from the twelfth-cent
Canterbury Psalter ra
the demon-possesse
black African men,
Christ as a white Eur

14. Huwawa (Humbaba) simultaneously provoked and embodied the fear felt in the innards. Images of his gut-filled face were used as protective amulets and haruspicy tools across Mesopotamia. Made c. 1800–1600 BCE, this example from Sippar bears an inscription on its reverse, written by a diviner called Warad-Marduk.

15. Now housed in Jerusalem's Israel Museum, this divine hand once reached into an eighth-century BCE tomb complex at Khirbet el-Qom, in the West Bank. A worn inscription running above petitions Yahweh and Asherah to bless and protect a certain Uriyahu in his tomb.

16. The high god El, holding up his right hand in a gesture of blessing. Fixture holes in the sides of his head indicate he was once endowed with bull horns. This late-fourteenth-century BCE bronze statue, covered in gold, is from Ugarit.

17. God's long arms parting the sea during the exodus from Egypt.
With one hand he casts Egyptians into the waters (right); with the other, he ushers the armed Israelites across the seabed (left). In the foreground, Moses appears twice, acting as God's agent. Detail from the frescos adorning the third-century CE synagogue in Dura Europos, Syria.

18. God's hand seizes Ezekiel by his hair and carries him to a cemetery in a Babylonian valley. Here, the deity's hands reassemble the disarticulated corpses of his exiles, who will be restored to life. Detail from the third-century CE synagogue frescos in Dura Europos, Syria.

19. A page from the Old English Hexateuch (eleventh century CE), depicting Moses' last day. Having delivered his farewell address (bottom), God permits him to see the Promised Land before he dies (top right). God then buries Moses on the mountaintop (top left) while the Israelites mourn.

Above left 20. A Sumerian figurine of a worshipper, his eyes wide and hands clasped in perpetual petition. Dated to about 2900–2300 BCE, this alabaster votive had been carefully repaired several times in antiquity.

Top right 21. This plastered skull from Jericho is about nine and a half thousand years old. Micro-CT scanning revealed that this individual's head had been tightly bound in infancy. Following his death, his denuded skull was given a new plaster face, complete with shell eyes. The skull became a type of being distinct from both the living and the dead.

Above right 22. The 'Lady of Uruk'. This beautiful marble face once topped the cult statue of a goddess in Uruk – probably Inanna, in whose temple complex it was found. Dated to about 3100 BCE, her lapis lazuli brows, inlay eyes and hair pieces have since been lost.

24. Minted in or around Persian-era Judah (Yehud) in the fourth century BCE, this silver coin shows a high god enthroned on a winged chariot-wheel. While the coin adapts divine motifs common across the western Persian empire and eastern Mediterranean, the deity was likely identified as Yahweh.

Fragment of an enthroned god from c. 1850–1750 BCE. With his vibrant red n and beautifully groomed dark beard, e deity embodies an idealized, hyper- sculine beauty vaunted across ancient south-west Asian cultures.

Inscribed with appeals for Yahweh's blessing and protection, these tiny ver scrolls were originally rolled up and worn on the body as amulets. ated to the late seventh century BCE, ney were discovered in a network of ombs at Ketef Hinnom, Jerusalem.

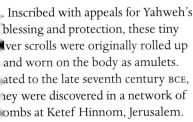

26. A gold amulet bearing the image of a high goddess, her attentive face framed by the caprids she holds in her hands. Against a starry backdrop, serpents appear at her waist, and she is positioned atop a lion. Dated c. 1450–1365 BCE, this striking object was found in excavations at Ugarit's port, Minet el-Beida.

27. Adopting the pose of a teacher or orator, Christ sits among his disciples or stude
His portrayal as a short-haired, beard-free beauty is typical of early Christian art. Dat
the fourth century CE, this fresco appears in the Catacomb of Domitilla, Rome.

28. An early portrayal of Christ as *Pantokrator*, the 'all powerful' ruler of the
cosmos, in the Church of Santa Pudenziana, Rome. Dated to the end of the fourt
century CE, this sumptuous mosaic depicts Christ as a Mediterranean high god, equip
with a thick beard and shimmering robes.

29. Adam's creation 'in the image of God' is reflected in this scene on a fourth-century CE Roman sarcophagus. Here, the faces of God and the first man are deliberately alike [...]. On the other side of Eden's tree, standing next to Eve, a youthful Christ performs miracles indexing the wonders of a paradisiacal afterlife (right).

30. This remarkable portrayal of the Trinity (left) appears on a fourth-century CE Roman sarcophagus. Overseeing the creation of Eve, God the Father sits enthroned, God the Son rests his hand on a child-sized Eve, pulled from the body of a tiny, sleeping Adam. Behind the divine throne, God the Holy Spirit looks on. All three members of the Trinity share the same facial features.

31. Christ is the white-haired Ancient of Days on this late-sixth-century CE icon from
St Catherine's Monastery, Sinai. The name Emmanuel ('God with us') hovers about h
while the frame bears a votive dedication: 'For the salvation and pardon of
the sins of your servant Philochristos'.

32. An aged, pot-bellied Christ sits enthroned as the Ancient of Days, flanked by Peter and Paul. Detail from a fifth- or sixth-century CE ivory panel, likely once part of a diptych, and later recycled as a Gospel book cover.

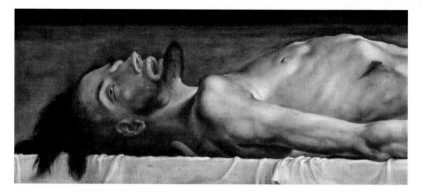

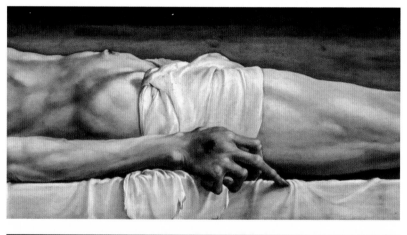

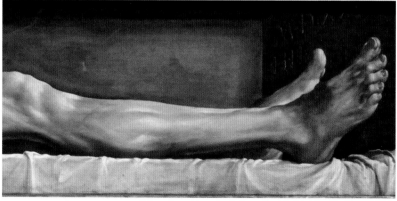

33. Christ's rotting corpse in Holbein's *The Body of the Dead Christ in the Tomb* (1521). The gulf between the divine body and the human body could not be wider.

was a god, and who was not.[10] To consume sacred food without divine permission (like Adam and Eve), or to serve the wrong portion of food (like Cain), was to neglect this carefully constructed distinction, and throw the world into disarray by dishonouring the divine.

It had long been known that the way to any deity's changeable heart (or 'mind') was through the stomach. As one Hittite priest put it, in the thirteenth century BCE, 'Is the mind of man and those of the gods somehow different? No! The mind is indeed one and the same . . . [the priest] gives his master something to eat or he gives him something to drink. And since he, his master, eats and drinks, he is of a tranquil state, and he is therefore attached to him'.[11] Like mortals, the gods took great sensory pleasure in eating and drinking. In addition to quenching their thirsts and filling their bellies, deities enjoyed the taste and texture of good food and drink: sacrificial meat is frequently praised as succulent and tender; sacred wine is sweet, spiced, or smooth; bread and grain is pleasingly salted. But it was the smell of roasting flesh, and the fragrant seasoning of incense, that whetted divine appetites, drawing the gods to the altar – and into a social relationship with the worshipper. A mythic precedent for this was to be found in the great flood stories circulating ancient south-west Asia, in which the broken bond between the gods and humanity was restored after the deluge by a sacrifice of ark animals offered by the flood hero. In a Mesopotamian version, dated to the eighteenth century BCE, the fabled Atrahasis is cast in the lead role. His offering proves irresistible to the gods, who 'smell the fragrance' and 'gather like flies around the sacrifice' before sitting down to eat with him. A later version in the Epic of Gilgamesh names the hero as Utnapishtim, who adds aromatic incense to his post-diluvial sacrifice. Again, the gods 'gather like flies', but this time they swarm about the 'one who had made the sacrifice', emphasizing the social function of the feast.[12] A millennium or so later, in the book of Genesis, it is Noah who emerges from the ark to offer a grateful sacrifice. The smoky scent of animal sacrifice not only draws God to Noah's newly built altar, but triggers his change of heart towards all mortal creatures: 'When Yahweh smelled the pleasing odour, Yahweh said in his heart, "I will never again curse the ground because of humankind . . . nor will I ever again destroy every living creature"'.[13] The sensory pleasures of sacrifice bring the deity into a binding relationship with all life in the earthly realm.

Divine Dining

It is no surprise to find that meat heavily flavours most biblical accounts of sacrifices offered to Yahweh. In the Jerusalem temple, the altar was sprinkled and smeared with the blood of sacrificial animals, cleansing Yahweh's dining table before he ate, while the 'pleasing odour' of their roasting flesh alerted the busy deity to mealtimes. Pork, of course, was off the menu – not because it harboured potentially deadly bacteria, as is often supposed, but because the pig tended to be regarded as a dangerously liminal animal. With the feet of a cud-eater, the diet of a scavenger, the habits of a dirt-dweller and the cunning of a human, it exhibited an unsettling combination of characteristics, rendering it culturally inedible for some (but not all) southern Levantine peoples, for whom pigs were often associated with the underworld or malevolent supernatural powers.[14] But there was plenty of other meat for Yahweh to enjoy. Twice a day, he consumed at least one roast lamb or goat, along with braised birds, breads and cakes, seasonal fruit and grain, flour mixed with oil, and several jugs of wine and beer. Additional snacks – a bird, a basket of fruit, bread or a cake – were brought to the temple by worshippers, who might be offering thanks to the deity, hoping for a special blessing, or seeking divine forgiveness. Once a week, on Shabbat, Yahweh's daily portions were doubled and supplemented with twelve loaves of bread, which were served on a special offering table dressed with a tablecloth, a seven-branched candelabra and fine dinnerware.[15] Special occasions, monthly feast-days and annual festivals offered the deity a welcome opportunity to binge. On the new moon, Yahweh ate two roast bulls, a ram and seven lambs, plus the usual trimmings of flour, oil and wine, with a goat for afters. During the week-long harvest festival of Sukkot, the deity consumed a total of 71 bulls, 15 rams, 105 lambs and a goat. A yearly festival commemorating the construction of the Jerusalem temple is said to have ncluded Yahweh and his worshippers gorging themselves on 22,000 oxen and 120,000 sheep in a fortnight.[16]

Within the religious imagination, the excessive nature of divine dining reflected the enormous size of God's body, so that his huge appetite matched his gigantic frame. In practice, however, the ritual menus of the Jerusalem temple were far more modest than the biblical writers would allow. After all, the sheer scale and expense demanded of some biblical sacrifices, and the logistics of managing such copious volumes of blood, flesh, dung and bones, would have been wildly impractical and wholly improbable. But behind the Bible's sacrificial texts were elitist, urban writers who were naturally regurgitating the ideological tastes of their social circles, in which conspicuous consumption (and its associated rhetoric) played a crucial role in the theatre of religious, economic and political performance. Whether big or small, the spectacle of sacrifice and feasting with the patron deities of cities and states communicated the status, power, wealth and provision on which all ancient south-west Asian kings and priesthoods relied.[17] Onto this temple-centric view of the world religious specialists mapped a spatial framework of an ordered cosmos. The temple altar not only served as the dining table around which God and favoured mortals shared food, but it was the centrepiece of the ordered, built environment managed by city-dwelling elites. Surrounding the urban centre were the fertile, cultivated soils of the villages and farmsteads that fed the deity and his worshippers in the city. At the edges of the fertile world were the dry expanses of the unworked, dangerous wilderness. And beyond that were the raging waters of disruptive disorder. All members of society, mortal and divine, were placed within this framework, from its privileged centre to its dreaded margins. Firmly fixed at the core of the cosmos, temple sacrifice fed not only the deity, but the political appetites of elites.

The God of the Bible was well aware of the ideological dynamics of sacrifice, and quick to chastise those making offerings for the sake of their own reputations, rather than his. 'What to me is the multitude of your sacrifices?' bellows an exasperated Yahweh in the book of Isaiah. 'I've had enough of burnt offerings of rams, and the fat of fed beasts; I do not delight in the blood of bulls, or lambs, or goats . . .

trample my temple-courts no more!' He goes even further in the book of Amos: 'I hate, I despise your festivals! I take no delight in your solemn assemblies! Even though you offer me your burnt offerings and grain offerings, I will not accept them; the well-being-offerings of your fatted animals I will not look upon'.[18] These oracles, dated to about the eighth century BCE, would eventually come to fuel an unpleasant Christian history of anti-ritual rhetoric, attacking first the 'superstitious' practices of Judaism, and later, for Protestants, the 'idolatry' of traditional Roman Catholicism. But in their ancient, biblical contexts, the divine rejection of sacrifice in these and similar oracles was not a wholesale rejection of food offerings. It was a pointed critique of wealthy urbanites, whose self-centred, grandiose sacrifices had become empty gestures, fuelled by the economic exploitation of the poor and the marginalized, on whose backs they had built their fortunes: 'Learn to do good! Seek justice! Rescue the oppressed, defend the orphan, plead for the widow!' Yahweh continues in the book of Isaiah. 'You trample on the poor, and take from them levies of grain . . . Seek good, and not evil!' he similarly cries in the book of Amos.[19]

The divine rejection of sacrifices was an age-old threat across ancient south-west Asia. Deities might decide to fast in mournful response to catastrophe, or they might punish religious and social transgressions by withdrawing from their worshippers. Withdrawal meant social dislocation: the gods abandoned their statues and temples, leaving their food un-smelled and untouched. Sometimes the rejection of a sacrifice was clear to see: a burnt offering refusing to flame, a loaf falling from a plate, spoiled fruit, spilled beer, or wine swimming with sediment. But more esoteric skills were required to spot the signs invisible to the untrained eye, for divine consumption was an inherently – inevitably – ambiguous process. Although all sacrificial food was offered to the gods, they ate only their portion; the deity's leftovers were divided between the priests, the sacrificial donor and the donor's household, who ate their share in the ordinary way in which humans do. But gods, of course, ate their sacrificial portions differently. Burning on the altar, their portion of fatty meat, oil, flour, or grain was engulfed by the radiance emanating from the divine body, and devoured by its fiery force. As the flaming food was transformed into scented smoke, it was further consumed by the gods as they inhaled its fragrant new form. Divine food was less toasted and roasted, than torched, scorched and burnt to a crisp.[20] But this was a process complicated by its more unpredictable aspects: the changing direction of the smoke's progress; the precise moment at which incinerated-food remains collapsed on the altar; the length of time an offering took to turn to ash. It thus fell to priests and seers to discern the difference between a rejected sacrifice and the mysterious mechanics of divine consumption.

Sharing the gods' meals in the cult place better enabled some religious specialists to perceive this information. As they are ingested, food and drink become embodied materials. Within religious contexts, this embodiment lends ritual comestibles a heightened significance and power: swallowing sacred substances temporarily transforms the body by incorporating something of the divine or holy within it.[21] It is a notion on which the Christian consumption of sanctified bread and wine rests – whether the ritual is taken to be a transubstantiation, substitution, or commemoration of the body and blood of Christ – which is itself a practice echoing something of the ingestion of sacred food in Yahweh's temple in Jerusalem. Here, the holiness of the deity's priests was not only maintained by an adherence to ritual distinctions between the sacred and the profane, but by the regular consumption of the god's food and drink. In the books of Exodus and Leviticus, sacrificial meat is to be eaten and enjoyed by priests because 'whatever touches its flesh shall become holy'.[22] Mortal holiness was not simply a social status, but a somatic state of being, enhancing or transforming the priest's religious perceptions. The same was true of other religious specialists, for whom the ingestion of divine matter functioned as oracular food, triggering visions and utterances. In the book of Jeremiah, the prophet's career as a diviner of visions begins when he eats the 'words' or 'things' Yahweh places in his mouth, while the prophet Ezekiel eats a honeyed scroll of oracles given to him by God so as to regurgitate its words to the people. Even in the hands of hated enemies, the contagious, oracular potency of sacred food clung to Yahweh's dinnerware. In the book of Daniel, Belshazzar of Babylon drinks from the vessels looted by King Nebuchadnezzar from the

Jerusalem temple, and experiences a vision of doom when he suddenly sees a heavenly hand writing words of destruction on the palace wall.[23] The transformative power of sacred food and drink enabled priests, prophets and other ritual specialists to perceive otherworldly realities more clearly: visions were seen, oracles were communicated and divine decisions were revealed.

Sacred alcohol was an especially effective agent of divination. Its psychoactive properties enhanced religious perception, freeing the body from the constraints of mortal control to be taken over by divine powers. The gods themselves were familiar with the ways in which beer and wine offered access to alternative realities, for they used alcohol as a means of transforming or transgressing their own cosmic rules of order to which they more usually adhered. A Sumerian myth tells of a drunken competition between the wise god Enki and the 'Lofty Lady' Ninmah, the top birth-goddess of the pantheon. Celebrating the creation of the first mortal, the two deities drink beer to the point of intoxicated elation, prompting Ninmah to boast that she has the power to decide the fate of humans, good or bad, because it is she who shapes the mortal form. In response, Enki wagers that no matter what kind of ill-fated mortal she creates, he will find it good fortune. The contest begins. Ninmah pinches off clay to create a range of humans whose bodies deviate from the paradigmatic human Enki has already devised. But each time, competitive, cunning Enki finds a good place for the new life in the world: the mortal unable to use his arms or hands is set on his feet to stand with honour next to the king; a man deprived of sight is to be a gifted musician; the mortal who is lame in the feet becomes a skilled artisan; the man afflicted with an ever-leaking penis is healed of his sickness; the woman unable to give birth is given a career in the royal household; the human created with neither male nor female sex organs is appointed chief courtier to the king. Enki then plays his winning hand: he creates a human form so helpless its fate can only remain uncertain. It is a newborn baby.[24]

If divine drunkenness enabled the gods to bring diversity and uncertainty to the human world, it also empowered them to turn their own world temporarily upside down by experiencing alternative states of being. In a fantastically vivid myth detailed on a clay tablet from fourteenth-century BCE Ugarit, the high deity El hosts a lavish feast for his pantheon in his temple. 'Eat, O gods, and drink! Drink wine until satiety, foaming wine until intoxication!' he commands. The dinner guests appear to do precisely this, and disorder ensues: the moon god Yarih, normally responsible for calendrical, ritual order, refills his wine goblet and drags it under the dinner table 'like a dog', where the goddesses Anat and Athtart gleefully treat him as such by throwing him choice cuts of sacrificial meat – much to the disapproval of the divine bouncer on the door, who yells at the goddesses, and then at El himself. But the party isn't over. El gathers his drinking companions and they move on to the next venue – an exclusive drinking club known as the *marzeah*, of which El was divine patron. There, it is said, 'he drank wine to satiety, new wine until intoxication'. It is time to go home. But as he 'stumbles off towards his dwelling', supported on either side by the junior deities Thukamun and Shanim, he is suddenly approached by 'a creeping monster', who has two horns and a tail. Scholars are uncertain as to the identity of this monster, but it is likely some sort of scorpion deity, charged with guarding the portal to the dangerous netherworld. It is into this other world that El passes, for the encounter prompts El to transgress taboos around divine contact with muck and filth as he loses complete control of his body:

> He floundered in his own faeces and urine,
> El fell down like a corpse;
> El was like those who go down into the underworld.

To the modern eye, this might read like a slop scene from a bawdy pantomime. But this is the language of myth. Dead drunk, El descends to the underworld – a realm constructed in such stark opposition to the heavenly plane that only the sun deity was permitted to pass through it safely each night. But in his intoxicated state, El undergoes a bodily transformation so intense he experiences an alternate reality: he transcends the boundary between the heavenly and netherworldly realms, his bodily excretions cloaking him with a protective disguise as he enters a dank world of mud and muck. His return from this state appears to have been facilitated by the earliest known use of the hair of the dog to cure a hangover – although its ingredients differ from the alcoholic versions with which we are more familiar today. Inscribed on the same clay tablet, the recipe calls for the hair of a dog and the knot of a vine shoot to be blended in virgin olive oil, and then rubbed on the patient's forehead. El is cured, and awakens. Sobriety and order are restored.[25]

Like his divine predecessor at Ugarit, the God of the Bible was well acquainted with the private drinking club known as the *marzeah*, for his own high-status worshippers were said to be its members. According to the book of Amos, these members are the wealthy urbanites of late eighth-century BCE Samaria, who 'drink wine from bowls and anoint themselves with the finest oils'; later, in the book of Jeremiah, they are the citizens of sixth-century BCE Jerusalem who share ritual meals with their deified ancestors in the underworld.[26] But not everyone approved of the use of alcoholic intoxication as a means of accessing otherworldly knowledge. 'The priest and the prophet reel with strong drink', an appalled seer declared at about the same time. 'They are confused with wine, they stagger with strong drink'. This loss of bodily control brings not divine revelation, he claims, but distorted religious perception: 'They err in vision, they stumble in giving judgement'. Worse still, their excessive drunkenness rendered the cult places in which they worked dangerously impure: 'All tables are covered with vomit and excrement; no sacred place is clean!'[27] As far as this seer was concerned, it was just one of many cultic corruptions to bring disaster upon Jerusalem in the sixth century BCE in the form of military invasion and destruction, orchestrated by God himself.

It was a view shared by other divinely inspired critics of the city's temple cult, whose visions would find their way into the texts of the Hebrew Bible. Yahweh no longer tolerated ritual intoxication among his temple personnel, they claimed. Instead, the divinatory wine he once shared with his elite worshippers would become a toxic cup of wrath, poisoning the temple community from the inside, leaving them unable to maintain the sanctity of God's house and unfit to defend against bullying empires. 'Drink, get drunk and vomit! Fall, but rise no more – because of the sword I'm sending you', Yahweh declares.[28] The cup would remain a stock feature of God's ritual arsenal of divine judgement, ever in hand, ready to be passed to those in the earthly realm as he saw fit. It is the cup he forces on his battered wife in the book of Ezekiel, commanding her to drink deep of shame. It is the cup he gives to the kings of enemy nations, forcing its scorching liquid down their throats. And in a place called Gethsemane, it is the cup a frightened Jesus of Nazareth begs God to remove as the darkness of night moves towards the day of his death.[29]

Divine Dirt

Sacred wine was not the only feature of ritual consumption to be weaponized by the God of the Bible. Sacrificial animals themselves would also be used against his own people. By the beginning of the fifth century BCE, the Jerusalem temple had been rebuilt. Yahweh had returned, his priesthood had been restored and divine dining in the sacred heart of the city had resumed. According to the book of Malachi, however, the new temple was beset with sacrificial irregularities. And Yahweh was furious. 'You have offered polluted food on my altar!' he bellows at his priests. 'You bring what has been taken by violence or is lame or sick, and this you bring as your offering! Shall I accept that from your hand? Cursed be the cheat who has a male in the flock and vows to give it, and yet sacrifices to the Lord what is blemished!'[30] Like any other economic establishment, a temple was not immune to corner-cutting and corruption. But the sacrifice of limping, mange-ridden animals was beyond unethical. It was physically repellent to Yahweh, triggering disgust so visceral that he would do unto others as was done unto him: 'I will smear shit on your faces – the shit of your festal animals'.[31] As far as Yahweh was concerned, blemished animals were not food at all, but the antimatter of consumption, equivalent to the stinking, inedible faeces expelled by the body. If his priests put this filth in his face, he would thrust shit into theirs.

God's earthy language – more usually sanitized as 'dung' or 'dirt' in translations – reflects the depth of his disgust and the foul physicality of his attack. It is a gut response to an inedible meal. And his decision to weaponize the dung of sacrificial animals underscores this. Whether dropped from their bodies or scooped from their butchered innards, the excrement of sacred animals was of a special status. Its association with the temple demanded its careful desacralization by means of ritual burning at a site in Jerusalem's Hinnom Valley, just beyond the city's inevitably named Dung Gate. Like any other form of excrement, the faeces of sacrificial animals were not inherently defiling. Some biblical texts instruct priests to burn the dung of sacrificed bulls and cows as an offering, while, in the everyday world, faeces of various forms (including human) were commonly used as a fertilizer and fuel. Even the dung beetle, complete with a ball of excrement between its claws, had been a sacred, solar emblem of the kingdom of Judah since at least the eighth century BCE. But excrement of any sort might trigger social and ritual anxieties if it was 'out of place', as the anthropologist Mary Douglas famously put it. It is God's deliberate displacement of faeces that renders his attack on his cult officials so shocking in its ancient cultural context: he transforms sacrificial scat into a priestly pollutant, forcing his priests' removal from the sanctuary, just like the muck with which they are covered.[32]

Contrary to common perceptions about biblical constructs of the divine, Yahweh of Jerusalem was not always averse to getting his hands (or feet) dirty. Nor was he unfamiliar with human excrement. As was usual in the Iron Age Levant, most urban households were not equipped with a privy or cesspit. People relieved themselves in alley-ways and stairwells, or walked through the city to use a communal cesspit or open sewer, often located just beyond the city walls. If they were caught short at home, some sort of chamber pot would be available, the contents of which would be thrown out into the street. Either way, defecation was often a public, rather than private activity, and everyone was unflappably familiar with the ever-present sight and smell of human excrement.[33] Even so, it was to be kept out of ritual space and away from the gods – unless the gods decided otherwise. Like other deities, the God of the Bible would often exhibit seemingly transgressive social behaviours and flout his own cultic regulations, whether to discipline and horrify others, or simply to demonstrate his godly ability to bend and transcend boundaries. In the Bible, he can be found ankle-deep in faeces as he tramples the Moabite enemies into a

vast dung-heap; he vows to dispose of the royal house of King Jeroboam I of Israel by clearing it away as he would household excrement;
after a military attack on Jerusalem, he washes the excrement and
blood from the traumatized, brutalized women of Zion.[34]

Given his apparent familiarity with human faeces, the temple
priests who ended up with a face full of filth should have counted
themselves lucky that the shit God spread was merely animal excrement. A century or so earlier, in the book of Nahum, he had deployed
faeces far fouler as a material and psychological weapon of warfare.
Nahum may be a small text, but its three short chapters are bloated
with the violence and brutality of Yahweh in his role as a divine warrior. Falsely claiming responsibility for the fall of the Assyrian city of
Nineveh in 612 BCE, the deity describes his assault on it as a sexual
attack on a woman – likely a thinly disguised manifestation of the
goddess Ishtar, the city's powerful patron. Wrenching her skirts over
her head, he displays her genitalia to onlooking nations and says, 'I will
throw shit all over you, and disfigure you, and make you a spectacle'.
Combined with graphic corporeal imagery, the excremental language
he uses strongly suggests that this is not animal dung.[35]

In behaving in this way, God was mimicking some of the more
concrete ways in which human aggressors sought to disempower other
people's deities and their urban centres. According to the books of
Kings, when King Jehu of Israel came to power, he not only tore down
a temple of Baal in the city of Samaria, but permanently desecrated its
holy ground by turning it into a public dung-heap.[36] It is a biblical story
with an astonishing archaeological parallel. In 2016, the Israel Antiquities Authority announced an extraordinary discovery at late eighth-
century BCE Lachish, one of the most important cities in the ancient
kingdom of Judah, besieged and destroyed by the Assyrians in about
701 BCE. A shrine had been found inside the city's six-chambered gateway, which served (like other city gates) as a ritual space in which
political, judicial and civic matters were managed under the watchful
eyes of the gods. Two large stone altars in the shrine had been desacral-
ized, while, in its holiest heart, a toilet seat had been installed. It was a
large block of stone, a sizable hole cut through its centre and bisected
at the front by a deep aperture well suited for a dangling, urinating penis

Fig. 27. The stone toilet seat found in a former shrine in a city gate at
Lachish. Dated to about 701 BCE, it appears to have been unused,
indicating it served as a ritual installation marking the shrine's
decommissioning or desecration.

(fig. 27). Chemical tests suggest that neither the toilet seat nor the
ground around it had been used for urination or defecation. This was
a magical installation, manifesting the deliberate desecration of the
shrine: the toilet not only invited impurity into its sacred space, but
effectively replaced its altars – the gods' own dining tables. It might as
well have been daubed with the slogan, 'Eat shit'. This was a high-status
desecration. Only the more affluent or powerful of elites enjoyed the
luxuries of a privy – a cesspit or basin, topped by a wooden frame or a
bore-holed stone seat, in a small room or enclosure. Lachish's gate
shrine had been decommissioned at the command of someone with
the wealth, authority and audacity to displace the city's gods, among
whom was a local version of Yahweh himself. The likely culprit is a
king – either Sennacherib of Assyria, who destroyed the city shortly
afterwards, or Jerusalem's own Hezekiah (as the shrine's excavators
propose), who is thought to have imposed a short-lived economic
measure during the Assyrian invasion to divert religious revenues to
Jerusalem by closing competing sanctuaries in his kingdom.[37]

The defiling power of human excrement turned not only on ritual
concerns about the purity of sacred space, but emotional responses to

faeces. In many cultures, including our own and those of Yahweh's ancient worshippers, what is most abject is simultaneously what is and is not the stuff of self. Our own faeces, vomit, urine and blood can manifest this abjection in the most corporeal and sensory of ways, so that in their excreted state, they can trigger disgust – in spite and because of the fact that they are and are not a part of us. Indeed, in the book of Ezekiel, it is this visceral disgust that the God of the Bible exhibits when he casts his own disobedient worshippers as shit, from whom he distances himself by expelling them from his temple and territory – much as the Promised Land had done when it 'vomited up' its 'abhorrent' indigenous inhabitants to make room for the incoming Israelites.[38]

While the biblical writers stop short at depicting their god as a defecating deity, it was far from an alien idea. These ancient thinkers were accustomed to drawing on scatology for their theology. Usually, however, it took the form of toilet humour as a means of mocking religious opponents. It is a tactic employed in a story in the books of Kings about the legendary prophet Elijah, who stages a competition between Yahweh and Baal in a time of drought to decide which deity is to be petitioned for fertile rains.[39] He invites all 450 prophets of Baal to the altar on top of Mount Carmel, where each deity is to be offered a bull – the high-status sacrificial animal beloved to both. The deity whose lightning ignites the pyre is to be declared the winner. Baal's prophets prepare the bull, arrange its butchered parts on the altar and, from morning to midday, cry out, 'O Baal, answer us!' But the god is absent. And his thunder stays silent. 'Shout in a loud voice – after all, he's a god!' Elijah taunts. 'Maybe he's on a journey, or he's asleep and must be awakened!' Or perhaps, the prophet suggests, Baal is answering a different sort of call: 'Maybe he's defecating!'[40] For Elijah, Baal is a hapless god, too busy straining at stool to attend to the needs of his worshippers. By contrast, Yahweh instantly responds to Elijah's offering. Fire falls from the heavens, consuming the sacrifice, wood and stones of the altar, and the ashes. It even licks up the water with which Elijah had confidently drenched the cult place. A downpour swiftly follows, breaking the drought. Yahweh has won.

By the end of the sixth century BCE, Yahweh of Jerusalem had apparently decided he could no longer tolerate other deities. His scribes intensified their excremental excoriation of his divine competitors, moving from scatological attacks to full-on faecal defamation. The smears stain biblical texts of this period: deities other than Yahweh become known as *gillulim* – 'shitgods'. This deliberately derogatory designation is usually rendered 'idols' in English (from the Greek Bible's *eidola*), but its more accurate translation reflects its derivation from a Hebrew term for excrement.[41] The Bible's shitgods are repeatedly described as man-made abominations. They are merely material lumps – whether of wood, metal, or stone. They are not responsive divine beings, but inanimate objects. Their materiality condemns them: they are reduced in name and essence to the basest form of matter, so that shitgods are rendered the waste of this world, rather than the holy host of heaven. Scholars often suppose this intense attack on cult statues in the sixth and fifth centuries BCE reflects a rejection of the traditional theology of divine bodies in favour of an increasingly immaterial, body-free God. But this was not the case. Shitgods and other divine statues were inferior to Yahweh not because they had bodies, but because they were dysfunctional and disabled. They were 'other gods made by human hands, objects of wood and stone that neither see, nor hear, nor eat, nor smell',[42] unlike the able-bodied, responsive God of the Bible, who had seeing eyes, hearing ears, a consuming mouth and an inhaling nose.

But shit sticks. And the association of faeces with the ungodly or unholy would become ever more pervasive among some religious literati, who spent much of their time reflecting and expanding upon the traditions of the Torah and the Prophets. By the first century CE, a Palestinian Jewish group known as the Essenes was said to be so stringent in honouring God's sacred time that they would avoid defecating on Shabbat. Any other day of the week, they would take themselves off to an isolated spot and carefully wrap their behinds in a garment while defecating, so that 'they may not affront the divine rays of light' of God's sight.[43] In the scrolls of the sect living near the western shore of the Dead Sea, the idealized city of God was portrayed as a place in which human defecation would be prohibited; citizens would have to walk at least 2,000 cubits (just over a kilometre) to desert cesspits housed in purpose-built, roofed enclosures.[44] These attitudes were considered extreme by other Jewish groups, for whom defecation was unproblematic unless it directly risked soiling sacred space or diminishing ritual activities. Accordingly, it was later said that, below the courtyard of the Jerusalem temple, there was a private toilet, screened by a door, for the benefit of the priests – along with a *mikveh* for ritual cleansing, should they experience a 'nocturnal emission' while on night duty.[45]

Even outside sacred space, the pious carefully regulated their toilet habits. Early rabbinic debates about a peculiar biblical verse gave rise to a series of regulations in antiquity about the correct deportment for excretion. In Ezekiel 8.16, God had complained about idolatrous worshippers facing away from him as they bowed down to the rising sun outside his temple in Jerusalem, raising their buttocks towards his house. God did not want to see backsides, whether clothed or exposed, the rabbis decided. Consequently, good Jews across and beyond Palestine were encouraged to orient their bodies in spatial relation to the Jerusalem temple when urinating or defecating – even though the building itself had been destroyed back in 70 CE. Assuming (of course) male anatomy, rabbis decreed that people were to turn their backs to the direction of the temple when urinating, shielding God from their penises, and face the direction of the temple when defecating, so as to hide their buttocks.[46] Some rabbis also encouraged the distancing of excrement from religious activities unrelated to sacred space. Personal prayers were not to be uttered in public spaces in which urination or defecation were common, and blessings were not to be said over the perfumes and oils used to fragrance the privies of those wealthy enough to have them. As the Roman Empire neared its end, purpose-built, communal public toilets and private lavatories were relatively more common in cities across south-west Asia, but they came with certain hazards. Along with cockroaches, flies and vermin, disruptive demons and disaffected ghosts were thought to lurk in toilets – especially at night – but warding off their dangerous presence was problematic. Many rabbis in Jewish communities across the empire commanded that the amulets and holy inscriptions ordinarily worn on the body to protect people from supernatural harm were not to be taken into privies, for fear of defiling their sacred forms. Hasty, pre-defecation rituals and noisy rattles might be used instead to scare off malevolent forces, but most relied on the presence of another to keep guard. One particularly nervous rabbi is said to have had a pet lamb trained to accompany him to the toilet, while another installed a small opening in the wall of his privy so that his wife could rest a comforting, protective hand on his head while he was in there.[47]

Ancient Jewish regulations about defecation were inextricably tied to theological distinctions between divinity and humanity. By the end of the first century CE, God had stopped eating with his worshippers. The Jerusalem temple had been destroyed, bringing an end to the sacrificial meals Yahweh had once enjoyed. Not that he missed or needed them, he apparently insisted. 'If I were hungry, I wouldn't tell you', he had once threatened, for 'the world and all that is in it is mine [to eat]'.[48] For those still mourning the loss of the temple and its sac-rifices, it was reassuring scriptural proof that God did not miss his daily barbecues. Henceforth, it was decided that he neither desired nor ate food. And if there was no food in heaven, there was certainly no excrement – of this, the ancient rabbis were now sure. By now, God's body was growing ever more distant and distinct from those of his worshippers, who naturally continued eating and excreting. And it was the very naturalness of defecation, early rabbis argued, that served to remind humans that they were earthly creatures akin to animals – and not gods. It was a religious perspective on the human body attributed to several important teachers, including Simeon ben Azzai, a Jewish sage of the second century CE: 'A human is beautiful and praiseworthy, and also casts out an ugly thing from his opening', he is reported to have said. 'If he were to cast out from his bowels foliatum or balsam or any sort of scented oil, how much the more would he exalt himself over the created beings!' For this sage, defecation was a daily humbling reminder of the raw and stinking realities of being human – no matter the divinely appointed, privileged position humans clearly enjoyed over other animals in the created earthly order.[49]

The need to defecate also served to distinguish humans from angels, by now a common feature of the heavenly realm. There was some debate as to whether angels – like God – had no need to eat (a notion encouraged by fleeting biblical references to divine messengers refusing food while on duty), or whether – unlike God – they ate only manna or the bread of heaven, which by this point was assumed to be a supernatural foodstuff, a little like the ambrosia of Greek gods, that was entirely absorbed by the body without triggering waste matter.[50] Either way, the rabbis decided, angels did not produce excrement, and had no need to defecate. But as faeces-free mediators between the heavenly and earthly realms, angels set a high bar for those privileged enough to enjoy direct interaction with God. Accordingly, there arose a series of rabbinic debates exploring the practicalities of Moses' meetings with God on Mount Sinai: Moses must have emptied his bowels before ascending to the summit to receive the Torah, it was said; he fasted for the forty days and nights he was there to avoid soiling sacred space, it was conjectured. In these ways, Moses attained and maintained the celestially somatic sanctity necessary to meet God and carry his holy commandments down to his worshippers below.[51]

If ancient Jewish teachers found themselves musing on the toilet habits of Moses, some early Christians were agonizing over the excretory activities of Christ. According to the Gospels, Jesus had made a point of eating and drinking with his followers – both before his death and after his resurrection. But missing from these stories was any clear steer from the Saviour as to whether or not he actually digested his food and defecated. For many in the earliest centuries of the faith, it was a worrying theological lacuna in their most authoritative religious texts. After all, this was a time in which Christian leaders of all stripes were fiercely debating the question of Christ's humanity and his relationship to God. Was he a mortal so pure he was granted divinity? Or was he an angelic being? Was he a divine being clothed in the body of a mortal? Or a human who sensed and suffered like others? Was he an offshoot of God? A second, lesser god? Or was he one and the same as God – as would eventually be doctrinally decreed? Whatever he was, the question of whether or not Christ digested and defecated was loaded with theological ramifications, for it impacted ideas about his 'true' nature. Most agreed that Christ ate and drank. This was important proof of his fleshy mortality, which was itself essential to his salvific death. But could God-as-Jesus really have had an ordinary body 'stuffed with excrement', as the second-century Christian thinker Marcion objected? Would digesting corruptible, decaying matter render Christ a 'shit-eating' god, as the philosopher Celsus scandalously observed?[52] For many, the idea that Christ's body might produce, contain and excrete faeces was either unbearable or nonsensical.

One way around the problem, as Clement of Alexandria saw it, was to suppose that Christ's body did not process food and drink in the usual way. Instead, Clement declared, it was sustained and nourished by the Holy Spirit; Christ ate and drank only to dispel future accusations that his perfect human body was a phantasm.[53] But this proved not to be a lasting solution to the problem of Christ's bowels. Liberating him from his digestive tract stripped him too clean of his humanity. Relatively short-lived, too, was the pious premise, echoed into the fourth century, that Christ's body was essentially and miraculously constipated. 'Jesus performed divinity: he ate and drank in his own way, without defecating', the highly influential second-century theologian Valentinus is reported to have written. 'Such was the power of self-control in him', Valentinus continued, 'that the nourishment in him did not become waste, since he did not possess corruption'.[54] This was not as extraordinary a suggestion as might be imagined. Valentinus was a highly educated Roman citizen who shared the widespread scientific view that the body's four elements (fire, earth, air and water), and their related qualities (hot, cold, dry and wet) and humours (blood, black bile, yellow bile and phlegm), could be perfectly balanced by disciplined self-control to keep it ticking over, rendering food-as-fuel and its resultant waste almost redundant. In a world in which the complete mastery of one's own body was celebrated as a superlative form of Graeco-Roman masculinity, digestive self-control was similarly attributed to other great men of the past, including Pythagoras and Epimenides.[55] Given Jesus' exemplary and enduring self-control, Valentinus seems to have reasoned, he had no need to excrete.

To the modern eye, the image of a Christ incapable of defecating is just as strange as the image of a Christ who does. This strangeness is due in part to the relative speed with which questions about Jesus' excrement quickly fossilized like coprolites. In 451 CE, an ecumenical council was convened at Chalcedon, in what is now Turkey, in yet another attempt to disentangle, once and for all, the knotty relationship between Christ's divinity and his humanity. The assembled Church leaders agreed that Christ was to be confessed as perfectly human, and purely divine. Anything else was heretical. But the very strangeness of a defecating deity also testifies to the success of those ancient Jewish and Christian thinkers early in the first millennium CE, who worked so hard to distance the divine from the dirty. The Jewish God abandoned his muck-raking, scat-slinging activities in favour of a cleaner, purified presence – with or without a temple – while Christ the man-god was delicately shrouded in a cloud of incarnational doctrine transcending probing questions. Ultimately, the divine body was sanitized of the controversies wrought by what was, after all, a human rather than godly anxiety about the most abject, stinking stuff of selfhood.

Part IV

ARMS AND HANDS

12

HANDEDNESS

The bodies were discovered in a heap in the dark and dirt of a collapsed tunnel. Sixteen, seventeen, maybe twenty dead. Rotted down to their bare bones, some were yellow with age, others charred black, or white as ash. One skull was split, exposing the remnants of its desiccated brain. Nuggets of iron mail, dislocated shield bosses and a jade-tipped sword hilt had fallen into empty ribcages. Lying amid a tangle of long thigh bones were leather purses, filled with coins. The dead had been paid, but they had clearly not been robbed. Instead, they had been piled up as a barricade, fresh in the flesh, and hurriedly abandoned. Their bones showed no signs of bludgeoning, hacking, or dismemberment. But in the tunnel, there were ample traces of sulphur crystals, bitumen and pitch. Death had come to this place not in bloody combat, but in the noxious cloud of a chemical attack.

In 256 CE, the eastern Syrian city known to some as Dura and to others as Europos had been braced for military assault. The city had been founded five centuries earlier, in about 300 BCE, as a small fortress settlement of the Seleucid Empire – one of the Hellenistic powers to emerge in the aftermath of the death of Alexander the Great. Strategically positioned on the western bank of the mighty Euphrates, Dura had quickly expanded in size and strength, becoming home to a culturally rich and diverse population drawn from across the eastern Mediterranean, Levant and Mesopotamia. It was an obvious target for competing regional powers seeking control of the busy, prosperous trade of the river. Within just a couple of centuries of its founding, the new city had been subjugated by the powerful Parthians, from what is now Iran, before falling to Rome under Lucius Verus (r. 161–9 CE) in the latter half of the second century CE. But a resurgent Persia was extending its territory westwards under the ambitious Sasanian dynasty, which had overthrown the Parthians and pushed ever onwards towards Roman territory. By 254 CE, they had already sacked Antioch. Now, two years later, the Sasanians had their sights on Dura.

The citizens readied themselves for the inevitable attack. Temples dedicated to deities of Greek, Syrian, Mesopotamian, Phoenician and Roman origin were carefully de-sanctified; homes were turned into munitions stores; treasures were hidden or removed as most of the city's wealthier inhabitants packed up and left, hoping to return once the enemy had been defeated – as it surely would. After all, the city sat at the edge of a steep cliff cut by the course of the river, and its northern and southern sides were hugged by deep wadis. The city's only vulnerability was its desert-facing western wall, but this had been shored up with a hastily built, thick mud-brick bank on its outer side, while the narrow lane, halls and houses on its other side had been filled, at great expense, by a deep-packed earthen rampart. As a crucial garrison guarding the trading waterway below, the city was also home to over three thousand Roman soldiers, crack troops of Syrians from nearby Palmyra, and a civilian militia, all tasked with maintaining control of this small pocket of the Roman Empire's eastern frontier. The city seemed inviolable. And yet, camped in the desert beyond its western gate, a Sasanian army was quite literally digging in.

Within a few short weeks, long low tunnels braced with timber had reached the city's western wall. Inside, small teams of Sasanian troops were hacking the large ashlar blocks into rubble, sapping the stone fortifications of their strength. On the other side of the wall, the Romans were burrowing too, hoping to capture their assailants and the tunnels. Beneath the wall, a Roman tunnel broke into a long narrow chamber from which a Sasanian tunnel descended into blackness. Crouching inside the chamber, a team of at least twenty Romans listened for the enemy. All was suspiciously quiet – until poisonous smoke rose up from below, prompting panicked, terrified cries as it filled the chamber. A few likely managed to scramble back into the city, but it was too late for the rest, who swiftly – horribly – choked to death. Below, the Sasanians had used bellows to fan the toxic fumes of burning sulphur and bitumen up into the chamber. Now, they waited for the screaming to stop and the smoke to clear, before climbing into the chamber. There, they hurriedly heaped the dead into a pile to block the inevitable Roman counter-attack, and scattered straw and scraps of linen laced with more sulphur and bitumen as they retreated, pausing only to set it alight as they reached the tunnel's exit.[1]

This chemical attack was just one of a number of coordinated assaults that would quickly overwhelm Dura. Abandoned and broken, the vibrant city disappeared into the dust of the desert for over a millennium and a half – until the impacted earth of those emergency mudbanks was carefully cut away by archaeologists in a series of excavations running from 1920 to 1937. Their work revealed that the defensive embankments had not only entombed the war dead, but protected the buildings just inside the city wall from centuries of erosion. As the dried mud was gently removed, the houses of what became known as Wall Street emerged. Nestled among them were religious buildings boasting airy courtyards and spacious rooms, their interiors decorated with brightly coloured frescos, stone statues and multilingual inscriptions. At the southern end of Wall Street there was a sanctuary dedicated to the deity Aphlad, who came from the nearby village of Anath; next door was a small temple to the Palmyrene high god known both as Zeus Kyrios and Baal Shamin; a block further was a Christian building – perhaps the earliest known church – rich in frescos depicting scenes from the life of Jesus. And then, just a few minutes up the street, the hand of God appeared.

The discovery of a synagogue at Dura in 1932 overturned the long-held assumption that Roman-era Judaism was strictly iconophobic, for the building's sensational floor-to-ceiling frescos were not only peopled with characters from the Hebrew Bible, but showcased the outstretched arms and busy hands of God himself. His hand was there on the niche in which the Torah scrolls had been housed, reaching down from heaven to halt Abraham's sacrifice of Isaac; there it was again, this time above the niche, stretched out to Moses standing barefoot at the burning bush. Higher up the wall, God's long brown arms could be seen spanning the skies over the waterway commonly remembered as the Red Sea, one open palm casting the Egyptian army into the waves, the other ushering the Israelites across the dried-up seabed (Plate 17). On another wall, the hand of God plunged out of the skies to grasp his prophet Ezekiel by the hair and carry him off to a Babylonian valley filled with the desiccated, disarticulated corpses of Jerusalem's exiles, where the hand conjured body parts back together (Plate 18). For the excavators, the artwork in the synagogue was so staggering that the dig's director, Clark Hopkins, likened the impact of the discovery to surviving a train crash. 'Once, when I was involved in a train wreck, I had no recollection of the moment between the shock when I was thrown from my seat and when I began to pick myself up from the bottom of the overturned car', he later wrote. 'So it was at Dura. All I can remember is the sudden shock and then the astonishment, the disbelief, as painting after painting came into view'. The images floored the team, leaving them wondering how an ancient Jewish community could so flagrantly – if beautifully – violate its own religious injunction against 'graven' images.[2]

For most scholars today, the hand of God in the ancient synagogue is best understood as an appropriated Graeco-Roman motif of divine authority, more usually seen in images of emperors and rulers being garlanded with a laurel wreath by a heavenly hand. The hand of God in the synagogue is simply assumed to be a conventional symbol, rather than a representation of a corporeal deity. But a rethink is in order. Although the Jewish community of Dura was as cosmopolitan as any other urban population in the Roman Empire, the portrayal of God's hands in their synagogue was not just an artistic device, but a remarkably faithful reflection of the biblical texts and traditions the frescos depict. Throughout the Hebrew Bible, the hand of God is presented as a powerful part of God's anatomy, manifesting his intervention in the human world. The Jewish community of third-century CE Dura inherited this biblical understanding of God's body: he was a hands-on deity, who had repeatedly reached into the earthly realm to shape the lived experiences of his people. In a diverse and vibrant city on the edge of empires, this small Jewish community celebrated God's handedness on the walls of their synagogue, painting a picture of a highly sociable, corporeal deity.

Of all parts of his body, God's hands had long been the most socially active – because our own are, too. Our hands are the body parts with which each of us is most familiar: they are the features we first encounter and explore in the womb, raising them to our mouths to sense their feel and form; throughout our lives, they are the parts of ourselves we see most often, most of the time, most days. Along with our faces, our hands are the bits of our bodies we tend to leave bare, simply because they are so very helpful to our social participation in the world. But while we make things, hold things, touch things and take things, it is with our hands that we also grasp our sense of reality – our sense of being in the world. Our hands are not simply tools, but sensing organs. With them, we can feel shape, weight, texture, pressure, temperature, vibrations and stillness. We can perceive comfort and pleasure, discomfort and pain. We can differentiate between substance and emptiness, materiality and immateriality. Our instinctive, habitual act of touching, feeling and perceiving with our hands is so constant that we are often unaware of it. We don't just use our hands, we sense, 'see' and 'think' with them, too: when we look at an object, we automatically anticipate touch. As one scholar puts it, a knife looks sharp, an icicle looks cold, a hammer looks graspable.[3] As sight- and hearing-impaired people know, it is with the touch of a hand, a press of a finger, that we experience the world in ways rather more profound than those elicited by our other enquiring senses. 'Without vision or hearing', writes the philosopher Matthew Ratcliffe, 'one would inhabit a very different experiential world, whereas one would not have a world at all without touch'.[4]

Our handedness not only renders us a species of creative action – doers – but beings of tactile perception, relation and reaction – feelers. I touch, therefore I am. Within the ancient religious imagination, the God of the Bible was no different. He touched, therefore he was. By contrast, a god with unfeeling hands was no god at all. As far as some biblical writers were concerned, any such god could be dismissed as a non-being: an insensate, incomplete, incoherent, unholy idol. In short, a mortal-made, hand-crafted object devoid of divine essence, like the powerless, incapacitated gods worshipped by foreigners:

> They have mouths but do not speak,
> they have eyes but do not see,
> they have ears but do not hear,
> they have noses but do not smell,
> they have hands but do not feel,
> they have feet but do not walk.[5]

It is no wonder God's hands are all over the Bible and the world it presents. And it is usually his right hand that is most active, rendering him a right-handed god – just like most deities of the ancient Levant. These gods tended to exhibit the same body language: enthroned in their temples, the gods' statues would hold an open-palmed, right hand up to their worshippers. It is a pose beautifully illustrated by the god El in one of his cult statues from Ugarit. Now housed in a museum in Damascus, it is only a little over twenty centimetres tall, but it is an object communicating immense status and power. Constructed of bronze, and overlaid with gold, El is in a seated position, dressed in a long, narrow robe falling neatly to his ankles. On his head is a tall conical crown typical of divine kings, adorned with two stylized curving horns; on his feet, he wears delicate sandals. His eyes are large and lined; his gaze is fixed ahead; his face is composed but serene. His left hand is clasped, suggesting he once held an accessory, now lost. But his right hand is raised up – palm open, fingers together – in a sign of blessing (Plate 16). This gesture of benevolent, divine engagement and sociability was common to deities across south-west Asia, both in literary and iconographic portrayals. It is a gesture inviting and anticipating touch; looking at the statue of El, it feels almost instinctive to raise a hand in polite, grateful greeting, to press it against the glass of the curator's cabinet, to reach for the touch of a welcoming god of old.

As a religious motif, the raised right hand of a deity is a symbol that has survived across millennia, from the tomb paintings of ancient Egypt, to the iconography of Christ in both Eastern Church and Western Church traditions. And it is nearly always the right hand that is raised. Social anthropologists have long observed that, across many traditional cultures past and present, the right hand is associated with life and all its blessings: eating, friendship, birth, high status and good luck. The left hand, by contrast, is often associated with death, danger and misfortune. For many communities, both ancient and modern, this is the hand which does not carry food to the mouth, but instead wipes away faeces and urine. In Western societies, this is the hand which gives its name, via Latin, to all that is sinister (literally, 'left').

Like El of Ugarit, the God of the Bible was rooted in a culture in which the right hand was righteous. It is with his right hand that Yahweh rescues his people from slavery in Egypt; it is with his right hand and arm that he clears the Promised Land of its indigenous inhabitants to make space for the Israelites; it is with his right hand that he grasps his worshippers; it is at the right hand of God that Christ will sit in heaven. The hands of the divine body thus index a cosmic orientation of the world and its workings. But they also craft that world, and shape its workings. Theologically, God is understood to have a hand in the world precisely because he made the world. Biblical writers describe God using his hands to stretch out the heavenly skies like a tent; he moulds landscapes, scoops out waterways, and plants forests and gardens. It is with his hands that he lays the foundations of the earth like brickwork, measures the pitch and height of mountains, weighs the winds and pours out rain. And it is with his hands, of course, that he also shapes the first human from clay.[6]

These images conjure the delicate craftsmanship of a gentle-handed deity – and yet, within the Bible's mythology of cosmic origins, they are secondary to his first, violent act of creation, in which Yahweh uses his hands and arms as powerful weapons to shatter, smite, pierce, strike, smash, crush, crack, sever, or punch the chaos monster into submission, before pinning its watery body beneath his feet. The violence of this battle, and its creative consequences, are vividly attested in a biblical poem of the sixth century BCE. Here, a description of Yahweh's role as the maker of day and night, summer and winter, and the boundaries of the world, is naturally prefaced by his fight with chaos and the repurposing of its watery body:

> You are the one who smashed Yam [Sea] with your might,
> cracked the heads of the dragons in the waters;
> you are the one who crushed the heads of Leviathan,
> you gave him as food for the wild beasts;
> you are the one who cut openings for springs and streams,
> you are the one who dried up the mighty rivers.[7]

The sea dragon was the most prominent of a primordial cohort of rebellious or disruptive divine monsters at once loved and feared by the ancient gods of south-west Asia. Born of the oldest generation of deities, long before the earthly, mortal realm had been formed, these monsters embodied all that was uncontrollable, undomesticated and uncertain in the cosmos. In the world of myth, where the lines of time did not run straight, but looped about in misshapen circles, battling a chaos monster in hand-to-hand (or hand-to-head) combat was essential to the story of the universe, in which an ordered world was necessarily built and sustained upon the gods' ongoing management of disruptive disorder. And as we've seen, it was a conflict far older than the biblical God himself.

Yahweh inherited both the battle and its body language from his older cultural cousins, Baal and Anat, both of whom laid claim to vanquishing the aqueous enemy. In mythological texts from Late Bronze Age Ugarit, Anat's victory is only briefly mentioned: 'Surely I fought Yam, the Beloved of El', she boasts; 'Surely I bound Dragon and destroyed him; I fought the Twisty Serpent, the Seven-headed Encircler! '[8] By contrast, Ugarit's citizens placed greater emphasis on the triumph of their patron deity, Baal. Embodied in the Baal myths of Ugarit as the sea god Yam (also known as Nahar, 'River'), the fearsome foe is finally vanquished when Baal smashes him on the head with magical clubs acting as extensions of his arms and hands. Baal further subjugates Yam's wet body with his own by gathering his splattered parts to drink him down and dry him up.[9] Conquered, contained and constrained, Yam is materially subsumed into the world order the storm god Baal has bludgeoned into being. The cosmic dynamics of his victory are celebrated on the Louvre's famous Baal Stela, originally located in or near the deity's temple in Ugarit, showing a triumphant Baal striding across the reordered universe. Under his feet are the mountains of the earthly realm, beneath which are locked the subdued, undulating waters of disorder. His right arm is raised above his head, club in hand, ready to strike should the waters rise up again. In his left hand is a downward-pointing, lightning-tipped spear, its wooden staff budding into leafy life as its blade pierces the boundary between the heavenly and earthly realms (fig. 28).

This was the strong-armed pose of menacing might common to warrior gods across ancient south-west Asia, including the very ancient storm deities Tishpak, god of the city of Eshnunna, and Ninurta, protector of Nippur. Each deity had long been a central character in the monster myths circulating around Mesopotamia. Among the earlier of these, dated to between 2340 and 2200 BCE, is a story in which the gods petition Tishpak to kill a 'raging dragon' terrorizing the land. Tishpak is said to have 'stirred up the clouds' and 'created a storm' as he threw his weapons at the terrifying being. Once dead, the dragon's enormous body – seemingly measuring a staggering fifty miles long – gushes blood for three years and three months, day and night. Tishpak's reward appears to be kingship over the gods or the city in which he was worshipped as patron.[10]

But his impressive victory was eclipsed by the more prominent successes of Ninurta, who described himself as 'the strong arm in battle'.[11] Among Mesopotamia's many deities, it was Ninurta who was most frequently credited with defeating monstrous disorder, often depicted as a seven-headed serpent-dragon. The battle itself was a stock feature of Mesopotamian art, whether exhibited in monumental form on the walls and stelae of high-status buildings, or carried by worshippers in smaller, portable forms, such as cylinder seals, stamp seals and protective tokens. An especially characterful example is a little plaque or amulet, dated to about 2500 BCE (fig. 29). Although only 1.5 inches wide, it captures well the cosmic scale of the conflict: Ninurta is down on one knee, straight-backed and determined, weapon in hand, ready to batter the second of the serpent-dragon's seven heads – the first is already slumped in defeat, a net or throw-stick on its neck, while the other heads rear up aggressively above the god. In literary portrayals of the aftermath of the battle, Ninurta straps the dismembered

Fig. 28. Baal of Ugarit, as shown on a limestone stela (*c.* 1700–1400 BCE) discovered near his temple in the city. As a storm deity, Baal was both a mighty warrior and a god of fertility, much as his leafy, lightning-tipped spear suggests. The small figure on a pedestal or platform beneath the deity's left arm is probably a king or a priest.

Fig. 29. Dated to about 2500 BCE, this little shell plaque shows a
Mesopotamian warrior god battling a seven-headed monster.
A fiery force radiates from its back as the deity quells one of
its serpentine heads. The vegetation springing from the deity's
horned headwear suggests this is Ninurta.

serpent-dragon to his chariot, harnessing its ongoing destructive force
for his own use – so much so, he appropriates the name and power of
the monster as he brandishes a weapon in his upraised hand: 'Deluge,
indefatigable serpent hurling yourself at the rebel land, Hero striding
formidably into battle; Lord, whose powerful arm is fit to bear the
mace, reaping like barley the necks of the insubordinate!'[12]

By the time the Babylonian epic Enuma Elish had been composed,
probably in the twelfth century BCE, Babylon's patron deity Marduk
had acquired Ninurta's victories for himself.[13] Included among these
was the battle with ferocious chaos, here named as the primordial
salt-sea mother goddess Tiamat, who attempts to put a stop to an
ongoing argument in the heavens by birthing an army of monsters,
led by her lover Qingu, to overwhelm the world of the gods. The
ultimate Babylonian warrior god, Marduk's body blazes with his
stifling, fiery aura, while his mighty arms and hands are almost indistinguishable from his weapons of war: 'He made the bow, appointed
it his weapon; he mounted the arrow, set it on the string; he took up

the mace, held it in his right hand; bow and quiver he hung on his arm'.[14] Like Ninurta, Marduk's weapons are cosmic chaos themselves: 'Deluge', of course, is his phallic war bow, while the high winds of a sea storm are his arrows, and captive monsters of disruption and disorder are among the beasts pulling his war chariot. When he finally smashes Tiamat's skull with a staff, the battle comes to an end, but the brutality of Marduk's attack is matched only by the violence wrought upon her dead body. He not only tramples her, but roofs the skies and floors the earth with watery fillets cut from her corpse, makes dewy mountains from her fluid-filled breasts, crafts rainclouds from her saliva, and brings forth the surging Euphrates and Tigris from her gouged-out eyes.

The overpowering of this unruly, malicious sea monster marked its domestication at the hand of the triumphant warrior god, who not only subdued chaos, but redeployed its formerly disruptive powers within a newly ordered cosmos. It was a mythic constellation distilled into a single, powerful image Marduk himself wore. In the ninth century BCE, the god's statue in Esagila, his primary temple in Babylon, was accessorized with a lapis lazuli cylinder seal hung around his neck. Commissioned by King Marduk-zakir-shumi I as an offering, the cylinder was to be rolled into the wet clay sealing the deity's missives. Its imprint showed Marduk towering over a subdued scaly dragon, and its message was clear: Marduk brought domesticated order to the world, transforming chaos from a monstrous enemy into an obedient companion (fig. 30).[15]

Like Ninurta and Marduk, Yahweh harnessed the powers of defeated chaos to take on other enemies – including the disruptive humans drowned by the great Flood, and the anonymous pharaoh reputed to have enslaved the Israelite tribes in Egypt. The biblical story of Israel's escape from Pharaoh is best known for the miraculous parting of a raging sea. It is a place misremembered in later tradition as the Red Sea, but named in the Hebrew Bible as the mythic *yam suf*, 'Sea of Reeds' – a deadly body of cosmic water equipped with dangerous twisting limbs or tails to ensnare its enemies.[16] At first, the parting of the sea seems to be one of a series of magical actions performed by Moses' own upraised hand, along with turning wooden staffs into

Fig. 30. Marduk and his monster. Detail from a large lapis lazuli cylinder seal, gifted to the deity by the ninth-century BCE Babylonian king Marduk-zakir-shumi I. An accompanying inscription suggests the seal was to be hung around the neck of Marduk's cult statue.

serpents and the waters of the Nile into blood. But it is the 'great hand' of Yahweh that the Israelites are said to have seen at the *yam suf*,[17] just as a much older, poetic form of the tradition embedded within the narrative in Exodus makes clear. Extolling the deity with the cry 'Yahweh is a warrior!' it makes no mention of Moses, and instead focuses on Yahweh's victory over watery chaos – here named as the primeval enemies Yam (Sea) and Tehom (Deep) – and his weaponizing of its parts to defeat the Egyptian army:

> Pharaoh's chariots and his army he cast into the Sea/Yam,
> his picked officers were sunk in the Sea of Reeds.
> Deep/Tehom covered them over,
> down they went in the depths like a stone.
> Your right hand, O Yahweh, is glorious in strength,
> your right hand, O Yahweh, smashes the enemy . . .
> At the snort of your nostrils the waters piled up,
> the streams stood up in a heap . . .
> You blew with your breath,

Sea/Yam covered them over;
they sank like lead in the mighty waters.[18]

The contours of the chaos myth shaped not only the biblical story of
God, but the frame of his body, too. Throughout the Hebrew Bible,
Yahweh's 'strong hand' and 'outstretched arm' are repeatedly praised
in ways evoking the powerful stance of a typical divine warrior, whose
iconography was so well known across the Levant. Yahweh is presented
as a deity of menace, whose arm is raised above his head, his fist
clenched, poised to strike: 'Yours is an arm with might! Your hand is
strong, your right hand raised!'[19] More than a biblical turn of phrase,
the 'strong hand and outstretched arm' of the God of the Bible was
not only a mythic memory of his battle with chaos, but a literary
reflection of the Levantine iconography of warrior deities.

But the chaos myth was as political as it was cosmic. Warrior gods
endorsed the power and might of their chosen earthly kings, who
imitated their divine patrons in visual and literary descriptions of their
own military prowess. Since at least 3000 BCE, Egypt's pharaohs had
portrayed themselves in the threatening pose of the gods, brandishing
a mace above their heads while grasping their cowering enemies by
the hair. These images were emblazoned on public monuments and
private royal furnishings, and verbally communicated in letters dispatched to Egypt's neighbours and enemies, in which pharaohs
boasted of their 'outstretched arm' and 'mighty hand' – just as the God
of the Bible would later come to do. The godlike menace of Egypt's
pharaohs is captured well in a temple inscription at Karnak celebrating
Tuthmosis III's important victory at Megiddo, in what is now Israel,
in 1457 BCE. 'His majesty set off on his electrum chariot, equipped with
an impressive array of weapons, like a strong-armed Horus, Lord of
Action, like Montu of Thebes, his father Amun strengthening his
arms'.[20] Although Megiddo would come to host other battles, it is no
surprise that it would forever be remembered as a site of cosmic
combat. This was the place at which an Egyptian god had laid waste
his enemies, and a place which would later become known as
Armageddon – the very name of which would morph into a cipher
for the final apocalyptic war between good and evil.[21]

Meanwhile, across ancient south-west Asia, kings were not only decorating their temples and palaces with imposing images of their gods subduing cosmic monsters, but asserting their own corresponding mastery of chaos in the earthly realm in staggering depictions of their military conquests. Inscriptions refer to kings sluicing their weapons in seawater following a successful military campaign, ceremonially re-enacting the divine defeat of a watery foe.[22] This correspondence between earthly kingship and divine warfare is clearly articulated in the early seventh century BCE by King Sennacherib of Assyria in an inscription describing his restoration of a temple. He tells of an image commissioned to adorn the temple gates, showing the high god Ashur going into battle against 'Tiamat and her brood'. Ashur is accompanied by a dizzying host of deities, alongside whom Sennacherib seems to imagine himself, riding in the high god's war chariot, as he proudly declares: '[This is] the image of Ashur as he advances to battle into the midst of Tiamat, the image of Sennacherib, king of Assyria . . . I am the one who conquers, stationed in Ashur's chariot'.[23]

This royal posturing was beyond symbolic, for a king's weapons were those of the gods. Mesopotamian annals spill over with the boasts of kings claiming to have slain their earthly enemies with the bow, lance, or sword of a patron warrior deity; images of a divine hand descending from the heavens to gift a king the cosmic war bow point to the ritual use of divine weapons in the earthly cult of kingship, while ritual texts suggest these precious objects, imbued with a magical power, were housed in temples. This was a very ancient aspect of royal religion, and is attested across ancient south-west Asian cultures. Evidence includes diplomatic correspondence between an ambassador in Aleppo and King Zimri-Lim of Mari, an eighteenth-century BCE city-state in what is now Syria. In a letter to the king, the ambassador confirms that the formidable storm god Adad was arranging for his weapons in Aleppo to be dispatched to a temple in Mari: 'The weapon with which I struck the Sea I have given to you', the deity is reported as telling Zimri-Lim.[24] Several centuries later, at Ugarit, a prayer for the security of the city was not only directed to El, Athirat and the other members of the pantheon, but directly appealed to the gods' own weapons, addressed as 'divine spear', 'divine axe' and 'divine mace'.[25]

Like Yahweh's footstool, these heavenly weapons were so closely associated with the bodies of the gods that they were themselves rendered divine.

The religious ideologies underlying human kingship were potently lofty – even in the tiny Iron Age kingdom of Judah. In an oracle seemingly recited at each king's enthronement in Jerusalem, Yahweh promised that the divine arms and hands that could subdue chaos would empower the king himself, so that he too would have a hand in maintaining order in the cosmos: 'My hand shall always remain with him, my arm also shall strengthen him', Yahweh declared. 'I will crush his foes before him and strike down those who hate him . . . I will set his hand on Sea, his right hand on River'.[26] Mythically seated at the right hand of Yahweh, with enemies pinned beneath their feet, Judah's kings were coached by the deity himself in the art of divine warfare. 'He trains my hands for war, so that my arms can bend a bow of bronze', the king proclaims in the temple, before gratefully addressing Yahweh himself: 'Your right hand has supported me; your help has made me great'.[27]

No wonder Jerusalem's kings boasted of their power to 'smite kings' and 'shatter heads' among enemy nations, smashing them into pieces using the 'forged weapon' and 'rod of iron' given to them by their god.[28] Some biblical texts hint at a royal cult of divine weapons housed within a sacred building adjacent to the temple in Jerusalem. Known as the 'house' or 'temple' of the Forest of Cedars, its name recalls the mythical mountaintop woodland of the oldest gods, which had once been guarded by the terrifying Huwawa. According to the book of Isaiah, the Forest of Cedars was the sanctuary to which citizens would look when the threat of attack loomed, hoping that Yahweh and the king would arm themselves with their magical weapons should the need arise.[29] And arise it did. In Judah, this distinctively royal ideology of divine warfare would become increasingly difficult to sustain – and threaten to disarm God himself.

13

ARM'S REACH

Families file out of the city, their belongings bundled into bags on their backs, or stacked high on ox-drawn carts. Small children toddle alongside their parents, some hanging onto their mother's skirts, others clutching their father's legs. Those too young or too tired to walk are carried on adults' shoulders. The women and children of one household are squeezed into a cart, balanced on their baggage; one woman cradles an infant on her lap, while the arms of an older child, sitting behind her, are clasped around her waist. The motley procession makes its way across the hilly landscape, past trees and vines heavy with fruit. But this is no liberating exodus. Soldiers force the long line of men, women and children from their city, taking them past impaled corpses, flayed bodies, and a local dignitary, forced onto his knees to have his throat slit. The traumatized families are being marched towards their fate: incorporation into Assyria. The supreme power of the empire is embodied by King Sennacherib himself, who sits upon a lofty throne, upheld by divine beings, overseeing the sack of the city and the parade of the spoils of war (figs. 31 and 32).

The fall of the Judahite city of Lachish at the end of the eighth century BCE barely gets a mention in the Bible, yet it was a city significant enough that its sack was monumentalized in a vast frieze in Sennacherib's Southwest Palace in Nineveh, celebrating the subjugation of his far-flung territories.[1] The Assyrian attack on Judah, an imperial vassal, had been triggered by the rebellion of its king,

Fig. 31. A family forced out of Lachish by Assyrian troops, filing past a corpse stretched out for flaying. Detail from a series of wall reliefs from Nineveh's Southwest Palace (*c.* 700–690 BCE), commissioned by Sennacherib to celebrate his destruction of the city in 701 BCE.

Fig. 32. Sennacherib enthroned in his royal encampment outside Lachish, surrounded by officials and attendants. His face was deliberately damaged in antiquity. The cuneiform inscription (top left) reads: 'Sennacherib, king of the world, king of Assyria, set up a throne and the booty of Lachish passed before him'. Detail from the Lachish reliefs of Nineveh's Southwest Palace, *c.* 700–690 BCE.

Hezekiah. Encouraged by promises made by a resurgent Egypt and a deal struck with the flashy Babylonian king Marduk-apla-iddina II (known in the Bible as Merodach-baladan), Hezekiah withheld the imperial tribute. It was a reckless decision. Just twenty years before, Judah's northern neighbour, the kingdom of Israel, had been annihilated for rebelling against its Assyrian emperor. Its gods were captured, their temples emptied, and King Hoshea imprisoned. The kingdom was snuffed out and replaced with an Assyrian province called Samerina, taking its name from the fallen capital, Samaria. Now, Judah itself was on the brink of oblivion. 'Do not be afraid or dismayed before the king of Assyria!' Hezekiah reportedly said to his people. 'With him is an arm of flesh, but with us is Yahweh our god, to help us and to fight our battles!'[2] It was an overconfident declaration. Judah was decimated. Jerusalem was left standing alone 'like a booth in a cucumber field', with Hezekiah trapped in the besieged city 'like a bird in a cage', as Sennacherib mockingly declared in his war reports.[3] Cut down to size and cowed into remorseful obedience, Hezekiah paid the heavy tribute the empire demanded, which included his own daughters. Jerusalem was spared. Slowly, its inhabitants recovered their confidence, crediting the city's escape from annihilation to the protective presence of Yahweh in his temple: 'God is in the midst of the city! It shall not be moved!' cult singers proclaimed. 'Great is Yahweh and greatly to be praised in the city of our god . . . Within its citadels God has shown himself a sure defence!'[4]

By the middle of the seventh century BCE, Assyria was beset by a series of civil wars, weakening the empire's hold on its territories – much to the delight of its rivals, Egypt and Babylonia. Judah was now caught between these warring powers, bending and buckling in the changing tides of empire. One after another, Judahite kings were killed, captured, or exiled at the command of competing foreign powers. In 612 BCE, King Nabopolassar of Babylon captured Nineveh, the imperial seat of Assyria, and with it the empire's heartlands. Having gained control of Mesopotamia, the newly expanded Babylonian Empire set its sights on driving Egypt back from its incursions into the Levant by taking these territories for itself. In 597 BCE, the Babylonians invaded Judah and seized Jerusalem. Judah's king, Jehoiachin, was exiled to

Babylon, along with key members of his court and some of the city's religious leaders. Others wealthy enough or lucky enough to flee made their way to Egypt. Babylon placed a more malleable member of Judah's royal family, Zedekiah, on the throne. But Egypt kept up the pressure on its southern Levantine targets, and Zedekiah proved a pushover. In 587 BCE, he rebelled against King Nebuchadnezzar of Babylon, who immediately attacked. Jerusalem was sacked and the kingdom destroyed. Fettered like an animal, Zedekiah was carted off to Babylon, along with most of the city's remaining political and religious elites. Monstrous chaos had overwhelmed the kingdom of Judah. 'He has devoured me, he has crushed me', Jerusalem cried of Nebuchadnezzar. 'He has swallowed me like the Dragon; he has filled his belly with my delicacies, he has spewed me out! '[5] Yahweh blamed the machinations of Egypt's king, whose disorder had been as repugnant as it was disruptive: 'You are like the Dragon in the seas, thrashing about in your streams, stirring up the water with your feet, fouling your streams', he is said to have declared.[6] But some worshippers blamed Yahweh himself, casting him as their inexplicably angry attacker: 'We have not forgotten you, or been false to your covenant; our heart has not turned back, nor have our steps departed from your way – yet you have crushed us in place of the Dragon!'[7]

Whoever was to blame, Judah's kings had proved themselves unable or unworthy in their divinely ordained task to subdue earthly chaos. But Yahweh's role as the monster-slayer lived on. Exiled elites drew on their ancient myths to petition their divine warrior to free them from captivity and restore them to their homeland. 'Bow your heavens, O Yahweh, and come down', they prayed, 'make the lightning flash and scatter them, send out your arrows and rout them! Stretch out your hand from on high! Set me free and rescue me from the mighty waters!'[8] For these worshippers, God's cosmic conflicts not only painted the turbulent world in vivid technicolour, but illustrated the profound personal distress of those drowning in the chaos of cultural trauma. From the depths of misery emerged some of the most heart-wrenching pleas in the Bible. 'Save me, O God, for the waters have come up to my neck . . . I have come into deep waters, and the flood sweeps over me', sobs one poet. 'I am weary with my crying, my throat is parched; my eyes grow dim with waiting for my God'.[9]

The interrelation of the mythic and the personal was more than notional. One of the most artfully crafted poems in the Bible reflects the prayers of an exiled community of Judahites in sixth-century BCE Babylon, who imagined their return as a second exodus, crossing the dangerous Sea of Reeds into the promised homeland. Moving from the mythic, to the political, to the personal, the poem shifts from the brutality of Yahweh's battle with the sea dragon, to escape from oppression in a foreign land, to the emotional salve of a pilgrim's journey to the Jerusalem temple. And it is specifically the arm of Yahweh that is addressed, transforming the deity's limb of brute force into a guiding hand of comfort:

> Awake, awake, put on strength, O arm of Yahweh!
> Awake, as in the days of old,
> the generations of long ago!
> Was it not you who cut Rahab in pieces,
> who pierced the Dragon?
> Was it not you who dried up the sea/Yam,
> the waters of great deeps/Mighty Tehom?
> Who made the depths of the sea/Yam
> a way for the redeemed to cross over?
> So the ransomed of Yahweh shall return,
> and come to Zion with singing . . .[10]

The idea that God's powerful arm was merely sleeping, rather than weakened or broken, was typical of ancient religious devotion. Despite the destruction of his temple in Jerusalem, Yahweh was not a god who had been defeated by Babylon, but a deity who had deliberately abandoned his people, withdrawing his powerful, protective arm. 'Why do you hold back your hand?' went the plaintive cry. 'Why do you keep your hand in your bosom?'[11] If the divine arm was sleeping, it was because Yahweh was, too. Across the ancient world, restful sleep was as normal an activity for gods as it was for humans, and some temples were equipped with ornate beds to which their divine residents would retire at night.[12] Like their worshippers, however, deities might also take to their beds as a means of retreating from the social world, whether because they were sulking, depressed, or punishing their people. According to a Sumerian lament, this is precisely what the great god Enlil did. Having afflicted his land with a famine, the old god shut himself up in his temple at Nippur, whereupon he pretended to be asleep while his punished people starved. Swift measures – and a certain degree of flattery and mollycoddling – were required. The goddess Inanna travelled from her temple in Uruk to Nippur in the hope of rousing Enlil. 'Feigning, my father feigns lying down!' she cried. 'May I soothe his heart! May I pacify his liver! May I direct my words to his distressed heart!' Sitting on his lap, she sings him awake with the refrain, 'O sleeping one, how long will you sleep?'[13] Inanna's lament was considered so powerful that her cult singers recited it in her temple at Uruk on the seventh day of each month in the hope of appeasing the gods for any unknown misdemeanour which might prompt untimely or simulated slumber. Precautionary measures were only sensible: discerning the difference between a sleeping god and a sulking god was not always easy.

Many centuries later, in the sixth century BCE, Yahweh's worshippers were singing petitions to awaken him to the devastating aftermath of the Babylonian attack. 'Rouse yourself! Why do you sleep, O Yahweh? Awake! Do not cast us off forever!'[14] For those left in Jerusalem, Yahweh's prolonged sleep likely marked the relatively short period in which his broken temple was completely out of action. But for Jerusalem's former elites, now living in exile, Yahweh's sleep endured for several generations. Most eventually got on with their new lives, reconfiguring their god into a deity easily accessible in the diaspora. On Elephantine, an island in the Nile, a mixed community of Yahweh worshippers – some exiles and refugees, some economic migrants – built a temple to their god and two companion deities, about whom we know very little: the god Eshum-Bethel, and the goddess Anat-Yahu (perhaps a consort of Yahweh himself). There, they offered sacrifices once again.[15] But some exiles in and around Babylon – Marduk's own city – believed that Yahweh of Jerusalem remained firmly territorial, and only their return to Zion could reunite them with their god. And yet this was a theological position fraught with anxiety. What if Yahweh's mighty arm was simply too weak or too short to reach into an enemy territory to rescue his scattered citizens?

It was a claim Yahweh vociferously denied, drawing on his subjugation of watery chaos to prove his point: 'Is my hand shortened, that it cannot redeem? Or have I no power to deliver? By my rebuke I dry up the sea, I make the rivers a desert!'[16] It was also a claim seemingly put to rest when King Cyrus II of Persia toppled Babylon in 539 BCE, and decreed the return of displaced peoples to their homelands, where they were to rebuild their temples and restore their gods – a canny political move designed to pitch the new emperor as a benevolent patron of the oppressed. Suddenly, Yahweh awoke 'like a warrior shaking off wine'[17] and 'opened his armoury and brought out the weapons of his wrath'.[18] Furious at any implication that he had been disarmed or sedated by Babylon, or even rescued by Persian Cyrus, Yahweh adorned himself with the regalia of a champion fighter – itemized in the book of Isaiah as a breastplate, a helmet and ceremonial robes. He then raised his mighty arm, ready to avenge his people, rescue his exiles – and salvage his godly reputation:

> His own arm saved him,
> and his righteousness upheld him.[19]

The idea that a god might need to rescue his own reputation was not uncommon – but it did give rise to one of the most extraordinary verses in the Bible. According to a poem in Deuteronomy, Yahweh had always planned to use foreign nations to wipe out his people altogether, 'young man and woman alike; nursing child and old grey head'. But he reversed this decision upon realizing that foreign nations might claim the genocidal massacre as the work of their own hands, rather than his – and he confesses he was afraid of the potential humiliation: 'I might have reduced them to naught, and blotted out the memory of them from mankind; but I feared the taunts of the foe, their enemies who might misunderstand and say, "Our own hand is triumphant; it was not Yahweh who did all this".'[20]

In the aftermath of the exile, Yahweh simply had to wake up and arm himself like a warrior again. Glimpses of his return to form are offered in prophetic oracles embedded in biblical texts of the Persian period: he flexes his muscular arm like a bodybuilder as he accompanies his repatriated exiles in triumphal procession back to Jerusalem; lookouts in the city spy him covered in blood, his holy arm held aloft, as he returns from a quick detour to punish the Edomites, who had helped the Babylonians to destroy his temple.[21] Back in his city, worshippers sang praises to his right hand and holy arm, raised in victory like a champion boxer in the rebuilt sanctuary, while the chastened waters of chaos and its monstrous inhabitants were encouraged to cheer and applaud their oppressor: 'His right hand and his holy arm have saved him! Yahweh has made known his victory! . . . Let the sea roar, and all that fills it . . . let the rivers clap their hands!'[22]

The Hebrew Bible gives the impression of a vast return of exiles to Judah, following in the train of God. But the reality was rather different. While most remained in Babylonia and Egypt, only a few hundred would trickle back to the homeland in the late sixth and early fifth centuries BCE. The former kingdom of Judah was now the tiny Persian satrapy of Yehud, governed by civil servants within a much larger imperial province given the no-frills moniker 'Beyond the River'. Jerusalem itself had a population of little more than two and a half thousand, while its newly rebuilt sanctuary would remain only a relatively modest structure until well into the Hellenistic period. Even so, the initial rebuilding of Jerusalem's temple in the late sixth and early fifth centuries BCE, and the imagined return of its divine warrior, marked a new chapter in the story of Yahweh and the sea monster. For the returnees, God had proved himself perfectly capable of recruiting the powerful Cyrus as his messianic ('anointed') servant, moving into foreign lands to bring his worshippers home and facilitating the Persian sponsorship of his new temple.[23] With a guiding hand in international politics, Yahweh's reach was increasingly perceived by many of his devotees to be ever greater: his power was unmatched by foreign gods; his control over chaos supreme. Worshippers looked forward to his imminent punishment of those who had revelled in the suffering of his people. Prophets declared it would be a day of unbridled ferocity, climaxing in the slaying of the dragon once and for all: 'On that day, Yahweh with his cruel and great and strong sword will punish Leviathan the fleeing serpent, Leviathan the twisting serpent; he will kill the dragon that is in the sea!'[24]

As Jerusalem's priests and literati grew increasingly comfortable amid the relative calm and economic stability of Persian imperial rule, Yahweh's primeval, fearsome foe became ever easier to subdue. In the myths upholding his mighty arm, overpowering his old enemy was now less of a violent battle, and rather more like trapping a flapping fish: 'Can you draw out Leviathan with a fishhook, or press down its tongue with a cord?' God now boasted in a lengthy monologue in the book of Job. Losing none of its formidable form, the chaos monster moved from disempowered enemy, who spoke 'soft words' of supplication to its captor, to a tamed animal, whom Yahweh could 'play with as a bird' and 'put on a leash' as a toy for young girls.[25] Just as Babylon's Marduk had once domesticated a monster, rendering it a faithful companion, so too Yahweh found himself the owner of a pet dragon. The monster was now cast as a creature of God, divinely formed on the fifth day of creation to fill the great sea; a monster Yahweh had tended on the day of its watery birth, wrapping the boisterous baby in swaddling bands to calm its writhes and wriggles.[26] The monster's revised role in creation gave it a renewed purpose: Yahweh had made the monster precisely to enjoy spending time with it, as his worshippers declared with delight: 'There is the sea, great and wide . . . and Leviathan whom you formed to play with!'[27]

This was less a reinvention of the south-west Asian combat myth than a re-emphasis of some of its oldest themes, in which cosmic monsters were born of the gods themselves, who felt great affection for their skittish, troublesome offspring. The notion that Yahweh enjoyed playing with his sea monster would endure well into the Common Era, and proved so appealing that rabbis would subsequently confirm he had timetabled this activity into his daily programme: after a busy morning working on the Torah and sitting in worldly judgement, followed by an industrious afternoon meting out mercy and feeding the earth's inhabitants, God would relax in the evening by playing with Leviathan.[28] It was a divine pastime which spoke as much

to the gentle-handedness of the biblical God as to his effortless control
of the forces of disorder in the cosmos. Either way, the warrior god
was increasingly disinclined to fight, for he was effortlessly able to keep
chaos in check. If disaster befell his worshippers again, it would be a
just punishment, orchestrated from a heavenly distance and with a
heavy heart by God himself – so heavy a heart, some rabbis later
assumed, that God would bind his own right arm behind his back to
prevent his instinctive intervention. Disarmed and constrained, he
would suffer in solidarity with his punished people.[29]

The cultural memory of a violent cosmic battle did not disappear,
however. Instead, it shapeshifted like ancient Tiamat herself, taking on
new forms as the political world changed around Yahweh's worshippers. As the relative stability of the Persian era gave way to more
unsettled, divisive and often oppressive conditions during the Hellenistic and Roman periods, some Jewish seers saw the waters of chaos
rising again, embodied this time by the monstrous forms of their
unrighteous opponents or foreign overlords. Their anxieties would be
articulated in some of the Bible's most esoteric literature, including
the second-century BCE book of Daniel, which drew on the rise and
fall of empires to announce the impending ascent of a glorious new
world order. Here, the pseudonymous seer presents a carefully controlled version of the chaos myth to describe the downfall of successive
oppressive nations, portrayed as terrifying beasts crawling out of a
whipped-up primordial sea. They are to be usurped by a heavenly
figure of human-like shape, described as 'one like a son of man', who
would appear riding on a cloud chariot and be appointed to kingship
over a new world order by an aged deity enthroned in the divine council, called the Ancient of Days.[30] This mystical narrative is best known
for its subsequent use as a proof-text endorsing the New Testament
portrayal of Christ as 'the Son of Man coming on the clouds of
heaven'.[31] But in Daniel, this vision was just one expression of a persistent mythic constellation which would find its way into other Jewish
writings of the Hellenistic and Roman periods. Some similarly
described a divine Son of Man riding on the clouds of heaven, this time
over the primeval sea, causing it to shrivel or tremble; others envisaged
an angelic mediator exercising God-given dominion over Leviathan,

who was painfully pinned beneath the divine throne.[32] These writers' worldviews were fundamentally shaped by the traditional south-west Asian dragon myth, the kernel of which told of a young warrior god winning kingship having vanquished or tamed monstrous, aqueous chaos.

This mythic paradigm also framed the religious perspectives of some early Jewish groups of a more sectarian or mystical nature, who responded to the political and cultural changes wrought by the upheavals between the second century BCE and the first century CE with end-time ('eschatological') visions. They looked forward to the end of the traumatic world, when the created realm would be destroyed entirely and a new cosmic order would arise. And if the old world had been made from the slaying of the chaos monster, its end was to come the same way. For many, the new death of chaos would be marked by the divine violence of old, with God or one of his divine agents – usually the archangel Michael or Gabriel – hunting out the dragon and smashing its heads.[33] For these anxious communities, watery chaos was no longer a dangerous force inclined to wayward disruption, but a cosmic evil actively set upon repeated rebellion against God, and intent on inciting mortals to do the same through the provocations of its supernatural envoys, Belial ('Wickedness') and Mastemah ('Hostility'). God would wipe out this toxic presence by stretching the heavens high and low, like a cosmic concertina, and crashing them into the corrupted earthly realm, which would be sent hurtling into the abyss. Only the righteous would survive this apocalyptic terror to witness the staggering wonder of the new cosmic order.

Early Jewish eschatology would shape the frightening visions of the great apocalypse in the early Christian book of Revelation. Dated to the end of the first century CE or the beginning of the second, the book is self-ascribed to a seer named John – a figure traditionally but erroneously identified with the apostle John. Whoever he was, he wrote with a fervent desperation to Christian communities in Roman Asia Minor (modern-day Turkey), urging them to hold fast to their faith, for the end of the world was imminent. John reports that his visions transported him to the heavenly throne room of God, where he witnessed Christ's army of archangels battling a seven-headed, flood-spewing, frog-phlegmed chaos dragon – now named as 'that ancient serpent, who is called the Devil and Satan, the deceiver of the whole world'.[34] After several nasty skirmishes, the dragon was finally overpowered, bound with chains and sealed into a bottomless pit. This triggered a new creation: 'Then I saw a new heaven and a new earth', John writes, 'for the first heaven and the first earth have passed away – and the Sea is no more'.[35] Transcendentally distanced from the battle as an unseen presence, God himself had kept his hands clean of the conflict. Instead, a series of angels had grappled with the dragon until Christ appeared, equipped with a sword, a warhorse and a bloody tunic, ready to take the glory of the young warrior god. His reward would be divine kingship over God's universal empire.

Not everyone imagined God would remain at arm's length. For many other early Jewish and Christian communities, the apocalyptic defeat of the cosmic sea dragon would not come with the messy shattering of the monster's many heads, its wrestling into chains, nor even its imprisonment in darkness. Instead, it would be marked by a more civilized end-of-times banquet. Summoning his most righteous

Fig. 33. The divine battle with a seven-headed monster remained a potent mythological motif in early Jewish and Christian traditions. Its recycling in the New Testament book of Revelation is vividly illustrated in this image from a medieval manuscript known as the Silos Apocalypse (1091–1109 CE).

worshippers to dinner in heaven, God would cater the final feast. Quickly and cleanly, he would dish up his pet dragon in salted slivers for his most righteous worshippers to consume.[36] It was an image drawn on what was by now an ancient claim in the Psalms that Yahweh had crushed Leviathan's heads and fed him to wild beasts. Now, this was recast as a salvific last supper to be hosted by God at a time of his choosing.[37] Having imprisoned Leviathan at the beginning of creation, God would fetch him from his watery store and serve him up as fishy fillets – a dish that would be both physically nourishing and reassuringly kosher, as some rabbis would later confirm.[38] God's mastery of chaos had become so thoroughly domestic that the monster was no longer a humbled servant, ferocious guardian, or beloved companion. Now, Leviathan was an animal raised to be cooked and eaten in a ritual meal, like a prized beast sacrificed from the sacred stall. This culinary twist on an old mythic trope offered God the renewed opportunity to show-case his more delicate, dexterous skills – a divine touch that had long shaped the lives of his worshippers.

14

Divine Touch

Towards the end of his life, shortly after 1000 CE, a learned English monk known as Ælfric of Eynsham wrote to his wealthy patron, an ealdorman called Æthelweard, reminding him that scripture was to be read responsibly, lest its literal sense be mistaken for its deeper, spiritual truths. The letter formed the preface to Ælfric's translation of Genesis 1–24, from the Latin of the Western Church into Anglo-Saxon – the vernacular English of his day. The translation was commissioned for what is now known as the Old English Hexateuch, which also contains Ælfric's versions of Numbers 13–26 and the book of Joshua, alongside anonymous translations of Genesis 25–50, Exodus, Leviticus, Numbers 1–12 and Deuteronomy. This Hexateuch is the oldest surviving Anglo-Saxon translation of the Bible's first six books, and is illustrated with hundreds of brightly coloured miniature paintings, filling the large spaces carefully left in the manuscripts as the work was compiled.[1] Not merely eye-catching images dressing the page, the paintings offer their own commentaries on the biblical books, enriching the sacred narratives with an iconography of Anglo-Saxon theology. We cannot know quite what Ælfric thought of the expensive illustrations accompanying the volume – if indeed he lived long enough to see any of them. But their bold, unflinching portrayal of biblical stories suggests the artist was far more comfortable with a literal interpretation of the Bible than Ælfric himself. And one painting in particular offers a remarkably close reading of a story more usually fudged by translators and theologians – both ancient and modern.

An entire page is devoted to a painting of Moses' last day, as told at the end of Deuteronomy. Set within a thick, muddy-red frame, the image invites the viewer to watch as Moses delivers his final address to the Israelites, and then ascends Pisgah, a peak atop Mount Nebo, in what is now Jordan. Cloaked and barefoot, both God and Moses tiptoe daintily across the mountain peaks, the deity pointing into the distance towards Canaan as he talks over his shoulder to Moses, who holds up his hands in wondrous astonishment. Having journeyed through the wilderness for over a generation to get there, this is the first time Moses has seen the Promised Land. But it will also be the last. 'I have let you see it with your eyes', Yahweh tells Moses in Deuteronomy, 'but you will not cross over there'. Moses promptly drops dead – not out of shock, but in obedience to 'the command of Yahweh'.[2] The moment of Moses' death goes unrepresented in the accompanying illustration, but its aftermath is clear to see: crowned with a blue and yellow halo, his robes fluttering behind him, God bends down to grasp Moses' shrouded corpse, manoeuvring it from the top of the mountain towards a cleft in the landscape, where he will bury it. Below him, the Israelites hold their hands to their faces, wiping away their tears (Plate 19).[3]

In the book of Deuteronomy, Moses' gravedigger is God himself. And yet this is a little-known feature of the biblical story of Moses, for it rarely appears in modern translations. But the Anglo-Saxon artist has captured well the words of the Latin Bible from which Ælfric and his colleagues were working – a text known as the Vulgate, which itself offers a faithful reflection of the Hebrew of Deuteronomy 34.6, which reads: 'Moses, the servant of Yahweh, died there in the land of Moab, at Yahweh's command. And he buried him in a valley in the land of Moab'. Thanks to the theological sensibilities of ancient scribes and translators, this verse has long been censored by pious emendation. Appalled by the idea that God could contaminate himself with the impurity of a corpse – even the corpse of so holy a man as Moses – some Jewish and Christian translators corrected what they perceived to be an error in the text: 'he buried him' simply became 'he was buried' or 'they buried him', leaving generations of readers to assume that mourning Israelites or weeping angels had performed Moses' mortuary rites, rather than God himself.

The idea that God would behave in such a way might have been unthinkable for some, but it was in keeping with older, traditional ideas about Yahweh. Like his divine peers, the God of the Bible was a deity who was neither averse to getting his hands dirty, nor unaccustomed to performing the ceremonies of life and death with which his worshippers were themselves familiar. From the birthing of a baby to the burial of a body, Yahweh was understood by many as a tactile deity, who expressed his relationship with his worshippers by means of a body language rich in ritual forms.

Yahweh's burial of Moses was one of a number of encounters the deity undertook with the material remains of the dead. Although his priests in Jerusalem would eventually come to impose a strict separation between the sacred and the sepulchral, fearing the cultural 'dirt' of death would contaminate the ritual cleanliness of holiness, the segregation of the divine from the dead was a relatively late incursion into the life of Yahweh. According to some biblical books, he had already proved himself an experienced corpse-wrangler and bone-handler. In some, he brags of his ability to reach into the underworld – a place known as Sheol – and draw out its inhabitants. This bragging is often couched as a threat, warning that Yahweh can punish the dead for their misdemeanours by displacing them from the relative comfort of their post-mortem existence: 'Though they dig into Sheol, from there my hand shall take them!'[4] But God's role as a tomb raider was not always malevolent. In the famous vision attributed to the sixth-century BCE prophet Ezekiel, Yahweh walks about a Babylonian valley housing the tombs of his exiled worshippers, picking his way through an overspill of bones littering the valley floor. Opening the tombs, he disinters the buried dead, bringing out their bones to join the others. Magically, the bones fuse back together; flesh, sinews and skin coat the newly articulated skeletons. The divine breath of life is blown into them, and the revivified dead stand on their feet, ready to return to Jerusalem.[5] Theologically, the vision promises the restoration of the diaspora people of God, but the deity's actions in the valley are modelled on the traditional bone rituals of his worshippers in ancient Israel and Judah, who would disinter their dead once the flesh had rotted away, and reorganize the bones into repositories within the tomb, effectively reinterring them. In this way, the deceased were re-socialized as ancestors, securing their afterlife in the underworld.

Yahweh's ability to reach into the underworld is graphically attested in a rock-cut tomb in a cave at Khirbet el-Qom, near Hebron, dated to the eighth century BCE. At the bottom of a small flight of steps, excavators discovered four burial chambers stretching off from a central room – an architectural configuration much like a domestic house for the living. Each burial chamber was equipped with three 'beds' for the dead, while in the main room, ritual objects used by the dead and their mourners were gathered: lamps, cups and bowls, plus amulets, rattles and figurines to scare off malevolent demons and would-be grave robbers. On the chambers' walls were scratched the names of some of the dead. But dominating the underworld vista was a protective godly hand, incised deep and wide into a doorpost, stretching down into the subterranean darkness. Its divine nature is suggested by the partially legible inscription positioned above it, petitioning Yahweh and Asherah to protect one of the tomb's residents: 'Blessed be Uriyahu by Yahweh! Now from his enemies deliver him by his Asherah . . . by his Asherah!' (Plate 15).[6] Marks in the soft rock known as 'ghost letters' indicate that the words of the inscription, and especially Asherah's name, had been traced over by mourners – again and again, as if to reiterate or extend the efficacy of the inscription as they paid repeated visits to the tomb. The divine hand, too, appears to bear the gentle ablations of ritual touch on its palm and fingers, as though the living had marked their mourning on the hand of God. Touching the inscribed walls in the dim lamplight of the underworld, the living physically connected with the dead and the deities looking over them.[7] This tomb was not only an otherworldly portal, but a place at which the divine touch could be felt.

The idea that the gods could extend a protective hand into the personal lives and deaths of their worshippers was far from new – particularly for those elite individuals who enjoyed the benefits of a more direct relationship with the high gods. Just as a divine hand could gift weapons from the heavens to mighty kings, so too the gods could reach down to caress the heads of faithful worshippers. Some of the most striking examples of this already ancient idea are evident in the iconography of the Egyptian king Akhenaten (c. 1352–1336 BCE). The artwork produced during this pharaoh's reign is remarkable not only for the delicate shapely forms of its subjects' bodies, but its intimate insights into the royal family's life. One particularly tender scene on a stela shows the king and his queen, Nefertiti, sitting opposite each other with three of their young daughters. The king cradles one child in his hands, lifting her to his face for a kiss; a baby girl nestles against the queen's shoulder, as a chatty toddler sits on her lap, holding her mother's hand and pointing to her father with the other. Positioned above them is the sun disc of the god Aten, his rays of light emblazoned with hands, reaching down to stroke the family with warm blessings (fig. 34). The same motif occurs on a wall panel in the royal family's tomb at Tel el-Amarna. Standing tall, arms reaching heavenwards, Akhenaten and Nefertiti offer up lotus blooms to the sun disc, while beams of divine light stretch down to touch the royal couple with gentle hands, some holding the *ankh* symbol of life.[8]

Fig. 34. Manifesting Aten's blessings, the rays of the sun disc extend gentle hands to Akhenaten, Nefertiti and their daughters. Detail from a limestone house altar from Tel el-Amarna, Egypt, c. 1352–1336 BCE.

Standing with outstretched arms, reaching up to the beaming embrace of the deity, the royal couple's pious posture anticipates that of Yahweh's own worshippers at Kuntillet 'Ajrud in northern Sinai, over six hundred years later. There, drawings inked onto a large storage jar, with Hebrew inscriptions, show a group of men standing in profile, their faces lifted towards the sky; raising their arms into the air, they appear to be performing a petitionary rite, reaching out to the divine (fig. 35).[9] It is a ritual gesture well attested in the Hebrew Bible, in which worshippers variously raise up, spread, or reach out their hands to Yahweh as they invoke his name. 'I will bless you as long as I live; I will lift up my hands and call on your name', vows one psalmist. 'Every day I call on you, O Yahweh; I spread out my hands to you', declares another.[10] This was a gesture anticipating the responsive touch of the deity, who similarly reached out to his worshippers: 'I held out my hands all day long', Yahweh says.[11]

To the modern mind, this ritual might seem merely symbolic, or inherently futile – an inevitably empty gesture, as human hands searching for God's touch feel nothing but the gulf between them. But for worshippers across the ancient Levant, the tactility of touch was felt

Fig. 35. Worshippers holding their hands aloft in a gesture of petition or praise. Dating to the first half of the eighth century BCE, these figures were inked in red onto a large storage jar at Kuntillet 'Ajrud in northern Sinai.

in the action itself. Within the religious imagination, the hand-raising ritual was a potent performance, creating otherworldly realities. In raising their hands in prayer or petition, worshippers described themselves as 'taking hold' of their god.[12] For those privileged enough to behold a cult image of the high god, his open-palmed right hand raised up in a motion of blessing, the divine touch was felt as a palm-press of promise or a hand-clasp of commitment: raising their own right hand in ritual salutation, kings, priests and prophets felt the deity take hold of their hand, and hold it tight, as Yahweh himself insisted: 'I am Yahweh your god, who holds your right hand'.[13]

The intimacy of the hand-raising ritual spoke to the intensity of the relationship between God and his worshippers. This was a deity who not only held his worshippers' hands, but drew them into his arms – sometimes as a lover, and sometimes as a father or a mother. 'When Israel was a child, I loved him, and out of Egypt I called my son . . . I taught Ephraim to walk, I took him up in my arms', the deity declares of his people in the book of Hosea.[14] It is a vivid snapshot of a tender divine love, similarly picked out with a delicate poetic beauty in the book of Isaiah. Vowing never to forget his worshippers, Yahweh asks, 'Can a woman forget her nursing child? Or show no compassion for the child of her womb?'[15] Speaking the promises whispered by countless generations of parents, he declares, 'You have been carried by me from birth, lifted from the womb; even to your old age I am he, even when you turn grey I will carry you'.[16]

Theologians and scholars alike have made much of the maternal imagery attributed to God throughout the Bible. For many, it is a sought-after sign that God is both male and female; for others, it points reassuringly to God's sexless, gender-free transcendence. More recently, and just as optimistically, biblical portrayals of God-as-woman have been held to signal the pan-gendered, transgendered, or gender-queer nature of the divine creator. And yet the biblical God is neither birth mother, nor female, nor womanly in these texts. Within the elite circles in which the traditions of the Hebrew Bible arose, motherhood and its attendant activities was as much a social construction of kinship as a biological, physiological state. To claim parenthood over others was a widespread cultural trope of power and protection, conventionally expressed in the language of tender hands and loving arms. It is vividly illustrated in a Phoenician inscription from the ancient city of Sam'al, now named Zincirli Höyük, in southern Turkey. Dated to about 825 BCE, the inscription was set up by King Kulamuwa of Sam'al, who cast his relationship with a people known as the Mushkabim as an intimately familial bond: 'I was to some a father; and I was to some a mother; and to some I was a brother . . . I took the Mushkabim by the hand, and they showed [me] affection like the affection of a fatherless child towards [its] mother'.[17] A similar ideology underlies Yahweh's mothering of his people in the Hebrew Bible. But it is tinged with a polemical hue, painted in the colours of the biblical writers' theological agenda: in asserting his role as divine kin to his people, Yahweh was also usurping the roles of the birth goddesses, divine midwives and heavenly wet nurses more usually invoked to protect a babe in arms.

In ancient Israel and Judah, birthing, nursing and weaning were collaborative responsibilities, shared by the women of the household and their extended families. The rituals accompanying pregnancy, birth and childcare not only wrapped the mother and infant into a magical web of otherworldly protection, but bound the mother, baby and women of the family into a close kinship network. This was not a network from which men were necessarily excluded, but it was predominantly a world of women, within which breastfeeding was a particularly important shared activity. From elite to lowly households, it was not unusual for mothers to nurse other women's children, often as a form of practical support in a culture in which children were not usually weaned until they were three or four years old. Together, these women raised what scholar Cynthia Chapman calls 'milk siblings' – one or two generations of children socialized into the extended household by shared nursing.[18] Within this world of women, breastmilk was a substance of social as well as physical nourishment, sustaining women's social networks and the children enmeshed in them – much as the ritual blood of male circumcision imparted a shared identity to men and boys within the household and the wider community. This might explain why inexpensive clay figurines depicting women supporting or offering their heavy, milk-filled breasts were among the most common of ritual objects in the home and the tomb.

Fig. 36. A late eighth-century BCE clay figurine of a heavy-breasted
woman, excavated in Jerusalem. Hundreds of examples have been found
in homes and tombs across ancient Judahite sites, spanning the period
from the early eighth to the late sixth century BCE. They seem to have
played a role in the well-being of the household.

Hundreds of examples have been found in Judahite sites dating from
the early eighth to the late sixth century BCE. Whether they specifically
served to petition goddesses for successful lactation, as some scholars
suggest, or functioned more generally to protect the household, as
others contend, they seem to have been closely associated with the
social identities and well-being of family members across the generations, both living and dead.[19]

Overseeing these women's nursing networks were not only the
gods of fertility with whom the biblical writers were so familiar –
Yahweh, El and Baal – but the traditional goddesses of birth, midwifery
and lactation (likely including Asherah), who have been marginalized
or ignored in the Bible's story of the past. Images of these divine
women have been unearthed in archaeological excavations in modern-
day Palestine and Israel, and they illustrate well the tender arms and
hands of a nursing deity. A figurine fragment from twelfth-century BCE
Shechem adapts the highly influential iconography of the Egyptian
goddess Isis and the infant Horus to cast a local goddess as a birth deity.
Only the woman's torso, arms and hands can be seen, but the long

curls of a goddess's hairstyle sit just below her shoulders, and she wears
thick bangles on her wrists. She holds a baby in her lap, who looks out
at the viewer with big eyes as he lifts his little hands to her breasts. A
tenth-century BCE example from the city of Beth-shean depicts the
torso of a nude woman with thickly incised labia. She is ornamented
with the accessories of a goddess – a jewelled belt, armlets, bracelets
and thick necklaces – and holds a baby on her left hip, her right hand
gently cupping his chin (fig. 37).[20] These clay figurines offer a fleeting
glimpse into the worlds of ordinary women, for whom divine assistance in birthing and nursing likely played a valuable role in their
religious lives. But higher-status households enjoyed the care of the
gods, too.

In royal households across ancient south-west Asia, the deities of
fertility, birth and lactation functioned not only as divine guardians,
but as the heavenly family of a newborn heir – a divine kinship celebrated in the ceremonies and statecraft of kingship. This was a
long-lived ideology, reaching into the distant past. In about 2460 BCE,
Eannatum, ruler of the Sumerian city-state of Lagash, described his
divine infancy in an inscription adorning a monument now known as

Fig. 37. A fragment of a clay figurine depicting a woman holding an infant
(tenth century BCE). The visibility of the woman's labia, combined with
her studded belt and elaborate jewellery, suggests this is a goddess.

the Stela of Vultures. He boasts he was implanted in the womb by Ningirsu, the city's warrior god, and joyfully delivered by Ninhursaga, the great birth goddess. Inanna then 'took him on her own arm' and named him, and then 'set him down on Ninhursaga's knee . . . and Ninhursaga suckled him'.[21] A century or so later, the Sumerian king Lugal-zagesi of Uruk was describing himself as a 'son born of Nisaba' (a goddess of grain and writing), who had 'suckled on the milk of Ninhursaga' and was 'reared by Ningirim' (a goddess skilled in incantations).[22] Raised by their divine kin, kings could claim the ongoing protection and endorsement of the gods. So potent was this royal ideology that it extended across ancient south-west Asia for millennia. In the seventh century BCE, King Esarhaddon of Assyria was reassured of his status as a man-child of the gods in an oracle from the deities Ishtar and Bel (a title of both Ashur and Marduk):

> Fear not, Esarhaddon! I am Bel. [Even as] I speak to you, I
> watch over the beams of your heart. When your mother gave
> birth to you, sixty great gods stood with me and protected you.
> [The moon deity] Sin was at your right side, [the sun deity]
> Shamash at your left; sixty great gods were standing around
> you and girded your loins. Do not trust in man. Lift up your
> eyes, look to me! I am Ishtar of Arbela; I reconciled Ashur
> with you. When you were small, I took you to me. Fear not!
> Praise me![23]

Esarhaddon's son and successor, Ashurbanipal, clearly understood the political power of divine conception and birth. Beset by rebellions orchestrated by his older brother, Shamash-shum-ukin (whom Esarhaddon had appointed king of Babylon), Ashurbanipal underscored his divine right to rule by piously denying his mortal family in favour of the cosmic origins of his kingship. In a hymn to the goddesses Ishtar of Nineveh and Ishtar of Arbela, he says, 'I knew no father or mother, I grew up in the lap of my goddesses. As a child the great gods guided me, going with me on the right and the left . . . The Lady of Nineveh, the mother who bore me, endowed me with unparalleled kingship; the Lady of Arbela, my creator, ordered everlasting life [for me].'[24] The king's claims to a divine mother are further endorsed in a conversation between Ashurbanipal and Nabu, the scribe god, in which we learn that the hyper-potency of Ishtar's breasts gave her double the nipples of an ordinary deity: 'You were a baby, Ashurbanipal, when you sat in the lap of the Queen [Ishtar] of Nineveh!' Nabu says. 'Her four teats were placed in your mouth; two you sucked, and two you milked to your face'.[25]

Across the Levant, the divine suckling of a child was a similarly fixed feature of royal ideologies. According to an Ugaritic legend, the dynastic ambitions of a fabled royal ancestor, King Kirta, were assured by the divinely ordained birth of his son Yasib, an heir gifted to Kirta by the high god El. The new baby, it was said, would 'drink the milk' of Athirat and 'drain the breasts' of Anat, much as El's own offspring are wet-nursed by Athirat in another Ugaritic myth.[26] The divine suckling of heirs at Ugarit is reflected in the iconography of a beautiful carved ivory frieze which once framed a royal bed, empowering its mortal occupants to conceive a divinely begotten child. Beneath a sacred tree of life, flanked by mythical winged guardians, a goddess wearing a horned headdress and long robe wraps her arms around two young princes standing in her embrace. Lifting their faces and hands to her breasts, they suckle from the goddess beneath the protective shade of her outstretched wings.[27]

Set against this rich cultural backdrop, it is no surprise to find the God of the Bible taking on the traditional roles of birth and lactation goddesses to endorse the reign of his kings. 'It was you who took me from the womb, you kept me safe on my mother's breast; on you I was cast from my birth, and since my mother bore me you have been my god', a poet declares in a psalm traditionally attributed to King David.[28] Yahweh was already perceived as the divine father of the kings of Israel and Judah – a relationship he powerfully reiterated at the point of the monarch's enthronement as the Son of God: 'You are my son; this day I have begotten you'.[29] A king's divine nature was similarly celebrated in oracles about royal births. Two such oracles appear in the book of Isaiah. Although they would later be co-opted into early Christian theology to herald the birth of Jesus, they are dated to about the eighth century BCE, and originally played a part in the dynastic cult of Judahite kingship. The first concerns an unnamed queen, who will birth a divinely given heir: 'The Lord himself will give you a sign: Look! The young woman is with child, and she will give birth to a son, and she will name him Immanu El ["God is with us"]'.[30] The second is longer, but no less exalted in its claims about the royal baby:

> For a child has been born to us,
> a son has been given to us,
> and leadership is on his shoulders.
> And his name is called Wondrous Counsellor,
> Divine Warrior, Eternal Ancestor, Prince of Peace.
> His authority shall grow continually,
> and there shall be endless peace
> for the throne of David and his kingdom.[31]

This high-status kinship with the gods was extended in the Hebrew Bible to Yahweh's people, rendering Israel his 'beloved son' – itself a mythological title which would eventually come to be recycled in the New Testament to describe the divinity of Jesus. But in performing the roles of heavenly midwife and divine suckler, Yahweh gradually displaced the powerful goddesses of old, inserting himself deeper into the household religion of his worshippers. From now on, Yahweh would parent alone, forcing his worshippers – his 'children' – to be wholly reliant upon him, and him alone. Faint echoes of the lost goddesses' birthing, nurturing skills would reverberate in later Jewish myths about both Lady Wisdom and the Shekhinah, and in Christian portrayals of Mary. But the traditional goddesses would never recover their prestigious roles.

In the Bible, the goddesses' absence is perhaps most starkly felt in the hands-on role Yahweh increasingly played in the creation of his worshippers. Across ancient south-west Asia, it was the birth goddesses who had more usually shaped mortals from clay, pinching off pieces of wet mud to craft the human form. But for the biblical writers, Yahweh was the divine clay-shaper, who not only formed the first man in Eden, but engineered the birth of all his worshippers from the fertile earth. 'Now, O Yahweh, you are our father; we are the clay, and you are our potter; we are all the work of your hand'.[32] But the divine touch could be as destructive as it was creative. 'Your hands fashioned and made me; and now you turn and destroy me!' Job cries, as his body begins to crumble through the afflictions Yahweh has imposed upon him. 'Remember that you fashioned me like clay; will you turn me to dust again?'[33]

Clay-shaping bodies had long been a ritual activity undertaken by both gods and mortals. In a Sumerian myth, the ingenious god Enki and the birth goddess Ninmah had crafted the first humans from clay, peopling their temples, farms and fields with worshippers devoted to their service. In a related tradition, the goddess Mami chanted an incantation as Enki trod the clay for her to shape into people.[34] At Ugarit, it was a process similarly performed by El, who had made an exorcism goddess from clay to cure King Kirta: ' "I shall create a remover of sickness, an expeller of disease!" He fills [his] hands . . . with the best of clay; he pinches off that which is [used] by a potter'.[35] Meanwhile, in Egypt, the god most frequently associated with the creation of humans was Khnum, who crafted all living things, including some gods, on his potter's wheel: 'You are the master of the wheel, who is pleased to model on the wheel . . . you have made humans on the wheel, you have created the gods; you have modelled the small and large cattle; you have formed everything on your wheel each day, in your name Khnum the potter'.[36]

In all these processes, clay-shaping is cast as a magical act – which is precisely the way it was understood by humans when they made terracotta images of their gods for use in their rituals. And just as worshippers moulded images of the gods in human-like form, so the gods moulded images of humans in godlike form – as the creation traditions in Genesis attest: 'Then God said, "Let us make humankind in our image, according to our likeness . . ." And so God created humankind in his image, in the divine image he created them; male and female he created them'. The mechanics of this divine creation are spelled out in the Eden story: 'Yahweh-God fashioned the man from the dust of the ground, and he breathed into his nostrils the breath of life, and the man became a living being'.[37] When the God of the Bible created people from clay, he was performing a specialized magical craft, conjuring new life in his hands.

*

From birth to death, the God of the Bible reached into the lives of his worshippers, performing the ritual actions essential to the ongoing existence, well-being and protection of his people. But these were not the only rituals he performed. God also enjoyed a rich inner-life of religious activity – a personal piety played out with his hands. One of the rituals he most frequently performs in the Bible is vow making. Like mortals, who raise a hand heavenwards and swear an oath by their god, Yahweh too raises his hand to the heavens – and invokes himself, rather than any other deity, as his witness: 'I lift up my hand to [the] heavens, and swear: As I live forever, when I whet my flashing sword, and my hand takes hold on judgement, I will take vengeance on my adversaries, and will repay those who hate me'.[38] Warfare inevitably demanded further religious activities, and so, in preparation for battle, Yahweh also performs a hand-clapping ritual. In contrast to joyful clapping or celebratory applause, ritual clapping served an apotropaic function, exorcising any malevolent powers bringing misfortune. On the battlefield, clapping rendered the enemy a demonic presence to be expunged. The efficacy of the ritual is confidently claimed by God in an oracle on the eve of a war: 'I too will strike hand to hand; I will satisfy my fury; I, Yahweh, have spoken!'[39]

Perhaps most remarkably of all, the God of the Bible is also a deity who offers sacrifice. Like many of their scribal forebears across the Levant, the biblical writers are careful to avoid the impression that a deity might offer up a blood sacrifice to another god – to do so would be to compromise the divine sacrificer's godly status. Instead, when the gods prepare and offer a sacrifice, it is quite literally a self-serving ritual, often set within a context of warfare. Casting the human enemy's destruction as a celebratory ritual slaughter, the gods' butchering of bodies, evisceration of innards and splattering of blood functions much like an animal sacrifice: the blood purifies and empowers the space of sacrifice, while the innards and fat are divinely devoured. This is graphically illustrated in a description of Yahweh's onslaught against the citizens of Bozrah, in Edom:

> Yahweh has a sword; it is sated with blood,
>   it is gorged with fat, with the blood of lambs and goats,

with the fat of kidneys and rams.
For Yahweh has a sacrifice in Bozrah,
a great slaughter in the land of Edom.
Wild oxen shall fall with them,
and young steers with the mighty bulls.
Their land shall be soaked with blood,
and their soil made rich with fat.[40]

In many ways, Yahweh's ritual activities were not so different from those of other deities across the ancient world, who not only swore vows, offered sacrifices and poured out libations, but purified themselves, experienced visionary dreams, performed exorcism rites and uttered magical incantations. But as time went on, and as the religious lives of his worshippers were increasingly aligned to the regulations set out in their sacred texts, so too God's personal piety fell into line with his worshippers' ritual practices. By the time the highly authoritative book of Jubilees had been composed in the second century BCE, God himself was keeping Shabbat every week with his angels and his people – as he had always done, apparently.[41] After all, these Jewish scribes appear to have thought, it was not without good reason that God had created a day of rest. It was a day on which space and time was given over to focused reflection on the close bond between God and his worshippers. Underlying this intimate notion was the sense that God was very much with his worshippers in their religious activities in their homes – an understanding that was already dear to diaspora communities, and would become increasingly important in the aftermath of the Jerusalem temple's final destruction in 70 CE. Keeping Shabbat would become as powerful as offering sacrifice in the temple: both provoked the glad and willing presence of God.

If Shabbat had its origins in the creation, and an archetypal adherent in God himself, then so too did other rituals common to early Jewish practice. According to a midrashic text, God's first ritual action occurred at the very beginning of the creation of the world, when he built the archetypal *sukkah* in Jerusalem – a prayer hut used in the Jewish festival of Sukkot (also known as Tabernacles). Inside this first *sukkah*, God had prayed his people would always remain obedient to him, so that he would not have to destroy the Jerusalem temple. When the people eventually sinned, some rabbis said, he tore down the *sukkah*, marking the destruction of his temple, and prayed again for his people's obedience so that he could rebuild it once more.[42]

The notion that God self-reflexively prayed and kept Shabbat reflects the ancient rabbinic tendency to align God so closely with the religious activities of his people that he came to be understood as subject to the strict ritual regulations he had set for his own worshippers. As he would come to declare in a Talmudic text, he is not like a mortal ruler who makes and then breaks his own laws. Rather, he says, 'I am he who is first to observe the commandments of the Torah'.[43] It was a commitment to his own commandments now evident in his daily activities. Since the early centuries of the Common Era, many rabbis had equated Torah observance with studying and teaching its precepts. Of course, they reasoned, God himself had already taken up this important activity, reading the Torah in the mornings and joining his students in specialized study houses as they worked on understanding and expounding the sacred scrolls.[44] By this time, God's commitment to his own commandments was also demonstrated in his body language. Gone were the bloodied arms of a fearsome warrior, the dusty hands of a mortuary worker, or the tender touch of a sacred suckler. Now, some rabbis deduced, God covered his head with a long prayer shawl and dressed his arm with texts from the Torah.

Evidence for the former was creatively extrapolated from the account of God's appearance to Moses in Exodus 34. Here, the deity incants his own divine attributes as though he were one of his own priests, declaring himself merciful, gracious, abounding in steadfast love across a thousand generations, forgiving of wrongdoing, but just in holding the guilty to account for four generations. Moses immediately bows down and prays. For Rabbi Yohanan, a revered sage of the second century CE, this must have been the moment at which God himself inaugurated the liturgy for a prayer service – and he was thus appropriately dressed for the occasion. 'This verse teaches us that the Holy One, blessed be He, drew his robe around him like the reader of a congregation and showed Moses the order of prayer'.[45] Just as prayer readers in ancient synagogues would cover their own heads and shoulders with the *tallit* – a fringed shawl made of wool or linen – so too did God when he instituted prayer itself.

But the *tallit* was not God's only ritual accessory. Some rabbis also claimed God wore *tefillin* – small pouches or boxes containing tiny scrolls bearing holy words found in portions of Exodus and Deuteronomy. Fixed to the head and the left arm (or the right for left-handed people), they appear to have been in use among Jewish groups from as early as the second century BCE, and are still worn in prayer by Jewish men (and, increasingly, some women) today. These sacred objects manifest obedience to one of the most authoritative of divine instructions in the book of Deuteronomy – an instruction which itself appears in one of the tiny scrolls contained in the *tefillin* boxes: 'Hear, O Israel: Yahweh is our God, Yahweh is one. And you shall love Yahweh your God with all your heart, and with all your being, and with all your might. Keep these words that I am commanding you today in your heart. Recite them . . . Bind them as a sign on your hand and they shall be as emblems between your eyes.'[46]

According to teaching passed on by the fourth-century CE Rabbi Avin, evidence indicating that God wore *tefillin* was to be found in selected verses in Deuteronomy, Isaiah and the Psalms, in which certain references to God vowing by his arm and hand, and allusions to his holding the Torah, were best understood to signal the presence of *tefillin* on his body. The teaching is typically complex and creative:

> Rabbi Avin son of Rabbi Ada in the name of Rabbi Yitzhak says: How do you know that the Holy One, blessed be He, puts on *tefillin*? For it is said: *The Lord hath sworn by His right hand, and by the arm of His strength* [Isaiah 62.8]. '*By His right hand*': this is the Torah; for it is said: *At His right hand was a fiery law unto them* [Deuteronomy 33.2]. '*And by the arm of His strength*': this is the *tefillin*; as it is said: *The Lord will give strength unto His people* [Psalm 29.11]. And how do you know that the *tefillin* are a strength to Israel? For it is written: *And all the peoples of the earth shall see that the name of the Lord is called upon thee, and they shall be afraid of thee* [Deuteronomy 28.10], and it has been

taught: Rabbi Eliezer the Great says: This refers to the *tefillin* of the head.[47]

To a reader unfamiliar with the interpretative gymnastics of rabbinic scriptural exposition, Rabbi Avin's argument looks impenetrably eso-teric. But it is the dynamic corporeal image of God's body, conjured by the rabbi's comfortable insistence that God wears *tefillin*, that is more striking. It is highly unlikely the rabbis of antiquity would have imagined these sacred objects magically appearing on God's body in a sudden blinding flash or a mysterious puff of smoke. Instead, they naturally assumed that God did what they did: he bound a pouch containing a portion of the Torah onto his upper arm with a long strip of leather, winding the strap down his arm and around his hand. Then he tied another Torah pouch to his forehead with another long leather strip, knotting it at the nape of his neck.

Fixed onto his own body like an amulet, the written word of God was not simply his literary output, nor solely an object of study in his daily schedule. It was a potent form of body modification – just as it was for his male worshippers, then as now. Torah became a part of God's person. It was the ultimate expression of the binding, formative and divine status of God's commandments – a status he had set in stone long ago, with his very finger.

15

Holy Handbooks

In the early hours of 3 March 2019, a fierce fire broke out at a small non-denominational church in Daniels, West Virginia. It reportedly took several hours for firefighters to bring the blaze under control and extinguish the flames. As the smoke cleared, the extent of the damage was revealed: the building was gutted, its burnt, blackened core a mass of rubble and ash. And yet the congregation's twenty or so Bibles had survived, seemingly unscathed. On its Facebook page, the attending fire department uploaded photographs of the Bibles in the detritus of the devastation – some paperback, some hardback, some leather-bound. 'Though odds were against us, God was not', read the accompanying message. 'Picture this, a building so hot that at one point in time, fire-fighters had to back out. In your mind, everything should be burned, ashes. Not a single bible [*sic*] was burned and not a single cross was harmed!! Not a single firefighter was hurt!' The post went viral. A reporter from the *Washington Post* was so taken with the story that she contacted Zondervan, the publishing house whose Bibles appeared in the photographs, for comment. 'There is nothing in the production process that would protect them from fire,' confirmed Zondervan's Melinda Bouma, who offered a theological explanation instead: 'It burned down,' she said of the church, 'and nothing really survived, but the word of our Lord survived.' It was a view the church's pastor, the Reverend Phil Farrington, also shared: 'In the midst of the fire, God's word will always stand,' he told the newspaper.[1]

Stories like this are not so unusual as to be astonishing – people perceive miracles at the most testing of times. More remarkable, perhaps, is the emphasis on the indestructible nature of the 'word of God' as a material object – a printed book, bought and sold in its millions every year. Within a religion in which the 'word of God' is professed to have been made flesh in the body of Christ, the Bible is an authoritative but supporting prop, rather than a sacred icon in and of itself. The Bible might be a holy book, but as a material object, it tends not to enjoy quite the same sanctified status as the Quran or the Torah scroll. But in Daniels, West Virginia, as in countless Christian communities of any stripe across the world, the Bible's materiality still matters. The 'word of God' is an extraordinary object, as well as an account of divine revelation.

In Christianity's older iterations, especially (but not exclusively) Eastern Orthodoxies and Roman Catholicism, the Bible's status as a sacred object is still evident in its specialized decoration, procession, exhibition and veneration in church services. Distinct from the Bibles of lay worshippers, the ceremonial scriptures of ritual tend to be large, ornate objects, clad in jewelled covers. Paraded around the church in a procession of clergy and crucifixes, the book is variously perfumed with incense, placed on the altar, kissed by a priest and held aloft before the congregation. As its pages are opened and read, many worshippers stand in reverence, ritually bow or nod their heads, or prostrate themselves before it. In church, the Bible is not simply read aloud, but adored, like a cult statue of old.

The sacred status of the written word is similarly evident in the rituals of Jewish services, in which reading aloud from the Torah scroll takes centre stage in synagogues. Enshrined behind a curtain in the ark – the specialized cupboard facing the direction of Jerusalem – the scroll is lifted from its dwelling place and carried upright around the congregation. Like the ceremonial scriptures of Christianity, the Torah scroll is heavily accessorized. Wearing a mantle and miniature breastplate (in the Ashkenazi tradition) or an ornate wooden or silver case (in the Sephardic tradition), the scroll is processed to the reading table, where it is undressed and unrolled. As the scroll is read aloud, the cantor uses a *yad* – a hand-shaped pointer – to follow the words of the text, preventing direct contact with its inked letters. During the reading, blessings are uttered over the scroll, and kisses transferred to its margins via the corner of the worshipper's prayer shawl, which is pressed to the lips and touched to the parchment's edge. The open scroll is then held high and shown to the congregation, before being rolled up, re-dressed and returned to its ark.

Within both Judaism and Christianity, the ritual use of an authoritative text as a sacred object is not only a matter of ceremonial tradition, but a reflection of the ancient status of scripture as divine revelation. This is writing which is not simply religious in content and character, but sacralized as a revelatory product of God: its origins are heavenly, whether inscribed by the deity himself, hand-delivered by divine beings, transcribed by humans who have spoken with God, or written by those he has mysteriously seized. In synagogues and churches, scripture is a 'power object', giving worshippers what scholar David Morgan describes as 'sight and sound' of God's voice.[2]

Earliest Christianity inherited its notion of sacred writing from the founding members of the Jesus movement in the first century CE. Originally a thoroughly Jewish sect, the Jesus movement held dear those writings which had become particularly authoritative for most other Jewish groups. And prime among these was the Torah – the five scrolls comprising the religious 'law' or 'teaching' (torah) found in Genesis, Exodus, Leviticus, Numbers and Deuteronomy. Although the stories, poems and religious regulations it contained were older, the Torah's textualized form as the 'books of Moses' had attained a special status as the continuous revelation of God, delivered on Mount Sinai. As a literary collection, the Torah was already in wide circulation by the time of Alexander the Great. But this was a textualized Torah centuries away from being fixed in form. Even in the first century CE, the Torah was still an unstable, fluid anthology. Multiple versions were in existence across Roman Palestine, Asia Minor, Greece, Macedonia, Egypt, Syria and Mesopotamia. Some scrolls differed in only their smaller details, while others varied in their sequence of narratives and books; still others contained expansions and distinct material. Some were Hebrew, others were Greek, and others would be written in Aramaic and, in the second century, Syriac. But no matter its precise form, the special status of the Torah was assured by its now regular exposition in worship and study, and its close association with Moses, which, for Jewish intellectuals like Philo and Josephus, gave the Torah a prestigious pedigree comparable to that of the works of the great Greek philosophers.

Although the Torah enjoyed a privileged status, it was one among many works in a Jewish literary world teeming with sacred manuscripts, variously described as 'holy scrolls' or 'oracles of God'.[3] These scrolls were revelatory, in the purest sense: they contained the wisdom and teaching of God as disclosed by him to his chosen mediators – a divine knowledge so potent that its careful study could continue to reveal further heavenly secrets. Among these scrolls were not only the books which would come to be included in the Tanakh, but important scriptures such as Jubilees and the books of Enoch, which had enjoyed a wide circulation for several generations and would remain highly influential, even though they would not eventually be classified as 'biblical'. Others were less well known but no less authoritative for the communities curating or creating them, such as some of the religious writings found among the Dead Sea Scrolls. Still others were reputed to have been hidden or lost – whether by divine design or mortal misfortune – so that only tantalizing, mysterious memories of them remained. According to one famous legend, Moses had not only recorded God's speeches in the Torah, but in a further ninety-four texts, which had been lost. It was only when Jerusalem's temple had been rebuilt in the fifth century BCE that the famous Ezra, who had led a group of exiles back to Jerusalem, was divinely inspired to dictate their contents to five scribes; God allowed twenty-four of these texts to be made available to worshippers, but insisted the remaining seventy would be kept back for a future group known only as 'the wise'.[4] As one Jewish writer had already complained in the third century BCE, 'Of making many books there is no end, and much study is a weariness of the flesh'.[5]

Whether real or imagined, all these sacred texts were products of a world in which holy writing had long played a formative role in the relationship between Yahweh and his worshippers – not least because the deity had handwritten some of them himself, as he had already confirmed in Hosea, declaring, 'I write the multitude of my teachings'.[6]

Fig. 38. The Temple Scroll is one of the best-preserved manuscripts found in caves near Qumran, by the Dead Sea. Produced in stages between the late first century BCE and the early first century CE, it is thought to be a copy of a late second-century BCE work. The scroll sets out Yahweh's regulations for his temple, presenting itself as a composition originally crafted by the deity himself. The sheer number and variety of 'holy scrolls' at Qumran reflects the fluidity and diversity of authoritative Jewish texts in this period.

God's best-known compositions, of course, are the Ten Commandments. In the Bible, these religious regulations are said to have been written 'with his finger' on tablets of stone, which he gave to Moses. The story has something in common with much older Mesopotamian tales, in which kings or prophets enter temples where the gods show them written decrees or temple blueprints, which serve as heavenly archetypes for religious regulations and activities in the earthly realm. A brisk version of the story of the Ten Commandments is found in Deuteronomy, but its longer form occurs in Exodus. As with so many stories in this complicated book, the narrative arc is difficult to trace: Yahweh first issues the Ten Commandments (literally, 'ten words' or 'ten utterances') to Moses as an oral instruction, then later tells Moses to ascend Mount Sinai again, where, he says, 'I will give you stone tablets, the teaching (torah) and the commandment, which I have written'.[7] The precise nature of the relationship between the stone tablets, the teaching and the commandment is unclear. Are they distinct? Or identical? The uncertainty only deepens as Yahweh carries on speaking to Moses: he proceeds to talk at great length (seven fulsome chapters) about the architectural and ritual features of the mobile, tented temple – or tabernacle – he expects Moses to make upon his descent from the mountain. At this point in the story, it is also unclear just how many stone tablets the deity has prepared. Will there be only two, inscribed with the Ten Commandments Yahweh has already spoken? Or a shelf-ful, to accommodate the lengthy monologue detailing Yahweh's instructions about the collapsible, pack-away tabernacle? It is difficult not to imagine Moses' relief when the deity reaches the end of his speech and gives him two stone tablets bearing the covenant between the Israelites and their god, which are later confirmed to bear the 'ten utterances' written with 'the finger of God'.[8]

The biblical narrator has no need to spell out the mechanics of God's writing process, for God requires neither stylus nor chisel. Instead, his finger is to be understood as an organ of creative power: it is the finger that was pointedly said to have conjured the great plagues in Egypt and inscribed the very moon and stars into the heavens.[9] Now, with the touch of a finger, Yahweh makes his mark in stone. And it is as much a mark of identity as instruction. Although humans might press stamp seals or cylinder seals into wax or clay to sign their declarations and binding agreements, they might also press the tip of a finger into the writing surface, their fingernail not only leaving a crescent-shaped confirmation of the document's declarations, but a visible imprint of their physical presence. Something of this practice lurks within the story of the stone tablets. As Yahweh's fingertip crafts the commandments by which his worshippers are to live, he inscribes his physical presence into his covenant with his people. This divine touch is at the heart of the story of the Ten Commandments, for the religious regulations binding worshippers to their deity are not just divine instructions but sacred objects, handcrafted and handwritten by God, as the biblical writer is so keen to insist: 'the tablets were the work of God, and the writing was the writing of God, engraved upon the tablets'.[10]

Thanks in no small part to Hollywood's Charlton Heston, we are accustomed to imagining the tablets as large single-sided plaques, akin

to the flattened commemorations of the Ten Commandments custom-
arily displayed on the walls of churches and US courthouses. But in
Exodus, Yahweh's tablets are 'written on both sides, written on the
front and the back', much like the smaller, double-sided clay tablets on
which scribes had long inscribed their texts.[11] Unlike the soft clay used
by mere mortals, however, Yahweh's tablets are hewn from stone – a
monumental material befitting the permanence of divine revelation.
Or, at least, that was the plan. When Moses descends from the mountain with the tablets, he walks straight into a party. Having camped at
Sinai's base for forty days and nights, the Israelites had grown tired of
waiting for Moses to bring messages from Yahweh. Taking matters
into their own hands, they had made an alternative form of divine
revelation: the notorious 'golden calf' – better understood as a statue
of Yahweh as a young bull god – in whose honour they were now
offering sacrifices and holding a raucous feast. Moses is unimpressed.
They have already transgressed one of Yahweh's freshly minted commandments ('You shall not make for yourself an image'). The covenant
is broken. And so too are the tablets of stone: Moses hurls them to the
ground in a ceremonial act more commonly used to mark the breaking
of a treaty between a king and his vassal.[12]

The breaking of the heavenly tablets is often thought to undermine
the sacred materiality of the holy handwriting. Some scholars have
even gone so far as to describe Moses as an iconoclast. But the smashed
tablets serve a more pragmatic purpose. They helpfully afford Yahweh
the opportunity to sanction the practices on which the Bible's writers
and compilers relied: the recrafting of older texts. All scribal cultures
depended on copied texts. And copying was rarely a matter of simple
duplication. Rather, it was an inherently creative process. Authoritative
works of all genres – whether myths, law codes, religious regulations,
state reports, or accounts ledgers – were routinely reproduced, updated
and amended. This not only extended the shelf life of literature as clay
tablets, waxed boards, papyrus documents and parchment scrolls aged,
but enabled important texts to be revised, consulted and circulated far
beyond the confines of archives and libraries. Accordingly, Yahweh
commissions copies of the Ten Commandments to be made. But this
time, the tablets are not hewn in heaven, but crafted on earth. Moses

must cut them himself from the base of the mountain and carry them up to God, where they will be written again. Once complete, they will be sealed into the ark of the covenant and enshrined, first in the tabernacle, and then – according to other biblical writers – in the Jerusalem temple, never to be seen again.[13]

The tantalizing hiddenness of God's written revelation was carefully countered in the Bible by stories emphasizing the proliferation of its words. Yahweh repeatedly tells Moses to write down 'all the words' of his *torah*, which he was to disseminate by transcribing them onto standing stones and ceremonial scrolls at which the people could gaze in wonder. These copies are not so much compositions to be read, but powerful icons by which the people are to be held accountable, as Moses makes plain when he has finished logging all his conversations with God: 'Take this scroll of the *torah* and put it beside the ark of the covenant of Yahweh your god; let it remain there as a witness against you. For I know well how rebellious and stubborn you are'.[14] Later, so the story goes, great heroes, including Moses' deputy, Joshua, and Ezra the scribe, would read aloud to the people 'all the words' of the *torah*, marking the renewal of the binding agreement between God and his people from the moment they first entered the Promised Land under Joshua's command to the moment they returned to Jerusalem from exile with Ezra. And the people would respond to the *torah* with religious awe, as though in the presence of a god, raising their hands and chanting, 'Amen, amen,' before bowing down in worship before it. Even the later Jewish priest and revolutionary leader Judah Maccabee is said to have unrolled the Torah scroll to discern 'those things which the Gentiles search out in the images of their gods'.[15] Like a cult statue in a temple, divine law was neither unreachable nor inaccessible. 'It is not in heaven', as Moses is reported to have said; rather, 'the word is very near to you'.[16] The deity's handwritten tablets might well have been sealed away in the ark, but his revelation didn't come to an end. And nor did God's writing career.

The stone tablets were not God's only compositions. He also had a book – or, more literally, a scroll – in which he kept a register of people,

Fig. 39. 'It is not in heaven . . . the word is very near to you'
(Deuteronomy 30.12). The Torah's emphasis on the accessibility of God's
written regulations is reflected in this miniature from the Regensburg
Pentateuch (*c.* 1300 CE). It shows Moses receiving and then transmitting
the Ten Commandments to the Israelites.

much like a census. 'Yahweh records the peoples in a book: "This one
was born there" '.[17] But the book's administrative purpose was not quite
as anodyne as it might seem. Following the unfortunate incident with
the golden calf, Moses had hastened back up the holy mountain to beg
God's forgiveness. 'Alas, this people has sinned a great sin', he says to
Yahweh, 'now if you will only forgive their sin – but if not, blot me out
of the book that you have written!' Moses is offering to take more than

a mark against his name; he is willing for his name to be struck from God's book altogether, in place of the names of the people. But the deity is not in the mood for negotiations. 'Whoever has sinned against me I will blot out of my book', he declares.[18] Yahweh was not simply a bookkeeper, but a creative writer. Inscribing the names of mortals into his heavenly book wrote them into social existence – both in the eyes of the deity, and in the sight of the religious community. In a world in which death was a subsequent state of existence for mortals, to be blotted out of Yahweh's book was not simply to be killed, but to be forever unknown to Yahweh and forgotten by the living. In short, it was to be without identity. And that was a fate worse than death.

Across ancient south-west Asia, the potential erasure of names was an anxiety felt especially by those privileged enough to exercise the power of their identity over others. Inscriptions on commemorative monuments, wall reliefs, memorial stelae and tombs urge their readers not to chip away or write over the names of those exhibited upon them. Public and private royal records typically warned readers against erasing kings' names. In Babylonia, King Hammurabi's famous law code was inscribed with curses both upon those who might violate his laws and anyone who might remove Hammurabi's name from the monument and replace it with their own. In Assyria, King Ashurbanipal inscribed a similar threat into one of his own books, warning that, 'whoever erases my written name and writes his own name, may [the god] Nabu, the scribe of all, erase his name'.[19] It was an understandable anxiety, for the deliberate destruction of a name could bring disaster on its owner, whether in life or in death. Even Yahweh commanded his worshippers to smash the religious monuments dedicated to other gods so that he could 'put his name there'.[20] And he too worried his own name might disappear in the face of competition from other gods and the machinations of false prophets: 'They plan to make my people forget my name by their dreams that they tell one another, just as their ancestors forgot my name for Baal'.[21] As in many societies today – including our own – exclusion or erasure from an official register, public record, or government list essentially amounts to non-existence: the anonymous and the unidentifiable are unseen and unknown.

To be recorded in God's Book of Life, as it eventually came to be called, was not only to be written into the world, but to acquire a divinely decreed life. 'In your book were written all the days that were formed for me, when none of them as yet existed!' enthuses one psalmist.[22] This was not so much a testament to scripted predestination, but a sense that Yahweh's writing was as creative as the hand that produced it – a hand that could also spell disaster for mortals. 'Why do you count me as your enemy?' cries Job as his flesh begins to rot. 'You write bitter things against me, and make me reap the iniquities of my youth!'[23] It was a complaint any mortal suffering misfortune might have made to their god, for Yahweh's book was modelled on a much older heavenly text, which had originally belonged to the Sumerian high god Enlil. The famed Tablet of Destinies was a lapis lazuli tablet recording in cuneiform the agreed decisions of the gods, impressed with cylinder seals to mark the fixed and binding nature of its words. In Enlil's role as the 'decreer of fates', the tablet bore the destinies of gods and mortals as Enlil wrote into being events in the heavenly and earthly realms. Clutching the tablet in his hand or wearing it on his chest, Enlil held the cosmos in his control. As rebellious divine forces sought to disrupt the cosmos, or as younger gods ascended the mythological ranks, the Tablet of Destinies would change hands several times across the centuries. But by the first millennium BCE, the divine Tablet of Destinies was in the steady curatorial care of Marduk's son, the scribe god Nabu, to whom mortals appealed for favourable fortunes. A well-known example is found in an early sixth-century BCE inscription commissioned by King Nebuchadnezzar II of Babylon (605–562 BCE) to memorialize his refurbishment of Nabu's temple in Borsippa: 'On your reliable writing board which establishes the border of heaven and the netherworld, decree the lengthening of my days, inscribe for me extreme old age. Cause my deeds to find acceptance before Marduk, the king of heaven and the netherworld, the father your begetter.'[24]

In order to ascertain whether or not his prayer had been answered, Nebuchadnezzar might have called upon his diviners, among whose tasks it was to look for divinely revealed reflections of Nabu's writing hidden in the creases of animal innards. After all, the gods not only wrote their judgements into the heavenly records of their meetings, but into the very stuff of the world, in which their handwriting might be discerned. From the microcosm of the internal organs to the macrocosm of shifting constellations, the cryptic communications of the gods were everywhere. But reading and interpreting these signs required a specialized form of divination – a highly erudite technology, curated by professional scribes and learned through careful study. In Mesopotamia, these experts systematized and consulted archives of divine decrees, past events, natural phenomena and medical conditions to explain prophecies and omens, ascertain future events, and advise their patrons of a preferred course of action. One of the largest archives was the royal library at Nineveh, in Assyria. Under the direction of King Ashurbanipal, who himself boasted of a highly advanced scribal education, the library's holdings had expanded significantly during the seventh century BCE, as written works from archives and private collections across and beyond the Assyrian Empire were industriously copied, catalogued, consulted, recopied and reworked. Although the material age of the library's oldest holdings was only about two hundred years old (the average lifespan of a clay tablet, scroll, or writing board), the intellectual and administrative traditions within the library stretched back at least a thousand years, and likely totalled something in the region of 30,000 texts – double the number later held in the famous library at Alexandria.[25] Working hand in hand with literary experts like those employed at Nineveh, diviners could interpret the words of the gods written into the stars of the skies, the births of babies, or sacrificial offal.

Divination was a mantic science with which the God of the Bible was familiar. He too communicated in birth omens and celestial signs, but he preferred to inscribe the internal organs of his worshippers, rather than those of animals destined for his dinner plate. This preference was motivated by his insistence that his worshippers adhere to his much-publicized *torah* – his binding teaching – rather than the secret knowledge of professional scribes and diviners in the pay of the wealthy and powerful. 'I will put my *torah* within them, and I will write it on their hearts', he declares in the book of Jeremiah.[26] The internalization of divine teaching was beyond metaphor. Like the diviners of Mesopotamia, Yahweh's worshippers understood that heavenly writing might find its earthly mirror within the fleshy folds of mortal bodies. Being written into God's heavenly book imprinted divine writing into human intestines, to the delight of his worshippers. 'Here I am! In the scroll of the book it is written of me; I delight to do your will, O my God; your *torah* is within my innards', enthuses one psalmist. But if Yahweh could inscribe his life-affirming directives into his peoples' bodies, he could also write their destructive destiny: 'The sin of Judah is written with an iron pen; with a diamond point it is engraved on the tablet of their hearts', he declares before the Babylonian attack on Jerusalem.[27]

On Mount Sinai, Yahweh had warned he could afflict mortal bodies with his hand-written curses, for they were transcribed into the treaty terms of his covenant. Should his worshippers break the covenant, these penalty clauses would be triggered, and the transgressors' names would be erased from God's heavenly ledger. 'All the curses written in this book will descend on them', Moses tells the Israelites, 'and Yahweh will blot out their names from under heaven'.[28] The verse conjures an image of inky curse-words leaking from the heavens, coating the perpetrators with the horrors of punishment promised by Yahweh: a pestilence that clings to the body; consumption, fever and swelling; boils, ulcers and itches; blindness, madness and confusion; infertility, unhappiness and misfortune; stolen wives, enslaved children and slaughtered livestock; blight, mildew and pests to ravage the crops; scorching heat and drought to kill the land.

By the fourth century BCE, God's scripted, dripping curses had given way to a winged scroll, gliding in the skies above Jerusalem. 'What do you see?' a divine being asks the prophet Zechariah. 'I see a flying scroll; its length is twenty cubits, and its width ten cubits', he replies. 'This is the curse that goes out over the whole land', the divine being explains, 'for everyone who steals shall be cut off according to the writing on one side, and everyone who swears falsely shall be cut off according to the writing on the other side'.[29] Measuring something in the region of nine metres by four, this enormous double-sided scroll can only have been written by a gigantic god. Yahweh is quick to confirm his authorship. 'I have sent it out', he says, 'and it shall enter the house of the thief, and the house of anyone who swears falsely by my name; and it shall abide in that house and consume it, both timber and stones'.[30] Like the Ten Commandments, written front and back with religious and ethical injunctions – including the prohibition of theft and the misuse of Yahweh's name – the scroll descends from the heavens to hold the deity's people to account. But this time, Yahweh's composition is not crafted as an icon, but morphs into a demon, akin to the Destroyer which had once passed over the houses of Egypt, killing all unprotected firstborns. The winged scroll will settle inside the homes of wrongdoers to kindle a punishing conflagration, trans-forming houses to dust.

The prophet Zechariah was not the first to have seen a heavenly scroll. Two hundred years earlier, by the waters of Babylon, the exiled priest Ezekiel had seen Yahweh's hand stretched out to him, holding another double-sided scroll. The divine hands unrolled the scroll and spread it before Ezekiel. 'It had writing on the front and on the back, and written on it were words of lamentation and mourning and woe', reports Ezekiel. 'Open your mouth', commands Yahweh; 'eat this scroll that I give you and fill your stomach with it . . . go to the house of Israel, and speak my very words to them'. In Ezekiel's mouth, bitter words of lamentation, mourning and woe become 'sweet as honey'; they infuse his internal organs with a divine power, transforming the priest into a prophet who speaks the 'very words' God has written.[31] Six centuries before Christians claimed Christ as the incarnate Word of God, the divine word was already enfleshed in Ezekiel.

The transformative power of God's scrolls spoke as much to the numinous quality of writing as to the otherworldly agency of their divine author. Whether a curse or a blessing, the written word had a magical power. As we've already seen, in the biblical regulation con-cerning women accused of adultery, the ink of a priest's written curse, mixed in holy water with the dust of the temple floor, becomes a magical ingredient in a potion concocted to trigger the miscarriage of an illegitimate pregnancy. Magic writing could also offer protection from God himself. Just before one of his attacks on his idolatrous worshippers in Jerusalem, Yahweh sent a divine scribe, equipped with a writing case, into the city. 'Go through the city, through Jerusalem, and put [the X-shaped letter] *taw* on the foreheads of those who sigh and groan over all the abominations that are committed in it', the deity commands in the book of Ezekiel – before coldly instructing his heavenly assassins to 'cut down old men, young men and girls, little children and women, but touch no one who has the mark. And begin at my sanctuary'. It was a protective measure Yahweh's own high priests adapted: in Exodus, the high priest is commanded to wear on his forehead a gold seal or amulet engraved with the words 'Holy to Yahweh', which was likely understood to guard the high priest from the dangerous gaze of God as he ministered in the temple's holy of holies. As far as Yahweh was concerned, this was a tried and tested protective measure: back at the beginning of human history, he had already put a similar mark on the killer Cain to shield him from retributive attack as he wandered the earth.[32]

These magical practices were not confined to specialist religious practitioners and their places of work. For upper-class residents of Jerusalem in the late seventh century BCE, written blessings functioned as powerful amulets in life and death. In a network of tombs at Ketef Hinnom, where the city's Kidron and Hinnom valleys meet, two tiny silver scrolls were discovered in a bone repository inside a burial chamber. The larger of the two measured only two centimetres tall, the other just half that. Each little scroll was likely worn on a necklace, next to the skin. When the scrolls were carefully unrolled, they were found to be inscribed with miniature appeals to Yahweh for his blessings and protection from demonic harm (Plate 25). When their owners were alive, these delicate little scrolls are unlikely to have been unrolled and read. What mattered was their material presence on the body – their words, unseen but there, protecting the wearer from harm, much as the sealed-up parchment scripts of the *tefillin*, and the ornamental scraps of gospels, worn – but unread – by early Christians, would later come to do.[33] In a world in which writing was not simply a tool of communication, but a prized material art, the written word was a powerful icon – whether or not it would or could be read.

Writing itself had always been associated with the divine. As a technology born of administrative necessity, it developed alongside the temple economies of the earliest Sumerian cities, where the careful juxtaposition of written symbols emerged not as a scripted form of sounds or language, but as a memory aid for accountants. Glimpses of this early form of writing can be seen on fragments of clay tablets recovered from the remains of Inanna's temple in Uruk. Dated to about 3100 BCE, these small tablets record the movement of goods and services in and out of the temple-district, which in earlier ages had been tracked using a system of tokens. Using a form of writing scholars now call proto-cuneiform, the tablets combine signs representing ideas, numbers, places and things. Grouped together, these signs form a 'pictographic' account. One example appears to record the receipt of livestock. It is incised with two half-ovals, each signifying the number one; a square with sharp lines stretching off from a corner, representing a temple or house; a quartered circle, the sign for 'sheep'; a star, symbolizing the concept of divinity or a deity, and a combination of large wedge-shapes, forming the sign for 'Inanna' (fig. 40). When this tablet was inscribed, two sheep had been delivered to the temple in Uruk as an offering to the goddess Inanna.[34]

By the time this pictographic system had given way to the complexities of full-blown cuneiform, the temple origins of writing had

Fig. 40. Drawing of a proto-cuneiform tablet from Inanna's temple-district in Uruk, recording the receipt of two sheep (c. 3100 BCE). From this bookkeeping system, writing would emerge.

been endowed with mythic and narrative shape. The Sumerian tale of
Enmerkar and the Lord of Aratta is perhaps the oldest known myth
about writing. Dated to about 2000 BCE, the story tells of a semi-divine
priest-king of Uruk, called Enmerkar, who lived in the very remote
past, when Uruk was known as Kullab. As a priest of Inanna, Enmerkar
is keen to refurbish the goddess's temple, and so, at the deity's suggestion, he sends an emissary to the priest-king of the distant mountain
city of Aratta, requesting precious stones and building materials. The
king of Aratta is reluctant to devalue his own temple to Inanna by
complying, ultimately leading to a war of words as their relayed oral
messages grow increasingly convoluted in their attempt to outwit one
another. When the royal emissary finally finds himself unable to mem-
orize one of Enmerkar's complicated communications, the priest-king
invents writing:

> Since the envoy
> – his words being difficult –
> was unable to render them,
> the lord of Kullab
> smoothed clay with the hand
> and set down the words on it
> in the manner of a tablet.
> While up to then
> there had been no one
> setting down words on clay,
> now, on that day,
> under the sun,
> thus it verily came to be;
> the lord of Kullab
> set down wo[rds on clay,]
> thus it verily
> came to be![35]

In another Sumerian myth, Inanna's temple city of Uruk is again the
earthly home of writing. This time, writing is one of the divine qualities of civilization belonging to the clever god Enki, who has them

stored in his underwater temple, known as the Abzu House, in the primordial city of Eridu. Inanna decides she wants to bestow these civilized attributes upon her beloved Uruk, and devises a way to talk Enki into gifting them to her. Sweet words give way to sweet wine – and a drinking competition. In an alcoholic stupor, Enki agrees to give Inanna writing, and she stows it away on her boat, along with carpentry, metalwork, weaponry, leather-work, prostitution, textile production, lovemaking, beer brewing, basket weaving and decision making. After a series of contests with sea storms and cosmic monsters – sent by a regretful, sober Enki – Inanna docks at Uruk, and the temple city learns to write.[36]

Underlying both these myths was the notion that writing was as much an extraordinary object as a type of civilized skill. The gods, of course, had always been in possession of objects such as these – and they frequently crafted their own. Like Yahweh, they wrote books of blessings and curses, indexed as the oracles and omens which might appear in the material world. According to a library catalogue at Nineveh, nine of the omen books within the archives were composed by the god Ea (Enki) himself, while others were said to have been dictated by Ea and written by scribes. Crafted before the great Flood, these were the divine books to which the most learned of scribes turned in seeking to discern the secrets of the heavens. But they were also the hardest to understand, as King Ashurbanipal himself declared: 'I have learned the hidden secret of the complete scribal art. With my own eyes I have seen the tablets of heaven and earth . . . I have carefully examined inscriptions on stone from before the Deluge that are sealed, stopped up, [and] confused.'[37]

By their very nature, divine books were impenetrable to all but the most gifted – those mortals especially favoured by the gods themselves. Yahweh might have made his Torah accessible, but it still required the mediatory role of Moses to make its words plain in the earthly realm. His other writings, however, would remain in the hands of the heavenly executive, their mystic meanings revealed to mortals only on a need-to-know basis. Indeed, by the end of the Persian period, Yahweh's writing process had become far more imperial in style, for he now engaged angelic courtiers to transcribe his words onto scrolls and tablets. Eavesdropping on his worshippers' conversations, Yahweh decided who was loyal to him and who was unfaithful, dictating their names to his heavenly scribes, who wrote them up in the deity's special 'book of remembrance'.[38] Although he might occasionally deign to inscribe stone peace treaties with his subjugated cosmic enemies – as he does in one of the Dead Sea Scrolls – by the second century CE, he would be outsourcing his written work altogether. According to an early Jewish text known as the Testament of Abraham, a group of angels was now in charge of the heavenly register, which was kept in God's throne room. One pair wrote up the good deeds of mortals, while another wrote up their bad deeds. Meanwhile, an angel much like the Egyptian scribe god Thoth weighed mortals' souls in a balance to determine where in the book their recorded deeds were to be filed.[39] The precise placement of a mortal's name in the heavenly ledger determined their fate in the world to come.

One of the most challenging problems for Yahweh's diviners had always been accounting for the apparent earthly success of the wicked. Life itself taught that those whose names were entered into the cursed side of God's book did not always suffer the fate they deserved – especially those foreign powers holding sway over God's own people. Their punishment was surely imminent, and yet God's time was not the same as mortal time. It bent and stretched and sprang back on itself in mysterious ways, giving the blessings and curses of God's book a similarly elastic quality. By the time the Hellenistic world had come to dominate south-west Asia and Egypt, Yahweh's book had become a time-bending cryptic catalogue of preordained destinies and end-of-days judgement. Crafted by God before the separation of the heavens from the earth, the book was inscribed with the divinely decreed fates of whole kingdoms and nations, from their rise to their fall, and from the past to the future. But those privileged enough to access it required angelic assistance to read and understand it.

In the biblical book of Daniel, it is called a Book of Truth, and in it are written the fates of the monstrous earthly empires Daniel sees emerging from the sea of chaos when he journeys in a vision to the heavenly throne room. There, he also sees all the scrolls of heaven lying unrolled before God, ready to be inscribed with his judgements.

But the Book of Truth also contains the fate of God's own people, as Daniel discovers when he is subsequently presented with the scroll itself by an archangel. 'There shall be a time of great anguish, such as has never occurred since nations first came into existence', the angel explains, 'but at that time your people shall be delivered, everyone who is found written in the book'. Daniel is instructed to keep the words of the scroll a secret, and to seal it until the impending end-of-days, when its inscribed prophecies would be fulfilled.[40]

Daniel is entrusted with God's book because he can already read some of the secrets of heaven – and God's handwriting. Although the biblical story of Daniel is a composition of the second century BCE, it is set four hundred years earlier, during the period of the Babylonian exile, with Daniel himself cast as a deportee serving in the court of Babylon's viceroy, 'King' Belshazzar. During a drunken party, a disembodied divine hand suddenly appears in Belshazzar's palace and inks a message on the wall: *'MENE MENE TEKEL PARSIN '*. Although Belshazzar calls on his diviners and magicians, they are unable to read the inscription. But Daniel is endowed with a 'divine spirit' and a God-given wisdom. He can read the writing on the wall. It is an Aramaic list of weights related to decreasing monetary values – a seemingly dull message for a divine hand to bother inscribing. And yet it is loaded with meaning, for it is a divine omen concerning Babylonia's destiny that only Daniel can interpret: God has measured out the days of the kingdom, Belshazzar himself is outweighed by fate, and Babylonia will be divided between the Medes and the Persians. The omen will prove true – after all, the biblical author is writing with the benefit of hindsight, centuries after the fall of Babylon. But the sudden manifestation of divine handwriting reassuringly affirmed that, even in the courts of the most powerful empires, God remained the author of earthly fates.[41]

Like Daniel, other legendary figures of the past were now said to have been in possession of God's heavenly books. Throughout the Hellenistic period and into the Roman era, copies of dispatches from heaven made by the fabled Enoch were in wide circulation – and wildly popular among scribal specialists. Enoch had long been known as the righteous sage who had walked with God for three hundred years before being taken up to heaven, just as a fleeting tradition in Genesis claimed.[42] Despite his brief biblical cameo, he was a figure around whom myths had been spun for centuries. He was known in scribal circles as the sage who had been taught to write when he ascended into the heavens, from where he had been taken on a grand tour of the cosmos and shown the secrets of the universe – including God's own archive of books, in which these secrets were written. 'Look, Enoch, at these heavenly tablets, and read what is written on them, and learn every individual fact', he is commanded. One of these tablets appears to be God's register – now a vast encyclopaedia of 'all the deeds of men and all the sons of the flesh that will be upon the earth until the generations of eternity'.[43] In a narrative dated to the first century CE, but likely reflecting older traditions, Enoch's dispatches are confirmed to be authorized copies of God's books. On his trip to the highest heaven, so the story goes, Enoch is transformed into an angelic executive later known as Metatron, whereupon God shows him his library of books, before commanding him to transcribe their copious contents: 'The Lord summoned one of his archangels, Vrevoil by name, who was swifter in wisdom than the other archangels, who records the Lord's deeds. And the Lord said to Vrevoil, "Bring out the books from the storehouses, and fetch a pen for speed-writing, and give it to Enoch and read him the books"'.[44]

Equipped with his special pen, Enoch wrote for thirty days and nights, and produced 366 books, which he delivered to his son, Methuselah. It is in this way, some believed, that copies of God's heavenly books reached the earthly realm – long before Moses received the Torah on Sinai. Although some had mysteriously disappeared, those copies that remained in human hands were regarded as divine compositions by many Jewish and Christian communities of the first and second centuries CE, including the group who produced the New Testament epistle of Jude, in which a book of Enoch is quite naturally cited as scripture.[45] Within a couple of centuries, however, the status of Enochic literature had waned. For influential rabbinic groups, God's secret lore had not been revealed in written form alongside the open revelations of the Torah, but was passed on as oral tradition via Moses – a tradition they themselves curated and later compiled in the Mishnah. They had also grown increasingly uncomfortable with the eclipsing of God's written law – the Torah – by the literary output of the angelic Enoch. After all, the Torah texts contained the most sacred name of God – Yahweh – which the books of Enoch, written when that name was too divine to use, did not. This gave the Torah scrolls a material sanctity unlike any other books of divine teaching. Meanwhile, some Christian communities (particularly in the Roman West) had become increasingly aware of Jewish discomfort with Enoch's books, and ever more unsettled by his role as a heavenly figure too akin to their own revelatory hero, Christ. The Christian theologian Tertullian (c. 160–225 CE) was one among many who felt compelled to argue for the divine status of the books of Enoch as authentic antediluvian compositions – just as Ashurbanipal of Assyria had claimed of the texts he had studied in his library at Nineveh, hundreds of years earlier.[46] But Tertullian's opinion on this was soon discounted. By the fourth century CE, the rabbinic movement had downgraded Enoch's books, while the Western Christian canon would eventually be closed without them.

If rabbis of the early Common Era tended to privilege the Torah over other sacred texts, then so too did their deity, who now routinely engaged in studying the heavenly prototype of the Torah, much as he expected his worshippers to study its earthly counterpart. For some early Christians, God's scholarly activities as both a writer and reader would come to be replicated in the figure of Christ, whose self-penned Gospels, letters and teachings were reputedly circulating around Christian communities into the fifth century CE.[47] But even before then, an authoritative scriptural literacy was a crucial skill the Jesus movement had been keen to ascribe to Christ. The New Testament Gospels not only depict Jesus as a charismatic preacher, but as a learned rabbi: he debates the interpretation of the Torah with experts, teaches in synagogues and Jerusalem's temple, gives a public reading from the scroll of Isaiah, and can quickly quote a dazzling array of scriptural texts in an effort to outwit Satan himself. Like other celebrated men of the Graeco-Roman world, he is said to have been a precociously clever child, whose learning quickly eclipsed that of his astonished teachers.[48] As an adult, he even has the divine authority (or, for some, the mortal audacity) to overwrite the Torah in God's own house, the Jerusalem temple. In a tradition later inserted into the Gospel of John, a group of Torah experts brings an adulterous woman to Jesus in the temple. 'In the Law [Torah], Moses commanded us to stone such women', they explain. 'Now what do you say?' they ask, inviting Jesus to compare himself to God's very own scribal representative.[49] Instead of engaging her accusers, Jesus bends down to write with his finger in the dust of the temple floor. Like the finger of God, Jesus' finger is an organ of divine power, which can heal the afflicted and cast out demons.[50] But this time, it seems to write a new commandment into being: 'Let any among you who is without sin be the first to throw a stone at her', Jesus announces, reaffirming his words by writing on the temple floor again.[51] His actions seem to upend that very ritual in the Torah in which a woman suspected of adultery is given a toxic potion of written curses and holy dust from the temple floor to drink. Now, written words and temple dust save a woman accused of adultery from bodily harm: one by one, her accusers shuffle off, and not a single stone is thrown.

If the Jesus of this tradition sought to supersede the Torah, other traditions had arisen in which he took control of God's heavenly books completely, as the iconography of Christ Pantokrator ('all powerful') would regularly come to show. For many early Jewish and Christian writers, God's heavenly register, now known as the Book of Life, remained a heavenly work in progress, to which they would make frequent reference.[52] As far as they were concerned, God continued to enter names into the book, and to erase them as and when he saw fit. But in the book of Revelation, it is Christ who has the power to record and blot out names in the heavenly register. This power is affirmed in a scene in God's throne room, where God ceremonially presents Christ with the double-sided, sealed-up scroll of destinies. It is the scroll Daniel had once seen – the scroll which was to remain rolled up and unread until the end times. That time has now come. The scroll's seven seals are to be broken, and its cosmic catastrophes unleashed. And Christ is the only one worthy enough to do this. In his guise as the Bloody Lamb, Christ approaches the throne and takes the scroll from God's right hand. He breaks the seals, and the scroll unrolls its devastating judgements into the universe: four horsemen of the apocalypse suddenly appear, bringing with them mass slaughter, famine, pestilence, animal

attack, an earthquake, a hurricane, a solar eclipse and a blood moon –
omens any ancient diviner would have understood to spell cosmic
disaster. And so they do. The heavens and the earth themselves are
obliterated. The scroll's curses are fulfilled.[53] The Lamb's scroll might
well have contained destructive writing, but it is a double-sided work.
After a brief interlude, during which the dead are resurrected and
judged, and the satanic chaos dragon is defeated by archangels, the
scroll's blessings are triggered. A glittering new Jerusalem descends
from a new heaven to a new earth. Only those who have been saved
from the apocalypse or judged favourably upon rising from their graves
are 'written in the Lamb's Book of Life' and thereby enrolled as the
inhabitants of the heavenly city.[54] In Genesis, God might have spoken
the first creation into being, saying, 'Let there be light', but in the book
of Revelation, it is Christ who writes the new creation into existence.

As the New Testament closes, the God of the Bible is no longer a
hands-on deity. Deputizing to his army of archangels in the great
apocalypse, his fighting days are over; handing his heavenly books to
Christ, so too are his writing days. And yet, in the book of Revelation,
there is one last inscription to write, and one last gesture to perform –
perhaps the most intimate of all. In the new Jerusalem, God's holy
name will be inscribed on the foreheads of his worshippers, enabling
them to safely approach his throne in the city and behold his dazzling
face for eternity.[55] It is to be the greatest revelation of all.

Part V

HEAD

16

FACE TO FACE

Nine and a half thousand years ago, just outside the place we now know as Jericho, a baby destined for a remarkable afterlife was born. To mark his special status, his head was bound from ear to ear, the tight strap pressing itself into the top of his soft skull. As he grew, the strap was periodically enlarged and lengthened, but its grip still bit into the hardening bone, rendering the very front and back of his head subtly but solidly swollen. He probably knew he was special – perhaps head-binding during childhood marked him out as such – but as an adult, he suffered the normal ills of an active, ageing body: toothache, abscesses, and a broken nose, which had healed at an angle. His faintly twisted nose gave him a rugged look, and his heavy brow and wide, high forehead only made his deep-set eyes look smaller. But his face was softened by the plump curve of his cheeks, his wide mouth and his sensuous lips. He died sometime in his thirties or forties, and – while his corpse was still fresh – a large hole was cut into the back of his skull, the sliver of bone set aside like a found jigsaw piece. But he was buried in the usual way, beneath the floor of a house. His new existence was about to begin.

Sometime after his burial, his head was retrieved. What was left of his skin and flesh was carefully stripped away, and his lower jaw was removed. Damp soil was pushed into the hole in the back of his skull and tightly packed into the cranial vault. The filling was left to dry, and then the packing process was repeated, this time with a finer wet mix, the artisan's fingers leaving their mark as the clay was pushed into place, until it eventually plugged the hole. Strengthened and weighted from the inside, the skull was ready for the next stage of its transformation. The puzzle piece of bone removed from the back of the head was fitted into place; a plaster stopper was used to seal the natural gap where the spinal cord had once entered the head. The bottom of the skull was then thickly plastered and shaped into a chin, enabling the skull to sit upright on its own. Further layers of plaster were added to give the skull a rounded face, and facial features were made anew: mouth, nose, cheeks, ears and eyelids. White shells from a far-off sea were inserted into the eye sockets, and a smoothing tool was used to polish the plaster to an iridescent shine. The skull had become a gleaming face (Plate 21).[1]

The Jericho skull was one among several plastered heads to enjoy a rich social life in its community, and one among many more created from the skulls of men, women and children across the Levant during the Neolithic period. Some were painted on top of the plaster, giving them red skin; others were equipped with painted eyelashes, or headbands, or moustaches, or tattoos. Some were accessorized with wigs made of organic materials – perhaps dried river reeds or basket weave – and some were replastered and remodelled several times over, suggesting each facial incarnation was transitory, to be made and remade for particular events or ritual activities.[2] Fusing human bone with both local materials and shells and mineral pigments from distant places, a new being was created. Crafted, displayed, handled and cared for by the living, these plastered skulls were not simply the deceased restored to life, but the heads of the dead transformed into a different category of person altogether. These new faces had a social power and status unlike the faces of the living, and distinct from the skeletal faces of the ordinary dead, buried beneath their homes. They were the faces of those who knew a world beyond the everyday. The living gazed upon the white-eyed faces of these extraordinary beings as the heads sat up and looked back at them – something surviving examples still do today in museum displays. Plastered skulls were not simply objects, but otherworldly social performers.

While we cannot be sure why certain individuals were selected for this remarkable afterlife, these artefacts reflect a very human tendency to give a face to imagined realities. From shapes in the clouds to the headlights and bumper of a car, even the vaguest suggestion of two eyes set above a mouth or a nose can become a face. For some, this might speak to an all too human self-centredness, so that we inevitably see ourselves reflected back at us as we walk in the world. But our tendency to find faces in non-human places more plausibly attests to our inherent sociality as a species, so that we are seeking and seeing not ourselves, but other people. As one visual theorist puts it, 'Our perception is most highly attuned to that which is most important and stimulating to us: other human bodies'.[3] We naturally find human faces especially stimulating, for they are so very crucial to our social relationships. Framed by our ears, the face is the site of our most informative, communicative senses: vision, hearing, smelling, tasting and speaking. It is a fleshy site of fixed features, and yet the face is the most malleable and expressive of our body parts. Eyes dart, water and weep. Eyelids blink, flutter, open wide and close tight shut; eyebrows rise, drop, curve and knit; noses wrinkle or drip. Nostrils flare, shrink and blow, and our noisy, moving mouths stretch, purse, pout, narrow and gape, offering flashes of teeth, gums and a thick, flitting tongue. When we are face to face, it is an intensely social experience – whether or not a word is exchanged or a touch is felt. Even seemingly still, expressionless faces are socially active by virtue of their very presence. A face-to-face encounter is never a passive experience. Faces are simply too stimulating.

God-Gazing

Throughout the Hebrew Bible, it is the intensity of a face-to-face encounter with God that worshippers most desire. 'When shall I come and behold the face of God?' one plaintively asks in the book of Psalms. 'I shall behold your face, I shall take my fill, wide awake, of your image!' promises another.[4] It is easy to dismiss the longing to see God's face as mere fantasy. But this was no hyperbolic fancy of an enraptured imagination. Worshippers hoped for the privilege of pilgrimage to a temple, where they might be lucky enough – or important enough – to see a statue of the deity in all its glory. In a world in which divine statues were manifestations of the gods, to look upon a divine image in a temple was to come face to face with a god. It was to lock eyes with the deity, to see and be seen in the most profound and physical of ways.

The artisans of ancient south-west Asia have left us some tantalizing glimpses of what it might have been like to come face to face with a deity in the temple. During the Early Dynastic period of Sumerian culture (c. 2900–2334 BCE), wealthy worshippers commissioned representations of themselves to stand in the presence of their gods in temples. Carved from alabaster or limestone, these votive statuettes of worshippers stand unsupported, their feet together and their hands demurely clasped at their waists. Their mouths are closed in pious silence, but their enlarged eyes are open wide, their pupils like saucers, their eyebrows raised. They were entranced by the deity before whom they stood. Just as their gods were manifest in their temple statues, so too were these Sumerian worshippers. Face to face with the divine, they stood in a state of permanent, awed adoration, gazing at the gods before them (Plate 20).[5]

The emotional intensity of a face-to-face encounter with a divine statue continued to be experienced by generations of worshippers across south-west Asia. Over a thousand years after Sumerian statuettes had gazed at their gods, kings across Mesopotamia were continuing to be bowled over by the religious experience of beholding a cult statue. It is an experience recounted on a stone tablet produced during the reign of King Nabu-apla-iddina of Babylon (r. 887–855 BCE). It describes the king's restoration of the cult statue of the sun god Shamash, which had been looted from the deity's main sanctuary in Sippar some two centuries earlier during an attack by the Sutians from the Syrian desert. In the absence of the cult statue, the god's symbol, a blazing sun disc, had instead received offerings while worshippers waited for Shamash to grant permission to refashion his image. Permission came in the form of a miraculous discovery: a canny high priest called Nabu-nadin-shumi fortuitously 'found' a baked clay model of the original statue from which a new lapis and gold-plated version could be crafted. The result was staggering, as the sublime illustration carved into the top of the tablet suggests. It shows the giant new statue of Shamash enthroned within his ornate, canopied shrine in his temple. The over-exaggerated scale of the cult statue celebrates Shamash's divinity, but also points to the overwhelming experience of finally coming face to face with the god: the new statue dwarfs the high priest, the king, and even the goddess who accompanies them into the god's throne room, adopting a diminutive pose in the overwhelming presence of Shamash. Only the two divine attendants, positioned beyond the god's line of sight as they helpfully reposition his solar disc, look vaguely comfortable (fig. 41). The inscription emphasizes that, upon seeing the god's image, the king's face was transformed by euphoria, so that he beamed with delight at the high priest: 'His heart rejoiced, and shining was his face . . . with his bright face, his ruddy countenance [and] his beautiful eyes, happily he looked at him'.[6]

In the biblical story of Moses, the physiological transformation triggered by a visual encounter with a deity is far more extreme, as we have already seen. Of all the Bible's characters, it is Moses who is

Fig. 41. The Babylonian king Nabu-apla-iddina is led into the presence of the sun god Shamash, whose cult statue had been newly restored to his temple in Sippar. Divine attendants hold ropes attached to the deity's cult object, a solar disc. This image tops an inscribed tablet produced between 860 and 850 BCE.

repeatedly said to have enjoyed a face-to-face relationship with the deity: 'Yahweh would speak to Moses face to face, as one speaks to a friend'.[7] It is a point about which the deity himself is unequivocal, highlighting the physical intimacy of their conversations: 'With him I speak mouth to mouth – an appearance, not in riddles; and he gazes at the form of Yahweh'.[8] Moses does not simply see Yahweh, but *looks* at him: he talks to him, he listens to him and engages with him. And having spent forty days and nights with Yahweh on Sinai, it is the corporeal, visual intensity of this social bond with the deity which is understood to transfigure Moses' face in the book of Exodus.[9]

Other Yahweh worshippers also felt the visceral, transformative power of seeing their god. In a psalm, one describes the encounter as the stark difference between famine and feast: 'My throat thirsts for you, my flesh faints for you, as in a dry and weary land where there is no water', he exclaims, 'so I looked upon you in the sanctuary, beholding your strength and glory . . . my throat is sated with fat and fatness'.[10] The deity, too, was likely sated by this meeting, for worshippers were not to turn up to temples without gifts of food. 'Three times a year all your males shall see the face of Yahweh your god at the cult-place that he shall choose', Moses commands the Israelites. 'They shall not see the face of Yahweh empty-handed; all shall give as they are able'.[11] Looking upon the face of God was the very purpose of a temple, as Yahweh makes clear in the ancient Greek translation of the book of Exodus: 'You shall make me a sanctuary and I shall be seen among you'.[12]

Written into the Torah, the command to see Yahweh's face was a formalized reflection of the deity's long-held desire to be seen. 'Seek my face!' he called to his worshippers. 'Come before his countenance!' his ritual singers urged.[13] In one psalm, worshippers who 'ascend the hill of Yahweh' and 'stand in his sacred standing-place' will receive blessings as they behold the deity's face.[14] And yet God's calls for face-to-face encounters with his worshippers often surprise modern readers of the Bible. As so often, the theological preferences of ancient and modern translators are partly to blame – translators who tend to soften the firm instruction to 'seek his face' into the more mealy-mouthed 'seek his presence'. But these translators have also been heavily influenced by certain biblical claims that seeing the radiant face of a divine being might be deadly dangerous or impossible. According to the book of Deuteronomy, the Israelites heard God's voice, but were unable to see his body.[15] In the Gospel of John, the narrator insists that 'No one has ever seen God', while the writer of 1 Timothy claims that 'God dwells in unapproachable light and no one has ever seen him or can see him!'[16] And yet several characters in the Bible – including Moses himself – do indeed see God's face and live to tell the tale.

These biblical inconsistencies likely derive from competing religious traditions about the extent to which Yahweh might render himself visible to mortals beyond the bounds of his temples. Across the ancient world, deities were understood to be innately dangerous, particularly when they were on the move. Whether betwixt and between temples, or the heavens and the earth, or the city and the wilderness, divine behaviour was far more unpredictable in liminal space. But even when worshippers entered temples, face-to-face encounters with the gods were carefully choreographed. In the regulated environment of sacred space, those people fortunate – or powerful – enough to be granted an audience with a deity were safeguarded from the potential dangers of the divine gaze by the rituals and furnishings structuring the meeting: mortal bodies were carefully cleansed, dressed and accessorized; sacred unguents, ceremonial clothing and offerings cloaked them with the aura of holiness, transfiguring earthly bodies into bodies fit for sacred space. Iconographic images of worshippers before the cult statues of their gods suggest that altars, offering tables, lamp stands and the scented clouds of incense burners served as security barriers separating mortals and gods, controlling their encounters. A beautifully detailed example is found on an Assyrian seal from the Phoenician city of Tyre. A woman in a fringed ceremonial robe stands before the imposing statue of a storm god on his pedestal; her clean, bare arms are raised towards the deity, and between them is an incense burner throwing up smoke and flames, and an offering table laden with rich fabrics and libations (fig. 42).

Ritual safeguarding in Yahweh's temples was no different. In the Hebrew Bible, priestly directives about temple practice suggest that clouds of fragrant incense not only called the god to his meals, but

Fig. 42. Imprint of an Assyrian cylinder seal (thirteenth century BCE)
showing a worshipper standing before the cult statue of a storm god.
Between them, an active incense burner and furnished offering
table act as a security barrier, controlling the potentially
dangerous dynamics of the encounter.

served as a smokescreen, blurring direct visual contact with the deity.
These smokescreens were easily associated with the thick clouds
thought to be wrapped about the god as he thundered through the
heavens. Although southern Levantine temples usually had windows
through which daylight could pass, some biblical writers insist Yahweh
of Jerusalem preferred to dwell in deep darkness. The darkness of the
temple's inner rooms, tempered only by lamplight, was likely thought
to function as a palpably protective layer, cushioning the impact of the
encounter between the deity and his priests.[17] Deep-dyed blue and
purple fabrics hanging around Yahweh's shrine in the temple's holy of
holies similarly enveloped the deity with a degree of privacy, akin to
that he was believed to have enjoyed in the old days, camping out in
the wilderness with the Israelite tribes.[18] At the same time, the temple
curtains shielded worshippers from the overwhelming sight of God –
an idea later repurposed by some early Christians, who sensationally
claimed the curtains had been ripped asunder by the world-changing
death of the new, more accessible face of divinity, Jesus himself.[19]

Not even Yahweh's most important attendants were entirely safe from the potential hazards of a direct audience with their god. In Jerusalem, the high priest was to be transfigured by holy oil, don sacred vestments and wear protective amulets and tinkling bells on his body to shield him from the deity as he entered the holy of holies.[20] But an unexpected encounter with a deity, away from the safety of a temple, was inevitably fraught with danger – as both Jacob and Moses are said to have discovered. In Genesis, Jacob spends a night wrestling a super-naturally powerful man, who later reveals himself to be a god, while, in Exodus, Yahweh tries to kill Moses when they suddenly meet in the dead of night on the road from Midian to Egypt. In these circum-stances, emergency measures are required. Moses is rescued by the rituals performed by his quick-thinking wife Zipporah, who anoints him with the protective, sacred blood of a hastily circumcised penis. Jacob's life is saved by his sensible decision to let go of his assailant before daybreak and humble himself before the newly revealed deity, vowing to transform their makeshift wrestling ring into a cult place devoted to him. He names it Peniel ('Face of God'), for, as Jacob says, 'I have seen God face to face, and my life is preserved'.[21]

Both stories suggest that Jacob and Moses had unwittingly strayed into the path of a dangerous deity of the night, subsequently glossed by biblical writers as Yahweh himself. Their trespassing had triggered a ferocious attack – which was a perfectly understandable reaction. The gods were easily irritated or unsettled by the impropriety of an unin-vited visitor or an unexpected encounter. The God of the Bible particularly disapproved of mass gawping. Stories about his early encounters with the Israelite tribes are keen to emphasize the protocols protecting the deity from crowds, busybodies and rubberneckers. Setting a boundary at the foot of his holy mountain in the Sinai wil-derness, he explains to Moses that the Israelites are not to rush up the mountain to see him until they have been invited by the sound of a heavenly horn.[22] As his desert temple is being packed away in readiness for its onward journey to the Promised Land, Yahweh warns that those priests without appropriate security clearance are not to sneak a peek inside the holy of holies in its state of undress ('not even for a moment') because they will die.[23] Even Yahweh's furniture – his throne, his footstool, his incense burners, his curtains – is imbued with a divinity that is not to be looked upon in its transitory state. It is a basic principle of religious etiquette forgotten or ignored by seventy citizens of Beth-shemesh in 1 Samuel; their enthusiasm at seeing Yahweh's footstool spills over into voyeurism when they attempt to look inside the ark – and are promptly struck dead.[24]

Gawping at Yahweh might have prompted divine offense, but stories like these also served very human purposes, both profound and pragmatic. Theologically, staring at a deity was to be discouraged, to prevent the reductive objectification of the god. No matter how noble the longing to behold a cult statue or sacred object, the divine was not to be regarded as a mere spectacle for the curious mortal gaze. As a deity, Yahweh was a category of being wholly unlike any other, and was to be treated neither as an oddity nor a luxury commodity for those lucky enough to enjoy privileged access to him. But the ancients were just as capable of cognitive dissonance as we are. Stories warning against ogling Yahweh also shored up the powerful positions enjoyed by his priests and temple personnel, with whom the authority to offer access to the deity lay – and whose theologies came to dominate much of the Bible. Like many powerful forms of visual culture today – be it religious relics, films, or pornography – permission to see or not to see is often in the gift of those socially sanctioned to curate, mediate, regulate, or propagate images. And the priests of ancient gods were no different. They not only controlled access to the temples in which the gods resided, but handled larger public-relations events, when a deity's statue might process about the outer courtyards of their house, or parade about the streets of their city. Although these more public viewings of the deity were crucial events in the religious calendar, the optics were still carefully stage-managed.

A lively example comes from the small but venerable city of Emar in north-western Syria, where, from at least the fourteenth to the twelfth centuries BCE, the city's patron, the fertile god Dagan, ceremonially showed himself to his people in an annual renewal of his devotion to the city. Accompanied by a stream of worshippers, Dagan left his urban temple to visit the ancient standing stones beyond the city walls. There, he and his citizens feasted on hundreds of sacrificial animals, before the god mounted his wagon and returned to the city to take up residence once again in his temple. Although the people accompanied Dagan's wagon while he was out and about, their access to him was still restricted, for the cult statue's face was veiled for much of the festival – guarding his privacy and cranking up the crowds' anticipation. It was only at key junctures in the proceedings that Dagan's priests revealed his face. The first occasion was as he passed among the stones, enabling him to socialize with the divine powers there, while the second was when he sat down to feast, allowing the assembled citizens to enjoy a glimpse of their patron deity. Finally, Dagan's face was unveiled again for his joyous homecoming, so that as he travelled, the fields surrounding the city were drawn into his beneficent, life-giving gaze.[25]

The power of the veil to shield or distance a deity's face from their worshippers was not only a device employed among large crowds. It also served to shut out the individual petitioner from socializing with their god in their prayers – sometimes in the most devastating way. This is distressingly portrayed in an Assyrian elegy discovered in the remains of Ashurbanipal's library in Nineveh. Its subject is a young woman dying in childbirth, who cries out in fear to the great Mesopotamian mother goddess, by now commonly known as Belet-ili, 'Lady of the gods'. Although the tablet on which this poem was inscribed is damaged, rendering some of its lines unreadable, the pain of its poetry is all too easily felt:

> During the days I was with child, how happy I was!
> Happy I was, and happy was my husband!
> The day my pains began, a shadow fell across my face,
> the day my labour started, brightness faded from my eyes.
> I besought Belet-ili, fists unclenched:
> 'O Mother, you that bore me, spare my life!'
> Belet-ili heard, then veiled her face:
> '[Who are] you, and why beseech me so?' . . .
> . . . Then to our bedroom stealthy Death did creep,
> from my house he drove me forth,
> from my husband cut me off;
> my footfall here he planted, in a place of no return.[26]

The intimate visual bond between the young woman and her goddess is distressingly reflected in their faces, even as their relationship breaks down. As the darkness of death dulls her vision and obscures her face, the woman reaches out with open, pleading, praying hands. But the goddess has covered her own face, so that it too is darkened. With unseeing eyes, she will no longer recognize her worshipper. Deity and devotee become faceless to one another. And in their facelessness, they are estranged.

Hide and Seek

The God of the Bible was similarly accustomed to obscuring his face in an effort to sever relationships with his own worshippers. In language conjuring an image of the deity covering his face with his hands, Yahweh is said to hide his face from those he once cared for, and now rejects: 'When you give to them, they gather it up; when you open your hand, they are filled with good things; when you conceal your face, they are dismayed'.[27] Dismayed – and cursed. In obscuring his own face, Yahweh exposes unworthy worshippers to the predations of malevolent beings: 'I will forsake them and hide my face from them, and they will be devoured; many evil troubles will find them'.[28] But hiding his face also renders Yahweh remote. He cannot – will not – acknowledge their distress. 'They will cry to Yahweh, but he will not answer them; he will hide his face from them at that time, for they have acted wickedly'.[29] Like Belet-ili veiling her face from a dying woman, Yahweh envelops himself in a heavenly garment, dulling his senses: 'You have wrapped yourself with a cloud, so that no prayer can pass through', sobs personified Jerusalem as she laments her destruction at the hands of the Babylonians.[30] The fault, of course, lies with Yahweh's wayward worshippers, whose sins had coagulated about their god's head like a miasma, shrouding his face and muffling his ears: 'Your sins have become barriers between you and your god', cries a prophet among the exiles in Babylon; 'your sins have hidden his face from you, so that he does not hear'.[31] God's face-covering not only rendered him ritually inaccessible, but theologically unapproachable, worryingly remote, and virtually imperceptible to the worshipper.

Should a deity hide their face, appeals to an appropriately powerful intercessor were essential. And across the Levant, there was none more appropriate than a senior goddess. In Phoenician cities and their colonies around the Mediterranean, the powerful goddess Tanit was often known as the 'Face of Baal', signalling her role as a mediator between the local high god and his worshippers. But one of the most successful intercessors in the heavenly realm was the mother of the gods herself, who was well placed to intervene on behalf of others, whether mortal or divine. In Ugarit, this role fell to Athirat, wife and consort of El, and mother to their seventy divine children. Naturally, it is to Athirat that Baal turns when he seeks El's permission to build himself a palace. It is a reasonable request, given that all the other gods have their own palaces, as he repeatedly complains. And yet, as much as Baal has groaned and cried to El, permission has not been forthcoming. At first, Baal's sister Anat intervenes on his behalf, but the excessive aggression of her demand does little to help Baal's cause – an unsurprising result, given that anyone threatening to smash in their father's head and cleave his skull in two would likely receive similarly short shrift. It is then that Baal and Anat appeal to Athirat to put the case to her husband, bringing her fine furniture as ritual gifts to win her favour. Athirat's approach is more tactful, her manner more gracious, and her influence over her all-powerful husband far greater.[32]

Thanks to Athirat, Baal not only got his palace, but Ugarit's citizens had their ideal divine intercessor. It was a role reflected in the golden amulets worn by the wealthy as pendants around their necks, hoping she would champion their causes before the other gods. In stark contrast to the darkened, hidden faces of those gods who chose not to respond to their worshippers, these amulets emphasized the goddess's friendly face – her gentle features, her eyes and ears open wide to prayers and petitions, her golden countenance radiating blessings (Plate 26).[33] Worn next to the skin, the reassuring warmth of the goddess's beaming face could be felt.

Athirat's role as power broker extended to Israel and Judah, where she was known, of course, as Asherah. As the wife of Yahweh, she was instrumental in securing her husband's blessings for his worshippers. It is a skill suggested by that remarkable inscription from an eighth-century BCE tomb in Khirbet el-Qom, in the modern West Bank, in which Yahweh's protection of the tomb's occupant is mediated by Asherah.[34] But whether in life or death, appeals to another deity to intercede were not always successful – at least, not as far as some biblical writers were concerned. In the wake of the Babylonian invasion of Judah in the sixth century BCE, desperate exiles and refugees had made offerings beseeching the help of a goddess anonymized in the Hebrew Bible as the 'Queen of Heaven' (a title later recycled for the Virgin Mary), whom worshippers had long credited with helping to ensure state security, economic prosperity and agricultural plenty. And yet Yahweh was only enraged by their appeals.[35] When the harried protagonist of the book of Job found his desperate cries to Yahweh had gone unanswered, his woefully unsupportive (and slightly stupid) friend Eliphaz counselled against appeals to any divine intercessor: 'Call now; is there anyone who will answer you? To which of the Holy Ones will you turn?' he asks. 'If it was me', he remarks, with all the condescension of someone who has failed to grasp the point, 'I would seek God, and to God I would commit my cause'.[36]

Some worshippers might have found divine intercessors to be too unpredictable or unhelpful, but as he became increasingly reclusive, Yahweh would come to rely upon them. By the fourth century BCE, divine messengers were taking on a more distinctively ambassadorial role, for their task was to interface with mortals on Yahweh's behalf – quite literally: one is called his 'Face Messenger', and another Yahweh simply names 'My Face'.[37] Meanwhile, Yahweh's breath-born daughter, Lady Wisdom, was pitching herself as the most successful heavenly intercessor. 'Whoever finds me finds life and obtains favour from Yahweh!' Wisdom proudly boasts in the book of Proverbs. At the same time, parents were advising their children to wear Wisdom on their throats like a necklace – an allusion to amulets bearing a goddess's image, akin to those golden pendants once worn by Ugarit's citizens, emphasizing the deity's welcoming, radiant face and her prominent, listening ears, ready to respond to worshippers' petitions.[38] An old proverb embedded in Ecclesiastes (known in Jewish tradition as

Qoheleth) suggests the radiant blessings conveyed by Lady Wisdom's face could be as viscerally transformative as those of her divine father: 'Wisdom makes one's face shine, and the harshness of his face is changed'.[39] This biblical aphorism might well read today as a saccharine platitude, reassuring worshippers of the faintly fluffy idea that religious understanding makes people happy. But the cultural backdrop to this little proverb is rather more precise. It recalls the iconography of the gods' faces. Bright blessings shone upon those fortunate enough to behold divine images, bathing worshippers in a warm glow akin to the touch of the sun.

This was the shining face of divine favour Yahweh's worshippers had always longed to see, as an ancient prayer in the book of Numbers so beautifully illustrates:

> May Yahweh bless you and guard you;
> may Yahweh make his face to shine upon you
>   and be gracious to you;
> may Yahweh lift up his face upon you and give you peace.[40]

It was virtually the same ritual refrain as that inscribed on the rolled-up silver amulets from Ketef Hinnom, and the same liturgical incantation as was sung in the Jerusalem temple, which would continue to be uttered in prayers long after the temple's final destruction in 70 CE. When they beseeched their god to 'make his face shine' upon them, worshippers were not simply hoping for a beatific vision, but longing for the highly social, intimate encounter manifest in a face-to-face relationship with their god – much as they or their ancestors might have experienced in his temples. There, the light of oil lamps had danced on the polished glow of the statue's golden countenance, enlivening it with wondrous movement. Bedazzled by the divine, awestruck worshippers had beheld their god's responsive, shining face. And what a face it was.

17

HEADSTRONG BEAUTY

On 23 September 2003, a small team of Iraqi police and US military personnel made its way to a farmhouse north of Baghdad. Armed with weapons, shovels and a tip-off, they were on the hunt for one of the most treasured artefacts plundered from the National Museum of Iraq in the aftermath of the US-led invasion. Following what was reported to be a brisk but intense interrogation of the householder, the team began digging beneath fruit trees behind the house. They soon unearthed a plastic bag. Inside, wrapped in cloth, was an almost life-sized marble face. Large almond-shaped eye-sockets sat under long, stylized brows. Neat, scalloped waves curled on the forehead. Gently rounded cheeks framed a regal nose, albeit chipped in an ancient accident. A small, delicate mouth was set above a petite chin. They had found the famed Lady of Uruk (Plate 22).[1]

Dated to about 3100 BCE, this striking face originally belonged in the vast temple complex of the Sumerian goddess Inanna, at Uruk, perhaps the world's earliest city. Located in the desert plain between the Tigris and Euphrates in southern Mesopotamia, the site had been a home to both humans and otherworldly beings since at least 5000 BCE, but by 3100 BCE, it housed thousands of mortals and a plethora of gods, among whom Inanna was one of the most prominent. Her temple precinct was known as Eanna, 'house of heaven' – and it really was heavenly. On three terraced platforms stood perfectly proportioned limestone temples and cool, airy buildings, interlinked by shady pavilions of colourful brickwork, wide monumental staircases and a large courtyard open to the skies. A fat-columned portico rose from one terrace to the next, each of its giant pillars decorated with a geometric mosaic of coloured cones, painted black, red and white. For Inanna's worshippers, there was nothing else like it on earth – nor indeed in heaven. Excavated in 1939 from a sacred deposition pit within the temple precinct, the pale marble face probably belonged to a cult statue of Inanna herself, the body of which was likely made of sacred wood (perhaps tamarisk) that had been ritually carved, smoothed and overlaid with precious materials, and dressed in the finest fabrics. Positioned on a podium in her temple, Inanna would have stood higher than a human, her large-eyed, flawless face turned towards her worshippers.[2]

For Western art historians raised on a rich European diet of Greek and Roman statuary, the face of the Lady of Uruk is especially prized for its remarkable realism. It is the earliest known work to capture in stone the naturalness of the human face, predating the 'high' art of the classical world by millennia. But this marble face was never intended to be the lifelike image of a mere mortal. It was created instead to manifest a more expansive imagined reality. It made visible what was usually hidden. This was the face of a goddess whose corporeal form transcended that of a human, and whose divine perfection eclipsed any earthly beauty. In its heyday, the face of the Lady of Uruk was staggeringly otherworldly. Now empty sockets, her wide eyes were once alive with the pearlescent shine of seashells or mineral paste, their pupils picked out with lapis lazuli or bitumen. Her gaze was framed by the lapis that had filled her stylized brows. The carefully sculpted curls on her forehead had probably been traced in gold, and an ornate carved hairpiece or luxuriant wig fixed into the grooves and perforations on the flat back of the marble. And crowning her beauty, curving around a turban set upon her head, there had been two proud bull-horns, rising up from the sides of her forehead.[3]

Inanna's beautiful divinity was manifest in the composite nature of her image – its repleteness – so that substance, form, style and ornamentation were combined in ways coded as divine. Just as our own heads and faces are prominent sites of enculturation – the parts of our bodies we especially highlight, modify, or decorate to express something of our social status, gender, occupation, age and personhood – so too the gods were coiffed, capped, contoured and coloured by their own cultural contexts. But the enculturation of the gods went beyond our own in one important way. While modern Westerners remain wholly human without hair, a hat, or jewellery, the very essence of divinity was completed or perfected by what might look to us to be mere (if elaborate) ornamentation. Replete with their cultural trappings, the gods were aesthetically perfect in form – and hence perfect in divinity. They were wholly holy.

The encultured, corporeal completeness of divinity is perhaps nowhere better expressed than in a Sumerian myth about Inanna herself. It tells of her descent to the underworld, the realm ruled by her sister Ereshkigal. It is an aggressively ambitious attempt to claim the underworld for herself, and she confidently plans to defy its nature as the 'land of no return' by leaving again. But when she arrives, she is appalled to learn that she must be ceremonially stripped of her seven powers of divinity as she passes through the seven gateways leading to her sister's throne room. At the first gate, her horned turban is removed. At the second, her lapis lazuli necklace. At the third, the string of egg-shaped beads decorating her breast. By the time she has passed through the sixth gate, she has lost her glittering pectoral, her golden finger-ring and her lapis lazuli toolkit – the measuring rod and line with which she apportions justice. Finally, at the seventh gateway, she is deprived of her robe, the 'garment of ladyship'. Crouching and naked, she has been robbed of her upright, forthright divinity – the very essence of her heavenly personhood. She is wholly diminished. But things are about to get worse. Although she seats herself on her sister's throne, she is not there for long. The divine denizens of the underworld assault her body further: they stare at her with the look of death; they speak to her with words of anger; and they bellow at her with the shout of shame. Bludgeoned by these incantations, she is turned into a corpse – and in a nightmarish detail, her corpse is hung on a hook.

But all is not lost. The wise god Enki crafts a rescue party from the clay caught under his fingernails, who retrieve Inanna's corpse from its hook and revive her with the balm of Enki's life-giving plant and a sprinkling of his life-giving water. As she leaves, Inanna secures her release with a promise she will be replaced in the land of death by a substitute. She decides it will be her lover, the fertile shepherd-god Dumuzi, who had rather foolishly failed to grieve for her sufficiently. He will spend half the year in the underworld in her place, much as Persephone will do in later Greek versions of the myth. Mournful but resolute, Inanna returns from the underworld to ornamented glory in the heavenly realm.[4]

It is within this context that the beautifying accoutrements of the gods are best understood. Every layer of divine radiance, every hair-style and headdress, every ornament and every prop solidified and certified a deity's divinity. And the God of the Bible was no exception. It is all too easy to dismiss those brisk references to his clothing and weaponry as cartoon features of a theologically unsophisticated one-dimensional deity. But whenever we encounter God's ornamentation and accessories in the Bible – whether his headdress, robes and sandals, or weapons, measuring rod and writing equipment – we are privy to a fleeting glimpse of an ancient wardrobe essential to his divine nature. He is not simply human-like in his penchant for decoration and display, but a deity complete in divinity. From head to toe, God's bodily decorations and personal possessions were imbued with their own heavenly power, augmenting the core divinity of his body.

A Crown of Horns

The oldest of God's bodily augmentations was the pair of bull-horns crowning his head: 'God, who brought [Israel] out of Egypt, has horns like a wild ox! He destroys nations who oppose him! He crushes their bones!' declares the prophet Balaam in an ancient oracle in the book of Numbers.[5] It is an image that modern-day readers of the Bible might find unsettling. In the Western imagination, a horned being tends to conjure images of the diabolical and the grotesque. From the man-eating bull-headed Minotaur of Greek myth to the cloven-hooved goat-faced Devil of Christianity, horns have long served as a hallmark of horror. But in the world of the very ancient gods, horns were the most prestigious and alluring manifestations of divinity, and most deities would be equipped with them.

Wrapped about these heavenly horns were deeply rooted ideas about cosmic order. The gods' horns marked them out as a species innately distinct from humans; they were beings of bullish virility and ferocious strength, whose sharp, majestic weapons were built into their bodies. But the horns of the gods manifested life as well as death: they mirrored the pointed horns of the crescent moon as it waxed and waned, pulling and pushing at the great rivers watering life in the desert plains of southern Mesopotamia.[6] It was here in Sumer that horns had first sprouted on the ancient gods as we know them. From as early as the late fourth millennium BCE, the horned cap was already the distinctive marker of divinity – so much so, the loss of the horned cap could mark death for a deity.

It is an idea vividly expressed on a cylinder seal showing a group of minor deities busily building a temple gate. In front of them, two higher-status gods are about to perform a ritual killing. They have thick beards, neatly styled hair, and impressive bull-horns stretching out and up from their headwear. Both wear the belt of a warrior around their waists. One raises his arms to the heavens as he looks at his companion, who is wielding a mace at a smaller god, crouched on the ground in submission. He wears nothing except for his beard and his horned cap, which is about to be ripped from his head (fig. 43).[7] This is the violent act that will strip him of divine immortality, much as Inanna's forced undressing had led to her own temporary 'death'.

The horns of the gods were not confined to Sumer, but soon sprouted on the heads, hats and turbans of deities across Mesopotamia, Anatolia, Syria and the Levant, passing from one generation of gods to the next, like a genetic carrier of divinity, travelling down the ages. By the middle of the second millennium BCE, the pedigreed horns of heaven were atop the head of the Levantine high god El, the cultural father of the God of the Bible. At Ugarit, El's horns were fashionably changeable, depending on the skills, influences and location of the artisans crafting his cult images. Sometimes his horns hugged the contours of his conical headdress with a graceful, controlled curve, mimicking the well-known *atef* crown of the pharaohs – a tall hat

Fig. 43. Drawing of a cylinder-seal impression showing a group of deities building a temple gate. To the left, a deity wielding a mace grasps the horned cap of another. This Mesopotamian seal has been dated to about 2340–2159 BCE.

framed by two long, large feathers. But sometimes El's horns looked as though they had sprung from his head with a sudden wild vigour. An especially lively example is the image of El carved into a stela found in a private house in Ugarit. It was probably intended as an offering to the god himself, but it was never finished. The deity sits on a stylish, low-backed throne, his feet on his footstool and his arms gesticulating, as though in animated conversation with the priest or king standing opposite him. El's horns branch out wide and high above his ears, while his crown – a tall turban – is ribbed with smaller pairs of tightly meshed horns, emphasizing his supreme divinity.[8]

Like many of his peers across south-west Asia, El was frequently titled 'Bull', and he quite naturally expected his divine children to inherit his horns of divinity: 'May they have horns like bulls, and humps like steers!' he cries when his two young wives go into labour with his offspring. His older children already bear the bull-horns of heaven. Anat's are particularly praised by her brother Baal, who excitedly anoints and blesses them: 'The horns of your power, Girl Anat, the horns of your power let Baal anoint!'[9] As a storm deity, Baal's own horns are said to be especially radiant, and closely identified with the lightning bolts flashing about his head as he moves through the skies or thunders in his mountaintop temple.[10] Images of both deities frequently show them wearing horns – as befitting any Levantine god, but especially those associated with the storm of war, or the rains of fertility.

It is no surprise, then, that in the older traditions embedded in the Hebrew Bible, God himself is not only portrayed as the divine Bull, equipped with horns, but fully expects his own progeny to inherit them.[11] It is an image applied to the tribe of Joseph in an ancient poem, in which God's divine blessings rain down on his 'son':

> Let them come on the head of Joseph,
> on the brow of the head of the prince among his brothers!
> The firstborn of his [divine] Bull – majesty is his!
> His horns are the horns of a wild ox;
> with them he gores peoples,
> driving them to the ends of the earth![12]

God's horns were remembered not only in ancient poems, but in the rituals and iconography of his temples, too. The prophet Zedekiah ben Chenaanah is said to have crafted a pair of iron horns to enact Yahweh's promise to the kings of Israel and Judah that the neighbouring Aramaeans would be gored to death in battle.[13] It is a tradition pointing to the widespread practice of ritualized prophetic performance, in which the diviner embodied the oracle by physically enacting the deity's decreed actions. We should probably imagine Zedekiah snorting and bellowing as he charges about the sanctuary, wearing a specially made horned headdress like those crowning the statues of gods.

But in some of Yahweh's temples, the deity was not simply crowned with heavenly horns, but took the form of a divine bull. According to the books of Kings, Yahweh's temples in Bethel and Dan were each said to have housed a golden statue of a young bull-god, while in the book of Hosea, a gold and silver statue of a bull was said to have been worshipped in Samaria, the capital of the kingdom of Israel. Despite his exasperated critique of worshippers fawning over the statue, the prophet can barely disguise the clear implication that it manifested the city's patron deity, Yahweh of Samaria himself.[14] These

Fig. 44. This beautifully wrought bronze bull was discovered at an early Iron Age cult place near ancient Dothan, in the Samarian hills. As a cult statue, it manifested one of the prominent deities of the region – whether El, Baal, or Yahweh himself.

statues might have been similar in style to the little bronze bull archaeologists found at an older, twelfth-century BCE shrine, in the hill country in which the kingdom of Israel would emerge (fig. 44), or perhaps they looked more like the bull-headed warrior god portrayed on an eighth-century BCE stela from the nearby Aramaean city of Bethsaida (fig. 45). Either way, Yahweh's militarized bull horns were particularly venerated in the religious iconography of his most powerful northern temples – which made these statues an obvious target for derision after Assyria captured them and destroyed the kingdom of Israel in the eighth century BCE.* Looking back at the humiliating calamity that had befallen their northern neighbours, later scribes in Jerusalem deliberately cast the statues in these rival temples simply as abominable images of an animal – giving rise to the story of the

---

* In his description of the kingdom's conquest, the Assyrian king Sargon II refers to the cult statues taken into captivity: 'I counted as spoil 27,280 people, together with their chariots *and the gods in whom they trusted*' (*COS* 2.118D; italics added).

Fig. 45. A basalt stela of a bull-headed god with a sword strapped to his waist, originally positioned in an eighth-century BCE gate-shrine in Bethsaida (likely the Aramaean city-state of Geshur). The image combines warrior-deity motifs with those of a lunar god.

infamous golden calf of Sinai.[15] These scribes naturally imagined that Yahweh had been as appalled by his animalized presence as they were. 'They exchanged my glory for the image of a bull that feeds on grass!' he is later said to have spluttered.[16] Why else, scribes reasoned, would the deity have abandoned his northern worshippers to foreign invasion?

God's horned headdress would gradually fade from view, leaving only glancing traces in the biblical literature – including the 'horns' sprouting from the forehead of his most venerable representative, Moses. But God's beauty was undiminished. Like the horns worn by his divine forebears, the horned hat of Yahweh had towered over a face carefully calibrated to exhibit the alluring aesthetics of heavenly perfection. And it was his face that would continue to entrance his worshippers.

Desiring the Divine

'One thing I asked of Yahweh, that I will seek ever after: to live in the house of Yahweh all the days of my life, to behold the beauty of

Yahweh . . . your face, Yahweh, I do seek! '[17] Sighing with longing, the author of these love lyrics in the book of Psalms yearns to dwell in the Jerusalem temple and feast his eyes on God – a deity so alluring that adoration borders on desire. This ancient poet was not the only one to be swept up by God's beauty. 'Praise Yahweh, for he is lovely looking!' another psalmist cries. 'Praise Yah, for Yahweh is good-looking!' yet another exclaims.[18] In these songs of worship, God's aesthetic qualities are more usually veiled in translation by the mistaken assumption that no one believed God had a body to be seen. His magnetic good looks are recast instead as immaterial moral virtues, so that, in most Bibles today, God is described not as 'good-looking', but 'good'; he is not 'lovely looking', but 'gracious'. And yet the Hebrew terms used in these psalms – *tob* and *na'im* – carry with them a strong sense of the aesthetic, and they are often used to describe attractive people, pretty places and wondrous sights, rather than abstract qualities.[19] God may well have embodied praiseworthy values, but he was also staggeringly beautiful.

This was a world in which beauty was perceived in the purity or intensity of its forms: the clarity of shape, the richness of colour, the brightness of light, the heaviness of scent. But the beauty of form was not to be distinguished from the beauty of function. From temple architecture to the good looks of the gods, beauty was as much about role, status, purpose and action, as shape, colour, tone and composition. Whether with an alluring being or an attractive building, an encounter with beauty was an emotional experience, overwhelming whoever was lucky enough to behold it. In this sense, beauty was understood not as a passive abstraction, but as a divinely derived, otherworldly intoxicant, so that even the most surprising objects could give rise to a deep desire dancing on that fine line between religious magnetism and physical attraction.[20] This is precisely what Gilgamesh is said to have experienced when he had a dream about an unusual copper axe, seemingly fallen from heaven. Describing the dream the next morning, he is overwhelmed by his desire for the extraordinarily alluring object: 'I saw it, and I felt [such] joy; I loved it as a woman', he tells his mother. Power tools were clearly as coveted in Gilgamesh's world as they are to some in our own. But Gilgamesh's desire for the axe was no work-shed fetish; it was a deeply emotional response to a purposeful object of such perfection, in both form and function, that he could not help but fall in love with it.[21]

Like Gilgamesh, the God of the Bible had himself experienced the powerful allure of beautiful things. In Genesis, the deity finishes creating the world, and then takes a moment to admire his handiwork: 'he saw everything that he had made, and indeed, it was very beautiful'.[22] The sense of this verse is that God himself marvelled both at the workings of the world and its attractive form. Even in God's garden, the fruit of the forbidden tree, set apart for God alone, was not only to be desired for the wisdom it would impart, but because it was pleasant tasting and 'a delight to the eyes'.[23] The garden itself is named 'Delight' (eden), and it is the language of delight that Yahweh often uses to express his physical attraction to beautiful things – just as his love song to the rebuilt Jerusalem, personified as his bride, vividly describes:

> You shall be a crown of beauty in Yahweh's hand,
> and a royal diadem in the hand of your God . . .
> You shall be called 'My Delight Is in Her',
> and your land 'Wedded One',
> for Yahweh delights in you,
> and your land shall be married.
> For as a young man marries a young woman,
> so shall your builder marry you.[24]

Beauty was in the gift of the gods, and so the appeal of Yahweh's holy city, the delights of his garden and the beauty of the created world were derived from the deity himself, for he was the artisan who had crafted them. And nothing could compare to the staggering beauty of Yahweh himself. As one early Jewish poet would soon come to put it, 'much better than these is their Lord, for the author of beauty created them'.[25]

Something of Yahweh's astonishing good looks can be glimpsed in the description of the most beautiful man in the Bible. He is found in the Song of Songs, where a young woman cannot help but use the

sensuous language of awestruck wonder to explain exactly why her
lover is so deliciously desirable:

> My beloved is radiant and ruddy,
> standing out among ten thousand.
> His head is gold, pure gold,
> his locks are curls,
> black as a raven.
> His eyes are like doves,
> by watercourses,
> bathed in milk,
> fitly set.
> His cheeks, like beds of spices,
> pouring forth perfumes.
> His lips are lilies,
> dripping liquid myrrh.
> His arms are rounded gold,
> inlaid with jewels.
> His genitalia are fine-worked ivory,
> with inlaid lapis lazuli.
> His legs are alabaster columns,
> set upon bases of gold.
> Like Lebanon is his look,
> choice as the cedars.
> His mouth is sweet,
> and all of him desirable.[26]

Here is a beautiful man exhibiting the facial features long admired by
both men and women across the ancient Levantine and Mesopotamian
worlds. And yet, adorned in gold and jewels, and anointed with fragrant oils, the woman's lover is no ordinary man. He is not even an
Adonis. He is a divine statue in a temple. He is a god. This is the way
in which some early rabbis understood these ancient love lyrics. For
them, the overwhelming beauty of that ruddy face and muscular body,
that black, lustrous hair and perfumed beard ('cheeks, like beds of
spices'), could only be understood as their beautiful God who had first

revealed himself to their ancestors as they fled Egypt; the deity who
had dwelt among them in sacred space, adorned with the gleaming
treasures and spiced scents of worship; the youthful god for whom
Solomon had built the Jerusalem temple.[27] In seeing God in this poem,
the rabbis were not simply wrestling prized love lyrics into a new
theological form, but drawing on a deeply ingrained cultural memory
of the beauty of Yahweh.

God's beauty incorporated those features traditionally associated
with idealized masculine beauty: reddened skin, thick locks of dark
hair and a carefully styled beard. One of the most exquisite examples
of masculine divine beauty was found at the city of Ur. Excavations
revealed a painted terracotta statuette of an enthroned god, which had
once been positioned before a small altar in a house in a wealthy residential area. Crafted sometime between 1850 BCE and 1750 BCE, the
deity wears a magnificent multi-tiered horned hat, coloured yellow to
represent the shiny gold of the horned crowns adorning divine statues
in the city's temples. The skin of his face and body has been painted
a rich red, and his hair a deep black, a shade conflated with the dark
blue hues of lapis lazuli which coloured the hair of the gods. Neat,
tight curls sit on his forehead, while larger ringlets, loosely pinned at
the nape of his neck, fall behind his shoulders. His facial hair is a
geometrically patterned thatch of more tight black curls, his thick,
tidy sideburns meeting the sculpted moustache and impressive beard
hugging his mouth. Although his beard extends well beyond his chin
and onto his chest, its length is tamed into immaculate zigzagged
locks, as though carefully crimped. He wears a wide, flat necklace,
painted yellow and red to represent gold-set gemstones, and his left
shoulder is draped with a white robe decorated with black lines
(Plate 23).[28]

Although this small statue predates the God of the Bible by several
centuries, its features would remain typical of masculine beauty across
Mesopotamia and the Levant. And one of the most alluring markers
of the gods' magnetic masculinity was ruddy-red, shining skin. Underlying this colour symbolism were the enlivening red pigments that had
been used for millennia to transform special objects into living beings,
and living beings into supercharged forces – much as the red tints given

to Neolithic plastered skulls might suggest. This age-old aesthetic found its way into the religions of subsequent societies across the broader region, so that divine bodies were generally understood to be red. It was a ruddiness of ritual power: in Egypt, the red resins used in mummification processes transformed a corpse into a newly 'living' being; in Mesopotamia, the ideal material for statues of the gods was reddish gold, which manifested the blazing divine light of their radiant skin.[29]

If the reddened skins of the gods manifested their otherworldly vitality, it also signalled their alluring virility and terrifying ferocity. In a world in which an overtly masculine sex appeal was mapped closely onto idealized tropes of aggressive virility and physical dominance, red-stained skin was particularly associated with what is best described as warrior erotica. Before going into battle, fighters might ritually prepare their bodies by staining their skin red, empowering them not only with the life-giving and death-bringing colour of blood, but with the ruddy hues of the clay from which the first earthly life was created, and to which all mortals returned in death. Ready to penetrate bodies on the battlefield, red-stained warriors marked themselves out as masters of mortality, sparing or severing lives, like the divine patrons they served. Sexually irresistible, and yet deadly dangerous, these intimidating fighters channelled the charismatic beauty of the gods.

The sex appeal of the red-stained warrior was especially divinized in the bodies of the goddesses for whom they fought. Unencumbered by the more rigid gender roles of mortals, many goddesses were themselves fierce fighters, whose magnetic sexuality straddled both masculine and feminine ideals, giving expression to a gender-queerness or fluidity more hesitantly explored in other aspects of society. In Mesopotamia, the goddess Ishtar (Inanna) was a favourite among warriors. She was not only celebrated for the beauty of her face, the entrancing gaze of her eyes and the sweet-scented warm wetness of her vulva, but also for her terrifying brute force in battle, her superlative martial skills and her voraciously masculine appetite for sex. Known in Sumerian literature as 'she of the red face', the goddess was closely identified with the red hues of cosmic forces, from the red-gold of her skin and the magical carnelian stones she particularly prized, to the red skies of the morning and evening, when her celestial body, the planet we know as Venus, was at its brightest.[30]

Like Ishtar, the ferocious Levantine goddess Anat had a reputation for both a very feminine beauty and a hyper-masculine violence. She too was the deity most beloved of local warriors, who inscribed her name on their arrowheads and counted themselves her sons and servants. In Ugaritic mythology, Anat is the goddess who not only reddens her body bathing in the blood of her enemies, but after purifying herself, she colours her skin with a red cosmetic to make herself even more sexually alluring. It is a bodily transformation also undertaken by a beautiful woman called Pughat, who mimics Anat's dangerous sex appeal by staining her body red, donning the clothing and weapons of war, and throwing her womanly robe over the top as she sets out to captivate and assassinate the killer of her beloved brother.[31]

This ruddy, charismatic beauty and bloody empowerment was well known to the God of the Bible. He not only commands his mortal fighters to adorn their skin, belts and sandals with blood, but is himself the alluring red-stained warrior, handsomely clothed in blood when he returns from battle in the book of Isaiah. When a sentry in Jerusalem spots the deity striding home from trampling his enemies in the red desert sands of Edom, he asks, 'Who is this so splendidly robed?'[32] His question is no mere formality. It is the exclamation of a man stunned at the sight of a beautiful blood-soaked warrior – a reaction Plutarch would similarly report of the women of Sparta, who realize their own victorious king, Akrotatos, is even better looking drenched in blood.[33] Yahweh's prophets were just as bowled over by the terrifying glamour of blood-red warriors. Nahum can barely contain his excitement in his heavily sexualized account of the destruction of Nineveh in 612 BCE. 'The shields of his warriors are red! His soldiers are clothed in crimson!' he gushes. 'The battering ram has come up against you . . . Gird your loins!' he cries, using a turn of phrase that might be more literally rendered, 'Harden your balls!'[34]

Even God himself is unmanned by the sexualized threat of invading armies when he accuses his abused wife, Jerusalem, of lusting after the 'desirable young men' of invading armies who are 'clad in vermilion'.[35] Not that Yahweh's own head had never been turned by the godlike beauty of a good-looking man. Having seen that the young shepherd-boy David was 'ruddy, and had beautiful eyes, and was good-looking', Yahweh promptly decided to set him up as king: 'Anoint him; this is the one'.[36] God was not the only one to fall for the beautiful young man. David's enticing appeal not only captivated Michal, the daughter of King Saul, but Saul's son and heir, the warrior Jonathan, who takes an erotically charged 'delight' in David, and whose love for him, David famously declares, was 'greater than the love of a woman'.[37] Like the ruddy, divine statue envisaged in the Song of Songs, David exhibits the same irresistible, sexually potent masculinity of a beautiful warrior.[38]

Today, we may not have the remnants of a polychrome statue of Yahweh, but we can come face to face with a deity or divinized being who looked very much like him. Excavations have revealed a number of striking limestone heads from the Iron Age kingdom of the Ammonites, just across the river from ancient Israel and Judah, in what is now northern Jordan. Dated from the ninth to the seventh centuries BCE, many of these heads once topped the statues of venerable dead kings, divinized in the afterlife. But some look decidedly higher status in their divinity, and are likely the high god Milkom, the patron deity of Ammonite kings – and Yahweh's opposite number.[39] Time has not been kind to these artefacts. But something of their allure remains – an allure most forcefully emanating from one particular example, now on prominent public display in Jerusalem's Israel Museum. And yet it is a scandal that this divine face can even be seen at all. Illegally excavated in or around Amman, Jordan, in the mid twentieth century, this artefact was likely smuggled into Israel, where it spent several years sitting on a bookshelf in the home of Moshe Dayan (1915–81) – a high-ranking Israeli politician, military leader, and notoriously corrupt antiquities collector.[40] One among a number of unprovenanced pieces controversially acquired by the museum, its status is tainted by its sordid journey into public view.*

* Untrained and unethical in his 'archaeological' endeavours, Dayan looted, traded and illegally excavated his way to amassing a vast collection of artefacts from ancient sites across the Middle East, as detailed in Raz Kletter's important 2003 article in the *Journal of Hebrew Scriptures*. While Dayan

But its divine beauty is still arresting. Traces of a vibrant red pigment
stain the deity's face and neck. Large eyes, now empty of their bright
inlays, are set beneath patterned eyebrows arching across his forehead,
their delicate hairs feathered like the fine veins of a green leaf. A neat,
combed moustache stretches over his mouth, and a luxuriant beard,
tamed into beautiful elongated curls, hugs his cheeks and chin. Clay
representations of gemstones, suspended from the small hoops he wears
in his ears, are nestled in his thick, corkscrew locks of hair. On his head
is a tall horned crown, its band blossoming with flowers. Virility, fertility,
ferocity and majesty are the hallmarks of his beauty. And it was a beauty
once reflected in the face of Yahweh himself.

Godly Grooming

Whether mortal or divine, a male face framed and furnished with
lustrous hair manifested masculine virility and physical dominance.
This cultural marker of bodily power was so pervasive that a goddess
or a queen might occasionally don a ceremonial prosthetic beard to
underscore her own supremacy.[41] Just as the hair of goddesses might
be described as the leaves of a palm tree or flowing water, and their
pubic hair as a flock of ducks or lush lettuces, the luxuriant hair of the
gods manifested the fertile abundance of the natural world in all its
generative, precious forms. In Mesopotamian literature, Marduk's hair
is a cultivated field, his topknot is tamarisk and his beard a frond. On
other male deities, hairy armpits are described as leeks, chest hair is a
thorn bush and pubic hair is boxwood.[42]

Across ancient south-west Asia, hairiness had long been associated
with an unfettered hyper-masculinity and a correspondingly raw sexuality. In early Mesopotamian art, the ferocious strength and untamed

---

claimed to have acquired a number of pieces as 'gifts', in his 1978 book *Living
with the Bible*, he states he had bought the Ammonite head from a dealer in
Jerusalem (p. 215). To the best of my knowledge, nothing of this artefact's
recent life is explicitly communicated to visitors to the Israel Museum beyond
the acknowledgement that it forms a part of the Moshe Dayan collection.

sexuality of the semi-divine heroes of old was evident in their long locks of hair, springing from their heads in six curling ropes as they wrestled ferocious monsters and wild beasts. They looked very much like the appropriately named Lahmu ('Hairy'), a minor deity who guarded the foundations and doorways of buildings from demonic attack.[43] In Mesopotamian myth, the ultimate hairy warrior was Enkidu – the wild man created by the gods to distract the semi-divine warrior-king Gilgamesh from brawling and bedding his way through the exhausted population of his city. Enkidu embodied the fertile wildness of the supreme warrior: 'His whole body was shaggy with hair, he was furnished with tresses like a woman, his locks of hair grew luxuriant like grain'. It is only once a beautiful sex-worker called Shamhat has taught Enkidu to eat bread instead of grass, to have languid, pleasurable sex, rather than rutting like an animal, and to engage in some personal grooming, that he is sufficiently civilized for urban life with Gilgamesh. Enkidu's newly tamed hair scares the wild animals with whom he had once roamed, for 'Enkidu had stripped [his hair]; his body was too clean'. His transformation into a beautiful warrior is complete. 'You are handsome!' exclaims Shamhat. 'You are just like a god!'[44]

Civilized but hegemonic masculinity was a powerfully hairy man appropriately coiffed and styled, his powerful control of the world matched by the taming and styling of his long hair and magnificent beard. The celebrated palace reliefs of late Assyrian kings illustrate well the cultural value of male grooming: whether a god or a king, the mightiest men of the Assyrian world wear their shoulder-length hair in tight curls, carefully pinned or plaited into disciplined shape. Their upper cheeks are neatly shaved, their short, sculpted sideburns and tidy moustaches delineated with patterned precision. Their long beards, sitting on their broad chests, are sharply squared off and intricately styled into a cross-hatch of curled rows and columns. This not only gives their faces an architectural aesthetic of geometric precision, but mimics the interlocking bark leaves of the date-palm tree, which stood at the symbolic heart of religious and economic life in Mesopotamia. By deliberate contrast, eunuchs are beardless, while dead or captive enemies either wear much shorter, rounded, or dishevelled beards, or are humiliatingly barefaced.[45]

The biblical writers, too, were familiar with the power and politics of male grooming. One of the most famous heroes of ancient Israel and Judah is the long-haired Samson, whose story is told in the book of Judges. He is the child born to be set apart for special service to Yahweh: 'You will conceive and bear a son', a divine messenger tells Samson's unnamed mother, 'and no razor will pass over his head, for the boy will be a Nazir of God from the womb'.[46] As a Nazir, Samson is to be classed among a special group of temporary 'dedications' to Yahweh – living, unsacrificed offerings to the deity, whose displacement from mainstream society was marked by their uncut hair, their holiness growing like their lengthening locks. 'When locks grow long in Israel, when people [ritually] offer themselves willingly – bless Yahweh!' ran an ancient song.[47] But Samson is remembered not so much for his religious service, but his superhuman strength.

Like Enkidu, the wild man of Mesopotamian myth, Samson's hyper-masculinity is marked by his long hair. He is the strong man who kills a lion with his bare hands, slaughters a thousand men with a donkey bone and carries a city gate on his shoulders. Unlike Enkidu, however, Samson is born a man of culture: he wears his long hair in seven plaits, braided and bound into order. His emasculation comes at the hands of his girlfriend, Delilah, who arranges for his hair to be shaved clean off by enemy Philistines while he sleeps in her lap. Baldness brings powerlessness, both physical and divine: Yahweh abandons him, as does his superhuman strength. Imprisoned, shackled, blinded and shaved, Samson is as helpless as a swaddled, bare-headed newborn. But as his hair grows back, Samson's powerful masculinity returns. Brought up from his prison as party entertainment at a temple festival, he is chained and displayed between two giant columns like a stricken baited bear, his long hair untamed and unbound. Samson brings the pillars of the Philistine temple crashing down upon his enemies, killing himself in the process. In a sense, his story ends much as Enkidu's had begun. With the return of Samson's long hair comes a raw, dehumanized and deadly wildness, set in stark opposition to the socialized sophistication of city living.[48]

Yahweh's apparent preference for carefully groomed, long-haired, bearded mortal men went beyond Samson. His priests were instructed not to shave their heads, cut back the hair on their cheeks, nor remove their sideburns – not even in grief, when men commonly divested themselves of their ordinary clothing and stripped themselves of their vivifying hair in solidarity with their rotting dead.[49] It was a mourning custom El himself had performed on learning of the death of Baal:

> He poured the ashes of mourning on his head,
> the dust of grovelling on his skull;
> for clothing he put on a loincloth.
> His skin with a stone he scored,
> his sidelocks with a razor.
> He cut his [hairy] cheeks and chin . . .[50]

It is a remarkable display of ritual self-abasement, for the deliberate shortening or shaving of a senior god's beard might sap his strength, stripping the deity of his authority, as well as his masculinity. It was a widespread cultural anxiety powerfully attested by a much earlier Mesopotamian cylinder seal, showing one god, horn-capped and heavily robed, mutilating the beard of another (fig. 46).

This form of emasculating mutilation was well known to kings across south-west Asia, whose law codes regularly decreed that political enemies, rebellious vassals and domestic criminals would be divested of those body parts most closely associated with generative power: their hair, beard, hands and genitals would be chopped off. In the Hebrew Bible, Yahweh levels a similar threat against his own people. Virtually brandishing a razor blade, he warns he will join the king of Assyria in cutting his people down to shameful size: 'The Lord will shave with a razor hired beyond the Euphrates River, with the king of Assyria, the head and the hair of the feet [genitals], and the beard, too, it will take off'. Humiliatingly, Yahweh's male worshippers will not only lose their hair and their beards, but they will be shorn of their pubic hair, too.[51] The God of the Bible clearly understood that a carefully groomed beard and a thick head of hair were potent markers of masculine virility. Not that he was necessarily insensitive to the potential socio-sexual humiliation inherent in natural male baldness, as his prophet Elisha was pleased to discover. According to a collection

Fig. 46. Detail from a Mesopotamian cylinder seal (*c.* 2350–2150 BCE), showing one horn-capped deity mutilating the beard of another.

of folk tales in the books of Kings, Elisha might have inherited Elijah's hairy animal-skin cloak, but it failed to make up for his baldness. When he is teased by a gang of small boys ('Go away, Baldy! Go away, Baldy!'), he might as well have been mocked for erectile dysfunction. But Yahweh heeds Elisha's call for a curse to fall upon the children – and responds with a sardonic, gender-bending flourish: two hairy she-bears suddenly appear, and attack the children, shredding a staggering forty-two of them.[52]

Given the cultural cachet of long, lustrous hair and muscular beardedness among divine and mortal men, it is almost unthinkable that Yahweh himself, the paradigmatic alpha-male, could ever have been imagined to be bald-headed or beard free. Before the cultural upheavals following the destruction of the kingdom of Judah in the sixth century BCE, his hair and beard was probably imagined to look very much like that of the mortal kings who ruled in his name. As the earthly doppelgänger of the heavenly king, the authority of the human king rested on his ideological or schematic likeness to Yahweh, in both form and function – so much so, one psalmist could describe the mortal king as a 'divine being', and 'the most beautiful of men . . . forever blessed by God'.[53] And a remarkable image of a king of Judah offers a tantalizing glimpse of this divinely derived royal beauty. Inked in red and black on a potsherd (the ancient equivalent of notepaper), it had likely served as an artist's preparatory sketch for a more costly image. Dated to the seventh century BCE, the potsherd was uncovered during the excavation of what is thought to be a royal residence in Ramat Rahel, just north of Bethlehem. It depicts a wide-eyed, muscular man, richly robed and sitting on an ornate throne, a benevolent smile dancing at his mouth. Thick, carefully groomed locks of hair fall to his shoulders, and his long black beard is shaped into a thrusting point – a style common to artistic representations of elite males across the southern Levant (fig. 47). In an age in which portraiture was highly unusual, this was not so much a portrayal of a specific ruler, but a recognizable representation of Judah-ite kingship, embodied by the requisite physical features of that alluring, idealized masculinity kings shared with their gods.[54]

If this little painting offered a mortal mirroring of the face of Yahweh, three hundred years later another would reveal the face of the deity himself. A storeroom in the British Museum is now home to a small silver coin, minted in the first half of the fourth century BCE, in or around Judah, which was now a Persian satrapy called Yehud. The obverse shows the profile of the local Persian governor,

Fig. 47. A thickly bearded king of Judah, embodying a divinely derived male beauty. This image was inked onto a potsherd at Ramat Rahel, near Bethlehem, in the seventh century BCE.

stereotypically presented as a bearded.military man wearing a crested helmet. On the reverse of the coin is a muscular god, wearing an ankle-length tunic or cloak. He is seated on a winged wheel, an emblem which had come to be used of solar high-gods across the eastern Mediterranean and the Levant. One hand rests comfortably on his lap, but the other is stretched out in front of him, a hunting bird perched on his hand. The god has thick side locks, a shapely beard and a luxuriant head of hair. Neatly styled and pinned, it reaches almost to his shoulders. Behind the god and his bird, the word 'Yehud' ('Judah'), is inscribed in Aramaic, the language dominating commerce and administration in the western half of the empire (Plate 24).

The coin was produced at a time when minting workshops in the southern Levant tended to imitate or adapt motifs influenced by the Greek, Phoenician and Egyptian imagery commonly found on money, weights and tokens across the wider region. But this example was locally produced for use in Judah itself, where the coin's constellation of symbols would have left little doubt about the identity of the seated deity on the coin's reverse. Adopting the now widespread Hellenized pose of the supreme god of the heavens, and sitting alongside the name of his homeland, it is Yahweh himself. To his worshippers in Judah, his winged wheel was easily identified both with Yahweh's winged chariot throne, and the winged solar disc which had long served as a religious emblem of the former kingdom of Judah. In contrast to the mysterious balding head and unkempt whiskers of the bulbous-nosed, ageing face positioned at his feet – a face that continues to baffle scholars – Yahweh is adorned with the thick hair and groomed beard of an attractively vigorous, virile deity.[55]

On this coin, the deity's traditional long locks and pointed black beard might well have morphed in style from distinctively Levantine to fashionably Greek, but it was a relatively minor wardrobe alteration. Over the course of the first millennium BCE, from its early centuries to the dawning of the Hellenistic era, the proud horns adorning Yahweh's head had already faded from view, and his youthful, ruddy beauty had matured into a seemingly more rugged, battle-stained glamour. But an even bigger change to God's good looks was on its way. He was about to go grey.

18

PROFILE

On the ceiling of the Vatican's Sistine Chapel, God reaches out to Adam in what is probably the most famous image of the biblical deity in Western art. Rippling with muscle, and surrounded by a gaggle of golden-haired angels and rosy-cheeked putti, God is the all-powerful cosmic Creator, sweeping through the heavenly skies to bless his new-made mortal with a touch of his finger. There are silver streaks in his pale grey hair, and frost-white curls in his cloud-coloured beard. Deep creases line his forehead, and wrinkles crinkle around his eyes. This is a god older than the universe.

Of course, when he painted *The Creation of Adam* in the early sixteenth century, Michelangelo was far from the first to imagine God in this way. The Western God had already been cast as the white-haired sovereign elder of the cosmos, because this was precisely the way he was portrayed in a highly influential passage in the second century BCE book of Daniel, giving rise to a wealth of early Jewish and Christian literature featuring an aged patriarchal deity enthroned at the apex of a multi-tiered heaven crowded with angels and archangels.[1] But when God's hair first turned white in the book of Daniel, it signalled his holiness as much as his age.

Throughout the first millennium BCE, the dazzling light emanating from Yahweh's body had manifested his innate purity as well as his divine radiance. Simply put, he was sparkling clean. In his temples, Yahweh's presence imparted the same purity to the space itself, hence

347

the need to keep temples ritually clean of the polluting 'dirt' of religious malpractice and spiritual impiety. But in the mid second century BCE, the temple in Jerusalem was defiled by Antiochus IV Epiphanes, a Hellenistic king of the Seleucid Empire under whose control the Levant had fleetingly fallen. Antiochus not only helped himself to the temple treasury, but reputedly appointed a deeply unpopular high priest, installed a statue of Zeus in Yahweh's sanctuary and offered sacrifices to him there. It was a short-lived measure, for Antiochus would soon be dead, killed by disease or war in 164 BCE, and Jerusalem's temple would be purged of its trespassing Greek god.

But this was the defiling horror the biblical book of Daniel sought in part to address. Composed shortly after Antiochus' incursion into the temple, the book's eponymous, legendary hero is cast as the visionary who foresees the punishment of Antiochus and his horde of 'dirty' foreigners, who are collectively presented as a ravenous, rampaging chaos monster equipped with iron teeth and eleven horns, the last of which – Antiochus himself – has human eyes and a 'mouth speaking arrogantly'.[2] Daniel is transported to the heavenly throne room, where he witnesses God decreeing the execution of the monstrous foe, which is promptly killed and set alight, before a younger divine figure in human form ('one like a son of man') rides in on the clouds of heaven to be given eternal kingship over all peoples.[3] It is a cataclysmic end-of-times vision, which promises the cosmos will made anew. But in the face of such defiling monstrosity and urgent cosmic reordering, God himself remains the picture of perpetual purity: enthroned in fiery splendour, and surrounded by thousands of divine courtiers, he is called 'an Ancient of Days', dressed in robes 'white as snow', with hair 'like lamb's wool'.[4] These verses conjure an image of a primordial, white-haired sovereign of the universe, directing the end-of-times events Daniel witnesses.

Underlying this biblical vision was a much older, long-lived mythic image of the aged high-god El, who had granted the young cloud-rider, Baal, kingship in the heavens. In the Ugaritic myths, El's status as the oldest of the gods was corporeally conveyed by the greyness of his hair and beard – a colour serving as a symbol of perpetuity, rather than a sign of physical degeneration. To his daughter Anat, El's grey hair and beard represented the very authority she sometimes sought to challenge: 'I shall strike the top of your skull!' she screams at El (albeit from a prudent distance). 'I shall make your grey hair run [with blood], the grey hair of your beard with gore!' To El's chief wife Athirat, his long grey beard, sitting on his chest, manifested the hoary wisdom of experience: 'The greyness of your beard indeed makes you wise, the compassion from your breast indeed instructs you!' she tells him. No wonder El was known as the 'Father of Years' – a title which spoke as much to his time-free eternal nature as to his seniority. As the younger gods themselves declared, El was 'the ageless one who begot us'.[5] In ancient Israel and Judah, Yahweh had gradually usurped El's status as the high god of the cosmos and taken his titles for himself. By the time the book of Genesis had been compiled, sometime in the fifth

Fig. 48. A small limestone statue of El of Ugarit, dated to about the thirteenth century BCE. His long beard rests on his chest. Although his eyes and arms have been lost, something of his dignified authority remains.

century BCE, Yahweh had already been called 'El the Everlasting'. Poets had declared 'no end' to his years, and that their number was simply 'unsearchable'.[6] Now, in the second century BCE, Yahweh was the Ancient of Days, whose hair and beard had acquired the greyness of El's own, his radiant purity rendering it a dazzling white.

The changing face of the biblical God inevitably raised questions for early Jewish scholars. Had their ancestors encountered God as a beautiful youth, a fearsome warrior, or a wise old man? For many rabbis, the answer lay hidden in plain sight in their holy scrolls. In the *Pesiqta de-Rab Kahana,* a collection of midrashic traditions dated to the third to fifth centuries CE, these old scriptural proofs were laid bare. Alluding to key biblical verses (including those describing the beautiful male lover in the 'Solomonic' Song of Songs and the Ancient of Days in the book of Daniel), the midrash explains how God could appear in many modes and yet remain unchangingly constant:

> . . . the Holy One, blessed may he be, appeared to them in the Sea like a warrior conducting a war; he revealed himself to them at Sinai, like a scribe who teaches the Torah, and he appeared to them in the time of Daniel like an old man who teaches the Torah; he appeared to them in the time of Solomon [like] a young man. The Holy One, blessed may he be, said to them: It is not that you deserved to see me in different forms, but it is I who was in the Sea, it is I who was at Sinai, [for] 'I am the Lord thy God'.[7]

For these rabbis, God was able to change his appearance at will – but not because he was like those shape-shifters of Greek and Roman myth, nor because he was a polymorphic phantasm like Jesus, whose own followers had struggled to recognize him after his miraculous resurrection. Rather, the rabbis argued, the aesthetics of God's form were innately bound to the specifics of his revelatory performance. When he fought to liberate his people from Egypt, he was a youthful warrior; when he instructed his people in the Torah on Sinai, he was a wise old teacher. Just as the Romans themselves celebrated the young man who conducted himself as an experienced elder, and the old man who displayed a youthful verve, so too the rabbis vaunted their unchanging God for his capacity for apparent paradox: the aged Torah scribe at Sinai was as youthfully vigorous as a warrior, while the young warrior who fought at the Sea was as sage as an elderly scholar.[8]

It was a rabbinic position carefully explicated to allay any suggestion that the Jewish God was either subject to the ravages of time, or that he was not even one god at all, but two. These were understandable anxieties. The image of God as the white-haired Ancient of Days had already found a place in much earlier Jewish traditions about the legendary Enoch, who had ascended into the heavens and been transformed into a celestial scribe. And by the first century CE, Enoch had been elevated further still in status. It was said that, when he had ascended to heaven, he was not simply one looking like a 'son of man' (human), but *the* Son of Man – a divine figure on whom the white-haired high god conferred cosmic kingship:

> There came out of that house [in heaven] Michael and Gabriel
> and Raphael and Phanuel, and many holy angels without
> number. And with them was the Head [Ancient] of Days,
> and his head was white and pure as wool, and his garments
> were indescribable . . . And he came to me and greeted me
> with his voice and said to me, 'You [are] that Son of Man who
> was born for righteousness, and righteousness dwells on you,
> and the righteousness of the Head [Ancient] of Days will not
> forsake you'.[9]

In this collection of visions in 1 Enoch, the eponymous seer not only learns he is the divine Son of Man, but foresees his enthronement in the heavens alongside God, where he will preside over the last judgement at the end of times.[10] No wonder some rabbis of the early centuries of the Common Era felt the need to assert the oneness of God. At the same time, of course, they were also contending with the very similar claims many Jews and Gentiles had been making about Jesus. In various early Christian writings, some of which would come to be canonical, Jesus was said to have identified himself as the Son of Man who would ascend to his divine Father on lightning-lit storm clouds, where he would be enthroned in the heavens at God's right hand, oversee the last judgement and be given an eternal kingdom.[11] As the heavenly Son of Man, Christ was given the white-wool hair and dazzling face of a divinity, aligning him in look and function with God himself, as the book of Revelation illustrates: 'I saw one like the Son of Man, clothed with a long robe and with a golden sash across his chest. His head and his hair were white as white wool, white as snow; his eyes were like a flame of fire . . . and his face was like the sun shining with full force.'[12]

As these traditions indicate, Daniel's vision of the white-haired Ancient of Days and the Son of Man was easily transposed onto the theological distinction between God the Father and his divine Son, while at the same time suggesting the two were to be closely identified. 'I am the Alpha and the Omega, the beginning and the end', the eternal God declares from his throne towards the end of Revelation, only for the same claim to be made by Christ at the book's close: 'I am the Alpha and the Omega, the first and the last, the beginning and the end!'[13] For the writer of this influential early Christian work, God and his Son were presented as identical in looks and equals in power. An early Christian insistence upon the visual likeness of the Son to his Father was similarly expressed in what appears to have been formulaic or ritual confessions of faith: 'Though he was in the form of God, he did not regard equality with God as something to be exploited', sang some. 'He has spoken to us by a Son, whom he appointed heir of all things, through whom he also created the worlds! He is the reflection of God's glory and the exact imprint of God's very being!' intoned others.[14]

As early as these ideas were, portrayals of a cosmic Christ in the likeness or image of God would take some time to filter into the visual cultures of his early devotees. The earliest identifiable Christian art is attested in the catacombs of Rome (from the beginning of the third century CE), the house-church in the eastern Syrian town of Dura Europos (mid third century) and on decorated Roman sarcophagi of the third and fourth centuries. These works usually depict Christ not as a mystical, bright-white, heavenly being, nor even as the suffering, crucified Son of God, but as a vivacious, beard-free and brown-haired

Graeco-Roman beauty (Plate 27). Whether seated in the authoritative pose of a learned teacher, performing miraculous wonders of healing and magic, or shepherding humanity with a lost lamb upon his shoulders, Christ was initially drawn in the image of youthful deities and semi-divine heroes like Apollo, Dionysus, Hermes and Orpheus, rather than mirroring the rugged majesty of the thickly bearded high gods like Zeus, Jupiter, Sarapis, Asclepius and Neptune.[15] In some early artworks, depictions of Christ as an orator, clutching a scroll, would give him the beard of a learned philosopher, as might be seen on depictions of Paul and Peter. But his youthful vigour was still proudly displayed in his athletic body and muscular chest (fig. 50).

With the explosion of church-building in the fourth century CE came the longer-haired, big-bearded haloed heavenly Christ with whom we are more familiar. Up until this point, Christian worship had tended to be a relatively low-profile communal activity. Across the Roman Empire, minority religious groups had often been subject to both sporadic and extended periods of persecution, when they might find themselves harassed, arrested, punished, or killed. Ostensibly, these measures were prompted by a refusal to sacrifice to the gods of Rome, or a perceived failure to conform to the broader norms of civility. But political machinations were also at work. Since the reign of Diocletian (284–305 CE), Rome's vast empire had been precariously divided between at least two (and usually four) emperors, each of whom often chose to target or ignore minority groups within their provinces as a part of their wider power play. But in 313 CE, the co-emperors Constantine and Licinius had signed the Edict of Milan, which endorsed (among other things) a more accommodating attitude to Christians and their freedom to worship, and decreed the restitution of their communally owned property.

Formally freed from persecution, Christians across the empire refashioned old house-churches, and new churches sprang up – many financed by Constantine himself. As a worshipper of Christ, Constantine siphoned money from the estates of Graeco-Roman temples to construct magnificent Christian basilicas not only in Rome, but in Antioch, Jerusalem, and his new imperial capital, Byzantion (in Latin, Byzantium), which was quickly renamed Constantinople. Local

Fig. 49. Christ's golden-haired, youthful good looks contrast with those of Peter and Paul in this mosaic from the Church of Santa Constanza, Rome. Dated to about the fourth century CE, this depiction of Christ echoes older portrayals of solar deities in the Graeco-Roman world.

Fig. 50. On this slab from an elaborately decorated sarcophagus (c. 300 CE), Christ is presented as a bearded philosopher, his students sitting obediently at his feet. While philosophers tended to be portrayed as unkempt, older men, Christ has the muscular build of a more youthful man.

Christian dignitaries east and west increasingly enjoyed the privileges accorded other higher-profile citizens, and were soon elevated into positions of civic, administrative and political power. Life for promi-nent and ordinary Christians alike became more stable in the care of their churches. Although Christianity would not become the 'official' religion of the Roman Empire until 381 CE, Constantine's policies were continued by all but one of his successors, and would have a lasting impact. Favoured with imperial largesse, urban Christianity prospered, and the magnificence of its art reflected this.

Out and proud in public buildings, Christ acquired the more clas-sical features of a Mediterranean high god, enthroned in splendour. It is a visual shift attested in a mosaic adorning the apse of Santa Puden-ziana in Rome, the city's oldest surviving church. Dated to the end of the fourth century, the mosaic shows Christ as *Pantokrator* – the 'all powerful' ruler of the universe. Dressed in shimmering robes, he sits on a huge golden throne studded with jewels and lined with scarlet silks. He holds an open book, which is inscribed in Latin with the words 'Lord and Preserver of the Church of Pudenziana'. Behind him is an enormous golden cross, encrusted with precious gemstones. Standing on Golgotha, the hill of Jesus' crucifixion, the cross reaches up into the multicoloured heavens, where God's cherubim gather about it. Here in Santa Pudenziana, Christ has inherited his divine Father's supreme glory, and brought the very kingdom of heaven into the church (Plate 28).

In some ways, the loftier portrayal of Christ not only reflected his exalted divine status, but also compensated for an absence of images of God himself. In keeping with what was by now a widespread Jewish convention, Christians had tended to avoid figurative images of the deity's face. While God's hand might be seen in Christian art plunging down from the heavens to direct the action in visual tableaus, his presence was more usually signalled by his cherubim, angels, or a sun chariot, hijacked from Helios. In this, Christian visual culture was little different from its Jewish counterparts across the empire, in which God's presence tended to be rendered visible only by means of his hands, a Torah ark, or symbols of the Jerusalem temple – be it a menorah, an altar, or an image of the lost building itself. But whether viewed through a Jewish or Christian lens, God's face persisted in the religious imagination, and by the fourth century CE, it had come to acquire the qualities of a cosmic prototype.

Fuelled by older traditions about the tangible, transformative impact of seeing God face to face, religious thinkers imagined God's face might not only leave a visible trace on the faces of those exceptional enough to behold him, but on the faces of those spiritually or scripturally equipped to perceive him. Jewish scholars and teachers had long been arguing that the way to truly perceive God was to study the mysteries embedded in the Torah – which is why some of the most beautiful rabbis reportedly had the look of God about them. In a series of Talmudic traditions collated during the third to fifth centuries CE, the best-looking rabbis across the generations had looked like God himself, for their beauty was ultimately derived from his, via Adam and Jacob: 'The beauty of Rabbi Kahana was like the beauty of Rav, the beauty of Rav was like the beauty of Rabbi Abbahu, the beauty of Rabbi Abbahu was like the beauty of Father Jacob, the beauty of Father Jacob was like the beauty of Adam, the beauty of Adam was like the beauty of the Divine Presence.'[16]

Hearing this list, some rabbinic students were perplexed about the absence of another famously beautiful sage, Rabbi Yohanan, until they were reminded that he was beardless – and thus rather too feminine and decidedly ungodly in his allure. But another gorgeous teacher would come to be included in this legendary beauty pageant. Rabbi Ishmael ben Elisha ha-Kohen was reported to have been among ten sages martyred by Rome, where the flayed skin of his lovely face became a magical relic. Before his death, the rabbi was said to have been taken up to the heavens, where the archangel Gabriel asked him, 'Are you the Ishmael in whom the Creator prides himself each day, saying that he has a servant on earth whose looks are like his facial features?'[17] Underscoring all these ancient rabbinic traditions was the biblical insistence that the first man had been created in God's image and likeness – so much so, early rabbis had said, that the angels in Eden were unable to distinguish Adam from his divine Creator.[18]

The idea that God's face served as a cosmic prototype is a point on which many Christians likely agreed, as one of the earliest, identifiably Christian depictions of his face suggests. Dated to the fourth century CE, it is found on a sarcophagus in the Vatican Museums' Pio Cristiano collection. This impressive marble coffin had clearly housed the remains of a wealthy Roman citizen, for its costly friezes are beautifully detailed and exquisitely carved. As with most early Christian funerary art, its focus is the alleviation of earthly ills and the promise of a paradisiacal post-mortem future, when believers would come face to face with the divine. As such, alongside scenes of a youthful, beardless Christ performing miracles, the sarcophagus offers an image of Eden. Adam and Eve appear either side of the garden's tree, around which is coiled a docile serpent. But Adam's face is turned towards that of a beautifully bearded figure standing next to him. Robed in the long toga of a Roman dignitary, he leans in to Adam, his right hand pressed on Adam's shoulder in a gentle gesture of affectionate blessing. It is God. And his face is identical to Adam's. The first man is God's mirror image (Plate 29).

Some scholars have proposed that this scene reflects certain theological claims about the nature of Christ as the incarnate *Logos* or 'Word' of God, through whom the world was created, as the opening verses of the Gospel of John urge its readers to believe. Certainly, prominent theologians of different stripes had repeatedly argued that it was not God the Father who had been with Adam and Eve in Eden, nor God the Father who had appeared to Abraham, Jacob, Moses and the prophets. Instead, they asserted, it was God the Son in his pre-existent, pre-incarnational state as the divine *Logos* who had rendered himself visible to select mortals in the past. This was the Son whom bishops upholding the decisions made at Constantine's Council of Nicaea in 325 CE had subsequently declared to be 'God from God, light from light' and 'one substance' with the Father – a claim that would have to be formally decreed at the Council of Constantinople in 381 CE and asserted yet again at the Council of Chalcedon in 451 CE given the strength of ongoing opposition from other theologians.[19] And yet, the extent to which this highbrow, esoteric theology might have been either assumed or fully comprehended by even wealthy, reasonably educated Christians of either Jewish or Gentile cultural identity, let alone identified on this marble coffin, is far from certain. After all, the

very fact that successive theologians and bishops would still feel the
need to insist that it was the pre-incarnate Son, and not God the Father,
whom various biblical figures had seen rather suggests their arguments
tended to fall on deaf ears. Instead, it was the deeply ingrained tradition
that God had made Adam in his own image and likeness that was more
pervasive and persuasive. In the fourth century CE, mourners and
pilgrims visiting Rome's Christian cemeteries were already accustomed
to seeing Christ as a beardless figure in funerary art – especially when
he appeared on sarcophagi. Looking at this particular sarcophagus,
they would be far more likely to recognize the figure standing next to
Adam simply as God, and to distinguish him from his more youthful,
beardless Son busily performing wonders in the same frieze. It was
God's face that was reflected in Adam's in the Garden of Eden, not
Christ's.

Another fourth-century sarcophagus in the Vatican Museums'
collection similarly displays the prototypical quality of God's face,
although this time it is not Adam he looks at. It too is decorated with
finely wrought friezes, showcasing snapshots from the life of Jesus,
who has the beard-free face of a young man. But at its upper left edge,
the creation of Eve is shown. Neatly coiffed and thickly bearded, God
sits enthroned, his feet resting on an ornate footstool. Behind him
stands another bearded figure, clutching the back of the divine throne.
With his curly hair and thick beard, he has the distinct look of God
about him. In front of the throne is a third figure, who has turned his
enquiring face to the deity, appealing for approval. And he too has the
face of God. His hand rests on the newly made Eve he has just pulled
from Adam's side, who is shown both as a small childlike sleeping
figure and as a grown-up, dwelling in a verdant paradise. The enthroned
God holds up his right hand, his forefingers raised, in a gesture of
blessing endorsing the invention of humanity (Plate 30).

This is an early figurative representation of the Trinity. It is God
the Father who sits enthroned, directing and approving the actions of
God the Son as he makes Eve. Looking on is the Holy Spirit, the third
member of the Trinity, emanating from the throne, his face turned to
the Father and the Son. As the writer of the Epistle to the Hebrews
had put it at the end of the first century CE, the Son was 'the reflection

of God's glory and the exact imprint of God's very being'. Now, on this fourth-century coffin, God's face could be seen imprinted on both the Son and the Spirit.[20] But if their near-identical faces served to unify the three, their body language implies a hierarchical relationship: the enthroned God enjoys a higher status than his divine companions, while the seemingly privileged, attendant position of the Spirit is rendered passive by the creative activity of the Son. Looking at the sarcophagus, it is difficult to decide how we are to understand the divine nature and status of the Son and the Spirit, in relation both to each other and to the Father God.

In some ways, this striking imagery sums up the theological problems at the heart of Christianity during the first four hundred years of the faith. Since the first century CE, baptism had been widely accepted as the first, crucial step to the believer's eternal salvation, and everyone agreed that Jesus himself had commanded his apostles to baptize 'in the name of the Father and of the Son and of the Holy Spirit'.[21] This was the threefold formula by which new members continued to be initiated into the faith. But quite what this formula meant was up for debate. Everyone knew the Son and the Holy Spirit were to be identified in some way with God, as the Vatican's Trinity sarcophagus itself illustrates, but there was disagreement about the precise nature of this identification and difficulty in establishing how they each related to one another.

By the fourth century, two broad camps had formed. One group tended to emphasize the distinctiveness of Father, Son and Spirit as three 'persons' (in Greek, *hypostases*) of one God as a means of explaining the different ways in which God acted within and beyond the created world. But the other group ardently believed this fragmented the oneness of God's nature—his 'essence' or 'substance' (in Greek, *ousia*). And for them, this fragmentation was deeply problematic: it either cast God not as one but three deities, or it subordinated the Son and the Spirit to the Father, relegating their theological roles to glorified assistants to the 'true' God. And yet, in emphasizing the oneness of God, their own position risked casting Father, Son and Spirit merely as unstable 'modes' or manifestations of God, thereby destabilizing the Father, Son and Spirit as permanent *hypostases* of God – those in whose distinct names Jesus had commanded his followers to be baptized. Falling between these camps were various others. Some held the Son and the Spirit were mediators or conduits to the Father, from whom they derived; some believed the Father and the Son shared the same 'substance' and were equal 'persons', but the Spirit, though of God, was not equal to the Father and the Son; others asserted Father, Son and Spirit all shared the same substance, but still recoiled at describing the Spirit as 'God'.[22] As is often the case with differences of opinion between Christian groups, the highly creative reinterpretation of scripture enabled everyone to claim biblical support for their own position – despite the fact that the idea of a triune God appears nowhere in the Jewish scriptures, and is staggeringly far from being a solid notion in the writings of the New Testament. A compromise of sorts ostensibly appears to have been reached at the Council of Chalcedon in 451 CE, where, in the course of revisiting the credal confessions drawn up at Nicaea and Constantinople, it was agreed that Father, Son and Spirit were one singular, eternal, divine 'substance', and were distinguishable as three 'persons' only by the manner in which each possessed that substance: the Father possessed the divine substance 'without cause' from himself; the Son possessed the divine substance in his being 'begotten from' the Father; and the Spirit possessed the divine substance by 'proceeding' from the Father. The Godhead was one substance, and three persons.[23]

Ultimately, theologians across the empire had been struggling to reconcile both the early deification of Christ and the divine agency of the 'Spirit' with the ostensibly monotheistic Jewish roots of their faith, headlined by God's own insistence in the scriptures that he was the one and only true God. Despite the expert philosophical craftsmanship of the early Church Fathers, it was a classic square-peg-in-a-round-hole dilemma – except there were three pegs of shifting form, shape and size, and the hole was variously too small, too big, too rigid, or too fragile to hold them all in one place. The rapprochement at Chalcedon would not resolve matters, for Trinitarian disputes continued to dog the faith and divide Christians – and still do today.

No matter how the Father, Son and Spirit were understood to relate to one another in their Trinitarian form, Christ continued to be made in God's image in religious art. And it was in the Roman East that Christ himself would eventually come to be portrayed as the aged, eternal God of the cosmos, complete with the dazzling white hair and hoary white beard of the Ancient of Days. Here, well-established early Christian communities in Asia Minor, Syria, Egypt and Palestine appear to have adopted the painted wood-panel portraits of the young gods and heroes of the older Hellenistic era for their own icons of Christ, as descriptions in early stories about the miraculous healing powers of Christ's picture suggest. The iconography of these portraits would later morph into the familiar face 'imprinted' on famous relics, such as the Mandylion of Edessa, the Handkerchief of Veronica and the Turin Shroud. But the first portraits of Christ in the Roman East probably looked very much like earlier Hellenistic artworks. Short haired and beardless, Christ tended to bear the dark good looks and big brown eyes of a more distinctively Middle Eastern or North African man, much like the older funerary portraits of wealthy young men common in Hellenistic Egypt long before the emergence of Christianity.[24]

The wood-panel portrait was a type of icon that would itself become iconic. As the vast eastern provinces of the Roman Empire gradually transformed into the powerful Byzantine Empire, the artistic conventions of their Christian communities not only swept westwards to colour the visual cultures of late antique and early medieval Europe, but fixed the form of Christian icons as we still find them in Eastern Orthodox churches today. But early examples of these icons are rare. As delicately painted wooden objects, they were prone to damp, damage and decay, while the aggressive, reactionary iconoclasm of Byzantine emperors in the eighth and ninth centuries would wipe out treasured collections in monasteries and churches across the region. But in the remote, arid environment of St Catherine's Monastery in Sinai, some remarkable examples have survived. And one in particular attests to a pointedly Eastern Church image of Christ.

Measuring a sizeable seventy-six centimetres in height, the large wooden icon is encased by a thick frame, on which a votive declaration is inscribed: 'For the salvation and pardon of the sins of your servant Philochristos'. Enthroned on a rainbow amid a galaxy of stars, Christ wears the golden robes of majesty, his sandalled feet resting on an orb, a pre-Christian emblem of overarching heavenly power. His head is crowned with a golden halo encircled by a red-hot beam of light, and the divine name 'Emmanuel', spelled out in golden Greek letters, hovers next to him. His right hand is authoritatively raised, and his left holds an open, golden-leaved book, in which traces of the words 'I am the light of the world' have been detected.[25] He is surrounded by a mandorla, around which two of an original four cherubim discreetly hover against the thick golden light enshrining his presence. This is Christ Pantokrator – but unlike his darker-haired manifestation in Western iconography of the age, his youthful face is adorned with the white hair and white beard of the supreme God of the heavens (Plate 31). Although the icon tends to be dated to the late sixth or early seventh century, its sophisticated imagery and expert execution suggests it is of a pre-existing type, rather than a new-fangled, experimental genre.[26] And the theological heft of the icon would support this.

The conflation of imagery and inscriptions in this icon points to several biblical motifs on which its iconology of Christ has been drawn: the white-haired deity is the aged Ancient of Days from the book of Daniel, his rainbow is ultimately taken from Ezekiel's vision of God enthroned above the cherubim, and the Greek inscription 'Emmanuel' ('God is with us') names the divinely promised baby born to a young woman in the book of Isaiah.[27] But this is not a heavy-handed pick-and-mix theology. Instead, it is a graphic reflection of more complex ideas about the divine nature of Christ, filtered through the lens of the book of Revelation, in which he is given the white hair of God the Father. On this icon, Christ himself is the Ancient of Days. He is God himself, the eternal ruler of the universe, who was made flesh and born of the Virgin. 'For my sake the Ancient of Days has become a babe!' worshippers in the Eastern Church of the period sang in celebration of the incarnation. 'Today the Ancient of Days, he that once gave the law on Mount Sinai to Moses, is seen as a babe!'[28]

In the Latin West, the aged features of the Ancient of Days tended to be reserved for images of God the Father, rather than Christ. But in the old library of Saint-Lupicin, a village in the Jura region of France, there was found a remarkable image of Christ on the cover of a Gospel book. The book itself dates to the ninth century CE, but the ivory panels serving as its front and back covers were once a Byzantine diptych, which was probably made in Constantinople in the fifth or sixth century CE.[29] Surrounded by scenes from legends about Jesus, Mary and the saints, the centrepiece on one of the panels shows Christ seated on an ornate throne, his feet on a pretty footstool. His right hand is raised in a gesture of blessing, while in his left he holds up a book, emblazoned with a cross. Behind him, looking over his shoulders, are Peter and Paul. Despite their cropped pudding-bowl hairstyles, they are elderly men, with wrinkled foreheads and bushy beards. And so too is Christ. Hunched in his chair, he has the loose pot-belly of an old man. His face is lined with age, his cheeks have sagged into jowls, and his long, almost scraggy, beard sits on his chest (Plate 32). There is no trace of Christ the divine Son. He has become the Ancient of Days in form as well as name. Like the high god El of the very distant past, whose own grey beard rested on his chest when he put his feet up on a footstool, Christ is the aged god of the cosmos. And it shows.

This was an iconology of Christ distinct to the Byzantine world, and it persists today in Eastern Orthodox churches, where, occasionally, images of a white-haired, heavenly Christ are still made in the likeness of his Father. By contrast, the Western churches of late antiquity preferred to cast God the Father as the eternal white-haired patriarch of the cosmos. So pervasive was this Western tendency that, by the tenth century CE, the God of the Bible had become the old man of the universe with whom we are so familiar. From the delicate deity gracing the pages of early medieval illuminated manuscripts to Michelangelo's muscular Creator whirling in the clouds in the Sistine Chapel, God's snow-white hair and bleach-bright beard would be forever fixed in the religious imagination.

19

SENSE AND SENSITIVITY

Shaking in terror, the young man clenches his teeth, forcing his screams to stay silent, as giant talons seize his scalp, puncturing his head with pain. 'He felt the claws bore far down, crack open his skull, touch his brain . . . "He's come again, he's come again," he murmured, trembling'. In *The Last Temptation of Christ*, his tender, tormented novel about the life and death of Jesus of Nazareth, Nikos Kazantzakis understands well the ancient sound of God. This is a deity whose voice is wholly unhuman. A divine word that rips into the flesh and bone of his chosen prophets and holy men, snatching them away like a ravenous bird of prey, to carry them off to a hyper-sensory, otherworldly plane. It is a far cry from the gentle dove of the Gospels, fluttering above Jesus' head as a voice from the heavens declares, 'This is my son, the Beloved, with whom I am well pleased'.[1]

In Kazantzakis' novel, the voice of God is the same razor-sharp sound that more usually clawed at his prophets in the Bible – an ear-splitting voice tearing its way through flesh and bone, assaulting mortal bodies with a noise so uncontainable, and so violent, it is all they can do to spit out his words like blood. For Amos, the sound of God's voice was the terrifying, guttural cry of a predator mauling its catch. 'The lion has roared, who is not frightened? The Lord God has spoken, who can but prophesy?' he helplessly asks.[2] God's roar blasted out of the Jerusalem temple, scorching its way across the land with a fire-hot force: 'Yahweh roars from Zion, and utters his voice from Jerusalem;

the pastures of the shepherds wither, and the top of Carmel dries up'.[3]
The same ferocious voice of God burns Jeremiah's mouth, forcing him
to breathe rhetorical fire on Yahweh's worshippers – and devastating
the prophet himself with the brutality of the divine attack on his body:
'You have overpowered me, you have prevailed', he sobs, 'whenever
I speak, I must cry out, I must shout, "Violence and destruction!"'[4]
The impact could be physically devastating for those around prophets,
too. As mortal vehicles of divine speech, the urgent screams of prophets savaged by God's voice ripped through startled, frightened
communities – much to the deity's delight. 'I have split them by the
prophets! I have murdered them with the words of my mouth!'[5]

In the Bible, the sound of God is concretely physical. Even when
the deity hides his body from the world, his noise materializes, sweeping, rumbling, roaring, or reverberating through the earthly realm,
disrupting any delicate differences drawn between the tangible and the
incorporeal. It is for this reason that God's prophets are often said to
'see', rather than hear, the spoken words of the deity. And it is why
the Israelite tribes assembled at Sinai are said to have 'seen the sounds'
of Yahweh's thunderous presence on the mountain.[6] These biblical
portrayals of sound were not unusual. The peoples of ancient south-
west Asia understood that sound is not immaterial. Although they
framed the mechanics of noise in ways vastly different from the tech
talk of modern-day physicists, who explain that sound comes into
being, in both its source and sensing, through the vibration of something material, they knew full well that sound is an inherently material
phenomenon, whether or not its source was visible to humans. The
gods were not always seen, but they could be heard, and in being heard,
their physical presence was known.

Across the ancient world, the most primordial otherworldly sound
was the boom of thunder or the roar of the sea. As loud noises emanating just beyond the edges of the mortal world, these were the
sounds most naturally identified with the voices of gods and monsters,
around which cosmological myths were spun. One of the most vivid
of mythological motifs was the shout of a storm god, whether he was
raging in battle or bellowing his victory from his mountaintop throne.
In the Levant, Baal's voice could be heard blasting through the open

window of his new heavenly palace, installed on the sage advice of his builder, the deity Kothar-wa-Hasis:

> Kothar-wa-Hasis laughed;
> he opened his voice and cried:
> 'Did I not say to you, O Valiant Baal,
> that you would return, Baal, to my suggestion?
> Let a window be opened in the house,
> a casement in the midst of the palace!'
> Baal opened a rift in the clouds,
> his holy voice Baal gave forth;
> Baal repeated the issue of his lips.
> At his holy voice the underworld quaked,
> at the issue of his lips the mountains were afraid.
> The ancient mountains were afraid;
> the hills of the earth tottered.[7]

This vivid mythic vignette hints at the anatomical mechanics of divine speech. The voices of the gods were physical entities, with their own heft, properties and dimensions. Stored in the deity's throat, ready for release, the divine voice was ever-present and ever-resonant – so much so that deities might talk to themselves without uttering a sound, much as Baal's adversary Mot (Death) does when he speaks to himself by 'calling out in his throat'.[8] By contrast, and as one biblical writer would put it, false gods were those who had 'no sound in their throats' at all.[9] Opening first their throats and then their mouths, the gods were heard as their voices continued to break through openings in divine space – a temple, or the clouds – to make their way into the earthly realm, where their splitting force might cleave mountains, pierce the ears of mortals and prise open the mouths of prophets. The sense that divine sounds were tangible material forms was reflected in the idea that divine messengers could even contain and 'carry' a deity's voice to another god or to a human, as though they were delivering a parcel – the original voicemail. But when Baal wanted to make his voice heard, messengers were rarely required. Atop his holy mountain, his booming voice was stored within his body, much as thunder, lightning and rain were understood to be stored in heavenly vaults and chambers, ready to be released. Just as Kothar-wa-Hasis' open, laughing mouth unleashed his voice, so Baal's open window in the clouds gave forth his voice, which repeats on his lips like the rolling rumble of thunder, shaking the earthly realm from its underworld foundations to the tops of its mountains.

Not one to be outdone by his older cultural sibling, the God of the Bible would also utter his booming voice from his own mountain-top palace – a heavenly building similarly furnished with windows, so that when God thundered, 'the windows of heaven opened, and the foundations of the underworld trembled!'[10] A more detailed description of God's voice occurs in Psalm 29, one of the oldest poems in the Psalter. Here, Yahweh sits enthroned over the defeated flood of chaos, while his 'divine sons' – the junior deities – assembled in his palace cry out in awe as his voice flashes, crackles and thunders through the world. Convulsing everything in its path, the voice of God was a visual, as well as audible, phenomenon:

> The voice of Yahweh is over the waters,
> the God of Glory thunders,
> Yahweh is over the mighty waters.
> The voice of Yahweh in power,
> the voice of Yahweh in majesty.
> The voice of Yahweh breaks the cedars,
> Yahweh breaks the cedars of Lebanon . . .
> The voice of Yahweh flashes forth flames of fire.[11]

These are the same fearsome sounds the Israelites are said to have 'seen' at Mount Sinai. Here, the silent stillness of the wilderness is smashed apart by Yahweh's thundering voice as he lists aloud his Ten Commandments. As he talks in thunderclaps, the deity's voice gener-ates flashes of lightning and ferocious flames, much as the Babylonian god Marduk is said to have kindled a fire 'when he moved his lips'.[12] Yahweh's body is hidden by a thick black cloud while streams of smoke swirl about the mountaintop to the ethereal sound of a shofar – a ram's horn seemingly trumpeted by a heavenly musician to herald the deity's presence. The cacophony of cosmic, mystical sounds is quite literally spectacular – and so terrifying that the Israelites back away from the mountain, shaking with fear. 'Do not let God speak to us', they beg Moses, 'or we will die!'[13] The mortal danger posed by God's voice would give rise to a myth weaving its way through rabbinic expositions of this biblical story: the Israelites were so frightened by the sound and sight of God's voice, some rabbis explained, they not only backed off from the mountain, but ran, and ran, and ran some more – until they all suffered heart attacks and dropped dead. The Torah itself had to step in. 'Master of the Universe! Are you giving me to the living or the dead?' Torah asked. 'To the living', God replied. 'But they're all dead', came the rather obvious response. God hastily revived the dead with life-giving dew from heaven, but the resurrected Israelites were still so frightened they could neither stand on their feet nor look up at God. Worrying that their hearts would fail again, God appointed a pair of angels to minister to each quaking worshipper: one to place a hand over each man's heart to keep it calm, and another to tilt each man's head heavenward, so that he could behold God.[14]

The sound of the gods was supernatural not only because it was divine in nature, but because it disrupted the natural noise of day-to-day life. And daily life was already very noisy. Just as we are accustomed to the hubbub of the everyday – the chatter of human voices, the hum of traffic, our blaring screens and radios, and the pings and rings of mobile phones – so too our ancestors were used to a world in which noise was the norm. But a noise that disturbed, unsettled, or invaded the soundscapes of everyday life was a rip in the mysterious membrane separating the world of mortals from the realm of the gods. A noise sounding in spaces where it should not be heard was especially frightening, and potentially signalled a divine disturbance of special significance.[15]

In a biblical story about the prophet Elijah, it is the wrong sort of sound that reveals the corporeal presence of Yahweh – but in a highly unexpected way. Across the Levant, gods were usually thought to have loud voices – they were, after all, superhuman, rendering everything about them bigger, better and louder than mere mortals. But Elijah's experience is rather different. Like Moses, he is said to ascend the holy mountain in the wilderness (here called Horeb), where a message from

Yahweh tells him that the deity will pass by. On his divine mountain, we might expect Yahweh to reveal himself in a show-stopping perform-ance of thunder, lightning and earth-shaking splendour. But the deity has other ideas. A ferocious stormy wind suddenly rips through the air, splitting mountains and shattering rocks – but Yahweh has not yet arrived. It is immediately followed by a tremendous earthquake – still, Yahweh does not appear. Suddenly, there is fire – but Yahweh is not in the crackling flames. Instead, after the cacophony of noise at the mountainous edge of heaven, there is a quietness. This is not the sound of sheer silence, as some modern translators would have it, but 'a quiet voice'.[16] It is the sound of God, and on this occasion, this is how he chooses to reveal himself – although Elijah cannot see him, for he is so unnerved he has wrapped his face in his mantle, sensibly shielding his eyes from the expected dangerous glare of the deity. For all his bellowing and bluster in his more public appearances, Yahweh speaks privately to his prophet, in a whisper. It is an image of intense intimacy as the gigantic deity, whose physical approach had shattered and burned the mountaintop, murmurs softly into the prophet's ear. But it may be that Yahweh rather enjoyed the opportunity for quieter moments like this, for the divine realm itself was a noisy place.

Selective Hearing

Long before the Devil came to have the best tunes, the God of the Bible was listening to music and song. 'Praise Yah!' (in Hebrew, *hallelu-yah*) was the repeated, rapturous refrain on the lips of his worshippers, and sing his praises they did – taking their lead from the junior gods in Yahweh's retinue, whose noisy adulation had started at the creation of the world, 'when the morning stars had sung together, and the divine sons had shouted with joy'.[17] Ever since, the heavenly chorus praising God's every move had continued to sound. Thanks to the privileged place of melodious chanting, choral singing and organ music in the religious traditions of the West, we tend to imagine the heavens were filled with the euphonious sound of angelic hymning and close-harmony choirs. But the everyday sounds of the ancient heavens tended to be rather more cacophonous. Yahweh himself, of course, was naturally noisy: in the Bible, he can not only be found thundering from his temple, but laughing at human hubris, screaming 'like a woman in labour' as he creates new marvels, whistling up punishing plagues of insects to ravage crops, and singing with unbridled joy at the top of his voice.[18] But his divine attendants were similarly clamorous. The cherubim flanking his throne made quite the racket, for when they moved with God, their enormous beating wings emitted deafening noises: the roar of a stormy sea, the crash and clamour of battle, the rumble and boom of thunderclaps.[19] The seraphim were little better. When Isaiah sees them in the Jerusalem temple, these winged, fiery serpents are busy chanting, 'Holy, holy, holy is Yahweh of Hosts!' as they wheel about God – and yet they are not singing, but shouting, and at such a volume that the very temple shakes. Even away from his sacred buildings, the noise of God and his divine companions could be heard. Later in the book of Isaiah, a prophet among the exiles in far-off Babylon can overhear the conversation between Yahweh and his council of gods in the heavens, who not only talk at considerable volume, but shout blessings to Yahweh's worshippers in the earthly realm below.[20]

Loud voices were an asset in a world in which worshippers' music and song enveloped sacred space, filling temples and sanctuaries with a sacral soundtrack, often accompanying the screams of sacrificial animals. Although musical performance in Yahweh's older temples had tended to be a more exclusive activity, likely undertaken by specialized players trained to please the deity in private, communal music took on a more prominent, public role from the fifth century BCE onwards, following the rebuilding of the Jerusalem temple. Worshippers and pilgrims alike were enjoined to sing and dance as they praised God with all manner of musical instruments: 'Praise him with blasts of the horn, praise him with harp and lyre! Praise him with timbrel and dance, praise him with strings and pipe! Praise him with clanging cymbals, praise him with loud clashing cymbals! '[21]

Against this sonic backdrop, the music and song of communal worship in the Second Temple era was increasingly understood to be an earthly reflection of the looping soundtrack of the divine realm, where God was now surrounded by the near-perpetual sound of the music and song of his divine entourage. As rabbinic legend would later have it, the noise was so constant that God had occasionally felt the need to tell the heavenly host to shut up. 'Do not sing today', he had apparently said to the angels as he submerged Egyptians in the Sea of Reeds. 'How can I listen to singing when the works of my hands are drowning in the sea?'[22] There was some debate among rabbis as to whether God's call for quiet was motivated by a dignified pang of sympathy for his victims, or a vengeful desire to ensure he could hear their screams as he thrust them under the waters. Either way, God's world had already become so noisy that the seer of the book of Revelation would feel the need to remark that there was silence in heaven 'for about half an hour' so that God could hear the prayers of the persecuted ascending with the smoke of incense towards his throne. Of course, once the prayers had reached God's ears, the thunder, trumpeting, shouting, roaring and singing of the heavenly realm began again.[23]

No wonder the God of the Bible had occasionally demanded the sound of silence. Given his human-like anatomy, Yahweh's ears were ever open (for not even gods had earlids), which meant he either had to cover them or command quietude if he wanted respite from the clamour of worship. 'Take away from me the noise of your songs! I will not listen to the melody of your harps!'[24] Yahweh's refusal to listen to songs of praise was often intended to punish his wayward worshippers, but it risked undermining his perceived ability to respond to those in dire need, who were painfully aware that, in covering his ears, God might miss their urgent prayers. 'Do not shut your ear to my cry for help, but give me relief!' pleaded one fretful petitioner. 'Do not hide your face from me in the day of my distress – incline your ear to me, answer me speedily!' begged another.[25]

Like his divine peers across the ancient world, Yahweh's hearing was crucial to his social relationships with his worshippers. It was not with his eyes or mouth that he acknowledged his people on a day-to-day basis (a privilege more usually gifted to religious elites), but with his ears, into which the prayers and pleas of his devotees were directed. But those prayers might need help in reaching God's ears. Across ancient south-west Asia, temple priests offered up daily petitions for the well-being of their local communities, but special requests stood a better chance of being heard if religious specialists could be persuaded to relay the petition to the deity's cult statue. A fleeting detail in the story of Samuel, a legendary prophet from Yahweh's venerable temple in Shiloh, seems to reflect this ritual: Samuel has to repeat the Israelite tribes' noisy appeal for a king directly into Yahweh's ears before the deity can agree to their demands.[26]

But one of the most effective ways to target a deity's ears was to turn a petition, prayer, or plea into a sacred object gifted to the god or goddess. In Egypt, for example, these votive offerings often took the form of little models of the deity's ear, or small stelae engraved with godly ears (fig. 51). As Egyptologist Emily Teeter remarks, these objects functioned 'much like an ancient mobile phone with a dedicated line to the deity'.[27] And Yahweh's worshippers were employing similar strategies. Suggestive archaeological evidence comes from the late Persian and Hellenistic periods. For those in and around fourth-century BCE Jerusalem, coins marked with Yahweh's ear (fig. 52) not only publicized his willingness to listen to his people, but paid to the temple,

Fig. 51. A painted limestone stela, engraved with five pairs of divine ears, from Medinet Habu, Luxor (c. 945–656 BCE). Dedicated to a deity, the stela petitioned the god to hear the prayers or pleas of their worshipper.

Fig. 52. Drawing of a coin from fourth-century BCE Yehud (Judah). The coin's obverse bears the image of an ear, while its reverse shows a bird of prey in flight. The ear was probably understood to be Yahweh's, ever-ready to hear the prayers of his worshippers. In a world in which temples also served as economic and administrative hubs, coins often bore theological symbols.

might have been more likely to ensure worshippers' petitions were both heard and seen by the deity himself – just as he is said to have promised Solomon when the Jerusalem temple had first been built: 'My eyes will be open and my ears attentive to the prayer from this place'.[28] In Yahweh's temple on Mount Gerizim, however, worshippers were more proactive in ensuring their prayers would reach God. Here, in the second century BCE, a man called Delayah was one of many to solidify his personal appeal to Yahweh into a permanent petition by paying for it to be inscribed into the stone brickwork of the sanctuary itself: 'This is [the stone] which Delayah son of Shimon offered for himself and his sons, [this] stone [for] good remembrance before the god in this place'.[29] Delayah was asking Yahweh not to forget about him or his children, which would inevitably bring them misfortune, but to favour them instead with his ongoing care and attention. The inscribed petition transformed the mute brick into a speaking stone – an audio text on constant repeat, serving as a permanent reminder to the deity dwelling in the temple.[30]

As far as his worshippers were concerned, confirmation of God's hearing had long been understood to come in the form of an answer to a prayer – recovery from illness, perhaps, or a new pregnancy, a successful harvest, or a smooth journey. But an unanswered prayer was not always as easy to identify and understand. Had the deity heard, but rejected the petition? Had he listened, but forgotten to reply? Or had he missed the prayer altogether? Some shouted their prayers louder, some ritually fasted, and some turned their prayers into mourning, all in the effort to draw the deity's attention to their petition. The anxiety is painfully attested in a heart-wrenching psalm:

> My God, my God, why have you forsaken me?
> Why are you so far away from helping me,
> and from the words of my groaning?
> O my God, I cry by day, but you do not answer;
> and by night, but find no rest.[31]

In the Gospels of Matthew and Mark, it is the opening line of this extract that is shouted by Jesus as he dies upon the cross. Having offered up prayers to be spared the night before his execution, these early Gospel writers are in no doubt their hero felt abandoned by his god.[32] But the psalm itself suggests Yahweh might simply be too far away to hear human noises, which is why he is so often asked in the Hebrew Bible not simply to 'incline' his ear towards his worshippers, but more literally to 'stretch' or 'extend' his ear, much as we might extend our own by cupping a hand or leaning into the direction of a sound we are grasping to hear. God's hearing was superhuman, but it was not limitless. It is for this reason that one ancient poet marvels that his distressed cries could reach Yahweh's ears in the heavenly heights of his mountaintop temple.[33] But even inside the building itself, God's hearing could be restricted. As we have already seen, ritual regulations in the book of Exodus reveal that the high priest's robes were fringed with bells, so that as he approached the deity's private room (the holy of holies), Yahweh could hear him coming. It was a precautionary measure intended to prevent the god from being so startled or angered by the sudden intrusion that he might attack and kill the priest.[34] But during sustained periods of calamity, when Yahweh appeared to be worryingly ignorant of his worshippers' pleas, the fear arose that he might have gone deaf – a deeply damaging condition for any deity tasked with responding to the voices of their people. 'His ear is not too dull to hear!' one prophet had found himself insisting to those exiled to Babylonia.[35]

But if Yahweh's ears were in good working order, his hearing was clearly selective. According to Genesis, when Abraham's slave wife Hagar was banished to the desert with her son to die, her desperate prayers to God went unheard. Instead, it was the cries of her son the deity could hear – the boy tellingly named Ishmael ('God hears'). 'What troubles you, Hagar?' says a divine messenger dispatched to her aid. 'Do not be afraid, for God has heard the voice of the boy'.[36] By contrast, Yahweh's hearing was far sharper when people moaned about him behind his back. The Israelite tribes are said to have grumbled among themselves about the hardships of the journey to the Promised Land, but Yahweh had overheard every word – and was livid. 'How long shall this wicked congregation complain against me?' he demands of Moses and Aaron. 'I have heard the complaints of the Israelites, which they complain against me!' he says, vowing to kill the naysayers before the journey's end.[37]

Theologically, God's ears were particularly sensitive to the sound of insincerity. Those suspected of prayers and rituals empty of conviction were frequently reprimanded: 'Look', Yahweh says, with the exasperation of a frazzled parent, 'you fast only to quarrel and to fight and to strike with a wicked fist; such fasting as you do today will not make your voice heard on high'.[38] Ostentatious performances of piety similarly rang hollow in God's ears. One group of worshippers soon came to realize their panting, pained petitions had done nothing to gain Yahweh's favour: 'Like a woman with child, who writhes and cries out in her pangs when she is near her time, so were we', confesses one poet; 'we were with child, we writhed, but we gave birth only to wind'.[39] Subsequent generations of prophets and rabbis would similarly warn against flatulent faith – including, apparently, Jesus of Nazareth, who is reported to have said, 'When you are praying, do not heap up empty phrases as the Gentiles do, for they think that they will be heard because of their many words'.[40]

God's aversion to excessive human noise was not simply a matter of religious propriety. It was an inherited condition, shared by almost all deities. Across ancient south-west Asia, the gods were naturally unsettled by loud noises emanating from other beings in the cosmos – be it the roar of an unruly monster, the iron-clad sound of an army, or the rumble of complaints from their worshippers. But some sounds were simply unbearable because they were so distressing. A particularly poignant example occurs in a Mesopotamian incantation invoking the high god Anu and his wife and consort Antu. It was to be recited three times by parents desperate to calm the cries of their newborn baby:

> Why does he scream until his mother sobs?
> Till, in heaven, Antu herself is in tears?
> 'Who is this, that makes such a racket on earth?
> If it's a dog, someone give it food!
> If it's a bird, someone fling a clod at it!
> If it's a human child that's angry,
> someone cast the spell of Anu and Antu over him!
> Let his father lie down to get the rest of his sleep!
> Let his mother, who has her chores to do, get her
>   chores done!'[41]

The noise of a crying baby disturbed the gods in more ways than one. Like us, they felt the double-edged stab of compassion and frustration at the sound of an infant's unexplained distress, and they too worried it signalled the onset of illness – although they were more likely to assume its cause was a baby-maiming demon, rather than colic. But the gods were also highly attuned to a baby's cry because it announced the ongoing multiplication of humans in the earthly realm. And more humans invariably meant a greater risk of overpopulation, draining the fragile earth's resources, and the consequent rise of disobedience and disorder in the cosmos.[42] According to some Mesopotamian traditions, the gods had necessarily been forced to create barrenness, disease, famine, flood and deadly demons in an effort to control human numbers.

In the Bible, echoes of this mythic mindset can be heard in God's hypersensitivity to the noise of humans busy with their own affairs, rather than his. Prophetic oracles threaten unruly communities not only with infertility, famine, disease and death, but with the cessation of the very sounds of human fertility and fruitfulness – from the voices of a newly-wed couple and the cry of a baby, to the clamour of loud singing and drunken parties celebrating the harvests.[43] God's episodic culling of human fruitfulness might have been spun as a punishment for religious misdemeanours, but it also helpfully silenced the racket mortal productivity created. In the ears of the deity, the din of an emboldened humanity was dangerously akin to the tumultuous, rebellious upsurge of the waters of chaos, and regularly needed muffling. 'You silence the roaring of the seas, the roaring of their waves, the tumult of the peoples!' one psalmist enthusiastically acknowledges.[44]

Indeed, among God's creatures, there were none louder than those industrious city-dwelling humans, whose noisy activities threatened to overwhelm the heavens were they not kept in check. Crowd control was essential, as the biblical story about the Tower of Babel illustrates. In the very distant past, so the story goes, all humans shared one language, enabling them to gang together to build themselves a city with a tower high enough to access the heavenly realm. Seemingly unnerved, Yahweh descended from the heavens to inspect the new construction and report back to the divine council. 'Look', he said, 'they are one people, and they all have one language; and this is only the beginning of what they might do; nothing that they propose to do will now be impossible for them'. The only solution was to restrict the extent to which humans could communicate and cooperate with one another. 'Come, let us go down and confuse their language there, so that they will not understand one another's speech', Yahweh instructed.[45] At Babel, human voices were to become a background babble – noisy, but neutered.

Eye of the Beholder

Across ancient south-west Asia, artisans ritually tasked with bringing the gods' statues into being used an age-old technique to capture the eyes of the divine. Set within almond-shaped ivory or alabaster, the huge irises of the gods' eyes were crafted from precious materials imbued with the divine hues of the primeval cosmos: onyx, obsidian, or lapis lazuli. Polished to an iridescent shine, the dark eyes of the divine glistened, their gaze intensified by the thick eyeliner – often a matching strip of gemstone – edging their upper and lower lids. Powerful incantations were whispered to the statue, inviting its newly resident deity to 'open the eyes', so that the gleam of the irises was no longer the lustre of stone or glass, but the shine of eyes alive with divinity.[46]

Literary reflections of God's glistening eyes can be glimpsed in the Bible. And in a poem that was already very ancient when it was appended to an early form of Deuteronomy, we suddenly get a vivid close-up of one of his eyeballs. It briefly looms into view in a description of Yahweh looking after his baby son Jeshurun (representing Israel) in the wilderness, although English translations can often obscure it. In the New Revised Standard Version of the Bible, for example, we read that God 'guarded him as the apple of his eye'.[47] This standard translation replaces an old Hebrew idiom with an English alternative, so that the baby boy is described as the 'apple' of God's eye – a metaphorical reference to the eye's pupil. But although the English expression captures the intensity of God's love for Jeshurun, it masks the anatomical dynamics of the Hebrew idiom itself, which refers to the eye's pupil as 'the little man' – a vivid allusion to the tiny reflection we can see of ourselves when we look closely into someone's eyes. Translated more carefully, this ancient poem portrays the deity gazing at his baby so intently that the boy is imprinted onto God's shiny black pupil: 'he watched him as the little man in his eye'. A similar expression is used of the people of Israel in a much later biblical book, in which Yahweh promises his worshippers that he will destroy any invader who would despoil their land: 'Truly, one who touches you touches the little child in my eye!'[48] For God, the plundering of his people was akin to a poke in the eye.

But God's language in this text went beyond metaphor. His eyes were not simply seeing organs, but feeling organs. And in this, he was no different from mortals. In a post-Enlightenment world, we are accustomed to setting our sense of sight within a context of spatial and conceptual distance: what we see is either near or far from us, and it remains separate from us. Our eyes have become corporeal cameras, rendering our optic lenses panes of glass through which we view the 'outside' world. But in ancient south-west Asian cultures (as in many others), seeing was not a remote, objective process operating distinctively or independently of the body's other senses. Instead, it was perceived as a reflexive, haptic (or tactile) sensation: the eyes could receptively feel what was seen, and actively affect or touch what they saw. Seeing, and being seen, were bodily encounters, rendering visual contact a form of physical contact – especially when seeing took on the intensity of looking or gazing.

These visual dynamics pervade the Bible. In Genesis, for example, Noah is the victim of a palpable visual assault: sprawled naked in his tent after a drinking session, he is oblivious to his son Ham looking at his 'nakedness' (genitals). It is tantamount to Ham touching his father's penis – an illicit act his brothers are so keen to avoid that, when they hasten into the tent to throw a garment over Noah, they not only avert their eyes, but walk backwards. Sober, Noah senses he has been physically violated: 'Noah awoke from his wine and he knew what his youngest son had done to him'.[49] This is the crime that had led Noah to curse the fruit of Ham's own loins. Anxieties about tactile vision cluster about women's bodies in the Bible, too. In several passages across both the Hebrew Bible and New Testament, the veiling of women often serves a protective function, shielding them from the penetrating 'touch' of the violating male gaze – even when it came from the heavens, as Paul appears to suggest when he insists women should cover their heads 'on account of the angels', who had been known to take a dangerous fancy to mortal women in the distant past.[50] Even the famous story of Doubting Thomas, which seems so concerned with physical touch, plays on the notion that the eyes were tactile organs. When the risen Jesus suddenly materializes before the disciples, Thomas cannot believe Christ's body is the same fleshy form that was crucified. 'Put your finger here and see my hands; reach out your hand and put it in my side', Jesus says, inviting him to touch his wounds. Contrary to centuries of Christian art showing Thomas sticking his finger into a gaping hole in Jesus' torso, he is not said to touch him with his hands at all. Instead, he uses his eyes to feel: looking

Fig. 53. Unlike their brother Ham, Shem and Japheth cover their eyes to avoid looking at Noah's genitalia in this miniature from a Biblia Pauperum produced in the Netherlands (*c.* 1405 CE).

at the wounds appears to confirm for Thomas the reality of the resurrected body, his astounded gasp ('My lord and my god!') prompting Jesus to ask, 'Have you believed because you have seen me?'[51]

Something of the divine power of heavenly beings and sacred objects could be absorbed or imprinted into the body via the eyes of those lucky enough to gaze upon them. Following Yahweh's careful instructions, Moses makes a bronze figurine of a snake and sets it up as a cult statue so that 'whenever a serpent bit someone, that person would look at the serpent of bronze and live'. Elijah's numinous power can only be transferred onto Elisha's body when Elisha watches him ascending into the heavens as a divinized being. And when Moses sees God on Sinai, of course, his face acquires something of God's own features, prompting him to veil himself from the eyes of the Israelites when he descends back into the ordinary world.[52]

If mortal eyes could 'touch' what they saw, so too could those of the gods. Casting their eyes over the earthly realm, deities looked upon their favoured peoples with a benevolent, life-giving gaze, so that fields and farms were rendered fertile, streams and rivers teemed with life, and cities prospered. Under their watchful care, humanity could physically flourish. As the patron deity of the Israelites, Yahweh's eyes were naturally fixed on the land he had given them: 'a land of hills and valleys, watered by rain from the heavens, a land that Yahweh your god surveys; the eyes of Yahweh your god are always on it, from the beginning of the year to the end of the year'.[53] Underlying this vivid image of God's gaze watering the land was the fundamental idea that, in both gods and mortals, the cranium was a well of water, rendering each eye a 'spring' (in Hebrew, the word *ayin* means both 'eye' and 'spring'). By looking upon the land, Yahweh's watery eyes fructified its soil.

The fertile touch of God's gaze naturally extended beyond the vista of the undulating landscape. Like most deities, Yahweh was also equipped with super-sight. But while the all-encompassing vision of other gods, like Marduk and Ishtar, was occasionally manifest in the doubling of their eyes, Yahweh's anatomy remained human-like: he had the standard two eyes – but they were telescopic. From a divine distance, the world's human inhabitants might have been like grasshoppers to God (as a verse in Isaiah puts it), but he could zoom in on the minutiae of human life, scrutinizing mortal bodies with an impressive attention to detail.[54] And that included taking note of whether or not his male worshippers were circumcised. As Yahweh tells Abraham in Genesis, the mark of circumcision was to be a 'sign' for the deity himself – a visual aide-mémoire akin to the rainbow 'sign' he set in the skies after the Flood – reminding Yahweh of his covenantal promise to bless his male worshippers with children, thereby perpetuating their dynastic line. When his worshippers had sex, Yahweh would look upon the circumcised penis and recall his promise, his fertile gaze supercharging the organ as it did its work.[55]

The God of the Bible appears not to have looked quite as carefully at women's reproductive organs – which is hardly surprising, given the androcentrism of the biblical writers. Having taken on the role of divine midwife, God's gynaecological interests tended to be limited to 'opening' the womb to form and deliver a child, should he so choose. And it was the child on whom he fixed his eyes. Switching from super-sight to X-ray vision, he looked through the wall of the womb – and often well past the mother – to focus on the foetus itself, his watchful gaze moulding the indistinct creature into a full-term baby, as one overwhelmed psalmist exclaims:

> It was you who formed my inward parts;
> you knit me together in my mother's womb . . .
> My frame was not hidden from you,
> when I was being made in secret,
> intricately woven in the depths of the earth.
> Your eyes beheld my unformed substance.[56]

On one of the rare occasions when the God of the Bible did look more closely at women, rather than looking through them, he still failed to see them properly. His eyes were caught only by the erotic sensuality of their bodies – and the dangerous power of their own gaze: 'They walk with outstretched necks, glancing wantonly with their eyes, mincing along as they go, tinkling with their feet', he says, scowling at the women of Jerusalem in the book of Isaiah.[57] It was a sight that irritated his masculinist, sensitive eyes – so much so that, as he glares at them, he envisages searing their hair from their heads and their genitalia, leaving them violated and exposed: 'The Lord will afflict with scabs the heads of the daughters of Zion; Yahweh will lay bare their private parts'. This horrific image is immediately followed by a warning that those women who draw attention to themselves with cosmetics will be dehumanized: they will be stripped, shaved and trussed up as slaves. 'Instead of perfume, there will be a stench, and instead of a sash, a rope', God growls. 'Instead of well-set hair, baldness; and instead of a rich robe, a binding of sackcloth; instead of beauty, shame'.[58]

By stark contrast, male beauty triggered a very different response.

Across much of the ancient world, the physical charms of a good-looking man were proof that he was favoured in the eyes of the gods, his features reflexively manifesting the blessings imparted by the enraptured stare of a smitten deity. And Yahweh appears to have been no different. In the biblical story explaining how Saul came to be the first king of the Israelites, his staggering good looks are cited as proof of Yahweh's favour. No man was more handsome, or taller, for he quite literally stood 'head and shoulders above everyone else'. He had clearly been chosen to reign by God himself.[59] And yet, as we have already seen, when the gorgeous teenaged David caught Yahweh's eye, the deity's head was easily turned, and the Israelites would have a new king. Saul was fated to be cut down to size: he will die on his knees on the battlefield, where his corpse will be decapitated, stripped and hung up on a city wall – his headless, naked torso transformed into a monstrous grotesque.[60]

Of course, Yahweh denied that David was chosen to replace Saul solely because of his looks. What was on the inside counted, too: 'Do not look on his appearance or on the height of his stature', Yahweh had said to Samuel as the faithful prophet was busy trying to establish exactly which beautiful boy Yahweh had selected to take Saul's place. 'Yahweh does not see as mortals see; they look on the outward appearance, but Yahweh looks on the heart', the deity had claimed.[61] God's X-ray vision gave him a piercing insight into whomever he chose to probe. Like a diviner examining the innards of a sacrificial animal, God scrutinized the cognitive workings of the heart, and the emotional heft of the liver and bowel, reading the hidden recesses of a person to discern between the virtuous and the villainous: 'His eyes behold, his eyelids scrutinize humankind; Yahweh examines the righteous and the wicked'.[62] In the stillness of the night, the devout could call on God in their prayers, inviting him to inspect them from head to toe, inside and out:

> From your face let my judgement come;
> let your eyes behold my righteousness.
> If you probe my heart, if you visit me by night,
> if you test me, you will find no wickedness in me,

> my mouth does not transgress . . .
> My steps have held fast to your paths,
> my feet have not stumbled . . .
> Watch over me as the little man [reflected] in the eye.[63]

For some worshippers, God's scrutiny was a wondrous, comforting encounter with a watchful, caring deity. For others, however, it was a brutal bodily invasion akin to a demonic attack.

Double Vision

Under God's unrelenting gaze, Job's skin burns, blisters and peels. His flesh disintegrates, his organs split and leak, his bones threaten to splinter and shatter. He is plagued with terrifying visions and monstrous nightmares. Job decides he has had enough of living – and he has had enough of God's suffocating scrutiny. 'Will you not look away from me for a while?' he begs his divine tormentor. 'You do not leave me alone while I swallow my spit! What sin have I done to you, you watcher of humanity? Why have you made me your target?'[64] As readers, we are in on God's game – a heavenly wager that, no matter the injustice and severity of his afflictions, Job will not curse God. We know Job's suffering is a false punishment for a non-existent sin; like Job himself, we know he is innocent of any wrongdoing. And so does God. And yet still Job suffers as God's eyes eat into his body, slowly devouring him, in a thoroughly corporeal way: 'He has gnashed his teeth at me, my adversary sharpens his eyes against me . . . he slashes open my kidneys, and shows no mercy; he has poured my gall out on the ground'.[65] God had become demonic.

When the bulk of the book of Job was composed, probably sometime in the late fifth or early fourth century BCE, malevolent demons were the more usual culprits of supernatural attacks. Like monsters, they were either servants of the gods or rebels against divine order. Whether they were dispatched from the heavens by an irritated deity, or came from the wilderness, the underworld, or a sorcerer's spell book, these vicious beings delighted in spreading sickness and disease, ravaging crops, and stealing the lives of new mothers and their babies. Some demons fell under the command of deities of plague and pestilence. Others were disembodied manifestations of hidden, noxious elements running riot in the cosmos, including destructive emotions emanating from the bodies of gods and mortals alike, the most common of which was the evil eye. A malicious look, or an envious stare, could conjure the evil eye into being, bringing the object of the ravenous gaze into its line of vision. Its victims could feel the bite or sting in their bodies – and in their pockets: the beautiful might experience hair loss; the affluent might find their rich food made them sick, or their fine clothes made their skin flake; landowners could discover that their vineyards had been attacked by insects; farmers that livestock had been mysteriously let loose from their pens. But a more studied, sinister stare could bring about far more serious symptoms: pregnant women might miscarry, newborns might die, and the outright cursed could find their bodies starting to rot like a corpse, much like Job. The close association of the evil eye with corrosive emotions like greed, envy and spite also rendered it internally damaging to those who triggered it, so that they might be eaten away on the inside should they not guard against it.[66]

Distinguishing between a straightforward demonic attack and the scourge of the evil eye was not always easy, but protection from both came in the form of amulets, which were worn on the body, attached to the windows and doorways of the home, and accompanied the dead into their tombs. The most common was the *udjat* amulet, better known today as the Eye of Horus, which in Egypt harnessed the health and protection of the falcon-eyed god Horus, but across the Levant and Mesopotamia had come to manifest the watchful gaze of benevolent deities guarding their worshippers. Whether engraved on small terracotta plaques, or wrought from semi-precious stones or ivory, *udjat* amulets brought the eyes of a god, edged with thick liner, into the earthly realm. For both gods and mortals, kohl eyeliner was itself an important magical tool against both the evil eye and the dangerous, penetrating stare of others: in emphasizing and enlarging the eyes, it simultaneously strengthened the gaze and repelled the glare of another.[67]

The heavily lined, unblinking gaze of Yahweh had long been understood to watch over his worshippers, protecting them from harm and misfortune. In the biblical imagination, the huge apotropaic eyes of God had not only looked down on the strange land of Canaan when the Israelites had first arrived, but more recently, 'the eye of God' had watched over those elders who had eventually returned to Jerusalem from exile in Babylonia, as though it were suspended in the skies like a celestial amulet.[68] But in the latter half of the first millennium BCE, as Yahweh's pantheon shrank and his portfolio of divine roles and functions correspondingly grew more expansive, discerning between the evil eye and the punishing, penetrating gaze of God became more difficult. Demons had long been known to roam through the mortal world, and now God's eyes increasingly did the same; in biblical texts from this later period, his seemingly disembodied eyeballs roved over the earth, his deadly glance flickering over humans, darting about, looking for misdemeanours so that he could fix them with a withering gaze.[69]

This is the deity who sets his sights on the protagonist of the book of Job. Stripped of his wealth, health and children (but not his furious wife), Job is left with nothing but the heap of dung on which he sits. As he scrapes the sores from his skin with a broken piece of pot, his friends insist he is either suffering the consequences of unconfessed offences, or he has been afflicted by demons. But throughout the book, Job knows he is under attack from the eyes of God himself. As he says to his nameless wife, 'Shall we receive the good from God and not receive the bad?'[70] If Yahweh was a sovereign deity, from whom all favour and misfortune equally came, his capacity for harm, whether serious or slight, was not only a theological certainty, but an evident reality in the day-to-day lives of his worshippers. But not everyone was comfortable with this position, as the book of Job itself attests: a second writer has appended a narrative introduction to its cycle of poems, reasserting the active presence of junior gods in Yahweh's divine council, and casting one of its members as 'the Satan' ('the Accuser') – a title, rather than the name, of a heavenly being appointed to bring charges of religious disobedience against mortals. It is the Satan who not only incites Yahweh to violence, as the deity himself claims, but is also directly responsible for attacking Job. Combining the roving gait of a bog-standard demon with the scrutinizing, all-seeing eyes of God himself, it is now the Satan who roams about Job's world, looking out for wrongdoing and punishing those who have sinned. He may have been a heavenly agent of God, but in the book of Job, the Satan served as a useful theological buffer between an all-seeing, all-powerful deity and the injustices of inexplicable human suffering.

Distancing God from his more malevolent attributes would not only give rise to a new satanic force in the cosmos, but would also give new life to evil. Although the God of the Bible had rid himself of the other high gods in his pantheon, he had retained the services of its lowest-ranking members – his divine messengers. But from about the third century BCE, they began to undergo a process of reinvention within certain circles: the anonymous divine messengers of old were soon a hierarchical organization of angelic beings, headed by powerful archangels with distinct roles and personalities – most prominently, Michael, Gabriel and Raphael. By means of a similar process, those scattered demons and malevolent forces which had long plagued humans, including the evil eye, were increasingly grouped together as a task-force of evil, capable of invading mortal bodies and inciting humans to sin. By the first century BCE, they were operating under the command of various supernatural adversaries of God, chief among them Belial, Mastemah and the Satan himself, who had been relocated from the heavenly realm to a sinister wasteland at the edges of the cosmos.[71] Not that most Yahweh worshippers were aware of the complexities of this cosmology. While angels and demons naturally continued to populate the religious landscape, an overtly dualistic worldview was not a widespread feature of ancient Jewish speculation. Instead, it was a specialist development within certain scribal circles, and a prominent feature of apocalyptic groups, who were convinced the end times were approaching, when the final battle between good and evil would be fought. By the end of the first century CE, these apocalyptic groups had come to include some of Jesus' devotees, many of whom held that humans were not only naturally inclined towards wrongdoing, but dangerously vulnerable to demon-induced sin, from which only Christ could deliver them.[72]

Against this shifting religious backdrop, the eyes of God had taken on a different hue. Culturally, the eye had already come to be perceived as an organ of light, much as it was in the Greek world. Like a little sun or a burning lamp, it emitted fiery rays of light that would touch whatever was within their path and transport its imprinted image back to the eye. As the historian Ruth Bielfeldt puts it, to see was to shine.[73] Healthy eyes were those which shone and sparkled, while damaged eyes were dull and devoid of light. Among God's worshippers, physical health was closely tied to spiritual health, so that the very optics of human righteousness and sinfulness were now coded in the same way: the bright eyes of the devout were physically and spiritually enlightened, while those who evil-eyed others with a look of greed, envy, or spite emitted not light, but darkness. As Jesus is reported to have said, repeating what was by then traditional Jewish teaching, 'The eye is the lamp of the body. So if your eye is healthy, your whole body will be full of light; but if your eye is evil, your whole body will be full of darkness'. It was better to rip out the evil eye than to risk the horrifying prospect of God's coming judgement, when the whole body would burn for eternity in the fires of Gehenna – a mythological place drawn on Jerusalem's Hinnom Valley (in Hebrew, *gehinnom*), which had once been an entryway into the underworld, but would later come to be known as hell.[74]

If the look of evil was darkness, God's gaze was now quite the opposite. His eyes blazed with a fiery light. According to the book of Sirach, his eyes were 'ten thousand times brighter than the sun'.[75] When Enoch had ascended into the heavens, it was said, he was overwhelmed when he locked eyes with God: 'I have seen the Lord's eyes, shining like the sun's rays, and filling the eyes of a man with awe!' he exclaimed.[76] For most Jewish communities in the Graeco-Roman world, God's watchful gaze was akin to the sun in the heavens, remotely surveying the world below with an all-seeing eye of warm benevolence or scorching heat as he meted out justice. But for those groups seized by a more eschatological or apocalyptic vision of the cosmos, including the earliest devotees of Christ, God's eyes were deadly. A mystical vision enshrined in the book of Daniel had described the archangels of a coming cosmic judgement as having eyes like 'flaming torches', and now God's eyes also burned with fire. In the book of Revelation, these are the eyes of the heavenly Christ and his army of archangels, who will destroy all those in the grip of Satan. Flaming eyes had once been a distinctive anatomical feature of primeval cosmic monsters and dangerous demons, their burning, noxious gaze repelled only by the dark, kohl-lined eyes of the watchful gods. But now, God's eyes embodied the terrifying gaze, so that even his most faithful servants could no longer look upon him. As one ancient Jewish mystic would later put it, 'no eyes of any being are able to gaze at him, neither eyes of flesh and blood nor the eyes of his [heavenly] attendants', for if anyone were to look at him, God's eyes would 'discharge and bring forth torches of fire, scorching and burning him'.[77] His gleaming lapis lazuli eyes and reflective black pupils had disappeared. Instead, God's eyes were now balls of fire, distancing him ever further from the world of his worshippers.

20

GASP AND GULP

It was a spring day in 1995. In the mountains above the village of Peqi'in in the Upper Galilee, not far from the Golan Heights, a bulldozer was suddenly stopped in its tracks. It had been cutting a new road into the bedrock when the mechanical teeth of the bulldozer's bucket bit into an empty hole in the hillside. Climbing down from the cab, the driver discovered his machine had eaten into the outer wall of a hidden cave. Inside, multicoloured stalagmites and stalactites enshrined a thick jumble of clay boxes, pots and human bones. When archaeologists from the Israel Antiquities Authority peered into the cavernous hole just a few hours later, they quickly realized that they were looking six and a half thousand years into the past. The cave was home to a Late Chalcolithic burial site (c. 4500–3600 BCE), housing the remains of at least six hundred adults, many of whose bones had been carefully interred in clay ossuaries – specialized boxes for the bones of the dead. Most of the ossuaries were decorated with red geometrical patterns, and nearly all had been given human features at one of their shorter ends: some had small clay eyes, little ears and a tiny mouth, and even miniature breasts or a painted beard; but most consistently, and most strikingly, each ossuary boasted a large, prominent nose – an iconographic motif representing the notion of 'breath' or 'life' in Late Chalcolithic cultures (fig. 54).[1]

These striking artefacts offer a vivid insight into the ways in which those privileged enough to have their bones ceremonially sealed into

Fig. 54. A clay ossuary from Peqi'in, equipped with a nose (*c.* 4500–3600
BCE). Re-interred in their bone boxes, the dead were effectively
re-embodied and given 'life' and 'breath' as a new type of being.

an ossuary were socially and materially transformed into ancestors or
divine beings. Experts are broadly agreed that the cave served as a
sacred burial site for several regional communities, who first dealt with
their dead locally, either by interring corpses or offering them to
vultures as a sky burial. Once the corpses were reduced to skeletal
form, the community gathered up the dry, clean bones and transferred
them to the cave at Peqi'in for a 'second' ritual internment. Tucked up
in their big-nosed ossuaries, which re-equipped them with nostrils, the
dead began to 'breathe' again in their new clay bodies, and settled into
their post-mortem lives.[2]

Breathing is a rhythm of life. The constant rise and fall of our
chests keeps us in motion, even when we are still. Our breath may be
invisible, but it is tangible. We can feel the movement of air in our
throats, in our noses, in our mouths – sometimes warm, sometimes
cold. We can hear its sound as we sniff and snore, as we sigh, gasp and
wheeze. And so can those around us. Those closest can feel our breath
moving across their skin, and sense its scent in their nostrils, just as we
can feel and smell theirs. More than a physiological process, breathing
is animatedly, palpably social. Breathing is not simply living. Breathing

is *being*. It is this sense of breathing-as-being that Late Chalcolithic communities in and around Peqi'in articulated in their mortuary practices. Death did not break their social bonds with the deceased; it brought about a transition in an ongoing relationship. The dead no longer looked like the living, nor sounded the same, but they continued to breathe – and in breathing, they continued to be.

Sacred Sniff

Like the people of Late Chalcolithic Peqi'in, the Bronze and Iron Age peoples of south-west Asia and Egypt imbued breathing with profound religious and social meanings. In ancient Egyptian art, breath is often represented by the *ankh* ('life') sign, which the gods hold to the noses and mouths of both the living and the dead. The *ankh* was also used in mummification rituals to enable the ritually reconfigured dead to breathe: as an amulet, it was positioned on the throat of the embalmed corpse and incorporated into the newly made body by means of the mummy's wrappings. Along with it was a *sema* ('to join') amulet, a schematic representation of the lungs, trachea and a wide, engorged throat – the airy chamber crucially connecting the nostrils and mouth to the windpipe. Strategically placed at the mummy's throat, the amulet vivified and protected the airways (fig. 55). A complex ritual known as the Opening of the Mouth was also performed by specialist priests, who touched the mummy's mouth with an amulet shaped like a *pesesh* knife – a birth tool used to cut the umbilical cord and clear mucus from the baby's mouth. The scent of aromatic incense and perfumed unguents further infused the mummy with the ability to breathe. Ritually transformed, the dead were alive, much like Osiris – the mummified, coffined deity known as 'he whose nose lives'.[3]

Across ancient Mesopotamia, similar rituals of transition were performed on newly crafted or refurbished divine images. This too was often known as the Opening of the Mouth ceremony, without which the deity manifest in the statue could neither breathe nor smell. Alongside incantations and incense, the statue's mouth was ritually washed in order to open its airways, enabling it to inhale the heady scent of

Fig. 55. An obsidian *sema* amulet, schematically cast as the lungs, trachea and throat (*c.* 664–343 BCE). In Egyptian mummification rituals, these amulets were placed on the corpse's throat to vivify and protect the airways in the afterlife.

juniper, cedar and cypress burning in braziers before it.[4] The deity's breathing was more than symbolic. Priests tasked with performing this highly technical and intimate sensory ritual were instructed not to eat leeks or fish before the event, for fear their bad breath might repel or offend the god. Following the successful completion of the ceremony, the gods were installed in their temples, where they continued to breathe in the scent of their worshippers' sacrifices and offerings.

Underpinning these rituals was the fundamental assumption that the gods, like the dead, were breathing beings. And this assumption is writ large in the Bible. False gods are described as those who can neither breathe nor smell.[5] By contrast, the God of the Bible is a deity who breathes, smells and sniffs his way through his worshippers' world. He is portrayed as a deity who pants, gasps, blows and snorts. He inhales the scent of burning incense, toasted grain and roasted meat placed 'before his nose' in his temples as offerings, and repeatedly remarks on its 'soothing' or 'pleasing' odour.[6] Not only was his fondness for incense reflected in its use as fragrant seasoning in his sacrificial food, but he also commanded that it be burned on its own in a special brazier at the

entrance to the innermost sanctum of the Jerusalem temple. An exclusive blend of sweet spices and frankincense, custom-made by the
temple's own parfumiers, its thick aroma fragranced the deity's private
room, distinguishing the air he inhaled from that of mortals. Even his
priests were to smell pleasingly distinctive. Anointed with their signa-
ture scent of olive oil infused with myrrh, cinnamon, cane and cassia,
their perfume not only embodied their sacred status as servants of
Yahweh, but also placated the potentially irritable deity as they moved
about his temple.[7]

Invisible but perceptible, expensive or exotic aromas carried on
moving air were naturally associated with the bodily presence of deities, who were rarely seen, but were there nonetheless. Much as fresh,
moving water (a spring, a river) was described as 'living', so the waft
of an aroma likely signalled the presence of 'living' air. And living air
was easily identified with the breath of a living, otherworldly being,
just as the movement of breath in and out of mortal bodies marked
'life' in the most visceral way. As scented, moving air, the billowing
smoke of incense was consequently prized as a more visible manifestation of the air which Yahweh himself inhaled and exhaled. It was an
ephemeral materialization of his presence in his worshippers' world.

The smoke and scent of incense also offered more accessible ways
to encounter the deity. Just as the smell of a tannery or a bakery could
waft from behind walls to spread across neighbourhoods, transcending
both social and physical boundaries, so the scent of worship could
bypass the need for priestly sanction within a temple, and reach Yahweh's nose no matter where his worshippers might be. Whether at
home or in a local holy place, and regardless of whether they were in
the deity's homeland or a diaspora community, those affluent enough
to afford incense offered it up in the hope its scent would carry their
prayers to God's nostrils, as well as his ears. Much as certain smells
might trigger powerful emotions in us, so too incense was known to
have a powerful and positive impact upon the deity, stimulating feelings
of pleasure, placidity and benevolence as he inhaled it. Its pleasing
scent encouraged him to be magnanimous in responding to the praise
and pleas of petitioners infused in its fragrance. But offer the wrong
kind of incense, or burn it in the wrong way or at the wrong place,

and the punishment could be severe. Legend had it that King Uzziah, a Judahite monarch of the eighth century BCE and a renowned favourite of Yahweh, had overstepped his sacral privileges: he had attempted to offer up incense on the deity's private brazier, a job reserved for the high priest. As a result, Uzziah had been struck with a nasty skin disease. His intimate relationship with Yahweh was over. Forced to retreat from public life altogether, he was also prevented from ever stepping into the Jerusalem temple, lest he defile it. The nature of this defilement was sensory: elsewhere in the Hebrew Bible, skin diseases tend to be associated with the offensive 'polluting' odours of corpses and genital infections.[8] It seems likely that the smell of Uzziah's afflicted flesh offended the deity's nose.

Even after the final destruction of the Jerusalem temple in 70 CE, God's sense of smell remained as keen as ever, and continued to frame his relationships with his worshippers. Daily animal sacrifice on a grand scale was no longer feasible nor permissible – at least, as far as Jerusalem's influential priestly families were concerned. But as the more pungent aromas of animal sacrifice began to fade from Yahweh's world, there was a new suggestion that God preferred scents that were distinctly more human in origin. According to the New Testament's letter to the Ephesians, written towards the end of the first century CE, Christ's crucified body was itself 'an offering and sacrifice for God as a pleasing odour'.[9] The implication was that the sacrificial scent of Christ's corpse would naturally trigger a favourable response from God. It represents a dramatic inversion of God's claimed aversion to the stench of death, from which the very heavens had once threatened to recoil ('rolling up like a scroll') should the stink of decaying corpses drift upwards.[10] But some later rabbis would be no less radical – nor any less graphic. In a midrash on the biblical story of mass circumcision in Abraham's household, it is not only the scarred penis that reminds God to be benevolent, but the welcome smell of rotting foreskins: 'Rabbi Aibu said: When Abraham circumcised those that were born in his house, he set up a hillock of foreskins; the sun shone upon them and they putrefied, and their odour ascended to the Lord like sweet incense. God then said: "When My children lapse into sinful ways, I will remember that odour in their favour and be filled with compassion for them".'[11]

As a trigger of divine memory, God's sense of smell marked more than the natural rhythms of his breathing. Much as we might press the clothes of a loved one to our faces, inhaling a lungful of their scent to bring them closer to us, so the sharp, deliberate in-breath of God was a sniff of commitment, responding to the ritual obedience of his worshippers, and celebrating the emotional bond between the deity and his people.

Snort and Swallow

The God of the Bible was particularly proud of his nose. In his lengthy monologue on Mount Sinai, he reels off a list of his best qualities, not only describing himself as merciful, gracious and abounding in stead-fast love and faithfulness, but 'long-nosed', too. Although some Jewish mystics would later insist his nose was perfectly proportioned (measuring the same as the length of his little finger), in the Bible, God's nose is admirably elongated.[12] In ancient Levantine cultures, the nose was not only an organ of pleasure, but an organ of anger: the physiological sensations of quickened, agitated breathing and snorts of fury pointed to the nasal cavity as the place in the body in which the heat of anger smouldered. But a long nose was equipped with deep nostrils, and deep nostrils meant slower, cooler breathing. Long-nosed Yahweh was a patient deity, naturally slow to lose his temper. At least, this is what he tells Moses on Sinai. Elsewhere in the Bible, his sensitive nose is easily irritated – particularly by religious malpractice. Reading across biblical texts, a preliminary sign of his growing annoyance is a blocked nose: his airways grow warm with his thickened, heavy breath as the scent of ritual deviancy reaches his nostrils, kindling what Yahweh describes as 'a smoke in my nostrils, a fire that burns all day long'.[13] A second stage is marked by the deity's rapid, noisy breathing as he threatens to lash out: 'I will cry out like a woman in labour, I will gasp and pant', he warns, promising that his howling, heated breath will scorch across the landscape, drying up its rivers and shrivelling its trees and plants.[14] When God finally explodes with rage, his anger 'pours out' like a molten stream of lava, casting his wrath as a nasal mucus streaming hot and thick with fiery fury, the flames and smoke of his wrathful breath consuming his enemies.[15] If the deity can sniff out deviant worship, he can snuff out the deviant worshipper. As one biblical poet put it, 'By the breath of God they perish, by the wind of his nose they come to an end'.[16]

The physiology of God's wrath was indistinguishable from his fighting fury as a warrior. It was with a snort of wrath, as well as his powerful arm, that Yahweh had defeated the Egyptians at the Sea of Reeds. And in one of the oldest poetic fragments in the Bible, Yahweh's weaponized breath had filleted aqueous chaos: 'The sources of Sea [Yam] were exposed; the foundations of the world laid bare, at the rebuke of Yahweh, at the blast of the breath of his nostrils'.[17] But it is in a complex passage in the book of Isaiah that the terrifying spectacle of Yahweh's consuming anger is most vividly drawn. A seer is shown an unlit sacrificial pyre in a deep valley, ready for its victim. He sees Yahweh approaching from afar, his nose burning and smoking. The deity's gaping, gasping mouth is also ablaze with the heat of wrath, 'his lips full of fury, his tongue a devouring fire; his breath an overflowing stream reaching up to the neck!' As Yahweh draws closer, the sacrificial victim comes into view: it is an unnamed Assyrian king whom the deity himself is offering up in a macabre caricature of a sacred rite. The deity's worshippers have gathered with music and song to witness the burning. As they dance, the deity's sulphurous breath kindles the pyre, and Yahweh prepares to feast.[18]

This horrifying passage is one of many ancient texts to artfully blur the boundaries between human sacrifice and the ritualized execution of an opponent or offender. But the startling close-up of the deity's ravenous mouth, and the vivid description of his scorching, lethal breath, also plays on widespread monster myths, which themselves gave shape to the primeval human fear of being eaten. Whether the monster was a writhing sea dragon, a horrifying Humbaba (Huwawa), or a sharp-toothed demon, all had scorching, toxic breath, powerful jaws and a wide mouth, ready to consume their helpless targets. But the most terrifying monster of them all was the most familiar and inevitable: death itself.

In a world in which the dead continued to live as ancestors, their post-mortem well-being was dependent upon the very materiality and care of their remains, reflected in their living descendants' concern to ensure the physical integrity of their bones and preserve the tranquillity and security of their tombs. By contrast, those whose corpses or bones were eaten by scavenging animals, or whose graves were desecrated and destroyed, were fated to disappear forever. In the Levant, something of death-as-disappearance was embodied by Mot ('Death'), the fearsome divine being who swallowed his victims into a hostile, barren netherworld. He cowed even the most powerful gods, for when he opened his mouth, one lip touched the earth, the other touched the heavens, and his tongue extended to the stars, threatening the very existence of those deities in whom life itself was manifest. Even Baal of Ugarit had disappeared down Mot's gullet 'like a roasted olive', spurring his devoted sister Anat to launch a daring rescue mission to battle Mot, retrieve Baal's corpse and facilitate his restoration to life.[19] Mot's appetite was as enormous as his maw, his hunger never satisfied. 'My throat consumes in heaps', he boasted, 'I eat by double handfuls!'[20] Unlike the flesh-shredding bite of a demon, the ultimate terror of Mot's mouth was not his powerful jaws, but the back of his throat: rather than ripping his prey into pieces like a predatory animal, he simply annihilated his victims by swallowing them down in one big gulp. Just as our own food disappears when we swallow it, so too the living vanished in Mot's maw.

Mot makes occasional cameo appearances in the biblical literature, usually in tandem with his underworld domain, known by its Hebrew name Sheol. Both are equipped with an insatiable appetite, a mouth beyond measure and a cavernous, swallowing throat. In keeping with the exclusionary theological preferences of the biblical writers, only fleeting glimpses of Mot's older mythic role as a larger-than-life adversary of the heavenly gods appear. In Isaiah, Yahweh accuses his rebellious worshippers in Judah of making a covenant with Mot in a foolhardy attempt to stave off foreign invasion, while in Hosea, he wonders whether it is worth rescuing his unruly worshippers from

Mot, taking the opportunity to incite the underworld king into bringing forth his plague-carrying assistants ('O Mot, where is your
Pestilence? O Sheol, where is your Scourge?').[21] More usually, however,
God himself appropriates Mot's voracious appetite by threatening to
devour his enemies, or pressing Sheol into service as a weapon of
punishment, so that the ground itself can open up and swallow his
targets – sometimes with startling efficiency. In the book of Numbers,
the entire households of three disobedient priests suddenly disappear
into the underworld when the ground beneath their feet splits apart
and swallows them up – adults and infants alike – before closing its
mouth, leaving everyone else in a panic lest the underworld decides to
swallow them too.[22]

But it is in an oracle in the book of Isaiah that Yahweh himself
becomes the great swallower. In a vision of a utopian future, a seer
envisages Yahweh preparing a ritual banquet on Zion, his holy mountain. Covered by a shroud, the guests at his dinner party are the dead,
who have been invited to dine on aged wines and rich food flavoured
with marrow, caricaturing the mortuary feasts the elite dead were
traditionally imagined to share with their patron deities. But Yahweh's
appetite will be sated in an entirely different way: 'He will destroy the
shroud that is cast over all peoples . . . he will swallow up Mot forever'.[23]
Turning the tables on Mot, Yahweh will defeat Death himself in one
great gulp.

Christians would later seize on this oracle in their scriptures and
claim that Death had indeed been 'swallowed up' by God. In one of
his letters to Christians in Corinth, Paul argued that the resurrection
of Christ was not only proof of God's destructive ingestion of Death,
but a guarantee of eternal life – immortality – for Christ's followers.
For Paul, it was not Satan who was the ultimate enemy of God, but
Death himself, whom Paul seems to have considered a terrifying
supernatural being: in his Greek guise as Thanatos, Death was the
otherworldly power who had ruled humanity from Adam's disobedience until the coming of Christ, and it was Death who was marked
out as the 'last enemy' to be destroyed at the end times.[24] Paul insisted
Christ's resurrection disempowered Death of his earthly rule and
signalled the new cosmic order in which Christ's followers were now

living. Paraphrasing the oracle in Isaiah, Paul declared that 'Death has been swallowed up in victory' – a victory God had achieved by means of Jesus' resurrection.[25]

Death might have been defeated, but cultural memories of Mot's throat endured. In the earliest known Christian art, the divine victory over Death was marked not by images of the crucified or resurrected Christ, but by images of the prophet Jonah, who had been swallowed not by a whale, but by a giant fish (a mythic descendant of the sea monster), and spewed back out into the land of the living.[26] For Jesus' devotees, Jonah's three-day stay in the belly of the fish prefigured Christ's time in the tomb, so that the vomiting fish marked the violent reversal of the swallow of Death, recasting Jonah himself as a prophet of Christ's resurrection (fig. 56). In later medieval art, Mot's maw would be regurgitated in more startling ways. With the transformation of the ancient underworld into an eternal hell came a gradual but graphic re-emphasis of the primal fear of being eaten. From about 1000 CE, sinners were shown their fates in illustrated devotional texts, church murals and dramatic performances. Blending the iconography of

Fig. 56. A sea monster vomits up Jonah in a fourth-century CE mosaic in the Patriarchal Basilica in Aquileia, Italy. For early Christians, Jonah's regurgitation prefigured Jesus' resurrection, rendering this biblical scene particularly popular in ancient Christian art.

pre-Christian, northern-European myths with scriptural stories and their theological reinterpretation, the gaping, sharp-fanged mouth of a bestial hell stretched high, low and wide as demons herded the wicked towards its cavernous gullet (fig. 57).

But there can be no death without life. And the God of the Bible had always promoted himself as a god of the living.

Fig. 57. Hairy demons round up sinners to be thrown into a gaping Hellmouth. A popular motif in medieval European art, the Hellmouth is a distant descendant of Mot, who swallowed his victims into the netherworld. This example appears in the Apocalypse of Isabella of France (*c.* 1313 CE), a commentary on the book of Revelation.

Life Breath

In ancient Israel and Judah, the gulp of death was pitched in opposition to the 'breath of life'. Far from a theological abstraction, the breath of life was rooted in the realities of human anatomy as the rush of air we can feel at the back of the throat every time we breathe in, rendering the throat (in Hebrew, *nephesh*) a life-sustaining organ. As the place at which the passage of air, food and the voice was manifest, the throat materialized the sociality of being – of living, existing – in and of itself. So close was the association of life with the throat that the term *nephesh* named not only the visible part of the body, but by extension, the very life force and selfhood of an individual – be it a human or a deity. Although Bible translators tend to render this use of *nephesh* as 'soul', this imparts a later, dualistic conception of a person as a composite of a bodily shell and an immortal, metaphysical essence that was alien to ancient Levantine cultures. Instead, the *nephesh* was usually understood to be the *social* aspect of an individual: their very personhood.

Mythologically, the breath of life was the air Yahweh himself exhaled. It was with his own breath that he enlivened the inanimate bodies of all creatures to bring them into existence as living beings, just as the story of Adam's creation so vividly describes: 'Yahweh-God formed the man from the dust of the ground, and breathed into his nostrils the breath of life, and the man became a living *nephesh*'.[27] By breathing into Adam's nose, the deity effectively opens his airways and vivifies the little figurine he has made, much as statues of the gods themselves were ritually enlivened. Yahweh's breath – in Hebrew, *nishmah*, or (more commonly) *ruah* – was the creative force in the universe, which could also be manifest as a vivifying wind (also termed *ruah*). This proves particularly useful later in the Bible's story of Israel, when God decides to restore full, fleshy life, en masse, to the bones of all those who have died in exile in Babylonia, so that they can make the journey back to Jerusalem. Addressing the vast jumble of bones, Yahweh says, 'I will lay sinews on you, and cause flesh to come upon you, and cover you with skin, and put breath in you, and you shall live'.[28] Once the bones have become bodies, equipped with nostrils and mouths, his powerful breath blows in as cosmic wind and infuses the newly built bodies with life.

Underlying these biblical images of the breath of life was the widespread notion that the human body was far from a self-contained entity, bound and sealed by a relatively impermeable skin barrier. Instead, the body was understood to be far more porous and permeable, and easily affected by external influences. The breath of life moved within it, but it was vulnerable to changes triggered by magically charged climatic airs and supernatural winds. A bad wind might carry dangerous toxic properties, triggering maladies ranging from bloating to depression, while a good wind might be freighted with divine favours, bestowing blessings of renewed health or specialist skills. However forceful or fleeting, these potent airs and winds were often personified or embodied as divine 'spirits' or 'offspring' of the gods – otherworldly entities who could touch, lift, carry, or enter mortal bodies.[29] The physiological dynamics of these encounters seem to have been rooted in the sensation many of us have felt in a strong blast of wind as its weight and strength pushes against our bodies, throwing us off balance and filling our airways with its suffocating presence. We register it as an invisible force of nature, but in ancient south-west Asia, the same experience was easily perceived as an otherworldly encounter. Whether cast as divine spirits or supernatural forces, these hyper-charged airs and winds derived from the gods themselves, whose very exhalations could transform the embodied experiences of mortals.

In the Bible, this transformation is given a heightened religious significance in stories about God's favourite humans, whom he tasks with particular roles. As with all living beings, the breath of life already moved within his chosen warriors, kings, prophets, scribes and artisans, but they were blessed with an additional, concentrated dose of divine breath, often cast as a wind or supernatural 'force' or 'spirit' (also termed *ruah*), which endowed them with superhuman powers and skills, enabling them to fight, rule, prophesy, write, or build on behalf of the deity. This is divine 'inspiration' in the more concrete sense of the term: an in-spiration of God's own breath. In an oracle in Isaiah, the impact of this 'in-breathing' is said to shape the ideal king of a utopian future: the *ruah* of Yahweh will settle upon the king, filling his body with a panoply of divine qualities and attributes (wisdom, insight, counsel, valour and knowledge), and the ability to sniff out the will of Yahweh, correspondingly empowering him to smell his way to making sound judgements on the deity's behalf: 'By his smelling in awe of Yahweh, and not by [what] his eyes see, will he judge, and not by [what] his ears hear, he will decide'.* Like Yahweh himself, the promised king will use his nose to mete out justice.[30]

Other passages present this extra helping of God's *ruah* as a palpable force that rushes, falls, or rests upon his chosen human, seemingly wrapping itself into the body like a thick vapour or heavy scent, while still others suggest it manifests itself as an invisible but tangible power or entity possessing the body. 'I am filled with power, with the *ruah* of Yahweh!' declares the prophet Micah.[31] Should those empowered by Yahweh's *ruah* fall out of divine favour, as so many do, another breath, wind, or divine spirit soon comes upon them, infecting them with the qualities or behaviours which will lead to their downfall, be it poor judgement, false prophecy, jealousy, or madness. In this way, God's *ruah* is a powerfully elastic phenomenon: it is simultaneously an exhalation, a wind and an otherworldly entity or force, which is expelled from his own body to take up residence within or upon that of a mortal.

The same conceptual fluidity pervades the opening verses of Genesis, as God's *ruah* sweeps over the primeval waters before he begins to create the heavens and the earth. Thanks to the Jewish intellectual Philo of Alexandria, a thoroughly Greek-minded thinker of the first century CE, this famous biblical verse is usually taken to refer to God's 'Spirit' – not a divine wind, nor breath, nor even an ephemeral supernatural entity, but an abstract essence or intellectual quality of God, which Christian theologians would later come to identify with the 'Holy Spirit' of their Trinity. But when it was composed in the fifth

---

* The Hebrew here in Isaiah 11.1–4 is difficult to translate, but it indicates that the king is to be filled with a 'breathing' or 'smelling', which he will prioritize over seeing and hearing as the senses by which he navigates his role as God's chosen ruler.

century BCE, this is not what this passage indicated. Instead, God's *ruah* before the creation is the powerful exhalation of the deity, moving as a wind across the primordial waters, and ready to reappear in the story of the Flood, when God blows his *ruah* across the earth to supress the tumultuous waters of the deluge.[32]

But in the first chapter of Genesis, God's breath does not only manifest itself as a cosmic wind in an unconstructed cosmos. In the very next breath, the deity begins to create by speaking the world into being ('Let there be light'), saying aloud the name of each new component ('And God called the light Day'), and then uttering a series of blessings upon his new creation. Just as human speech is a physiological extension of breathing (as air pushed up the trachea moves across our vocal cords), so too divine speech was naturally understood to be a corporeal extension of the deity's breathing, as one biblical psalmist makes plain: 'By the word of Yahweh the heavens were made, and all their host by the breath of his mouth!'[33]

More than simply commanding the created world to appear, like a king issuing orders, God's speaking in creation reflected a wider world of divine incantations – the gods' own specialized form of 'magical' ritual speech. Far more powerful than human incantations, but anatomically articulated in similar ways, the potent breath of the gods was carefully shaped and sounded by the movement of their throats and mouths, and expelled as 'power words', conjuring new realities into being. It was with the help of incantations, blasted from his mouth as a cosmic wind, that Marduk of Babylon had both spoken a constellation into existence and disarmed the primeval salt-sea goddess Tiamat at the beginning of creation. Baal and Athtart of Ugarit had similarly used incantations to capture and destroy the sea god Yam, while El himself had used power words to enliven a new goddess from clay, recycling the ancient technologies of the Mesopotamian gods, who had used incantations to vivify the clay bodies of the first humans.[34] Mythologically, then, power words had always been closely associated with inventive acts of divine creation and cosmic management, and when the God of the Bible recrafted the primeval cosmos and populated it with mortal beings, he used them, too.

But all that talking was a tiring business. As is well known, after six days of speaking the heavens and earth into existence, Yahweh is said to have 'rested from all the work he had done' on the seventh day. Jewish and Christian theologians are so accustomed to imagining God as a deity unfettered by physical limitations that the idea of divine rest tends to be reverently cast as a day of reflection and contemplation. But the Bible itself offers a more pragmatic reason for God's day of rest: he was running out of puff. As the deity himself tells Moses in the book of Exodus, 'in six days Yahweh made the heavens and the earth, and on the seventh day he rested, and caught his breath'.[35]

Recycled Air

Crafting new realities, the potent force of Yahweh's breath-borne words can even create new supernatural beings. Eliphaz, one of Job's so-called friends, appears to experience an embodied word of God in a terrifying night-time encounter, when an utterance from Yahweh manifests itself as a tangible being. In the darkness, Eliphaz hears a whispered word, and then feels it as a *ruah* gliding across his face – a sensation so unsettling (if not ticklish) that it causes the hairs on his skin to bristle. When the *ruah* stands still, he is unable to discern its precise appearance, but he can see it has a form and shape. And then it speaks again, delivering a rather beautiful but faintly menacing reminder that the human body is innately fragile, its clay easily reduced to dust and crushed like a moth, in an instant.[36] The revelatory word of God, more usually spoken by his *ruah*-powered prophets, had bypassed the need for a mortal mouthpiece and taken on a life of its own as an otherworldly being.

But God's breath-borne speech did not always manifest itself in such eerily sinister ways. Old myths and traditions about the goddess figure Wisdom were reworked in some religious circles to cast her as a manifestation of Yahweh's breath. Called Hokmah in Hebrew works and Sophia in Greek texts, Wisdom was already cast as a cosmic care-taker: she was closely associated with universal and moral law – the very principles of righteousness and justice undergirding the orderly workings of the heavenly and earthly realms. In this, she was not unlike the much older Egyptian goddess Maat, the beloved daughter and companion of the creator deity Re, whose intimate relationship with her father was expressed in her role as the one who gave 'life to his nostrils'. Like Maat, Wisdom was naturally assumed to be a permanent fixture at her father's side – so much so, she even assisted him in building and organizing the cosmos, as she explains in the book of Proverbs (c. fifth century BCE): 'Yahweh begot me at the beginning of his work', she declares. 'When he established the heavens, I was there; when he drew a circle on the face of the Deep . . . then I was beside him, like a master worker'.[37] But it is in the later book of Sirach that the mechanics of this intimate relationship are spelled out: she is the very air God had exhaled when he blew upon the chaotic primeval ocean and spoke the world into being. 'I came forth from the mouth of the Most High, and covered the earth as a mist . . . Alone I compassed the vault of heaven, and traversed the depths of the [watery] abyss'. Within the ordered cosmos, she remained an eternal presence, dwelling in a holy tent ('tabernacle') and ministering to God as the intoxicating, incense-laden air he inhaled.[38] Wisdom was the very in-breath and out-breath of God.

Written in the second century BCE, when Yahweh's supremacy left no room for fully fledged deities as his companions, Sirach's portrayal of Wisdom marks a tension in her nature as a divine entity: despite her exalted status, she was no longer a goddess-like figure, but a personification of God's breath, manifest as the Torah, so that when the Torah was read or heard, it was Wisdom giving voice to Yahweh's words.[39] By the end of the first century BCE, some had further disembodied her, casting Wisdom as a reflection of an increasingly abstract form of divine power: 'She is a breath of the power of God, and a pure emanation of the glory of the Almighty . . . a spotless mirror of the working of God, and an image of his goodness'.[40] But if Wisdom could be disembodied, she could be re-embodied, too. For many Jewish groups in the first and second centuries CE, Wisdom's role as the creative word of God marked her out as a highly specialized type of divine messenger, manifesting his commandments, teachings and self-revelation, giving rise to the phrase *bat qol*, 'daughter of [the] voice', to refer to God's speech. For some, she continued to be identified with the Torah itself, while Philo of Alexandria, writing in Greek, would describe her as the divine *Logos* ('Word', 'Reason'). But for others, Wisdom re-emerged as a supernatural being – a second 'power' in the heavens, filtered through Greek philosophical frames to be understood as both separate from God and a part of him.

It is this thoroughly Jewish notion that underlies the casting of Christ as the divine Word (*Logos*) in the prologue to John's Gospel. Here, the *Logos* is the one who 'was with God' and who 'was God'; it is by means of the *Logos* that the created world came into being 'in the beginning', and it is the *Logos* who dwells in a holy tent ('tabernacle') among God's people.[41] Just as Jesus' followers drew on myths and legends about Moses, Elijah, Enoch, Gabriel, Michael and the Son of Man to elaborate on what they perceived to be his status as a holy mediator or divinized being, so too some recycled older traditions about God's breath-born daughter to render Christ divine. In John's Gospel, the ancient goddess has been regendered and turned into both a man and a god. Although the highly specialized, esoteric ideas of John's prologue would come to dominate Christian theology, they differ – often markedly – from other early Christian ideas about Jesus' relationship to God. And in the first century CE, this relationship often turned on the power of God's breath as 'spirit'.

Early traditions embedded in New Testament texts suggest Jesus' status as a holy, divinized, or deified figure began when the 'spirit' of God empowered him. The oldest of these appear in the writings of Paul (mid first century CE), whose utter disinterest in telling stories about the earthly life of Jesus renders the resurrection the definitive moment in Christ's career. This is, of course, the central claim of Christianity, and one of its earliest, for soon after his execution, some of Jesus' followers believed they had seen him. While some interpreted these visions as encounters with Jesus' underworld shade, others contended that he had been physically raised from the dead (a claim some had made of John the Baptist). These believers appear to have credited Jesus' resurrection to the power of God's 'spirit', as Paul does in his letter to the community in Rome. He opens by citing what scholars broadly agree to have been a pre-existing formulaic or ritual confession of faith: 'Jesus Christ . . . who was descended from the seed of David according to the flesh, and who was declared to be Son of God with power according to a spirit of holiness by his resurrection from the dead, Jesus Christ our Lord.'[42]

Writing in Greek, Paul's term for 'spirit' is *pneuma*, which was as elastic as its Hebrew and Aramaic counterparts, so that it could also mean 'breath' or 'wind'. For most first-century philosophers, *pneuma* was not the abstract immateriality of Platonic theory, but an airy yet material substance pervading the cosmos, much as Stoic thinkers imagined. Its fiery heat and dynamism gave it a generative quality easily qualified as divine in origin.[43] In this early ritual confession in Romans, the *pneuma* that resurrects Christ is identified as being 'holy', and it is the powerful divine force that not only reboots but upgrades Christ's body in a process of extraordinary corporeal transformation. While this portrayal of holy *pneuma* evokes something of the generative nature it was accorded in some philosophical circles, it also reflects a specialized outworking of what were already very ancient scriptural traditions about the bodily transformation of Yahweh's kings and prophets, and the divine breath that had enlivened the clay figurine of Adam. For Paul himself, the transformation of Christ's corpse was a substantive corporeal change, so that his risen body was composed entirely of *pneuma*: 'Thus it is written, "The first man, Adam, became a living being", the last Adam [Christ] became enlivening *pneuma*'.[44]

For other first-century Christians, it was Jesus' baptism that marked the moment at which he was empowered by God's *pneuma*. This was the divine power, they claimed, that had enabled Jesus to exorcise demons, perform healings and utter prophecies before his death. New Testament reflections of these traditions cast the *pneuma* as a visible, material entity that had descended onto Jesus 'like' or 'as' a dove – an image both invoking an ancient symbol of a divine messenger and evoking the sensation of moving air. In the ancient religious imagination, this was likely understood as God's spoken breath, which could be heard appointing the newly baptized Christ his 'Son' and 'Beloved' as the *pneuma* descended. Others preferred to believe Jesus had been born already equipped with a holy *pneuma* – another attribute he shared with John the Baptist, whose birth to a barren mother and an elderly father had been miraculous, and whose *pneuma* was said to have derived from Elijah.[45] In deliberate contrast to John the Baptist, however, the bestowal of Jesus' holy *pneuma* was not a foetal gift from a heavenly mediator, but the direct result of his divine conception, as the tradition incorporated into the Gospels of Matthew and Luke attests. In Matthew, the child in Mary's womb is only briskly described as being 'from holy *pneuma*'.[46] But in Luke, the bodily dynamics of this conception are spelled out: the archangel Gabriel informs a flabbergasted Mary that 'holy *pneuma* will come upon you and power of the Most High will overshadow you; therefore the one to be born will be called holy, Son of God'.[47] Drawing on already ancient ideas about the permeability of the human body and Yahweh's 'spirit' as a forceful climatic air, Mary is to be impregnated when God's power 'overshadows' her. It is a deliberately loaded term. In Matthew, Mark and Luke, it describes the divine cloud from which God speaks on the mountain of Jesus' transfiguration, while in the older Greek translations of the Hebrew scriptures, it is used to refer to the dark storm cloud which had once veiled God's body on Mount Sinai. Gabriel is telling Mary that God's storm cloud will cover her body, filling her womb with new life.* The extent to which she has any choice about the matter is far from ambiguous. 'Here I am, the slave of the Lord', she says in response. 'Let it be with me according to your word'.[48] Contrary to centuries of Christian teaching, this is no joyful assent. Describing herself as a 'slave' (*doule*), Mary articulates not her willingness to be impregnated, but her powerlessness to object.[49]

However Christ was understood to have acquired the divine power manifest as a holy *pneuma*, many early Christians understood it to be a potent exhalation of God, which blew through their communities soon after Christ's resurrection. Its arrival is vividly portrayed in the book of Acts. Having watched the risen Christ ascend into the heavens on a cloud, the disciples had decamped to Jerusalem for the harvest festival of Shavuot (Pentecost). A sound from heaven suddenly bursts into the house in which they are gathered. It is described as 'the rush

---

*   Writing at about the same time as the author of Luke, Plutarch ascribed a similarly climatic mode of pneumatic conception to Plato, who was held by some to have been the son of Apollo (*Table Talk* 717d–e, 718a).

of a mighty wind', and brings with it 'tongues of fire', which rest on the disciples as *pneuma* penetrates their bodies. It is a transformative encounter: 'All of them were filled with holy *pneuma* and began to speak in other languages as *pneuma* gave them utterances'.[50] All the noise attracts a crowd. Some are astounded that these Galileans can speak foreign languages, while others assume the disciples are drunk on harvest wine – a suggestion Peter roundly rejects ('It's only nine o'clock in the morning!' he protests). Instead, he interprets their experience as the fulfilment of a prophecy in the ancient book of Joel, in which Yahweh had promised he would pour out his 'spirit' (in Hebrew, *ruah*; in Greek, *pneuma*) onto all mortals, empowering sons and daughters to prophesy, old men to dream oracular dreams, and young men to see visions.[51]

In Acts, the noisy rush of *pneuma* is an outpouring of a fiery but favourable exhalation of God himself. But in the later Gospel of John, the holy *pneuma* that penetrates the disciples' bodies is Christ's own breath. Following Jesus' appearance to Mary Magdalene at his empty tomb, the disciples are gathered in a locked room, hiding from their enemies. Jesus suddenly materializes before them. He shows off the wounds of his crucifixion, tells them he is sending them on a divine mission, and then breathes 'on' or 'into' his disciples. 'Receive holy *pneuma*', he says in the next breath.[52] Earlier in the Gospel, Jesus had described this mysterious *pneuma* as an audible wind, 'blowing where it chooses'.[53] Now, that airy *pneuma* is identified as the very breath of the risen Christ. Breathing onto or into his disciples, Jesus mimics the way Yahweh had vivified not only Adam in Genesis, but the scattered bones of diaspora worshippers in Ezekiel. 'Indeed, just as the Father raises the dead and gives them life, so also the Son gives life to whomever he wishes', Jesus had said earlier in the story.[54] But in John's Gospel, as in other early Christian works, the life bestowed by *pneuma* is not simply regenerative or empowering, but eternal. Shockingly, Christ's breath imparts a new form of life: a pneumatic immortality, surpassing the vivifying 'breath of life' of God himself.[55]

As John's Jesus mimicked God, so Christians mimicked the risen Christ. At least, that is what they would come to understand. The story in John either reflects or inspired a key ritual in early Christian communities: along with baptism, anointing and the laying on of hands, breathing or blowing into the face played a sensory role in the transmission of *pneuma* when believers were initiated into the faith. By at least the fourth century CE, this practice was often understood to exorcise sin-inciting demons residing in the bodies of believers, whose foreheads, ears and nostrils were then anointed and 'sealed' with oil, leaving the body ready for the spiced waters of baptism and a second, perfumed layer of anointing oil.[56] Implicit in these rituals were memories of God's respiratory system, for their aromatic ingredients were pointedly similar to those prescribed in the Jewish scriptures for use in the Jerusalem temple. As the theologian and bishop Ambrose of Milan put it (*c.* 339–397 CE), Christians themselves became 'a sweet odour' to God.[57]

But for those early Church Fathers whose works would shape the crafting of Christian doctrine, and who were so appalled at the very idea of God's body, the divine nose was now itself pneumatic – like the rest of him. 'God is *pneuma*', Jesus is said to have proclaimed.[58] In its original context, this declaration referred only to God as the source of life-giving *pneuma* – a mysterious but material cosmic substance. But it would later be reinterpreted as Christ's confirmation of the immaterial, incorporeal nature of the God of the Bible. Philosophically and doctrinally, the body of God would eventually disappear, leaving in its place the incarnate Christ. And yet the religious realities of God's body would be impossible to erase. God's breath would be materialized and enshrined for all to see, hear and touch in the 'in-spirational' Christian Bible itself, as one of its sacred texts declared:

All scripture is God-breathed.[59]

Like the grin of the Cheshire Cat, it was the breath of God that would remain, as his body gradually vanished.

EPILOGUE

21

AN AUTOPSY

The Bible is bunkum. Its God is dead. At least, that's what myriad thinkers and writers have told us. Since the Enlightenment, prominent Western intellectuals have not only rendered the biblical God lifeless, but reduced him to a mere phantom, conjured by the human imagination. And yet the God of the Bible looks nothing like the deity dissected and dismissed by modern atheism. The God killed off by the rationalist intellectuals of Western philosophy and science is not to be found in the Bible. Their dead deity is a post-biblical, hybrid being, a disembodied, science-free Artificial Intelligence, assembled over the course of two thousand years from selected scraps of ancient Jewish mysticism, Greek philosophy, Christian doctrine, Protestant iconoclasm and European colonialism. In the contemporary age, this composite being has become a god who forgot to create dinosaurs and failed to account for evolution; a god who allows cancer to kill children, but hates abortion; a god who is everywhere and sees everything, but remains absent and says nothing. But the modern God of the West and the ancient God of the Bible are very different beings.

If it were the corpse of the biblical God laid out on a slab before us, what would we see? A supersized, human-shaped body with male features and shining, ruddy-red skin, tinged with the smell of rainclouds and incense. His broad legs suggest he was accustomed not only to striding, leaping and marching, but sitting and standing resolutely stiff, posing like a ceremonial statue. His biceps bulge. His forearms are as hard as iron. There are faint indentations around his big toes, left by thonged sandals. Beneath his toenails there are traces of human blood, as though he has been trampling on broken bodies, while the remnants of fragrant grass around his ankles suggest strolls through a verdant garden. The slightly lighter tone of the skin on his thighs indicates he was most often clothed, at least down to his knees, if not his ankles. Minute fibres of fine fabric – a costly linen and wool mix – indicate that his clothing was similar to the vestments of high-status priests. His penis is long, thick and carefully circumcised; his testicles are heavy with semen. His stomach is swollen with spiced meat, bread, beer and wine. The chambers of his heart are deep and wide. His fingers are stained with an expensive ink, and there are remnants of clay under his fingernails. On his arms are faint scars left from the grazes of giant fish-scales, and the crooks of his elbows, slightly sticky with a salty oil, bear the imprint of swaddling bands, suggesting he has cradled newborn babies. Traces of the tannery fluid used by hide-workers wind in a stripe around his left arm and down to the palm of his hand – a residual substance left by a long leather *tefillin* strap.

His thick hair is oiled with a sweet-smelling ointment, and shows evidence of careful styling: the hair-shafts suggest it was once separated and curled into thick ropes, while slight marks on the back of his scalp indicate it has been partly pinned beneath some sort of headgear – and his forehead is marked with the faint impression of a tight band of metal. Although his beard reaches beyond his chin, it has been neatly groomed, while his moustache and eyebrows are thick but tidy. The hair on his head and face shimmers – first dark with blue hues, like lapis lazuli, then white and bright, like fresh snow. In one glance, he has the beard of his aged father, the ancient Levantine god El; in another, it is the stylized beard of a youthful warrior, like the deity Baal. His ears are prominent, and their lobes are pierced. His eyes are thickly lined with kohl. His nose is long, its nostrils broad – the scent of burnt animal flesh and fragrant incense lingers inside them. His lips are full and fleshy, his mouth large and wide. It is at once the mouth of a devourer and a lover. His teeth are strong and sharp, his tongue is red hot. His saliva is charged with a blistering heat. The back of his throat is a vast, airy chamber, once humming with life. Below it is the opening of a cavernous gullet. Shadowy scraps of another powerful being, the dusty underworld king, cling to its walls.

If we were to diagnose a cause of death, we might find the early blows were struck at the end of the eighth century BCE, when the Assyrians destroyed the northern kingdom of Israel, and at the beginning of the sixth century BCE, when the Babylonians sacked Jerusalem. With the destruction of Yahweh's temples came the loss of its sacred objects – including what were probably statues of Yahweh himself.[1] In Judah, the fall of Jerusalem marked a decisive rupture in traditional religious practice, from which the body of God would never really recover. By the time the Jerusalem temple had been rebuilt, in the early fifth century BCE, the city was under the religious control of powerful families newly returned from Babylonia, whose own experience had taught them that Yahweh had no need for a cult statue: to them, he was a deity transcending the bounds of temple and homeland – a hidden but powerful presence among his displaced people. Accordingly, some worshippers would come to see material images of the deity as religiously dangerous: in ritual terms, they were evidently vulnerable to displacement, disabling, or destruction, but in broader theological terms, they constrained an increasingly transcendent deity in ways some now found worryingly immobilizing.

In Jerusalem, Yahweh was back in his newly built temple, dining at his altar and inhaling the sweet scent of sacrifice and incense, but he was increasingly cast as an unseen presence, mysteriously shrouded from view behind a smoky screen of sacrifice and the impenetrable darkness of sacred space in the holy of holies. It is at this point that the explicit prohibition of images of Yahweh or any other divine being within his downsized retinue appears to have found its way into the Ten Commandments: 'You shall not make for yourself a carved image'.[2] Instead, the Torah itself – the written word of God – would take the place of a cult statue.

But although Yahweh's body was no longer to be seen, it did not vanish altogether. During this Second Temple period, material images of deities would become increasingly reviled precisely because their bodies were not like Yahweh's: their feet were immovable, their eyes blind, their ears deaf and their mouths mute, while their nostrils could

neither smell nor breathe. Yahweh's body, of course, functioned perfectly well. He was hidden, but he was far from disembodied. Instead,
God became ever more transcendent. The Jerusalem temple had once
been the meeting place of heaven and earth. Now, heaven would begin
to stretch away, further from the world, taking the deity deeper into
its highest heights, leaving only God's Torah, his inscribed 'name', or
increasingly ephemeral traces of his 'holiness' and 'glory', in residence.
The temple would no longer be the dwelling place of God, but an
earthly reflection of his far-off heavenly home. From now on, only
seers and mystics who travelled to the heavens in a rapturous daze
were able to catch a glimpse of his form. To them, God's corporeality
became increasingly, gigantically cosmic: it bore the semblance of a
human shape, but it projected bright light, fire, noise and wind so
spectacular that, even in the heavens, it was almost impossible to
comprehend it. For some, God's body was simply too overwhelming
to behold. For others, it would become mysteriously invisible.

It was the cultural heft of certain forms of philosophical abstraction that would strike the deadly blow to God's body. But it was a slow
death. In some communities, the emergence of Greek versions of the
Hebrew scriptures in the third and second centuries BCE had encouraged the gradual – and seemingly natural – metamorphosis of ancient
Levantine mythology into cutting-edge Jewish metaphysics. In a
Graeco-Roman world in which Judaism and its subsequent Christian
inflections were minority religions, some Jewish and Christian intellectuals were keen to demonstrate the erudite, sophisticated truths of
their own theologies by identifying the God of their scriptures with
constructs of the supreme Divine in Greek philosophy. Qualities and
attributes of the Jewish and Christian God were instinctively but insistently mapped onto broadly Platonic abstractions: in Greek, scriptural
references to God's breath (*pneuma*) and word (*logos*) became the divine
Spirit and Reason of the higher, immaterial world, while references to
God's anatomical features, such as his head, hands and feet, became
increasingly complex metaphors and multi-layered allegories, pointing
to higher, esoteric truths. Just as there was believed to be an intellectual
or spiritual realm beyond the physical, so too the scriptures conveyed

intellectual and spiritual meanings far beyond what was immediately apparent.

Early Jewish proponents of this position included the Egyptian scholars Aristobulus (second century BCE) and Philo of Alexandria (first century CE), who each suggested that the great Greek philosophers, including Plato himself, had learned the secrets of the universe, and the divine world beyond it, from Moses via the Torah.[3] While most Jewish scholars agreed that the careful exposition of the scriptures could reveal hidden truths about God, the majority remained comfortable with more traditional ideas about divine corporeality – especially during the rabbinic period (c. 100–600 CE), and continuing in the mystical tradition, which would give rise to medieval forms of Kabbalah. In mainstream Jewish circles, the full force of the philosophical denial of God's body was articulated by the twelfth-century Sephardic scholar Rabbi Moses ben Maimon – better known as Maimonides or Rambam. Maimonides' rationalist abstractions mirrored similar constructs of the divine in contemporaneous Islamic philosophy. 'God is not a body', he insisted; 'there is absolutely no likeness in any respect whatever between Him and the things created by Him'.[4] For Maimonides, anthropomorphic portrayals of God in the Hebrew Bible simply served as a means of instructing worshippers by speaking to them about God in the language of ordinary people. The point of Jewish worship, Maimonides argued, was intellectual and spiritual transformation, so that by keeping the commandments of the Torah, the enlightened worshipper would not only better understand the commandments, but learn to dispense with the 'ordinary language' of their scriptures and come to comprehend the true nature of God as a timeless, changeless, immaterial deity wholly unlike anything in the created realm.[5] Although his views were contested by many other influential rabbis – whether Sephardic or not – his influence on the shaping of Jewish thought was profound, as one well-known refrain, which began circulating a century after his death, celebrated: 'From Moses to Moses there was none like to Moses'.[6]

Among certain Christian thinkers, the eradication of God's body was relatively – and necessarily – quicker. Within the first few centuries of Christianity, the hiddenness and invisibility of God would give

rise to declarations that God is without a body – although many
Christian authorities would continue to disagree (vehemently, and
often violently). Philosophically, the winning side had been persuaded
by the Platonic insistence on the incorporeality and immateriality of
the divine.[7] But theologically, it was the claim that Christ himself was
God incarnate ('in the flesh') that was uppermost in learned minds.
This, the Church Fathers finally agreed, was the only way in which
God had truly revealed his formerly hidden self: for a short time, the
immaterial, invisible God had become a mortal man, born to die,
resurrect, and ascend back to heaven in order to bring eternal life
to humanity (although quite what this meant still remained up for
debate). Now, worshippers could continue to encounter the incarnation in the Eucharist, in which the divine body was ritually materialized
as bread and wine. For these theologians, so keen to assert the unique
truth of their faith, it was Christ who had the exclusive monopoly on
divine corporeality. In essence, God's body was simply replaced with
another.

But it was the insistence that God was at once Father, Son and
Holy Spirit, rather than three separate entities or a deity comprising
three parts, that would ultimately destroy God's body. At the Council
of Chalcedon (451 CE), assembled bishops from east and west had
finally agreed that, as Father, Son and Spirit, God was a singular divine
nature or 'substance', distinguishable as three 'persons' only by the
manner in which each possessed that substance. Theologically, this
put Father, Son and Spirit on an equal divine footing (about which
Christians had long disagreed), guarded against tritheism (theoreti-
cally, at least) and defended the Christian God against charges of
polymorphism. Philosophically, however, the insistence that God was
one substance who was distinguishable but not *divisible* as three persons relied on the Platonic premise that God was neither divisible nor
changeable: if he were, God would not be God at all. And if God
could not be divided into three separate entities or parts, neither could
he be divisible any other way. Ultimately, this meant that God could
not have a body. Although the incorporeality of God would not be
formally declared at Chalcedon, and earlier theologians had already
arrived at this conclusion, the council's explication of the triune God

prioritized and endorsed a Platonic framework for early Christian theology, according to which God was necessarily assumed to be an absolute, simple entity: the supreme, single and permanent ultimate principle, by which the universe and everything within it should be accounted. As the source of the universe, God transcended it, and was therefore utterly unlike it. This rendered God immutable, in contrast to the fluctuating, changeable universe, and non-composite, unlike the universe, which was comprised of parts. As an immutable, non-composite entity (upon which mainstream Trinitarian theology now insisted), it was impossible that God could have a body, for a body is mutable and composite, which can not only be divided and separated into its constituent parts, but presupposes an external 'composer' to put it together in the first place, as Aquinas would later emphasize. As the ultimate principle and source, God could have neither a body nor a composer. The divine is inherently simple, not composite.[8] When hundreds of Church patriarchs, bishops, abbots and royal representatives from across the Latin West gathered in Rome for the Fourth Lateran Council of 1215, this dogma would be plainly stated: God is *substantia seu natura simplex omnino* – a substance or nature that is absolutely simple.[9]

Early Christian thinkers were not alone in drawing on the philosophical notion of divine simplicity to challenge deeply rooted assumptions about the corporeality of God: it had already shaped the work of some Jewish intellectuals, of course, and would later play a dominant role in early Islamic theologies, too. But it is primarily the Christianized, philosophically inflected notion of the immateriality and incorporeality of the divine that has shaped Western ideas about God – and humans. Once upon a time, in the book of Genesis, humans were made in the visual image and likeness of God. It was a social, as well as corporeal correspondence, celebrating both the fleshy wonders of the human body and the personable presence of the deity. But it was also a correspondence granting humans a special status in the cosmos, for their god-shaped bodies placed them in a superior position within the created realm, as one biblical poet, reflecting on the wondrous craftsmanship of God's hands, had once enthused:

> When I look at your heavens, the work of your fingers,
> the moon and the stars that you have established;
> what are humans that you are mindful of them,
> mortals that you care for them?
> Yet you have made them a little lower than gods,
> and crowned them with glory and honour.
> You have given them dominion over the works of your hands;
> you have put all things under their feet . . . [10]

But with the Christianized separation of the divine from the material, and spirit from matter, the body was no longer a point of correspondence between God and humans. Instead, that function passed solely to the enlivening breath of God, now recast as the 'spirit' or 'soul' the deity magnanimously bequeathed to mortal beings. The human body itself could not be further from the image of God, just as Hans Holbein's 1521 portrayal of Christ's all-too-human corpse so powerfully suggests (Plate 33). In the oppressive enclosure of the tomb, the moment of death is frozen on Christ's face: his eyes have glazed and rolled back into his head, his motionless mouth hangs open. The hollow airlessness of the body is marked by its bony frame jutting under collapsing skin. Lifeless blood has crusted over the wounds of crucifixion. The corpse's feet are already blackened by decomposition, and the right hand and face are turning green as the flesh rots. The very transience of human life is pointedly memorialized by the prominence of Christ's belly button – a trace of birth at the end of the fleeting journey from womb to tomb. Holbein's startling, repulsive image of Christ confronts us with the material realities of mortality. In the fetid frame of the tomb, Christ's bodilyness is entirely, uncompromisingly human. There is no trace of his divinity. The theological gulf between the divine and the human could not be wider.

And yet the distance between God and humanity is light years from the image of God in the Bible. The Christian construct of God as a transcendent, invisible and incorporeal being is a distorted refraction, not a reflection, of the biblical image of God. The real God of the Bible was an ancient Levantine deity whose footsteps shook the earth, whose voice thundered through the skies and whose beauty and radiance dazzled his worshippers. This was a deity who crafted god-shaped humans from clay, and breathed life into their nostrils. But this was also a god who wept and talked and slept and sulked. A god who felt and fought and loved and lost. A god who sometimes failed and sometimes triumphed. This was a god more like the best of us and the worst of us. A god made in our own image.

Glossary

Adad	The Akkadian name of an ancient south-west Asian storm god of particular significance in Assyria. Also known as Hadad; his name probably means 'thunderer'.
Akkadian	A language used across ancient south-west Asia.
Anat	A warrior goddess worshipped across the Levant and Egypt, but best known from Ugarit. She is the sister of Baal.
Antu	A Babylonian goddess and wife of Anu.
Anu	The Babylonian name for the primeval god of the sky, known in Sumerian traditions as An ('heaven').
Aqhat	The hero of an Ugaritic myth. He is the divinely promised son of King Kirta, and the proud owner of a magical bow, fashioned by the god Kothar-wa-Hasis.
Aramaic	A language used across ancient south-west Asia.
Asherah	The Hebrew name of a major Levantine goddess, worshipped in ancient Israel and Judah alongside Yahweh. In the Hebrew Bible, her name is also used of her cult object.
Ashur	The name of both a major high god and an important city in Assyria.
Aten	A form of the sun god in ancient Egypt, often represented as a solar disc or sphere.
Athirat	The most senior goddess at Ugarit. She is the consort of El and mother of the gods. Her name later appears in Hebrew texts and inscriptions as 'Asherah'.
Athtar	A warrior deity at Ugarit and a son of El.
Athtart	A warrior goddess at Ugarit, sometimes associated with hunting. The Hebrew version of her name occurs in the Bible as a generic label for 'goddess', but in translations often appears as 'Astarte'.

425

Atrahasis	A name or epithet of the flood hero in Mesopotamian traditions.
Atum	An Egyptian creator deity, often portrayed as the primordial divine power.
Baal	A major storm god across ancient south-west Asia, whose name means 'lord'. At Ugarit, he is the divine patron of the city and brother of the goddess Anat.
Bel	An Akkadian title or epithet of high-ranking male deities in Mesopotamia, used especially of Marduk. It means 'lord'.
Belet-ili	A name or title of the Mesopotamian mother goddess, meaning 'Lady of the gods' or 'Mistress of the gods'. She is also known as Mami and Ninmah.
Belial	Derived from the Hebrew term for 'wickedness', this is the name of a supernatural envoy or personification of cosmic evil.
canon	A term derived from the Greek word *kanon* ('rule' or 'standard'), used by early Christians to refer to the list of religious writings they 'ruled' to be holy.
cherubim	Composite, mythological beings who serve as divine attendants and the guardians of sacred places. The singular form is rendered in English as 'cherub'.
covenant	A formal agreement or treaty between two parties.
cuneiform	A wedge-shaped script used in ancient south-west Asia.
Dagan	A Levantine grain god worshipped across ancient south-west Asia. His Hebrew name is Dagon.
Deber	The Hebrew name of a minor deity or supernatural personification of pestilence.
Dumuzi	The Mesopotamian shepherd god, often cast as the lover of Inanna (Ishtar).
Ea	The Akkadian name of the Sumerian god Enki.
El	The Levantine father of the gods. His name means 'deity'.
Elyon	Translated 'Most High', this is a Hebrew epithet or title of the head of the pantheon. It is used of both El and Yahweh in biblical texts.
Enki	The Sumerian name of the Mesopotamian god of wisdom, cunning and the subterranean freshwater ocean. His Akkadian name is Ea.

Enkidu	The companion and friend of the eponymous hero of the Epic of Gilgamesh.
Enlil	The Sumerian name of the father of the gods in Mesopotamia. His Akkadian name is Ellil.
Ereshkigal	The goddess and ruler of the Mesopotamian underworld. Her Akkadian name is Allatu. In some traditions, she is the sister of Inanna (Ishtar).
Gula	A Mesopotamian healing goddess. Her name means 'great'.
Hebrew Bible	A modern designation for the collection of books known in Jewish tradition as Tanakh, and in Christian tradition as the Old Testament.
Hittites	A people living in Anatolia (modern-day Turkey) and parts of Syria in the second millennium BCE. Their myths often reflect Hurrian traditions.
Hokmah	The Hebrew name of a goddess-like manifestation or personification of Wisdom. In Greek, her name is Sophia.
Humbaba	The Akkadian name of Huwawa, a divine guardian.
Hurrians	A people living in north-eastern Mesopotamia and parts of Syria in the late third and second millennia BCE.
Huwawa	The monstrous guardian of the Forest of Cedars, killed by Gilgamesh and Enkidu. His Akkadian name is Humbaba.
Inanna	The Sumerian name of the most important goddess in Mesopotamia, who is typically cast as a patron of both warfare and sexuality. Her Akkadian name is Ishtar.
Ishtar	The Akkadian name of the goddess Inanna.
kabod	A Hebrew term often used in the Bible to mean 'glory' or 'radiance'.
Khnum	An Egyptian creator deity, often cast as a potter and associated with the annual Nile flood.
Kothar-wa-Hasis	A craft god at Ugarit, occupying a lower-ranking position in the pantheon.
Kumarbi	A Hurrian god who usurps his father to become the high god of the pantheon. His son is the warrior god Teshub (also known as Tarhun).

Lahmu	Meaning 'hairy', this is the name of a protective Mesopotamian deity, whose image was used in the foundations of buildings to ward off evil.
Levant	A common name for the region encompassing what we know today as Palestine, Israel, Jordan, Lebanon and western Syria.
Leviathan	The biblical name of a monster associated or identified with the primeval cosmic sea.
Maat	An Egyptian goddess personifying truth, justice and cosmic order. She is often cast as the daughter of Re.
Mami	A name or title of the Mesopotamian mother goddess, meaning 'Mother' or 'Mommy'. She is also known as Belet-ili and Ninmah.
Mandylion	Derived from a Greek term for a 'cloth' or 'towel', this is the name of a famous relic believed to bear the imprint of Christ's face.
Marduk	The patron deity of Babylon, often identified as the son of Enki (Ea) and the father of Nabu.
massebah	A Hebrew term for a sacred standing stone.
Mastemah	Derived from the Hebrew term for 'hostility', this is the name of a supernatural envoy or personification of cosmic evil.
melammu	An Akkadian term used to refer to the radiance of divinity.
menorah	A seven-branched lampstand or candelabrum.
messiah	'Anointed one' (in Hebrew, *mashiah*). It is rendered in Greek as *christos*.
midrash	A form of commentary on the Hebrew scriptures and other important Jewish texts.
mikveh	A specially constructed bathing pool for ritual washing.
Milkom	The chief god of the Ammonites. His name is derived from the word meaning 'king'.
Min	An Egyptian god of fertility and male sexuality, endowed with a permanent erection.
Mishnah	A collection of rabbinic opinions and rulings, compiled in the third century CE.
monolatrous	A modern term describing a religious culture or theological system in which a number of deities are known, but only one is worshipped.

Mot	The god or supernatural king of the Levantine underworld. His name means 'death'.
Nabu	The Mesopotamian scribe god, sometimes cast as the son of Marduk. He is known as Nebo in the Hebrew Bible.
Nahar	A name or title of the sea god Yam, meaning 'river' or 'river-flood'.
Nammu	The Sumerian name of a primeval goddess who birthed heaven (the god An) and earth (a goddess named Ki). She is often cast as the mother of Enki.
Nanna	The Sumerian name of the moon god, sometimes identified as the father of Inanna (whom other traditions cast as the daughter of Enlil).
Nergal	A Mesopotamian warrior god closely associated with the underworld. He is often cast as the husband of Ereshkigal.
Ningirsu	A warrior god and divine patron of the Sumerian city-state of Lagash.
Ninhursaga	The Sumerian name of a Mesopotamian mother goddess responsible for the birth of many deities.
Ninlil	A Mesopotamian goddess and wife of the god Enlil. In Assyrian sources, she is known as Mullissu and held to be the wife of Ashur.
Ninmah	A name or title of the Mesopotamian mother goddess, meaning 'Lofty Lady'. She is also known as Mami and Belet-ili.
Ninurta	An important Mesopotamian warrior god and a patron of Nippur. He is often associated with agriculture.
Nisaba	Originally a grain goddess, this Mesopotamian deity is also a divine scribe and accountant, sometimes cast as the wife of Nabu.
Nut	The Egyptian sky goddess, daughter of the air god Shu and his sister Tefnut, the goddess of sweet moisture.
Pesach	The religious festival of Passover.
pneuma	A Greek term that can mean 'breath', 'wind' or 'spirit'.
Rahab	A name or title of a monster associated with the primeval sea.
Re	An important Egyptian creator god, closely associated with kingship. His name means 'sun'.

Resheph	A deity of warfare and disease, well known across ancient south-west Asia and Egypt.
ruah	A Hebrew term that can mean 'breath', 'wind' or 'spirit'.
Second Temple	A label commonly used to refer to the temple rebuilt in Jerusalem in the late sixth or early fifth century BCE and destroyed in 70 CE.
Semitic	The label given to a large family of languages spoken across ancient south-west Asia, unrelated to European languages. The term derives from the name of Noah's son Shem who was said to be the ancestor of Levantine and Mesopotamian peoples.
Septuagint	The Greek translation of the Hebrew scriptures, which emerged in the third and second centuries BCE. The name is derived from the Latin word for 'seventy', reflecting an ancient tradition that over seventy Jewish scholars were commissioned to translate the Torah into Greek.
seraphim	Fiery winged serpents of the divine realm.
Shabbat	The sabbath day.
Shadday gods	A class or group of wilderness deities in the southern Levant.
Shamash	The Akkadian name of the Mesopotamian sun deity, a god of justice. His Sumerian name is Utu.
Shapsh	The sun goddess at Ugarit.
Shavuot	A religious festival, also known as the Feast of Weeks or Pentecost.
Shekhinah	In Jewish tradition, the 'indwelling' or 'presence' of God in the world.
Sheol	A Hebrew name for the underworld.
shofar	A ram's horn, used as a ritual trumpet.
Shu	The Egyptian god of airy space. He is the brother and partner of the goddess Tefnut.
Sin	The Akkadian name of the Mesopotamian moon god. His Sumerian name is Nanna.
Sophia	The Greek name for the goddess-like manifestation or personification of Wisdom in biblical texts.
Sukkot	A religious festival, also known as Tabernacles or the Festival of Booths.

tabernacle	The portable sanctuary or 'tent' of Yahweh, also known as the 'tent of meeting'.
tallit	A prayer shawl.
Talmud	A collection of commentaries on the Mishnah, compiled in the third to sixth centuries CE. There are two versions: the Babylonian Talmud (*Bavli*) and the Palestinian (Jerusalem) Talmud (*Yerushalmi*).
Tanakh	Acronym for the Jewish Bible drawn from its three main parts: Torah, *Neviim* (Prophets) and *Ketuvim* (Writings).
tannin	A Hebrew term for a sea monster or dragon.
Tarhun	A Hittite name for the Hurrian storm god Teshub.
Tashmetu	Divine wife of the Mesopotamian god Nabu.
tefillin	Small leather pouches or boxes containing excerpts from the Torah, worn on the head and arm during prayer. Also known as phylacteries.
Tefnut	The Egyptian goddess of sweet moisture. She is the sister and partner of the air god Shu.
Tehom	A Hebrew name of the primeval 'Deep' or cosmic sea.
Telipinu	An Anatolian deity associated with agriculture and fertility, best attested in Hittite traditions.
Teshub	A Hurrian storm god who usurps his father, Kumarbi.
Thanatos	The Greek name for the deity-like manifestation or personification of Death.
Thoth	The Egyptian god of writing, wisdom and secret knowledge.
Tiamat	A goddess or divine personification of the primeval salt sea, cast in the Babylonian epic Enuma Elish as the dangerous opponent of Marduk.
Tishpak	A Mesopotamian warrior god and divine patron of the city of Eshnunna.
Torah	The first five books of the Hebrew Bible, traditionally understood to contain divine 'teaching' (*torah*).
Ugarit	An ancient city-state located at Ras Shamra on the Mediterranean coast of Syria.
Utnapishtim	A name or epithet of the flood hero in Mesopotamian traditions.
votive	A dedication or gift to a deity.
Vulgate	Jerome's Latin translation of the Hebrew scriptures.
Yahweh	The most important god in ancient Israel and Judah. Also known as Yah, Yaho or Yahu.

Yam	The sea god at Ugarit, and a cosmic enemy of Yahweh in biblical traditions.
yam suf	The 'sea of reeds' through which Moses leads the Israelites in the book of Exodus. Greek versions of Exodus render it the 'Red Sea'.
Yarih	The moon god at Ugarit.
Yom Kippur	The Day of Atonement, a religious festival.
Zoroastrianism	A Persian religion emerging from the teachings of the prophet Zoroaster (also known as Zarathustra) in the sixth century BCE. At its heart is the worship of the supreme god Ahura Mazda.

Notes

ANF   The Ante-Nicene Fathers series (Grand Rapids, MI: Eerdmans)

b.   Babylonian Talmud (*Bavli*)

COS   *The Context of Scripture*, 4 vols. Edited by W. W. Hallo and K. Lawson Younger, Jr. (Leiden: Brill, 1997–2017)

ETCSL   The Electronic Text Corpus of Sumerian Literature (http:// etcsl.orinst.ox.ac.uk/). Edited by J. A. Black, G. Cunningham, J. Ebeling, E. Flückiger-Hawker, E. Robson, J. Taylor and G. Zólyomi (University of Oxford, 1998–2006)

IPIAO 3   Silvia Schroer, *Die Ikonographie Palästinas/Israels und der Alte Orient. Eine Religionsgeschichte in Bildern, Band 3: Die Spätbronzezeit* (Fribourg: Academic Press, 2010)

IPIAO 4   Silvia Schroer, *Die Ikonographie Palästinas/Israels und der Alte Orient. Eine Religionsgeschichte in Bildern, Band 4: Die Eisenzeit bis zum Beginn der achämenidischen Herrschaft* (Basel: Schwabe Verlag, 2018)

KTU   *Die keilalphabetischen Texte aus Ugarit*. Third enlarged edition. Edited by M. Dietrich, O. Loretz and J. Sanmartín (Münster: Ugarit-Verlag, 2013)

m.   Mishnah

t.   Tosefta

y.   Palestinian Talmud (*Yerushalmi*)

CHAPTER 1: DISSECTING THE DIVINE

1. Joshua Conrad Jackson, Neil Hester and Kurt Grey, 'The Faces of God in America: Revealing Religious Diversity across People and Politics', in *PLoS ONE* 13(6), 2018, article e0198745. The news headlines I cite can be found online here: https://www.express.co.uk/news /science/973117/God-face-photograph-Christianity-what-does-god-look -like-study; https://www.nbcnews.com/news/us-news/face-god-eye -beholder-researchers-say-n882491; https://www.forbes.com/sites /ericmack/2018/06/14/elon-musk-really-is-god-at-least-in-the-minds -eye-of-christian-believers/#72a350af6afd.

2. Xenophanes, fragments 29, 32 and 33 in Daniel W. Graham (trans. and ed.), *The Texts of Early Greek Philosophy: The Complete Fragments and Selected Testimonies of the Major Presocratics, Part I* (Cambridge: Cambridge University Press, 2010); Maria Michela Sassi, 'Where Epistemology and Religion Meet: What Do(es) the God(s) Look Like?', in *Rhizomata* 1(2), 2013, pp. 283–307.

3. See Genesis 1.26–27; 5.1, 3; 9.6; Numbers 33.52; 2 Kings 11.18; Isaiah 40.18–20. Here, the key Hebrew terms are *tselem* ('image') and *demut* ('likeness'). For further discussion, see Stephen L. Herring, *Divine Substitution: Humanity as the Manifestation of Deity in the Hebrew Bible and the Ancient Near East* (Göttingen: Vandenhoeck & Ruprecht, 2013), especially pp. 96–127; Anne K. Knafl, *Forming God: Divine Anthropomorphism in the Pentateuch* (Winona Lake, IN: Eisenbrauns, 2014), pp. 53–67; Catherine L. McDowell, *The Image of God in the Garden of Eden: The Creation of Humankind in Genesis 2:5–3:24 in Light of the* mīs pî pīt pî *and* wpt-r *Rituals of Mesopotamia and Ancient Egypt* (Winona Lake, IN: Eisenbrauns, 2015), pp. 117–77.

4. For an accessible overview of these matters, see Lester L. Grabbe, *Ancient Israel: What Do We Know and How Do We Know It?* (revised edition) (London: T&T Clark, 2017).

5. 1 Kings 16.27. See further Francesca Stavrakopoulou, 'The Historical Framework: Biblical and Scholarly Portrayals of the Past', in John Barton (ed.), *The Hebrew Bible: A Critical Companion* (Princeton, NJ: Princeton University Press, 2016), pp. 24–53.

6. Tero Alstola, *Judeans in Babylonia: A Study of Deportees in the Sixth and Fifth Centuries BCE* (Leiden: Brill, 2020).

7. For an overview of the composition and compilation of Hebrew Bible and New Testament texts, there is no better guide than John Barton, *A History of the Bible: The Book and Its Faiths* (London: Allen Lane, 2019). For the Jesus movement as a Jewish sect, see Paula

Fredriksen, *When Christians Were Jews: The First Generation* (New Haven, CT: Yale University Press, 2018).

8. Exodus 24.9–10; 33.11.

9. Here, I refer to Genesis 18.1–33; 32.22–30 (*cf.* Hosea 12.1); Isaiah 6.1–4; Ezekiel 1.1–28; Amos 9.1; Mark 16.19; John 6.46 (*cf.* John 1.18; 5.36–38); Acts 7.54–56; Revelation 4.1–5.14.

10. In the Bible, this assumption is reflected in Colossians 1.15; 1 Timothy 1.17; Hebrews 11.27.

11. Exodus 20.4; *cf.* Deuteronomy 5.8.

12. Herbert Niehr, 'In Search of YHWH's Cult Statue in the First Temple', in Karel van der Toorn (ed.), *The Image and the Book: Iconic Cults, Aniconism, and the Rise of Book Religion in Israel and the Ancient Near East* (Leuven: Peeters, 1997), pp. 73–95; Christoph Uehlinger, 'Anthropomorphic Cult Statuary in Iron Age Palestine and the Search for Yahweh's Cult Images', in Karel van der Toorn (ed.), *The Image and the Book: Iconic Cults, Aniconism, and the Rise of Book Religion in Israel and the Ancient Near East* (Leuven: Peeters, 1997), pp. 97–155; Matthias Köckert, 'Vom Kultbild Jahwes zum Bilderverbot. Oder: Vom Nutzen der Religionsgeschichte für die Theologie', in *Zeitschrift für Theologie und Kirche* 106(4), 2009, pp. 371–406; Joachim Schaper, *Media and Monotheism: Presence, Representation, and Abstraction in Ancient Judah* (Tübingen: Mohr Siebeck, 2019), especially pp. 65–70.

13. Christopher Walker and Michael B. Dick, 'The Induction of the Cult Image in Ancient Mesopotamia: The Mesopotamian *mīs pî* Ritual', in Michael B. Dick (ed.), *Born in Heaven, Made on Earth: The Making of the Cult Image in the Ancient Near East* (Winona Lake, IN: Eisenbrauns, 1999), pp. 55–121.

14. Benjamin D. Sommer, *The Bodies of God and the World of Ancient Israel* (Cambridge: Cambridge University Press, 2009), pp. 12–57; Beate Pongratz-Leisten and Karen Sonik (eds.), *The Materiality of Divine Agency* (Berlin: de Gruyter, 2015).

15. Tryggve N. D. Mettinger, *No Graven Image? Israelite Aniconism in Its Ancient Near Eastern Context* (Stockholm: Almqvist & Wiskell, 1995); Tallay Ornan, *The Triumph of the Symbol: Pictorial Representations of Deities in Mesopotamia and the Biblical Image Ban* (Fribourg/Göttingen: Academic Press/Vandenhoeck & Ruprecht, 2005); Brian R. Doak, *Phoenician Aniconism in Its Mediterranean and Near Eastern Contexts* (Atlanta, GA: Society of Biblical Literature, 2015).

16. Deuteronomy 4.11–16.

17. Thomas Römer (trans. Raymond Geuss), *The Invention of God* (Cambridge, MA: Harvard University Press, 2015), pp. 24–34; Josef Tropper, 'The Divine Name *Yahwa', in Jürgen van Oorschot and Markus Witte (eds.), *The Origins of Yahwism* (Berlin: de Gruyter, 2017), pp. 1–21.

18. Deuteronomy 32.8–9. Thanks to ancient scribal emendations seeking to 'correct' the polytheism of these verses, this reading (variously reflected in the Greek and the Dead Sea Scrolls) is not always found in modern Bibles. For further discussion, see the literature cited in the note below.

19. Mark S. Smith, *The Origins of Biblical Monotheism: Israel's Polytheistic Background and the Ugaritic Texts* (Oxford: Oxford University Press, 2001), pp. 48–9; Innocent Himbaza, 'Dt 32,8, une correction tardive des scribes: Essai d'interprétation et de datation', in *Biblica* 83(4), 2002, pp. 527–48.

20. Deuteronomy 33.2–3; Judges 5.4–5; Habakkuk 3.3–15. See Martin Leuenberger, 'YHWH's Provenance from the South: A New Evaluation of the Arguments pro and contra', in Jürgen van Oorschot and Markus Witte (eds.), *The Origins of Yahwism* (Berlin: de Gruyter, 2017), pp. 157–79.

21. Numbers 22–24.

22. For an accessible translation and discussion, see Carl S. Ehrlich, 'Balaam the Seer: From the Bible to the Deir 'Alla Inscription', TheTorah.com (2018), https://thetorah.com/article/balaam-the-seer -from-the-bible-to-the-deir-alla-inscription. For a more detailed discussion, including the role of Balaam in the book of Numbers, see Baruch A. Levine, *Numbers 21–36: A New Translation with Introduction and Commentary* (New York, NY: Doubleday, 2000), pp. 135–275.

23. Genesis 17.1–2.

24. Genesis 35.11.

25. Genesis 33.20.

26. Herbert Niehr, 'The Rise of YHWH in Judahite and Israelite Religion: Methodological and Religio-Historical Aspects', in Diana Edelman (ed.), *The Triumph of Elohim: From Yahwisms to Judaisms* (Kampen: Kok Pharos, 1995), pp. 45–72; Seth L. Sanders, 'When the Personal Became Political: An Onomastic Perspective on the Rise of Yahwism', in *Hebrew Bible and Ancient Israel* 4(1), 2015, pp. 78–105; Omer Sergi, 'State Formation, Religion and "Collective Identity" in the Southern Levant', in *Hebrew Bible and Ancient Israel* 4(1), 2015, pp. 56–77.

27. Exodus 6.2–3.
28. For an accessible overview, see Israel Finkelstein, *The Forgotten Kingdom: The Archaeology and History of Northern Israel* (Atlanta, GA: Society of Biblical Literature, 2013).

CHAPTER 2: GROUNDED

1. Elizabeth C. Stone and Paul E. Zimansky, *The Iron Age Settlement at 'Ain Dara, Syria: Survey and Soundings* (Oxford: British Archaeological Reports, 1999). On the Turkish airstrike, see the UNESCO-approved report by Michael D. Danti, Darren P. Ashby, Marina Gabriel and Susan Penacho, 'Special Report: Current Status of the Tell Ain Dara Temple', American Society of Overseas Research Cultural Heritage Initiatives (CHI): Safeguarding the Heritage of the Near East Initiative. Released online 2 March 2018; updated 7 March 2018. Available at https://www.asor.org/chi/reports/special-reports/tell-ain-dara-temple.
2. Matthew R. Bennett and Sarita A. Morse, *Human Footprints: Fossilised Locomotion?* (London: Springer, 2014), pp. 1–2.
3. See further David Summers, *Real Spaces: World Art History and the Rise of Western Modernism* (London: Phaidon, 2003), p. 27; Tim Ingold, 'Footprints through the Weather-World: Walking, Breathing, Knowing', in *Journal of the Royal Anthropological Institute* 16(1), 2010, pp. 121–39.
4. For these and further examples, see Janet Bord, *Footprints in Stone: Imprints of Giants, Heroes, Holy People, Devils, Monsters and Supernatural Beings* (Loughborough: Heart of Albion, 2004); Margo DeMello, *Feet and Footwear: A Cultural Encyclopedia* (Santa Barbara, CA: Greenwood Press, 2009).
5. Herodotus, *Historiae*, 4.82, trans. A. D. Godley, *Herodotus II: Books 3 and 4* (Loeb Classical Library, 118; Cambridge, MA: Harvard University Press, 1921); Lucian, *Vera historia*, 1.7, trans. A. M. Harmon, *Lucian I* (Loeb Classical Library, 14; Cambridge, MA: Harvard University Press, 1913).
6. Katherine Dunbabin, '*Ipsa deae vestigia* . . . Footprints Divine and Human on Graeco-Roman Monuments', in *Journal of Roman Archaeology* 3, 1990, pp. 85–109; Sarolta A. Takács, 'Divine and Human Feet: Records of Pilgrims Honouring Isis', in Jaś Elsner and Ian Rutherford (eds.), *Pilgrimage in Graeco-Roman and Early Christian Antiquity: Seeing the Gods* (Oxford: Oxford University Press, 2005), pp. 353–69.

7. Jacob N. Kinnard, *Places in Motion: The Fluid Identities of Temples, Images, and Pilgrims* (Oxford: Oxford University Press, 2014), pp. 76–7.

8. Brannon Wheeler, *Mecca and Eden: Ritual, Relics, and Territory in Islam* (Chicago, IL: University of Chicago Press, 2006), pp. 78–80; Kathryn Blair Moore, *The Architecture of the Christian Holy Land: Reception from Late Antiquity* (Cambridge: Cambridge University Press, 2017), pp. 251–3.

9. Genesis 3.8; 18.1–2, 16, 22, 33; 28.13.

10. Exodus 24.9–10.

11. Isaiah 60.13.

12. Ezekiel 43.7.

13. Tim Ingold, 'Culture on the Ground: The World Perceived Through the Feet', in *Journal of Material Culture* 9(3), 2004, pp. 315–40.

14. Ann Andersson, 'Thoughts on Material Expressions of Cultic Practice: Standing Stone Monuments of the Early Bronze Age in the Southern Levant', in Nicola Laneri (ed.), *Defining the Sacred: Approaches to the Archaeology of Religion in the Near East* (Oxford: Oxbow, 2015), pp. 48–59.

15. See the entries for these sites in Ephraim Stern (ed.), *The New Encyclopedia of Archaeological Excavations in the Holy Land* (4 vols.) (Jerusalem/New York, NY: Israel Exploration Society/Simon and Schuster, 1993); plus Lawrence E. Stager, 'The Shechem Temple – Where Abimelech Massacred a Thousand', in *Biblical Archaeology Review* 29(4), 2003, pp. 265–6, 269; Elizabeth Bloch-Smith, 'Will the Real *Massebot* Please Stand Up: Cases of Real and Mistakenly Identified Standing Stones in Ancient Israel', in Gary M. Beckman and Theodore J. Lewis (eds.), *Text, Artifact, and Image: Revealing Ancient Israelite Religion* (Providence, RI: Brown Judaic Studies, 2006), pp. 64–79.

16. Genesis 28.11–22.

17. Genesis 31.13.

18. For the identification of present-day Beitin with ancient Bethel, see Anson F. Rainey, 'Looking for Bethel: An Exercise in Historical Geography', in Seymour Gitin, J. Edward Wright and J. P. Dessel (eds.), *Confronting the Past: Archaeological and Historical Essays on Ancient Israel in Honor of William G. Dever* (Winona Lake, IN: Eisenbrauns, 2006), pp. 269–73.

19. This explains the hostility towards the Bethel temple in the pro-Jerusalem traditions embedded in the books of Kings. In particular, Bethel is portrayed as a hotbed of idolatry, polytheism and political rebellion (1 Kings 12–13; 2 Kings 23.15–20).

20. Isaiah 60.13; Ezekiel 43.7.
21. Meir Malul, 'Foot Symbolism in the Ancient Near East: Imprinting Foundlings' Feet in Clay in Ancient Mesopotamia', in *Zeitschrift für Altorientalische und Biblische Rechtsgeschichte* 7, 2001, pp. 353–67; Carlo Zaccagnini, 'Feet of Clay at Emar and Elsewhere', in *Orientalia* 63(1), 1994, pp. 1–4; Yoram Cohen, 'Feet of Clay at Emar: A Happy End?', in *Orientalia* 74(2), 2005, pp. 165–70.
22. Meir Malul, *Studies in Mesopotamian Legal Symbolism* (Kevelaer: Butzon & Bercker, 1988), pp. 381–91; Christine Palmer, 'Unshod on Holy Ground: Ancient Israel's "Disinherited" Priesthood', in Leonard J. Greenspoon (ed.), *Fashioning Jews: Clothing, Culture, and Commerce* (West Lafayette, IN: Purdue University Press, 2013), pp. 1–17.
23. E.g., Deuteronomy 25.5–10; Ruth 3.7–10.
24. Genesis 13.17; Deuteronomy 11.24.
25. Job 2.2.
26. Psalms 60.8; 108.9.
27. Tallay Ornan, '"Let Ba'al Be Enthroned": The Date, Identification, and Function of a Bronze Statue from Hazor', in *Journal of Near Eastern Studies* 70(2), 2011, pp. 253–80.
28. *COS* 1.111, tablet 4, lines 104, 129–31, 136–40 (trans. Benjamin R. Foster).
29. Psalms 74.13–15; 89.9–10; Isaiah 51.9; Job 26.12–13.
30. Job 41.1–34.
31. Psalm 29.10.
32. Psalm 93.1–4.
33. Exodus 14.21–29; Mark 6.45–52; John 6.15–21 (*cf.* Matthew 14.23–26); Revelation 12.1–9.
34. See further Timothy K. Beal, *Religion and Its Monsters* (London: Routledge, 2002); Natasha O'Hear and Anthony O'Hear, *Picturing the Apocalypse: The Book of Revelation in the Arts over Two Millennia* (Oxford: Oxford University Press, 2015), pp. 131–54.
35. The classic study of this motif is Richard J. Clifford, *The Cosmic Mountain in Canaan and the Old Testament* (Cambridge, MA: Harvard University Press, 1972).
36. Amos 4.13.
37. See Michael B. Hundley, *Gods in Dwellings: Temples and Divine Presence in the Ancient Near East* (Atlanta, GA: Society of Biblical Literature, 2013).
38. 1 Kings 6–7 (compare the cult objects' dimensions in the Greek versions); 2 Chronicles 4.1 (*cf.* 1 Kings 8.63–64). See further Elizabeth Bloch-Smith, 'Solomon's Temple: The Politics of Ritual Space', in

Barry M. Gittlen (ed.), *Sacred Time, Sacred Place: Archaeology and the Religion of Israel* (Winona Lake, IN: Eisenbrauns, 2002), pp. 83–94.

39. 1 Kings 6.19, 23–28; 8.4–8.
40. 1 Chronicles 28.2.
41. Psalm 99.1–5.

CHAPTER 3: FOOTLOOSE

1. Heinrich Piening, 'Examination Report: The Polychromy of the Arch of Titus Menorah Relief', in *Images: A Journal of Jewish Art and Visual Culture* 6, 2012, pp. 27–32; Steven Fine, 'Polychromy and Jewish Visual Culture of Roman Antiquity', in Rubina Raja and Jörg Rüpke (eds.), *A Companion to the Archaeology of Religion in the Ancient World* (Chichester: Wiley Blackwell, 2015), pp. 133–43.
2. 1 Kings 22.19.
3. Daniel 7.9–10.
4. *COS* 1.110 (trans. Stephanie Dalley). This version of the myth was found at Tel el-Amarna in Egypt. A much later and longer version comes from seventh-century BCE Sultantepe, in what is now Turkey. Interestingly, in this later version, Nergal's initial offence is not refusing to stand in the presence of the divine queen's representative, but refusing to kneel (*COS* 1.109).
5. Isaiah 14.13–14.
6. Isaiah 14.19.
7. *KTU* 1.6 i 43–62. Accessible translations of Ugarit's myths can be found in Simon B. Parker (ed.), *Ugaritic Narrative Poetry* (Atlanta, GA: Society of Biblical Literature, 1997); Nicolas Wyatt, *Religious Texts from Ugarit* (second edition) (Sheffield: Sheffield Academic Press, 2002).
8. For a discussion of this myth, and its corresponding texts, see Mary R. Bachvarova, 'Wisdom of Former Days: The Manly Hittite King and Foolish Kumarbi, Father of the Gods', in Ilona Zsolnay (ed.), *Being a Man: Negotiating Ancient Constructs of Masculinity* (New York, NY: Routledge, 2017), pp. 83–111; *cf.* Harry A. Hoffner, *Hittite Myths* (second edition) (Atlanta, GA: Scholars Press, 1998), pp. 42–3.
9. Apollodorus, *Bibliotheca*, 1.6.3–4, trans. J. G. Frazer, *Apollodorus: The Library, Volume I* (Loeb Classical Library, 121; Cambridge, MA: Harvard University Press, 1921).
10. Genesis 25.21–34; Hosea 12.3.
11. 1 Samuel 4.3.

12. 1 Samuel 4.7. On the probability that a cult statue of Yahweh is assumed in this story, see Thomas Römer, 'Y avait-il une statue de Yhwh dans le premier temple? Enquêtes littéraires à travers la Bible hébraïque', *Asdiwal* 2, 2007, pp. 41–58 (here, pp. 49–50).
13. 1 Samuel 5.4.
14. Numbers 10.35–36.
15. 1 Kings 8.9.
16. Psalm 132.8.
17. See the examples in Steven D. Fraade, 'Facing the Holy Ark: In Words and Images', in *Near Eastern Archaeology* 82(3), 2019, pp. 156–63.
18. For an accessible overview, see David Gurevich, 'Magdala's Stone of Contention', published online in August 2018 at https://www.bibleinterp.com/articles/2018/08/gur428008.shtml. See further Lutz Doering, 'The Synagogue at Magdala: Between Localized Practice and Reference to the Temple', in Lutz Doering and Andrew R. Krause (eds.), *Synagogues in the Hellenistic and Roman Periods: Archaeological Finds, New Methods, New Theories* (Göttingen: Vandenhoeck & Ruprecht, 2020), pp. 127–54; Judith H. Newman, 'Contextualizing the Magdala Synagogue Stone in its Place: An Exercise in Liturgical Imagination', in Lutz Doering and Andrew R. Krause (eds.), *Synagogues in the Hellenistic and Roman Periods: Archaeological Finds, New Methods, New Theories* (Göttingen: Vandenhoeck & Ruprecht, 2020), pp. 155–74.
19. *Mekhilta de-Rabbi Ishmael* 11.47–49, adapting the translation in Jacob Z. Lauterbach (ed.), *Mekhilta de-Rabbi Ishmael: A Critical Edition*, vol. 1 (second edition) (Philadelphia, PA: Jewish Publication Society, 2004).
20. Aharon Oppenheimer, 'Babylonian Synagogues with Historical Associations', in Dan Urman and Paul V. M. Flesher (eds.), *Ancient Synagogues: Historical Analysis and Archaeological Discovery* (Leiden: Brill, 1998), pp. 40–48 (here, pp. 41–2); Steven Fine, 'From Meeting House to Sacred Realm: Holiness and the Ancient Synagogue', in Steven Fine (ed.), *Sacred Realm: The Emergence of the Synagogue in the Ancient World* (Oxford: Oxford University Press, 1996), pp. 21–47.
21. 2 Kings 5.15–17.
22. A. Kirk Grayson and Jamie Novotny, *The Royal Inscriptions of Sennacherib, King of Assyria (704–681 BC), Part 2* (Winona Lake, IN: Eisenbrauns, 2014), p. 268.
23. *KTU* 1.4 iv 23–30.
24. *KTU* 1.5 vi 23–25. For similar translations of these lines (and those immediately below), see *COS* 1.86 (trans. Dennis Pardee) and Wyatt, *Religious Texts*, pp. 126–39.

25. *KTU* 1.6 iii 22–iv 5.
26. *KTU* 1.6 iii 14–20.
27. Psalm 99.1–5.
28. Isaiah 66.1.
29. 2 Kings 24.13.
30. Psalm 74.3–7.
31. Lamentations 2.1.
32. Ezekiel 1.4–28; 10.1–22; 11.22–25.
33. Ezekiel 1.1.
34. Psalm 18.9–13.
35. Psalm 68.4.
36. Ezekiel 11.16.
37. Isaiah 66.1.
38. Matthew 5.34–37. For rabbinic parallels, see Dennis C. Duling, ' "[Do Not Swear . . .] by Jerusalem Because It Is the City of the Great King" (Matt. 5:35)', in *Journal of Biblical Literature* 110(2), 1991, pp. 291–309.
39. Clement, *Stromateis*, 5.11.71.4. I borrow the translation in G. L. Prestige, *God in Patristic Thought* (London: Society for the Promotion of Christian Knowledge, 1952), p. 9.
40. E.g., Theophilus, *Ad Autolycum*, 2.22; Irenaeus, *Epideixis*, 12. For English translations of these works, see Robert H. Grant (trans.), *Theophilus of Antioch: Ad Autolycum* (Oxford: Oxford University Press, 1970); Joseph P. Smith (trans.), *St. Irenaeus: Proof of the Apostolic Teaching* (Mahwah, NJ: Paulist Press, 1952). For other early Christian strategies to combat biblical anthropomorphism, see Mark Sheridan, *Language for God in Patristic Tradition: Wrestling with Biblical Anthropomorphism* (Downers Grove, IL: InterVarsity Press, 2015).
41. Origen, *Homiliae in Genesim*, 1.13, trans. Ronald E. Heine, *Origen: Homilies on Genesis and Exodus* (The Fathers of the Church, 7; Washington, DC: Catholic University of America Press, 1982). On these ways of reading scripture, see John C. Cavadini, 'From Letter to Spirit: The Multiple Senses of Scripture', in Paul M. Blowers and Peter W. Martens (eds.), *The Oxford Handbook to Early Christian Biblical Interpretation* (Oxford: Oxford University Press, 2019), pp. 126–48.

CHAPTER 4: SENSATIONAL FEET

1. Exodus 21.24; Deuteronomy 19.21.
2. *KTU* 1.3 ii 5–30.
3. Isaiah 63.1–6.

4. Revelation 14.19–20; 19.11–15.

5. On the biblical book of Revelation as a key text for Crusader ideologies, see Elizabeth Lapina and Nicholas Morton (eds.), *The Uses of the Bible in Crusader Sources* (Leiden: Brill, 2017). On the red cross of Crusader symbol-systems, see Michel Pastoureau (trans. Jody Gladding), *Red: The History of a Color* (Princeton, NJ: Princeton University Press, 2017), pp. 64–8; William J. Purkins, ' "Zealous Imitation": The Materiality of the Crusader's Marked Body', in *Material Religion* 14(4), 2018, pp. 438–53.

6. Genesis 3.8.

7. Deuteronomy 23.12–14.

8. For El, see *KTU* 1.23 in Wyatt, *Religious Texts*, pp. 324–35. For Enlil and Ninlil, see ETCSL 1.2.1 (lines 1–23). Key texts in this electronic corpus can also be found in Jeremy Black, Graham Cunningham, Eleanor Robson and Gábor Zólyomi, *The Literature of Ancient Sumer* (Oxford: Oxford University Press, 2004).

9. Genesis 5.22–24; 6.9; 18.16–33; Habakkuk 3.3–6. Yahweh is not the only deity to have perceived walking with male mortals in this way: in the Cyrus Cylinder inscription, the Persian king Cyrus the Great describes the Babylonian god Marduk walking alongside him on the road to Babylon 'like a companion and friend'. For a translation of the Cyrus Cylinder, see *COS* 2.124.

10. Genesis 18.16–33. In the preceding verses (1–15), Yahweh is not only human-shaped, but human-sized – and he looks so much like an ordinary mortal that the other characters in the story are unaware that he is a deity. For some scholars, it is the most human-like portrayal of God in the Hebrew Bible. See Esther J. Hamori, '*When Gods Were Men*': The Embodied God in Biblical and Near Eastern Literature* (Berlin: de Gruyter, 2008).

11. Genesis 5.22–24. On the Enoch traditions, see Peter Schäfer, *The Origins of Jewish Mysticism* (Tübingen: Mohr Siebeck, 2009); John C. Reeves and Annette Yoshiko Reed, *Enoch from Antiquity to the Middle Ages, Volume 1: Sources from Judaism, Christianity, and Islam* (Oxford and New York: Oxford University Press, 2018).

12. Leviticus 26.12.

13. Genesis 3.8–10.

14. Judges 5.4–5.

15. 2 Samuel 5.24.

16. *KTU* 1.17 vi 44–46. Here, I borrow the lively translation in Michael D. Coogan and Mark S. Smith (eds.), *Stories from Ancient Canaan* (second edition) (Louisville, KY: Westminster John Knox, 2012), p. 42.

17. *b. Berakhot* 59a.

18. In the Epic of Gilgamesh, this is what the eponymous hero instructs his friend Enkidu to do, so as to avoid capture when he creeps into the underworld to steal back the precious ball and stick Gilgamesh had lost. See Stephanie Dalley, *Myths from Mesopotamia: Creation, the Flood, Gilgamesh, and Others* (Oxford: Oxford University Press, 1989), pp. 120–22.

19. Emily Teeter, *Religion and Ritual in Ancient Egypt* (Cambridge: Cambridge University Press, 2011), pp. 46–51.

20. This appears to be the sense of the exorcism of the temple in the Babylonian Akitu (New Year) festival, in which the temple was symbolically reduced to rubble, purified and rebuilt. See further Benjamin D. Sommer, 'The Babylonian Akitu Festival: Rectifying the King or Renewing the Cosmos?', in *Journal of Ancient Near Eastern Studies* 27(1), 2000, pp. 81–95; *cf.* Julye Bidmead, *The Akitu Festival: Religious Continuity and Royal Legitimation in Mesopotamia* (Piscataway, NJ: Gorgias Press, 2002); Isabel Cranz, *Atonement and Purification: Priestly and Assyro-Babylonian Perspectives on Sin and Its Consequences* (Tübingen: Mohr Siebeck, 2017).

21. For priestly foot-washing and toe rituals, see Exodus 29.20; 30.21; Leviticus 8.23–24; 14.14, 17, 25, 28. For priestly vestments, see Exodus 28.1–43; 39.1–31; Leviticus 8.6–9. See further Joachim J. Krause, 'Barefoot before God: Shoes and Sacred Space in the Hebrew Bible and Ancient Near East', in Christoph Berner, Manuel Schäfer, Martin Schott, Sarah Schulz and Martina Weingärtner (eds.), *Clothing and Nudity in the Hebrew Bible* (London: T&T Clark, 2019), pp. 315–22; Michael D. Swartz, 'The Semiotics of the Priestly Vestments', in Albert I. Baumgarten (ed.), *Sacrifice in Religious Experience* (Leiden: Brill, 2002), pp. 57–80; Nathan MacDonald, 'The Priestly Vestments', in Christoph Berner, Manuel Schäfer, Martin Schott, Sarah Schulz and Martina Weingärtner (eds.), *Clothing and Nudity in the Hebrew Bible* (London: T&T Clark, 2019), pp. 435–48.

22. Jodi Magness, *Stone and Dung, Oil and Spit: Jewish Daily Life in the Time of Jesus* (Grand Rapids, MI: Eerdmans, 2011), pp. 16–17.

23. Philo, *De specialibus legibus*, 1.207, trans. F. H. Colson, *Philo: On the Decalogue. On the Special Laws, Books 1–3* (Loeb Classical Library, 320; Cambridge, MA: Harvard University Press, 1937).

24. Philo, *Quaestiones et solutiones in Exodum*, 1.2, trans. Ralph Marcus, *Philo: Questions on Exodus* (Loeb Classical Library, 401; Cambridge, MA: Harvard University Press, 1953).

25. Psalms of Solomon 2.1–2.

26. Josephus, *Jewish War*, 4.3.6, trans. H. St. J. Thackeray, *Josephus: The Jewish War*, vol. 2 (Loeb Classical Library, 487; Cambridge, MA: Harvard University Press, 1927).

27. P. Oxy. 840, trans. J. K. Elliott, *The Apocryphal New Testament: A Collection of Apocryphal Christian Literature in an English Translation Based on M. R. James* (Oxford: Clarendon Press, 1993), pp. 33–4.

28. See further Michael J. Kruger, *The Gospel of the Saviour: An Analysis of P.OXY. 840 and Its Place in the Gospel Traditions of Early Christianity* (Leiden: Brill, 2005).

29. Dalley, *Myths from Mesopotamia*, p. 18.

30. Hellmut Brunner, *Altägyptische Weisheit. Lehren für das Leben* (Zurich: Artemis, 1988), p. 228.

31. Plato, *Phaedrus*, 15, trans. R. Hackforth in Edith Hamilton and Huntington Cairns (eds.), *The Collected Dialogues of Plato* (Princeton, NJ: Princeton University Press, 1961), p. 486. For the accusations against Socrates, see the discussion in Tim Whitmarsh, *Battling the Gods: Atheism in the Ancient World* (London: Faber & Faber, 2016), pp. 129–34.

32. Ecclesiastes 5.1–2. See further Marjo C. A. Korpel and Johannes de Moor, *The Silent God* (Leiden: Brill, 2011), pp. 78–109.

33. Josephus, *Jewish War*, 5.5.2, trans. H. St. J. Thackeray, *Josephus: The Jewish War*, vol. 3 (Loeb Classical Library, 210; Cambridge, MA: Harvard University Press, 1928). For the inscription, see Hannah M. Cotton, Leah Di Segni, Wener Eck, Benjamin Isaac, Alla Kushnir-Stein, Haggai Misgav, Jonathan Price, Israel Roll and Ada Yardeni (eds.), *Corpus Inscriptionum Iudaeae/Palaestinae, Volume 1.1* (Berlin: de Gruyter, 2010), pp. 42–7.

34. Andrew R. George, *Babylonian Divinatory Texts Chiefly in the Shøyen Collection* (Bethesda, MD: CDL Press, 2013), p. 234; Meir Malul, 'Foot Symbolism in the Ancient Near East: Imprinting Foundlings' Feet in Clay in Ancient Mesopotamia', in *Zeitschrift für Altorientalische und Biblische Rechtsgeschichte* 7, 2001, pp. 353–67 (here, p. 360).

35. Numbers 5.11–31. In an early Christian work known as the Protoevangelium of James, which enjoyed wide circulation from the late second century to the fifth century CE, Jesus' mother Mary endures a similar 'drink test' to prove her miraculous pregnancy is not the result of an adulterous (or sexual) encounter.

36. Exodus 3.1–6 (*cf.* Joshua 5.13–15). Scholars tend to agree that the reference to a divine messenger in Exodus 3.2 is a later gloss.

37. Exodus 3.5–6.

38. Available online at http://catholicherald.co.uk/foot-washing-is-too
    -important-to-be-dragged-into-a-feminist-debate/.

39. The bishop's comments were reported on a number of traditionalist
    Roman Catholic websites, including catholicculture.org and rorate
    -caeli.blogspot.com. See further https://cruxnow.com
    /church/2016/01/not-all-are-on-board-with-pope-francis-decision-to
    -include-women-in-foot-washing/. For the statement issued by the
    Latin Mass Society of England and Wales, see http://www
    .lmschairman.org/2016/01/statement-on-allowing-washing-of-feet
    .html.

40. John 13.7–8.

41. John 13.8.

42. Matthew L. Bowen, ' "They Came and Held Him by the Feet and
    Worshipped Him": Proskynesis before Jesus in Its Biblical and Ancient
    Near Eastern Context', in *Studies in the Bible and Antiquity* 5, 2013,
    pp. 63–89.

43. Psalm 2.11–12; *cf.* 1 Kings 19.18.

44. Luke 7.36–50. In John 12.1–8, the woman who anoints Jesus' feet is
    Mary of Bethany.

45. Petronius, *Satyricon*, 69, trans. Michael Heseltine, *Petronius, Seneca:
    Satyricon, Apocolocyntosis* (Loeb Classical Library, 15; Cambridge, MA:
    Harvard University Press, 1913). On the erotic dynamics of Luke's
    story, see Elaine Wainwright, 'Unbound Hair and Ointmented Feet:
    An Ecofeminist Reading of Luke 7.36–50', in Natalie K. Watson and
    Stephen Burns (eds.), *Exchanges of Grace: Essays in Honour of Ann
    Loades* (London: SCM Press, 2008), pp. 178–89.

46. Ruth 3.3–14; 4.11–17.

47. 2 Samuel 11.8; Jeremiah 13.26; Nahum 3.5; Isaiah 3.16–17; Proverbs 7.11–12.

48. *COS* 1.128 (trans. Alasdair Livingstone). See further Martti Nissinen,
    'Love Lyrics of Nabû and Tašmetu: An Assyrian Song of Songs?', in
    Manfried Dietrich and Ingo Kottsiepier (eds.), *'Und Mose schrieb dieses
    Lied auf': Studien zum Alten Testament und zum Alten Orient* (Münster:
    Ugarit-Verlag, 1998), pp. 585–634 (here, pp. 588–90).

49. Song of Songs 7.1.

50. Jerome, *Epistulae*, 22.7, trans. F. A. Wright, *Jerome: Select Letters* (Loeb
    Classical Library, 262; Cambridge, MA: Harvard University Press,
    1933); Paulinus, *Letters*, 23.38, trans. P. G. Walsh, *Letters of St. Paulinus
    of Nola*, vol. 2 (Paramus, NJ: Paulist Press, 1967).

51. Mark S. Burrows, 'Foundations for an Erotic Christology: Bernard
    of Clairvaux on Jesus as "Tender Lover" ', in *Anglican Theological
    Review* 80(4), 1998, pp. 477–93; Anthony Bale (trans.), *The Book of*

Margery Kempe (Oxford: Oxford University Press, 2015), pp. 83, 186. See further Louise Nelstrop, 'Erotic and Nuptial Imagery', in Edward Howells and Mark A. McIntosh (eds.), *The Oxford Handbook of Mystical Theology* (Oxford: Oxford University Press, 2020), pp. 328–46.

52. E.g., *b. Qiddushin* 31a; *b. Berakhot* 43b. See further Elliot R. Wolfson, 'Images of God's Feet: Some Observations on the Divine Body in Judaism', in Howard Eilberg-Schwartz (ed.), *People of the Body: Jews and Judaism from an Embodied Perspective* (Albany, NY: State University of New York Press, 1992), pp. 143–81.

53. Here, I cite the translation in Pieter W. van der Horst, 'The Measurement of the Body: A Chapter in the History of Ancient Jewish Mysticism', in Dirk van der Plas (ed.), *Effigies Dei: Essays on the History of Religions* (Leiden: Brill, 1987), pp. 56–68.

54. Wolfson, 'Images of God's Feet', pp. 162–73.

CHAPTER 5: COVER UP

1. Irene Baldriga, 'The First Version of Michelangelo's Christ for S. Maria Sopra Minerva', in *Burlington Magazine* 142(1173), 2000, pp. 740–5. An earlier publication had mistakenly identified the statue as an early-seventeenth-century derivation of Michelangelo's work: Silvia Danesi Squarzina, 'The Collections of Cardinal Benedetto Giustiniani. Part II', in *Burlington Magazine* 140(1139), 1998, pp. 102–118 (here, p. 112).

2. Norman E. Land, 'A Concise History of the Tale of Michelangelo and Biagio da Cesena', in *Source: Notes in the History of Art* 32(4), 2013, pp. 15–19. Aretino's letter appears in John T. Paoletti and Gary M. Radke, *Art in Renaissance Italy* (third edition) (London: Lawrence King, 2005), p. 505, following John Addington Symonds, *The Life of Michelangelo Buonarroti*, vol. 1 (London: J. C. Nimmo, 1899), pp. 333–36.

3. John O'Malley, 'Art, Trent, and Michelangelo's "Last Judgement"', in *Religions* 3(4), 2012, pp. 344–56. On the wider contexts of the Council of Trent, see Diarmaid MacCulloch, *A History of Christianity: The First Three Thousand Years* (London: Allen Lane, 2009), pp. 655–88.

4. In thinking about this, I have been helped particularly by the essays collected in Joanne Entwistle and Elizabeth Wilson (eds.), *Body Dressing* (Oxford: Berg, 2001).

5. Genesis 3.1–24.

6. Augustine, *De Genesi ad litteram*, 11.31.41, trans. Edmund Hill, *On Genesis* (Works of Saint Augustine, Part 1, Volume 13; Hyde Park, NY: New City Press, 2002). See further Pier Franco Beatrice (trans. Adam Kamesar), *The Transmission of Sin: Augustine and the Pre-Augustinian Sources* (Oxford: Oxford University Press, 2013).

7. Genesis 3.22.

8. Genesis 4.1–26.

9. Galatians 5.16–17.

10. 1 Corinthians 7.2–9, 25–38.

11. Luke 14.26.

12. Matthew 5.27–28; Mark 12.25.

13. Acts of Thomas 12; Gospel of Thomas 79. Both are translated in Elliott, *Apocryphal New Testament*, pp. 144, 452.

14. Luke 21.23.

15. Deuteronomy 24.5.

16. David Biale, *Eros and the Jews: From Biblical Israel to Contemporary America* (Berkeley and Los Angeles, CA: University of California Press, 1997), pp. 53–4.

17. Genesis 1.28.

18. On the difficulties of dating the Song of Songs, see J. Cheryl Exum, *Song of Songs: A Commentary* (Louisville, KY: Westminster John Knox Press, 2005), pp. 66–7.

19. E.g., Exodus 28.42; Ezekiel 44.18. On the symbolic 'neutering' of priests by means of their underpants, see Deborah W. Rooke, 'Breeches of the Covenant: Gender, Garments, and the Priesthood', in Deborah W. Rooke (ed.), *Embroidered Garments: Priests and Gender in Biblical Israel* (Sheffield: Sheffield Phoenix, 2009), pp. 19–37.

20. Tarja S. Philip, *Menstruation and Childbirth in the Bible: Fertility and Impurity* (New York, NY: Peter Lang, 2006); Charlotte Elisheva Fonrobert, *Menstrual Purity: Rabbinic and Christian Reconstructions of Biblical Gender* (Stanford, CA: Stanford University Press, 2000).

21. See further Laurie Guy, '"Naked" Baptism in the Early Church: The Rhetoric and the Reality', in *Journal of Religious History* 27(2), 2003, pp. 133–42; Juliette J. Day, 'Women's Rituals and Women's Ritualizing', in Risto Uro, Juliette J. Day, Richard E. DeMaris and Rikard Roitto (eds.), *The Oxford Handbook of Early Christian Ritual* (Oxford and New York, NY: Oxford University Press, 2019), pp. 644–60; Teresa Berger, 'Women's Liturgical Practices and Leadership Roles in Early Christian Communities', in Joan E. Taylor and Ilaria L. E. Ramelli (eds.), *Patterns of Women's Leadership in Early Christianity* (Oxford and New York, NY: Oxford University Press, 2021), pp. 180–94.

22. See Naomi Koltun-Fromm, *Hermeneutics of Holiness: Ancient Jewish and Christian Notions of Sexuality and Religious Community* (Oxford and New York, NY: Oxford University Press, 2010); Teresa Berger, *Gender Differences and the Making of Liturgical History: Lifting the Veil on Liturgy's Past* (Burlington, VT: Ashgate, 2011), pp. 95–126; David Brakke, 'The Problematization of Nocturnal Emissions in Early Christian Syria, Egypt, and Gaul', in *Journal of Early Christian Studies* 3(4), 1995, pp. 419–60.

23. Ezekiel 1.27–28.

24. Roland Boer, *The Earthy Nature of the Bible: Fleshy Readings of Sex, Masculinity, and Carnality* (London: Palgrave Macmillan, 2012), p. 51; Howard Eilberg-Schwartz, *God's Phallus – and Other Problems for Men and Monotheism* (Boston, MA: Beacon Press, 1994), pp. 180–81.

25. Isaiah 6.3. On the seraphim (and examples of their images on stamp seals), see Izaak J. de Hulster, 'Of Angels and Iconography: Isaiah 6 and the Biblical Concept of Seraphs and Cherubs', in Izaak J. de Hulster, Brent A. Strawn and Ryan P. Bonfiglio (eds.), *Iconographic Exegesis of the Hebrew Bible/Old Testament: An Introduction to Its Method and Practice* (Göttingen: Vandenhoeck & Ruprecht, 2015), pp. 147–64.

26. Isaiah 6.1, 5.

27. G. R. Driver, 'Isaiah 6:1 "his train filled the temple"', in Hans Goedicke (ed.), *Near Eastern Studies in Honor of William Foxwell Albright* (Baltimore, MD: Johns Hopkins University Press, 1971), pp. 87–96; Lyle Eslinger, 'The Infinite in a Finite Organical Perception (Isaiah VI 1–5)', in *Vetus Testamentum* 45(2), 1995, pp. 145–73; cf. Gerlinde Baumann, *Love and Violence: Marriage as Metaphor for the Relationship between YHWH and Israel in the Prophetic Books* (Collegeville, MN: Liturgical Press, 2003), pp. 52–55. For examples of the term's genital use, see Jeremiah 13.22, 26; Nahum 3.5; Lamentations 1.9.

28. *KTU* 1.23.

29. *KTU* 1.4 iv 35–39.

30. ETCSL 1.1.3 (lines 250–58).

31. E.g., Genesis 49.24; Exodus 32; Numbers 23.21–22; 24.8; 1 Kings 12.28–32; 2 Kings 10.29; 17.16; Isaiah 1.24; 49.26; Hosea 8.5–6; 10.5; 13.2; Psalm 132.2, 5. For further discussion, see most recently Theodore J. Lewis, *The Origin and Character of God: Ancient Israelite Religion through the Lens of Divinity* (Oxford and New York, NY: Oxford University Press, 2020), pp. 197–8, 317–33. A fragmentary votive inscription, dated to the

seventh century BCE, refers to a person named Abbiryahu ('Yahu is a Bull'); see *COS* 2.49.

32. Hosea 2.20–23. This translation draws on the discussion in Mayer I. Gruber, *Hosea: A Textual Commentary* (London: T&T Clark, 2017), pp. 154–61.

CHAPTER 6: PHALLIC MASCULINITIES

1. https://twitter.com/realDonaldTrump/status/948355557022420992 [last accessed 7 February 2019].

2. Fiona Bowie, *The Anthropology of Religion: An Introduction* (second edition) (Oxford: Blackwell, 2006), pp. 47–9; drawing on Peter C. Reynolds, *Stealing Fire: The Atomic Bomb as Symbolic Body* (Palo Alto, CA: Iconic Anthropology Press, 1991); Hugh Gusterson, 'Nuclear Weapons Testing: Scientific Experiment as Political Ritual', in Laura Nader (ed.), *Naked Science: Anthropological Inquiry into Boundaries, Power, and Knowledge* (New York, NY: Routledge, 1996), pp. 131–47.

3. *COS* 1.111 (trans. Benjamin R. Foster). See the discussion in Jerrold S. Cooper, 'Female Trouble and Troubled Males: Roiled Seas, Decadent Royals, and Mesopotamian Masculinities in Myth and Practice', in Ilona Zsolnay (ed.), *Being a Man: Negotiating Ancient Constructs of Masculinity* (New York, NY: Routledge, 2017), pp. 112–24 (here, p. 115).

4. Habakkuk 3.9. My translation draws on J. J. M. Roberts, *Nahum, Habakkuk, and Zephaniah: A Commentary* (Louisville, KY: Westminster John Knox Press, 1991), p. 129.

5. Isaiah 13.7–8; Jeremiah 51.56; Ezekiel 21.6; Nahum 2.10.

6. Lamentations 3.12–13, 16. On these verses and their contexts, see Emma Nagouse, ' "To Ransom a Man's Soul": Male Rape and Gender Identity in *Outlander* and "The Suffering Man" of Lamentations 3', in Caroline Blyth, Emily Colgan and Katie B. Edwards (eds.), *Rape Culture, Gender Violence, and Religion: Biblical Perspectives* (London: Palgrave Macmillan, 2018), pp. 143–58 (here, p. 151); Chris Greenough, *The Bible and Sexual Violence Against Men* (Abingdon: Routledge, 2021); Rhiannon Graybill, *Texts After Terror: Rape, Sexual Violence, and the Hebrew Bible* (Oxford: Oxford University Press, 2021), ch. 5. I am grateful to Dr Graybill for sharing this chapter with me ahead of her book's publication.

7. Psalm 18.13–15; Habakkuk 3.8–10; *cf.* Isaiah 51.9–10; Job 26.13.

8. Genesis 9.13–15.

9. Ezekiel 1.28. See further Sandra Jacobs, 'Divine Virility in Priestly Representation: Its Memory and Consummation in Rabbinic Midrash', in Ovidiu Creangă (ed.), *Men and Masculinity in the Hebrew Bible and Beyond* (Sheffield: Sheffield Phoenix Press, 2010), pp. 146–70; Alan Hooker, ' "Show Me Your Glory": The Kabod of Yahweh as Phallic Manifestation?', in Ovidiu Creangă and Peter-Ben Smit (eds.), *Biblical Masculinities Foregrounded* (Sheffield: Sheffield Phoenix Press, 2014), pp. 17–34.

10. Megan Cifarelli, 'Gesture and Alterity in the Art of Ashurnasirpal II of Assyria', in *Art Bulletin* 80(2), 1998, pp. 210–28.

11. Julia Assante, 'Men Looking at Men: The Homoerotics of Power in the State Arts of Assyria', in Ilona Zsolnay (ed.), *Being a Man: Negotiating Ancient Constructs of Masculinity* (New York, NY: Routledge, 2017), pp. 42–82 (here, p. 50).

12. Ann Kessler Guinan, 'Auguries of Hegemony: The Sex Omens of Mesopotamia', in *Gender & History* 9(3), 1997, pp. 462–79 (here, p. 465); M. Stol, *Birth in Babylonia and the Bible: Its Mediterranean Setting* (Groningen: Styx, 2000), p. 2; Biale, *Eros and the Jews*, p. 51.

13. Judith R. Baskin, *Midrashic Women: Formations of the Feminine in Rabbinic Literature* (Hanover, NH: Brandeis University Press, 2002), p. 59; Howard Schwartz, *Tree of Souls: The Mythology of Judaism* (Oxford: Oxford University Press, 2004), pp. 216–17.

14. Ancient south-west Asian gender constructs included a variety of non-binary forms, some of which encompassed intersex persons (both mortal and divine) and those of composite, intersectional, transitional, multiple, fluid, ambiguous or modified genders, including those persons conventionally termed 'eunuchs'. See Ilan Peled, *Masculinities and Third Gender: The Origins and Nature of an Institutionalized Gender Otherness in the Ancient Near East* (Münster: Ugarit-Verlag, 2016); Sophus Helle, ' "Only in Dress?" Methodological Concerns Regarding Non-Binary Gender', in Stephanie L. Budin, Megan Cifarelli, Agnès Garcia-Ventura and Adelina Millet Albà (eds.), *Gender and Methodology in the Ancient Near East: Approaches from Assyriology and Beyond* (Barcelona: Edicions de la Universitat de Barcelona, 2018), pp. 41–53.

15. Martha T. Roth, *Law Collections from Mesopotamia and Asia Minor* (second edition) (Atlanta, GA: Society of Biblical Literature, 1997), p. 160; Martti Nissinen (trans. Kirsi Stjerna), *Homoeroticism in the Biblical World: A Historical Perspective* (Minneapolis, MN: Fortress Press, 1998), pp. 24–8; Susan Ackerman, *When Heroes Love: The*

Ambiguity of Eros in the Stories of Gilgamesh and David (New York, NY: Columbia University Press, 2005), pp. 76–8.

16. Leviticus 18.19–23; 20.13. On 'wasted' semen, see the story of Tamar, Onan and his brothers in Genesis 38 and Howard Eilberg-Schwartz, *The Savage in Judaism: An Anthropology of Israelite Religion and Ancient Judaism* (Bloomington, IN: Indiana University Press, 1990), pp. 182–4; Eve Levavi Feinstein, 'Sexual Pollution in the Hebrew Bible: A New Perspective', in S. Tamar Kamionkowski and Wonil Kim (eds.), *Bodies, Embodiment, and the Theology of the Hebrew Scriptures* (London and New York, NY: T&T Clark, 2010), pp. 114–45. On the biblical prohibition of homoerotic relationships, see especially Saul M. Olyan, ' "And with a Male You Shall Not Lie the Lying Down of a Woman": On the Meaning and Significance of Leviticus 18:22 and 20:13', in *Journal of the History of Sexuality* 5(2), 1994, pp. 179–206; Nissinen, *Homoeroticism in the Biblical World*, pp. 37–44.

17. Samuel Auguste David Tissot (trans. A. Hume), *Onanism: or, a Treatise upon the Disorders Produced by Masturbation: or, The Dangerous Effects of Secret and Excessive Venery* (London: J. Pridden, 1766). An initial – and much shorter – form of Tissot's study was published in Latin in 1758.

18. Genesis 38.8–9.

19. It was a point Augustine made repeatedly in his writings. For references and discussion, see Beatrice, *Transmission of Sin*, pp. 68–70.

20. Tissot, *Onanism*, pp. 26–7.

21. Job 10.9.

22. Gwendolyn Leick, *Sex and Eroticism in Mesopotamian Literature* (London: Routledge, 1994), p. 92.

23. Stol, *Birth in Babylonia and the Bible*, pp. 9–13.

24. Deuteronomy 30.9.

25. ETCSL 6.1.9.a8.

26. Robert D. Biggs, *ŠÀ.ZI.GA. Ancient Mesopotamian Potency Incantations* (Locust Valley, NY: J. J. Augustin, 1967), p. 33; Leick, *Sex and Eroticism*, pp. 206–7.

27. *COS* 1.57 (trans. Gary Beckman).

28. *KTU* 1.6 iii 12–13; 1.6 iv 1–3, 12–14. See *COS* 1.86 (trans. Dennis Pardee).

29. Hosea 9.11–14.

30. One exception is the goddess Nammu, cast in a Sumerian myth as the self-procreating, primeval womb who births heaven and earth; see Leick, *Sex and Eroticism*, pp. 13–14.

31. *COS* 1.9 (trans. James P. Allen). See further Lynn M. Meskell and Rosemary A. Joyce, *Embodied Lives: Figuring Ancient Maya and Egyptian Experience* (London: Routledge, 2003), pp. 95–7.

32. ETCSL 1.1.1. Given the fluidity of divine names and epithets in this text, the precise identity of Enki's first sexual 'partner' is ambiguous. Here, I follow Keith Dickson, 'Enki and Ninhursag: The Trickster in Paradise', in *Journal of Near Eastern Studies* 66(1), 2007, pp. 1–32. See also Thorkild Jacobsen, *The Harps That Once . . . Sumerian Poetry in Translation* (New Haven, CT: Yale University Press, 1987), pp. 181–204.

33. Bachvarova, 'Wisdom of Former Days', pp. 83–111; Jaan Puhvel, '*Genus* and *Sexus* in Hittite', in Simo Parpola and Robert Whiting (eds.), *Sex and Gender in the Ancient Near East* (Helsinki: Neo-Assyrian Text Corpus Project, 2002), pp. 547–50; Stephanie Lynn Budin, 'Phallic Fertility in the Ancient Near East and Egypt', in Nick Hopwood, Rebecca Flemming and Lauren Kassel (eds.), *Reproduction: Antiquity to the Present Day* (Cambridge: Cambridge University Press, 2018), pp. 25–38.

34. An overview can be found in Ilona Zsolnay, 'Gender and Sexuality: Ancient Near East', in Julia O'Brien (ed.), *The Oxford Encyclopedia of the Bible and Gender Studies*, vol. 1 (New York, NY: Oxford University Press, 2014), pp. 273–87.

35. Genesis 2.7.

36. Sirach 24.2–4.

37. Deuteronomy 32.18.

CHAPTER 7: PERFECTING THE PENIS

1. Koons' remarks were reported in Jonathan Jones, 'Jeff Koons: Not Just the King of Kitsch', in the *Guardian*, 30 June 2009, https://www.theguardian.com/artanddesign/2009/jun/30/jeff-koons-exhibition-serpentine.

2. Genesis 17.10–11.

3. Genesis 6.9.

4. Judah Goldin (ed. and trans.), *The Fathers According to Rabbi Nathan* (New Haven, CT: Yale University Press, 1955), p. 23.

5. *KTU* 1.23. Here, I follow Wyatt, *Religious Texts*, pp. 326–27. See further Nicolas Wyatt, 'Circumcision and Circumstance: Male Genital Mutilation in Ancient Israel and Ugarit', in *Journal for the Study of the Old Testament* 33(4), 2009, pp. 405–31.

6. John 15.1–8.

7. Genesis 22.1–19 (note the term 'beloved' in the Greek version); Eusebius, *Praeparatio evangelica*, 1.10.33, trans. E. H. Gifford, *Eusebii Pamphili evangelicae praeparationis*, vol. 3, part 1 (Oxford: Oxford University Press, 1903). In another manuscript, El's sacrificed son is called 'Ieoud' ('Only Begotten'). See further Harold W. Attridge and

Robert A. Oden, *Philo of Byblos: The Phoenician History* (Washington, DC: Catholic Biblical Association of America, 1981), p. 94; Francesca Stavrakopoulou, *King Manasseh and Child Sacrifice: Biblical Distortions of Historical Realities* (Berlin: de Gruyter, 2004), pp. 290–92.

8. Naguib Kanawati and Ali Hassan, *The Teti Cemetery at Saqqara, Volume II: The Tomb of Ankhmahor* (Warminster: Aris & Philips, 1997), p. 49; John F. Nunn, *Ancient Egyptian Medicine* (Norman, OK: University of Oklahoma Press, 1996), pp. 170–71.

9. Francesca Stavrakopoulou, 'Making Bodies: On Body Modification and Religious Materiality in the Hebrew Bible', in *Hebrew Bible and Ancient Israel* 2(4), 2013, pp. 532–53.

10. Herodotus, *Historiae*, 2.37, adapting A. D. Godley (trans.), *Herodotus I: Books 1 and 2* (Loeb Classical Library, 117; Cambridge, MA: Harvard University Press, 1920).

11. Genesis 17.5–6.

12. Leviticus 19.23–25. See Eilberg-Schwartz, *Savage in Judaism*, pp. 149–54.

13. Exodus 22.29–30.

14. For the ritual 'rescue' of the firstborn, see Exodus 13.12–13; 34.19–20; Numbers 18.15–18. Further discussion can be found in Stavrakopoulou, *King Manasseh and Child Sacrifice*, pp. 179–206; Jon D. Levenson, *The Death and Resurrection of the Beloved Son: The Transformation of Child Sacrifice in Judaism and Christianity* (New Haven, CT: Yale University Press, 1993).

15. Genesis 1.28.

16. See, for example, Exodus 4.10; 6.12, 30; Deuteronomy 10.16; Isaiah 6.5–7; Jeremiah 4.4; 6.10. For further discussion, see Saul M. Olyan, *Disability in the Hebrew Bible: Interpreting Mental and Physical Differences* (Cambridge: Cambridge University Press, 2008), pp. 36–38.

17. See T. M. Lemos, 'Shame and Mutilation of Enemies in the Hebrew Bible' in *Journal of Biblical Literature* 125(2), 2006, pp. 225–41; David Tabb Stewart, 'Sexual Disabilities in the Hebrew Bible', in Candida R. Moss and Jeremy Schipper (eds.), *Disability Studies and Biblical Literature* (New York, NY: Palgrave Macmillan, 2011), pp. 67–87; Nicole J. Ruane, 'Bathing, Status and Gender in Priestly Ritual', in Deborah W. Rooke (ed.), *A Question of Sex? Gender and Difference in the Hebrew Bible and Beyond* (Sheffield: Sheffield Phoenix, 2007), pp. 66–81.

18. On the varied social and gendered constructs of 'eunuchs' in ancient south-west Asian contexts, see T. M. Lemos, ' "Like the Eunuch who does not Beget": Gender, Mutilation, and Negotiated Status in the Ancient Near East', in Candida R. Moss and Jeremy

Schipper (eds.), *Disability Studies and Biblical Literature* (New York, NY: Palgrave Macmillan, 2011), pp. 47–66; Assante, 'Men Looking at Men', pp. 64–73; Omar N'Shea, 'Royal Eunuchs and Elite Masculinity in the Neo-Assyrian Empire', in *Near Eastern Archaeology* 79(3), 2016, pp. 214–21.

19. Isaiah 56.3–5. This passage employs the Hebrew term *yad*, which can mean both 'stela' and 'penis' (as well as 'hand'). Eunuchs are probably a target of the regulations in Leviticus 21.20 and Deuteronomy 23.1, in which men whose penises have been 'cut off', or whose testicles are 'crushed', are banned from sacred space.

20. Shaye J. D. Cohen, *Why Aren't Jewish Women Circumcised? Gender and Covenant in Judaism* (Berkeley, CA: University of California Press, 2005), pp. 56–58; Rogaia Mustafa Abusharaf, 'Introduction: The Custom in Question', in Rogaia Mustafa Abusharaf (ed.), *Female Circumcision: Multicultural Perspectives* (Philadelphia, PA: University of Pennsylvania Press, 2006), pp. 1–24; Bret L. Billet, *Cultural Relativism in the Face of the West: The Plight of Women and Female Children* (New York, NY: Palgrave Macmillan, 2007), pp. 19–51.

21. Leviticus 18.19; *cf.* 15.19–24.

22. Leviticus 12.2–5.

23. A point similarly made by Joan E. Taylor, *What Did Jesus Look Like?* (London: Bloomsbury T&T Clark, 2018), pp. 1–2, following S. G. F. Brandon, 'Christ in Verbal and Depicted Imagery: A Problem of Early Christian Iconography', in Jacob Neusner (ed.), *Christianity, Judaism and Other Greco-Roman Cults: Studies for Morton Smith at Sixty, Part 2* (Leiden: Brill, 1975), pp. 165–72.

24. Luke 2.21.

25. Luke 2.21–24. See further Andrew S. Jacobs, *Christ Circumcised: A Study in Early Christian History and Difference* (Philadelphia, PA: University of Pennsylvania Press, 2012), pp. 29–34.

26. John 15.1–8; Colossians 2.9–11.

27. 1 Maccabees 1.11–15; Josephus, *Antiquities*, 12.5.1, trans. Ralph Marcus, *Josephus: Jewish Antiquities*, vol. 5 (Loeb Classical Library, 365; Cambridge, MA: Harvard University Press, 1943).

28. 1 Corinthians 7.18.

29. Nissan Rubin, 'Brit Milah: A Study of Change in Custom', in Elizabeth Wyner Mark (ed.), *The Covenant of Circumcision: New Perspectives on an Ancient Jewish Rite* (Lebanon, NH: Brandeis University Press, 2003), pp. 87–97.

30. Aristophanes, *Clouds*, lines 1010–14, trans. Jeffrey Henderson, *Aristophanes II: Clouds. Wasps. Peace* (Loeb Classical Library, 488;

Cambridge, MA: Harvard University Press, 1998). On the Graeco-
Roman penis, see Frederick M. Hodges, 'The Ideal Prepuce in
Ancient Greece and Rome: Male Genital Aesthetics and Their
Relation to Lipodermos, Circumcision, Foreskin Restoration, and
the Kynodesmē', in *Bulletin of the History of Medicine* 75(3), 2001,
pp. 375–405.

31. For a recent discussion, see Shaun Tougher, *The Roman Castrati:
     Eunuchs in the Roman Empire* (London: Bloomsbury Academic, 2021).

32. Galatians 3.28–29.

33. 1 Corinthians 7.17.

34. For further discussion, see Candida R. Moss, *Divine Bodies:
     Resurrecting Perfection in the New Testament and Early Christianity* (New
     Haven, CT: Yale University Press, 2019), pp. 67–72.

35. For an English translation of the Arabic Infancy Gospel, see
     Alexander Walker (ed. and trans.), *Apocryphal Gospels, Acts and
     Revelations* (Ante-Nicene Library, 16; Edinburgh: T&T Clark, 1873),
     pp. 100–24. It is available online via e-Clavis: Christian Apocrypha, at
     http://www.nasscal.com/e-clavis-christian-apocrypha/arabic-infancy
     -gospel/.

36. Amy G. Remensnyder, *Remembering Kings Past: Monastic Foundation
     Legends in Medieval Southern France* (Ithaca, NY: Cornell University
     Press, 1995), pp. 172–82; Robert B. Palazzo, 'The Veneration of the
     Sacred Foreskin(s) of Baby Jesus: A Documentary Analysis', in James
     P. Helfers (ed.), *Multicultural Europe and Cultural Exchange in the Middle
     Ages and Renaissance* (Tunhout: Brepols, 2005), pp. 155–76; Jacobs,
     Christ Circumcised, pp. ix–x.

37. David Farley, *An Irreverent Curiosity: In Search of the Church's Strangest
     Relic in Italy's Oddest Town* (New York, NY: Gotham Books, 2009).

38. Marc Shell, 'The Holy Foreskin; or, Money, Relics, and Judeo-
     Christianity', in Jonathan Boyarin and Daniel Boyarin (eds.), *Jews and
     Other Differences: The New Jewish Cultural Studies* (Minneapolis, MN:
     University of Minnesota Press, 1997), pp. 345–59.

39. Ulrike Wiethaus (ed. and trans.), *Agnes Blannbekin, Viennese Beguine:
     Life and Revelations* (Cambridge: D. S. Brewer, 2002), p. 35.

40. Prayer 25 in Suzanne Noffke (ed. and trans.), *The Prayers of Catherine
     of Siena* (second edition) (Lincoln, NE: Authors Choice Press, 2001),
     pp. 254–65 (here, p. 256).

41. Here, I borrow the translations in Caroline Walker Bynum, *Holy Feast
     and Holy Fast: The Religious Significance of Food to Medieval Women*
     (Berkeley, CA: University of Los Angeles Press, 1987), pp. 174–75;
     Caroline Walker Bynum, *Fragmentation and Redemption: Essays on*

Gender and the Human Body in Medieval Religion (New York, NY: Zone Books, 1991), pp. 185–86.

42. On the iconography of 'Jewishness' in this period, see Sara Lipton, *Dark Mirror: The Medieval Origins of Anti-Semitic Iconography* (New York, NY: Metropolitan Books, 2014); *cf.* Eric Silverman, *A Cultural History of Jewish Dress* (London: Bloomsbury, 2013), pp. 47–67.

43. Henry Abramson and Carrie Hannon, 'Depicting the Ambiguous Wound: Circumcision in Medieval Art', in Elizabeth Wyner Mark (ed.), *Covenant of Circumcision: New Perspectives on an Ancient Jewish Rite* (Lebanon, NH: Brandeis University Press, 2003), pp. 98–113.

44. This is the manner in which the third-century saint Catherine of Alexandria is presented in Filippino Lippi's lavishly styled *Mystic Marriage of Saint Catherine* (1501) – another celebrated female devotee who was believed to have been wedded to the heavenly Christ. As Catherine kneels at the Christ child's groin, her eyes are fixed on his genitals – as are the eyes of John the Baptist and Saint Sebastian, who stand alongside the throne on which the Madonna and child are seated.

45. Leo Steinberg, *The Sexuality of Christ in Renaissance Art and in Modern Oblivion* (second revised and expanded edition) (Chicago, IL: University of Chicago Press, 1996). A number of the European artworks I discuss here are examined in Steinberg's important book. On erotic celibacy and its queering of gender in Christian art and theology, see Lisa Isherwood, *The Power of Erotic Celibacy: Queering Heteropatriarchy* (London: T&T Clark, 2006), pp. 1–29.

CHAPTER 8: DIVINE SEX

1. E.g., Isaiah 57.3–5; Jeremiah 2.20; 3.1–13; Ezekiel 16; 23; Hosea 2.2–13; 4.12–13.

2. It was a view encouraged by the equally problematic stories of sex and religion peddled by ancient writers including Herodotus, Lucian and Strabo, who sexed-up their accounts of the 'exotic' religions of foreigners with salacious tales of temple-led prostitution and ritualized sex. See further Stephanie Lynn Budin, *The Myth of Sacred Prostitution in Antiquity* (Cambridge: Cambridge University Press, 2008).

3. See, for example, Deuteronomy 16.21; 1 Kings 15.13; 18.19; 2 Kings 21.6; 23.6–7. Modern Bibles often gloss over the name of the goddess and her cult object in these texts by rendering the Hebrew term *asherah* as 'sacred pole'.

4. *COS* 2.47 and 2.52. For an accessible overview of these inscriptions and their religious contexts, see William G. Dever, *Did God Have a Wife? Archaeology and Folk Religion in Ancient Israel* (Grand Rapids, MI: Eerdmans, 2005).

5. Genesis 49.25–26. My translation draws on that in Mark S. Smith, *The Early History of God: Yahweh and the Other Deities in Ancient Israel* (second edition) (Grand Rapids, MI: Eerdmans, 2002), pp. 49–50.

6. Mark S. Smith, *How Human Is God? Seven Questions about God and Humanity in the Bible* (Collegeville, MN: Liturgical Press, 2014), p. 61.

7. Genesis 6.1–4.

8. 1 Corinthians 11.5–10.

9. 2 Peter 2.4–5; Jude 6 (*cf.* 1 Peter 3.18–20). See further Annette Yoshiko Reed, *Fallen Angels and the History of Judaism and Christianity: The Reception of Enochic Literature* (Cambridge: Cambridge University Press, 2005).

10. Genesis 4.1.

11. David E. Bokovoy, 'Did Eve Acquire, Create, or Procreate with Yahweh? A Grammatical and Contextual Reassessment of קנה in Genesis 4:1', in *Vetus Testamentum* 63(1), 2013, pp. 19–35.

12. Genesis 3.20.

13. Hosea 2.14–15.

14. Mayer I. Gruber, *Hosea: A Textual Commentary* (London: Bloomsbury T&T Clark, 2017), p. 147.

15. Ezekiel 16.4–6.

16. Ezekiel 16.7–8. The Hebrew indicates that the girl's hair has 'sprouted' or 'sprung up', implying it is pubic growth.

17. Ruth 3.9.

18. My analysis of Ezekiel 16 (and 23, as I go on to discuss) draws particularly on Fokkelien Van Dijk-Hemmes, 'The Metaphorization of Woman in Prophetic Speech: An Analysis of Ezekiel XXIII', in *Vetus Testamentum* 43(2), 1993, pp. 162–70; Linda M. Day, 'Rhetoric and Domestic Violence in Ezekiel 16', in *Biblical Interpretation* 8(3), 2000, pp. 205–30 (especially pp. 214–16); Gale Yee, *Poor Banished Children of Eve: Woman as Evil in the Hebrew Bible* (Minneapolis, MN: Fortress Press, 2003), pp. 111–134; Sharon Moughtin-Mumby, *Sexual and Marital Metaphors in Hosea, Jeremiah, Isaiah, and Ezekiel* (Oxford: Oxford University Press, 2008); Aaron Koller, 'Pornography or Theology? The Legal Background, Psychological Realism, and Theological Import of Ezekiel 16', in *Catholic Biblical Quarterly* 79(3), 2017, pp. 402–21.

19. Ezekiel 16.20–21; *cf.* 23.37.

20. Ezekiel 16.32–36. See Moshe Greenberg, *Ezekiel 1–20* (Garden City, NY: Doubleday, 1983), pp. 285–86; David Halperin, *Seeking Ezekiel: Text and Psychology* (University Park, PA: Pennsylvania State University Press, 1993), p. 146; S. Tamar Kamionkowski, 'Gender Reversal in Ezekiel 16', in Athalya Brenner (ed.), *Prophets and Daniel: A Feminist Companion to the Bible* (second series) (London: Sheffield Academic Press, 2001), pp. 170–85 (here, p. 177); Paul M. Joyce, *Ezekiel: A Commentary* (London: T&T Clark, 2007), p. 132.

21. Ezekiel 16.37–42. My language here is deliberately loaded. Biblical scholars frequently describe this material in Ezekiel (and similar iterations in Hosea, Isaiah and Jeremiah) as 'pornoprophetic' or 'prophetic pornography', following T. Drorah Setel, 'Prophets and Pornography: Female Sexual Imagery in Hosea', in Letty M. Russell (ed.), *Feminist Interpretation of the Bible* (Louisville, KY: Westminster John Knox Press, 1985), pp. 86–95. See too Athalya Brenner, 'Pornoprophetics Revisited: Some Additional Remarks', in *Journal for the Study of the Old Testament* 28, 1990, pp. 63–89.

22. Ezekiel 23.5–8, 19–21. See Kamionkowski, 'Gender Reversal in Ezekiel 16', pp. 174–7.

23. Ezekiel 23.22, 28, 37.

24. Ezekiel 23.9–10.

25. Ezekiel 23.22–29.

26. Ezekiel 23.31–34.

27. *m. Megillah* 4.10; *t. Megillah* 3.34.

28. Origen's homilies on Ezekiel have reached us via Jerome's Latin translation, a critical edition of which is published as Marcel Borret, SJ. (ed. and trans.), *Homélies sur Ézéchiel: Text Latin, Introduction, Traduction et Notes* (Paris: Éditions du CERF, 1989). Here, I cite Andrew Mein's translation in 'Ezekiel's Women in Christian Interpretation: The Case of Ezekiel 16', in Andrew Mein and Paul M. Joyce (eds.), *After Ezekiel: Essays on the Reception of a Difficult Text* (London: T&T Clark, 2011), pp. 159–83 (here, p. 162).

29. Bryan Bibb, 'There's No Sex in Your Violence: Patriarchal Translation in Ezekiel 16 and 23', in *Review and Expositor* 111(4), 2014, pp. 337–45.

30. 2 Corinthians 11.2.

31. Romans 7.1–4.

32. Ephesians 5.23–24.

33. Matthew 9.14–17; Mark 2.18–20; John 3.28–30.

34. See further Antti Marjanen, *The Woman Jesus Loved: Mary Magdalene in the Nag Hammadi Library and Related Documents* (Leiden: Brill, 1996),

pp. 94–121, 147–69; Christopher Tuckett, 'The Gospel of Mary', in *Revista catalana de teologia* 37(1), 2012, pp. 111–29.

35. Jane Schaberg, *The Resurrection of Mary Magdalene* (London and New York, NY: Continuum, 2004); Ann Graham Brock, 'Mary Magdalene' in Benjamin H. Dunning (ed.), *The Oxford Handbook of New Testament, Gender, and Sexuality* (Oxford and New York, NY: Oxford University Press, 2019), pp. 429–47.

36. April D. DeConick, *Holy Misogyny: Why the Sex and Gender Conflicts in the Early Church Still Matter* (New York, NY: Continuum, 2011), pp. 129–45; see also Anthony Le Donne, *The Wife of Jesus: Ancient Texts and Modern Scandals* (London: Oneworld, 2013).

Chapter 9: Back and Beyond

1. *Itinerarium Egeriae* 4.1–3, trans. M. L. McClure and C. L. Feltoe, *The Pilgrimage of Etheria* (London: Society for the Promotion of Christian Knowledge, 1919), p. 4.

2. Given Egeria's use of scripture as her own guidebook, the 'cave' she saw is likely to be the huge boulder on Sinai's peak, rather than the small cavern known today as the Cave of Moses. Note Anne McGowan and Paul F. Bradshaw (ed. and trans.), *The Pilgrimage of Egeria: A New Translation of the* Itinerarium Egeriae *with Introduction and Commentary* (Collegeville, MN: Liturgical Press, 2018), p. 107, n. 5.

3. Exodus 33.22–23.

4. Jeremiah 2.27; 18.17; 32.33.

5. *KTU* 1.2 iv 25–26.

6. *KTU* 1.3 iii 32–35; 1.4 ii 16–20. See further *COS* 1.86, n. 89.

7. Ezekiel 1.27; Daniel 7.9–10.

8. Exodus 24.17.

9. Jean Bottéro (trans. Teresa Lavender Fagan), *Religion in Ancient Mesopotamia* (Chicago, IL: University of Chicago Press, 2001), p. 61; Francesca Rochberg, ' "The Stars Their Likeness": Perspectives on the Relation between Celestial Bodies and Gods in Ancient Mesopotamia', in Barbara Nevling Porter (ed.), *What Is a God? Anthropomorphic and Non-Anthropomorphic Aspects of Deity in Ancient Mesopotamia* (Winona Lake, IN: Eisenbrauns/Casco Bay Assyriological Institute, 2009), pp. 41–91 (here, p. 49); Dalley, *Myths from Mesopotamia*, p. 236.

10. Shiyanthi Thavapalan, 'Radiant Things for Gods and Men: Lightness and Darkness in Mesopotamian Language and Thought', *Colour Turn*

1(7), 2018, pp. 1–36; Kim Benzel, ' "What Goes In Is What Comes Out" – But What Was Already There? Divine Materials and Materiality in Ancient Mesopotamia', in Beate Pongratz-Leisten and Karen Sonik (eds.), *The Materiality of Divine Agency* (Berlin: de Gruyter, 2015), pp. 89–118; David Wengrow, 'Art and Material Culture', in Ann C. Gunter (ed.), *A Companion to Ancient Near Eastern Art* (Hoboken, NJ: Wiley, 2019), pp. 25–48.

11. Victor Avigdor Hurowitz, 'What Goes In Is What Comes Out: Materials for Creating Cult Statues', in Gary M. Beckman and Theodore J. Lewis (eds.), *Text, Artifact, and Image: Revealing Ancient Israelite Religion* (Providence, RI: Brown Judaic Studies, 2010), pp. 3–23 (here, p. 9).

12. Mark E. Cohen, *The Canonical Lamentations of Ancient Mesopotamia*, vol. 2 (Potomac, MD: Capital Decisions, 1988), p. 582; Shawn Zelig Aster, *The Unbeatable Light: Melammu and Its Biblical Parallels* (Münster: Ugarit-Verlag, 2012), p. 44, n. 42.

13. Text K2652 (line 19) in Rykle Borger, *Beiträge zum Inschriftenwerk Assurbanipals: Die Prismenklassen A, B, C = K, D, E, F, G, H, J und T sowie andere Inschriften* (Wiesbaden: Harrossowitz, 1996), p. 102; Stephanie Dalley, *Esther's Revenge at Susa: From Sennacherib to Ahasuerus* (Oxford: Oxford University Press, 2007), p. 77.

14. Dalley, *Myths from Mesopotamia*, p. 96.

15. E.g., Deuteronomy 33.2; Isaiah 60.1–2; Ezekiel 1.27–28; Job 37.22; 40.10; Psalm 104.2.

16. Habakkuk 3.3–4, 10–12; *cf.* Deuteronomy 33.2–3. Similar translations and further discussions of this difficult text can be found in Aster, *The Unbeatable Light*, pp. 337–51; Michael Fishbane, *Biblical Myth and Rabbinic Mythmaking* (Oxford: Oxford University Press, 2003), pp. 53–4; Theodore J. Lewis, 'Divine Fire in Deuteronomy 33:2', in *Journal of Biblical Literature* 132(4), 2013, pp. 791–803.

17. Isaiah 2.10.

18. William H. Propp, *Exodus 19–40: A New Translation with Introduction and Commentary* (New York, NY: Doubleday, 2006), p. 608. See further Avraham Grossman, 'The School of Literal Jewish Exegesis in Northern France', in Magne Sæbø (ed.), *Hebrew Bible/Old Testament: The History of Its Interpretation, Vol. 1, Part 2 – Middle Ages* (Göttingen: Vandenhoeck & Ruprecht, 2000), pp. 321–71 (here, pp. 367–69).

19. Exodus 34.29–35. See William H. Propp, 'The Skin of Moses' Face – Transfigured or Disfigured?', in *Catholic Biblical Quarterly* 49(3), 1987, pp. 375–86; Seth L. Sanders, 'Old Light on Moses' Shining Face', in *Vetus Testamentum* 52(3), 2002, pp. 400–6.

20. Daniel 7.9; 10.6; 1 Enoch 14.18–23.
21. Manuscript 1QS 3.18–25, trans. Florentino García Martínez and Eibert J. C. Tigchelaar, *The Dead Sea Scrolls: Study Edition*, vol. 2 (Leiden: Brill, 1998). See further Cecilia Wassen, 'Angels in the Dead Sea Scrolls', in Friedrich Reiterer, Tobias Nicklas and Karin Schöpflin (eds.), *Deuterocanonical and Cognate Literature Yearbook 2007. Angels: The Concept of Celestial Beings – Origins, Development and Reception* (Berlin: de Gruyter, 2007), pp. 499–523.
22. Luke 2.9; Matthew 28.3.
23. Luke 24.4; John 20.12.
24. Revelation 1.12–16.
25. 2 Corinthians 11.14.
26. Matthew 17.2; Mark 9.3; Luke 9.31–32.
27. Acts of John 90, trans. Elliott, *The Apocryphal New Testament*, p. 317.
28. John 8.12; 9.5.
29. John 1.3–5, 9.
30. 1 Corinthians 15.54.
31. Revelation 3.4–5; 4.4; 6.10–11; 7.9, 13. See also Candida R. Moss, *Divine Bodies: Resurrecting Perfection in the New Testament and Early Christianity* (New Haven, CT: Yale University Press, 2019), pp. 97–109. On Paul's language, see Martin F. Connell, 'Clothing the Body of Christ: An Inquiry about the Letters of Paul', in *Worship* 85(2), 2011, pp. 128–46; M. David Litwa, *We Are Being Transformed: Deification in Paul's Soteriology* (Berlin: de Gruyter, 2012), especially pp. 119–71.
32. J. N. D. Kelly, *Early Christian Doctrines* (fifth revised edition) (London: A&C Black, 1977), p. 232.
33. Thomas F. Mathews, *The Clash of Gods: A Reinterpretation of Early Christian Art* (revised edition) (Princeton, NJ: Princeton University Press, 1993), pp. 115–19.
34. E.g., Mathews, *Clash of Gods*, pp. 116–17; Taylor, *What Did Jesus Look Like?* p. 72.
35. Bissera V. Pentcheva, *The Sensual Icon: Space, Ritual, and the Senses in Byzantium* (University Park, PA: Penn State University Press, 2010); Anna Kartsonis, 'The Responding Icon', in Linda Safran (ed.), *Heaven on Earth: Art and the Church in Byzantium* (University Park, PA: Penn State University Press, 1998), pp. 58–80.
36. John 1.5; 13.27–30; 18.1–3. In John 3.1–21, a Pharisee named Nicodemus visits Jesus at night, but appears to remain 'in the dark' when he fails to grasp Jesus' enlightening teaching, prompting Jesus to retort, 'Are you a teacher of Israel, and yet you do not understand these things?'

37. Acts 26.12–18; *cf.* 9.3–9; 22.4–16.

38. Some of the roots of modern discourse about 'race' and racism (sometimes termed 'proto-racism') may lie, nonetheless, in the ancient world. See Denise E. McCoskey, *Race: Antiquity and Its Legacy* (Oxford: Oxford University Press, 2012); Benjamin H. Isaac, *The Invention of Racism in Classical Antiquity* (Princeton, NJ: Princeton University Press, 2004); Benjamin Isaac, Joseph Zingler and Miriam Eliav-Feldon (eds.), *The Origins of Racism in the West* (Cambridge: Cambridge University Press, 2009). On race and the Bible, see Rodney S. Sadler Jr, *Can a Cushite Change His Skin? An Examination of Race, Ethnicity, and Othering in the Hebrew Bible* (London and New York, NY: T&T Clark, 2005); Brian Rainey, *Religion, Ethnicity, and Xenophobia in the Bible: A Theoretical, Exegetical and Theological Survey* (Abingdon: Routledge, 2019); David G. Horrell, *Ethnicity and Inclusion: Religion, Race, and Whiteness in Constructions of Jewish and Christian Identities* (Grand Rapids, MI: Eerdmans, 2020).

39. Gay L. Byron, *Symbolic Blackness and Ethnic Difference in Early Christian Literature* (London and New York, NY: Routledge, 2002); Denise Kimber Buell, *Why This New Race? Ethnic Reasoning in Early Christianity* (New York, NY: Columbia University Press, 2005).

40. Homily 18 in Marie Ligouri Ewald (trans.), *The Homilies of Saint Jerome: Volume I (1–59 On the Psalms)* (Washington, DC: Catholic University of America, 1964), pp. 135–45 (here, p. 140).

41. Acts of Peter 8, trans. Elliott, *Apocryphal New Testament*, p. 406. For the Epistle of Barnabas (here, 4.9–14 and 20.1–2), see the translation in Michael W. Holmes, *The Apostolic Fathers in English* (third revised edition) (Grand Rapids, MI: Baker Academic, 2006), pp. 172–301. For further discussion, see Robert E. Hood, *Begrimed and Black: Christian Traditions on Blacks and Blackness* (Minneapolis, MA: Fortress Press, 1994), pp. 76–77; Clare K. Rothschild, 'Ethiopianising the Devil: ὁ μέλας in Barnabas 4', in *New Testament Studies* 65(2), 2019, pp. 223–45.

42. The translation is taken from Carolinne White (ed. and trans.), *Early Christian Lives* (London: Penguin, 1998), pp. 7–70 (here, pp. 12–13).

43. Genesis 10.6.

44. I have found the following works particularly helpful: David M. Goldenberg, *The Curse of Ham: Race and Slavery in Early Judaism, Christianity, and Islam* (Princeton, NJ: Princeton University Press, 2003); Sylvester A. Johnson, *The Myth of Ham in Nineteenth Century American Christianity: Race, Heathens, and the People of God* (New York, NY: Palgrave Macmillan, 2004); David M. Whitford, *The Curse of Ham in the Early Modern Era: The Bible and the Justifications for Slavery*

(Farnham: Ashgate, 2009); Geraldine Heng, *The Invention of Race in the European Middle Ages* (Cambridge: Cambridge University Press, 2018); Nyasha Junior, 'The Mark of Cain and White Violence', in *Journal of Biblical Literature* 139(4), 2020, pp. 661–73.

45. See especially Sylvester A. Johnson, *African American Religions, 1500–2000: Colonialism, Democracy, and Freedom* (New York, NY: Cambridge University Press, 2015); Mukti Barton, 'The Bible in Black Theology', in *Black Theology* 9(1), 2011, pp. 57–76; J. Kameron Carter, *Race: A Theological Account* (New York, NY: Oxford University Press, 2008); Alejandro F. Botta and Pablo R. Andiñach (eds.), *The Bible and the Hermeneutics of Liberation* (Atlanta, GA: Society of Biblical Literature, 2009); Musa W. Dube, 'The Scramble for Africa as the Biblical Scramble for Africa: Postcolonial Perspectives', in Musa Dube, Andrew M. Mbuvi and Dora R. Mbuwayesango (eds.), *Postcolonial Perspectives in African Biblical Interpretations* (London and New York, NY: Routledge, 1997), pp. 1–26; Edward J. Blum and Paul Harvey, *The Color of Christ: The Son of God and the Saga of Race in America* (Chapel Hill, NC: University of North Carolina Press, 2012); Traci C. West, 'When a White Man-God Is the Truth and the Way for Black Christians', in George Yancy (ed.), *Christology and Whiteness: What Would Jesus Do?* (London and New York, NY: Routledge, 2012), pp. 114–27.

46. On the intersection and history of Christian antisemitism, racialized blackness and white supremacy, it is essential to read James H. Cone, *The Cross and the Lynching Tree* (Maryknoll, NY: Orbis, 2011). For the intersection of Christian whiteness and its antisemitic and Islamophobic agendas, see also Nasar Meer, 'Racialization and Religion: Race, Culture and Difference in the Study of Antisemitism and Islamophobia', in *Ethnic and Racial Studies* 36(3), 2013, pp. 385–98. On science and racism, see Angela Saini, *Superior: The Return of Race Science* (Boston, MA: Beacon Press, 2019); Adam Rutherford, *How to Argue with a Racist: History, Science, Race and Reality* (London: Weidenfeld & Nicolson, 2020).

CHAPTER 10: INSIDE OUT

1. For Von Hagen's description of his work as 'edutainment', see Stuart Jeffries, 'The Naked and the Dead', in the *Guardian*, 19 March 2002, https://www.theguardian.com/education/2002/mar/19/arts.highereducation. Global attendance figures for the 'Body Worlds' exhibition can be found at https://bodyworlds.com.

2. ETCSL 1.8.1.5 (lines 126–129).
3. Sarah B. Graff, 'The Head of Humbaba', in *Archiv für Religionsgeschichte* 14(1), 2013, pp. 129–42.
4. Mark S. Smith, 'The Heart and Innards in Israelite Emotional Expressions: Notes from Anthropology and Psychobiology', in *Journal of Biblical Literature* 117(3), 1998, pp. 427–36; Thomas Staubli and Silvia Schroer (trans. Linda M. Maloney), *Body Symbolism in the Bible* (Collegeville, MN: Liturgical Press, 2001), pp. 68–81.
5. Anat's visceral response occurs in *KTU* 1.3 ii 25–27. For Marduk's response, and the translation I cite, see Daniel I. Block, 'Divine Abandonment: Ezekiel's Adaptation of an Ancient Near Eastern Motif', in Margaret S. Odell and John T. Strong (eds.), *The Book of Ezekiel: Theological and Anthropological Perspectives* (Atlanta, GA: Society of Biblical Literature, 2000), pp. 15–42 (here, pp. 84–5).
6. Jeremiah 4.19–20; cf. 8.18–22; 9.1–3, 10–11, 18–19; 14.31–32. Here, I follow J. J. M. Roberts, 'The Motif of the Weeping God in Jeremiah and Its Background in the Lament Tradition of the Ancient Near East', in *Old Testament Essays* 5(3), 1992, pp. 361–4. Further support for the view that Yahweh is speaking in Jeremiah 4.19–22 can be found in K. M. O'Connor, 'The Tears of God and the Divine Character in Jeremiah 2–9', in Timothy Beal and Todd Linafelt (eds.), *God in the Fray: A Tribute to Walter Brueggemann* (Minneapolis, MN: Fortress Press, 1998), pp. 172–85; cf. David A. Bosworth, 'The Tears of God in the Book of Jeremiah', in *Biblica* 94(1), 2013, pp. 24–46.
7. See, for example, the sensory dynamics expressed in Isaiah 16.11; 42.14; Jeremiah 8.18; 31.20.
8. Isaiah 63.15–17.
9. Anne Löhnert, 'Manipulating the Gods: Lamenting in Context', in Karen Radner and Eleanor Robson (eds.), *The Oxford Handbook of Cuneiform Culture* (Oxford: Oxford University Press, 2011), pp. 402–17 (here, p. 412). In this quotation, I have glossed '*gudu*-priest' as 'cultic expert' in the light of the discussions in Graham Cunningham, '*Deliver Me from Evil': Mesopotamian Incantations 2500–1500 BC* (Rome: Pontifical Biblical Institute, 2007), p. 14, and Joan Goodnick Westenholz, 'In the Service of the Gods: The Ministering Clergy', in Harriet Crawford (ed.), *The Sumerian World* (London: Routledge, 2013), pp. 246–74 (especially pp. 262–3).
10. Adapted from Samuel N. Kramer, 'BM 29616: The Fashioning of the Gala', in *Acta Sumerilogica* 3, 1981, pp. 1–11.
11. Dahlia Shehata, 'Sounds from the Divine: Religious Musical Instruments in the Ancient Near East', in Joan Goodnick Westenholz,

Yossi Maurey and Edwin Seroussi (eds.), *Music in Antiquity: The Near East and the Mediterranean* (Berlin: de Gruyter, 2014), pp. 102–28; Uri Gabbay, 'Drums, Hearts, Bulls, and Dead Gods: The Theology of the Ancient Mesopotamian Kettledrum', in *Journal of Ancient Near Eastern Religions* 18(1), 2018, pp. 1–47.

12. Jeremiah 9.17–18.

13. Sarit Paz, *Drums, Women, and Goddesses: Drumming and Gender in Iron Age II Israel* (Fribourg/Göttingen: Academic Press/Vandenhoeck & Ruprecht, 2007); Raz Kletter and Katri Saarelainen, 'Judean Drummers', in *Zeitschrift des Deutschen Palästina-Vereins* 127(1), 2011, pp. 11–30.

14. *COS* 1.147 (trans. Tremper Longman III). See further C. J. Gadd, 'The Harran Inscriptions of Nabonidus', in *Anatolian Studies* 8, 1958, pp. 35–92.

15. Hosea 11.8.

16. 1 Kings 3.26.

17. E.g., Jeremiah 7.31; 19.5; 32.35.

18. Genesis 6.5–7.

19. Deuteronomy 29.4.

20. For Yahweh's remark about a heart 'after my own', see Jeremiah 3.15; *cf.* 1 Samuel 13.14. For a 'heart of flesh', see Ezekiel 11.19; 36.26. David's ritual title 'shepherd' is attested in 2 Samuel 5.2 and Ezekiel 34.23. The fanciful story of his origins as shepherd-boy can be found in 1 Samuel 16–17. Other biblical characters ideologically cast as the royal shepherd include Jesus (John 10.11; Hebrews 13.20; Revelation 7.17) and God himself (Genesis 48.15; 49.24; Psalms 23; 80.1).

21. Following P.-R. Berger, 'Der Kyros-Zylinder mit dem Zusatzfragment BIN II Nr. 32 und die akkadischen Personennamen in Danielbuch', in *Zeitschrift für Assyriologie* 64(2), 1975, pp. 192–234. For an English translation of the inscription, see *COS* 2.124. See further Irving L. Finkel (ed.), *The Cyrus Cylinder: The King of Persia's Proclamation from Ancient Babylon* (London: I. B. Tauris, 2013).

22. Isaiah 43–45. Here, Yahweh declares Cyrus his 'messiah' in 45.13, and his 'shepherd' in 44.28.

23. 2 Chronicles 36.23.

24. 1 Chronicles 28.9; Psalm 7.9. Yahweh's comment about the evil inclinations of humans' hearts occurs in Genesis 6.5.

25. 1 Samuel 2.35.

26. Diana Edelman, 'The "Seeing God" Motif and Yahweh as a God of Justice', in Oliver Artus (ed.), *Loi et justice dans la littérature du Proche-Orient ancien* (Wiesbaden: Harrassowitz, 2013), pp. 197–224;

Christophe Nihan and Julia Rhyder, 'Aaron's Vestments in Ezekiel 28 and Priestly Leadership', in Katharina Pyschny and Sarah Schulz (eds.), *Debating Authority: Concepts of Leadership in the Pentateuch and the Former Prophets* (Berlin: de Gruyter, 2018), pp. 45–67.

27. Exodus 28.15–30.
28. John 1.18.
29. Matthew 9.4; Mark 2.8; Luke 5.22; Revelation 2.23.
30. Romans 10.9.
31. Proverbs 14.33.
32. 1 Kings 3.9; 4.29–34.
33. ETCSL 4.07.3. I quote the more poetic translation in Charles Halton and Saana Svärd, *Women's Writing of Ancient Mesopotamia: An Anthology of the Earliest Female Authors* (Cambridge: Cambridge University Press, 2018), pp. 79–87.
34. Job 10.13; 28.14, 22.
35. Jeremiah 10.11–12. In this passage (as elsewhere in the Hebrew Bible), the Hebrew term *eretz* can mean both 'earth' and 'underworld'. The latter is more appropriate in these verses, given that they evoke the tripartite structure of the universe (underworld, earthly realm, heavens).
36. Manuscript 11Q5, column 26, lines 10–12, trans. Florentino García Martínez and Eibert J. C. Tigchelaar, *The Dead Sea Scrolls: Study Edition*, vol. 2 (Leiden: Brill, 1998).
37. Ezekiel 28.2, 6–9.
38. Ezekiel 28.12–13. On biblical reflections of the ritual ascent of the king, see Nicolas Wyatt, *Myths of Power: A Study of Royal Myth and Ideology in Ugaritic and Biblical Tradition* (Münster: Ugarit-Verlag, 1996).
39. Ezekiel 28.17. The breastplate is the gemstone 'covering' described in verse 13.
40. On the relationship between these traditions in Genesis and Ezekiel, see Dexter E. Callender, *Adam in Myth and History: Ancient Israelite Perspectives on the Primal Human* (Winona Lake, IN: Eisenbrauns, 2000).
41. Genesis 3.22–24. On the muddle of trees in the garden, see Ziony Zevit, *What Really Happened in the Garden of Eden?* (New Haven, CT: Yale University Press, 2013), pp. 93–95; Nicolas Wyatt, 'A Royal Garden: The Ideology of Eden', in *Scandinavian Journal of the Old Testament* 28(1), 2014, pp. 1–35.
42. Genesis 3.14, 16–19. On the loss of the serpent's wings, see Philip J. King and Lawrence E. Stager, *Life in Biblical Israel* (Louisville: Westminster John Knox, 2001), p. 84.

CHAPTER 11: FROM BELLY TO BOWEL

1. Reinhard Pummer, *The Samaritans: A Profile* (Grand Rapids, MI: Eerdmans, 2016); Gary N. Knoppers, *Jews and Samaritans: The Origins and History of Their Early Relations* (Oxford: Oxford University Press, 2013).
2. Exodus 11–12.
3. Michael Dietler, 'Feasting and Fasting', in Timothy Insoll (ed.), *The Oxford Handbook of the Archaeology of Ritual and Religion* (Oxford: Oxford University Press, 2011), pp. 179–94 (here, p. 179).
4. Rebekah Welton, *'He Is a Glutton and a Drunkard': Deviant Consumption in the Hebrew Bible* (Leiden: Brill, 2020), pp. 29–66.
5. *COS* 1.159 (trans. Jacob Klein).
6. *COS* 1.111 (trans. Benjamin R. Foster).
7. The classic study of the king as the divinely appointed gardener is Geo Widengren, *The King and the Tree of Life in Ancient Near Eastern Religion* (Wiesbaden: Harrassowitz, 1951). See also Mirko Novák, 'The Artificial Paradise: Programme and Ideology of Royal Gardens', in Simo Parpola and Robert M. Whiting (eds.), *Sex and Gender in the Ancient Near East* (Helsinki: Neo-Assyrian Text Corpus Project, 2002), pp. 443–60.
8. Genesis 4.1–16.
9. Genesis 4.3–4.
10. Yvonne Sherwood, 'Cutting Up "Life": Sacrifice as a Device for Clarifying – and Tormenting – Fundamental Distinctions between Human, Animal and Divine', in Jennifer L. Koosed (ed.), *The Bible and Posthumanism* (Atlanta, GA: Society of Biblical Literature, 2014), pp. 247–97.
11. Translated by Jared L. Miller, *Royal Hittite Instructions and Related Administrative Texts* (Atlanta, GA: Society of Biblical Literature, 2013), pp. 244–65.
12. *COS* 1.130 and 1.132 (both translated by Benjamin R. Foster).
13. Genesis 8.20–21.
14. Seth Kunin, *We Think What We Eat: Neo-Structuralist Analysis of Israelite Food Rules and Other Cultural and Textual Practices* (London: T&T Clark, 2003), pp. 83–98; Emmanuelle Vila and Anne-Sophie Dalix, 'Alimentation et idéologie: la place du sanglier et du porc à l'Âge du Bronze sur la côte levantine', in *Anthropozoologica* 39(1), 2004, pp. 219–36; Welton, *He Is a Glutton and a Drunkard*, pp. 87–91; Lidar Sapir-Hen, 'Food, Pork Consumption, and Identity in Ancient Israel', in *Near Eastern Archaeology* 82(1), 2019, pp. 52–59.

15. E.g., Numbers 4.7; 28.1–15; Leviticus 24.5–9. Here, I borrow Stuart Weeks' playful language in 'Man-Made Gods? Idolatry in the Old Testament', in Stephen C. Barton (ed.), *Idolatry: False Worship in the Bible, Early Judaism, and Christianity* (London and New York, NY: T&T Clark, 2007), pp. 7–21.
16. 1 Kings 8.63; 2 Chronicles 15.11.
17. See Dietler, 'Feasting and Fasting', pp. 179–94; *cf.* Stefan M. Maul, 'Den Gott ernähren. Überlegungen zum regelmässigen Opfer in altorientalischen Tempeln', in Eftychia Stavrianopoulou, Axel Michaels and Claus Ambos (eds.), *Transformations in Sacrificial Practices: From Antiquity to Modern Times* (Berlin: Lit Verlag, 2008), pp. 75–86; Stefania Ermidoro, *Commensality and Ceremonial Meals in the Neo-Assyrian Period* (Venice: Edizioni Ca' Foscari, 2015).
18. Isaiah 1.11–12; Amos 5.21–22.
19. Isaiah 1.17; Amos 5.11, 14.
20. Christian A. Eberhart, 'A Neglected Feature of Sacrifice in the Hebrew Bible: Remarks on the Burning Rite on the Altar', in *Harvard Theological Review* 97(4), 2004, pp. 485–93; Anne Katrine de Hemmer Gudme, '"If I were hungry, I would not tell you" (Ps 50, 12): Perspectives on the Care and Feeding of the Gods in the Hebrew Bible', in *Scandinavian Journal of the Old Testament* 28(2), 2014, pp. 172–84.
21. Finbarr Barry Flood, 'Bodies and Becoming: Mimesis, Mediation, and the Ingestion of the Sacred in Christianity and Islam', in Sally M. Promey (ed.), *Sensational Religion: Sensory Cultures in Material Practice* (New Haven, CT: Yale University Press, 2014), pp. 459–93.
22. Leviticus 6.27.
23. Jeremiah 1.9; 15.16; Ezekiel 2.8–3.4; Daniel 5.1–31.
24. *COS* 1.159 (trans. Jacob Klein). While some have argued Enki's winning creature is a person with disabilities, most agree it is a baby – perhaps born prematurely.
25. *KTU* 1.114. See further Wyatt, *Religious Texts*, pp. 404–13. On the tablet itself, a dividing line separates the myth from the cure, but the implication is that El's recovery was facilitated by the recipe (part of which is missing).
26. Amos 6.4–7; Jeremiah 16.5–9.
27. Isaiah 28.7–8.
28. Jeremiah 25.27.
29. Ezekiel 23.31–34; Jeremiah 25.15–29; Habakkuk 2.16; Obadiah 1.16; Psalm 75.16; Matthew 26.39–45; Mark 14.36; Luke 22.42. In John 18.11, Jesus is resolved to drink from God's cup.

30. Malachi 1.7–14.
31. Malachi 2.3.
32. Malachi 1.7, 13–14; 2.3. On the 'defiling' nature of excrement, see Ezekiel 4.12–15. For 'matter out of place', see Mary Douglas, *Purity and Danger: An Analysis of Concepts of Pollution and Taboo* (London: Routledge & Kegan Paul, 1966).
33. Estēe Dvorjetski, 'Public Health in Ancient Palestine: Historical and Archaeological Aspects of Lavatories', in Ann Killebrew and Gabriele Faßbeck (eds.), *Viewing Ancient Jewish Art and Archaeology* (Leiden: Brill, 2015), pp. 48–100.
34. 1 Kings 14.10; Isaiah 4.4; 25.10. See further Gershon Hepner, 'Scatology in the Bible', in *Scandinavian Journal of the Old Testament* 18(2), 2004, pp. 278–95. On Yahweh's scatological attacks (including that in Malachi), see Yvonne Sherwood, *Biblical Blaspheming: Trials of the Sacred for a Secular Age* (Cambridge: Cambridge University Press, 2012), pp. 143–75.
35. Nahum 3.5–6. On the abused woman as Ishtar, see Aron Pinker, 'Descent of the Goddess Ishtar to the Netherworld and Nahum II 8', in *Vetus Testamentum* 55(1), 2005, pp. 89–100; Laurel Lanner, *'Who Will Lament Her?' The Feminine and Fantastic in the Book of Nahum* (London and New York, NY: T&T Clark, 2006), especially pp. 37–43; Gregory D. Cook, 'Nahum and the Question of Rape', in *Bulletin for Biblical Research* 26(3), 2016, pp. 341–52.
36. 2 Kings 10.18–27.
37. On eating excrement as a biblical motif of siege, warfare and displacement, see 2 Kings 18.27; Isaiah 36.12; Ezekiel 4.12. For the Lachish toilet, see Saar Ganor and Igor Kreimerman, 'Going to the Bathroom at Lachish', in *Biblical Archaeology Review* 43(6), 2017, pp. 56–60; Saar Ganor and Igor Kreimerman, 'An Eighth-Century B.C.E. Gate Shrine at Tel Lachish, Israel', in *Bulletin of the American Schools of Oriental Research* 381(1), 2019, pp. 211–36; Yosef Garfinkel, 'The Cultic Reform in the Gate Shrine of Lachish', in *Strata: Bulletin of the Anglo-Israel Archaeological Society* 38, 2020, pp. 31–44.
38. Leviticus 18.25, 28 (*cf.* 20.22); Lamentations 3.45; Ezekiel 22.15–16. See further Thomas Staubli, 'Feces: The Primary Disgust Elicitor in the Hebrew Bible and in the Ancient Near East', in Annette Schellenberg and Thomas Krüger (eds.), *Sounding Sensory Profiles in the Ancient Near East* (Atlanta, GA: Society of Biblical Literature Press, 2019), pp. 119–43. On the most abject as the stuff of self, see Julia Kristeva (trans. Leon S. Roudiez), *Powers of Horror: An Essay in Abjection* (New York, NY: Columbia University Press, 1982), especially pp. 90–112.

39. 1 Kings 18.20–40.

40. 1 Kings 18.27. Here, my translation draws on Gary A. Rendsburg, 'The Mock of Baal in 1 Kings 18:27', in *Catholic Biblical Quarterly* 50(3), 1988, pp. 414–17.

41. Daniel Bodi, 'Les *gillûlîm* chez Ézéchiel et dans l'Ancien Testament, et les différentes pratiques cultuelles associées à ce terme', in *Revue Biblique* 100(4), 1993, pp. 481–510.

42. Deuteronomy 4.28. See further Nathaniel B. Levtow, *Images of Others: Iconic Politics in Ancient Israel* (Winona Lake, IN: Eisenbrauns, 2008); Saul M. Olyan, 'The Ascription of Physical Disability as a Stigmatizing Strategy in Biblical Iconic Polemics', in *Journal of Hebrew Scriptures* 9(14), 2009, pp. 1–15.

43. Josephus, *Jewish War*, 2.8.9, trans. H. St. J. Thackeray, *Josephus: The Jewish War*, vol. 1 (Loeb Classical Library, 203; Cambridge, MA: Harvard University Press, 1927). For further discussion, see Ian Werrett, 'A Scroll in One Hand and a Mattock in the Other: Latrines, Essenes, and Khirbet Qumran', *Revue de Qumrân* 23(4) 2008, pp. 475–89.

44. Manuscript 11Q19 46.13–16, trans. Florentino García Martínez and Eibert J. C. Tigchelaar, *The Dead Sea Scrolls: Study Edition*, vol. 2 (Leiden: Brill, 1998), p. 1265.

45. *m. Tamid* 1.1; *cf.* Leviticus 15.16. See further Jodi Magness, 'Toilet Practices, Purity Concerns, and Sectarianism in the Late Second Temple Period', in Benedict Eckhardt (ed.), *Jewish Identity and Politics between the Maccabees and Bar Kokhba: Groups, Normativity, and Rituals* (Leiden: Brill, 2012), pp. 51–70.

46. Rachel Neis, ' "Their Backs toward the Temple, and Their Faces toward the East": The Temple and Toilet Practices in Rabbinic Palestine and Babylonia', in *Journal for the Study of Judaism* 43(3), 2012, pp. 328–68.

47. These rabbinic toilet tales can be found in Dvorjetski, 'Public Health in Ancient Palestine', pp. 79–80.

48. Psalm 50.12.

49. *Derekh Eretz Rabbah* 3.3, as discussed in Jonathan Wyn Schofer, *Confronting Vulnerability: The Body and the Divine in Rabbinic Ethics* (Chicago, IL: University of Chicago Press, 2010), pp. 58–59.

50. David Goodman, 'Do Angels Eat?', in *Journal of Jewish Studies* 37(2), 1986, pp. 160–75.

51. *b. Yoma* 4a–b, as discussed in Magness, *Stone and Dung*, p. 137.

52. Marcion's words are reported in Tertullian, *Adversus Marcionem*, 3.10.1. I borrow Jaraslov Pelikan's translation in *The Christian Tradition: A History of the Development of Doctrine*, vol. 1 (Chicago, IL: Chicago

University Press, 1971), p. 75. Celsus' frank critique has reached us via Origen, *Contra Celsum*, 7.13, available in Henry Chadwick (trans.), *Origen: Contra Celsum* (Cambridge: Cambridge University Press, 1953). In his translation, Chadwick politely sanitizes the term *skatophagein* ('shit-eating') as 'eating filth' (p. 405).

53. Clement, *Stromateis*, 6.71.2, in Alexander Roberts and James Donaldson (eds.), *The Ante-Nicene Fathers: Translations of the Writings of the Fathers Down to A.D. 325*, vol. 2 (Edinburgh: T&T Clark, 1885).

54. Valentinus, fragment 3 in Geoffrey S. Smith (trans. and ed.), *Valentinian Christianity: Texts and Translations* (Oakland, CA: University of California Press, 2020), p. 13. For fourth-century claims that Christ remained excrement-free, see Kelley Spoerl's articles 'Eustathius of Antioch on Jesus' Digestion', in *Studia Patristica* 74, 2016, pp. 147–57; 'Epiphanius on Jesus' Digestion', in *Studia Patristica* 96, 2017, pp. 3–10.

55. The digestive control of Epimenides and Pythagoras is described in Diogenes Laertius, *Philosophoi bioi*, 1.114 and 8.19, trans. R. D. Hicks, *Diogenes Laertius: Lives of Eminent Philosophers*, 2 vols (Loeb Classical Library, 184–5; Cambridge, MA: Harvard University Press, 1925). On the human body in the Greek and Roman worlds, see Laura M. Zucconi, *Ancient Medicine: From Mesopotamia to Rome* (Grand Rapids, MI: Eerdmans, 2019).

Chapter 12: Handedness

1. My reconstruction draws on Simon James, 'Stratagems, Combat, and "Chemical Warfare" in the Siege Mines of Dura-Europos', in *American Journal of Archaeology* 115(1), 2011, pp. 69–101, and Clark Hopkins (ed. Bernard Goldman), *The Discovery of Dura-Europos* (New Haven, CT: Yale University Press, 1979).

2. Hopkins, *The Discovery of Dura-Europos*, p. 131.

3. Jesse J. Prinz, 'Foreword: Hand Manifesto', in Zdravko Radman (ed.), *The Hand, an Organ of the Mind: What the Manual Tells the Mental* (Cambridge, MA: MIT Press, 2013), pp. ix–xvii. All the essays in this excellent volume have helped me with my observations on human handedness here.

4. Matthew Ratcliffe, 'Touch and the Sense of Reality', in Zdravko Radman (ed.), *The Hand, an Organ of the Mind: What the Manual Tells the Mental* (Cambridge, MA: MIT Press, 2013), pp. 131–57 (here, p. 132).

5. Psalm 115.5–7.

6. God plants a garden and shapes the first man from clay in Genesis 2.4–8. In this paragraph, I also allude to examples of the deity's

creative handiwork in Numbers 24.6; Isaiah 40.12, 22; Amos 4.13; Job
38.4–6; Psalms 95.4; 104.2; Proverbs 30.4.

7. Psalm 74.13–15. My translation draws on Smith, *Origins of Biblical
Monotheism*, p. 36; and K. Williams Whitney, *Two Strange Beasts:
Leviathan and Behemoth in the Second Temple* (Winona Lake, IN:
Eisenbrauns, 2006), pp. 170–71.

8. *KTU* 1.3 iii 40–41; following Wyatt, *Religious Texts*, p. 79.

9. *KTU* 1.1–1.2.

10. For the text and translation, see Theodore J. Lewis, '*CT* 13.33–34 and
Ezekiel 32: Lion-Dragon Myths', in *Journal of the American Oriental
Society* 116(1), 1996, pp. 28–47.

11. ETCSL 1.6.1 (lines 165–167). Here, I cite the translation in Jerrold S.
Cooper, *The Return of Ninurta to Nippur* (Rome: Pontifical Biblical
Institute, 1978), pp. 86–89.

12. ETCSL 1.6.2 (lines 10–16).

13. On the dating of Enuma Elish, see W. G. Lambert, *Babylonian
Creation Myths* (Winona Lake, IN: Eisenbrauns, 2013), pp. 439–65.

14. *COS* 1.111, tablet 4, lines 35–40 (trans. Benjamin R. Foster).

15. Ornan, *The Triumph of the Symbol*, pp. 66–67.

16. See further Nicolas Wyatt, *Space and Time in the Religious Life of the
Near East* (Sheffield: Sheffield Academic Press, 2001), p. 86.

17. Exodus 14.31.

18. Exodus 15.1–18 (here, verses 4–10).

19. Psalm 89.13.

20. *COS* 2.2A, lines 84b–89 (trans. James K. Hoffmeier).

21. See further Eric H. Cline, *The Battles of Armageddon: Megiddo and the
Jezreel Valley from the Bronze Age to the Nuclear Age* (Ann Arbor, MI:
Michigan University Press, 2000).

22. Abraham Malamat, *Mari and the Bible* (Leiden: Brill, 1998), pp. 24–32.

23. Daniel David Luckenbill, *Ancient Records of Assyria and Babylonia,
Volume II: Historical Records of Assyria (from Sargon to the End)*
(Chicago, IL: Chicago University Press, 1927), pp. 186–88; Tallay
Ornan, 'The Godlike Semblance of a King: The Case of
Sennacherib's Rock Reliefs', in Jack Cheng and Marian H. Feldman
(eds.), *Ancient Near Eastern Art in Context: Studies in Honor of Irene
J. Winter by Her Students* (Leiden: Brill, 2007), pp. 161–78 (here, p. 170).
Sennacherib's vivid description has been classed as an ancient form of
'virtual reality' in Allison Karmel Thomason, 'From Sennacherib's
Bronzes to Taharqa's Feet: Conceptions of the Material World at
Nineveh', in *Iraq* 66, 2004, pp. 151–62 (here, p. 156).

24. J.-M. Durand, 'Le mythologeme du combat entre le Dieu de l'orage et le mer en Mésopotamie', in *MARI: Annales de recherches interdisciplinaires* 7, 1993, pp. 41–61 (here, pp. 43–45); Joanna Töyräänvuori, 'Weapons of the Storm God in Ancient Near Eastern and Biblical Traditions', in *Studia Orientalia* 112, 2012, pp. 147–80. For a similar translation, see *COS* 4.47.
25. *KTU* 1.65. For a translation, see Wyatt, *Religious Texts*, pp. 363–65.
26. Psalm 89.21–25. My translation draws on that in Lewis, *The Origin and Character of God*, p. 457.
27. Psalm 18.34–35. For the mythological positioning of kings at Yahweh's right hand, and for the enemies at their feet, see (for example) Psalms 18.38–39; 45.3–5; 110.1–2; *cf.* 2.6, 9; 1 Chronicles 28.5.
28. Psalms 2.8–9; 110.1–6.
29. Isaiah 22.8; *cf.* 1 Kings 7.2; 10.14–15; 2 Chronicles 9.16, 20. For further discussion, see Philippe Guillaume and Martha Hellander, 'The House of the Forest of Lebanon: A Temple Silenced', in *Biblische Notizen* 180, 2019, pp. 15–29.

CHAPTER 13: ARM'S REACH

1. 2 Kings 18.13–17 (echoed in 2 Chronicles 32.9; Isaiah 36.1–3). On the fall of Lachish, see Christoph Uehlinger, 'Neither Eyewitnesses, Nor Windows to the Past, but Valuable Testimony in Its Own Right: Remarks on Iconography, Source Criticism, and Ancient Data-Processing', in Hugh G. M. Williamson (ed.), *Understanding the History of Ancient Israel* (Oxford: Oxford University Press, 2007), pp. 173–228; David Ussishkin, *Biblical Lachish: A Tale of Construction, Destruction, Excavation, and Restoration* (Jerusalem: Israel Exploration Society, 2014).
2. 2 Chronicles 32.7–8.
3. Isaiah 1.8; *COS* 2.119B (trans. Mordechai Cogan).
4. Psalms 46.5; 48.3.
5. Jeremiah 51.34.
6. Ezekiel 32.2.
7. Psalm 44.17–19. Like many other scholars, I follow those biblical manuscripts presupposing a reference to a 'dragon' (*tannin*) here, rather than 'jackals' (*tannim*).
8. Psalm 144.5–7.
9. Psalm 69.1–3.
10. Isaiah 51.9–11
11. Psalm 74.11.

12. Barbara Nevling Porter, 'Feeding Dinner to a Bed: Reflections on the Nature of Gods in Ancient Mesopotamia', in *State Archives of Assyria Bulletin* 15, 2006, pp. 307–31.

13. Here, Enlil is known by the specialized form Mullil (reflecting a particular Sumerian dialect). For the text and its translation, see Mark E. Cohen, *Balag-Compositions: Sumerian Lamentation Liturgies of the Second and First Millennium BCE* (Malibu, CA: Undena Publications, 1974), pp. 20–2.

14. Psalm 44.24.

15. Karel van der Toorn, *Becoming Diaspora Jews: Behind the Story of Elephantine* (New Haven, CT: Yale University Press, 2019), pp. 89–114. For the goddess, see also Collin Cornell, 'The Forgotten Female Figurines of Elephantine', in *Journal of Ancient Near Eastern Religions* 18(2), 2018, pp. 111–32.

16. Isaiah 50.2.

17. Psalm 78.65.

18. Jeremiah 50.25.

19. Isaiah 59.16. God's warrior clothing is described in the following verse.

20. Deuteronomy 32.25–27.

21. Isaiah 52.8; 63.1–6. I borrow the image of God as a bodybuilder from Stephen D. Moore, *God's Gym: Divine Male Bodies of the Bible* (New York, NY: Routledge, 1996), especially pp. 75–138.

22. Psalm 98.1–8.

23. Isaiah 44.28; 45.1–15, 13; Ezra 1.1–11; 2 Chronicles 36.22–23.

24. Isaiah 27.1.

25. Job 38.8–9; 41.1–5.

26. Genesis 1.21; Job 38.8–9.

27. Psalm 104.26.

28. *b. Aboda Zara* 3b.

29. Fishbane, *Biblical Myth and Rabbinic Mythmaking*, pp. 144–9.

30. Daniel 7.1–27.

31. E.g., Matthew 24.30; 26.64; Mark 13.26; 14.62; Luke 21.27; *cf.* John 1.51; 3.13.

32. For examples, see the discussion in Fishbane, *Biblical Myth and Rabbinic Mythmaking*, pp. 112–31.

33. See the discussion in Whitney, *Two Strange Beasts*, pp. 31–142.

34. Revelation 12.9; 20.1.

35. Revelation 21.1; Jonathan Moo, 'The Sea That Is No More: Rev. 21:1 and the Function of Sea Imagery in the Apocalypse of John', in *Novum Testamentum* 51(2), 2009, pp. 148–67.

36. E.g., 4 Ezra 6.49–52; 2 Baruch 29.4; 1 Enoch 60.7–10.
37. Psalm 74.14 (*cf.* Ezekiel 32.4); 4 Ezra 6.52.
38. Doak, *Religion and Its Monsters*, pp. 57–70; Michael Mulder, 'Leviathan on the Menu of the Messianic Meal: The Use of Various Images of Leviathan in Early Jewish Tradition', in Koert van Bekkum, Jaap Dekker, Henk van de Kamp and Eric Peels (eds.), *Playing with Leviathan: Interpretation and Reception of Monsters from the Biblical World* (Leiden: Brill, 2017), pp. 115–30.

CHAPTER 14: DIVINE TOUCH

1. Rebecca Barnhouse and Benjamin Withers (eds.), *The Old English Hexateuch: Aspects and Approaches* (Kalamazoo, MI: Medieval Institute Publications, 2000); Andrew Scheil, 'Ælfric of Eynsham', in James Simpson (ed.), *Oxford Handbooks Online* (Oxford: Oxford University Press, 2014). Available at www.oxfordhandbooks.com/.
2. Deuteronomy 34.4–5.
3. Cotton MS Claudius B IV, f. 139v (British Library).
4. Amos 9.2.
5. Ezekiel 37. 1–14.
6. For the inscription, see *COS* 2.52. For the hand motif, see Siegfried Mittmann, 'Das Symbol der Hand in der altorientalischen Ikonographie', in R. Kieffer and J. Bergman (eds.), *La Main de Dieu. Die Hand Gottes* (Tübingen: Mohr Siebeck, 1997), pp. 19–48.
7. Brian B. Schmidt, *The Materiality of Power: Explorations in the Social History of Early Israelite Magic* (Tübingen: Mohr Siebeck, 2016), pp. 155–62; Alice Mandell and Jeremy Smoak, 'Reading and Writing in the Dark at Khirbet el-Qom: The Literacies of Ancient Subterranean Judah', in *Near Eastern Archaeology* 80(3), 2017, pp. 188–95.
8. For a high-quality image of the artefact, see Zahi Hawass, *Inside the Egyptian Museum with Zahi Hawass* (Cairo: American University in Cairo, 2010), pp. 140–1.
9. On this site, see Ze'ev Meshel, *Kuntillet 'Ajrud (Ḥorvat Teman): An Iron Age II Religious Site on the Judah–Sinai Border* (Jerusalem: Israel Exploration Society, 2012).
10. Psalms 44.21–22; 63.4; 88.9; 119.48; 141.2; *cf.* Exodus 9.29, 33; 1 Kings 8.22, 38, 54; Lamentations 2.19; 3.4; Ezra 9.5; Nehemiah 8.6; 2 Chronicles 6.12–13, 29–30.
11. Isaiah 65.2.
12. Isaiah 64.7.

13. Isaiah 41.9, 13; 42.6; 45.1; 64.7; Jeremiah 31.32; Job 8.20; Psalms 73.23; 139.10.

14. Hosea 11.1–3.

15. Isaiah 49.15.

16. Isaiah 46.3–4; *cf.* Isaiah 1.2; 66.9; Psalms 22.9–10; 71.6.

17. *COS* 2.30, lines 10–13 (trans. K. Lawson Younger, Jr.).

18. Cynthia R. Chapman, *The House of the Mother: The Social Roles of Maternal Kin in Biblical Hebrew Narrative and Poetry* (New Haven, CT: Yale University Press, 2016), pp. 125–49.

19. Francesca Stavrakopoulou, 'Religion at Home: The Materiality of Practice', in Susan Niditch (ed.), *The Wiley Blackwell Companion to Ancient Israel* (Chichester: Wiley, 2016), pp. 347–65; Erin Darby, *Interpreting Judean Pillar Figurines: Gender and Empire in Judean Apotropaic Ritual* (Tübingen: Mohr Siebeck, 2014).

20. *IPIAO*4, nos. 1179, 1182.

21. Jerrold S. Cooper, *Reconstructing History from Ancient Inscriptions: The Lagash-Umma Border Conflict* (Malibu, CA: Undena Publications, 1981), pp. 45–47; Irene J. Winter, 'After the Battle Is Over: The *Stele of Vultures* and the Beginning of Historical Narrative in the Art of the Ancient Near East', in Herbert L. Kessler and Marianna Shreve Simpson (eds.), *Pictorial Narrative in Antiquity and the Middle Ages* (Washington, DC: National Gallery of Art, 1985), pp. 11–32.

22. J. N. Postgate, *Early Mesopotamia: Society and Economy at the Dawn of History* (Abingdon: Routledge, 1992), p. 35.

23. Tablet K4310 (lines 16′–33′), adapting the translation in Simo Parpola (trans. and ed.), *Assyrian Prophecies* (State Archives of Assyria, 9; Helsinki: Helsinki University Press, 1997), pp. 4–11.

24. Tablet K1290 (obverse, lines 13–15 and recto, lines 14–16), in Alasdair Livingstone (trans. and ed.), *Court Poetry and Literary Miscellanea* (State Archives of Assyria, 3; Helsinki: Helsinki University Press, 1989), pp. 10–13.

25. Tablet K1285 (recto, lines 6–8), adapting the translation in Livingstone, *Court Poetry*, pp. 33–35.

26. *COS* 1.87 and 1.102.

27. *IPIAO* 3, nos. 829, 957. See also Marguerite Yon, *The City of Ugarit at Tell Ras Shamra* (Winona Lake, IN: Eisenbrauns, 2006), p. 136.

28. Psalm 22.9–10.

29. Psalm 2.7.

30. Isaiah 7.14.

31. Isaiah 9.6–7.

32. Isaiah 64.8.

33. Job 10.8–9.
34. For Enki and Ninmah, see ECTSL 1.1.2. For Enki and Mami (a story told in Atrahasis), see Dalley, *Myths from Mesopotamia*, pp. 16–17.
35. *KTU* 1.16 v 25–30. On the magic of clay-shaping, see Theodore J. Lewis, 'The Identity and Function of Ugaritic Sha'tiqatu: A Divinely Made Apotropaic Figure', in *Journal of Ancient Near Eastern Religions* 14(1), 2014, pp. 1–28.
36. Ronald A. Simkins, 'The Embodied World: Creation Metaphors in the Ancient Near East', *Biblical Theology Bulletin* 44(1), 2014, pp. 40–53 (here, p. 46), citing Serge Sauneron and Jean Yoyotte, 'La naissance du monde selon "Égypte ancienne"', in *La Naissance du Monde* (Paris: Seuil, 1959), pp. 17–91 (here, p. 73).
37. Genesis 1.24–27; 2.7.
38. Deuteronomy 32.40–41.
39. Ezekiel 21.17.
40. Isaiah 34.6–7.
41. Jubilees 2.1–30.
42. *m. Tehillim* 76.2–3.
43. *y. Rosh Hashanah* 1.2. On God keeping his own commandments (much like other deities performing acts of 'worship'), see Kimberley Christine Patton, *Religion of the Gods: Ritual, Paradox, and Reflexivity* (Oxford and New York, NY: Oxford University Press, 2009), pp. 249–81; Dov Weiss, *Pious Irreverence: Confronting God in Rabbinic Judaism* (Philadelphia, PA: University of Pennsylvania Press, 2017), especially pp. 155–7.
44. *Pesiqta de-Rab Kahana* 5.16; *b. Berakhot* 6a.
45. *b. Rosh Hashanah* 17b.
46. Deuteronomy 6.6–8. See also Exodus 13.9, 16; Deuteronomy 11.18–20. For the early history of *tefillin*, see Yehuda B. Cohn, *Tangled Up in Text: Tefillin and the Ancient World* (Providence: Brown University, 2008).
47. *b. Berakhot* 6a.

CHAPTER 15: HOLY HANDBOOKS

1. Lindsey Bever, 'In a church's ashes, firefighters find unexpected survivors: Bibles, untouched by flame', in *Washington Post*, 5 March 2019, https://www.washingtonpost.com/religion/2019/03/05/churchs -ashes-firefighters-find-unexpected-survivors-bibles-untouched-by -flame/?utm_term=.0c5099ff1288. For the fire department's Facebook post, see https://www.facebook.com/CCVFD105/posts

/on-march-3-around-1258am-our-department-was-dispatched-to-assist
-beaver-vfd-with/1508634686013394/.

2. David Morgan, *The Forge of Vision: A Visual History of Modern
Christianity* (Oakland, CA: University of California Press, 2015),
pp. 105–34.

3. On sacred texts in early Judaism, see Eva Mroczek, *The Literary
Imagination in Jewish Antiquity* (Oxford: Oxford University Press, 2016).

4. 1 Esdras 14.44–46.

5. Ecclesiastes 12.12.

6. Hosea 8.12.

7. Exodus 24.12.

8. Exodus 31.18. God verbally decrees the Ten Commandments in
Exodus 20.1–17; the story is also told (with variations) in
Deuteronomy 5. The stone tablets are described as the 'ten words' in
Exodus 34.28; Deuteronomy 4.13; 10.4.

9. Exodus 8.19; Psalm 8.4.

10. Exodus 32.15–16.

11. Exodus 32.15.

12. Exodus 32.1–24.

13. Exodus 34.1–4, 27–28; 40.20–21; 1 Kings 8.9; 2 Chronicles 5.10; *cf.*
Hebrews 9.4.

14. Deuteronomy 31.26–27.

15. Nehemiah 8.5–6; 1 Maccabees 3.48. See further Karel van der Toorn,
'The Iconic Book: Analogies between the Babylonian Cult of Images
and the Veneration of the Torah', in Karel van der Toorn (ed.), *The
Image and the Book: Iconic Cults, Aniconism, and the Rise of Book Religion
in Israel and the Ancient Near East* (Leuven: Peeters, 1997), pp. 229–48;
Dorina Miller Parmenter, 'The Bible as Icon: Myths of the Divine
Origins of Scripture', in Craig A. Evans and H. Daniel Zacharias
(eds.), *Jewish and Christian Scripture as Artifact and Canon* (London:
T&T Clark, 2009), pp. 298–309.

16. Deuteronomy 30.11–14.

17. Psalm 87.6.

18. Exodus 32.31–33.

19. *COS* 1.113 (trans. Stephanie Dalley). Ashurbanipal's words appear at
the very end of this five-tablet composition.

20. Deuteronomy 12.1–5.

21. Jeremiah 23.27.

22. Psalm 139.16.

23. Job 13.24–28.

24. *COS* 2.122B (trans. Paul-Alain Beaulieu). Nebuchadnezzar's petition appears at the end of this inscription.
25. Irving Finkel, 'Assurbanipal's Library: An Overview', in Kim Ryholt and Gojko Barjamovic (eds.), *Libraries before Alexandria: Ancient Near Eastern Traditions* (Oxford: Oxford University Press, 2019), pp. 367–89; Eckart Frahm, 'Keeping Company with Men of Learning: The King as Scholar', in Karen Radner and Eleanor Robson (eds.), *The Oxford Handbook of Cuneiform Culture* (Oxford: Oxford University Press, 2011), pp. 508–32.
26. Jeremiah 31.33.
27. Psalm 40.7–8; Jeremiah 7.1.
28. Deuteronomy 29.20.
29. Zechariah 5.1–3.
30. Zechariah 5.4.
31. Ezekiel 2.8–3.4.
32. Genesis 4.13–15. The other texts to which I refer in this paragraph are Numbers 5.11–31 (the curse of miscarriage); Ezekiel 9.1–6 (protection from divine execution); Exodus 28.31–38 (marking the high priest). In the Ezekiel passage, the X-shaped *taw* reflects a traditional Iron Age Hebrew script, rather than the later 'square' script (adopted from Aramaic). On these scripts, see William M. Schniedewind, 'Aramaic, the Death of Written Hebrew, and Language Shift in the Persian Period', in Seth L. Sanders (ed.), *Margins of Writing, Origins of Culture* (Chicago, IL: Oriental Institute, 2007), pp. 141–52.
33. See further Jeremy D. Smoak, *The Priestly Blessing in Inscription and Scripture: The Early History of Numbers 6:24–26* (Oxford: Oxford University Press, 2015); Dorina Miller Parmenter, 'How the Bible Feels: The Christian Bible as Effective and Affective Object', in James W. Watts (ed.), *Sensing Sacred Texts* (Sheffield: Equinox, 2018), pp. 27–37, especially pp. 29–30.
34. Hans Nissen, 'The Archaic Texts from Uruk', in *World Archaeology* 17, 1986, pp. 317–34 (fig. 6); Amanda H. Podany, *The Ancient Near East: A Very Short Introduction* (Oxford: Oxford University Press, 2014), pp. 17–19.
35. *COS* 1.170 (trans. Thorkild Jacobsen).
36. *COS* 1.161 (trans. Gertrud Farber).
37. Alasdair Livingstone, 'Ashurbanipal: Literate or Not?', in *Zeitschrift für Assyriologie* 96(1), 2007, pp. 98–118 (here, p. 100); *cf. COS* 1.113.
38. Malachi 3.16.
39. Testament of Abraham 12.1–18 (recension A).
40. Daniel 12.1–4.

41. Daniel 5.1–30.
42. Genesis 5.21–24.
43. 1 Enoch 81.1–3; 103.2.
44. 2 Enoch 22.10.
45. Jude 14–15.
46. Tertullian, *De cultu feminarum*, 1.3, trans. S. Thelwall in Alexander Roberts and James Donaldson (eds.), *The Ante-Nicene Fathers: Translations of the Writings of the Fathers Down to A.D. 325*, vol. 4 (Edinburgh: T&T Clark, 1885).
47. Chris Keith, *Jesus' Literacy: Scribal Culture and the Teacher from Galilee* (London: T&T Clark, 2011), pp. 156–63.
48. E.g., Matthew 4.23; 9.35; 13.54–56; Mark 1.21–22, 39; 6.1–3; Luke 4.15, 31–32; John 6.59 (teaching in synagogues); John 18.19–20 (teaching in the Jerusalem temple); Matthew 7.28–29; 15.1–20; Mark 1.22–28; Luke 6.6–11; 13.10–17 (debating Torah experts); Luke 4.16–22 (reading from the Isaiah scroll); Matthew 4.1–11; Luke 4.1–13 (quoting scripture at Satan); Luke 2.41–49 (Jesus as a clever child; *cf.* Infancy Gospel of Thomas 6.1–8.3; 14.1–5; 15.1–7).
49. John 8.2–11. These verses, and the wider passage in which they occur (John 7.53–8.11), are not attested in the oldest surviving manuscripts, indicating the story is a later insertion. See Chris Keith, 'Recent and Previous Research on the *Pericope Adulterae* (John 7.53–8.11)', in *Currents in Biblical Research* 6(3), 2008, 377–404 (here, pp. 379–81).
50. Mark 7.31–37; Luke 11.19–20.
51. John 8.7–8.
52. E.g., Philippians 4.3; Hebrews 10.7; Odes of Solomon 23; Apocalypse of Zephaniah 3.6–7; Shepherd of Hermas 1.3.2. See further Leslie Baynes, *The Heavenly Book Motif in Judeo-Christian Apocalypses, 200 BCE–200 CE* (Leiden: Brill, 2012), especially pp. 171–96.
53. Revelation 5.1–14 (the Lamb receives the scroll); 6.1–17 (opening the first six seals); 8.1 (opening the seventh seal).
54. Revelation 21.27; *cf.* 3.5; 13.8; 17.8; 20.15.
55. Revelation 22.4; *cf.* Exodus 28.36–38.

Chapter 16: Face to Face

1. This reconstruction draws on the results of the micro-CT scanning and 3D printing of the skull by a team led by curators at the British Museum; see Alexandra Fletcher, Jessica Pearson, Theya Molleson, Richard Abel, Janet Ambers and Crispin Wiles, 'Beneath the Surface: Imaging Techniques and the Jericho Skull', in A. Fletcher,

D. Antoine and J. D. Hill (eds.), *Regarding the Dead: Human Remains in the British Museum* (London: Trustees of the British Museum, 2014), pp. 93–104. For an interactive image of the skull, see https://blog.britishmuseum.org/facing-the-past-the-jericho-skull/.

2. Karina Croucher, 'Keeping the Dead Close: Grief and Bereavement in the Treatment of Skulls from the Neolithic Middle East', in *Mortality* 23(2), 2018, pp. 103–20.

3. Daniel Black, 'What Is a Face?', in *Body & Society* 17(4), 2011, pp. 1–25 (here, p. 11). See also Stewart Guthrie, *Faces in the Clouds: A New Theory of Religion* (Oxford: Oxford University Press, 1993).

4. Psalms 17.15; 42.2.

5. Zainab Bahrani, *Mesopotamia: Ancient Art and Architecture* (London: Thames & Hudson, 2017), pp. 70–5.

6. *COS* 2.135 (trans. Victor Hurowitz).

7. Exodus 33.11.

8. Numbers 12.8.

9. Exodus 34.29–35.

10. Psalm 63.1–5.

11. Deuteronomy 16.16–17. Following a pious emendation in antiquity, modern Bibles translate these verses slightly differently, distorting the instruction to 'see' the face of the deity into the command to 'appear' before the deity. Biblical scholars are widely agreed that the former is the original sense of the Hebrew.

12. Exodus 25.8 (Septuagint).

13. E.g., 1 Chronicles 16.11; 2 Chronicles 7.14; Hosea 5.15; Psalms 27.8; 100.2; 105.4. See also Andreas Wagner (trans. Marion Salzmann), *God's Body: The Anthropomorphic God in the Old Testament* (London: T&T Clark, 2019), pp. 126–29.

14. Psalm 24.3–6.

15. Deuteronomy 4.12.

16. John 1.18; 1 Timothy 6.16.

17. 1 Kings 8.12; 2 Chronicles 6.1; *cf.* Exodus 20.21; Deuteronomy 5.22–23; Psalm 97.2. Divine darkness is palpable in Exodus 10.21–22.

18. Exodus 26.31–35. Produced in Phoenicia, blue and purple pigments were not only expensive, but credited with a protective function. See Astrid Nunn, *Die Wandmalerei und der glasierte Wandschmuck im Alten Orient* (Leiden: Brill, 1988), pp. 239–41. On windows in temples, see Yosef Garfinkel and Madeleine Mumcuoglu, 'The Temple of Solomon in Iron Age Context', in *Religions* 10(3), 2019, article 198 (here, p. 12), online at https://www.mdpi.com/2077-1444/10/3/198/htm.

19. Matthew 27.51; Mark 15.38; Luke 23.45; *cf.* Hebrews 10.20.
20. Exodus 28.31–35. See Jeremy Schipper and Jeffrey Stackert, 'Blemishes, Camouflage, and Sanctuary Service: The Priestly Deity and His Attendants', in *Hebrew Bible and Ancient Israel* 2(4), 2013, pp. 458–78 (here, pp. 472–4).
21. Genesis 32.22–32; Exodus 4.24–26.
22. Exodus 19.10–13, 21–24.
23. Numbers 4.20.
24. Numbers 4.17–20; 1 Samuel 6.1–7.1. See Simon Chavel, 'The Face of God and the Etiquette of Eye-Contact: Visitation, Pilgrimage, and Prophetic Vision in Ancient Israelite and Early Jewish Imagination', in *Jewish Studies Quarterly* 19(1), 2012, pp. 1–55.
25. Daniel E. Fleming, 'Seeing and Socializing with Dagan at Emar's *zukru* Festival', in Beate Pongratz-Leisten and Karen Sonik (eds.), *The Materiality of Divine Agency* (Berlin: de Gruyter, 2015), pp. 197–210.
26. I cite the translation in A. R. George, 'The Assyrian Elegy: Form and Meaning', in Sarah Melville and Alice Slotsky (eds.), *Opening the Tablet Box: Near Eastern Studies in Honor of Benjamin R. Foster* (Leiden: Brill, 2010), pp. 203–16.
27. Psalm 104.28–29.
28. Deuteronomy 31.17.
29. Micah 3.4.
30. Lamentations 3.44.
31. Isaiah 59.2.
32. *KTU* 1.3–1.4.
33. Izak Cornelius, 'The Iconography of Ugarit', in Wilfred G. E. Watson and Nicolas Wyatt (eds.), *Handbook of Ugaritic Studies* (Leiden: Brill, 1999), pp. 586–602; Izak Cornelius, *The Many Faces of the Goddess: The Iconography of the Syro-Palestinian Goddesses Anat, Astarte, Qedeshet, and Asherah c. 1500–1000 BCE* (Fribourg/Göttingen: Academic Press/ Vandenhoeck & Ruprecht, 2004), pp. 64–65.
34. Simon B. Parker, 'Divine Intercession in Judah?', in *Vetus Testamentum* 56(1), 2006, pp. 76–91.
35. Jeremiah 7.16–20; 44.17–19.
36. Job 5.1–8.
37. Isaiah 63.9; Malachi 3.1.
38. Proverbs 3.22; 8.35.
39. Ecclesiastes 8.1.
40. Numbers 6.24–26; *cf.* Psalms 67.1; 80.3, 7, 19.

CHAPTER 17: HEADSTRONG BEAUTY

1. Matthew Bogdanos, 'The Casualties of War: The Truth about the Iraq Museum', in *American Journal of Archaeology* 109(3), 2005, pp. 477–526.

2. Harriet Crawford, *Sumer and the Sumerians* (second edition) (Cambridge: Cambridge University Press, 1991), pp. 69–75.

3. Bahrani, *Mesopotamia*, pp. 48–50.

4. ETCSL 1.4.1.

5. Numbers 24.8.

6. Tallay Ornan, 'The Bull and Its Two Masters: Moon and Storm Deities in Relation to the Bull in Ancient Near Eastern Art', in *Israel Exploration Journal* 51(1), 2001, pp. 1–26. On the early history of the horned headwear of the gods, see Julia M. Asher-Greve, 'Reading the Horned Crown', in *Archiv für Orientforschung* 42/43, 1995/96, pp. 181–9.

7. Julia M. Asher-Greve and Deborah Sweeney, 'On Nakedness, Nudity, and Gender in Egyptian and Mesopotamian Art', in Silvia Schroer (ed.), *Images and Gender: Contributions to the Hermeneutics of Reading Ancient Art* (Fribourg/Göttingen: Academic Press/Vandenhoeck & Ruprecht, 2006), pp. 111–60 (here, p. 129).

8. *IPIAO* 3, no. 937.

9. *KTU* 1.10 ii 21–23; 1.12 i 30. See Wyatt, *Religious Texts*, pp. 157, 163.

10. Mark S. Smith and Wayne Y. Pitard, *The Ugaritic Baal Cycle, Volume II: Introduction with Text, Translation and Commentary of KTU/CAT 1.3–1.4* (Leiden: Brill, 2009), pp. 296–9.

11. Nicolas Wyatt, 'Bull El and His Avatars: The Iron Age Legacy of an Ugaritian Trope', in Carole Roche-Hawley and Robert Hawley (eds.), *Mélanges européennes en l'honneur de Dennis Pardee* (Louvain: Peeters, forthcoming). My thanks to Professor Wyatt for sharing this piece with me ahead of its publication.

12. Deuteronomy 33.16–17.

13. 1 Kings 22.11.

14. Hosea 8.1–6; *cf.* 10.5. For the statues at Bethel and Dan, see 1 Kings 12.27–29. Described in these texts as 'calves', scholars widely understand them to be divine bull images. See Lewis, *The Origin and Character of God*, pp. 317–33.

15. The story of the Golden Calf is told in Exodus 32. See further James W. Watts, 'Aaron and the Golden Calf in the Rhetoric of the Pentateuch', in *Journal of Biblical Literature* 130(3), 2011, pp. 417–30; Michael B. Hundley, 'What Is the Golden Calf?', in *Catholic Biblical Quarterly* 79, 2017, pp. 559–79.

16. Psalm 106.19–20.
17. Psalm 27.4, 8.
18. Psalms 135.3; 147.1.
19. James Alfred Loader, 'What Do the Heavens Declare? On the Old Testament Motif of God's Beauty in Creation', in *HTS Theological Studies* 67(3), 2011, article 1098; Athalya Brenner, *The Intercourse of Knowledge: On Gendering Desire and 'Sexuality' in the Hebrew Bible* (Leiden: Brill, 1997), pp. 43–51; Luke Ferretter, 'The Power and the Glory: The Aesthetics of the Hebrew Bible', in *Literature & Theology* 18(2), 2004, pp. 123–38; David Penchansky, 'Beauty, Power, and Attraction: Aesthetics and the Hebrew Bible', in Richard J. Bautch and Jean-François Racine (eds.), *Beauty and the Bible: Toward a Hermeneutics of Biblical Aesthetics* (Atlanta, GA: Society of Biblical Literature, 2013), pp. 47–68.
20. Irene J. Winter, 'Defining "Aesthetics" for Non-Western Studies: The Case of Ancient Mesopotamia', in Michael A. Holly and Keith Moxey (eds.), *Art History, Aesthetics, Visual Studies* (Williamstown, MA: Sterling and Francine Clark Art Institute, 2002), pp. 3–28.
21. Dalley, *Myths from Mesopotamia*, p. 57. See further Irene J. Winter, 'The Eyes Have It: Votive Statuary, Gilgamesh's Axe, and Cathected Viewing in the Ancient Near East', in Robert S. Nelson (ed.), *Visuality Before and Beyond the Renaissance* (Cambridge: Cambridge University Press, 2000), pp. 22–44.
22. Genesis 1.31.
23. Genesis 3.6.
24. Isaiah 62.3–5.
25. Wisdom of Solomon 13.3.
26. Song of Songs 5.10–16.
27. See especially Daniel Boyarin, ' "This We Know to Be the Carnal Israel": Circumcision and the Erotic Life of God and Israel', in *Critical Inquiry* 18, 1992, pp. 474–505; idem, 'The Song of Songs: Lock or Key? Intertextuality, Allegory and Midrash', in Regina M. Schwartz (ed.), *The Book and the Text: The Bible and Literary Theory* (Oxford: Blackwell, 1990), pp. 214–30; Jonathan Kaplan, *My Perfect One: Typology and Early Rabbinic Interpretation of Song of Songs* (Oxford: Oxford University Press, 2015), pp. 135–53.
28. Bahrani, *Mesopotamia*, pp. 197–8.
29. Shiyanthi Thavapalan, 'Radiant Things for Gods and Men: Lightness and Darkness in Mesopotamian Language and Thought', in *Colour Turn* 1(7), 2018, pp. 1–36; Duane E. Smith, 'The Color of Fortune: The Role of Color in Mesopotamian Divination', in Rachael B. Goldman

(ed.), *Essays in Global Color History: Interpreting the Ancient Spectrum* (Piscataway, NJ: Gorgias Press, 2016), pp. 9–29.

30. Caitlín E. Barrett, 'Was Dust Their Food and Clay Their Bread? Grave Goods, the Mesopotamian Afterlife, and the Liminal Role of Inana/Ishtar', in *Journal of Ancient Near Eastern Religions* 7(1), 2007, pp. 7–65.

31. *KTU* 1.3 ii 14–35; 1.3 iii 1–3; 1.3 iv 45; 1.19 iv 28–61. On Anat's arrowheads, see André Lemaire, 'From the Origin of the Alphabet to the Tenth Century BCE: New Documents and New Directions', in Meir Lubetski and Edith Lubetski (eds.), *New Inscriptions and Seals Relating to the Biblical World* (Atlanta, GA: Society of Biblical Literature, 2012), pp. 1–20.

32. Isaiah 63.1–3.

33. Plutarch, *Pyrrhus*, 28.3, trans. Bernadotte Perrin, *Plutarch: Lives IX* (Loeb Classical Library, 101; Cambridge, MA: Harvard University Press, 1920). For red-stained warriors, see 1 Kings 2.5; Psalms 58.11; 68.24. For further discussion, see Frank Ritchel Ames, 'The Red-Stained Warrior in Ancient Israel', in Brad E. Kelle, Frank Ritchel Ames and Jacob L. Wright (eds.), *Warfare, Ritual, and Symbol in Biblical and Modern Contexts* (Atlanta, GA: Society of Biblical Literature 2014), pp. 83–109.

34. Nahum 2.1–3.

35. Ezekiel 23.12–16.

36. 1 Samuel 16.12.

37. 2 Samuel 1.26.

38. Scott B. Noegel, 'Scarlet and Harlots: Seeing Red in the Hebrew Bible', in *Hebrew Union College Annual* 87(1), 2016, pp. 1–47; Stuart J. Macwilliam, 'Ideologies of Male Beauty and the Hebrew Bible', in *Biblical Interpretation* 17(3), 2009, pp. 265–87.

39. On the clay heads, see Craig W. Tyson, 'The Religion of the Ammonites: A Specimen of Levantine Religion from the Iron Age II (*ca.* 1000–500 BCE)', in *Religions* 10(3), 2019, no. 153; Joel S. Burnett, 'Iron Age Deities in Word, Image, and Name: Correlating Epigraphic, Iconographic, and Onomastic Evidence for the Ammonite God', in *Studies in the History and Archaeology of Jordan* 10, 2009, pp. 153–64; Joel S. Burnett, 'Ammon, Moab and Edom: Gods and Kingdoms East of the Jordan', in *Biblical Archaeology Review* 42(6), 2016, pp. 26–40, 66–7; Siegfried H. Horn, 'The Crown of the King of the Ammonites', in *Andrews University Seminary Studies* 11(2), 1973, pp. 170–80, and plates xvii–xx.

40. Raz Kletter, 'A Very General Archaeologist – Moshe Dayan and Israeli Archaeology', in *Journal of Hebrew Scriptures* 4(5), 2003, pp. 1–41 (here, pp. 20–21); Tallay Ornan, *A Man and His Land: Highlights from the Moshe Dayan Collection* (Jerusalem: Israel Museum, 1986), p. 38.

41. Kathleen McCaffrey, 'Reconsidering Gender Ambiguity in Mesopotamia: Is a Beard Just a Beard?', in Simo Parpola and Robert M. Whiting (eds.), *Sex and Gender in the Ancient Near East* (Helsinki: Neo-Assyrian Text Corpus Project, 2002), pp. 379–91, especially pp. 389–91; Uroš Matić, '(De)queering Hatshepsut: Binary Bind in Archaeology of Egypt and Kingship Beyond the Corporeal', in *Journal of Archaeological Method and Theory* 23, 2016, pp. 810–31.

42. See the texts collated in Alasdair Livingstone, *Mystical and Mythological Explanatory Works of Assyrian and Babylonian Scholars* (Winona Lake, IN: Eisenbrauns, 2007), pp. 92–112.

43. Jeremy Black and Anthony Green, *Gods, Demons and Symbols of Ancient Mesopotamia: An Illustrated Dictionary* (London: British Museum Press, 1992), p. 115.

44. Here, I quote from the translations in Dalley, *Myths from Mesopotamia*, pp. 52–53, and A. R. George, *The Babylonian Gilgamesh Epic: Introduction, Critical Edition and Cuneiform Texts*, vol. 1 (Oxford: Oxford University Press, 2003), pp. 548–51.

45. Assante, 'Men Looking at Men, pp. 65–67; Omar N'Shea, 'Royal Eunuchs and Elite Masculinity in the Neo-Assyrian Empire', in *Near Eastern Archaeology* 79(3), 2016, pp. 214–21.

46. Judges 13.5.

47. Judges 5.2.

48. Judges 13–16. See further Susan Niditch, '*My Brother Esau Is a Hairy Man': Hair and Identity in Ancient Israel* (Oxford: Oxford University Press, 2008).

49. Shaving rituals associated with mourning are prohibited in Leviticus 19.27–28 and Deuteronomy 14.1. See Saul M. Olyan, 'What Do Shaving Rites Accomplish and What Do They Signal in Biblical Ritual Contexts?', in *Journal of Biblical Literature* 117(4), 1998, pp. 611–22.

50. *KTU* 1.5 vi 15–19 (here, I adapt Wyatt, *Religious Texts*, p. 127).

51. Isaiah 7.20. In 2 Samuel 10.1–5, the Ammonite king Hanan is said to have emasculated David's envoys in a similar way: he shaves off half the beard of each man, and cuts their tunics off at the hips, exposing their genitals, before sending them home. Their humiliation is designed to shame David himself, who insists the men remain hidden in Jericho until their beards have grown back.

52. 2 Kings 2.23–24. For Elijah as a 'lord of hair' and his animal-skin clothing, see 2 Kings 1.8; *cf.* Zechariah 13.4. See further Niditch, *My Brother Esau*, pp. 112–14.

53. Psalm 45.2–6.

54. Izak Cornelius, 'Revisiting the Seated Figure from Ḥirbet Ṣaliḥ/ Rāmat Rāḫēl', in *Zeitschrift des Deutschen Palästina-Vereins* 131(1), 2015, pp. 29–43.

55. Michael Shenkar, 'The Coin of the "God on the Winged Wheel"', in *BOREAS* 30/31, 2007/8, pp. 13–23; Izaak J. de Hulster, 'A Yehud Coin with Representation of a Sun Deity and Iconic Practice in Persian Period Palestine: An Elaboration on TC 242.5/BMC Palestine XIX 29', September 2009, online at https://www.academia .edu/38727481/A_Yehud_coin_with_the_Representation_of_a_Sun _Deity_and_Iconic_Practice_in_Persian_Period_Palestine_An _Elaboration_on_TC_242.5_BMC_Palestine_XIX_29.

Chapter 18: Profile

1. Daniel 7.1–28.

2. Daniel 7.7–8.

3. Daniel 7.13–14.

4. Daniel 7.9.

5. *KTU* 1.3 v 1–4, 24–25; 1.4 v 1–5; 1.10 iii 5–6.

6. Genesis 21.33; Job 36.26; Psalm 102.27.

7. *Pesiqta de-Rab Kahana* 12.24 (Oxford Manuscript 151), following José Costa, 'The Body of God in Ancient Rabbinic Judaism: Problems of Interpretation', in *Revue de l'histoire des religions* 227(3), 2010, pp. 283–316 (here, p. 305).

8. Peter Schäfer, *The Jewish Jesus: How Judaism and Christianity Shaped Each Other* (Princeton, NJ: Princeton University Press, 2012), pp. 55–67.

9. 1 Enoch 71.9–14.

10. 1 Enoch 69.27.

11. Matthew 16.27; 19.28; 25.31; 26.64; Mark 13.26; 14.62; Luke 9.44; 21.27; 22.69; John 3.13; 24.30; *cf.* Acts 7.55–56.

12. Revelation 1.13–16.

13. Revelation 21.6; 22.13.

14. Philippians 2.6; Hebrews 1.2–3.

15. Robin M. Jensen, *Face to Face: Portraits of the Divine in Early Christianity* (Minneapolis, MN: Fortress Press, 2005), especially pp. 142–59; Taylor, *What Did Jesus Look Like?* especially pp. 88–98. See also Michele Bacci, *The Many Faces of Christ: Portraying the Holy in*

the East and West, 300 to 1300 (London: Reaktion Books, 2014), pp. 97–116.

16. *b. Bava Batra* 58a; *b. Bava Metzi'a* 84a. Standardized publications of these texts tend to omit the final link to God, or refer instead to 'the beauty of Adam the first man, who was created in the image of God'. I quote here the translation from manuscript readings in Shamma Friedman, 'Anthropomorphism and Its Eradication', in Willem van Asselt, Paul van Geest, Daniela Müller and Theo Salemink (eds.), *Iconoclasm and Iconoclash: Struggle for Religious Identity* (Leiden: Brill, 2007), pp. 157–78 (here, p. 173).

17. The legend about Rabbi Ishmael ben Elisha ha-Kohen is told in various recensions of an ancient anthology called *The Legend of the Ten Martyrs*. Here, I borrow the translation in Friedman, 'Anthropomorphism', p. 175, which follows Julius (Judah) D. Eisenstein, *Otzar Midrashim* (New York, NY: J. D. Eisenstein, 1915), p. 440. For an English translation of the *Ten Martyrs*, see David Stern, 'Midrash Eleh Ezkerah, or *The Legend of the Ten Martyrs*', in David Stern and Mark Jay Mirsky (eds.), *Rabbinic Fantasies: Imaginative Narratives from Classical Hebrew Literature* (New Haven, CT: Yale University Press, 1990), pp. 143–65.

18. *Genesis Rabbah* 8.10.

19. Robin M. Jensen, 'Theophany and the Invisible God in Early Christian Theology and Art', in Andrew B. McGowan, Brian E. Daley and Timothy J. Gaden (eds.), *God in Early Christian Thought* (Leiden: Brill, 2009), pp. 271–96.

20. Hebrews 1.3. See Robin M. Jensen, 'The Economy of the Trinity at the Creation of Adam and Eve', in *Journal of Early Christian Studies* 7(4), 1999, pp. 527–46. A similar image, in poor condition, is found on a contemporaneous sarcophagus now housed in the Musée de l'Arles Antique.

21. Matthew 28.19.

22. For an expert navigator through these debates, see Morwenna Ludlow, *The Early Church* (London: I.B. Tauris, 2009).

23. Franz Dünzl (trans. John Bowden), *A Brief History of the Doctrine of the Trinity in the Early Church* (London: T&T Clark, 2007), pp. 117–31. For the wider political contexts of the councils of Constantinople and Chalcedon, see Diarmaid MacCulloch, *A History of Christianity: The First Three Thousand Years* (London: Penguin, 2009), pp. 215–28.

24. Thomas F. Mathews (with Norman E. Muller), *The Dawn of Christian Art in Panel Paintings and Icons* (Los Angeles, CA: Paul J. Getty Trust,

2016). For the 'imprinted' relics I mention, see Taylor, *What Did Jesus Look Like?* pp. 43–67.

25. John 8.12.
26. Mathews, *Dawn of Christian Art*, pp. 149–51. See also Kurt Weitzmann, *The Monastery of Saint Catherine at Mount Sinai: The Icons, Vol. 1, From the Sixth to the Tenth Century* (Princeton, NJ: Princeton University Press, 1976), pp. 41–2.
27. In the order in which I refer to them: Daniel 7.9; Ezekiel 1.28; Isaiah 7.14.
28. Gretchen Kreahling McKay, 'Illustrating the Gospel of John: The Exegesis of John Chrysostom and Images of the Ancient of Days in Eleventh-Century Byzantine Manuscripts', in *Studies in Iconography* 31, 2010, pp. 51–68 (here, pp. 60–61).
29. John Lowden, 'The Word Made Visible: The Exterior of the Early Christian Book as Visual Argument', in William E. Klingshirn and Linda Safran (eds.), *The Early Christian Book* (Washington, DC: Catholic University of America Press, 2007), pp. 13–47.

CHAPTER 19: SENSE AND SENSITIVITY

1. Matthew 3.16–17; see also Mark 1.10; Luke 3.22; John 1.32. Kazantzakis' novel was first published under the title *Ο Τελευταίος Πειρασμός* (*The Last Temptation*) in 1955. I cite here an English translation: *The Last Temptation of Christ* (trans. P. A. Bein) (London: Faber, 1961), p. 31.
2. Amos 3.8.
3. Amos 1.2.
4. Jeremiah 20.7–8.
5. Hosea 6.5.
6. Isaiah 2.1; Amos 1.1; Micah 1.1; Exodus 20.18.
7. *KTU* 1.4 vii 21–35, trans. Wyatt, *Religious Texts*, p. 109.
8. *KTU* 1.4 vii 47–49.
9. Psalm 115.7.
10. Isaiah 24.18.
11. Psalm 29.3–7.
12. *COS* 1.111, tablet 1, line 96 (trans. Benjamin R. Foster).
13. Exodus 20.18.
14. Howard Schwartz, *Tree of Souls: The Mythology of Judaism* (Oxford: Oxford University Press, 2004), pp. 259–60.
15. For sound as a divine portent, see Anne-Caroline Rendu Loisel, 'When Gods Speak to Men: Reading House, Street, and Divination

from Sound in Ancient Mesopotamia (1st Millennium BC)', in *Journal of Near Eastern Studies* 75(2), 2016, pp. 291–309.

16. 1 Kings 19.11–12. See further Jyrki Keinänen, *Traditions in Collision: A Literary and Redaction-Critical Study on the Elijah Narratives 1 Kings 17–19* (Göttingen: Vandenhoeck & Ruprecht, 2001), pp. 142–55.

17. Job 38.7.

18. E.g., Psalms 2.4; 37.13; 59.8; Isaiah 7.18; 42.14; Zephaniah 3.17.

19. Ezekiel 1.23–25; *cf.* 10.5; Psalm 18.10.

20. Isaiah 6.3–4; 40.1–9.

21. Psalm 150.3–5.

22. Schwartz, *Tree of Souls*, pp. 385–6.

23. Revelation 5.8; 8.1–13.

24. Amos 5.23.

25. Lamentations 3.56; Psalm 102.2.

26. 1 Samuel 8.21.

27. Emily Teeter, 'Household Cults', in Emily Teeter and Janet H. Johnson (eds.), *The Life of Meresamun: A Temple Singer in Ancient Egypt* (Chicago, IL: Oriental Institute Museum, 2009), pp. 71–5. See also Lynn Meskell, *Object Worlds in Ancient Egypt: Material Biographies Past and Present* (Oxford: Berg, 2004), pp. 130–46.

28. 2 Chronicles 7.15. For the coin, see Yaakov Meshorer (trans. R. Amoils), *A Treasury of Jewish Coins: From the Persian Period to Bar Kokhba* (Jerusalem: Yad Ben-Zvi Press, 2001), pp. 11–13; Patrick Wyssmann, 'The Coinage Imagery of Samaria and Judah in the Late Persian Period', in Christian Frevel, Katharina Pyschny and Izak Cornelius (eds.), *A 'Religious Revolution' in Yehûd? The Material Culture of the Persian Period as a Test Case* (Fribourg/Göttingen: Academic Press/Vandenhoeck & Ruprecht, 2014), pp. 221–66 (here, p. 250); Izak Cornelius, 'The Study of the Old Testament and the Material Imagery of the Ancient Near East, with a Focus on the Body Parts of the Deity', in Louis C. Jonker, Gideon R. Kotzé and Christl M. Maier (eds.), *Congress Volume Stellenbosch 2016* (Leiden: Brill, 2017), pp. 195–227 (here, p. 214).

29. Anne Katrine de Hemmer Gudme, *Before the God in This Place for Good Remembrance: A Comparative Analysis of the Aramaic Votive Inscriptions from Mount Gerizim* (Berlin: de Gruyter, 2013), p. 85.

30. Today, a similar practice continues at the Western Wall in Jerusalem, where pilgrims leave their prayers on slips of paper inserted into the gaps between the large stone blocks.

31. Psalm 22.1–2.

32. Matthew 27.46; Mark 15–34.

33. Psalm 18.6.
34. Exodus 28.31–35.
35. Isaiah 59.1.
36. Genesis 21.17.
37. Numbers 14.26.
38. Isaiah 58.4.
39. Isaiah 26.17–18.
40. Matthew 6.7.
41. Benjamin R. Foster, *Before the Muses: An Anthology of Akkadian Literature* (third edition) (Bethesda, MD: CDL Press, 2005), p. 1012.
42. Yagmur Heffron, 'Revisiting "Noise" (*rigmu*) in *Atra-hasis* in Light of Baby Incantations', in *Journal of Near Eastern Studies* 73(1), 2014, pp. 83–93.
43. E.g., Isaiah 6.9–10; Jeremiah 7.34; 16.9; Lamentations 4.4; *cf.* Job 29.10.
44. Psalm 65.7; see also Isaiah 17.12–14; Ezekiel 5.7; Psalm 65.7; Habakkuk 2.20; Zephaniah 1.7; Zechariah 2.13.
45. Genesis 11.1–9.
46. Irene J. Winter, 'Opening the Eyes and Opening the Mouth: The Utility of Comparing Images in Worship in India and the Ancient Near East', in Michael W. Meister (ed.), *Ethnography and Personhood: Notes from the Field* (Jaipur and New Delhi: Rawat Publications, 2000), pp. 129–62; Walker and Dick, 'The Induction of the Cult Image', pp. 55–121.
47. Deuteronomy 32.10.
48. Zechariah 2.8 (in Hebrew, verse 12). Here, the unusual term *babah* (rendered 'little child') is used of the reflective pupil or eyeball. See further Ludwig Koehler, Walter Baumgartner and Johann J. Stamm (trans. Mervyn E. J. Richardson), *The Hebrew and Aramaic Lexicon of the Old Testament: Study Edition*, vol. 1 (Leiden: Brill, 2001), p. 107.
49. Genesis 9.20–27.
50. 1 Corinthians 11.10. I also discussed this passage in Chapter 8: Divine Sex (p. 155).
51. John 20.24–29.
52. Exodus 34.29–35 (Moses' face); Numbers 21.9; *cf.* 2 Kings 18.4 (serpent statue); 2 Kings 2.9–11, 15 (Elijah and Elisha). See Meir Malul, *Knowledge, Control, and Sex: Studies in Biblical Thought, Culture, and Worldview* (Tel Aviv: Tel Aviv-Jaffa Archaeological Center Publications, 2002), pp. 209, 286–7, 351; Nicole Tilford, 'The Affected Eye: Re-Examining a Biblical Idiom', in *Biblical Interpretation* 23(2), 2015, pp. 207–21.
53. Deuteronomy 11.11–12.

54. Isaiah 40.22.
55. Genesis 17.11; *cf.* 9.12–17. See Michael V. Fox, 'The Sign of the Covenant: Circumcision in the Light of the Priestly '*ôt* Etiologies', in *Revue Biblique* 81(4), 1974, pp. 557–96; Schipper and Stackert, 'The Priestly Deity', pp. 474–77. My thinking about this issue has also been helped by Rachel Neis, *The Sense of Sight in Rabbinic Culture: Jewish Ways of Seeing in Late Antiquity* (Cambridge: Cambridge University Press, 2013).
56. Psalm 139.13–16; *cf.* Jeremiah 1.5; Job 10.8–11.
57. Isaiah 3.16.
58. Isaiah 3.16–24.
59. 1 Samuel 9.2; 10.23–24.
60. 1 Samuel 31.1–10. For the transferral of divine approval from Saul to David, see 1 Samuel 16.12–14.
61. 1 Samuel 16.7.
62. Psalm 11.4–5.
63. Psalm 17.2–8.
64. Job 7.19–20.
65. Job 16.9, 13.
66. John H. Elliott, *Beware the Evil Eye: The Evil Eye in the Bible and the Ancient World*, vol. 3 (Eugene, OR: Cascade Books, 2016), pp. 1–110.
67. Francesca Stavrakopoulou, 'Making Bodies: On Body Modification and Religious Materiality in the Hebrew Bible', in *Hebrew Bible and Ancient Israel* 2(4), 2013, pp. 532–53 (here, pp. 543–47).
68. Deuteronomy 11.11–12; Ezra 5.5.
69. Zacharias Kotze, 'The Evil Eye of YHWH', in *Journal for Semitics* 17(1), 2008, pp. 207–18; Kristen Lee Helms, 'The Roaming Eyes of Yhwh: The Hypostatization of the Eyes of God in Persian Period Yehud', unpublished PhD dissertation (Princeton Theological Seminary, 2013).
70. Job 2.10.
71. See the entries for 'Belial' and 'Mastemah' in Karel van der Toorn, Bob Becking and Pieter W. van der Hoorst (eds.), *Dictionary of Deities and Demons in the Bible* (second extensively revised edition) (Leiden: Brill, 1999), pp. 169–71 and pp. 553–54. See also Dale B. Martin, 'When Did Angels Become Demons?', in *Journal of Biblical Literature* 129(4), 2010, pp. 657–77; Loren T. Stuckenbruck, 'The Demonic World of the Dead Sea Scrolls', in Ida Fröhlich and Erkki Koskenniemi (eds.), *Evil and the Devil* (London: T&T Clark, 2013), pp. 51–70; Annette Yoshiko Reed, *Demons, Angels, and Writing in Ancient Judaism* (Cambridge: Cambridge University Press, 2020).

72. See Eric Sorensen, *Possession and Exorcism in the New Testament and Early Christianity* (Tübingen: Mohr Siebeck, 2002); Miriam T. Brand, *Evil Within and Without: The Source of Sin and Its Nature as Portrayed in Second Temple Literature* (Göttingen: Vandenhoeck & Ruprecht, 2013); Loren T. Stuckenbruck, 'The Human Being and Demonic Invasion: Therapeutic Models in Ancient Jewish and Christian Texts', in Christopher C. H. Cook (ed.), *Spirituality, Theology and Mental Health: Multidisciplinary Perspectives* (London: SCM Press, 2013), pp. 94–123.
73. Ruth Bielfeldt, 'Sight and Light', in Michael Squire (ed.), *Sight and the Ancient Senses* (Abingdon: Routledge, 2016), pp. 123–42.
74. Matthew 5.29; 6.22–23; 18.9; *cf.* Mark 9.47; Luke 11.34–36.
75. Sirach 23.19.
76. 2 Enoch 39.4.
77. James R. Davila, *Hekhalot Literature in Translation: Major Texts of Merkavah Mysticism* (Leiden: Brill, 2013), pp. 62–3.

CHAPTER 20: GASP AND GULP

1. Zvi Gal, Dina Shalem and Howard Smithline, 'The Peqi'in Cave: A Chalcolithic Cemetery in Upper Galilee, Israel', in *Near Eastern Archaeology* 74(4), 2011, pp. 196–206; Dina Shalem, 'Do the Images on Chalcolithic Ossuaries Comprise Attributes?', in Piotr Bieliński, Michał Gawlikowski et al., *Proceedings of the Eighth International Congress on the Archaeology of the Ancient Near East, 30 April–4 May 2012, Volume I* (Wiesbaden: Harrassowitz Verlag, 2014), pp. 505–24.
2. David Ilan and Yorke M. Rowan, 'Expediting Reincarnation in the Fifth Millennium BCE: Interpreting the Chalcolithic Ossuaries of the Southern Levant', in *Oxford Journal of Archaeology* 38(3), 2019, pp. 248–70.
3. Lynn M. Meskell and Rosemary A. Joyce, *Embodied Lives: Figuring Ancient Maya and Egyptian Experience* (London: Routledge, 2003), pp. 70–4. For Osiris' epithet, see Adolf Erman and Hermann Grapow, *Wörterbuch der Ägyptischen Sprache*, vol. 1 (Berlin: Akademie-Verlag, 1926), p. 578; *cf.* Alexandre Alexandrovich Loktionov, 'May my nose and ears be cut off: Practical and "Supra-practical" Aspects of Mutilation in the Egyptian New Kingdom', in *Journal of the Economic and Social History of the Orient* 60(3), 2017, pp. 263–91.
4. Walker and Dick, 'The Induction of the Cult Image', pp. 55–121.
5. E.g., Deuteronomy 4.28; Psalms 115.6; 135.17; Jeremiah 10.14; 51.17; Habakkuk 2.19.

6. E.g., Genesis 8.21; Leviticus 26.31; Numbers 28.2. For examples of Yahweh as a breathing deity, see Genesis 2.7; 2 Samuel 22.16; Job 4.9; 37.10; Psalms 18.15; 33.6; Isaiah 42.14.

7. E.g., Exodus 30.22–37. See Cornelius Houtman, 'On the Function of the Holy Incense (Exodus XXX 34–38) and the Sacred Anointing Oil (Exodus XXX 22–33)', in *Vetus Testamentum* 42(4), 1992, pp. 458–64.

8. The story about Uzziah is told in 2 Chronicles 26.16–21 (compare that of Jeroboam ben Nebat in 1 Kings 13). See further Yitzhaq Feder, 'Contagion and Cognition: Bodily Experience and the Conceptualization of Pollution (*ṭum'ah*) in the Hebrew Bible', in *Journal of Near Eastern Studies* 72(2), 2013, pp. 151–67; Thomas Kazen, 'Dirt and Disgust: Body and Morality in Biblical Purity Laws', in Naphtali S. Meshel, Jeffrey Stackert, David P. Wright and Baruch J. Schwartz (eds.), *Perspectives on Purity and Purification in the Bible* (London and New York, NY: T&T Clark, 2008), pp. 43–64.

9. Ephesians 5.2. Other texts in which Jesus offers himself as a sacrifice include Hebrews 7.27; 9.25–26; 10.10–14. See Christian A. Eberhart, *The Sacrifice of Jesus: Understanding Atonement Biblically* (Philadelphia, PA: Fortress Press, 2011).

10. Isaiah 34.3–4.

11. *Genesis Rabbah* 47.7. Harry Freedman and Maurice Simon (trans. and ed.), *Midrash Rabbah: Genesis*, vol. 1 (London: Soncino, 1939), p. 403.

12. Exodus 34.6; cf. Numbers 14.18. For the matching measurements of God's nose and little finger, see van der Horst, 'Measurement of the Body', p. 62. See further Freidman, 'Anthropomorphism', pp. 165–68.

13. Isaiah 65.3, 5. On the assumed physiology of the language of anger (including God's), see further Yael Avrahami, *The Senses of Scripture: Sensory Perception in the Hebrew Bible* (London and New York, NY: T&T Clark, 2012), pp. 105, 149–50; Nicole L. Tilford, *Sensing World, Sensing Wisdom: The Cognitive Foundation of Biblical Metaphors* (Atlanta, GA: Society of Biblical Literature, 2017), pp. 142–5.

14. Isaiah 42.14–15.

15. Isaiah 30.27–28, 30, 33.

16. Job 4.9.

17. 2 Samuel 22.16; cf. Psalm 18.15. For Yahweh's weaponized snort at the Sea of Reeds, see Exodus 15.8.

18. Isaiah 30.27–33.

19. *KTU* 5 ii 2–5.

20. *KTU* 1.5 i 19–22.

21. Isaiah 28.14–22; Hosea 13.14. Other biblical references to Mot include Psalm 49.15; Jeremiah 9.21; Habakkuk 2.5.

22. Numbers 16.27–34; 26.9–10; *cf.* Deuteronomy 11.6; Psalm 106.17. For further examples of the swallowing underworld, see Exodus 15.12; Isaiah 5.14; Habakkuk 2.5; Proverbs 1.12; Psalm 69.15.

23. Isaiah 25.7.

24. 1 Corinthians 15.20–28; *cf.* Romans 5.14, 17.

25. 1 Corinthians 15.54. In the next verse, Paul also draws on Yahweh's taunting of Mot in Hosea 13.14. See further John F. Healey, '"Death Is Swallowed Up in Victory" (1 Corinthians 15:54): Canaanite Mot in Prophecy and Apocalypse', in Peter J. Harland and Robert Hayward (eds.), *New Heaven and New Earth: Prophecy and the Millennium* (Leiden: Brill, 1999), pp. 205–15.

26. Jonah 1.17–2.10.

27. Genesis 2.7.

28. Ezekiel 37.6.

29. See further Ingrid E. Lilly, 'Conceptualizing Spirit: Supernatural Meteorology and Winds of Distress in the Hebrew Bible and the Ancient Near East', in Joel Baden, Hindy Najman and Eibert J. C. Tigchelaar (eds.), *Sibyls, Scriptures, and Scrolls: John Collins at Seventy* (Leiden: Brill, 2016), pp. 826–44; Enrique Jiménez, 'Highway to Hell: The Wind as Cosmic Conveyors in Mesopotamian Incantation Texts', in Greta Van Buylaere, Mikko Luukko, Daniel Schwemer and Avigail Mertens-Wagschal (eds.), *Sources of Evil: Studies in Mesopotamian Exorcistic Lore* (Leiden: Brill, 2018), pp. 316–50.

30. See Arie Shifman, '"A Scent" of the Spirit: Exegesis of an Enigmatic Verse (Isaiah 11:3)', in *Journal of Biblical Literature* 131(2), 2012, pp. 241–9; Ian D. Ritchie, 'The Nose Knows: Bodily Knowing in Isaiah 11.3', in *Journal for the Study of the Old Testament* 87(1), 2000, pp. 59–73.

31. Micah 3.8. In Luke 4.14–21, Jesus casts himself as one of Yahweh's prophets, corporeally empowered by the deity's *ruah*, when he reads aloud Isaiah 61.1–2. 'Today, this scripture has been fulfilled in your hearing', he declares.

32. Genesis 1.2; 8.1.

33. Psalm 33.6.

34. See Lewis, 'The Identity and Function of Ugaritic Sha'tiqatu', pp. 1–28; *idem*, '"Athtartu's Incantations and the Use of Divine Names as Weapons', in *Journal of Near Eastern Studies* 70(2), 2011, pp. 207–27.

35. Exodus 31.17. Most English translations render the Hebrew 'he was refreshed' or 'he refreshed himself', but the use of the verb here points to the physiology of panting after laborious work, as Exodus 23.12 suggests. See Robert Alter, *The Hebrew Bible: A Translation with Commentary*, vol. 1 (New York, NY: W. W. Norton, 2019), pp. 310, 338,

following Hans-Walter Wolff, *Anthropology of the Old Testament* (Philadelphia, PA: Fortress Press, 1974), p. 13.

36. Job 4.12–21. Note the reference to God's toxic, angry breath shortly before, in verse 9. There are good reasons to suspect that older versions of the book of Job originally attributed this eerie encounter to Job himself, rather than Eliphaz. See Edward L. Greenstein, *Job: A New Translation* (New Haven, CT: Yale University Press, 2019), p. 16.

37. Proverbs 8.22–31.

38. Sirach 24.1–15.

39. Sirach 24.1, 23.

40. Wisdom of Solomon 7.25–26.

41. John 1.1–3, 14.

42. Romans 1.1–3.

43. In thinking about *pneuma* in early Christianity, I have found the following discussions particularly helpful: Troels Engberg-Pedersen, *Cosmology and Self in the Apostle Paul: The Material Spirit* (Oxford: Oxford University Press, 2010); M. David Litwa, *Iesus Deus: The Early Christian Depiction of Jesus as a Mediterranean God* (Minneapolis, MN: Fortress Press, 2014); Jörg Frey and John Levinson (eds.), *The Holy Spirit, Inspiration, and the Cultures of Antiquity: Multidisciplinary Perspectives* (Berlin: de Gruyter, 2014); Matthew W. Bates, *The Birth of the Trinity: Jesus, God, and Spirit in New Testament and Early Christian Interpretations of the Old Testament* (Oxford: Oxford University Press, 2015).

44. 1 Corinthians 15.45; see also 1 Peter 3.18; 1 Timothy 3.16; Acts 2.36.

45. Luke 1.13–19.

46. Matthew 1.18, 20.

47. Luke 1.35.

48. Luke 1.38. On climatic conception, including that of Plato, see Litwa, *Iesus Deus*, pp. 37–67. For Plutarch's *Table Talk* (717d–e, 718a), see Paul A. Clement and Herbert B. Hoffleit, *Plutarch: Moralia, Volume VIII* (Loeb Classical Library, 424; Cambridge, MA: Harvard University Press, 1969).

49. Betsy Bauman-Martin, 'Mary and the Marquise: Reading the Annunciation in the Romantic Rape Tradition', in Roberta Sterman Sabbath (ed.), *Sacred Tropes: Tanakh, New Testament, and Qur'an as Literature and Culture* (Leiden: Brill, 2009), pp. 217–31; *cf.* Stephen Benko, *The Virgin Goddess: Studies in the Pagan and Christian Roots of Mariology* (Leiden: Brill, 2004), pp. 10–11; Marianne Bjelland Kartzow,

The Slave Metaphor and Gendered Enslavement in Early Christian Discourse
(New York, NY: Routledge, 2018), pp. 47–70.

50. Acts 2.1–4.
51. Acts 2.6–21; Joel 2.28–29.
52. John 20.22.
53. John 3.8.
54. John 5.21.
55. My thinking about this has been helped particularly by James D. G.
Dunn, 'Baptism in the Holy Spirit: Yet Once More – Again', in *Journal of Pentecostal Theology* 19(1), 2010, pp. 32–43; Marianne Meye
Thompson, 'The Breath of Life: John 20:22–23 Once More', in
Graham N. Stanton, Bruce W. Longenecker and Stephen C. Barton
(eds.), *The Holy Spirit and Christian Origins: Essays in Honor of James D. G. Dunn* (Grand Rapids, MI: Eerdmans, 2004), pp. 69–78;
Jeannine K. Brown 'Creation's Renewal in the Gospel of John', in
Catholic Biblical Quarterly 72, 2010, pp. 275–90; Annette Weissenrieder,
'The Infusion of the Spirit: The Meaning of ἐμφυσάω in John 20:22–
23', in Jörg Frey and John Levinson (eds.), *The Holy Spirit, Inspiration, and the Cultures of Antiquity: Multidisciplinary Perspectives* (Berlin: de
Gruyter, 2014), pp. 119–51; Jeremy W. Barrier, 'Jesus' Breath: A
Physiological Analysis of πνεῦμα within Paul's Letter to the
Galatians', in *Journal for the Study of the New Testament* 37(2), 2014,
pp. 115–38.
56. Evidence is found in the so-called Apostolic Tradition (which
probably draws on much older traditions) and in the works of
theologians including Tertullian and Augustine. See further Robin
M. Jensen, *Baptismal Imagery in Early Christianity: Ritual, Visual, and
Theological Dimensions* (Grand Rapids, MI: Baker Academic, 2012),
pp. 35–38; Mary Thurlkill, *Sacred Scents in Early Christianity and Islam*
(Lanham, MD: Lexington, 2016), pp. 88–94; Susan Ashbrook Harvey,
Scenting Salvation: Ancient Christianity and the Olfactory Imagination
(Berkeley, CA: University of California Press, 2006).
57. Here (as elsewhere) Ambrose is alluding to Ephesians 5.2. Ambrose,
Sacraments 1.1.3, trans. Roy Joseph Deferrari, *Saint Ambrose, Theological and Dogmatic Works* (Washington, DC: Catholic University of America
Press, 1963).
58. John 4.24; *cf.* 2 Corinthians 3.17.
59. 2 Timothy 3.16.

CHAPTER 21: AN AUTOPSY

1. Bob Becking, 'The Gods, in Whom They Trusted . . . Assyrian
   Evidence for Iconic Polytheism in Ancient Israel?', in Bob Becking,
   Meindert Dijkstra, Marjo C. A. Korpel and Karel J. H. Vriezen (eds.),
   *Only One God? Monotheism in Ancient Israel and the Veneration of the
   Goddess Asherah* (London: Sheffield Academic Press, 2001), pp. 151–63;
   Römer, 'Y avait-il une statue de Yhwh dans le premier temple?', p. 56;
   Stéphanie Anthonioz, 'Le destruction de la statue de Yhwh', 2015,
   online at https://www.academia.edu/11719779/La_destruction_de_la
   _statue_de_Yhwh. See too the works cited on p. 435, n. 12.
2. Exodus 20.4; *cf.* Deuteronomy 5.8.
3. Aristobulus, fragments 2 and 4 in Carl R. Holladay (trans. and ed.),
   Fragments from Hellenistic Jewish Authors, vol. 3 (Atlanta, GA: Scholars
   Press, 1995). Philo's insistence on the philosophical priority of Moses
   and the Torah is threaded through his many works. For examples and
   further discussion, see Peter van Nuffelen, *Rethinking the Gods:
   Philosophical Readings of Religion in the Post-Hellenistic Period*
   (Cambridge: Cambridge University Press, 2011), pp. 200–16; Arthur
   P. Urbano, *The Philosophical Life: Biography and the Crafting of
   Intellectual Identity in Late Antiquity* (Washington, DC: Catholic
   University of America, 2013), pp. 100–105; Gregory E. Sterling,
   ' "The Jewish Philosophy": Reading Moses via Hellenistic Philosophy
   according to Philo', in Torrey Seland (ed.), *Reading Philo: A Handbook
   to Philo of Alexandria* (Grand Rapids, MA: Eerdmans, 2014), pp. 129–54;
   Erich S. Gruen, *The Construct of Identity in Hellenistic Judaism: Essays in
   Early Jewish Literature and History* (Berlin: de Gruyter, 2016), pp. 133–52.
4. Maimonides, *Guide*, 1.35, trans. Shlomo Pines, *The Guide of the
   Perplexed*, vol. 1 (Chicago, IL: University of Chicago Press, 1963).
5. See further Marc B. Shapiro, *The Limits of Orthodox Theology:
   Maimonides' Thirteen Principles Reappraised* (Oxford: Liverpool
   University Press, 2004), pp. 60–85; Daniel H. Frank, 'Maimonides and
   Medieval Jewish Aristotelianism' in Daniel H. Frank and Oliver
   Leaman (eds.), *The Cambridge Companion to Medieval Jewish Philosophy*
   (Cambridge: Cambridge University Press, 2006), pp. 135–56. On
   Maimonides' cultural contexts, see Sarah Stroumsa, *Maimonides in His
   World: Portrait of a Mediterranean Thinker* (Princeton, NJ: Princeton
   University Press, 2009).
6. Martin Goodman, *A History of Judaism* (London: Allen Lane, 2017),
   p. 331. As Herbert A. Davidson puts it in his book *Maimonides the
   Rationalist* (Oxford: Liverpool University Press, 2011), p. vii,

Maimonides' *Guide of the Perplexed* is 'the most widely read and influential Jewish philosophical work ever written'.

7. See further Christoph Markschies (trans. Alexander Johannes Edmonds), *God's Body: Jewish, Christian, and Pagan Images of God* (Waco, TX: Baylor University Press, 2019), pp. 182–282.

8. Jeffrey E. Brower, 'Simplicity and Aseity', in Thomas P. Flint and Michael C. Rea (eds.), *The Oxford Handbook of Philosophical Theology* (Oxford: Oxford University Press, 2011), pp. 105–28; Oliver D. Crisp, 'Incorporeality', in Chad Meister and Paul Copan (eds.), *The Routledge Companion to Philosophy of Religion* (second edition) (New York, NY: Routledge, 2013), pp. 344–55.

9. Ludwig Ott (trans. Patrick Lynch), *Fundamentals of Catholic Dogma* (second edition) (Cork: Mercier, 1957), pp. 31–32.

10. Psalm 8.3–6.

Bibliography

Abramson, Henry, and Carrie Hannon, 'Depicting the Ambiguous Wound: Circumcision in Medieval Art', in Elizabeth Wyner Mark (ed.), *The Covenant of Circumcision: New Perspectives on an Ancient Jewish Rite* (Hanover, NH: Brandeis University Press, 2003), pp. 98–113.

Abusharaf, Rogaia Mustafa, 'Introduction: The Custom in Question', in Rogaia Mustafa Abusharaf (ed.), *Female Circumcision: Multicultural Perspectives* (Philadelphia, PA: University of Pennsylvania Press, 2006), pp. 1–24.

Ackerman, Susan, *When Heroes Love: The Ambiguity of Eros in the Stories of Gilgamesh and David* (New York, NY: Columbia University Press, 2005).

Alstola, Tero, *Judeans in Babylonia: A Study of Deportees in the Sixth and Fifth Centuries BCE* (Leiden: Brill, 2020).

Alter, Robert, *The Hebrew Bible: A Translation with Commentary*, 3 vols (New York, NY: W. W. Norton, 2019).

Ambrose (trans. Roy Joseph Deferrari), *Sacraments*, in *Saint Ambrose, Theological and Dogmatic Works* (Fathers of the Church, 44; Washington, DC: Catholic University of America Press, 1963).

Ames, Frank Ritchel, 'The Red-Stained Warrior in Ancient Israel', in Brad E. Kelle, Frank Ritchel Ames and Jacob L. Wright (eds.), *Warfare, Ritual, and Symbol in Biblical and Modern Contexts* (Atlanta, GA: Society of Biblical Literature, 2014), pp. 83–109.

Andersson, Ann, 'Thoughts on Material Expressions of Cultic Practice: Standing Stone Monuments of the Early Bronze Age in the Southern Levant', in Nicola Laneri (ed.), *Defining the Sacred: Approaches to the Archaeology of Religion in the Near East* (Oxford: Oxbow, 2015), pp. 48–59.

Anthonioz, Stéphanie, 'Le destruction de la statue de Yhwh', 2015, online at https://www.academia.edu/11719779/La_destruction_de_la_statue_de_Yhwh.

Apollodorus (trans. J. G. Frazer), *The Library, Volume I: Books 1–3* (Loeb Classical Library, 121; Cambridge, MA: Harvard University Press, 1921).

Aristophanes (trans. Jeffrey Henderson), *Clouds. Wasps. Peace* (Loeb Classical Library, 488; Cambridge, MA: Harvard University Press, 1998).

Asher-Greve, Julia M., 'Reading the Horned Crown', in *Archiv für Orientforschung* 42/43, 1995/1996, pp. 181–9.

—— and Deborah Sweeney, 'On Nakedness, Nudity, and Gender in Egyptian and Mesopotamian Art', in Silvia Schroer (ed.), *Images and Gender: Contributions to the Hermeneutics of Reading Ancient Art* (Fribourg/Göttingen: Academic Press/Vandenhoeck & Ruprecht, 2006), pp. 111–60.

Assante, Julia, 'Men Looking at Men: The Homoerotics of Power in the State Arts of Assyria', in Ilona Zsolnay (ed.), *Being a Man: Negotiating Ancient Constructs of Masculinity* (New York, NY: Routledge, 2017), pp. 42–82.

Aster, Shawn Zelig, *The Unbeatable Light: Melammu and Its Biblical Parallels* (Münster: Ugarit-Verlag, 2012).

Athanasius (trans. Carolinne White), *Life of Antony* in Carolinne White, *Early Christian Lives* (London: Penguin, 1998).

Attridge, Harold W., and Robert A. Oden, *Philo of Byblos: The Phoenician History. Introduction, Critical Text, Translation, Notes* (Washington, DC: Catholic Biblical Association of America, 1981).

Augustine (trans. Edmund Hill), *The Literal Meaning of Genesis* in *On Genesis* (Works of Saint Augustine, 1/13; Hyde Park, NY: New City Press, 2002).

Avrahami, Yael, *The Senses of Scripture: Sensory Perception in the Hebrew Bible* (London and New York, NY: T&T Clark, 2012).

Bachvarova, Mary R., 'Wisdom of Former Days: The Manly Hittite King and Foolish Kumarbi, Father of the Gods', in Ilona Zsolnay (ed.), *Being a Man: Negotiating Ancient Constructs of Masculinity* (New York, NY: Routledge, 2017), pp. 83–111.

Bahrani, Zainab, *Mesopotamia: Ancient Art and Architecture* (London: Thames & Hudson, 2017).

Baldriga, Irene, 'The First Version of Michelangelo's Christ for S. Maria Sopra Minerva', in *Burlington Magazine* 142(1173), 2000, pp. 740–45.

Bale, Anthony (ed. and trans.), *The Book of Margery Kempe* (Oxford: Oxford University Press, 2015).

Barnhouse, Rebecca, and Benjamin Withers (ed.), *The Old English Hexateuch: Aspects and Approaches* (Kalamazoo, MI: Medieval Institute Publications, 2000).

Barrett, Caitlín E., 'Was Dust Their Food and Clay Their Bread? Grave Goods, the Mesopotamian Afterlife, and the Liminal Role of Inana/Ishtar', in *Journal of Ancient Near Eastern Religions* 7(1), 2007, pp. 7–65.

Barrier, Jeremy W., 'Jesus' Breath: A Physiological Analysis of πνεῦμα within Paul's Letter to the Galatians', in *Journal for the Study of the New Testament* 37(2), 2014, pp. 115–38.

Barton, John, *A History of the Bible: The Book and Its Faiths* (London: Allen Lane, 2019).

Barton, Mukti, 'The Bible in Black Theology', in *Black Theology* 9(1), 2011, pp. 57–76.

Baskin, Judith R., *Midrashic Women: Formations of the Feminine in Rabbinic Literature* (Waltham, MA: Brandeis University Press, 2002).

Bates, Matthew W., *The Birth of the Trinity: Jesus, God, and Spirit in New Testament and Early Christian Interpretations of the Old Testament* (Oxford and New York, NY: Oxford University Press, 2015).

Bauman-Martin, Betsy, 'Mary and the Marquise: Reading the Annunciation in the Romantic Rape Tradition', in Roberta Sterman Sabbath (ed.), *Sacred Tropes: Tanakh, New Testament, and Qur'an as Literature and Culture* (Leiden: Brill, 2009), pp. 217–31.

Baumann, Gerlinde, *Love and Violence: Marriage as Metaphor for the Relationship between YHWH and Israel in the Prophetic Books* (Collegeville, MN: Liturgical Press, 2003).

Baynes, Leslie, *The Heavenly Book Motif in Judeo-Christian Apocalypses, 200 BCE–200 CE* (Leiden: Brill, 2012).

Beal, Timothy K., *Religion and Its Monsters* (London: Routledge, 2002).

Beatrice, Pier Franco (trans. Adam Kamesar), *The Transmission of Sin: Augustine and the Pre-Augustinian Sources* (Oxford: Oxford University Press, 2013).

Becking, Bob, 'The Gods, in Whom They Trusted . . . Assyrian Evidence for Iconic Polytheism in Ancient Israel?', in Bob Becking, Meindert Dijkstra, Marjo C. A. Korpel and Karel J. H. Vriezen (eds.), *Only One God? Monotheism in Ancient Israel and the Veneration of the Goddess Asherah* (London: Sheffield Academic Press, 2001), pp. 151–63.

Benko, Stephen, *The Virgin Goddess: Studies in the Pagan and Christian Roots of Mariology* (Leiden: Brill, 2004).

Bennett, Matthew R., and Sarita A. Morse, *Human Footprints: Fossilised Locomotion?* (London: Springer, 2014).

Benzel, Kim, ' "What Goes In Is What Comes Out" – But What Was Already There? Divine Materials and Materiality in Ancient Mesopotamia', in Beate Pongratz-Leisten and Karen Sonik (eds.), *The Materiality of Divine Agency* (Berlin: de Gruyter, 2015), pp. 89–118.

Berger, P.-R., 'Der Kyros-Zylinder mit dem Zusatzfragment BIN II Nr. 32 und die akkadischen Personennamen in Danielbuch', in *Zeitschrift für Assyriologie* 64(2), 1975, pp. 192–234.

Berger, Teresa, *Gender Differences and the Making of Liturgical History: Lifting the Veil on Liturgy's Past* (Burlington, VT: Ashgate, 2011).

—— 'Women's Liturgical Practices and Leadership Roles in Early Christian Communities', in Joan E. Taylor and Ilaria L. E. Ramelli (eds.), *Patterns of Women's Leadership in Early Christianity* (Oxford and New York, NY: Oxford University Press, 2021), pp. 180–94.

Bever, Lindsey, 'In a church's ashes, firefighters find unexpected survivors: Bibles, untouched by flame', in *Washington Post*, 5 March 2019, online at https://www.washingtonpost.com/religion/2019/03/05/churchs-ashes-firefighters-find-unexpected-survivors-bibles-untouched-by-flame/.

Biale, David, *Eros and the Jews: From Biblical Israel to Contemporary America* (Berkeley, CA: University of California Press, 1997).

Bibb, Bryan, 'There's No Sex in Your Violence: Patriarchal Translation in Ezekiel 16 and 23', in *Review and Expositor* 111(4), 2014, pp. 337–45.

Bidmead, Julye, *The Akitu Festival: Religious Continuity and Royal Legitimation in Mesopotamia* (Piscataway, NJ: Gorgias Press, 2002).

Bielfeldt, Ruth, 'Sight and Light', in Michael Squire (ed.), *Sight and the Ancient Senses* (Abingdon: Routledge, 2016), pp. 123–42.

Biggs, Robert D. (ed.), *ŠÀ.ZI.GA. Ancient Mesopotamian Potency Incantations* (Locust Valley, NY: J. J. Augustin, 1967).

Billet, Bret L., *Cultural Relativism in the Face of the West: The Plight of Women and Children* (New York, NY: Palgrave Macmillan, 2007).

Black, Daniel, 'What Is a Face?', in *Body & Society* 17(4), 2011, pp. 1–25.

Black, Jeremy, and Anthony Green, *Gods, Demons and Symbols of Ancient Mesopotamia: An Illustrated Dictionary* (London: British Museum Press, 1992).

—— and Graham Cunningham, Jarle Ebeling, Esther Flückiger-Hawker, Eleanor Robson, Jonathan Taylor, Gábor Zólyomi, *The Electronic Text Corpus of Sumerian Literature* (University of Oxford, 1998–2006), online at http://etcsl.orinst.ox.ac.uk/.

—— and Graham Cunningham, Eleanor Robson, Gábor Zólyomi, *The Literature of Ancient Sumer* (Oxford: Oxford University Press, 2004).

Bloch-Smith, Elizabeth, 'Solomon's Temple: The Politics of Ritual Space', in Barry M. Gittlen (ed.), *Sacred Time, Sacred Place: Archaeology and the Religion of Israel* (Winona Lake, IN: Eisenbrauns, 2002), pp. 83–94.

—— 'Will the Real Massebot Please Stand Up: Cases of Real and Mistakenly Identified Standing Stones in Ancient Israel', in Gary M. Beckman and Theodore J. Lewis (eds.), *Text, Artifact, and Image: Revealing Ancient Israelite Religion* (Providence, NJ: Brown Judaic Studies, 2006), pp. 64–79.

Block, Daniel I., 'Divine Abandonment: Ezekiel's Adaptation of an Ancient Near Eastern Motif', in Margaret S. Odell and John T. Strong (eds.), *The Book of Ezekiel: Theological and Anthropological Perspectives* (Atlanta, GA: Society of Biblical Literature, 2000), pp. 15–42.

Blum, Edward J., and Paul Harvey, *The Color of Christ: The Son of God and the Saga of Race in America* (Chapel Hill, NC: University of North Carolina Press, 2012).

Bodi, Daniel, 'Les *gillûlîm* chez Ézéchiel et dans l'Ancien Testament, et les différentes pratiques cultuelles associées à ce terme', in *Revue Biblique* 100(4), 1993, pp. 481–510.

Boer, Roland, *The Earthy Nature of the Bible: Fleshly Readings of Sex, Masculinity, and Carnality* (London: Palgrave MacMillan, 2012).

Bogdanos, Matthew, 'The Casualties of War: The Truth about the Iraq Museum', in *American Journal of Archaeology* 109(3), 2005, pp. 477–526.

Bokovoy, David E., 'Did Eve Acquire, Create, or Procreate with Yahweh? A Grammatical and Contextual Reassessment of קנה in Genesis 4:1', in *Vetus Testamentum* 63(1), 2013, pp. 19–35.

Bord, Janet, *Footprints in Stone: Imprints of Giants, Heroes, Holy People, Devils, Monsters and Supernatural Beings* (Loughborough: Heart of Albion, 2004).

Borger, Rykle, *Beiträge zum Inschriftenwerk Assurbanipals: Die Prismenklassen A, B, C = K, D, E, F, G, H, J und T sowie andere Inschriften* (Wiesbaden: Harrossowitz, 1996).

Bosworth, David A., 'The Tears of God in the Book of Jeremiah', in *Biblica* 94(1), 2013, pp. 24–46.

Botta, Alejandro, and Pabo R. Andiñach (eds.), *The Bible and the Hermeneutics of Liberation* (Atlanta, GA: Society of Biblical Literature, 2009).

Bottéro, Jean (trans. Teresa Lavender Fagan), *Religion in Ancient Mesopotamia* (Chicago, IL: University of Chicago Press, 2001).

Bowen, Matthew L., ' "They Came and Held Him by the Feet and Worshipped Him': Proskynesis before Jesus in Its Biblical and Ancient Near Eastern Context', in *Studies in the Bible and Antiquity* 5(6), 2013, pp. 63–89.

Bowie, Fiona, *The Anthropology of Religion: An Introduction* (second edition) (Oxford: Blackwell, 2006).

Boyarin, Daniel, 'The Song of Songs: Lock or Key? Intertextuality, Allegory and Midrash', in Regina M. Schwartz (ed.), *The Book and the Text: The Bible and Literary Theory* (Oxford: Blackwell, 1990), pp. 214–30.

—— '"This We Know to Be the Carnal Israel": Circumcision and the Erotic Life of God and Israel', in *Critical Inquiry* 18(3), 1992, pp. 474–505.

Brakke, David, 'The Problematization of Nocturnal Emissions in Early Christian Syria, Egypt, and Gaul', in *Journal of Early Christian Studies* 3(4), 1995, pp. 419–60.

Brand, Miriam T., *Evil Within and Without: The Source of Sin and Its Nature as Portrayed in Second Temple Literature* (Göttingen: Vandenhoeck & Ruprecht, 2013).

Brandon, S. G. F., 'Christ in Verbal and Depicted Imagery: A Problem of Early Christian Iconography', in Jacob Neusner (ed.), *Christianity, Judaism and Other Greco-Roman Cults: Studies for Morton Smith at Sixty, Part 2* (Leiden: Brill, 1975), pp. 165–72.

Braude, William G., and Israel J. Kapstein, *Pěsikta dě-Rab Kahăna: R. Kahana's Compilation of Discourses for Sabbaths and Festal Days* (second edition) (Philadelphia, PA: Jewish Publications Society, 2002).

Brenner, Athalya, 'Pornoprophetics Revisited: Some Additional Reflections', in *Journal for the Study of the Old Testament* 21(70), 1996, pp. 63–86.

—— *The Intercourse of Knowledge: On Gendering Desire and 'Sexuality' in the Hebrew Bible* (Leiden: Brill, 1997).

Brock, Ann Graham, 'Mary Magdalene' in Benjamin H. Dunning (ed.), *The Oxford Handbook of New Testament, Gender, and Sexuality* (Oxford and New York, NY: Oxford University Press, 2019), pp. 429–47.

Brower, Jeffrey E., 'Simplicity and Aseity', in Thomas P. Flint and Michael C. Rea (eds.), *The Oxford Handbook of Philosophical Theology* (Oxford and New York, NY: Oxford University Press, 2011), pp. 105–28.

Brown, Jeannine K., 'Creation's Renewal in the Gospel of John', in *Catholic Biblical Quarterly* 72(2), 2010, pp. 275–90.

Brunner, Hellmut, *Altägyptische Weisheit. Lehren für das Leben* (Zurich: Artemis, 1988).

Budin, Stephanie Lynn, *The Myth of Sacred Prostitution in Antiquity* (Cambridge: Cambridge University Press, 2008).

—— 'Phallic Fertility in the Ancient Near East and Egypt', in Nick Hopwood, Rebecca Flemming and Lauren Kassel (eds.), *Reproduction: Antiquity to the Present Day* (Cambridge: Cambridge University Press, 2018), pp. 25–38.

Buell, Denise Kimber, *Why This New Race? Ethnic Reasoning in Early Christianity* (New York, NY: Columbia University Press, 2005).

Burnett, Joel S., 'Iron Age Deities in Word, Image, and Name: Correlating Epigraphic, Iconographic, and Onomastic Evidence for the Ammonite God', in *Studies in the History and Archaeology of Jordan* 10, 2009, pp. 153–64.

—— 'Ammon, Moab and Edom: Gods and Kingdoms East of the Jordan', in *Biblical Archaeology Review* 42(6), 2016, pp. 26–40, 66–67.

Burrows, Mark. S., 'Foundations for an Erotic Christology: Bernard of Clairvaux on Jesus as "Tender Lover"', in *Anglican Theological Review* 83(4), 1998, pp. 477–93.

Bynum, Caroline Walker, *Holy Feast and Holy Fast: The Religious Significance of Food to Medieval Women* (Berkeley, CA: University of Los Angeles Press, 1987).

—— *Fragmentation and Redemption: Essays on Gender and the Human Body in Medieval Religion* (New York, NY: Zone Books, 1991).

Byron, Gay L., *Symbolic Blackness and Ethnic Difference in Early Christian Literature* (London and New York, NY: Routledge, 2002).

Callender, Dexter E., *Adam in Myth and History: Ancient Israelite Perspectives on the Primal Human* (Winona Lake, IN: Eisenbrauns, 2000).

Carter, J. Kameron, *Race: A Theological Account* (Oxford and New York, NY: Oxford University Press, 2008).

Cavadini, John C., 'From Letter to Spirit: The Multiple Senses of Scripture', in Paul M. Blowers and Peter W. Martens (eds.), *The Oxford Handbook to Early Christian Biblical Interpretation* (Oxford and New York, NY: Oxford University Press, 2019), pp. 126–48.

Chapman, Cynthia R., *The House of the Mother: The Social Roles of Maternal Kin in Biblical Hebrew Narrative and Poetry* (New Haven, CT: Yale University Press, 2016).

Charlesworth, James H. (ed.), *The Old Testament Pseudepigrapha*, 2 vols (Garden City, NY: Doubleday, 1983–85).

Chavel, Simon, 'The Face of God and the Etiquette of Eye-Contact: Visitation, Pilgrimage, and the Prophetic Vision in Ancient Israelite and Early Jewish Imagination', in *Jewish Studies Quarterly* 19(1), 2012, pp. 1–55.

Cifarelli, Megan, 'Gesture and Alterity in the Art of Ashurnasirpal II of Assyria', in *Art Bulletin* 80(2), 1998, pp. 210–28.

Clifford, Richard J., *The Cosmic Mountain in Canaan and the Old Testament* (Cambridge, MA: Harvard University Press, 1972).

Cline, Eric H., *The Battles of Armageddon: Megiddo and the Jezreel Valley from the Bronze Age to the Nuclear Age* (Ann Arbor, MI: Michigan University Press, 2000).

Cohen, Mark E., *Balag-Compositions: Sumerian Lamentation Liturgies of the Second and First Millennium BCE* (Malibu, CA: Undena Publications, 1974).

—— *The Canonical Lamentations of Ancient Mesopotamia*, 2 vols (Potomac, MD: Capital Decisions, 1988).

Cohen, Shaye J. D., *Why Aren't Jewish Women Circumcised? Gender and Covenant in Judaism* (Berkeley, CA: University of California Press, 2005).

Cohen, Yoram, 'Feet of Clay at Emar – A Happy End?', in *Orientalia* 74(2),
2005, pp. 165–70.

Cohn, Yehuda B., *Tangled Up in Text: Tefillin and the Ancient World*
(Providence, RI: Brown University, 2008).

Cone, James H., *The Cross and the Lynching Tree* (Maryknoll, NY: Orbis,
2011).

Connell, Martin F., 'Clothing the Body of Christ: An Inquiry about the
Letters of Paul', in *Worship* 85(2), 2011, pp. 28–146.

Coogan, Michael D., and Mark S. Smith (eds. and trans.), *Stories from
Ancient Canaan* (second edition) (Louisville, KY: Westminster John
Knox, 2012).

Cook, Gregory D., 'Nahum and the Question of Rape', *Bulletin for Biblical
Research* 26(3), 2016, pp. 341–52.

Cooper, Jerrold S., *The Return of Ninurta to Nippur* (Rome: Pontifical
Biblical Institute, 1978).

—— *Reconstructing History from Ancient Inscriptions: The Lagash-Umma Border
Conflict* (Malibu, CA: Undena Publications, 1981).

—— 'Female Trouble, and Troubled Males: Roiled Seas, Decadent Royals,
and Mesopotamian Masculinities in Myth and Practice', in Ilona
Zsolnay (ed.), *Being a Man: Negotiating Ancient Constructs of Masculinity*
(New York, NY: Routledge, 2017), pp. 112–24.

Cornelius, Izak, 'The Iconography of Ugarit', in Wilfred G. E. Watson and
Nicolas Wyatt (eds.), *Handbook of Ugaritic Studies* (Leiden: Brill, 1999),
pp. 586–602.

—— *The Many Faces of the Goddess: The Iconography of the Syro-Palestinian
Goddesses Anat, Astarte, Qedeshet, and Asherah c. 1500–1000 BCE*
(Fribourg/Göttingen: Academic Press/Vandenhoeck & Ruprecht,
2004).

—— 'Revisiting the Seated Figure from Ḥirbet Ṣaliḥ/Rāmat Rāḥēl', in
Zeitschrift des Deutschen Palästina-Vereins 131(1), 2015, pp. 29–43.

—— 'The Study of the Old Testament and the Material Imagery of the
Ancient Near East, with a Focus on the Body Parts of the Deity', in
Louis C. Jonker, Gideon R. Kotzé and Christl M. Maier (eds.),
Congress Volume Stellenbosch 2016 (Leiden: Brill, 2017), pp. 195–227.

Cornell, Collin, 'The Forgotten Female Figurines of Elephantine', in
Journal of Ancient Near Eastern Religions 18(2), 2018, pp. 111–32.

Costa, José, 'The Body of God in Ancient Rabbinic Judaism: Problems
of Interpretation', in *Revue de l'histoire des religions* 227(3), 2010,
pp. 283–316.

Cotton, Hannah M., and Leah Di Segni, Wener Eck, Benjamin Isaac, Alla Kushnir-Stein, Haggai Misgav, Jonathan Price, Israel Roll, Ada Yardeni (eds.), *Corpus Inscriptionum Iudaeae/Palaestinae. Volume 1, Part 1: Jerusalem* (Berlin: de Gruyter, 2010).

Cranz, Isabel, *Atonement and Purification: Priestly and Assyro-Babylonian Perspectives on Sin and Its Consequences* (Tübingen: Mohr Siebeck, 2017).

Crawford, Harriet, *Sumer and the Sumerians* (second edition) (Cambridge: Cambridge University Press, 1991).

Crisp, Oliver D., 'Incorporeality', in Chad Meister and Paul Copan (eds.), *The Routledge Companion to Philosophy of Religion* (second edition) (New York, NY: Routledge, 2013), pp. 344–55.

Croucher, Karina, 'Keeping the Dead Close: Grief and Bereavement in the Treatment of Skulls from the Neolithic Middle East', in *Mortality* 23(2), 2018, pp. 103–20.

Cunningham, Graham, *'Deliver Me from Evil': Mesopotamian Incantations 2500–1500 BC* (Rome: Pontifical Biblical Institute, 2007).

Dalley, Stephanie, *Myths from Mesopotamia: Creation, the Flood, Gilgamesh, and Others* (Oxford: Oxford University Press, 1989).

—— *Esther's Revenge at Susa: From Sennacherib to Ahasuerus* (Oxford: Oxford University Press, 2007).

Danby, Herbert, *The Mishnah: Translated from the Hebrew with Introduction and Brief Explanatory Notes* (Oxford: Clarendon Press, 1933).

Danti, Michael D., and Darren P. Ashby, Marina Gabriel, Susan Penacho, 'Special Report: Current Status of the Tell Ain Dara Temple', American Society of Overseas Research Cultural Heritage Initiatives (CHI): Safeguarding the Heritage of the Near East Initiative. Released online 2 March 2018; updated 7 March 2018. Online at https://www.asor.org/chi/reports/special-reports/tell-ain-dara-temple.

Darby, Erin, *Interpreting Judean Pillar Figurines: Gender and Empire in Judean Apotropaic Ritual* (Tübingen: Mohr Siebeck, 2014).

Davidson, Herbert A., *Maimonides the Rationalist* (Oxford: Liverpool University Press, 2011).

Davila, James R., *Hekhalot Literature in Translation: Major Texts of Merkavah Mysticism* (Leiden: Brill, 2013).

Day, Juliette J., 'Women's Rituals and Women's Ritualizing', in Risto Uro, Juliette J. Day, Richard E. DeMaris and Rikard Roitto (eds.), *The Oxford Handbook of Early Christian Ritual* (Oxford and New York, NY: Oxford University Press, 2019), pp. 644–60.

Day, Linda M., 'Rhetoric and Domestic Violence in Ezekiel 16', in *Biblical Interpretation* 8(3), 2000, pp. 205–30.

Dayan, Moshe, *Living with the Bible* (London: Weidenfeld and Nicolson, 1978).

DeConick, April D., *Holy Misogyny: Why the Sex and Gender Conflicts in the Early Church Still Matter* (New York, NY: Continuum, 2011).

DeMello, Margo, *Feet and Footwear: A Cultural Encyclopedia* (Santa Barbara, CA: Greenwood Press, 2009).

Dever, William G., *Did God Have a Wife? Archaeology and Folk Religion in Ancient Israel* (Grand Rapids, MI: Eerdmans, 2005).

Dickson, Keith, 'Enki and Ninhursag: The Trickster in Paradise', in *Journal of Near Eastern Studies* 66(1), 2007, pp. 1–32.

Dietler, Michael, 'Feasting and Fasting', in Timothy Insoll (ed.), *The Oxford Handbook of the Archaeology of Ritual and Religion* (Oxford and New York, NY: Oxford University Press, 2011), pp. 179–94.

Dietrich, Manfried, and Oswald Loretz, Joaquín Sanmartín (eds.), *Die keilalphabetischen Texte aus Ugarit* (third enlarged edition) (Münster: Ugarit-Verlag, 2013).

Diogenes Laertius (trans. R. D. Hicks), *Lives of Eminent Philosophers*, 2 vols (Loeb Classical Library, 184 and 185; Cambridge, MA: Harvard University Press, 1925).

Doak, Brian R., *Phoenician Aniconism in Its Mediterranean and Near Eastern Contexts* (Atlanta, GA: Society of Biblical Literature, 2015).

Doering, Lutz, 'The Synagogue at Magdala: Between Localized Practice and Reference to the Temple', in Lutz Doering and Andrew R. Krause (eds.), *Synagogues in the Hellenistic and Roman Periods: Archaeological Finds, New Methods, New Theories* (Göttingen: Vandenhoeck & Ruprecht, 2020), pp. 127–54.

Douglas, Mary, *Purity and Danger: An Analysis of Concepts of Pollution and Taboo* (London: Routledge & Kegan Paul, 1966).

Driver, G. R., 'Isaiah 6:1 "his train filled the temple"', in Hans Goedicke (ed.), *Near Eastern Studies in Honor of W. F. Albright* (Baltimore, MD: Johns Hopkins University Press, 1971), pp. 87–96.

Dube, Musa W., 'The Scramble for Africa as the Biblical Scramble for Africa: Postcolonial Perspectives', in Musa Dube, Andrew M. Mbuvi and Dora R. Mbuwayesango (eds.), *Postcolonial Perspectives in African Biblical Interpretations* (London and New York, NY: Routledge, 1997), pp. 1–26.

Duling, Dennis C., ' "[Do Not Swear . . .] by Jerusalem Because It Is the City of the Great King" (Matt. 5:35)', in *Journal of Biblical Literature* 110(2), 1991, pp. 291–309.

Dunbabin, Katherine, '*Ipsa Deae Vestigia* . . . Footprints Divine and Human on Graeco-Roman Monuments', in *Journal of Roman Archaeology* 3, 1998, pp. 85–109.

Dunn, James D. G., 'Baptism in the Holy Spirit: Yet Once More – Again', in *Journal of Pentecostal Theology* 19(1), 2010, pp. 32–43.

Dünzl, Franz (trans. John Bowden), *A Brief History of the Doctrine of the Trinity in the Early Church* (London: T&T Clark, 2007).

Durand, J.-M., 'Le mythologeme du combat entre le Dieu de l'orage et le mer en Mésopotamie', in *MARI: Annales de recherches interdisciplinaires* 7, 1993, pp. 41–61.

Dvorjetski, Estēe, 'Public Health in Ancient Palestine: Historical and Archaeological Perspectives', in Ann E. Killebrew and Gabriele Faßbeck (eds.), *Viewing Ancient Jewish Art and Archaeology. Vehinnei Rachel: Essays in Honor of Rachel Hachlili* (Leiden: Brill, 2016), pp. 48–100.

Eberhart, Christian A., 'A Neglected Feature of Sacrifice in the Hebrew Bible: Remarks on the Burning Rite on the Altar', in *Harvard Theological Review* 97(4), 2004, pp. 485–93.

—— *The Sacrifice of Jesus: Understanding Atonement Biblically* (Philadelphia, PA: Fortress Press, 2011).

Edelman, Diana, 'The "Seeing God" Motif and Yahweh as a God of Justice', in Oliver Artus (ed.), *Loi et justice dans la littérature du Proche-Orient ancien* (Wiesbaden: Harrassowitz, 2013), pp. 197–224.

Ehrlich, Carl S., 'Balaam the Seer: From the Bible to the Deir 'Alla Inscription', in *TheTorah.com* (2018), online at https://www.thetorah.com/article/balaam-the-seer-from-the-bible-to-the-deir-alla-inscription.

Eilberg-Schwartz, Howard, *The Savage in Judaism: An Anthropology of Israelite Religion and Ancient Judaism* (Indianapolis, IN: Indiana University Press, 1990).

—— *God's Phallus – and Other Problems for Men and Monotheism* (Boston, MA: Beacon Press, 1994).

Eisenstein, Julius (Judah) D., *Otzar Midrashim* (New York, NY: J. D. Eisenstein, 1915).

Elliott, J. K., *The Apocryphal New Testament: A Collection of Apocryphal Christian Literature in an English Translation Based on M. R. James* (Oxford: Clarendon Press, 1993).

Elliott, John H., *Beware the Evil Eye: The Evil Eye in the Bible and the Ancient World*, vol. 3 (Eugene, OR: Cascade Books, 2016).

Engberg-Pedersen, Troels, *Cosmology and Self in the Apostle Paul: The Material Spirit* (Oxford and New York, NY: Oxford University Press, 2010).

Entwistle, Joanne, and Elizabeth Wilson (eds.), *Body Dressing* (Oxford: Berg, 2001).

Erman, Adolf, and Hermann Grapow, *Wörterbuch der Ägyptischen Sprache*, vol. 1 (Berlin: Akademie-Verlag, 1926).

Ermidoro, Stefania, *Commensality and Ceremonial Meals in the Neo-Assyrian Period* (Venice: Edizioni Ca' Foscari, 2015).

Eslinger, Lyle, 'The Infinite in a Finite Organical Perception (Isaiah VI 1–5)', in *Vetus Testamentum* 45(2), 1995, pp. 145–73.

Eusebius (trans. Edwin H. Gifford), *The Preparation for the Gospel* (Oxford: Clarendon Press, 1903; repr. Eugene, OR: Wipf and Stock, 2002).

Exum, J. Cheryl, *Song of Songs: A Commentary* (Louisville, KY: Westminster John Knox Press, 2005).

Farley, David, *An Irreverent Curiosity: In Search of the Church's Strangest Relic in Italy's Oddest Town* (New York, NY: Gotham Books, 2009).

Feder, Yitzhaq, 'Contagion and Cognition: Bodily Experience and the Conceptualization of Pollution (*ṭum'ah*) in the Hebrew Bible', in *Journal of Near Eastern Studies* 72(2), 2013, pp. 151–67.

Feinstein, Eve Levavi, 'Sexual Pollution in the Hebrew Bible: A New Perspective', in S. Tamar Kamionkowski and Wonil Kim (eds.), *Bodies, Embodiment, and the Theology of the Hebrew Scriptures* (London and New York, NY: T&T Clark, 2010), pp. 114–45.

Ferretter, Luke, 'The Power and the Glory: The Aesthetics of the Hebrew Bible', in *Literature & Theology* 18(2), 2004, pp. 123–38.

Fine, Steven, 'From Meeting House to Sacred Realm: Holiness and the Ancient Synagogue', in Steven Fine (ed.), *Sacred Realm: The Emergence of the Synagogue in the Ancient World* (Oxford: Oxford University Press, 1996), pp. 21–47.

—— 'Polychromy and Jewish Visual Culture of Roman Antiquity', in Rubina Raja and Jörg Rüpke (eds.), *A Companion to the Archaeology of Religion in the Ancient World* (Chichester: Wiley Blackwell, 2015), pp. 133–43.

Finkel, Irving (ed.), *The Cyrus Cylinder: The King of Persia's Proclamation from Ancient Babylon* (London: I. B. Tauris, 2013).

—— 'Assurbanipal's Library: An Overview', in Kim Ryholt and Gojko Barjamovic (eds.), *Libraries before Alexandria: Ancient Near Eastern Traditions* (Oxford and New York, NY: Oxford University Press, 2019), pp. 367–89.

Finkelstein, Israel, *The Forgotten Kingdom: The Archaeology and History of Northern Israel* (Atlanta, GA: Society of Biblical Literature, 2013).

Fishbane, Michael, *Biblical Myth and Rabbinic Mythmaking* (Oxford and New York, NY: Oxford University Press, 2003).

Fleming, Daniel E., 'Seeing and Socializing with Dagan at Emar's *zukru* Festival', in Beate Pongratz-Leisten and Karen Sonik (eds.), *The Materiality of Divine Agency* (Berlin: de Gruyter, 2015), pp. 197–210.

Fletcher, Alexandra, and Jessica Pearson, Theya Molleson, Richard Abel, Janet Ambers, Crispin Wiles, 'Beneath the Surface: Imaging Techniques and the Jericho Skull', in A. Fletcher, D. Antoine and J. D. Hill (eds.), *Regarding the Dead: Human Remains in the British Museum* (London: Trustees of the British Museum, 2014), pp. 93–104.

Flood, Finbarr Barry, 'Bodies and Becoming: Mimesis, Mediation, and the Ingestion of the Sacred in Christianity and Islam', in Sally M. Promey (ed.), *Sensational Religion: Sensory Cultures in Material Practice* (New Haven, CT: Yale University Press, 2014), pp. 459–93.

Fonrobert, Charlotte E., *Menstrual Purity: Rabbinic and Christian Reconstructions of Biblical Gender* (Stanford, CA: Stanford University Press, 2000).

Foster, Benjamin R., *Before the Muses: An Anthology of Akkadian Literature* (third edition) (Bethesda, MD: CDL Press, 2005).

Fox, Michael V., 'The Sign of the Covenant: Circumcision in the Light of the Priestly 'ôt Etiologies', in *Revue Biblique* 81(4), 1974, pp. 557–96.

Fraade, Steven D., 'Facing the Holy Ark: In Words and Images', in *Near Eastern Archaeology* 82(3), 2019, pp. 156–63.

Frahm, Eckart, 'Keeping Company with Men of Learning: The King as Scholar', in Karen Radner and Eleanor Robson (eds.), *The Oxford Handbook of Cuneiform Culture* (Oxford and New York, NY: Oxford University Press, 2011), pp. 508–32.

Frank, Daniel H., 'Maimonides and Medieval Jewish Aristotelianism' in Daniel H. Frank and Oliver Leaman (eds.), *The Cambridge Companion to Medieval Jewish Philosophy* (Cambridge: Cambridge University Press, 2006), pp. 135–56.

Fredriksen, Paula, *When Christians Were Jews: The First Generation* (New Haven, CT: Yale University Press, 2018).

Freedman, Harry, and Maurice Simon (trans. and ed.), *Midrash Rabbah: Genesis*, vol. 1 (London: Soncino, 1939).

Frey, Jörg, and John Levinson (eds.), *The Holy Spirit, Inspiration, and the Cultures of Antiquity: Multidisciplinary Perspectives* (Berlin: de Gruyter, 2014).

Friedman, Shamma, 'Anthropomorphism and Its Eradication', in Willem van Asselt, Paul van Geest, Daniela Müller and Theo Salemink (eds.), *Iconoclasm and Iconoclash: Struggle for Religious Identity* (Leiden: Brill, 2007), pp. 157–78.

Gabbay, Uri, 'Drums, Hearts, Bulls, and Dead Gods: The Theology of the Ancient Mesopotamian Kettledrum', in *Journal of Ancient Near Eastern Religions* 18(1), 2018, pp. 1–47.

Gadd, C. J., 'The Harran Inscriptions of Nabonidus', in *Anatolian Studies* 8, 1958, pp. 35–92.

Gal, Zvi, and Dina Shalem, and Howard Smithline, 'The Peqi'in Cave: A Chalcolithic Cemetery in Upper Galilee, Israel', in *Near Eastern Archaeology* 74(4), 2011, pp. 196–206.

Ganor, Saar, and Igor Kreimerman, 'Going to the Bathroom at Lachish', in *Biblical Archaeology Review* 43(6), 2017, pp. 56–60.

—— 'An Eighth-Century B.C.E. Gate Shrine at Tel Lachish, Israel', in *Bulletin of the American Schools of Oriental Research* 381(1), 2019, pp. 211–36.

García Martínez, Florentino, and Eibert J. C. Tigchelaar (eds.) *The Dead Sea Scrolls: Study Edition*, 2 vols (Leiden: Brill, 1998).

Garfinkel, Yosef, 'The Cultic Reform in the Gate Shrine of Lachish', in *Strata: Bulletin of the Anglo-Israel Archaeological Society* 38, 2020, pp. 31–44.

—— and Madeleine Mumcuoglu, 'The Temple of Solomon in Iron Age Context', in *Religions* 10(3), 2019, article 198.

George, A. R., *The Babylonian Gilgamesh Epic: Introduction, Critical Edition and Cuneiform Texts*, vol. 1 (Oxford: Oxford University Press, 2003).

—— 'The Assyrian Elegy: Form and Meaning', in Sarah C. Melville and Alice L. Slotsky (eds.), *Opening the Tablet Box: Near Eastern Studies in Honor of Benjamin R. Foster* (Leiden: Brill, 2010), pp. 203–16.

—— *Babylonian Divinatory Texts Chiefly in the Shøyen Collection* (Bethesda, MD: CDL Press, 2013).

Goldenberg, David M., *The Curse of Ham: Race and Slavery in Early Judaism, Christianity, and Islam* (Princeton, NJ: Princeton University Press, 2003).

Goldin, Judah (ed. and trans.), *The Fathers According to Rabbi Nathan* (New Haven, CT: Yale University Press, 1955).

Goodman, David, 'Do Angels Eat?', in *Journal of Jewish Studies* 37(2), 1986, pp. 160–75.

Goodman, Martin, *A History of Judaism* (London: Allen Lane, 2017).

Grabbe, Lester L., *Ancient Israel: What Do We Know and How Do We Know It?* (revised edition) (London: T&T Clark, 2017).

Graff, Sarah B., 'The Head of Humbaba', in *Archiv für Religionsgeschichte* 14(1), 2013, pp. 129–42.

Graham, Daniel W. (ed. and trans.), *The Texts of Early Greek Philosophy: The Complete Fragments and Selected Testimonies of the Major Presocratics, Part I* (Cambridge: Cambridge University Press, 2010).

Graybill, Rhiannon, *Texts After Terror: Rape, Sexual Violence, and the Hebrew Bible* (Oxford and New York, NY: Oxford University Press, 2021).

Grayson, A. Kirk, and Jamie Novotny, *The Royal Inscriptions of Sennacherib, King of Assyria (704–681 BC), Part 2* (Winona Lake, IN: Eisenbrauns, 2014).

Greenberg, Moshe, *Ezekiel 1–20: A New Translation with Introduction and Commentary* (Garden City, NY: Doubleday, 1983).

Greenough, Chris, *The Bible and Sexual Violence Against Men* (Abingdon: Routledge, 2021).

Greenstein, Edward L., *Job: A New Translation* (New Haven, CT: Yale University Press, 2019).

Grossman, Avraham, 'The School of Literal Jewish Exegesis in Northern France', in Magne Sæbø (ed.), *Hebrew Bible/Old Testament: The History of Its Interpretation. Volume 1, Part 2 – Middle Ages* (Göttingen: Vandenhoeck & Ruprecht, 2000), pp. 321–71.

Gruber, Mayer I., *Hosea: A Textual Commentary* (London: Bloomsbury T&T Clark, 2017).

Gruen, Erich S., *The Construct of Identity in Hellenistic Judaism: Essays in Early Jewish Literature and History* (Berlin: de Gruyter, 2016).

Gudme, Anne Katrine de Hemmer, *Before the God in This Place for Good Remembrance: A Comparative Analysis of the Aramaic Votive Inscriptions from Mount Gerizim* (Berlin: de Gruyter, 2013).

—— '"If I were hungry, I would not tell you" (Ps 50, 12): Perspectives on the Care and Feeding of the Gods in the Hebrew Bible', in *Scandinavian Journal of the Old Testament* 28(2), 2014, pp. 172–84.

Guillaume, Philippe, and Martha Hellander, 'The House of the Forest of Lebanon: A Temple Silenced', in *Biblische Notizen* 180, 2019, pp. 15–29.

Guinan, Ann Kessler, 'Auguries of Hegemony: The Sex Omens of Mesopotamia', in *Gender & History* 9(3), 1997, pp. 462–79.

Gurevich, David, 'Magdala's Stone of Contention', August 2018, online at https://www.bibleinterp.com/articles/2018/08/gur428008.shtml.

Gusterson, Hugh, 'Nuclear Weapons Testing: Scientific Experiment as Political Ritual', in Laura Nader (ed.), *Naked Science: Anthropological Inquiry into Boundaries, Power, and Knowledge* (New York, NY: Routledge, 1996), pp. 131–47.

Guthrie, Stewart, *Faces in the Clouds: A New Theory of Religion* (Oxford: Oxford University Press, 1993).

Guy, Laurie, '"Naked" Baptism in the Early Church: The Rhetoric and the Reality', in *Journal of Religious History* 27(2), 2003, pp. 133–42.

Hallo, William. W., and K. Lawson Younger, Jr. (eds.), *The Context of Scripture*, 4 vols (Leiden: Brill, 1997–2017).

Halperin, David, *Seeking Ezekiel: Text and Psychology* (University Park, PA; Pennsylvania University Press, 1993).

Halton, Charles, and Saana Svärd, *Women's Writing of Ancient Mesopotamia: An Anthology of the Earliest Female Authors* (Cambridge: Cambridge University Press, 2018).

Hamilton, Edith, and Huntington Cairns (eds.), *The Collected Dialogues of Plato* (Princeton, NJ: Princeton University Press, 1961).

Hamori, Esther J., *'When Gods Were Men': The Embodied God in Biblical and Near Eastern Literature* (Berlin: de Gruyter, 2008).

Harvey, Susan Ashbrook, *Scenting Salvation: Ancient Christianity and the Olfactory Imagination* (Berkeley, CA: University of California Press, 2006).

Hawass, Zahi, *Inside the Egyptian Museum with Zahi Hawass* (Cairo: American University in Cairo, 2010).

Healey, John F., '"Death Is Swallowed Up in Victory" (1 Corinthians 15:54): Canaanite Mot in Prophecy and Apocalypse', in Peter J. Harland and Robert Hayward (eds.), *New Heaven and New Earth: Prophecy and the Millennium* (Leiden: Brill, 1999), pp. 205–15.

Heffron, Yagmur, 'Revisiting "Noise" (*rigmu*) in Atra-hasis in Light of Baby Incantations', in *Journal of Near Eastern Studies* 73(1), 2014, pp. 83–93.

Helle, Sophus, '"Only in Dress?" Methodological Concerns Regarding Non-Binary Gender', in Stephanie L. Budin, Megan Cifarelli, Agnès Garcia-Ventura and Adelina Millet-Albà (eds.), *Gender and Methodology in the Ancient Near East: Approaches from Assyriology and Beyond* (Barcelona: Universitat de Barcelona, 2018), pp. 41–53.

Helms, Kristen Lee, 'The Roaming Eyes of Yhwh: The Hypostatization of the Eyes of God in Persian Period Yehud', unpublished PhD dissertation (Princeton Theological Seminary, 2013).

Heng, Geraldine, *The Invention of Race in the European Middle Ages* (Cambridge: Cambridge University Press, 2018).

Hepner, Gershon, 'Scatology in the Bible', in *Scandinavian Journal of the Old Testament* 18(2), 2004, pp. 278–95.

Herodotus (trans. A. D. Godley), *Herodotus, Volumes I–II* (Loeb Classical Library, 117–18; Cambridge, MA: Harvard University Press, 1920–21).

Herring, Stephen L., *Divine Substitution: Humanity as the Manifestation of Deity in the Hebrew Bible and the Ancient Near East* (Göttingen: Vandenhoeck & Ruprecht, 2013).

Himbaza, Innocent, 'Dt 32,8, une correction tardive des scribes: Essai d'interprétation et de datation', in *Biblica* 83(4), 2002, pp. 527–48.

Hodges, Frederick M., 'The Ideal Prepuce in Ancient Greece and Rome: Male Genital Aesthetics and Their Relation to Lipodermos,

Circumcision, Foreskin Restoration, and the Kynodesmē', in *Bulletin of the History of Medicine* 75(3), 2001, pp. 375–405.

Holladay, Carl R. (ed. and trans.), *Fragments from Hellenistic Jewish Authors*, vol. 3 (Atlanta, GA: Scholars Press, 1995).

Holmes, Michael W., *The Apostolic Fathers in English* (third revised edition) (Grand Rapids, MI: Baker Academic, 2006).

Hood, Robert E., *Begrimed and Black: Christian Traditions on Blacks and Blackness* (Minneapolis, MN: Fortress Press, 1994).

Hooker, Alan, ' "Show Me Your Glory": The Kabod of Yahweh as Phallic Manifestation?', in Ovidiu Creangă and Peter-Ben Smit (eds.), *Biblical Masculinities Foregrounded* (Sheffield: Sheffield Phoenix Press, 2014), pp. 17–34.

Hopkins, Clark (ed. Bernard Goldman), *The Discovery of Dura-Europos* (New Haven, CT: Yale University Press, 1979).

Horn, Siegfried H., 'The Crown of the King of the Ammonites', in *Andrew's University Seminary Studies* 11(2), 1973, pp. 170–80.

Horrell, David G., *Ethnicity and Inclusion: Religion, Race, and Whiteness in Constructions of Jewish and Christian Identities* (Grand Rapids, MI: Eerdmans, 2020).

Horst, Pieter W. van der, 'The Measurement of the Body: A Chapter in the History of Ancient Jewish Mysticism', in Dirk van der Plas (ed.), *Effigies Dei: Essays on the History of Religion* (Leiden: Brill, 1987), pp. 56–68.

Houtman, Cornelius, 'On the Function of the Holy Incense (Exodus XXX 34–38) and the Sacred Anointing Oil (Exodus XXX 22–33)', in *Vetus Testamentum* 42(4), 1992, pp. 458–64.

Hulster, Izaak J. de, 'A Yehud Coin with Representation of a Sun Deity and Iconic Practice in Persian Period Palestine: An Elaboration on TC 242.5/BMC Palestine XIX 29', September 2009, online at https://www.academia.edu/38727481/A_Yehud_coin_with_the_Representation_of_a_Sun_Deity_and_Iconic_Practice_in_Persian_Period_Palestine_An_Elaboration_on_TC_242.5_BMC_Palestine_XIX_29.

—— 'Of Angels and Iconography: Isaiah 6 and the Biblical Concept of Seraphs and Cherubs', in Izaak J. de Hulster, Brent A. Strawn and Ryan P. Bonfiglio (eds.), *Iconographic Exegesis of the Hebrew Bible/Old Testament: An Introduction to Its Method and Practice* (Göttingen: Vandenhoeck & Ruprecht, 2015), pp. 147–64.

Hundley, Michael B., *Gods in Dwellings: Temples and Divine Presence in the Ancient Near East* (Atlanta, GA: Society of Biblical Literature, 2013).

—— 'What Is the Golden Calf?', in *Catholic Biblical Quarterly* 79(4), 2017, pp. 559–79.

Hurowitz, Victor Avigdor, 'What Goes In Is What Comes Out: Materials for Creating Cult Statues', in Gary Beckman and Theodore J. Lewis (eds.), *Text, Artifact, and Image: Revealing Ancient Israelite Religion* (Providence, RI: Brown University, 2006), pp. 3–23.

Ilan, David, and Yorke Rowan, 'Expediting Reincarnation in the Fifth Millennium BCE: Interpreting the Chalcolithic Ossuaries of the Southern Levant', in *Oxford Journal of Archaeology* 38(3), 2019, pp. 248–70.

Ingold, Tim, 'Culture on the Ground: The World Perceived Through the Feet', in *Journal of Material Culture* 9(3), 2004, pp. 315–40.

—— 'Footprints through the Weather-World: Walking, Breathing, Knowing', in *Journal of the Royal Anthropological Institute* 16(1), 2010, pp. 121–39.

Irenaeus (trans. Joseph Smith), *Proof of the Apostolic Teaching* (Mahwah, NJ: Paulist Press, 1952).

Isaac, Benjamin H., *The Invention of Racism in Classical Antiquity* (Princeton, NJ: Princeton University Press, 2004).

—— and Joseph Zingler, Miriam Eliav-Feldon (eds.), *The Origins of Racism in the West* (Cambridge: Cambridge University Press, 2009).

Isherwood, Lisa, *The Power of Erotic Celibacy: Queering Heteropatriarchy* (London: T&T Clark, 2006).

Jackson, Joshua Conrad, and Neil Hester, Kurt Grey, 'The Faces of God in America: Revealing Religious Diversity across People and Politics', in *PLoS ONE* 13(6), 2018, article e0198745.

Jacobs, Andrew S., *Christ Circumcised: A Study in Early Christian History and Difference* (Philadelphia, PA: University of Pennsylvania Press, 2012).

Jacobs, Sandra, 'Divine Virility in Priestly Representation: Its Memory and Consummation in Rabbinic Midrash', in Ovidiu Creangă (ed.), *Men and Masculinity in the Hebrew Bible and Beyond* (Sheffield: Sheffield Phoenix Press, 2010), pp. 146–70.

Jacobsen, Thorkild, *The Harps That Once . . . Sumerian Poetry in Translation* (New Haven, CT: Yale University Press, 1987).

James, Simon, 'Stratagems, Combat, and "Chemical Warfare" in the Siege Mines of Dura-Europos', in *American Journal of Archaeology* 115(1), 2011, pp. 69–101.

Jeffries, Stuart, 'The Naked and the Dead', in the *Guardian*, 19 March 2002, online at https://www.theguardian.com/education/2002/mar/19/arts.highereducation.

Jensen, Robin M., 'The Economy of the Trinity at the Creation of Adam and Eve', in *Journal of Early Christian Studies* 7(4), 1999, pp. 527–46.

—— *Face to Face: Portraits of the Divine in Early Christianity* (Minneapolis, MN: Fortress Press, 2005).

—— 'Theophany and the Invisible God in Early Christian Theology and Art', in Andrew B. McGowan, Brian E. Daley and Timothy J. Gaden (eds.), *God in Early Christian Thought* (Leiden: Brill, 2009), pp. 271–96.

—— *Baptismal Imagery in Early Christianity: Ritual, Visual, and Theological Dimensions* (Grand Rapids, MI: Baker Academic, 2012).

Jerome (trans. F. A. Wright), *Select Letters* (Loeb Classical Library, 262; Cambridge, MA: Harvard University Press, 1933).

—— (trans. Marie Ligouri Ewald), *The Homilies of Saint Jerome: Volume I (1–59 On the Psalms)* (Washington, DC: Catholic University of America, 1964).

Jiménez, Enrique, 'Highway to Hell: The Wind as Cosmic Conveyors in Mesopotamian Incantation Texts', in Greta Van Buylaere, Mikko Luukko, Daniel Schwemer and Avigail Mertens-Wagschal (eds.), *Sources of Evil: Studies in Mesopotamian Exorcistic Lore* (Leiden: Brill, 2018), pp. 316–50.

Johnson, Sylvester A., *The Myth of Ham in Nineteenth Century American Christianity: Race, Heathens, and the People of God* (New York, NY: Palgrave Macmillan, 2004).

—— *African American Religions, 1500–2000: Colonialism, Democracy, and Freedom* (Cambridge and New York, NY: Cambridge University Press, 2015).

Jones, Jonathan, 'Jeff Koons: Not Just the King of Kitsch', in the *Guardian*, 30 June 2009, online at https://www.theguardian.com/artanddesign/2009/jun/30/jeff-koons-exhibition-serpentine.

Josephus (trans. H. St. J. Thackeray), *The Jewish War*, 3 vols (Loeb Classical Library, 203, 210, 487; Cambridge, MA: Harvard University Press, 1927–28).

—— (trans. Ralph Marcus), *Jewish Antiquities*, vol. 5 (Loeb Classical Library, 365; Cambridge, MA: Harvard University Press, 1943).

Joyce, Paul M., *Ezekiel: A Commentary* (London: T&T Clark, 2007).

Junior, Nyasha, 'The Mark of Cain and White Violence', in *Journal of Biblical Literature* 139(4), 2020, pp. 661–73.

Kamionkowski, S. Tamar, 'Gender Reversal in Ezekiel 16', in Athalya Brenner (ed.), *Prophets and Daniel: A Feminist Companion to the Bible* (second series) (Sheffield: Sheffield Academic Press, 2001), pp. 170–85.

Kanawati, Naguib and Ali Hassan, *The Teti Cemetery at Saqqara, Volume II: The Tomb of Ankhmahor* (Warminster: Aris & Philips, 1997).

Kaplan, Jonathan, *My Perfect One: Typology and Early Rabbinic Interpretation of Song of Songs* (Oxford: Oxford University Press, 2015).

Kartsonis, Anna, 'The Responding Icon', in Linda Safran (ed.), *Heaven on Earth: Art and the Church in Byzantium* (University Park, PA: Pennsylvania University Press, 1998), pp. 58–80.

Kartzow, Marianne Bjelland, *The Slave Metaphor and Gendered Enslavement in Early Christian Discourse* (New York, NY: Routledge, 2018).

Kawami, Trudy S., and John Olbrantz, *Breath of Heaven, Breath of Earth: Ancient Near Eastern Art from American Collections* (Salem, OR: Hallie Ford Museum of Art at Willamette University, 2013).

Kazantzakis, Nikos (trans. P. A. Bein), *The Last Temptation of Christ* (London: Faber, 1961).

Kazen, Thomas, 'Dirt and Disgust: Body and Morality in Biblical Purity Laws', in Naphtali S. Meshel, Jeffrey Stackert, David P. Wright and Baruch J. Schwartz (eds.), *Perspectives on Purity and Purification in the Bible* (London and New York, NY: T&T Clark, 2008), pp. 43–64.

Keinänen, Jyrki, *Traditions in Collision: A Literary and Redaction-Critical Study on the Elijah Narratives 1 Kings 17–19* (Göttingen: Vandenhoeck & Ruprecht, 2001).

Keith, Chris, 'Recent and Previous Research on the *Pericope Adulterae* (John 7.53–8.11)', in *Currents in Biblical Research* 6(3), 2008, pp. 377–404.

—— *Jesus' Literacy: Scribal Culture and the Teacher from Galilee* (London: T&T Clark, 2011).

Kelly, J. N. D. *Early Christian Doctrines* (fifth revised edition) (London: A&C Black, 1977).

Kessler, Herbert L., and David Nirenberg (eds.), *Judaism and Christian Art: Aesthetic Anxieties from the Catacombs to Colonialism* (Philadelphia, PA: University of Pennsylvania Press, 2011).

King, Philip J., and Lawrence E. Stager, *Life in Biblical Israel* (Louisville, KY: Westminster John Knox, 2001).

Kinnard, Jacob N., *Places in Motion: The Fluid Identities of Temples, Images, and Pilgrims* (Oxford and New York, NY: Oxford University Press, 2014).

Kletter, Raz, 'A Very General Archaeologist – Moshe Dayan and Israeli Archaeology', in *Journal of Hebrew Scriptures* 4, 2003, article 5.

—— and Katri Saarelainen, 'Judean Drummers', in *Zeitschrift des Deutschen Palästina-Vereins* 127(1), 2011, pp. 11–30.

Knafl, Anne K., *Forming God: Divine Anthropomorphism in the Pentateuch* (Winona Lake, IN: Eisenbrauns, 2014).

Knoppers, Gary N., *Jews and Samaritans: The Origins and History of Their Early Relations* (Oxford and New York, NY: Oxford University Press, 2013).

Köckert, Matthias, 'Vom Kultbild Jahwes zum Bilderverbot. Oder: Vom Nutzen der Religionsgeschichte für die Theologie', in *Zeitschrift für Theologie und Kirche* 106(4), 2009, pp. 371–406.

Koehler, Ludwig, Walter Baumgartner and Johann J. Stamm (trans. Mervyn E. J. Richardson), *The Hebrew and Aramaic Lexicon of the Old Testament: Study Edition* (Leiden: Brill, 2001).

Koller, Aaron, 'Pornography or Theology? The Legal Background, Psychological Realism, and Theological Import of Ezekiel 16', in *Catholic Biblical Quarterly* 79(3), 2017, pp. 402–21.

Koltun-Fromm, Naomi, *Hermeneutics of Holiness: Ancient Jewish and Christian Notions of Sexuality and Religious Community* (Oxford and New York, NY: Oxford University Press, 2010).

Korpel, Marjo C. A., and Johannes de Moor, *The Silent God* (Leiden: Brill, 2011).

Kotze, Zacharias, 'The Evil Eye of YHWH', in *Journal for Semitics* 17(1), 2008, pp. 207–18.

Kramer, Samuel N., 'BM 29616: The Fashioning of the *Gala*', in *Acta Sumerilogica* 3, 1981, pp. 1–9.

Krause, Joachim J., 'Barefoot before God: Shoes and Sacred Space in the Hebrew Bible and Ancient Near East', in Christoph Berner, Manuel Schäfer, Martin Schott, Sarah Schulz and Martina Weingärtner (eds.), *Clothing and Nudity in the Hebrew Bible* (London and New York, NY: T&T Clark, 2019), pp. 315–22.

Kristeva, Julia (trans. Leon S. Roudiez), *Powers of Horror: An Essay in Abjection* (New York, NY: Columbia University Press, 1982).

Kruger, Michael J., *The Gospel of the Saviour: An Analysis of P.Oxy. 840 and Its Place in the Gospel Traditions of Early Christianity* (Leiden: Brill, 2005).

Kunin, Seth, *We Think What We Eat: Neo-Structuralist Analysis of Israelite Food Rules and Other Cultural and Textual Practices* (London: T&T Clark, 2003).

Lambert, W. G., *Babylonian Creation Myths* (Winona Lake, IN: Eisenbrauns, 2013).

Land, Norman E., 'A Concise History of the Tale of Michelangelo and Biagio da Cesena', in *Source: Notes in the History of Art* 32(4), 2013, pp. 15–19.

Lanner, Laurel, *'Who Will Lament Her?' The Feminine and Fantastic in the Book of Nahum* (London and New York, NY: T&T Clark, 2006).

Lapina, Elizabeth, and Nicholas Morton (eds.), *The Uses of the Bible in Crusader Sources* (Leiden: Brill, 2017).

Lauterbach, Jacob Z., *Mekhilta de-Rabbi Ishmael: A Critical Edition, Based on the Manuscripts and Early Editions, with an English Translation, Introduction, and Notes* (second edition) (Philadelphia, PA: Jewish Publication Society, 2004).

Law, Timothy Michael, *When God Spoke Greek: The Septuagint and the Making of the Christian Bible* (Oxford and New York, NY: Oxford University Press, 2013).

Le Donne, Anthony, *The Wife of Jesus: Ancient Texts and Modern Scandals* (London: Oneworld, 2013).

Leick, Gwendolyn, *Sex and Eroticism in Mesopotamian Literature* (London: Routledge, 1994).

Lemaire, André, 'From the Origin of the Alphabet to the Tenth Century BCE: New Documents and New Directions', in Meir Lubetski and Edith Lubetski (eds.), *New Inscriptions and Seals Relating to the Biblical World* (Atlanta, GA: Society of Biblical Literature, 2012), pp. 1–20.

Lemos, T. M., 'Shame and Mutilation of Enemies in the Hebrew Bible', in *Journal of Biblical Literature* 125(2), 2006, pp. 225–41.

—— ' "Like the Eunuch who does not Beget": Gender, Mutilation, and Negotiated Status in the Ancient Near East', in Candida R. Moss and Jeremy Schipper (eds.), *Disability Studies and Biblical Literature* (New York, NY: Palgrave Macmillan, 2011), pp. 47–66.

Leuenberger, Martin, 'YHWH's Provenance from the South: A New Evaluation of the Arguments pro and contra', in Jürgen van Oorschot and Markus Witte (eds.), *The Origins of Yahwism* (Berlin: de Gruyter, 2017), pp. 157–79.

Levenson, Jon D., *The Death and Resurrection of the Beloved Son: The Transformation of Child Sacrifice in Judaism and Christianity* (New Haven, CT: Yale University Press, 1993).

Levine, Baruch A., *Numbers 21–36: A New Translation with Introduction and Commentary* (New York, NY: Doubleday, 2000).

Levtow, Nathaniel B., *Images of Others: Iconic Politics in Ancient Israel* (Winona Lake, IN: Eisenbrauns, 2008).

Lewis, Theodore J., '*CT* 13.33–34 and Ezekiel 32: Lion-Dragon Myths', in *Journal of the American Oriental Society* 116(1), 1996, pp. 28–47.

—— 'Athtartu's Incantations and the Use of Divine Names as Weapons', in *Journal of Near Eastern Studies* 70(2), 2011, pp. 207–27.

—— 'Divine Fire in Deuteronomy 33:2', in *Journal of Biblical Literature* 132(4), 2013, pp. 791–803.

—— 'The Identity and Function of Ugaritic Sha'tiqatu: A Divinely Made Apotropaic Figure', in *Journal of Ancient Near Eastern Religions* 14(1), 2014, pp. 1–28.

—— *The Origin and Character of God: Ancient Israelite Religion through the Lens of Divinity* (Oxford and New York, NY: Oxford University Press, 2020).

Lilly, Ingrid E., 'Conceptualizing Spirit: Supernatural Meteorology and Winds of Distress in the Hebrew Bible and the Ancient Near East', in Joel Baden, Hindy Najman and Eibert J. C. Tigchelaar (eds.), *Sibyls, Scriptures, and Scrolls: John Collins at Seventy* (Leiden: Brill, 2016), pp. 826–44.

Lipton, Sara, *Dark Mirror: The Medieval Origins of Anti-Semitic Iconography* (New York, NY: Metropolitan Books, 2014).

Litwa, M. David, *We Are Being Transformed: Deification in Paul's Soteriology* (Berlin: de Gruyter, 2012).

—— *Iesus Deus: The Early Christian Depiction of Jesus as a Mediterranean God* (Minneapolis, MN: Fortress Press, 2014).

Livingstone, Alasdair, *Court Poetry and Literary Miscellanea* (State Archives of Assyria, 3; Helsinki: Helsinki University Press, 1989).

—— 'Ashurbanipal: Literate or Not?', in *Zeitschrift für Assyriologie* 97(1), 2007, pp. 98–118.

—— *Mystical and Mythological Explanatory Works of Assyrian and Babylonian Scholars* (Winona Lake, IN: Eisenbrauns, 2007).

Loader, James A., 'What Do the Heavens Declare? On the Old Testament Motif of God's Beauty in Creation', in *HTS Theological Studies* 67(3), 2011, article 1098.

Löhnert, Anne, 'Manipulating the Gods: Lamenting in Context', in Karen Radner and Eleanor Robson (eds.), *The Oxford Handbook of Cuneiform Culture* (Oxford and New York, NY: Oxford University Press, 2011), pp. 402–17.

Loktionov, Alexandre Alexandrovich, 'May my nose and ears be cut off: Practical and "Supra-practical" Aspects of Mutilation in the Egyptian New Kingdom', in *Journal of the Economic and Social History of the Orient* 60(3), 2017, pp. 263–91.

Lowden, John, 'The Word Made Visible: The Exterior of the Early Christian Book as Visual Argument', in William E. Klingshirn and Linda Safran (eds.), *The Early Christian Book* (Washington, DC: Catholic University of America Press, 2007), pp. 13–47.

Lucian (trans. A. M. Harmon), *A True Story* in *Lucian I* (Loeb Classical Library, 14; Cambridge, MA: Harvard University Press, 1913).

Luckenbill, Daniel David, *Ancient Records of Assyria and Babylonia, Volume II: Historical Records of Assyria (from Sargon to the End)* (Chicago, IL: Chicago University Press, 1927).

Ludlow, Morwenna, *The Early Church* (London: I. B. Tauris, 2009).

McCaffrey, Kathleen, 'Reconsidering Gender Ambiguity in Mesopotamia: Is a Beard Just a Beard?', in Simo Parpola and Robert M. Whiting (eds.), *Sex and Gender in the Ancient Near East* (Helsinki: Neo-Assyrian Text Corpus Project, 2002), pp. 379–91.

McClellan, Daniel, 'The Gods-Complaint: Psalm 82 as a Psalm of Complaint', in *Journal of Biblical Literature* 137(4), 2018, pp. 833–51.

McClure, M. L., and C. L. Feltoe, *The Pilgrimage of Etheria* (London: Society for the Promotion of Christian Knowledge, 1919).

McCoskey, Denise E., *Race: Antiquity and Its Legacy* (Oxford and New York, NY: Oxford University Press, 2012).

MacCulloch, Diarmaid, *A History of Christianity: The First Three Thousand Years* (London: Allen Lane, 2009).

MacDonald, Nathan, 'The Priestly Vestments', in Christoph Berner, Manuel Schäfer, Martin Schott, Sarah Schulz and Martina Weingärtner (eds.), *Clothing and Nudity in the Hebrew Bible* (London: T&T Clark, 2019), pp. 435–48.

McDowell, Catherine L., *The Image of God in the Garden of Eden: The Creation of Humankind in Genesis 2:5–3:24 in Light of the* mīs pî *and* wpt-r *Rituals of Mesopotamia and Ancient Egypt* (Winona Lake, IN: Eisenbrauns, 2015).

McGowan, Anne, and Paul F. Bradshaw, *The Pilgrimage of Egeria: A New Translation of the* Itinerarium Egeriae *with Introduction and Commentary* (Collegeville, MN: Liturgical Press, 2018).

McKay, Gretchen Kreahling, 'Illustrating the Gospel of John: The Exegesis of John Chrysostom and Images of the Ancient of Days in Eleventh-Century Byzantine Manuscripts', in *Studies in Iconography* 31, 2010, pp. 51–68.

Macwilliam, Stuart J., 'Ideologies of Male Beauty and the Hebrew Bible', in *Biblical Interpretation* 17(3), 2009, pp. 265–87.

Magness, Jodi, *Stone and Dung, Oil and Spit: Jewish Daily Life in the Time of Jesus* (Grand Rapids, MI: Eerdmans, 2011).

—— 'Toilet Practices, Purity Concerns, and Sectarianism in the Late Second Temple Period', in Benedict Eckhardt (ed.), *Jewish Identity and Politics between the Maccabees and Bar Kokhba: Groups, Normativity, and Rituals* (Leiden: Brill, 2012), pp. 51–70.

Maimonides (trans. Shlomo Pines), *The Guide of the Perplexed*, 2 vols (Chicago, IL: University of Chicago Press, 1963).

Malamat, Abraham, *Mari and the Bible* (Leiden: Brill, 1998).

Malul, Meir, *Studies in Mesopotamian Legal Symbolism* (Kevelaer: Butzon & Bercker, 1988).

—— 'Foot Symbolism in the Ancient Near East: Imprinting Foundlings' Feet in Clay in Ancient Mesopotamia', in *Zeitschrift für altorientalische und biblische Rechtsgeschichte* 7, 2001, pp. 353–67.

—— *Knowledge, Control, and Sex: Studies in Biblical Thought, Culture, and Worldview* (Tel Aviv: Tel Aviv-Jaffa Archaeological Center Publications, 2002).

Mandell, Alice, and Jeremy Smoak, 'Reading and Writing in the Dark at Khirbet el-Qom: The Literacies of Ancient Subterranean Judah', in *Near Eastern Archaeology* 80(3), 2017, pp. 188–95.

Marjanen, Antti, *The Woman Jesus Loved: Mary Magdalene in the Nag Hammadi Library and Related Documents* (Leiden: Brill, 1996).

Markschies, Christoph (trans. Alexander Johannes Edmonds), *God's Body: Jewish, Christian, and Pagan Images of God* (Waco, TX: Baylor University Press, 2019).

Martin, Dale B., 'When Did Angels Become Demons?', in *Journal of Biblical Literature* 129(4), 2010, pp. 657–77.

Mathews, Thomas F., *The Clash of Gods: A Reinterpretation of Early Christian Art* (revised edition) (Princeton, NJ: Princeton University Press, 1993).

—— (with Norman E. Muller), *The Dawn of Christian Art in Panel Paintings and Icons* (Los Angeles, LA: Paul J. Getty Trust, 2016).

Matić, Uroš, '(De)queering Hatshepsut: Binary Bind in Archaeology of Egypt and Kingship Beyond the Corporeal', in *Journal of Archaeological Method and Theory* 23, 2016, pp. 810–31.

Maul, Stefan M., 'Den Gott ernähern. Überlegungen zum regelmässigen Opfer in altorientalischen Tempeln', in E. Stavrianopoulou, A. Michaels and C. Ambos (eds.), *Transformations in Sacrificial Practices from Antiquity to Modern Times* (Berlin: Lit Verlag, 2008), pp. 75–86.

Meer, Nasar, 'Racialization and Religion: Race, Culture and Difference in the Study of Antisemitism and Islamophobia', in *Ethnic and Racial Studies* 36(3), 2013, pp. 385–98.

Mein, Andrew, 'Ezekiel's Women in Christian Interpretation: The Case of Ezekiel 16', in Andrew Mein and Paul M. Joyce (eds.), *After Ezekiel: Essays on the Reception of a Difficult Text* (London and New York, NY: T&T Clark, 2011), pp. 159–83.

Meshel, Ze'ev, *Kuntillet 'Ajrud (Ḥorvat Teman): An Iron Age II Religious Site on the Judah–Sinai Border* (Jerusalem: Israel Exploration Society, 2012).

Meshorer, Yaakov (trans. R. Amoils), *A Treasury of Jewish Coins: From the Persian Period to Bar Kokhba* (Jerusalem: Yad Ben-Zvi Press, 2001).

Meskell, Lynn, M., *Object Worlds in Ancient Egypt: Material Biographies Past and Present* (Oxford: Berg, 2004).

—— and Rosemary A. Joyce, *Embodied Lives: Figuring Ancient Maya and Egyptian Experience* (London: Routledge, 2003).

Mettinger, Tryggve N. D., *No Graven Image? Israelite Aniconism in Its Ancient Near Eastern Context* (Stockholm: Almqvist & Wiskell, 1995).

Miller, Jared L., *Royal Hittite Instructions and Related Administrative Texts* (Atlanta, GA: Society of Biblical Literature, 2013).

Mittmann, Siegfried, 'Das Symbol der Hand in der altorientalischen Ikonographie', in R. Kieffer and J. Bergman (eds.), *La Main de Dieu. Die Hand Gottes* (Tübingen: Mohr Siebeck, 1997), pp. 19–48.

Mofokeng, Takatso, 'Black Christians, the Bible, and Liberation', in *Journal of Black Theology* 2(1), 1988, pp. 34–42.

Moo, Jonathan, 'The Sea That Is No More: Rev. 21:1 and the Function of Sea Imagery in the Apocalypse of John', in *Novum Testamentum* 51(2), 2009, pp. 148–67.

Moore, Kathryn Blair, *The Architecture of the Christian Holy Land: Reception from Late Antiquity* (Cambridge: Cambridge University Press, 2017).

Moore, Stephen D., *God's Gym: Divine Male Bodies of the Bible* (New York, NY: Routledge, 1996).

Morgan, David, *The Forge of Vision: A Visual History of Modern Christianity* (Oakland, CA: University of California Press, 2015).

Moss, Candida R., *Divine Bodies: Resurrecting Perfection in the New Testament and Early Christianity* (New Haven, CT: Yale University Press, 2019).

Moughtin-Mumby, Sharon, *Sexual and Marital Metaphors in Hosea, Jeremiah, Isaiah, and Ezekiel* (Oxford: Oxford University Press, 2008).

Mroczek, Eva, *The Literary Imagination in Jewish Antiquity* (Oxford and New York, NY: Oxford University Press, 2016).

Mulder, Michael, 'Leviathan on the Menu of the Messianic Meal: The Use of Various Images of Leviathan in Early Jewish Tradition', in Koert van Bekkum, Jaap Dekker, Henk van de Kamp and Eric Peels (eds.), *Playing with Leviathan: Interpretation and Reception of Monsters from the Biblical World* (Leiden: Brill, 2017), pp. 115–30.

Nagouse, Emma, ' "To Ransom a Man's Soul": Male Rape and Gender Identity in *Outlander* and "The Suffering Man" of Lamentations 3', in Caroline Blyth, Emily Colgan and Katie B. Edwards (eds.), *Rape Culture, Gender Violence, and Religion: Biblical Perspectives* (London: Palgrave Macmillan, 2018), pp. 143–58.

Neis, Rachel, ' "Their Backs toward the Temple, Their Faces toward the East": The Temple and Toilet Practices in Rabbinic Palestine and Babylonia', in *Journal for the Study of Judaism* 43(3), 2012, pp, 328–68.

—— *The Sense of Sight in Rabbinic Culture: Jewish Ways of Seeing in Late Antiquity* (Cambridge: Cambridge University Press, 2013).

Nelstrop, Louise, 'Erotic and Nuptial Imagery', in Edward Howells and Mark A. McIntosh (eds.), *The Oxford Handbook of Mystical Theology* (Oxford and New York, NY: Oxford University Press, 2020), pp. 328–46.

Newman, Judith H., 'Contextualizing the Magdala Synagogue Stone in its Place: An Exercise in Liturgical Imagination', in Lutz Doering and Andrew R. Krause (eds.), *Synagogues in the Hellenistic and Roman Periods: Archaeological Finds, New Methods, New Theories* (Göttingen: Vandenhoeck & Ruprecht, 2020), pp. 155–74.

Niditch, Susan, *'My Brother Esau Is a Hairy Man': Hair and Identity in Ancient Israel* (Oxford: Oxford University Press, 2008).

Niehr, Herbert, 'The Rise of YHWH in Judahite and Israelite Religion: Methodological and Religio-Historical Aspects', in Diana Edelman (ed.), *The Triumph of Elohim: From Yahwisms to Judaisms* (Kampen: Kok Pharos, 1995), pp. 45–72.

—— 'In Search of YHWH's Cult Statue in the First Temple', in Karel van der Toorn (ed.), *The Image and the Book: Iconic Cults, Aniconism, and the Rise of Book Religion in Israel and the Ancient Near East* (Leuven: Peeters, 1997), pp. 73–95.

Nihan, Christophe, and Julia Rhyder, 'Aaron's Vestments in Ezekiel 28 and Priestly Leadership', in Katharina Pyschny and Sarah Schulz (eds.), *Debating Authority: Concepts of Leadership in the Pentateuch and the Former Prophets* (Berlin: de Gruyter, 2018), pp. 45–67.

Nissen, Hans, 'The Archaic Texts from Uruk', in *World Archaeology* 17(3), 1986, pp. 317–34.

Nissinen, Martti (trans. Kirsi Stjerna), *Homoeroticism in the Biblical World: A Historical Perspective* (Minneapolis, MN: Fortress Press, 1998).

—— 'Love Lyrics of Nabû and Tašmetu: An Assyrian Song of Songs?', in Manfried Dietrich and Ingo Kottsiepier (eds.), *'Und Mose schrieb dieses Lied auf': Studien zum Alten Testament und zum Alten Orient* (Münster: Ugarit, 1998), pp. 585–634.

Noegel, Scott B., 'Scarlet and Harlots: Seeing Red in the Hebrew Bible', in *Hebrew Union College Annual* 87, 2016, pp. 1–47.

Noffke, Suzanne (ed. and trans.), *The Prayers of Catherine of Siena* (second edition) (Lincoln, NE: Authors Choice Press, 2001).

Novák, Mirko, 'The Artificial Paradise: Programme and Ideology of Royal Gardens', in Simo Parpola and Robert M. Whiting (eds.), *Sex and Gender in the Ancient Near East* (Helsinki: Neo-Assyrian Text Corpus Project, 2002), pp. 443–60.

N'Shea, Omar, 'Royal Eunuchs and Elite Masculinity in the Neo-Assyrian Empire', in *Near Eastern Archaeology* 79(3), 2016, pp. 214–21.

Nuffelen, Peter van, *Rethinking the Gods: Philosophical Readings of Religion in the Post-Hellenistic Period* (Cambridge: Cambridge University Press, 2011).

Nunn, Astrid, *Die Wandmalerei und der glasierte Wandschmuck im Alten Orient* (Leiden: Brill, 1988).

Nunn, John F., *Ancient Egyptian Medicine* (Norman, OK: University of Oklahoma Press, 1996).

O'Connor, Kathleen M., 'The Tears of God and the Divine Character', in Tod Linafelt and Timothy K. Beal (eds.), *God in the Fray: A Tribute to Walter Bruggemann* (Minneapolis, MN: Fortress Press, 1998), pp. 172–85.

O'Hear, Natasha, and Anthony O'Hear, *Picturing the Apocalypse: The Book of Revelation in the Arts over Two Millennia* (Oxford: Oxford University Press, 2015).

Olyan, Saul M., ' "And with a Male You Shall Not Lie the Lying Down of a Woman": On the Meaning and Significance of Leviticus 18:22 and 20:13', in *Journal of the History of Sexuality* 5(2), 1994, pp. 179–206.

—— 'What Do Shaving Rites Accomplish and What Do They Signal in Biblical Ritual Contexts?', in *Journal of Biblical Literature* 117(4), 1998, pp. 611–22.

—— *Disability in the Hebrew Bible: Interpreting Mental and Physical Differences* (Cambridge: Cambridge University Press, 2008).

—— 'The Ascription of Physical Disability as a Stigmatizing Strategy in Biblical Iconic Polemics', in *Journal of Hebrew Scriptures* 9(14), 2009, pp. 1–15.

O'Malley, John, 'Art, Trent, and Michelangelo's "Last Judgement" ', in *Religions* 3(2), 2012, pp. 344–56.

Oppenheimer, Aharon, 'Babylonian Synagogues with Historical Associations', in Dan Urman and Paul V. M. Flesher (eds.), *Ancient Synagogues: Historical Analysis and Archaeological Discovery* (Leiden: Brill, 1998), pp. 40–48.

Origen (trans. Henry Chadwick), *Contra Celsum* (Cambridge: Cambridge University Press, 1953).

—— (trans. Ronald E. Heine), *Homilies on Genesis and Exodus* (Fathers of the Church, 7; Washington, DC: Catholic University of America Press, 1982).

—— (trans. Marcel Borret, S.J.), *Homélies sur Ézéchiel: Text Latin, Introduction, Traduction et Notes* (Paris: Éditions du CERF, 1989).

Ornan, Tallay, *A Man and His Land: Highlights from the Moshe Dayan Collection* (Jerusalem: Israel Museum, 1986).

—— 'The Bull and Its Two Masters: Moon and Storm Deities in Relation to the Bull in Ancient Near Eastern Art', in *Israel Exploration Journal* 51(1), 2001, pp. 1–26.

—— *The Triumph of the Symbol: Pictorial Representations of Deities in Mesopotamia and the Biblical Image Ban* (Fribourg/Göttingen: Academic Press/Vandenhoeck & Ruprecht, 2005).

—— 'The Godlike Semblance of a King: The Case of Sennacherib's Rock Reliefs', in Jack Cheng and Marian H. Feldman (eds.), *Ancient Near Eastern Art in Context: Studies in Honor of Irene J. Winter by Her Students* (Leiden: Brill, 2007), pp. 161–78.

—— ' "Let Ba'al Be Enthroned": The Date, Identification, and Function of a Bronze Statue from Hazor', in *Journal of Near Eastern Studies* 70(2), 2011, pp. 253–80.

Ott, Ludwig (trans. Patrick Lynch), *Fundamentals of Catholic Dogma* (second edition) (Cork: Mercier, 1957).

Palazzo, Robert B., 'The Veneration of the Sacred Foreskin(s) of Baby Jesus: A Documentary Analysis', in James P. Helfers (ed.), *Multicultural Europe and Cultural Exchange in the Middle Ages and Renaissance* (Tunhout: Brepols, 2005), pp. 155–76.

Palmer, Christine, 'Unshod on Holy Ground: Ancient Israel's "Disinherited" Priesthood', in Leonard J. Greenspoon (ed.), *Fashioning Jews: Clothing, Culture, and Commerce* (West Lafayette, IN: Purdue University Press, 2013), pp. 1–17.

Paoletti, John T., and Gary M. Radke (eds.), *Art in Renaissance Italy* (third edition) (London: Lawrence King Publishing, 2005).

Parker, Simon B. (ed.), *Ugaritic Narrative Poetry* (Atlanta, GA: Society of Biblical Literature, 1997).

—— 'Divine Intercession in Judah?', in *Vetus Testamentum* 56(1), 2006, pp. 76–91.

Parmenter, Dorina Miller, 'The Bible as Icon: Myths of the Divine Origins of Scripture', in Craig A. Evans and H. Daniel Zacharias (eds.), *Jewish and Christian Scripture as Artifact and Canon* (London: T&T Clark, 2009), pp. 298–309.

—— 'How the Bible Feels: The Christian Bible as Effective and Affective Object', in James W. Watts (eds.), *Sensing Sacred Texts* (Sheffield: Equinox, 2018), pp. 27–37.

Parpola, Simo, *Assyrian Prophecies* (State Archives of Assyria, 9; Helsinki: Helsinki University Press, 1997).

Pastoureau, Michel (trans. Jody Gladding), *Red: The History of a Color* (Princeton, NJ: Princeton University Press, 2017).

Patton, Kimberley Christine, *Religion of the Gods: Ritual, Paradox, and Reflexivity* (Oxford: Oxford University Press, 2009).

Paulinus (trans. P. G. Walsh), *Letters of St. Paulinus of Nola, Volume 2: Letters 23–51* (Paramus, NJ: Paulist Press, 1967).

Paz, Sarit, *Drums, Women, and Goddesses: Drumming and Gender in Iron Age II Israel* (Fribourg/Göttingen: Academic Press/Vandenhoeck & Ruprecht, 2007).

Peled, Ilan, *Masculinities and Third Gender: The Origins and Nature of an Institutionalised Gender Otherness in the Ancient Near East* (Münster: Ugarit-Verlag, 2016).

Pelikan, Jaraslov, *The Christian Tradition: A History of the Development of Doctrine*, vol. 1 (Chicago, IL: Chicago University Press, 1971).

Penchansky, David, 'Beauty, Power, and Attraction: Aesthetics and the Hebrew Bible', in Richard J. Bautch and Jean-François Racine (eds.), *Beauty and the Bible: Toward a Hermeneutics of Biblical Aesthetics* (Atlanta, GA: Society of Biblical Literature, 2013), pp. 47–68.

Pentcheva, Bissera V., *The Sensual Icon: Space, Ritual, and the Senses in Byzantium* (Pennsylvania, PA: Pennsylvania State University Press, 2010).

Petronius (trans. Michael Heseltine), *The Satyricon* in *Petronius, Seneca: Satyricon, Apocolocyntosis* (Loeb Classical Library, 15; Cambridge, MA: Harvard University Press, 1913).

Philip, Tarja S., *Menstruation and Childbirth in the Bible: Fertility and Impurity* (New York, NY: Peter Lang, 2006).

Philo (trans. F. H. Colson), *On the Decalogue. On the Special Laws, Books 1–3* (Loeb Classical Library, 320; Cambridge, MA: Harvard University Press, 1937).

—— (trans. Ralph Marcus), *Questions on Exodus* (Loeb Classical Library, 401; Cambridge, MA: Harvard University Press, 1953).

Piening, Heinrich, 'Examination Report: The Polychromy of the Arch of Titus Menorah Relief', in *Images: A Journal of Jewish Art and Visual Culture* 6, 2012, pp. 27–32.

Pinker, Aron, 'Descent of the Goddess Ishtar to the Netherworld and Nahum II 8', in *Vetus Testamentum* 55(1), 2005, pp. 89–100.

Plutarch (trans. Bernadotte Perrin), *Pyrrhus* in *Lives, Volume IX* (Loeb Classical Library, 101; Cambridge, MA: Harvard University Press, 1920).

—— (trans. Paul A. Clement and Herbert B. Hoffleit), *Moralia, Volume VIII: Table Talk, Books 1–6* (Loeb Classical Library, 424; Cambridge, MA: Harvard University Press, 1969).

Podany, Amanda H., *The Ancient Near East: A Very Short Introduction* (Oxford: Oxford University Press, 2014).

Pongratz-Leisten, Beate, and Karen Sonik (eds.), *The Materiality of Divine Agency* (Berlin: de Gruyter, 2015).

Porter, Barbara Nevling, 'Feeding Dinner to a Bed: Reflections on the Nature of Gods in Ancient Mesopotamia', in *State Archives of Assyria Bulletin* 15, 2006, pp. 307–31.

—— (ed.), *What Is a God? Anthropomorphic and Non-Anthropomorphic Aspects of Deity in Ancient Mesopotamia* (Winona Lake, IN: Eisenbrauns/ Casco Bay Assyriological Institute, 2009).

Postgate, J. N., *Early Mesopotamia: Society and Economy at the Dawn of History* (Abingdon: Routledge, 1992).

Prestige, G. L., *God in Patristic Thought* (London: Society for the Promotion of Christian Knowledge, 1952).

Prinz, Jesse J., 'Foreword: Hand Manifesto', in Zdravko Radman (ed.), *The Hand, an Organ of the Mind: What the Manual Tells the Mental* (Cambridge, MA: MIT Press, 2013), pp. ix–xvii.

Propp, William H., 'The Skin of Moses' Face – Transfigured or Disfigured?', in *Catholic Biblical Quarterly* 49(3), 1987, pp. 375–86.

—— *Exodus 19–40: A New Translation with Introduction and Commentary* (New York, NY: Doubleday, 2006).

Puhvel, Jaan, '*Genus* and *Sexus* in Hittite', in Simo Parpola and Robert M. Whiting (eds.), *Sex and Gender in the Ancient Near East* (Helsinki: Neo-Assyrian Text Corpus Project, 2002), pp. 547–50.

Pummer, Reinhard, *The Samaritans: A Profile* (Grand Rapids, MI: Eerdmans, 2016).

Purkins, William J., ' "Zealous Imitation": The Materiality of the Crusader's Marked Body', in *Material Religion* 14(4), 2018, pp. 438–53.

Radman, Zdravko (ed.), *The Hand, an Organ of the Mind: What the Manual Tells the Mental* (Cambridge, MA: MIT Press, 2013).

Rainey, Anson F., 'Looking for Bethel: An Exercise in Historical Geography', in Seymour Gitin, J. Edward Wright and J. P. Dessel (eds.), *Confronting the Past: Archaeological and Historical Essays on Ancient Israel in Honor of William G. Dever* (Winona Lake, IN: Eisenbrauns, 2006), pp. 269–73.

Rainey, Brian, *Religion, Ethnicity, and Xenophobia in the Bible: A Theoretical, Exegetical and Theological Survey* (Abingdon: Routledge, 2019).

Ratcliffe, Matthew, 'Touch and the Sense of Reality', in Zdravko Radman (ed.), *The Hand, an Organ of the Mind: What the Manual Tells the Mental* (Cambridge, MA: MIT Press, 2013), pp. 131–57.

Reed, Annette Yoshiko, *Fallen Angels and the History of Judaism and Christianity: The Reception of Enochic Literature* (Cambridge: Cambridge University Press, 2005).

—— *Demons, Angels, and Writing in Ancient Judaism* (Cambridge: Cambridge University Press, 2020).

Reeves, John C., and Annette Yoshiko Reed, *Enoch from Antiquity to the Middle Ages, Volume 1: Sources from Judaism, Christianity, and Islam* (Oxford and New York, NY: Oxford University Press, 2018).

Remensnyder, Amy G., *Remembering Kings Past: Monastic Foundation Legends in Medieval Southern France* (Ithaca, NY: Cornell University Press, 1995).

Rendsburg, Gary A., 'The Mock of Baal in 1 Kings 18:27', in *Catholic Biblical Quarterly* 50(3), 1988, pp. 414–17.

Rendu Loisel, Anne-Caroline, 'When Gods Speak to Men: Reading House, Street, and Divination from Sound in Mesopotamia (1st Millennium BC)', in *Journal of Near Eastern Studies* 75(2), 2016, pp. 291–309.

Reynolds, Peter C., *Stealing Fire: The Atomic Bomb as Symbolic Body* (Palo Alto, CA: Iconic Anthropology Press, 1991).

Ritchie, Ian D., 'The Nose Knows: Bodily Knowing in Isaiah 11.3', in *Journal for the Study of the Old Testament* 87(1), 2000, pp. 59–73.

Roberts, J. J. M., *Nahum, Habakkuk, and Zephaniah: A Commentary* (Louisville, KY: Westminster/John Knox Press, 1991).

—— 'The Motif of the Weeping God in Jeremiah and Its Background in the Lament Tradition of the Ancient Near East', in *Old Testament Essays* 5(3), 1992, pp. 361–74.

Rochberg, Francesca, '"The Stars Their Likeness": Perspectives on the Relation between Celestial Bodies and Gods in Ancient Mesopotamia', in Barbara Nevling Porter (ed.), *What Is a God? Anthropomorphic and Non-Anthropomorphic Aspects of Deity in Ancient Mesopotamia* (Winona Lake, IN: Eisenbrauns/Casco Bay Assyriological Institute, 2009), pp. 41–91.

Römer, Thomas, 'Y avait-il une statue de Yhwh dans le premier temple? Enquêtes littéraires à travers la Bible hébraïque', *Asdiwal* 2, 2007, pp. 41–58.

—— (trans. Raymond Geuss), *The Invention of God* (Cambridge, MA: Harvard University Press, 2015).

Rooke, Deborah W., 'Breeches of the Covenant: Gender, Garments, and the Priesthood', in Deborah W. Rooke (ed.), *Embroidered Garments: Priests and Gender in Biblical Israel* (Sheffield: Sheffield Phoenix, 2009), pp. 19–37.

Roth, Martha T., *Law Collections from Mesopotamia and Asia Minor* (second edition) (Atlanta, GA: Society of Biblical Literature, 1997).

Rothschild, Clare K., 'Ethiopianising the Devil: ὁ μέλας in Barnabas 4', in *New Testament Studies* 65(2), 2019, pp. 223–45.

Ruane, Nicole J., 'Bathing, Status and Gender in Priestly Ritual', in Deborah W. Rooke (ed.), *A Question of Sex? Gender and Difference in the Hebrew Bible and Beyond* (Sheffield: Sheffield Phoenix, 2007), pp. 66–81.

Rubin, Nissan, 'Brit Milah: A Study of Change in Custom', in Elizabeth Wyner Mark (ed.), *The Covenant of Circumcision: New Perspectives on an*

Ancient Jewish Rite (Hanover, NH: Brandeis University Press, 2003), pp. 87–97.

Rutherford, Adam, *How to Argue with a Racist: History, Science, Race and Reality* (London: Weidenfeld & Nicolson, 2020).

Sadler, Rodney S. Jr, *Can a Cushite Change His Skin? An Examination of Race, Ethnicity and Othering in the Hebrew Bible* (London and New York, NY: T&T Clark, 2005).

Saini, Angela, *Superior: The Return of Race Science* (Boston, MA: Beacon Press, 2019).

Sanders, Seth L., 'Old Light on Moses' Shining Face', in *Vetus Testamentum* 52(3), 2002, pp. 400–6.

—— 'When the Personal Became Political: An Onomastic Perspective on the Rise of Yahwism', in *Hebrew Bible and Ancient Israel* 4(1), 2015, pp. 78–105.

Sapir-Hen, Lidar, 'Food, Pork Consumption, and Identity in Ancient Israel', in *Near Eastern Archaeology* 82(1), 2019, pp. 52–59.

Sassi, Maria Michela, 'Where Epistemology and Religion Meet: What Do(es) the God(s) Look Like?', in *Rhizomata* 1(2), 2013, pp. 283–307.

Satlow, Michael L., *How the Bible Became Holy* (New Haven, CT: Yale University Press, 2014).

Sauneron, Serge, *Le Temple d'Esna*, vol. 3 (Cairo: Institut Français d'Archéologie Orientale, 1968).

—— and Jean Yoyotte, 'La naissance du monde selon "Égypte ancienne"', in *La Naissance du Monde* (Paris: Seuil, 1959), pp. 17–91.

Schaberg, Jane, *The Resurrection of Mary Magdalene* (London and New York, NY: Continuum, 2004).

Schäfer, Peter, *The Origins of Jewish Mysticism* (Tübingen: Mohr Siebeck, 2009).

—— *The Jewish Jesus: How Judaism and Christianity Shaped Each Other* (Princeton, NJ: Princeton University Press, 2012).

Schaper, Joachim, *Media and Monotheism: Presence, Representation, and Abstraction in Ancient Judah* (Tübingen: Mohr Siebeck, 2019).

Scheil, Andrew, 'Ælfric of Eynsham', in James Simpson (ed.), *Oxford Handbooks Online* (Oxford: Oxford University Press, 2014), online at https://www.oxfordhandbooks.com/view/10.1093/oxfordhb/9780199935338.001.0001/oxfordhb-9780199935338-e-54?rskey=j5OoEb& result=1

Schipper, Jeremy, and Jeffrey Stackert, 'Blemishes, Camouflage, and Sanctuary Service: The Priestly Deity and His Attendants', in *Hebrew Bible and Ancient Israel* 2(4), 2013, pp. 458–78.

Schmidt, Brian B., *The Materiality of Power: Explorations in the Social History of Early Israelite Magic* (Tübingen: Mohr Siebeck, 2016).

Schniedewind, William M., 'Aramaic, the Death of Written Hebrew, and
    Language Shift in the Persian Period', in Seth L. Sanders (ed.),
    Margins of Writing, Origins of Culture (Chicago, IL: Oriental Institute,
    2007), pp. 141–52.
Schofer, Jonathan Wyn, *Confronting Vulnerability: The Body and the Divine in
    Rabbinic Ethics* (Chicago, IL: University of Chicago Press, 2010).
Schreckenberg, Heinz, *The Jews in Christian Art: An Illustrated History* (New
    York, NY: Continuum, 1996).
Schroer, Silvia, *Die Ikonographie Palästinas/Israels und der Alte Orient. Eine
    Religionsgeschichte in Bildern. Band 3: Die Spätbronzezeit* (Fribourg:
    Academic Press, 2011).
—— *Die Ikonographie Palästinas/Israels und der Alte Orient. Eine
    Religionsgeschichte in Bildern. Band 4: Die Eisenzeit bis zum Beginn der
    achämenidischen Herrschaft* (Basel: Schwabe Verlag, 2018).
Schwartz, Howard, *Tree of Souls: The Mythology of Judaism* (Oxford: Oxford
    University Press, 2004).
Sergi, Omer, 'State Formation, Religion and "Collective Identity" in
    the Southern Levant', in *Hebrew Bible and Ancient Israel* 4(1), 2015,
    pp. 56–77.
Setel, T. Drorah, 'Prophets and Pornography: Female Sexual Imagery in
    Hosea', in Letty M. Russell (ed.), *Feminist Interpretation of the Bible*
    (Philadelphia, PA: Westminster, 1985), pp. 86–95.
Shalem, Dina, 'Do the Images on Chalcolithic Ossuaries Comprise
    Attributes?', in Piotr Bieliński, Michał Gawlikowski, Rafał Koliński,
    Dorota Ławecka, Arkadiusz Sołtysiak and Zuzanna Wygnańska (eds.),
    *Proceedings of the Eighth International Congress on the Archaeology of the
    Ancient Near East, 30 April–4 May 2012*, vol. 1 (Wiesbaden: Harrassowitz
    Verlag, 2014), pp. 505–24.
Shapiro, Marc B., *The Limits of Orthodox Theology: Maimonides' Thirteen
    Principles Reappraised* (Oxford: Liverpool University Press, 2004).
Shehata, Dahlia, 'Sounds from the Divine: Religious Musical Instruments
    in the Ancient Near East', in Joan Goodnick Westenholz, Yossi
    Maurey and Edwin Seroussi (eds.), *Music in Antiquity: The Near East
    and the Mediterranean* (Berlin: de Gruyter, 2014), pp. 102–28.
Shell, Marc, 'The Holy Foreskin; or, Money, Relics, and Judeo-Christianity',
    in Jonathan Boyarin and Daniel Boyarin (eds.), *Jews and Other
    Differences: The New Jewish Cultural Studies* (Minneapolis, MN:
    University of Minnesota Press, 1997), pp. 345–59.
Shenkar, Michael, 'The Coin of the "God on the Winged Wheel"', in
    BOREAS 30/31, 2007/2008, pp. 13–23.

Sheridan, Mark, *Language for God in Patristic Tradition: Wrestling with Biblical Anthropomorphism* (Downers Grove, IL: InterVarsity Press, 2015).

Sherwood, Yvonne, *Biblical Blaspheming: Trials of the Sacred for a Secular Age* (Cambridge: Cambridge University Press, 2012).

——'Cutting Up Life: Sacrifice as a Device for Clarifying – and Tormenting – Fundamental Distinctions between Human, Animal, and Divine', in Jennifer L. Koosed (ed.), *The Bible and Posthumanism* (Atlanta, GA: Society of Biblical Literature, 2014), pp. 247–97.

Shifman, Arie, ' "A Scent" of the Spirit: Exegesis of an Enigmatic Verse (Isaiah 11:3)', in *Journal of Biblical Literature* 131(2), 2012, pp. 241–49.

Silverman, Eric, *A Cultural History of Jewish Dress* (London: Bloomsbury, 2013).

Simkins, Ronald A., 'The Embodied World: Creation Metaphors in the Ancient Near East', *Biblical Theology Bulletin* 44(1), 2014, pp. 40–53.

Smith, Duane E., 'The Color of Fortune: The Role of Color in Mesopotamian Divination', in Rachael B. Goldman (ed.), *Essays in Global Color History: Interpreting the Ancient Spectrum* (Piscataway, NJ: Gorgias Press, 2016), pp. 9–29.

Smith, Geoffrey S., *Valentinian Christianity: Texts and Translations* (Oakland, CA: University of California Press, 2020).

Smith, Mark S., 'The Heart and Innards in Israelite Emotional Expressions: Notes from Anthropology and Psychology', in *Journal of Biblical Literature* 117(3), 1998, pp. 427–36.

—— *The Origins of Biblical Monotheism: Israel's Polytheistic Background and the Ugaritic Texts* (Oxford and New York, NY: Oxford University Press, 2001).

—— *The Early History of God: Yahweh and the Other Deities in Ancient Israel* (second edition) (Grand Rapids, MI: Eerdmans, 2002).

—— *How Human Is God? Seven Questions About God and Humanity in the Bible* (Collegeville, MN: Liturgical Press, 2014).

—— *Where the Gods Are: Spatial Dimensions of Anthropomorphism in the Biblical World* (New Haven, CT: Yale University Press, 2016).

—— and Wayne Y. Pitard, *The Ugaritic Baal Cycle, Volume II: Introduction with Text, Translation and Commentary of KTU/CAT 1.3–1.4* (Leiden: Brill, 2009).

Smoak, Jeremy D., *The Priestly Blessing in Inscription and Scripture: The Early History of Numbers 6:24–26* (Oxford and New York, NY: Oxford University Press, 2015).

Sommer, Benjamin D., 'The Babylonian Akitu Festival: Rectifying the King or Renewing the Cosmos?', in *Journal of Ancient Near Eastern Studies* 27(1), 2000, pp. 81–95.

—— *The Bodies of God and the World of Ancient Israel* (Cambridge: Cambridge University Press, 2009).

Sorensen, Eric, *Possession and Exorcism in the New Testament and Early Christianity* (Tübingen: Mohr Siebeck, 2002).

Spoerl, Kelley, 'Eustathius of Antioch on Jesus' Digestion', in *Studia Patristica* 74, 2016, pp. 147–57.

—— 'Epiphanius on Jesus' Digestion', in *Studia Patristica* 96, 2017, pp. 3–10.

Squarzina, Silvia Danesi, 'The Collections of Cardinal Benedetto Giustiniani. Part II', in *The Burlington Magazine* 140(1139), 1998, pp. 102–118.

Stager, Lawrence E., 'The Shechem Temple – Where Abimelech Slaughtered a Thousand', in *Biblical Archaeology Review*, 29(4), pp. 265–6, 269.

Staubli, Thomas, 'Feces: The Primary Disgust Elicitor in the Hebrew Bible and in the Ancient Near East', in Annette Schellenberg and Thomas Krüger (eds.), *Sounding Sensory Profiles in the Ancient Near East* (Atlanta, GA: Society of Biblical Literature, 2019), pp. 119–43.

—— and Silvia Schroer (trans. Linda M. Maloney), *Body Symbolism in the Bible* (Collegeville, MN: Liturgical Press, 2001).

Stavrakopoulou, Francesca, *King Manasseh and Child Sacrifice: Biblical Distortions of Historical Realities* (Berlin: de Gruyter, 2004).

—— 'Making Bodies: On Body Modification and Religious Materiality in the Hebrew Bible', in *Hebrew Bible and Ancient Israel* 2(4), 2013, pp. 532–53.

—— 'The Historical Framework: Biblical and Scholarly Portrayals of the Past', in John Barton (ed.), *The Hebrew Bible: A Critical Companion* (Princeton, NJ: Princeton University Press, 2016), pp. 24–53.

—— 'Religion at Home: The Materiality of Practice', in Susan Niditch (ed.), *The Wiley Blackwell Companion to Ancient Israel* (Chichester: Wiley, 2016), pp. 347–65.

—— 'The Ancient Goddess, the Biblical Scholar, and the Religious Past: Re-imaging Divine Women', in Yvonne Sherwood (ed.), *The Bible and Feminism: Remapping the Field* (Oxford: Oxford University Press, 2017), pp. 495–513.

—— and John Barton (eds.), *Religious Diversity in Ancient Israel and Judah* (London: T&T Clark, 2010).

Steinberg, Leo, *The Sexuality of Christ in Renaissance Art and in Modern Oblivion* (second revised and expanded edition) (Chicago, IL: University of Chicago Press, 1996).

Sterling, Gregory E., '"The Jewish Philosophy": Reading Moses via Hellenistic Philosophy according to Philo', in Torrey Seland (ed.),

Reading Philo: A Handbook to Philo of Alexandria (Grand Rapids, MI: Eerdmans, 2014), pp. 129–54.

Stern, David, 'Midrash Eleh Ezkerah, or *The Legend of the Ten Martyrs*', in David Stern and Mark Jay Mirsky (eds.), *Rabbinic Fantasies: Imaginative Narratives from Classical Hebrew Literature* (New Haven, CT: Yale University Press, 1990), pp. 143–65.

Stern, Ephraim (ed.), *The New Encyclopedia of Archaeological Excavations in the Holy Land*, 4 vols. (Jerusalem/New York, NY: Israel Exploration Society/Simon and Schuster, 1993).

Stewart, David Tabb, 'Sexual Disabilities in the Hebrew Bible', in Candida R. Moss and Jeremy Schipper (eds.), *Disability Studies and Biblical Literature* (New York, NY: Palgrave Macmillan, 2011), pp. 67–87.

Stol, M., *Birth in Babylonia and the Bible: Its Mediterranean Setting* (Groningen: Styx, 2000).

Stone, Elizabeth C., and Paul E. Zimansky, *The Iron Age Settlement at 'Ain Dara, Syria: Survey and Soundings* (Oxford: British Archaeological Reports, 1999).

Stroumsa, Sarah, *Maimonides in His World: Portrait of a Mediterranean Thinker* (Princeton, NJ: Princeton University Press, 2009).

Stuckenbruck, Loren T., 'The Demonic World of the Dead Sea Scrolls', in Ida Fröhlich and Erkki Koskenniemi (eds.), *Evil and the Devil* (London and New York, NY: T&T Clark, 2013), pp. 51–70.

—— 'The Human Being and Demonic Invasion: Therapeutic Models in Ancient Jewish and Christian Texts', in Christopher C. H. Cook (ed.), *Spirituality, Theology and Mental Health: Multidisciplinary Perspectives* (London: SCM Press, 2013), pp. 94–123.

Summers, David, *Real Spaces: World Art History and the Rise of Western Modernism* (London: Phaidon, 2003).

Swartz, Michael D., 'The Semiotics of the Priestly Vestments', in Albert I. Baumgarten (ed.), *Sacrifice in Religious Experience* (Leiden: Brill, 2002), pp. 57–80.

Takács, Sarolta A., 'Divine and Human Feet: Records of Pilgrims Honoring Isis', in Jaś Elsner and Ian Rutherford (eds.), *Pilgrimage in Graeco-Roman and Early Christian Antiquity: Seeing the Gods* (Oxford: Oxford University Press, 2005), pp. 353–69.

Taylor, Joan E., *What Did Jesus Look Like?* (London: Bloomsbury T&T Clark, 2018).

Teeter, Emily, 'Household Cults', in Emily Teeter and Janet H. Johnson (eds.), *The Life of Meresamun: A Temple Singer in Ancient Egypt* (Chicago, IL: Oriental Institute Museum, 2009), pp. 71–5.

—— *Religion and Ritual in Ancient Egypt* (Cambridge: Cambridge University Press, 2011).

Tertullian (trans. S. Thelwall), *The Apparel of Women* in *The Ante-Nicene Fathers: Translations of the Writings of the Fathers Down to A.D. 325*, vol. 4 (Edinburgh: T&T Clark, 1885).

Thavapalan, Shiyanthi, 'Radiant Things for Gods and Men: Lightness and Darkness in Mesopotamian Language and Thought', in *Colour Turn* 1(7), 2018, pp. 1–36.

Theophilus (trans. Robert H. Grant), *Ad Autolycum* (Oxford: Oxford University Press, 1970).

Thomason, Allison Karmel, 'From Sennacherib's Bronzes to Taharqa's Feet: Conceptions of the Material World at Nineveh', in *Iraq* 66, 2004, pp. 151–62.

Thompson, Marianne Meye, 'The Breath of Life: John 20:22–23 Once More', in Graham N. Stanton, Bruce W. Longenecker and Stephen C. Barton (eds.), *The Holy Spirit and Christian Origins: Essays in Honor of James D. G. Dunn* (Grand Rapids, MI: Eerdmans, 2004), pp. 69–78.

Thurlkill, Mary, *Sacred Scents in Early Christianity and Islam* (Lanham, MD: Lexington, 2016).

Tilford, Nicole, 'The Affected Eye: Re-Examining a Biblical Idiom', in *Biblical Interpretation* 23, 2015, pp. 207–21.

—— *Sensing World, Sensing Wisdom: The Cognitive Foundation of Biblical Metaphors* (Atlanta, GA: Society of Biblical Literature, 2017).

Tissot, Samuel Auguste David (trans. A. Hume), *Onanism: or a Treatise upon the Disorders Produced by Masturbation: or The Dangerous Effects of Secret and Excessive Venery* (London: J. Pridden, 1766).

Toorn, Karel van der, 'The Iconic Book: Analogies between the Babylonian Cult of Images and the Veneration of the Torah', in Karel van der Toorn (ed.), *The Image and the Book: Iconic Cults, Aniconism, and the Rise of Book Religion in Israel and the Ancient Near East* (Leuven: Peeters, 1997), pp. 229–48.

—— *Becoming Diaspora Jews: Behind the Story of Elephantine* (New Haven, CT: Yale University Press, 2019).

—— and Bob Becking, Pieter W. van der Hoorst (eds.), *Dictionary of Deities and Demons in the Bible* (second extensively revised edition) (Leiden: Brill, 1999).

Tougher, Shaun, *The Roman Castrati: Eunuchs in the Roman Empire* (London: Bloomsbury Academic, 2021).

Töyräänvuori, Joanna, 'Weapons of the Storm God in Ancient Near Eastern and Biblical Traditions', in *Studia Orientalia* 112, 2012, pp. 147–80.

Tropper, Josef, 'The Divine Name *Yahwa', in Jürgen van Oorschot and Markus Witte (eds.), *The Origins of Yahwism* (Berlin: de Gruyter, 2017), pp. 1–21.

Tuckett, Christopher, 'The Gospel of Mary', in *Revista catalana de teologia* 37(1), 2012, pp. 111–29.

Tyson, Craig W., 'The Religion of the Ammonites: A Specimen of Levantine Religion from the Iron Age II (ca. 1000–500 BCE)', in *Religions* 10(3), 2019, article 153, online at https://doi.org/10.3390/rel10030153.

Uehlinger, Christoph, 'Anthropomorphic Cult Statuary in Iron Age Palestine and the Search for Yahweh's Cult Images', in Karel van der Toorn (ed.), *The Image and the Book: Iconic Cults, Aniconism, and the Rise of Book Religion in Israel and the Ancient Near East* (Leuven: Peeters, 1997), pp. 97–155.

—— 'Neither Eyewitnesses, Nor Windows to the Past, but Valuable Testimony in Its Own Right: Remarks on Iconography, Source Criticism, and Ancient Data-Processing', in H. G. M. Williamson (ed.), *Understanding the History of Ancient Israel* (Oxford: Oxford University Press, 2007), pp. 173–228.

Urbano, Arthur P., *The Philosophical Life: Biography and the Crafting of Intellectual Identity in Late Antiquity* (Washington, DC: Catholic University of America, 2013).

Ussishkin, David, *Biblical Lachish: A Tale of Construction, Destruction, Excavation, and Restoration* (Jerusalem: Israel Exploration Society, 2014).

Van Dijk-Hemmes, Fokkelien, 'The Metaphorization of Woman in Prophetic Speech: An Analysis of Ezekiel XXIII', in *Vetus Testamentum* 43(2), 1993, pp. 162–70.

Vila, Emmanuelle, and Anne-Sophie Dalix, 'Alimentation et idéologie: la place du sanglier et du porc à l'Âge du Bronze sur la côte levantine', in *Anthropozoologica* 39(1), 2004, pp. 219–36.

Wagner, Andreas (trans. Marion Salzmann), *God's Body: The Anthropomorphic God in the Old Testament* (London: T&T Clark, 2019).

Wainwright, Elaine, 'Unbound Hair and Ointmented Feet: An Ecofeminist Reading of Luke 7.36–50', in Natalie K. Watson and Stephen Burns (eds.), *Exchanges of Grace: Essays in Honour of Ann Loades* (London: SCM Press, 2008), pp. 178–89.

Walker, Alexander (ed. and trans.), *Apocryphal Gospels, Acts and Revelations* (Ante-Nicene Library, 16; Edinburgh: T&T Clark, 1873).

Walker, Christopher, and Michael B. Dick, 'The Induction of the Cult Image in Ancient Mesopotamia: The Mesopotamian *mīs pî* Ritual', in

Michael B. Dick (ed.), *Born in Heaven, Made on Earth: The Making of the Cult Image in the Ancient Near East* (Winona Lake, IN: Eisenbrauns, 1999), pp. 55–121.

Wassen, Cecilia, 'Angels in the Dead Sea Scrolls', in Friedrich V. Reiterer, Tobias Nicklas and Karin Schöpflin (eds.), *Deuterocanonical and Cognate Literature Yearbook 2007: Angels. The Concept of Celestial Beings – Origins, Development, and Reception* (Berlin: de Gruyter, 2007), pp. 499–523.

Watts, James W., 'Aaron and the Golden Calf in the Rhetoric of the Pentateuch', in *Journal of Biblical Literature* 130(3), 2011, pp. 417–30.

Weeks, Stuart, 'Man-Made Gods? Idolatry in the Old Testament', in Stephen C. Barton (ed.), *Idolatry: False Worship in the Bible, Early Judaism, and Christianity* (London and New York, NY: T&T Clark, 2007), pp. 7–21.

Weiss, Dov, *Pious Irreverence: Confronting God in Rabbinic Judaism* (Philadelphia, PA: University of Pennsylvania Press, 2017).

Weissenrieder, Annette, 'The Infusion of the Spirit: The Meaning of ἐμφυσάω in John 20:22–23', in Jörg Frey and John Levinson (eds.), *The Holy Spirit, Inspiration, and the Cultures of Antiquity: Multidisciplinary Perspectives* (Berlin: de Gruyter, 2014), pp. 119–51.

Weitzman, Kurt, *Monastery of Saint Catherine at Mount Sinai: The Icons, Volume 1, From the Sixth to the Tenth Century* (Princeton, NJ: Princeton University Press, 1976).

Welton, Rebekah, '*He Is a Glutton and a Drunkard': Deviant Consumption in the Hebrew Bible* (Leiden: Brill, 2020).

Wengrow, David, 'Art and Material Culture', in Ann C. Gunter (ed.), *A Companion to Ancient Near Eastern Art* (Hoboken, NJ: John Wiley, 2019), pp. 25–48.

Werrett, Ian, 'A Scroll in One Hand and a Mattock in the Other: Latrines, Essenes, and Khirbet Qumran', in *Revue de Qumrân* 23(4), 2008, pp. 475–89.

West, Traci C., 'When a White Man-God Is the Truth and the Way for Black Christians', in George Yancy (ed.), *Christology and Whiteness: What Would Jesus Do?* (London and New York, NY: Routledge, 2012), pp. 114–27.

Westenholz, Joan Goodnick, 'In the Service of the Gods: The Ministering Clergy', in Harriet Crawford (ed.), *The Sumerian World* (London: Routledge, 2013), pp. 246–74.

Wheeler, Brannon, *Mecca and Eden: Ritual, Relics, and Territory in Islam* (Chicago, IL: University of Chicago Press, 2006).

Whitford, David M., *The Case of Ham in the Early Modern Era: The Bible and the Justifications for Slavery* (Farnham: Ashgate, 2009).

Whitmarsh, Tim, *Battling the Gods: Atheism in the Ancient World* (London: Faber & Faber, 2016).

Whitney, K. William, *Two Strange Beasts: Leviathan and Behemoth in the Second Temple* (Winona Lake, IN: Eisenbrauns, 2006).

Widengren, Geo, *The King and the Tree of Life in Ancient Near Eastern Religion* (Wiesbaden: Harrassowitz, 1951).

Wiethaus, Ulrike (ed. and trans.), *Agnes Blannbekin, Viennese Beguine: Life and Revelations* (Cambridge: D. S. Brewer, 2002).

Winter, Irene J., 'After the Battle Is Over: The *Stele of Vultures* and the Beginning of Historical Narrative in the Art of the Ancient Near East', in Herbert L. Kessler and Marianna Shreve Simpson (eds.), *Pictorial Narrative in Antiquity and the Middle Ages* (Washington, DC: National Gallery of Art, 1985), pp. 11–32.

—— 'Opening the Eyes and Opening the Mouth: The Utility of Comparing Images in Worship in India and the Ancient Near East', in Michael W. Meister (ed.), *Ethnography and Personhood: Notes from the Field* (Jaipur and New Delhi: Rawat Publications, 2000), pp. 129–62.

—— 'The Eyes Have It: Votive Statuary, Gilgamesh's Axe, and Cathected Viewing in the Ancient Near East', in R. Nelson (ed.), *Visuality Before and Beyond the Renaissance* (Cambridge: Cambridge University Press, 2000), pp. 22–44.

—— 'Defining "Aesthetics" for Non-Western Studies: The Case of Ancient Mesopotamia', in Michael A. Holly and Keith Moxey (eds.), *Art History, Aesthetics, Visual Studies* (Williamstown, MA: Sterling and Francine Clark Art Institute, 2002), pp. 3–28.

Wolff, Hans Walter, *Anthropology of the Old Testament* (Philadelphia: Fortress Press, 1974).

Wolfson, Elliot R., 'Images of God's Feet: Some Observations on the Divine Body in Judaism', in Howard Eilberg-Schwartz (ed.), *People of the Body: Jews and Judaism from an Embodied Perspective* (Albany, NY: State University of New York, 1992), pp. 143–81.

Wyatt, Nicolas, *Myths of Power: A Study of Royal Myth and Ideology in Ugaritic and Biblical Tradition* (Münster: Ugarit-Verlag, 1996).

—— *Space and Time in the Religious Life of the Near East* (Sheffield: Sheffield Academic Press, 2001).

—— *Religious Texts from Ugarit* (second edition) (Sheffield: Sheffield Academic Press, 2002).

—— 'Circumcision and Circumstance: Male Genital Mutilation in Ancient
     Israel and Ugarit', in *Journal for the Study of the Old Testament* 33(4),
     2009, pp. 405–31.
—— 'A Royal Garden: The Ideology of Eden', in *Scandinavian Journal of
     the Old Testament* 28(1), 2014, pp. 1–35.
—— 'Bull El and His Avatars: The Iron Age Legacy of an Ugaritian
     Trope', in Carole Roche-Hawley and Robert Hawley (eds.), *Mélanges
     européennes en l'honneur de Dennis Pardee* (Louvain: Peeters,
     forthcoming).
Wyssmann, Patrick, 'The Coinage Imagery of Samaria and Judah in the
     Late Persian Period', in Christian Frevel, Katharina Pyschny and Izak
     Cornelius (eds.), *A 'Religious Revolution' in Yehûd? The Material Culture
     of the Persian Period as a Test Case* (Fribourg/Göttingen: Academic
     Press/Vandenhoeck & Ruprecht, 2014), pp. 221–66.
Yee, Gale, *Poor Banished Children of Eve: Woman as Evil in the Hebrew Bible*
     (Minneapolis, MN: Fortress Press, 2003).
Yon, Marguerite, *The City of Ugarit at Tell Ras Shamra* (Winona Lake, IN:
     Eisenbrauns, 2006).
Zaccagnini, Carlo, 'Feet of Clay at Emar and Elsewhere', in *Orientalia*
     63(1), 1994, pp. 1–4.
Zevit, Ziony, *What Really Happened in the Garden of Eden?* (New Haven,
     CT: Yale University Press, 2013).
Zsolnay, Ilona, 'Gender and Sexuality: Ancient Near East', in Julia O'Brien
     (ed.), *The Oxford Encyclopedia of the Bible and Gender Studies*, vol. 1
     (Oxford and New York, NY: Oxford University Press, 2014), pp. 273–87.
Zucconi, Laura M., *Ancient Medicine: From Mesopotamia to Rome* (Grand
     Rapids, MI: Eerdmans, 2019).

Acknowledgements

Writers often talk about the pain and pleasure of living with the subject of their book (and for this life-long atheist, it's always been a complicated relationship), but there are several people who've also had to live with God and his body. My deepest thanks go to my brilliant publisher and editor, George Morley. From the moment I met her, I not only knew I wanted to work with her, but I knew I had found a fearless ally. I'm very lucky. And it's thanks to my fantastic agent, Will Francis, that this book has even come into being. Obviously, I thought he was crazy when he first suggested I write a book for non-specialists, but it turns out he's always right about everything. Thank you, Will.

In the US, my lovely agent PJ Mark enabled me to work with the wonderful Robin Desser. I'll be forever grateful that she took a punt on me. My special thanks also to the stellar Dan Frank, whose response to the completed draft rendered me speechless in the best of ways. Although I only knew him for a short time, his sharp mind and emotional generosity made such a difference to me. Since his terrible loss, Vanessa Haughton has been tremendous in seeing the book into print – and I'm so grateful for her patience and care.

On both sides of the Atlantic, an army of people has worked hard on *God* with me, from the copy-editors to the design teams. But I'm especially grateful to Nicholas Blake, Marissa Constantinou and Gaby Quattromini. Cecilia Mackay is a legend – she not only hunted down the images in the book, but instinctively understood what I wanted those images to do. I also owe the mega-talented Daniel McClellan a huge thank-you (and a slap-up dinner) for drawing some of the artefacts shown in this book.

Much of the research was undertaken during a period of study leave funded by a generous grant from the Leverhulme Trust, for which I'm very grateful. I'm also very much indebted to John Barton, Susan Niditch and Nicolas Wyatt for writing in support of my application. Academia can be a brutal world (ivory towers come equipped with gate-keepers and corridor trolls), but I'm lucky to be able to call on the best in the business to ask for their wisdom, advice and support. My eternal thanks to Thomas Bolin, Jonathan Hill, David Horrell, Mark Leuchter, Adrian Thatcher and Nicolas Wyatt, each of whom read every word of the manuscript, and offered the constructive criticism I needed. I only hope I can go some way to returning the favour. Other friends and colleagues variously read draft material, shared their expertise and new research, answered my weird questions, or hunted down books and articles I couldn't access – especially when Covid hit. Massive thanks to Moudhy Al-Rashid, Sarah Bond, Joel Burnett, Dexter Callender, Izak Cornelius, James Crossley, Bea Fones, Rhiannon Graybill, Chris Greenough, Anne Katrine de Hemmer Gudme, Helen John, Nyasha Junior, Chris Keith, Louise Lawrence, Emma Loosley, Morwenna Ludlow, Aren Maeir, Andrew Mein, Lloyd Pietersen, Sarah Shectman, Arthur Urbano and Tim Whitmarsh. This book shouldn't be assumed to reflect their views, of course. (And I expect one or two might breathe a sigh of relief at that!)

Working with my undergraduate, MA and PhD students over the years has given me the chance to rabbit on about some of the ideas I've finally explored in this book, and I'm particularly grateful to Elisabeth Cook, Alan Bernthal-Hooker, Daniel McClellan, Bethany Wagstaff and Rebekah Welton for being such brilliant conversation partners. Love and thanks also to my clever friends (and tireless cheerleaders) Heather Baker, Natalie Haynes, Caroline Horrell, Salman Jafri, Ellena Lyell, Dominic Mattos, Catherine Nixey, Richard Osman and Adam Rutherford, each of whom has left their mark on this book in some way.

A bit like Egeria (but now with the added benefits of FaceTime and WhatsApp), I've spent a lot of time travelling about the Middle East, and Sinai remains particularly special to me. My love and gratitude to my brother-from-another-mother, Hadi Mohammed Elaaser, and sincere thanks to Rabia Gad, all the southern Sinai Bedouin, the monks of St Catherine's, and Kenneth Wolfe, who first took me and my class-mates to Sinai a million years ago when I was seventeen.

Finally, I'm so grateful to the people who have kept me on the straight and narrow(ish). My special love and thanks go to Stuart Macwilliam, and our beloved friend Geoff Urwin, who didn't live long enough to see the book completed, but who said he'd probably only read the dirty bits anyway. Thank you to my family – blood, blended, borrowed and extended – from Mykonos to Chesterfield and everywhere in between. Above all, my fiercest love and deepest thanks to my amazing mum, and to my partner, Andy. At this point in my career, I've already written hundreds of thousands of words about God, but there aren't enough words in the world to express how I feel about Andy. This book is dedicated to him.

Index

References in bold are to illustrations.

moon 328
  see also Nanna
mosaics 81, 100, 182, 325, **354**, 355, **400**
Moses 13, 23, 246–7, 357, 375, 396, 406, 408
  and adultery 305
  and the ark of the covenant 57–8
  bodily transformation of 177–8,
    313–14, 381
  and the burning bush 80, 81, 237–8
  death of 265–6
  and defecation 229
  and the divine power of sight 380, 381
  face-to-face encounters with God 16,
    32, 229, 313–14, 315, 317, 381
  first encounter with God 80–1
  and God's curses 295
  and God's feet 32, 167
  and God's voice 368
  and Greek philosophy 419
  and the heart 198
  horns of 177–8, 332
  leads the Israelites to the Promised
    Land 12
  oral tradition of 303
  and the parting of the sea 44
  and the prohibition of divine
    images 18
  request to see God's body 167–9, 171,
    177–9
  and the Ten Commandments 81,
    177–8, 287–90, **291**
  toilet habits of 229
  and the Torah 12, 229, 285, 286, 300
mosques 73, 167–8, 195
Mot 20, 60, 120–1, 203, 366, 398–400, **401**
mother goddesses 19, 24, **124**, 211,
  319–20
  see also Tiamat
motnayim (groin/genitals) 102–3
Mount of Olives 32, 45
mountains 45–6, 54–5
mourning customs 194–5, 343

mouths 392–3, 403
Muhammad 32
mummification 337, 392, **393**
Mushkabim people 271
music 369, 370–1, 397
Musk, Elon 7
Muslims 31
  see also Islam
mysticism 388–9
  Christian 142–4
  Jewish 63, 86–7, 261, 389, 396, 415, 419
mythological imagination 67

Naaman 60
Nablus (ancient Shechem) 35, 206, 207
Nabonidus of Babylon 195
Nabopolassar of Babylon 253
Nabu 85, 275, 292, 293
Nabu-apla-iddina of Babylon 312, **313**
Nabu-nadin-shumi 312
Nadab 32
Nahar ('River') 43, 242
  see also Yam
Nahum, book of 223
names, erasure 291–2
Nammu 211
Nanna (Sin) 201–2, **202**
Naram-Sin 42
National Museum of Iraq 209, 324
Nazir 342
NBC website 7
Nebo, Mount 265
Nebuchadnezzar II of Babylon 61,
  217–18, 254, 293
Nefertiti 268–9, **268**
Negev desert 21
  see also Arad
Nehardea 59–60
Neolithic period 310, 337
nephesh (throat/personhood) 402
Nephilim 154–5
Neptune 353

Illustration Credits

Colour plates

Plate 1. Divine footprints at an Iron Age temple in 'Ain Dara, north-western Syria. Photo: © Phillip Gorny.

Plate 2. Monument depicting Naram-Sin trampling his enemies, originally from Sippar, Mesopotamia, c. 2250 BCE. Musée du Louvre, Paris. Photo: Ali Meyer / Bridgeman Images.

Plate 3. Ceremonial sandals, from the tomb of Tutankhamun (KV62), Valley of the Kings, West Thebes. Egyptian Museum, Cairo. JE 62685. Photo: Laboratorio Rosso.

Plate 4. Figurine of a deity (El or Baal?) wearing wedged sandals, Hazor, Israel, fourteenth century BCE. Collection of the Israel Antiquities Authority. Photo: © Israel Museum, Jerusalem.

Plate 5. Moses removes his sandals at the burning bush, mosaic, sixth century CE. Basilica of St Catherine's Monastery, Sinai. Photo: Reproduced by permission of St Catherine's Monastery, Sinai, Egypt.

Plate 6. Michelangelo, *The Risen Christ*, Monastero San Vincenzo Martire, Bassano Romano. Photo: © Alessandro Vasari Photography.

Plate 7. Mosaic depicting the baptism of Christ, sixth century CE. Arian Baptistery, Ravenna. Photo: Boris Breytman/Dreamstime.com.

Plate 8. Willem Key (attrib.), *Pietà*, painting, early sixteenth century. Alte Pinakothek, Munich. Photo: Bridgeman Images.

Plate 9. Ludwig Krug, *The Man of Sorrows*, engraving, c. 1510–1532. British Museum, London. Photo: © The Trustees of the British Museum.

Plate 10. Terracotta plaque figurine of a goddess (usually identified as Asherah), c. 1250 BCE. Found near Kibbutz Revadim, Israel. Collection of the Israel Antiquities Authority. Photo: © The Israel Museum, Jerusalem / David Harris.

Plate 11. Tiered ritual object from Taanach, Israel, tenth century BCE. Staff Archaeological Officer, Civil Administration of Judea and Samaria. Photo: © The Israel Museum, Jerusalem.

Plate 12. Mosaic depicting Christ enthroned on a rainbow, early fifth century CE. Church of Hosios David, Thessaloniki. Photo: © David Hendrix/The Byzantine Legacy.

Plate 13. Miniature depicting Jesus' exorcism of the Gadarenes, from the Canterbury Psalter, English, twelfth century CE. Bibliothèque Nationale de France, Paris. MS lat. 8846, folio 3v (detail). Photo: © BnF.

Plate 14. Terracotta plaque depicting the face of Huwawa (Humbaba). Sippar, Mesopotamia, *c.* 1800–1600 BCE. British Museum, London. Photo: BibleLandPictures/Alamy.

Plate 15. Inscribed hand from a tomb complex at Khirbet el-Qom, in the West Bank, eighth century BCE. Collection of the Israel Antiquities Authority. Photo: © The Israel Museum, Jerusalem.

Plate 16. Bronze and gold statue of El. Ugarit, late fourteenth century BCE. National Museum of Syria, Damacus. Photo: Interfoto/Alamy.

Plate 17. Detail from a fresco showing God's parting of the sea, from the synagogue in Dura Europos, Syria, third century CE. National Museum of Syria, Damacus. Photo: Godong/Bridgeman Images.

Plate 18. Detail from a fresco showing God seizing Ezekiel by his hair, from the synagogue in Dura Europos, Syria, third century CE. National Museum of Damascus, Syria. Photo: Zev Radovan/Bridgeman Images.

Plate 19. Miniature showing Moses' last day, from the Old English Hexateuch, English, eleventh century CE. British Library, London. Cotton MS Claudius B IV, f. 139v. Photo: © British Library Board. All Rights Reserved/Bridgeman Images.

Plate 20. Alabaster votive figurine of a worshipper, Sumerian, *c.* 2900–2300 BCE. The Menil Collection, Houston. Photo: Paul Hester.

Plate 21. Plastered skull from Jericho, *c.* 8500–6000 BCE. British Museum, London. Photo: © The Trustees of the British Museum.

Plate 22. Marble face from a cult statue of a goddess (probably Inanna), Uruk, *c.* 3100 BCE. National Museum of Iraq, Baghdad. Photo: Osama Shukir Muhammed Amin FRCP(Glasg).

Plate 23. Fragment of a painted terracotta statuette of an enthroned god, Ur, *c.* 1850–1750 BCE. British Museum, London. Photo: Lanmas/Alamy.

Plate 24. Silver coin showing a male deity on a winged chariot-wheel. Yehud (Judah), fourth century BCE. British Museum, London. Photo: © The Trustees of the British Museum.

Plate 25. Silver scrolls originally worn as amulets, late seventh century BCE, found at Ketef Hinnom, Jerusalem. Collection of the Israel Antiquities Authority. Photo: © Israel Museum, Jerusalem/Nahum Slapak.

Plate 26. Gold amulet bearing the image of a high goddess atop a lion, found at Minet el-Beida, near Ras Shamra (Ugarit), c. 1450–1365 BCE. Musée du Louvre, Paris. Photo: DeAgostini/Getty Images.

Plate 27. Christ sits among his disciples or students, detail from a fresco in the Catacomb of Domitilla, Rome, fourth century CE. Photo: Held Collection/Bridgeman Images.

Plate 28. Christ as *Pantokrator*, detail from a mosaic, Church of Santa Pudenziana, Rome, late fourth century CE. Photo: Jozef Sedmak/Dreamstime.com.

Plate 29. Detail of a relief on a marble sarcophagus showing Adam facing God. Roman, fourth century CE. Pio Cristiano Collection, Vatican Museums. Photo: © Governatorato SCV - Museum Directorate. All Rights Reserved.

Plate 30. Detail from a relief on a marble sarcophagus showing the Trinity and the creation of Eve. Roman, fourth century CE. Pio Cristiano Collection, Vatican Museums. Photo: © Governatorato SCV - Museum Directorate. All Rights Reserved.

Plate 31. Icon depicting Christ as the Ancient of Days, late sixth century CE. St Catherine's Monastery, Sinai. Photo: Courtesy of the Michigan-Princeton-Alexandria Expeditions to the Monastery of St Catherine on Mount Sinai. Reproduced by permission of the Monastery of St Catherine, Sinai.

Plate 32. Ivory panel depicting Christ as the Ancient of Days, flanked by Peter and Paul. Byzantine, fifth or sixth century CE. Bibliothèque nationale de France, Paris. Latin 9384. Photo: © BnF.

Plate 33 (a–b). Hans Holbein the Younger, *The Body of the Dead Christ in the Tomb*, 1521. Kunstmuseum, Basel. Photo: Azoor/Alamy.

Illustrations in the text

Fig. 1. 'The face of God', composite computer-generated image, 2018. Jackson, J. C., Hester, N., and Gray, K. (2018). 'The Faces of God in America: Revealing Religious Diversity across People and Politics', *PloS One*, 13(6), article e0198745. Reproduced with permission.

Fig. 2. Standing stones, c. 2000–1500 BCE, Gezer, Israel. Photo: Lenazap/istockphoto.

Fig. 3. Reconstruction of the inner sanctum of an eighth-century BCE temple excavated at Arad, Israel. Collection of the Israel Antiquities Authority. Photo: © Israel Museum, Jerusalem/Laura Lachman.

Fig. 4. Drawings of two third-century CE coins from Byblos (left) and Tyre (right). Illustration: Daniel O. McClellan, 2021.

Fig. 5. Detail of an ivory plaque from Megiddo, Israel, *c.* 1350–1150 BCE. Collection of the Israel Antiquities Authority. Photo: © The Israel Museum, Jerusalem/Elie Posner.

Fig. 6. Detail from a relief commemorating the spoils of Jerusalem, from the Arch of Titus, Rome, *c.* 81 CE. Photo: Granger/Alamy.

Fig. 7. Detail from a palace relief from Kalhu (Nimrud), Assyria, *c.* 730 BCE. British Museum, London. Photo: © The Trustees of the British Museum.

Fig. 8. Carved stone block from a mid first-century CE synagogue in the ancient city of Magdala, Israel. Private collection. Photo: Zev Radovan/Bridgeman Images.

Fig. 9. Wall plaque depicting a deity on the back of a lion, from Ashur, Assyria, seventh century BCE. Vorderasiatisches Museum, Berlin. Photo: © 2021 Scala, Florence/bpk, Bildagentur für Kunst, Kultur und Geschichte, Berlin.

Fig. 10. Basin assumed to be a foot bath, from Lachish, Judah, late eighth century BCE. Collection of the Israel Antiquities Authority. Photo: © The Israel Museum, Jerusalem/Avraham Hay.

Fig. 11. *Mikveh*, Gamlah, Upper Galilee, Israel, probably first century CE. Photo: Dmitriy Feldman/Dreamstime.com.

Fig. 12. Greek inscription on a slab found at Temple Mount, Jerusalem, first century CE. Archaeological Museum, Istanbul. Photo: Bible-LandPictures/Alamy.

Fig. 13. Detail of Enki (Ea) issuing waters from a Mesopotamian cylinder seal, *c.* 2250 BCE. Illustration: Daniel O. McClellan, 2021.

Fig. 14. Relief depicting Amun-Re in his role as Amun-Kamutef, Temple of Karnak, Egypt, *c.* 1300–1100 BCE. Photo: Wikimedia Commons.

Fig. 15. Relief showing King Ashurnasirpal II in his chariot, from the Northwest Palace in Kalhu (Nimrud), Assyria, *c.* 865–860 BCE. British Museum, London. Photo: © The Trustees of the British Museum.

Fig. 16. Plaque depicting a birth goddess, from ancient Eshnunna, Mesopotamia, *c.* 1800 BCE. Illustration: Daniel O. McClennan, 2021.

Fig. 17. Relief depicting circumcision, from the tomb of Ankhmahor,

Saqqara, Egypt, Sixth Dynasty (*c.* 2345–2181 BCE). Reproduced by kind permission of the Wellcome Library, London.

Fig. 18. The circumcision of Christ, miniature from Guillaume de Digul- leville, *The Pilgrimage of Human Life, the Pilgrimage of the Soul and the Pilgrimage of Jesus Christ,* Flanders, *c.* 1400 CE. Royal Library, Brussels. MS 10176-8, fol. 222. Photo: KBR.

Fig. 19. Motif of a sacred tree from a storage jar discovered at Kuntillet 'Ajrud, Sinai, Egypt, eighth century BCE. Illustration: Daniel O. McClellan, 2021.

Fig. 20. Relief of a high-status goddess, excavated from a thirteenth- century BCE grave in Minet el-Beida, near Ras Shamra (Ugarit), Syria. Musée du Louvre, Paris. Photo: Peter Horree / Alamy.

Fig. 21. Ashur drawing back his war bow, detail from an enamelled brick from a temple in Ashur, Assyria, *c.* 890–884 BCE. British Museum, London. Illustration: Daniel O. McClellan, 2021.

Fig. 22. The goddess Ishtar (Inanna), Mesopotamian clay plaque, *c.* 1800 BCE. Yale University, Babylonian Collection. Photo: Klaus Wagensonner.

Fig. 23. Detail from a stela depicting King Hammurabi of Babylon standing before Shamash, Babylonian, *c.* 1760 BCE. Musée du Louvre, Paris. Photo: Ivy Close Images / Alamy.

Fig. 24. Terracotta figurines of female drummers, from Achzib, Phoenicia, eighth and seventh centuries BCE. Israel Museum, Jerusalem. Photo: Zev Radovan / Alamy.

Fig. 25. Detail from a votive lunar disc assumed to show Enheduanna, high priestess of the moon god Nanna, Ur, *c.* 2300 BCE. University of Penn- sylvania Museum of Archaeology & Anthropology. Photo: Courtesy of the Penn Museum, object no. B16665.

Fig. 26. Alabaster vessel found at Uruk, *c.* 3100 BCE. Iraq Museum, Baghdad. Photo: Wikimedia Commons / Osama Shukir Muhammed Amin.

Fig. 27. Stone toilet seat, Lachish, Judah (modern Israel) late eighth century BCE. Israel Antiquities Authority. Photo: BibleLandPictures / Alamy.

Fig. 28. Limestone stela depicting Baal, Ugarit, *c.* 1700–1400 BCE. Musee du Louvre, Paris. Photo: Granger / Alamy.

Fig. 29. Mesopotamian shell plaque showing a warrior god battling a seven-headed monster, *c.* 2500 BCE, Private collection. Photo: Zev Radovan / Alamy.

Fig. 30. Marduk and his monster. Detail from a large lapis lazuli cylinder seal, Babylonia, ninth century BCE. Illustration from F. Weissbach, *Bab- ylonische Miscellen* (Leipzig: Hinrichs, 1903), p. 16, fig. 1.

Fig. 31. Citizens leaving Lachish. Detail from the Lachish wall reliefs from the Southwest Palace, Nineveh, Assyria, *c.* 700–690 BCE. British Museum, London. Photos: © The Trustees of the British Museum.

Fig. 32. King Sennacherib of Assyria. Detail from the Lachish wall reliefs from the Southwest Palace, Nineveh, Assyria, *c.* 700–690 BCE. British Museum, London. Photo: © The Trustees of the British Museum.

Fig. 33. Image of a divine battle with a seven-headed monster, from Beatus of Liebana and Dominicus, the Silos Apocalypse (1091–1109 CE). British Library, London. © British Library Board. All Rights Reserved/Bridgeman Images.

Fig. 34. Limestone house altar depicting Akhenaten, Nefertiti and their daughters. Amarna, Egypt, *c.* 1352–1336 BCE. Neues Museum, Berlin. Photo: Paul Williams/Alamy.

Fig. 35. Worshippers holding their hands aloft, detail from storage jar found at Kuntillet 'Ajrud in northern Sinai, Egypt, eighth century BCE. Illustration: Daniel O. McClellan, 2021.

Fig. 36. Clay figurine of a heavy-breasted woman, Jerusalem, late eighth century BCE. Collection of the Israel Antiquities Authority. Photo: © The Israel Museum, by Ardon Bar-Hama.

Fig. 37. Drawing of a fragment of a clay figurine depicting a woman holding an infant, Beth-shean, Israel, tenth century BCE. Illustration: Daniel O. McClellan, 2021.

Fig. 38. The Temple Scroll, late first century BCE to early first century CE. Found near Qumran, Israel. Israel Antiquities Authority. Photo: BibleLandPictures/Alamy.

Fig. 39. Miniature depicting Moses receiving and then transmitting the Ten Commandments to the Israelites, from the Regensburg Pentateuch (*c.* 1300 CE). Israel Museum, Jerusalem. MS 180/052, fol. 154 v. Photo: © The Israel Museum, Jerusalem by Ardon Bar Hama.

Fig. 40. Drawing of a proto-cuneiform tablet from Inanna's temple-district in Uruk (*c.* 3100 BCE). Illustration: Daniel O. McClellan, 2021.

Fig. 41. Detail of a tablet showing of King Nabu-apla-iddina in the presence of the sun god Shamash. Babylonian, *c.* 860–850 BCE. British Museum, London. Photo: BibleLandPictures/Alamy.

Fig. 42. Drawing of a cylinder-seal impression showing a worshipper standing before the cult statue of a storm god. Assyrian, thirteenth century BCE. Illustration: Daniel O. McClennan, 2021.

Fig. 43. Drawing of a Mesopotamian cylinder-seal impression showing a group of deities building a temple gate, *c.* 2340–2159 BCE. Illustration: Daniel O. McClellan, 2021.

Fig. 44. Bronze bull from an eleventh-century BCE cult site near Dothan, Israel. Staff Archaeological Officer, Civil Administration of Judea and Samaria. Photo: © Israel Museum, Jerusalem, by Ardon Bar-Hama.

Fig. 45. Basalt stela of a bull-headed god, from Bethsaida, eighth century BCE. Collection of the Israel Antiquities Authority. Photo: © The Israel Museum, Jerusalem by Ilan Sztulman.

Fig. 46. Drawing of a Mesopotamian cylinder-seal impression showing a deity mutilating the beard of another, *c.* 2350–2150 BCE. Illustration: Daniel O. McClellan, 2021.

Fig. 47. Potsherd depicting a king of Judah. Ramat Rahel (modern Israel), seventh century BCE. Illustration: Daniel O. McClellan, 2021.

Fig. 48. Limestone statue of El, found at Ugarit, thirteenth century BCE. Latakia Museum, Syria. Photo: Philippe Maillard / akg-images.

Fig. 49. Mosaic depicting Christ, Peter and Paul, from the Church of Santa Constanza, Rome, *c.* fourth century CE. Photo: Independent Picture Service / Alamy.

Fig. 50. Christ with students, detail from a marble sarcophagus, *c.* 300 CE. Museo Nazionale Romano, Palazzo Messimo alle Terme, Rome. Photo: De Agostini / Getty Images.

Fig. 51. Painted limestone stela engraved with five pairs of divine ears, from Medinet Habu, Luxor (*c.* 945–656 BCE). Photo: Courtesy of the Oriental Institute of the University of Chicago.

Fig. 52. Coin marked with an ear, from fourth-century BCE Yehud (Judah). Illustration: Daniel O. McClellan, 2021.

Fig. 53. The drunkenness of Noah, miniature from a Biblia Pauperum, produced in the Netherlands, *c.* 1405 CE. British Library, London. Kings 5, fol. 15. © British Library Board. All Rights Reserved / Bridgeman Images.

Fig. 54. Clay ossuary with a nose, from a burial cave in Peqi'in, Israel, *c.* 4500–3600 BCE. Collection of Israel Antiquities Authority. Photo © The Israel Museum, Jerusalem, by Elie Posner.

Fig. 55. Obsidian *sema* amulet, Egyptian, *c.* 664–343 BCE. Brooklyn Museum, New York. Gift of Evangeline Wilbour Blashfield, Theodora Wilbour, and Victor Wilbour honoring the wishes of their mother, Charlotte Beebe Wilbour, as a memorial to their father Charles Edwin Wilbour, 16.580.60. Photo: Brooklyn Museum Creative Commons.

Fig. 56. Detail of a mosaic showing Jonah and a monstrous fish, fourth century CE. Patriarchal Basilica, Aquileia, Italy. Photo: AgeFotostock/ Getty Images.

Fig. 57. Miniature showing a Hellmouth, from an illustrated Apocalypse, Belgium, *c.* 1313 CE. Bibliothèque nationale de France, Paris. Français 13096, fol. 86r. Photo: BnF.

A Note About the Author

FRANCESCA STAVRAKOPOULOU is a graduate of Oxford University and chaired professor of Hebrew Bible and ancient religion at the University of Exeter, U.K. Her focus is on the history and religions of ancient Israel and Judah. She has also worked in television for the BBC, Channel 4 and the History Channel, presenting shows on the archaeology and history of the Bible. She lives in Exeter, England.

A Note About the Type

This book was set in Monotype Dante, a typeface designed by Giovanni Mardersteig (1892–1977). Modeled on the Aldine type used for Pietro Cardinal Bembo's treatise *De Aetna* in 1495, Dante is a modern interpretation of the venerable face.

Composed by North Market Street Graphics,
Lancaster, Pennsylvania

Printed and bound by Berryville Graphics,
Berryville, Virginia